The Secret Life of Oscar Wilde

The Secret Life
of
Oscar Wilde

Neil McKenna

Century · London

Published by Century in 2003

1 3 5 7 9 10 8 6 4 2

First published in the United Kingdom in 2003 by Century
The Random House Group Limited
20 Vauxhall Bridge Road, London SW1V 2SA

Random House Australia (Pty) Limited
20 Alfred Street, Milsons Point, Sydney,
New South Wales 2061, Australia

Random House New Zealand Limited
18 Poland Road, Glenfield,
Auckland 10, New Zealand

Random House South Africa (Pty) Limited
Endulini, 5A Jubilee Road, Parktown 2193, South Africa

The Random House Group Limited Reg. No. 954009

www.randomhouse.co.uk

A CIP catalogue record for this book is available
from the British Library

Papers used by Random House are natural, recyclable products
made from wood grown in sustainable forests. The manufacturing processes
conform to the environmental regulations of the country of origin.

The author and publisher have made all reasonable efforts to contact copyright holders
for permission and apologise for any omissions or errors in the form of credits given.
Corrections may be made to future printings.

ISBN 0 7126 6986 8

Typeset by SX Composing DTP, Rayleigh, Essex
Printed and bound in Great Britain by
Clays Ltd, St Ives plc

For Robert
in love and friendship

ACKNOWLEDGEMENTS

This book could not have been written without consulting some of the rich manuscript collections held in libraries. In Britain, I am grateful to the staff of the Public Record Office in Kew, the British Library in London and Boston Spa, the Bodleian Library in Oxford, the University of Reading Library, the library of King's College, Cambridge, the library of the Fitzwilliam Museum, Cambridge, and the National Library of Scotland in Edinburgh. In the Netherlands, I was greatly helped by the staff of Homodok, the excellent archive of gay and lesbian history. In the United States, I am indebted to the staff of the William Andrews Clark Library in Los Angeles, especially Suzanne Tatian and Jennifer Schaffner, and the staff of the Harry Ransom Humanities Research Center at the University of Texas, Austin.

I would also like to thank the many people who have helped me in ways large and small over the past three years: Val Allam, Charlotte Arnold, Hans Arnold, Neil Bartlett, Di Bennett, Jamie Buxton, Martin Bowley, John Cooper, Nancy Duin, Tim d'Arch Smith, Trevor Fisher, Jonathan Fryer, James Gardiner, Simon Garfield, Sandra Greaves, Emily Green, Peter Grogan, Judith Hawley, Terry Heath, Philip Horne, Pam T. Job, Ellen Jones, Marion Janner, Liane Jones, Neil Kydd, Marie-Jaqueline Lancaster, Marina Leopardi, Jayne Lewis, Leo McKinstry, Peter Millson, Roger Moss, Douglas Murray, Rictor Norton, Harold Pinter, Keith Raffan, Dr David Rose, Nic Rose, John Rubinstein, Charles Russell, Dee Searle, Diane Samuels, David Souden, Jane Scruton, Linda Semple, Paula Synder, Jan Speigel, Liz Sturgeon, Ian Small, Chris Smith MP, Ben Summerskill, Alex Sutherland, Peter Tatchell, Thomas Venning, Simon Watney, Pamela Lady Wedgwood, Fay Weldon, Jacqueline Wesley, Peter Wilby and Sarah Woodley.

I would particularly like to thank: Sally Cline for her unfailing optimism and encouragement; Sian Jones for her excellent translations; Angie Penfold for all her hard work; Siobhan Kilfeather for encouraging me to undertake this book; Professor Jules Lubbock, my tutor at Essex University, who taught me a great deal and continues to do so; Professor John McRae of Nottingham University who generously shared his insights and expert knowledge of *Teleny* with me; and Janice Stevenor Dale and her family for her generous hospitality in Los Angeles. I owe a debt of gratitude to John B. Thomas of the Humanities Research Center in Austin, Texas, who not only put at my disposal his unrivalled knowledge of the collections there, especially the George Ives materials, but who also became a friend.

I would also like to express my sincere appreciation of the way in which Hannah Black, Kate Watkins and other staff at Century have worked with me on this book with immense professionalism and great cheerfulness. I also want to acknowledge the huge contribution made by David Smith, my copy-editor, who has enthusiastically read and re-read the manuscript and made an enormous number of suggestions and improvements.

I was fortunate enough to have the opportunity of meeting and talking with the late Sheila Colman, who knew Bosie in his last years and who generously shared her knowledge with me. John Stratford was also extremely helpful and answered my many questions about Bosie. Caspar Wintermans, the biographer of Bosie, has put his knowledge of Bosie at my disposal, and I eagerly anticipate his forthcoming edition of Bosie's letters.

I am extremely grateful to Merlin Holland, Oscar Wilde's grandson, who has not only been extremely supportive of this project but has also answered my many questions with unfailing grace and charm. In our enjoyable and stimulating conversations about Oscar over the past three years, Merlin has generously pointed me in the direction of materials I did not know about and has made many acute observations about Oscar and his sexuality.

I want to thank my agent, Andrew Lownie, who took me and the idea of this book on, and who spent a long time and a great deal of energy in finding a publisher. Without Andrew, this book would not have seen the light of day. I also want to thank my publisher, Mark Booth, who has been a joy to work with. Mark entered enthusiastically into the spirit of the book and has been wonderfully encouraging and supportive. It would be hard to think of a nicer publisher, or, indeed, a nicer person.

Finally, I want to express my profound gratitude to Robert Jones without whose love and friendship this book could not have been written.

'There is nothing Wilde would desire more than that we should know everything about him.' – W.H. Auden

'What a lurid life Oscar does lead – so full of extraordinary incidents. What a chance for the memoir writers of the next century.' – Max Beerbohm

'Nothing is serious except passion.' – Oscar Wilde

CONTENTS

FOREWORD

Oscar Wilde always knew that the story of his emotional and sexual life, and especially the story of his disastrous affair with Lord Alfred Douglas, would one day be told in full. 'Some day the truth will have to be known: not necessarily in my lifetime or in Douglas's,' he wrote shortly before his release from Reading Gaol.

This biography sets out to tell that story, to chart Oscar's odyssey to find his true sexual self, from the troubled and uncertain first stirrings of his feelings for other men, to the joyous paganism of his last years in exile. It was a journey of self-discovery with more than its fair share of love and lust, joy and despair, comedy and tragedy.

Despite many excellent biographies and critical studies, comparatively little has been written about Oscar's sexuality and his sexual behaviour. Most accounts of Oscar's life present him as predominantly heterosexual, a man whose later love of men was at best some sort of aberration, a temporary madness and, at worst, a slow-growing cancer, a terrible sexual addiction which slowly destroyed his mind and his body.

But the truth, as Oscar famously remarked, is rarely pure and never simple. Like many men of his time, Oscar struggled long and hard against his overwhelming sexual feelings for young men, before he decided to surrender to them. As time went by, he not only surrendered to these sexual feelings, but embraced them, and eventually became a brave champion of 'the Love that dare not speak its name'.

For years, Oscar had a secret sexual and emotional life. He was a husband and a father, a poet and a playwright, a wit and a dandy, and a lover of young men. He was torn between the desire to proclaim the existence of his secret life and the need to conceal it. These conflicting imperatives fired Oscar's creativity and found expression in his writing.

In researching and writing this book, I wanted to go beyond the mythology and the misapprehensions about Oscar's sexuality, and seek to present a coherent and psychologically convincing account of his sexual journey, one which would examine his relationships with Constance, with Robbie Ross, with Bosie Douglas and with the host of other boys and young men whose lives became entwined, however briefly, with his.

I wanted to find answers to some of the puzzling questions about Oscar's life. When did he first realise that he was attracted to other men? If he knew himself to be attracted to men, why then did he marry Constance? How much did Constance know or suspect? And why, knowing that he was almost certain to be found guilty on charges of 'gross indecency', did Oscar choose to stay in England and face imprisonment? I have, I believe, found answers to these and many other unanswered questions.

Oscar's place in the history of the small but courageous band of men who strove to bring about the legal and social emancipation of men who loved men has rarely been acknowledged. To Oscar, Bosie, George Ives and others, 'the Cause', as they simply termed their social and political aspirations, was nothing short of sacred. Understanding Oscar's commitment to 'the Cause' helps to explain many of his otherwise inexplicable decisions.

I was also intrigued by the persistent but unproven rumour of a political conspiracy underpinning the vigorous prosecution of Oscar. Immediately after he was sentenced to two years imprisonment with hard labour, Bosie and one or two others made a series of wild allegations that senior members of the ruling Liberal Party had conspired together and sacrificed Oscar in order to protect the reputation of the Prime Minister, Lord Rosebery, himself a lover of men. It quickly became apparent to me that Bosie's allegations were far from wild and were founded on a solid basis of fact.

There is a surprising wealth of material about Oscar's sexual and emotional life. Some of it is new and exciting, like the recently discovered witness statements made by the boys Oscar had sex with, and to which I was fortunate enough to be granted exclusive access. The boys' statements bring Oscar's sexual behaviour vividly to life. Taken in conjunction with the publication, earlier this year, of the full and unexpurgated transcript of the trial of the Marquis of Queensberry for criminally libelling Oscar, these statements made it possible for me to reconstruct Oscar's immensely rich and complicated sexual life between 1892 and 1895, the years of his love affair with Bosie.

There are other materials – like the voluminous diaries of Oscar's friend and fellow lover of men, George Ives, and the scabrous and unpublished memoirs of Trelawny Backhouse – which have yielded important information and shed much light on Oscar's attitudes to sex and love.

I have re-examined much under-used material which has been published once and promptly forgotten, or never published at all, often because it was deemed inappropriate or obscene. And I have given due prominence to other materials, like Fred Althaus's poignant letters charting his unhappy love affair with Oscar, which have simply been overlooked.

Oscar's own writings are a rich biographical source. Nearly all his work – from the very early poems to his four great society comedies – is highly autobiographical, reflecting and revealing his secret life. And Oscar's letters, recently republished with many new additions, remain the single most important source of information about his life and his loves, especially about his affair with Bosie and his last years abroad.

Oscar Wilde lived more lives than one, and no single biography can ever compass his rich and extraordinary life and achievements. I hope that this book has succeeded in telling the story of one, and to me the most interesting, of Oscar's many lives.

Neil McKenna
London, 2003

May 1895

It was unusually hot that last Saturday in May, and the small, cramped and badly ventilated courtroom at the Old Bailey was stifling. It was the last day of the second trial of Oscar Wilde on charges of gross indecency with young men, and everyone confidently expected that a verdict would be reached by the end of the afternoon. Every available seat was occupied, and the courtroom was, the *Illustrated Police Budget* reported, 'crowded to suffocation'.

The jury retired at half past three. Oscar's small but gallant band of friends and supporters in the public gallery were hoping against hope that the jury would fail to reach a verdict, as they had done just three weeks earlier. If they did, Oscar would almost certainly go free. A second retrial would surely be out of the question. 'You'll dine your man in Paris tomorrow,' Sir Frank Lockwood, who had prosecuted Oscar, remarked to Sir Edward Clarke, Oscar's barrister. But Clarke was not so sure. 'No, no, no,' he replied, shaking his head sadly.

The trials of Oscar Wilde had been going on for two months, since the fateful day in early March when Oscar had applied for a warrant for the arrest of the Marquis of Queensberry, the father of his lover Bosie, for criminally libelling him as a 'ponce and sodomite'. Oscar had appeared – as either prosecutor or defendant – in no fewer than nine separate court proceedings, and had spent four gruelling days in the witness box being cross-examined by three of the greatest advocates of the day.

The wait for a verdict in the Old Bailey was interminable. An hour or so after the jury went out there was a ripple of excitement in the stuffy courtroom. Was the verdict imminent? But it turned out to be a false alarm. The jury had only requested some bottled water and some paper and pencils. Another hour dragged by and the atmosphere in the court became more and more tense, more and more expectant. A few minutes after five-thirty, Oscar was brought up from the cells below and took his place in the dock. As the jury filed back into court, he leant over the front of the dock, 'eagerly scanning the faces of the twelve good men and true, seemingly trying to read in their physiognomies his fate'.

No one spoke, no one hardly dared to breathe. 'The silence was so deep,' the *Times* reported, 'that it could almost be felt.' As the foreman of the jury rose to deliver the verdict, Oscar's face was as 'white as a miller's apron'. When the first of the seven verdicts of 'Guilty' rang out, Oscar 'clutched convulsively at the front rail of the dock':

His face became paler than before – if that was possible – his eyes glared and twitched from an unseen excitement within, and his body practically shook with nervous prostration, whilst a soft tear found a place in his eye.

There was a stunned silence after the verdict had been read, interrupted only by the heavy tread of Oscar's friend, Alfred Taylor, who had already been found guilty, as he climbed the wooden stairs that led directly into the dock. The judge, seventy-seven-year-old Mr Justice Wills, did not mince his words in passing sentence. 'It is the worst case I have ever tried,' he said:

That you, Taylor, kept a kind of male brothel, it is impossible to doubt. And that you, Wilde, have been the centre of a circle of extensive corruption of the most hideous kind among young men, it is equally impossible to doubt. I shall, under the circumstances, be expected to pass the severest sentence the law allows. In my judgement it is totally inadequate for such a case as this. The sentence of the court is that each of you be imprisoned and kept to hard labour for two years.

There were a few gasps at the severity of the sentence and some loud cries of 'Shame' from the public gallery. Oscar seemed temporarily stunned by the sentence. 'And I?' he said hoarsely. 'May I say nothing, my lord?' But Mr Justice Wills merely waved his hand dismissively to the warders who hurried the two prisoners down the stairs leading to the cells.

Later, Oscar and Alfred Taylor were taken by Black Maria to Pentonville, the first of three prisons where Oscar would serve his sentence. Oscar saw himself as a martyr to Love. He had chosen to go to prison rather than repudiate his love for Bosie and his love for men. 'It is perhaps in prison that I am going to test the power of love,' he had written in his last, achingly beautiful letter to Bosie before his conviction. 'I am going to see if I cannot make the bitter waters sweet by the intensity of love I bear you.'

Towards the end of his sentence, from the silence and solitude of his prison cell in Reading Gaol – 'this tomb for those who are not yet dead' – Oscar would reflect on the 'scarlet threads' of his life that Fate had woven into so strange and paradoxical a pattern. And it was there, beneath the flaring gas jets in his small brick cell, that Oscar wrote, night after night, *De Profundis*, the great *apologia* for his life and for his love affair with Bosie.

'The two great turning points in my life,' he wrote, 'were when my father sent me to Oxford, and society sent me to prison.' These two events were carefully chosen: they marked the beginning and the end of a long and eventful sexual odyssey, in the course of which he discovered the secret of his sexual nature and learned to speak its name with pride and with passion. His great journey from Oxford University to Reading Gaol took him twenty-one years, almost to the day. By May 1895, Oscar's love had come of age.

Wonder and remorse

'Oxford is the capital of romance . . . in its own way as memorable as Athens.'

There was something different, even remarkable, about Oscar Fingal O'Flahertie Wills Wilde when he arrived at Magdalen College, Oxford in October 1874. He was certainly striking to look at. He was tall – taller than most of his contemporaries – and athletically built, though he always claimed to spurn exercise. And he looked rather younger than he really was, more like a gawky seventeen-year-old than a young man of twenty. His hair was dark and slightly wavy, rather longer than was usual, or indeed acceptable, causing several of his friends and fellow students to comment on it. It was 'much too long', recalled G.T. Atkinson, and he wore it 'sometimes parted in the middle, sometimes at the side, and he tossed it off his face'.

Oscar's face was large and pale and putty-coloured – 'moonlike', Atkinson called it – with extraordinarily large and expressive greenish-yellow eyes of remarkable lustre and intelligence. His lips were dark and flat and rather noticeable, and his teeth were discoloured. But when he smiled or spoke or laughed, he radiated a captivating aura of geniality and openness. The novelist Julia Constance Fletcher, who met Oscar in Italy in 1877, described his expression as 'singularly mild yet ardent'.

Oscar was different in another way. He was Irish, and his Irishness was evident from the mellifluous and delightful lilt in his voice, which, as the years in England multiplied, would virtually vanish. It was not uncommon for students from wealthy Anglo-Irish families to go to Oxford, but it was comparatively rare for a student with a discernible Irish accent to study there. It made him an outsider. 'He did not come from an English public school, and so he was, in a way, detached from what is largely a continuance of school life and friendships,' Atkinson wrote perceptively. This sense of detachment and difference, of otherness and apartness, was with Oscar all his life. At Oxford and afterwards, he seemed to have as many enemies as he had friends, and, bewilderingly, his greatest friends could often turn abruptly into his deadliest enemies. Women liked him, and sometimes fell a little in love with him. Men, on the other hand, were often hostile, irrationally so.

Oscar's avowed lack of interest in games drove a wedge between him and many of his contemporaries. Sport – playing sport, watching sport, talking sport – was a major constituent of the social cement that bound Oxford men together. Many felt that there was something not quite right about a man who professed himself so profoundly bored with the subject of sport. And some found it distinctly odd that while Oscar ridiculed athleticism, he could at the same time profess his admiration for the bodies of athletes.

Oscar's obvious intelligence and superior knowledge – and his willingness to demonstrate them – both attracted and repelled. It was galling that a man who boasted that he never did a stroke of work should be so successful academically. He was an accomplished and energetic talker, already among the best in Oxford. His talk was intelligent, articulate and incisive and, at the same time, allusive, imaginative, profound and richly poetic. Julia Constance Fletcher said he spoke 'like a man who has made a study of expression', and, perhaps more importantly, 'listened like one accustomed to speak'.

Oscar had been studying the art of conversation ever since he was a child. He and his older brother, Willie, were allowed to sit at Sir William and Lady Wilde's large dinner table in their house in Merrion Square, Dublin, where the great, the good and the interesting assembled to talk. Sir William was a successful surgeon, as well as an acknowledged expert on Irish antiquities. His wife described him as 'a Celebrity – a man eminent in his profession, of acute intellect and much learning, the best conversationalist in the metropolis, and author of many books, literary and scientific'. Lady Wilde had become famous in her youth as an ardent Irish nationalist and poet. Writing under the *nom de plume* 'Speranza', she published revolutionary poems urging the Irish to rise up against the English oppressor. Oscar had continued his apprenticeship in the art of conversation at Trinity College, Dublin when he came into the orbit of the remarkable classical scholar, John Pentland Mahaffy. In a city of great talkers, Mahaffy was among the greatest, and he would go on to write *The Principles of the Art of Conversation*.

Oscar was different in another way too – a difference invisible to the naked eye, but nonetheless one that could be sensed, however imperfectly, by his contemporaries. By the time he arrived in Oxford he had almost certainly begun to experience within himself some vague, hard-to-pin-down feelings of warmth and attraction towards young men. But it was hard for him to isolate, define or articulate these faint emotional stirrings. All he knew was that, as time went by, they slowly, almost imperceptibly, resolved themselves into the first weak flutterings of something very like love.

How and when this long and sometimes painful process started is impossible to know, but it could well have begun when Oscar was sixteen – the time of his 'sex-awakening', he told his friend, the journalist, writer and celebrated womaniser, Frank Harris – and was about to leave Portora Royal School, the boarding school he and Willie attended near Enniskillen. Many years later, Oscar admitted that he had had some 'sentimental friendships' with boys at Portora, one of which struck him as particularly significant. 'There was one boy, and one peculiar incident,' he told Frank Harris towards the end of his life. Oscar had been very friendly with a boy who was a year or so younger. 'We were great friends,' he said. 'We used to take long walks together and I talked to him interminably.' On the day Oscar left Portora for the last time, his friend came to the railway station with him to say his goodbyes. As the Dublin train was about to depart, the boy suddenly turned and cried out 'Oh, Oscar!':

> Before I knew what he was doing he had caught my face in his hot hands, and kissed me on the lips. The next moment he had slipped out of the door and was gone.

Oscar was shocked and shaken. He became aware of 'cold, sticky drops' trickling down his face. They were the boy's tears. Oscar was strangely affected by the experience. It was a kind of epiphany, a moment of revelation. 'This is love,' he said to himself, trembling slightly. 'For a long while I sat,' he told Frank Harris, 'unable to think, all shaken with wonder and remorse.' This combination of wonder and remorse would characterise Oscar's complex and ambivalent attitudes towards his attraction to young men for many years to come.

There were no words that could accurately or adequately describe the feelings Oscar was beginning to experience in his first year at Oxford. Words like 'sodomy' and 'sodomite', derived from the Old Testament story of the city of Sodom which was destroyed by fire and brimstone because of the unnatural sexual practices of its inhabitants, did not apply. Oscar's feelings were emotional and were not – as yet – sexual. Any suggestion of sodomy, which in law explicitly meant anal sex, would have been utterly repugnant to him. Sodomy was taboo. It was the *crimen tantum horribile non inter Christianos nominandum*, 'the too horrible vice which is not to be named among Christians', and was regarded, if anything, as more horrible than murder. In 1828, in the lifetimes of Sir William and Lady Wilde, the penalty for sodomy had been increased from imprisonment to death, and was reduced to penal servitude for life only in 1861. When, in 1895, the Marquis of Queensberry publicly accused Oscar of being 'a ponce and sodomite', it was the worst insult that could be thrown at a man.

Nor could Oscar describe himself or his feelings as in any way 'homosexual', as the term had been coined only five years earlier in Germany by Karl Maria Kertbeny, and would not come into common usage in English until the turn of the century. By the time he went up to Oxford, Oscar could only invoke the concept of 'Greek love' to define his feelings for young men. As an outstanding Greek scholar, he would have known all about the tradition of friendship – 'the romantic medium of impassioned friendship', as he described it in his Commonplace Book at Oxford – between men and boys which was accepted as natural in ancient Greece.

Greek love was much on Oscar's mind in 1874. Before he went up to Oxford, he spent several weeks helping his friend and mentor Mahaffy with his forthcoming book, *Social Life in Greece*, which was the first book to contain a frank discussion of the phenomenon. Mahaffy took the bull by the horns, though he was careful to frame the discussion in conventional moral terms. Greek love was, he said:

> that strange and to us revolting perversion, which reached its climax in later times, and actually centred upon beautiful boys all the romantic affections which we naturally feel between opposite sexes, and opposite sexes alone.

'These things are so repugnant and disgusting that all mention of them is usually omitted in treating of Greek culture,' he wrote. Nevertheless, Mahaffy believed that it was worthwhile examining the social context of the 'peculiar delight and excitement felt by the Greeks in the society of handsome youths'. Though Greek love could sometimes lead to 'strange and odious consequences', it was, more often than not, a friendship of 'purity and refinement'. Oscar's exact role in Mahaffy's book is not known, though some have detected his youthful voice raised for the first time in defence of Greek love in the sentence: 'As to the epithet *unnatural,* the Greeks would answer probably, that all civilisation was unnatural.' Mahaffy certainly paid generous tribute to 'my old pupil Mr Oscar Wilde of Magdalen College' for his 'improvements and corrections all through the book'. Oscar reciprocated. Mahaffy was 'my first and my best teacher', Oscar said many years later, 'the scholar who showed me how to love Greek things'.

At Oxford, the word 'Greek' began to creep into Oscar's vocabulary, invariably to describe youthful male beauty, present and past. There was Armitage, 'who has the most Greek face I ever saw', the athlete Stevenson, whose 'left leg is a Greek poem', the poet Keats's 'Greek sensuous delicate lips', and Harmodious, 'a beautiful boy in the flower of Greek loveliness'. When he was a student, Oscar began to write poetry in earnest, and many of his poems written in Oxford invoke and celebrate great male lovers from Greek history and mythology. For the time being, at least, Oscar's Greek feelings towards other young men were spiritual and emotional, more than sexual. But, in the course of his four years at Oxford, the 'purity and refinement' of his Greek feelings gave way to a frankly more erotic interest in young men, and would soon result in the 'strange and odious consequences' that Mahaffy had spoken of. It was not long before there was unpleasant gossip. In October 1875, Oscar's friend John Bodley recorded in his diary that people were saying that 'old Wilde is a damned compromising acquaintance' and that he was in the habit of leaving 'foolish letters from people who are "hungry" for him . . . for his friends to read'.

A new word, brought over from Europe on the wind of intellectual change, entered Oscar's vocabulary halfway through his time in Oxford. 'Psychological' came to mean men who loved men, and reflected the wave of new thinking in Germany, Austria and France that love and sex between men was a disturbance, a disease of the mind to be treated by the physician, rather than a crime to be punished by the courts. In Britain, the word became a kind of shorthand to refer to anything pertaining to love and sex between men. Oscar started to use 'psychological' in this sense in 1876, in a letter to his Oxford friend William 'Bouncer' Ward – 'I want to ask your opinion on this psychological question' – about a love affair between an undergraduate and a boy. Another time, Oscar wrote that another Magdalen undergraduate, Cresswell Augustus Cresswell, or 'Gussy', 'is charming though not educated well: however he is "psychological" and we have long chats and walks'. Oscar also used the word 'spooning' to describe the attachment between a fellow undergraduate at Magdalen and a younger boy, a Magdalen chorister. The word is redolent of boarding school crushes between older and younger boys, where sex may or may not have been involved.

Oscar may have actually had – or at the very least aspired to – some sort of relationship with a choirboy at Oxford, as an unpublished and remarkably homoerotic poem, 'Choir Boy', makes clear. It was written at some point during his four years in Oxford, possibly in 1876. The poem opens with a quotation from Elizabeth Barrett Browning, 'Ah God, it is a dreary thing to sit at home with unkissed lips', and vividly describes how Oscar 'went out into the night' and 'waited under the lamp's light' for a young male lover to appear:

> And there came on with eyes of fire,
> > And a throat as a singing dove,
> And he looked on me with desire,
> > And I know that his name was Love.
>
> See what I found in the street
> > A man child lusty and fair
> With little white limbs and little feet
> > A glory of golden yellow hair
>
> Red and white as a mountain rose,
> > Little brown eyes so bright as wine
> Little white fingers and little white toes
> > O he is lovely, this boy of mine.

Oscar ended the poem by throwing down a gauntlet to those who would condemn his love for his 'lusty and fair' boy:

> What do ye say he's the child of sin
> > That God looks on him with angry eyes,
> And never will let him enter in
> > The holy garden of Paradise?

'Choir Boy' was never finished. Oscar may have decided that the poem was too explicit, too revealing of his secret self. It is, of course, entirely possible that Oscar's passion for his 'lovely' choirboy was chaste, that the delight he took in his beauty was just that: delight. The poet and writer John Addington Symonds, whom Oscar greatly admired and eventually started a correspondence with, had also fallen in love with a choirboy fifteen years earlier. Symonds was twenty-two when he fell in love with Alfred Brooke, the same age as Oscar at the time he wrote 'Choir Boy'. Symonds felt unable to express the love he felt for Alfred sexually:

> I had been taught that the sort of love I felt for Alfred Brooke was wicked. I had seen that it was regarded with reprobation by modern society. At the same time I knew it to be constitutional, and felt it to be ineradicable. What I attempted to do in these circumstances was to stifle it so far as outward action went. I could not repress it internally any more than I could stop the recurrence of dreams in sleep or annihilate any native instinct for the beauty of the world.

After one or two snatched kisses and some furtive hand-holding, the affair with Alfred ended badly and left Symonds ill with a variety of alarming psychosomatic complaints. In his *Memoirs*, Symonds recalled how he attempted to 'divert my passions from the burning channel in which they flowed for Alfred Brooke, and lead them gently to follow a normal course toward women'.

Symonds's attempt to channel his sexual desires for boys towards women may help to explain Oscar's several attempts to kindle love affairs with women. As with many of his contemporaries who shared his growing passion for other men, Oscar's path to erotic self-realisation was twisted and stony. In his published poems, he publicly celebrated the glories of Greek love, and in private he rhapsodised poetically over the physical charms of choirboys. Yet it seems that Oscar was able to successfully separate his sexual yearnings from his sexual identity. He could have sex with young men, and yet still cast himself as a conventional lover of women. And he could convince himself – even lie to himself – that his sexual contacts with men were of a different order to his sexual contacts with women. In the first place, sex with a man was not real sex. Real sex consisted of the act of coitus with a woman. It necessarily involved penetration. Sex with boys and with men rarely if ever, for Oscar at this time, involved penetration. There might be kissing, caressing and mutual masturbation. But fellatio and sodomy – or *pedicatio* as it was sometimes termed – were taboo. So Oscar could tell himself that, although what he might be doing gave him pleasure and satisfaction, it was not and could never be the same as real sex with a woman.

And sex with men was supposedly a passing phase. Sex between boys and between young men was common, and to a certain extent tolerated, in public schools and universities. The rule was never to get caught, and there was an expectation that young men would eventually grow out of these habits and marry. Men who continued to have sex with other men well into adult life could tell themselves that their behaviour was merely the continuation of a habit they had formed at school and university, a habit that met a need, a habit that could and would be broken when the right woman came along.

Such comforting doublethink could assuage but not entirely obviate the burden of guilt and self-doubt. There were also times when Oscar struggled against the 'burning channel' of his inclinations, when, like Symonds, he was severely distressed by what he saw as his 'wicked' desires. The wonder of sex with a young man would be followed by bitter remorse. Such storms of self-loathing and self-doubt would batter him over the next few years, and return, with hurricane force, during his imprisonment.

In the summer of 1875, Oscar flirted with at least two young women. The mother of one wrote to him to express her disapproval of Oscar's behaviour with her daughter:

> Dear Oscar, I was very much pained the last time I was at your house when I went into the drawing room and saw Fidelia sitting upon your knee. Young as she is, she ought to have had (and I told her) the instinctive delicacy that would have shrunk from it – but oh! Oscar, the thing was neither right, nor manly, nor gentlemanlike in you.

She went on to reproach Oscar for kissing Fidelia when her back was turned. 'As to kissing Fidelia . . . out of sight as it were,' she wrote:

> For instance the last day I saw you – you left me, a lady, to open the hall door for myself, you staying behind at the same time in the hall to kiss Fidelia. Did you think for a moment that I was so supremely stupid as not to know that you always kissed F. when you met her, if you had an opportunity?

There was also Eva, whose affection for Oscar prompted her aunt to write to him in October 1875, dropping a heavy hint that 'dear Eva' was minded to accept a proposal of marriage, if Oscar was 'truly in earnest'.

In the summer of 1876, Oscar was at home in Dublin and wrote to his Oxford friend Reginald 'Kitten' Harding with some exciting news:

> I am just going out to bring an *exquisitely pretty girl* to afternoon service in the Cathedral. She is just seventeen with the *most perfectly beautiful face I ever saw and not a sixpence of money*. I will show you her photograph when I see you next.

The name of this exquisitely pretty girl was Florence Balcombe. Oscar was quite smitten. He sketched her in pencil, a sketch which still survives and shows a slender young woman with long dark hair and large dark eyes with a thoughtful, faraway look. Two months after he met Florrie, Oscar presented her with a watercolour painting he had done of the 'View from Moytura House', the house built by his father as country retreat in County Mayo. And at Christmas that year, he gave her a small gold cross. There was no doubt that

Oscar and Florrie were courting. They wrote to each other frequently, though only a handful of Oscar's letters have survived.

Oscar's courtship of Florrie continued into 1878 and then, inexplicably, seemed to fade into friendship. Not long afterwards, Florrie met and fell in love with Bram Stoker, a young Irish civil servant who would go on to write *Dracula*. When he heard of her forthcoming marriage to Stoker, Oscar wrote to Florrie and asked her to return the 'little gold cross':

> It serves as a memory of two sweet years – the sweetest of all the years of my youth – and I should like to have it always with me.

Three years later, as Florrie was about to make her debut on the London stage, Oscar asked the actress Ellen Terry to give her a crown of flowers as if they were from herself:

> I should like to think that she was wearing something of mine the first night she comes on the stage, that anything of mine should touch her. Of course if you think – but you won't think she will suspect. How could she? She thinks I never loved her, thinks I forget. My God how could I!

On the face of it, Oscar's love for Florrie appeared to be real, passionate and heartfelt. And yet, at the time he met Florrie, and during the entire 'two sweet years' of their courtship, Oscar was involved in a relationship – a sexual relationship – with another man, Frank Miles. It was the start of a pattern of behaviour that was to last for nearly twenty years. Flirting with pretty girls, making love to beautiful young women, and eventually marrying were for Oscar always more than merely 'a cloak to hide his secret', as he would later memorably phrase it. Women were half of the equation of love: they represented purity and freshness, safety and security, and sometimes even sanctuary: boys and young men, on the other hand, were on the dangerous and dark side of the erotic moon, where forbidden pleasures tasted so much sweeter.

Tea and beauties

'It is a dreadful thing to have one's name in the papers. And still more dreadful not to.'

Oscar met Frank Miles in the spring of 1876. Frank was two years older and was living in London, where he was trying to establish himself as a portrait painter of society ladies. Photographs of Frank show a dashingly good-looking, blond-haired young man. He was, according to Frank Harris, 'a very pleasant, handsome young fellow who made a sympathetic impression on everyone'. By early summer, Oscar and Frank were good friends and were almost certainly already lovers. On a visit to Bosie at Oxford in 1892, Oscar would confess – in a fit of *nostalgie de la boue* – that he and Frank first had sex there.

In June 1876, Frank took his friend, the sculptor Lord Ronald Gower, to meet Oscar. 'By early train to Oxford with F. Miles,' Gower wrote in his diary for 4 June:

> There I made the acquaintance of young Oscar Wilde, a friend of Miles's. A pleasant cheerful fellow but with his long-haired head full of nonsense regarding the Church of Rome.

Gower was Frank's friend and patron. He was also a notorious sodomite, with a penchant for 'rough trade' in the form of soldiers, sailors and labourers. Not only did he introduce Frank to fashionable society ladies in need of one of the flattering pastel portraits that Frank specialised in, but Gower was also his guide to London's sexual underworld. Later, Oscar would base the character of Lord Henry Wotton, the corrupt and corrupting prophet of strange sins in *Dorian Gray*, on Gower.

Frank's father was rector of Bingham in Nottinghamshire, and it was not long before Frank, Oscar and Gower visited Bingham and spent a delightful week there. 'I came down here on Monday and had no idea it was so lovely,' Oscar wrote to his best friend in Oxford, Reginald 'Kitten' Harding, from Bingham Rectory. 'A wonderful garden with such white lilies in rose walks; only that there are no serpents or apples it would be quite paradise.' Eden was clearly never going to be enough. Oscar was already signalling his need to be tempted by forbidden fruit. 'Life's aim, if it has one,' he wrote later, 'is simply

11

to be always looking for temptations. There are not nearly enough of them. I sometimes pass a whole day without coming across a single one. It is quite dreadful. It makes one so nervous about the future.'

After 'dallying in the enchanted isle of Bingham Rectory, and eating the lotus flowers of Love', Oscar went to Ireland where he had arranged to spend a week or so in Moytura House with Frank, before they went into the mountains of Connemara to 'a charming little fishing lodge' where Oscar was determined to make Frank 'land a salmon and kill a brace of grouse'.

It was not love that Oscar felt for Frank, at least not the conventional love that he felt for Florrie Balcombe. Rather it was 'a richly impassioned friendship' which gave him and Frank both emotional stability and sexual expression. Like all his subsequent relationships with young men, Oscar's relationship with Frank is unlikely to have been monogamous. They had sex with each other, and with other people. But the sexual bond between them weakened as time passed. Frank wore a moustache, which was something that became anathema to Oscar: he preferred his young men to be beardless. From the outset, Oscar availed himself of his sexual freedom. In December 1876 he visited Lord Ronald Gower in Windsor, taking another young artist, Arthur May, as his companion. 'We had a delightful day,' he wrote to 'Kitten' Harding. 'I have taken a great fancy to May. He is quite charming in every way and a beautiful artist.' Oscar also wrote praising May to his other Oxford friend, William Ward, a few days later. 'I saw a great deal of Arthur May: he is quite charming in every way and we have rushed into friendship.' Over the next four years there would be several other young men with whom Oscar would rush into friendship equally precipitately.

Oscar was beginning to get his work published, poems mostly, and the occasional review. In July 1877, he reviewed an exhibition of paintings at the fashionable Grosvenor Gallery, dwelling lovingly, almost lasciviously, on the images of boys in the exhibition. There were references to the beautiful boys of the Greek islands, to St Sebastian, to a 'Greek Ganymede' and to other notable artistic examples of 'the bloom and vitality and the radiance of this adolescent beauty'.

When his review was published in the *Dublin University Magazine*, he sent a copy to Walter Pater at Oxford who, four years earlier, had published his notorious *Studies in the History of the Renaissance*. The book's controversial 'Conclusion' preached a dangerous gospel. Pater made a passionate appeal to his readers to drink fully from the heady cup of life, to consume every experience that was on offer. 'A counted number of pulses only is given to us of a variegated dramatic life,' he wrote. Ecstasy consisted of squeezing and consuming as many of these pulses as possible into a lifetime, of burning always with a 'hard, gemlike flame'. There were moments when Pater no longer seemed to be talking about art, but about sex:

> While all melts under our feet, we may well grasp at any exquisite passion, or
> any contribution to knowledge that seems by a lifted horizon to set the spirit

free for a moment, or any stirring of the senses, strange dyes, strange colours, and curious odours, or work of the artist's hands, or the face of one's friend.

Pater's invocation of strange and curious passions inspired by the beautiful face of a friend was profoundly homoerotic and gave rise to much speculation about his sexual tastes. Pater himself realised that he may have gone too far and removed the 'Conclusion' from later editions of the book, saying 'I conceived it might possibly mislead some of those young men into whose hands it might fall.' Oscar was one of those young men willingly misled by Pater's passionate advocacy. Not only were many of his ideas about the supremacy and sensuality of art imbibed from Pater, but his attitudes towards sex and promiscuity can also be traced back to Pater's 'Conclusion'. Pater's hard, gemlike flame became for Oscar the flame of sexual passion. 'All flames are pure,' he told his friend George Ives in a discussion on sex.

When Pater received Oscar's letter and a copy of his review, he recognised a fellow spirit and wrote a carefully coded reply. 'I hope you will give me an early call on your return to Oxford,' Pater wrote:

The article shows that you possess some beautiful, and, for your age, quite exceptionally cultivated tastes; and a considerable knowledge too of many beautiful things.

Oscar and Pater began a cautious friendship. For Oscar, Pater was always too hesitant, too secretive about his sexual tastes, while for Pater, Oscar was the opposite. According to Vincent O'Sullivan, who was a friend of both of them, Pater was 'timid and afraid that W. would compromise him'. John Bodley called at Oscar's rooms late one morning and found him delicately laying the table for luncheon. When Bodley asked if he could stay, Oscar refused point blank. 'No, no!' he said. 'Impossible to have a Philistine like you. Walter Pater is coming to lunch with me for the first time.' Bodley looked on with extreme concern at Oscar's developing friendship with Pater. He knew that, as recently as 1874, Pater had been implicated in a scandal with an undergraduate, William Money Hardinge, known as 'the Balliol Bugger'. Hardinge was extremely indiscreet about his interest in men and it was discovered that he had received letters from Pater signed 'Yours Lovingly'.

Bodley claimed later that it was Oscar's 'intimacy' with Pater which turned Oscar into an 'extreme aesthete'. Bodley's phrase was carefully chosen. He meant to convey that it was Pater who had corrupted Oscar into becoming a lover of men. He was mistaken: Oscar was already a lover of men. But it was true that Oscar was now an ardent convert to the Aesthetic movement which had emerged in opposition and reaction to the ugly certainties of Victorian Britain. Aestheticism seemed to spring into life, fully formed, towards the end of the 1870s and was a heady mix of art, idealism and politics which sought to propagate a new gospel of Beauty. Aestheticism was a hybrid which drew on diverse strands of radical thinking – the ideals of the Pre-Raphaelite

Brotherhood and John Ruskin, Pater's theories on art for art's sake, William Morris's Arts and Crafts movement, Socialism and the Trades Union movement. Aestheticism embodied many of the ideas and ideals of these movements and yet had a unique and distinct identity. The apostles of Aestheticism believed that the very idea of beauty – the simple, natural beauty of the arts and the crafts, of poetry and prose, of thoughts and ideas – was powerful enough to change the world.

'I find it harder and harder every day to live up to my blue china,' Oscar is reputed to have said. Whether he had indeed made the remark was, he quickly discovered, immaterial. The saying passed into the currency of Oxford myth, and Oscar was amused and delighted some weeks later when he heard that John Burgon, Vicar of St Mary's Church in Oxford, took it so seriously that he preached a sermon against it:

> When a young man says not in polished banter, but in sober earnestness, that he finds it difficult to live up to the level of his blue china, there has crept into these cloistered shades a form of heathenism which it is our bounden duty to fight against and crush out, if possible.

This was, Oscar said afterwards, the 'first time that the absolute stupidity of the English people was ever revealed to me'. It was also the first time that he had been so publicly talked about and talked against. It was a strangely pleasurable experience, and he felt that it conferred on him a species of celebrity.

Oscar continued to plough the furrow of his Paterian 'cultivated tastes' in boys and young men. In December 1877, his poem 'Wasted Days' was published in *Kottabos*, the magazine of Trinity College, Dublin. Oscar wrote the poem after seeing a tile painted, in the medieval manner by Violet Troubridge, of a beautiful slender boy. The poem is unashamedly homoerotic:

> A fair slim boy not made for this world's pain,
> With hair of gold thick clustering round his ears,
> And longing eyes half veiled by foolish tears
> Like bluest water seen through mists of rain;
> Pale cheeks whereon no kiss hath left its stain,
> Red under-lip drawn in for fear of Love.

Longing eyes, foolish tears, unkissed cheeks and lips drawn in for fear of love, 'Wasted Days' spoke 'scarlet volumes' about Oscar's artistic and sexual tastes. Boyish youths and youthful men, 'rose-red youth' and 'rose-white boyhood', were to become a sexual leitmotiv. 'Youth! Youth! There is absolutely nothing in the world but youth!' Lord Henry Wotton tells Dorian Gray. And at his trial Oscar would declare, 'To me youth, the mere fact of youth, is so wonderful.'

But Oscar's continuing wonder at the beauty of youth was interrupted by a storm of remorse and self-loathing. On 15 April 1878, he had a long interview

14

with the Catholic priest Father Sebastian Bowden at the Brompton Oratory. Bowden wrote a letter to Oscar the following day from which much of what Oscar said can be guessed at. Bowden described Oscar's visit with him as a 'confession'. Oscar had, he wrote, freely and entirely laid open his 'life's history' and his 'soul's state'. He had spoken at length of his 'present unhappy self' and about 'the aimlessness and misery' of his life. One sentence in Bowden's letter is especially revealing:

> You have like everyone else an evil nature and this in your case has become more corrupt by bad influences mental and moral, and by positive sin.

Reading between the lines, it seems clear that Oscar had confessed some or all of his sexual experiences, possibly with the anonymous choirboy, probably with Frank Miles and Arthur May, and perhaps with others, to Father Bowden. This was the 'positive sin' Bowden was referring to. And at least one of the 'bad influences, mental and moral' that Bowden mentioned was Lord Ronald Gower, who was increasingly playing Lord Henry Wotton to Oscar's Dorian Gray. Another bad influence was John Addington Symonds – 'Mr Soddington Symonds', as the poet Swinburne dubbed him – with whom Oscar was now in regular correspondence, and who was an indefatigable champion of Greek love.

Bowden fervently urged Oscar to take the plunge and convert to Catholicism. 'As a Catholic,' he told him:

> you would find yourself a new man in the order of nature as of grace. I mean that you would put from you all that is affected and unreal and a thing unworthy of your better self.

Father Bowden chose his words carefully. His phrase 'a new man in the order of nature' strongly suggests that, by becoming a Catholic, Oscar would not only enter a state of spiritual grace, but that he would also throw off the burden of his unnatural sexual desires – that 'thing unworthy of himself' – and take his assigned place in the natural order as a normal man, a man who loved women. He urged Oscar to visit him again for another talk. 'In the meantime pray hard and talk little' – the latter injunction difficult, if not impossible, for Oscar to obey. After his confession, Oscar appeared to recover his equilibrium as quickly as he had lost it. He cancelled his second appointment with Father Bowden, sending him a bunch of lilies in his stead.

The lily was the unofficial symbol of the Aesthetic movement. Oscar's bunch of lilies to Father Bowden clearly signalled his intentions. His spiritual and sexual crisis was over. He had chosen to worship Beauty, rather than God, and to put his faith in art, rather than religion. Six months later Oscar left Oxford for life in London, grandly styling himself 'Professor of Aesthetics and Art Critic'.

Oscar set up home with Frank Miles. They had two floors of an old and rambling house in Salisbury Street, leading off the Strand – 'this untidy but romantic house', Oscar called it. Oscar had a large sitting room, panelled and painted white, where he and Frank Miles would entertain, sending out invitations broadcast for 'Tea and Beauties' where Frank's pastel portraits of beautiful women would be prominently displayed in the hopes of picking up a commission or two. Their aim was not so much to break into the rigid and stuffy confines of high society, but to establish themselves as arbiters of taste among the more relaxed, more exciting and fashionable society of writers, artists and poets. Oscar once remarked that there were only three ways to get into society: feed it, amuse it or shock it. He used all three tactics simultaneously.

One of their early visitors at Salisbury Street was a young woman, Laura Troubridge, sister to Violet, who wrote a vivid sketch of her visit. 'Went to tea at Oscar Wilde's,' she wrote in her diary:

> Great fun, lots of vague 'intense' men, such duffers, who amused us awfully. The room was a mass of white lilies, photos of Mrs Langtry, peacock-feather screens and coloured pots, pictures of various merit.

Lillie Langtry was a professional beauty who had modelled for the greatest painters of the day and who was shortly to become the mistress of the Prince of Wales. She also agreed to model for Frank Miles, who drew numerous pastel portraits of her. It was through Frank that Oscar met the 'Jersey Lily' at a tea party one afternoon. Lillie later recorded her first, not entirely favourable, impressions of Oscar. 'How astonished I was at his strange appearance,' she wrote later:

> Then he must have been not more than twenty-two. He had a profusion of brown hair, brushed back from his forehead, and worn rather longer than was conventional, though not with the exaggeration which he afterwards affected. His face was large, and so colourless that a few pale freckles of good size were oddly conspicuous. He had a well-shaped mouth, with somewhat coarse lips and greenish-hued teeth. The plainness of his face, however, was redeemed by the splendour of his great, eager eyes.

Lillie and Oscar became friends. There were rumours that he was deeply in love with her, and that he presented her with a single pale lily every day. 'I would have rather discovered Mrs Langtry than have discovered America,' he remarked. He wrote a poem – 'The New Helen' – praising her beauty and sent her a copy inscribed 'To Helen, formerly of Troy, now of London.'

Oscar was prepared to do almost anything to further his career as a poet and a writer. He knew the value of publicity, and he knew too that nothing generated publicity like controversy. 'There is only one thing in the world worse than being talked about,' Lord Henry Wotton says in *Dorian Gray*, 'and that is not being talked about.' Oscar's hair grew longer and longer, and his clothes more and more *outré*. It was rumoured – falsely – that Oscar had walked down Piccadilly in Aesthetic costume of kneebreeches and a flowing velvet jacket reverently holding a lily in his hand. 'Anyone could have done that,' he said proudly. 'The great and difficult thing was what I achieved – to make the whole world believe that I had done it.'

Oscar's extravagant and very public devotion to Lillie Langtry, and to the actresses Ellen Terry and Sarah Bernhardt, was designed to get his name in the newspapers and in the minds of the public at large. He reputedly greeted the arrival of Sarah Bernhardt in England by throwing an armful of lilies at her feet. His efforts did not go unrewarded. When his Oxford friend William Ward called at Salisbury Street one morning, he found Oscar still in bed, his sitting-room a mess:

> He explained that he had given a supper party the night before, at which Sarah Bernhardt had been present and that she had tried to see how high she could jump and write her name with a charcoal on the wall. From the scrawl on the side of the room and not much below the ceiling it seemed that she had attained considerable success in her attempt.

Oscar's name was everywhere and it was not long before he achieved the dubious distinction of being satirised by *Punch*, 'a comic weekly' with a large circulation, which saw its role as puncturing pretension and pomposity wherever it occurred. Oscar and the Aesthetic craze were a prime target. Oscar personified the 'very aesthetic', 'supremely intense', 'long-haired and hyper-poetic' Apostle of Beauty:

> And many a maiden will mutter,
>   When OSCAR looms large on her sight,
> 'He's quite too consummately utter,
>   As well as too utterly quite.'

From 1880 onwards, Oscar was lampooned mercilessly in *Punch* as 'Jellaby Postlethwaite', the namby-pamby, limp-wristed poet, striking poetic attitudes for all he was worth and worshipping beauty in the most unlikely ways; and as 'Maudle', the painter with an unhealthy interest in youth. In one famous *Punch* cartoon, Maudle, looking exactly like an over-fed Oscar, admires Mrs Brown's teenage son:

> Maudle: How *consummately* lovely your son is, Mrs Brown!
> Mrs Brown (a Philistine from the country): What! He's a *nice, manly* Boy, if you mean *that*, Mr Maudle. He has just left school, you know, and wishes to be an Artist.
> Maudle: *Why* should he be an Artist?
> Mrs Brown: Well, he must be *something*!
> Maudle: Why should he *Be* anything? Why not let him remain for ever content to *Exist Beautifully*!

The caption to the cartoon closes with the words: *Mrs Brown determines that at all events her Son shall not study Art under Maudle.* *Punch* was clearly not fooled by Oscar's extravagant declarations of love for beautiful young women.

Oscar acknowledged that he was the inspiration behind Maudle. 'I suppose that I am the original of *Maudle*,' he reluctantly admitted in a newspaper interview. But he looked down with Olympian disdain on *Punch*'s caricatures:

> My attitude toward all this is that a true artist who believes in his art and his mission must necessarily be altogether insensible to praise or blame. If he is not a mere sham, he cannot be disturbed by any caricature or exaggeration. He has the truth on his side, and the opinion of the whole world should be of no consequence to him.

In 1881, Frank Burnand, the editor of *Punch*, decided to exploit the public fascination with all things Aesthetic and wrote a play, *The Colonel*, which featured the shamming poet and Aesthete, Lambert Streyke, who was clearly modelled on Oscar. Queen Victoria saw the play and wrote that it was:

> a very clever play, written to quiz and ridicule the foolish aesthetic people who dress in such absurd manner, with loose garments, puffed sleeves, great hats, and carrying peacock's feathers, sunflowers and lilies.

Oscar's own volume of poetry, simply entitled *Poems*, was published in the summer of 1881, further confusing him in the public mind with his alter egos Jellaby Postlethwaite and Lambert Streyke. It was poorly received. 'I see that Oscar Wilde, the utterly utter is bringing out 10s. 6d worth of poems,' the Jesuit and poet Gerard Manley Hopkins told a friend, while the translator and literary critic Edmund Gosse called the volume 'a curious toadstool' and 'a malodorous Parasitic growth'. *Punch* also produced a 'Fancy Portrait' of Oscar as a sunflower:

> Aesthete of Aesthetes!
> What's in a name?
> The poet is WILDE,
> But his poetry's tame.

'The cover is consummate, the paper is distinctly precious, the binding is beautiful, and the type is utterly too,' said *Punch* scathingly, describing *Poems* as 'a volume of echoes', 'Swinburne and water'. For the past decade, Algernon Charles Swinburne had been England's most controversial young poet, writing lushly sensual verse and leading a drunken, scandalous existence.

In a debate at the Oxford Union on whether to accept Oscar's present of a signed copy of *Poems*, the poems were savaged as both derivative and immoral.

'It is not that these poems are thin – and they *are* thin,' declared Oliver Elton:

> It is not that they are immoral – and they *are* immoral: it is not that they are
> this or that – and they *are* all this and all that: it is that they are for the most
> part not by their putative father at all, but by a number of better-known and
> more deservedly reputed authors.

The Union voted by a narrow margin to decline Oscar's gift. But despite the
almost universal criticism of *Poems*, Oscar was not unduly cast down. The book
went through five editions in as many months. It was true, there was no such
thing as bad publicity.

The publication of *Poems* had one unexpected consequence. It brought to an
abrupt – and perhaps not unwelcome – end Oscar's relationship with Frank
Miles. The sexual side of it had probably already died a death, though they
remained friends and continued living together. But Frank's sexual behaviour
was growing increasingly erratic. Perhaps the syphilis that he had already
contracted and that was to kill him ten years later was already beginning to
manifest itself. Frank had started to live dangerously, too dangerously for
Oscar. There was a succession of unpleasant and unsettling incidents. Frank
was blackmailed, almost certainly over an indiscretion with a young man. An
anonymous memoir of Oscar describes Frank's 'terror and misery' at the
blackmail. 'He revealed his trouble to his fellow tenant,' the memoir recorded,
'and Wilde immediately volunteered to do his best to rescue him from his
persecutor.' It was Oscar's first brush with the world of blackmailers and it
would not be his last. On another occasion the police tried to force an entry to
Keats House to arrest Miles on a charge of immorality, probably with a young
boy. Oscar is supposed to have held the police at bay until Frank could escape
over the rooftops and then to have let the police in, glibly explaining that he
thought the police raid was a practical joke and claiming that 'Mr Miles was
travelling on the continent'.

When Frank's father, Canon Miles, read a copy of *Poems* shortly after
publication, he wrote immediately to Oscar expressing his deep concern about
Oscar's continuing friendship with his son:

> If we seem to advise a separation for a time it is not because we do not believe
> you in character to be very different to what you suggest in your poetry, but
> it is because you do not see the risk we see in a published poem which makes
> all who read it say to themselves 'this is outside the pale of poetry', 'it is
> licentious and may do great harm to any soul that reads it'.

Oscar flew into a rage and demanded to know what Frank himself thought.
When Frank weakly agreed with his father, Oscar left the house they shared,
there and then, and moved into rooms in Charles Street in Mayfair. It was the
end of the friendship.

Oscar was far from inconsolable. There had been other young men in his life, like the young actor Norman Forbes-Robertson, to whom he had made overtures early in 1880. 'I don't know if I bored you the other night with my life and its troubles,' Oscar wrote to him:

> There seems something so sympathetic and gentle about your nature, and you have been so charming whenever I have seen you, that I felt somehow that although I knew you only a short time, yet that still I could talk to you about things, which I only talk of to people whom I like – to those whom I count my friends. If you will let me count *you* as one of my friends, it would give a new pleasure to my life.

Norman was attractive, with 'gold hair' and 'rose cheeks'. His was the classic, peaches-and-cream type of English boyish beauty to which Oscar would always be drawn.

There was also the poet James Rennell Rodd, who was four years younger than Oscar. Rodd had been awarded the Newdigate Prize for poetry in 1880, two years after Oscar had won it. Rodd was extremely handsome in a poetic sort of way. 'Nature has given him a poet's face, that thrills to the pathos and passion of his thought,' declared the *Daily Telegraph* after he declaimed his prize-winning poem in the Sheldonian Theatre. Although Oscar had known Rodd slightly at Oxford, their friendship really blossomed in London when Rodd was invited to Salisbury Street for tea and beauties. In the late summer of 1880 they decided to go on a walking tour of France, an idyllic trip which Oscar described to the son of George Lewis, the society solicitor who in due course was to get Oscar and Bosie out of several serious situations with blackmailing servants and outraged fathers:

> I had a very charming time in France and travelled among beautiful vineyards all down the Loire, one of the most wonderful rivers in the world, mirroring from sea to source a hundred cities and five hundred towers. I was with a delightful Oxford friend and, as we did not wish to be known, he travelled under the name of Sir Smith, and I was Lord Robinson.

Oscar and Rodd had a 'richly impassioned friendship' and – for the space of a summer – may have fancied themselves to be in love. Sex may well have entered the romantic equation, almost certainly at Oscar's instigation. But it probably consisted of little more than fervid hand-holding, snatched kisses and bed-sharing in French lodgings with some attendant, fumbling mutual masturbation.

But this was not the whole of Oscar's romantic life. As always, there were two sides to his erotic moon. During these first years in London – at the same time that he was involved in relationships with Frank Miles, Norman Forbes-Robertson and Rennell Rodd – Oscar was also seriously contemplating marriage.

A little in love

'*Men marry because they are tired; women, because they are curious; both are disappointed.*'

Marriage had been on Oscar's mind – if only intermittently – ever since Oxford. Speranza was constantly encouraging both her sons to make what she called 'a good marriage', a marriage with a young woman of fortune and family connections who could help her husband in his chosen career.

Oscar had proposed to at least two young women in the two years since he had left university. The first was Charlotte Montefiore, the sister of his Oxford friend Leonard Montefiore. Leonard died very suddenly in America in September 1879, at the age of twenty-six. Oscar was, he said, 'distressed beyond words' and wrote to Charlotte a few days later:

> I am so glad you are coming to town. I want to see you though the memories you will bring with you will be most bitter. Yet often I think when a friend dies those who are left become very close to one another, just as when an oak falls in the forest the other trees reach out and join branches over the vacant place.

Quite what the nature of Oscar's relationship with Charlotte was at the time of her brother's death is impossible to say. He signed his letter to her 'Your affectionate friend'. They had clearly met, probably on several occasions. Oscar's comments on Charlotte's courage in the face of her bereavement – 'Alfred Milner . . . tells me you are so brave – I knew you would be' – suggest that they knew each other really quite well. Charlotte may have visited Leonard at Oxford – just like the sister of Oscar's friend John Bodley who had spent a happy fortnight sampling the University's social delights and going for picnics and excursions with her brother and Oscar and assorted other undergraduates. Equally, Oscar may well have met Charlotte during a visit to the Montefiore family home.

What is clear from Oscar's letter is that his intentions towards Charlotte involved rather more than being just her affectionate friend. He hoped, he wanted, he aspired to 'become very close' to her, to share her grief for Leonard. 'I want to see you,' he wrote. 'If I called in on Wednesday evening would you see me?' These phrases have the ring of an impatient lover, of a suitor in waiting. A few days later he did call on Charlotte and initiated a discreet courtship of the grieving sister. And early in 1880, he proposed marriage.

Charlotte turned him down. She liked him, she was much attached to him. He was the close friend of her dear, departed brother. They had shared their grief. But she did not love him and therefore could not, would not marry him. It was also clear that he did not love her. During the courtship, Oscar wrote many letters to Charlotte, nearly all of which she later destroyed. In a brief note penned immediately after she had refused his offer, Oscar wrote: 'Charlotte, I am so sorry about your decision. With your money and my brain we could have gone far.' Charlotte Montefiore was almost certainly right to refuse Oscar. The flippancy of his note betrayed the ambition, the cynicism and the flagrantly mercenary motives that lay beneath his proposal.

There was no question of mercenary motives underpinning Oscar's next proposal. Violet Hunt was the captivatingly beautiful daughter of the Pre-Raphaelite landscape painter Alfred Hunt and his wife Margaret Raine Hunt, the popular novelist. In May 1879, Margaret Hunt received an invitation to 'Bellevue', the London home of W.B. Scott and his wife Letitia, to a party given to meet 'a wonderful young Irishman just up from Oxford'. Margaret's response was muted. 'Another of Letitia's young men!' she remarked, but nevertheless she accepted the invitation, taking seventeen-year-old Violet with her. Violet was a perfect Pre-Raphaelite beauty with her abundant auburn hair, large eyes and expressive mouth. 'Out of Botticelli by Burne-Jones' was Ellen Terry's response to Violet's beauty. 'You were a pretty child,' she told Violet. 'You will be a beautiful woman.' Violet had grown up in the company of artists and writers and was precociously confident and articulate. She was already writing fiction and poetry and was studying art at South Kensington Art School.

Oscar and Violet hit it off instantly. 'In ten minutes I was the fashion, wrapt into sudden glory by the fact that Mr Oscar Wilde allowed me to monopolise him for a couple of hours.' They sat together in a window seat which looked out over the Thames where there was hardly room for Violet – just a 'slip of a girl' as she described herself – and the 'big lusty fellow with the wide, white face, the shapely red mouth and the long lock of straight peasant-like black hair that fell across his fine forehead, and which he pushed away now and then with a full poetic gesture.'

Oscar told Violet how he had been to tea the day before with 'The Bernhardt', who had just made her first appearance on a London stage and how she had lain 'on a red couch like a pallid flame'. He recited from memory a sonnet he had written to Ellen Terry in his 'fine, true voice with its exquisite *timbre* and cadence'. Oscar laid flattery on with a trowel: 'Beautiful women like you,' he rather pointedly told Violet, 'hold the fortunes of the world in your hands to make or mar.' Then, bending forwards conspiratorially, he said, 'We will rule the world – you and I – you with your looks and I with my wits.' It was a dazzling performance and Violet was smitten. She went home, dazed and adoring – 'and a little in love to boot'. Oscar, it was clear, was seeking to make the most of his one great capital asset: his intelligence. He wanted to combine forces with Charlotte's money or with Violet's looks. His stated aim was to go far, to rule the world, and he saw a wife as an essential component in his manifest destiny.

For the next two years Oscar saw a great deal of Violet Hunt. On Sunday evenings, more often than not, he would visit the Hunts at their London home, Tor Villa. And Margaret and Violet were earnestly invited to tea with Oscar and Frank Miles at Salisbury Street. Oscar confessed to Margaret that he thought Violet 'the sweetest Violet in England . . . though you must not tell her so'. Violet was in love with Oscar, and Oscar was, according to Violet, 'really in love with me – for the moment and perhaps more than a moment'.

In her published memoirs, Violet says that she 'as nearly as possible escaped the honour of being Mrs Wilde'. Oscar broached the question of marriage obliquely by sending the sweetest Violet 'a single white Eucharist lily without a stalk, reposing on cotton wool in a box, ridiculed by my younger sisters'. Oscar's hesitancy may have been due to financial considerations. The Hunts were not wealthy and there would be no marriage settlement of any substance for her. Oscar's hesitation sealed the matter and his proposal was declined by Alfred Hunt, initially to Violet's chagrin, although she would later begin to see Oscar in a clearer, harder light.

There may have been another element in Alfred Hunt's rejection of Oscar's matrimonial overtures. What he made of Oscar living with Frank Miles, or of Oscar's puzzlingly intense, seemingly romantic friendship with the young poet Rennell Rodd can only be surmised. Speculation and gossip about Oscar were rife. *Punch* had repeatedly caricatured him as effeminate. There was a cloud of suspicion hanging over him, a cloud which Alfred Hunt as an affectionate and protective father surely could not ignore.

It was shortly after his failed bid for Violet Hunt, in the early summer of 1881, that Oscar met the woman who was to become his wife. Constance Mary Lloyd was twenty-three years old. She was tall by the standards of the day, slim and elegant with abundant wavy, auburn hair, piercing violet eyes and fine features. Oscar had met Constance's older brother Otho four years earlier. Although they were contemporaries at Oxford, they met first in Dublin, at the Wilde family home in Merrion Square. Otho Lloyd was staying with his Irish grandmother, 'Mama Mary' Atkinson, who knew the Wildes and encouraged Otho to call. Lady Wilde was probably not yet up. She never received anyone till 5pm, as she hated what she called 'the brutality of strong lights'. So the two young men were alone. According to Otho, 'Oscar . . . gave me a most amusing description of a journey he had recently returned from to Athens and by boat a voyage among the Aegean islands where they encountered a terrific storm with two or three men friends.' Although the two undergraduates subsequently bumped into each other at Oxford, and Oscar invited Otho to call on him at Magdalen College, it was an acquaintance which did not quite ripen into friendship.

Now, four years later, in June 1881, Oscar met Otho's younger sister Constance for the first time. Lady Wilde and her son had been invited to tea at Lancaster Gate, the home of Constance's grandfather, to meet Otho and Constance's aunt who was visiting from Dublin. Constance almost certainly knew more about Oscar than Oscar knew about her. Her great-uncle, Charles Hemphill, who knew Speranza well, had kept the Lloyds up to date on the Wilde family vicissitudes following the death of Sir William and Speranza's move to London two years earlier:

Lady Wilde has sold the Merrion Square house – everything was mortgaged to the hilt, including the country residence of Moytura and the row of houses at Bray – and is gone to launch herself on the great unheeding metropolis across the water. She wants Oscar to enter the Parliament when he settles – he would get in on his mother's name alone, I should think. Willie is living with her in London, but Oscar has taken rooms off the Strand.

Constance had heard stories of Oscar at Oxford from Otho and could not help but be aware also of his burgeoning fame as a 'Professor of Aesthetics', and now as a poet. Oscar's *Poems* were published sometime in June and Constance was evidently nervous at the prospect of meeting such a celebrity. The tea party went well. Oscar was dazzling and Constance was duly dazzled. She wrote to Otho the very next morning:

O.W. came yesterday at about 5.30 (by which time I was shaking with fright!) and stayed for half-an-hour, begged me to come and see his mother again soon, which little request I need hardly say I have kept to myself. I can't help liking him, because when he's talking to me alone he's never a bit affected, and speaks naturally, except that he uses better language than most people.

Constance also divined hidden depths in Oscar at this very first meeting which others could not always see: 'Grandpa, I think, likes Oscar, but of course the others laugh at him, because they don't choose to see anything but that he wears long hair and looks aesthetic.' For his part, Oscar was captivated by the beautiful, intelligent and receptive young woman he met. Her nervous blushes and shyness added to her quiet, modest charm. Ever one to make snap decisions in matters of the heart, Oscar remarked to his mother as they left Lancaster Gate, 'By the by, Mama, I think of marrying that girl.'

That Oscar exercised a fascination for women is beyond dispute. Many young women seemed to fall in love with him on the spot. Violet Hunt fell 'a little in love' with Oscar at their first meeting, as did Laura Troubridge, who confided to her diary how she 'fell awfully in love with him', and 'thought him quite delightful'. Unlike many young men of the period who suffered from stultifying shyness or a paralysing excess of etiquette in the presence of young women, Oscar had the gift of being able to instantly establish a rapport, a conversational intimacy, which allowed him to talk with women rather than to them. As a true son of the revolutionary Speranza, he was an unabashed champion of women's rights and believed women to be every bit as intelligent as men and equally worthy of what she called 'that higher culture and education which has been so tardily and, in some instances, so grudgingly granted to them'. He was charming, sympathetic and funny. He could flatter outrageously, but at the same time intelligently. He could talk knowledgeably about the loveliness of their clothes and wittily about the shortcomings of other people's. He was intimate with famous beauties, infamous mistresses, actresses and all manner of fascinating and deadly women. He could gossip about the Bernhardt and the Jersey Lily. He was a poet who could talk poetically – mesmerisingly even – about art and beauty and life, love and death. He was a literary lion, and the world was beginning to sit up and take notice. It would have been surprising if Constance had not fallen in love with him.

Constance no longer lived with her mother. Her father, Horace Lloyd, had died comparatively young of pulmonary disease when she had just turned sixteen. It was a difficult age for a girl to lose her father, particularly a father whose kindness and love for his daughter counteracted her mother's indifference and sometimes downright hostility. Horace Lloyd had been a successful barrister. His marriage to his Irish cousin, Adele, had been unhappy and, after the birth of Otho and Constance, the couple lived increasingly separate lives. Horace's career in law and his expansive – and expensive – social life in the Prince of Wales's set had kept him away from home, while Adele missed Ireland and made long visits with the children to Mama Mary Atkinson's house in Dublin.

Anyone meeting the quietly assured, beautiful and charming young woman that Constance appeared to be in 1881 might well have been surprised to learn that she had led a deeply unhappy life which would leave her permanently scarred. After Constance's premature death in 1898, Otho wrote:

> There are some lives that are evidently doomed to mistreatment, and hers was one; I doubt if she ever strictly knew what happiness was, at least for any long time together.

Constance's childhood seems to have been desperately, agonisingly unhappy as a result of her mother's mental instability. Adele abused Constance emotionally, and perhaps even physically. Writing privately towards the end of his life, Otho described Constance's childhood and adolescence as 'a tragedy, in consequence of her ill-treatment by her mother who was unfortunately of a very jealous and cruel temper'. His mother, he said, had been 'scarcely responsible' for her outbursts, implying obliquely that Adele was a victim of mental illness. There seems to have been a history of violent, uncontrollable outbursts of temper in the family, and Otho considered that his mother had inherited this terrible defect. He quotes a family tradition that those who suffered from this defect of temper 'were like devils when once roused'.

The presence of Constance's father had, it appears, in some way acted as a brake on the worst excesses of Adele's outbursts. But Horace's death in 1874 left the sixteen-year-old Constance exposed and totally unprotected. Otho was away at boarding school in Bristol and then at university in Oxford, leaving Constance alone and having to shift as best she could with an unstable and unpredictable mother: 'Two women cousins living,' Otho wrote, 'could testify to what she underwent at her mother's hands, especially from the time of her father's death.' And indeed, when Otho's daughter met one of these cousins in 1935, 'she could not say bad enough of my mother'.

Indeed, so appalling was the treatment meted out to Constance that Otho considered it a significant factor in her early death – even more of a factor than the trauma she would experience as the wife of Oscar: 'I shall always think,' he wrote in 1937, 'that her internal tumour was brought about in the first place by what she went through under her mother.' It was Otho who finally took matters into his own hands and decided to rescue Constance from her mother. He went to see his grandfather, John Horatio Lloyd, and demanded – 'at my instance and on my insistence' are the words he used – that he give Constance the protection of his home where Adele could not reach her.

Life with Grandpapa Lloyd was calm and well-regulated. His unmarried daughter, Constance's Aunt Emily, ran his opulent household in Lancaster Gate with extreme efficiency. She was strict with Constance but always scrupulously fair. If she could not love her niece, then she at least tried to protect her and look after her interests. And if there was any resentment at a pretty granddaughter becoming the centre of Grandpapa Lloyd's attention, while she, the spinster daughter, shouldered the generally thankless burden of nursing him, she tried not to show it. Grandpapa Lloyd was an indulgent grandfather and Constance wanted for nothing materially. Otho was a tower of strength, her protector, her champion. And like many children of unhappy and abusive parents, Constance had assuaged her unhappiness by creating close friendships with other adults, notably Georgiana, Lady Mount-Temple whom Constance significantly christened 'Mia Madre'.

Now Constance had found Oscar and the future seemed full of promise. We know very little about the early days of the courtship of Oscar and Constance. After Oscar's precipitate declaration of his intention to 'marry that girl', little seems to have happened. Oscar was busy promoting his *Poems*. No doubt Constance, chaperoned by Otho, attended at least one or two of Speranza's weekly salons in her cramped, darkened drawing room in Park Street, Chelsea. And Oscar almost certainly called again at Lancaster Gate and slowly improved his acquaintance with the family.

The discreet pace of the courtship was dramatically interrupted in September by an unexpected invitation. Five months earlier, Gilbert and Sullivan's operatic satire on Aestheticism, *Patience; or Bunthorne's Bride*, had opened. The 'hero' was the 'fleshly' and effeminate poet Bunthorne, inspired primarily by Swinburne, but with touches of Oscar thrown in for good measure. Bunthorne wears the regulation aesthetic garb of kneebreeches, silk stockings and long hair. He is:

> A most intense young man,
> A soulful-eyed young man,
> An ultra-poetical, super-aesthetical
> Out-of-the-way young man.

The success of *Patience* in London encouraged its producer, Richard D'Oyly Carte, to put on a production in New York which opened in September to rave reviews. New York audiences were fascinated by Bunthorne and wanted to find out more about the movement which *Patience* so brilliantly satirised. D'Oyly Carte and his business partner Colonel Morse decided that if New York could not go to Bunthorne, then Bunthorne must go to New York. On 30 September Oscar received a cable from New York. Would he consider undertaking a lecture tour in the United States with a minimum of fifty lectures? Oscar did not hesitate for a second. 'Yes, if offer good,' he replied.

Nothing but my genius

'Strange that a pair of silk stockings should so upset a nation.'

Oscar set sail for New York on Christmas Eve 1881 and arrived there on 2 January. It was late afternoon when the S.S. *Arizona* dropped anchor and a horde of reporters, unable to wait for him to disembark, travelled by tug to the ship and eagerly clambered aboard to catch their first glimpse of the rare and wonderful English Aesthete. Oscar did not disappoint. He had dressed carefully for the part and appeared in a striking new overcoat. 'His outer garment was a long Ulster, trimmed with two kinds of fur, which reached almost to his feet,' the *New York World* breathlessly reported:

> He wore patent-leather shoes, a smoking-cap or turban, and his shirt might be termed ultra-Byronic, or perhaps *décolleté*. A sky-blue cravat of the sailor style hung well down upon his chest. His hair flowed over his shoulders in dark-brown waves, curling slightly upwards at the end.

Oscar's rather pompous comments on art and Aestheticism were not what the reporters had hoped for, and they were forced to scurry around asking his fellow passengers for suitably utterly-utterly utterances. 'I am not exactly pleased with the Atlantic,' he is supposed to have remarked mid-voyage. 'It is not so majestic, or even as large, as I expected.' Apocryphal or not, the newspapers lapped it up: 'Mr Wilde disappointed with the Atlantic', the headlines blared. Thankfully, the newspapers did not print the comments of the captain of the *Arizona* who, like so many other men, had taken an immediate and visceral dislike to Oscar. 'I wish I had that man lashed to the bowsprit on the windward side,' he had said during the voyage.

When he was asked by US Customs officials if he had anything to declare, Oscar is supposed to have proclaimed in ringing tones, 'Nothing. I have nothing to declare but my genius,' but even Oscar was surprised at the extraordinary and intense level of interest he generated. He was fêted wherever he went, and his every utterance on art and life was dutifully scribbled down by the reporters who dogged his footsteps. By sustained and determined feats of self-publicity, Oscar had achieved a degree of mild notoriety in London which had helped him to scratch a precarious living from writing. But in New

York he found that he was not only famous, he was also – for the first time in his life – rich. It was a delightful sensation. Two weeks after his arrival, he wrote in great good humour to his friend Mrs George Lewis to announce that he was being treated like royalty wherever he went:

I stand at the top of reception rooms when I go out, and for two hours they defile past for introduction. I bow gracefully and sometimes honour them with a royal observation, which appears next day in all the newspapers. When I go to the theatre the manager bows me in with lighted candles and the audience rise. Yesterday I had to leave by a private door, the mob was so great. Loving virtuous obscurity as much as I do, you can judge how much I dislike this lionising, which is worse than that given to Sarah Bernhardt I hear.

Oscar gave his first lecture at New York's Chickering Hall exactly a week after his arrival. The night before, he attended a performance of *Patience* at the Standard Theatre, arrayed in a black velvet suit with kneebreeches, set off by a scarlet silk handkerchief. His costume was almost identical to that worn by Bunthorne the poet prancing on stage below, but Oscar seemed not to mind, merely remarking to his companions, 'Caricature is the tribute which mediocrity pays to genius.' Chickering Hall was a sell-out. At eight o'clock a placard announcing 'Standing Room Only' was placed outside, but the queues still grew. Inside there was a buzz of anticipation. New York was waiting to be dazzled. But New York was disappointed. Oscar's first attempt at a public lecture was received in stony silence. His subject was 'The English Renaissance of Art', but there was nothing artistic about Oscar's delivery. It was stiff and formal, and his voice struck many of those present as 'sepulchral'. Despite his external bravado, Oscar was extremely nervous. None of his warmth and wit shone through. It was a mistake he very quickly rectified, ruthlessly pruning the lecture by a quarter, making the content less theoretical and the language less grandiloquent. And as his confidence grew, Oscar's delivery became more relaxed and more assured.

Despite the general lionisation of Oscar, there were plenty of dissenting voices, and there were many sly, and not so sly, digs at him. He was variously described as 'maidenly', 'girlish' and 'womanish'. The *New York Times* called him a 'mamma's boy', and spoke of his 'affected effeminacy', while the *Newark Daily Advertiser* described his eyebrows as 'neat, delicate and arched, and of the sort coveted by women'. The *Boston Evening Transcript* was moved to verse:

> Is he manne, or woman, or childe?
> Either,
> and neither!
> She looks as much like a manne
> As ever shee canne;
> He looks more like a woman
> Than any feminine human.

Matters were not helped when Oscar's friend from Oxford, John Bodley, mounted an unexpected and vicious attack in the *New York Times* on 21 January, in which he described Oscar as 'epicene'. Henry James spoke of Oscar as a 'fatuous fool', 'a tenth-rate card' and 'an unclean beast', while James's friend and correspondent, Mrs Henry Adams, said that Oscar's sex was 'undecided'. When Oscar paid a visit to New York's Century Club, some members refused point blank to meet him. 'Where is *she*?' another member demanded to know. 'Well, why not say "she"? I understand she's a "Charlotte Ann".' A 'Charlotte Ann' was the American slang term for an effeminate sodomite, the equivalent of a 'Mary Ann' in England.

There were those who saw, or claimed they saw, New York's sexual underground – the city's 'Charlotte Anns' and 'Miss Nancys' – rallying to Oscar's banner. On the day after his arrival in New York, the *Brooklyn Daily Eagle* predicted that Oscar – 'the pallid and lank young man' – will find 'in the great metropolis (any fair day on Fifth Avenue) a school of gilded youths eager to embrace his peculiar tenets'. The use of the word 'embrace' was calculated to suggest sexual contact.

On the night of Oscar's lecture in Chickering Hall, the reporter for the New York *Tribune* observed 'many pallid and aesthetic young men in dress suits and banged hair' leaning 'in medieval attitudes against the wall'. His meaning was clear. 'Banged hair' was a way of dressing the hair and usually consisted of a deep fringe, with longer ringlets, waves or plaits on either side. Only women wore their hair in bangs. Towards the end of the month, the *Washington Post* spoke of Oscar in the same breath as the 'young men painting their faces . . . with unmistakable rouge on their cheeks'. New York had a thriving sub-culture of men who loved men. Greenwich Village was renowned as a resort of male prostitutes. And eighteen years after Oscar visited New York, a committee investigating the goings on at Paresis Hall on the Bowery recorded that the men there:

> act effeminately; most of them are painted and powdered, they are called Princess this and Lady So and So and the Duchess of Marlboro, and get up and sing as women, and dance; ape the female character; call each other sisters and take people out for immoral purposes.

Oscar's aesthetic costume and long hair were hardly designed to emphasise his vigorous masculinity. But the hostile press reports were not simply a case of smoke and no fire. Oscar was, it seems, indiscreet and incautious about his sexual tastes almost from the day he set foot in New York. On 8 January, he wrote an unguarded note to the politician and *bon vivant* Robert Barnwell Roosevelt to thank him for a hand-delivered message of welcome. 'What a little Ganymede you have sent me as your herald!' Oscar wrote. 'The prettiest thing I have yet seen in America.' In Greek mythology, Ganymede was the beautiful shepherd boy abducted and anally raped by Zeus in the form an eagle. Oscar's comments proclaimed an interest in Greek love that went far beyond the theoretical.

Oscar desperately wanted to meet Walt Whitman, whom he and many others considered to be America's greatest living poet. Oscar claimed that he had been weaned on Whitman. He had, he told a reporter from the *Philadelphia Press*, 'absorbed the Whitmanesque poetry from boyhood', when Lady Wilde used to read his poems aloud. Oscar also said that he and other 'Oxford boys' would bring Whitman's poems with them on their 'rambles' and read them to each other.

There was another, more compelling, reason behind Oscar's eagerness to meet Walt Whitman. Whitman's poetry spoke of the potency of friendship and love between men, particularly between working-class men, and positively oozed homoeroticism. Indeed, the 'Calamus' section of Whitman's great poetic cycle *Leaves of Grass* was so intensely homoerotic that it gave rise to the short-lived term 'calamite' to denote a man who loved men. Swinburne was to denounce 'the cult of the calamus' and 'calamites'. Whitman had a vision of what he called 'adhesiveness' between men, of a 'high towering love of comrades', which was somehow separate from and more noble than the love between men and women.

Men like John Addington Symonds and the socialist poet and writer Edward Carpenter, who were ardent campaigners for the social and legal emancipation of men who loved men, saw Whitman as a great prophet of a new erotic world order. 'The chief value of his work is in its prophecy, not in its performance,' Oscar was later to write of Whitman. 'He has begun a prelude to larger themes. He is the herald of a new era. As a man he is the precursor of a fresh type.' One or two 'Whitmanite fellowships' had already sprung up in the North of England, the first, cautious coming together of men – and a few women – to discuss male love. Symonds in particular had become obsessed with Whitman's poetry. He instituted a long correspondence with Whitman, probing him as to the exact nature of the 'manly love of comrades' he spoke about, but Whitman's replies were invariably and maddeningly evasive. Oscar and Symonds can hardly have failed to discuss Whitman in their correspondence before Oscar departed for America. Oscar was as intrigued as Symonds about Whitman's sexual tastes. 'There is something so Greek and sane about his poetry,' Oscar told the *Philadelphia Press*.

Oscar was indebted to the Philadelphia publisher Joseph Marshall Stoddart, who owned the US publishing rights to the Gilbert and Sullivan operas, for his meeting with Whitman. Stoddart befriended Oscar and may have been sympathetic to – and perhaps even shared – his sexual tastes. 'Oscar Wilde has expressed his great desire to meet you socially,' Stoddart wrote to Whitman:

> He will dine with me Saturday afternoon when I shall be most happy to have you join us. The bearer, Mr. Wanier, will explain at greater length any details which you may wish to know, and will be happy to bring me your acquiescence.

Whitman at first declined to meet Oscar, sending him instead his 'hearty

31

salutations and American welcome'. But he changed his mind after reading Oscar's admiring comments in the *Philadelphia Press* on 17 January, sending a note to Stoddart the next day. 'Walt Whitman will be in from two till three-thirty this afternoon, and will be most happy to see Mr Wilde and Mr Stoddart.'

The meeting at Whitman's untidy house in Camden, New Jersey was a roaring success. Oscar was suitably humble in the presence of Whitman, greeting him with the words, 'I have come to you as to one with whom I have been acquainted almost from the cradle.' The contrast between the two poets could not have been more marked. Oscar was young, tall, slender and clean shaven. Whitman was in his early sixties, but looked much older. He was shorter than Oscar and wore a long, bushy white beard. Oscar was highly educated, cultivated and still in his languid Aesthetic phase. Whitman was self-taught, and robustly masculine in manner.

Stoddart tactfully left the two poets alone. 'If you are willing – will excuse me – I will go off for an hour or so – come back again – leaving you together,' he said. 'We would be glad to have you stay,' Whitman replied. 'But do not feel to come back in an hour. Don't come for two or three.' Whitman opened a bottle of elderberry wine and he and Oscar drank it all before Whitman suggested they go upstairs to his 'den' on the third floor where, he told Oscar, 'We could be on "thee and thou" terms.' Whitman gave a detailed account of the meeting to a reporter from the *Philadelphia Press* the next day. 'We had a jolly good time,' he said. 'I think he was glad to get away from lecturing and fashionable society, and spend some time with an old rough':

> One of the first things I said was that I should call him 'Oscar.' 'I like that so much,' he answered, laying his hand on my knee. He seemed to me like a great big, splendid boy. He is so frank, and outspoken, and manly. I don't see why such mocking things are written of him.

They talked for two or three hours. Oscar had brought 'cordial messages' for Whitman from several English poets, almost certainly including John Addington Symonds. The mention of Symonds's name turned the conversation to love and sex with young men. Years later Stoddart was quoted as saying that:

> Everyone who knew Whitman even slightly was certain that he had these tastes and that, in free conversation with intimate friends, the poet did not trouble to conceal his liking for handsome youths.

Stoddart went on to say that 'after embracing, greeting each other as "Oscar" and "Walt", the two talked of nothing but pretty boys, of how insipid was the love of women, and of what other poets, Swinburne in particular, had to say about these tastes'. Stoddart's reminiscences accord with Oscar's later account of the meeting to his friend, George Ives. According to the voluminous diaries of Ives, Whitman told Oscar that he refused to answer Symonds's questions about his sexual inclinations because 'he just resented Symonds's curiosity and the way he put his questions'. Oscar told Ives that there was 'no doubt' about Whitman's sexual tastes. 'I have the kiss of Walt Whitman still on my lips,' he boasted.

Oscar's friendship with Stoddart took root and blossomed, and seven years later the publisher would commission Oscar to write his only novel, *The Picture of Dorian Gray*. But in Philadelphia, Oscar had a more immediate concern. Before leaving London, he had offered to look for a publisher in America for Rennell Rodd's first volume of poetry, *Songs in the South*. The book had been first published in England in a small edition in 1881 when Rodd had inscribed Oscar's copy with a prophetic verse in Italian:

> Unto thy martyrdom, eager and bold
> That crowd will gather to thine agony;
> Thee on thy cross they'll hasten to behold
> And of them all, not one will pity thee.

Oscar persuaded Stoddart to publish Rodd's poems under a new title of his own devising, *Rose Leaf and Apple Leaf*. Without consulting Rodd and much to his embarrassment, Oscar added an explicitly homoerotic dedication to himself: 'To Oscar Wilde – "Heart's Brother" – These few songs and many songs to come'. He added insult to injury by writing a lengthy introduction – an *Envoi* – to the poems which sailed dangerously close to the wind. It was a very public declaration of love: 'There is none whose love of art is more flawless,' he wrote of Rodd, 'none indeed who is dearer to myself.'

Back in London, Rodd was appalled. His career in the Diplomatic Service was in jeopardy. He wrote immediately to Stoddart saying the inscription was 'too effusive' and asking him to halt the distribution of the poems. But he was too late. The book was already in circulation. The *Saturday Review* in London mercilessly mocked Rodd and paraphrased the *Envoi* to suggest that Rodd was Oscar's lover:

> Among the 'many young men' who follow Mr Wilde, 'none is dearer to myself' than the beloved of Mr Wilde and of the Muses, Mr Rodd.

Swinburne immediately wrote maliciously to Theodore Watts-Dunton. 'Have you read the *Saturday* on Oscar Wilde's young man,' he asked, 'the Hephaestion of that all-conquering Alexander?' The reference to Hephaestion and Alexander was carefully and precisely meditated. Hephaestion was reputedly Alexander the Great's lover and catamite.

The relationship between the two poets, which had begun so well, now soured. Rodd chose social acceptability and his career as a diplomat. Later, when Oscar returned from America, Rodd would write to him to finish their friendship. 'My friends criticised the ascendancy which he began to exercise,' he recalled long afterwards, in a coded repudiation of the dominant love affair of his youth. But to Oscar, Rodd would always be 'the true poet and the false friend'.

In mid-February, Oscar delivered two lectures at the Central Music Hall in Chicago. Among his audience was John Donoghue, a penniless young sculptor. Donoghue later wrote to Oscar. His letter is lost, but whatever he said was sufficient to persuade Oscar to call on him at his studio. Oscar found an extraordinarily handsome young Irish-American sculptor with piercing blue eyes. Donoghue specialised in carving bas-reliefs in the style of ancient Greek sculpture. It is likely that Donoghue was Greek in another sense. Oscar was thrilled with his discovery and took up John Donoghue's cause, sending a photograph of one of Donoghue's sculptures to Charles Eliot Norton in an effort to win a commission. 'I send you the young Greek: a photograph of him,' he wrote. 'The young sculptor's name is John Donoghue: Pure Celt is he':

I feel sure he could do any of your young athletes, and what an era in art that would be to have the sculptor back in the palestra, and of much service too to those who separate athletics from culture, and forget the right ideal of the beautiful and healthy mind in a beautiful and healthy body.

In his lectures, Oscar praised Donoghue's work to such an extent that his fortunes took a spectacular turn for the better. The friendship with Donoghue endured, and Oscar met him two years later in Paris where he bought from him what Constance described as 'a lovely bas-relief . . . a nude figure full profile of a boy playing a harp, perfectly simple and quite exquisite in line and expression'.

Oscar crossed and re-crossed the United States for ten months, even venturing into Canada. He delivered nearly 150 lectures and was seen and heard by tens of thousands of Americans. By the time his tour ended in October he had become an accomplished and compelling lecturer. He spent the last weeks of his year in America in New York, trying to get *Vera, or the Nihilists* produced, a drama – almost a melodrama – about love and death among Russian anarchists, which he had written the previous year in London. And he also signed a contract with the actress Mary Anderson for a New York production of a new play he had begun during his travels, *The Duchess of Padua*. Oscar was back in New York in time to greet Lillie Langtry's arrival with an armful of lilies. She had come to make her début on the American stage, and Oscar was her guide and escort in the city.

Oscar was the victim of a curious and unsettling incident at this time. He was walking up Fifth Avenue late one morning when he was accosted 'by a thin-faced youth' who introduced himself as the son of a financier, Anthony J. Drexel, whom Oscar had met. Accounts of the incident are sketchy, but it appears that Oscar immediately invited the young man to lunch, over which he announced that he had won a lottery prize and asked Oscar to go with him to collect it. The youth took Oscar to a house where illegal dice games were going on. Oscar apparently started gambling and had soon written cheques for the enormous sum of $1,200. Realising afterwards that he had been fleeced, Oscar went to the bank to put a stop on the cheques and then went to the police.

It is quite possible that there was more to this incident than meets the eye. Fifth Avenue was the acknowledged haunt of male prostitutes, and the description of the youth as 'thin-faced' immediately conjures up images of the pallid and lank young men who frequented Oscar's lectures. The 'thin-faced youth' could easily have been one of the scores of 'gilded youths' earning a living from prostitution and blackmail. It was certainly odd that Oscar should not be able to differentiate between the scion of a fabulously wealthy banking family and a cheap confidence trickster. And it was odder still that Oscar should invite the young man to lunch, let alone go off with him afterwards to an unknown destination. Was it in reality a pick-up in Fifth Avenue, and had Oscar gone to the young man's rooms expecting, perhaps even getting, sex, only to be threatened with exposure unless he paid up there and then? It was a common enough trap for men to fall into. If there was a sexual dimension to the incident, then it marked the first of many occasions when Oscar would fall victim to crimes associated with his sexual tastes.

A few days later, Oscar boarded the S.S. *Bothnia* bound for England. He was ready to go home. He had been away from London for a year and was beginning to miss his family and his friends. The first giddying days of fame and fortune were over. Audiences for his lectures had dwindled dramatically in the last few months of his tour, and he was no longer the young lion of New York. 'America is a land of unmatched vitality and vulgarity,' he said later, and Americans 'a people who care not at all about values other than their own and, who, when they make up their minds, love you and hate you with a passionate zeal.' It was time to make a graceful exit from the New World and return to pick up the scattered threads of his life in the Old.

Freedom from sordid care

'The proper basis for marriage is a mutual misunderstanding.'

Constance was certainly one of the scattered threads that Oscar was anxious to weave back into his life. Though no letters between them survive, it is possible, perhaps probable, that they wrote to each other and that the courtship, if such a slow and ceremonial procedure could be called a courtship, continued across the Atlantic.

Throughout 1882, Constance could only wait patiently in London for Oscar to return. She must have been in a flurry of anxiety in July 1882 when reports filtered back to the London newspapers of his supposed engagement to a Miss Howe, the daughter of his friend and champion in the United States, Julia Ward Howe. Speranza wrote to Oscar immediately. 'Are you in love?' she demanded. 'Why don't you take a bride? Miss Howe was given to you by all the papers here.' Violet Hunt confided to her diary, a little ruefully, the rumour of an engagement to 'Miss Ward Howe, with a million of money'. Oscar promptly denied the rumour.

In December, anticipating Oscar's imminent return, Constance prompted her uncle, Charles Hemphill, to call on Lady Wilde. Constance may perhaps have felt unsettled by the rumours of Oscar's romantic attachments and engagements and wanted Uncle Charles to enquire discreetly how the land lay – and perhaps convey that she was still interested in Oscar. Uncle Charles despatched his errand with great tact and 'praised Constance immensely' to Lady Wilde who reciprocated by dropping heavy hints that she would be in favour of the match. She dutifully reported back to Oscar:

> I had nearly in mind to say I would like her for a daughter-in-law, but I did not. It was Constance told him where we lived. I thought the visit looked encouraging. He said you were quite a celebrity now.

Oscar was in London for just three weeks after his return from New York in January 1883, before he went to Paris for three months. He called at Lancaster

Gate at least once to re-establish his relationship with Constance. A month later, on 28 February, Constance and Otho were at Speranza's salon, whose eccentricities Otho described to his fiancée, Nellie Hutchinson:

I think she would kill you with laughing. I came away not quite certain whether I liked her or not. In appearance she is an enormous woman with a face like the face of an eagle and she talks like a book . . . what a talk we all had afterwards about the Irish though Lady Wilde would speak of little else than her son Oscar, whom she calls As-car.

After civilising America, Oscar had set his sights on conquering Paris. He arrived there towards the end of January, determined to use the money he had earned in America to keep him while he finished *The Duchess of Padua*. Oscar lived the writer's life in Paris, taking rooms in the Hôtel Voltaire, in the city's literary quarter. He turned down an invitation to visit his mother's friend Clarisse Moore in Rome. 'At present I am deep in literary work and cannot stir from my little rooms over the Seine till I have finished two plays,' he wrote:

This sounds ambitious, but we live in an age of inordinate personal ambition and I am determined that the world shall understand me, so I will now, along with my art work, devote to the drama a great deal of my time.

Oscar succeeded in finishing the play and had enough time to spare to look about him and crash the Parisian literary scene. He sent copies of his *Poems* to several well-known writers and arbiters of literary taste, accompanied by charming notes begging them to accept 'mes premières fleurs de poésies'. The diarist Edmond de Goncourt was among those to receive a copy. The two men met a few days later and de Goncourt recorded in his journal how Oscar had mounted an astonishing attack on Swinburne for deliberately posing as a sodomite and a pederast, when he was, in fact, no such thing. When de Goncourt met Oscar at a dinner a few days later, he described him scathingly as '*cet individu au sexe douteux, au langage de cabotin, aux récits blagueurs*' – 'this individual of doubtful sex, with the language of a third-rate actor, full of tall stories'.

It was during this stay in Paris that Oscar first met Robert Sherard, who was to become one of his great friends and champions and would eventually write several partisan accounts of Oscar's life and times. Sherard was a great-grandson of William Wordsworth and, like Oscar, had gone to Paris to find literary fame and fortune. He wrote poetry and dabbled, not very successfully, in journalism. But he was young, with longish blond hair – 'honey-coloured', Oscar called it – and he was passionate about life and literature. Oscar was instantly attracted to him, though nothing seems to have ever come of the attraction. Sherard was a red-blooded heterosexual with a penchant for prostitutes, the younger the better. Some years later, the French writer Pierre Louÿs described a night on the tiles with Sherard which culminated in a dawn breakfast of oysters and bacon with two sixteen–year–old prostitutes who had 'suppurating syphilitic sores the size of walnuts'.

Sherard felt uncomfortable when Oscar used to greet him with a kiss on the lips and disliked Oscar's use of Christian names. But they spent the greater part of every day together for almost two months and Oscar would recall fondly their 'moonlit meanderings' and 'sunset strolls'. He was enormously flattered when Sherard asked if he would accept the dedication of his forthcoming volume of poetry. 'How could I refuse a gift so musical in its beauty and fashioned by one whom I love so much as I love you?' Oscar replied extravagantly. Sherard was not so much devoted to Oscar as obsessed by him. It was an obsession that was to last to the end of his life. At the time of Oscar's trials, Sherard found it almost impossible to accept that Oscar was indeed guilty of the crimes he was charged with. And during Oscar's imprisonment, Sherard sought to drive a wedge between Oscar and Bosie so that he could bring about a reconciliation between Oscar and Constance.

Sherard did record Oscar's single encounter with a female prostitute in Paris. Oscar announced one evening that 'Priapus was calling' and left Sherard to visit the Eden, a notorious music hall where he met the famous demi-mondaine Marie Aguétant, whose lover later slit her throat as she bestrode him during sex. 'What animals we all are, Robert!' Oscar remarked to Sherard the next morning. Sherard – himself a regular patron of prostitutes – was only surprised that Oscar used prostitutes so rarely: 'The only reflection I made to myself on the morning when I heard of the Eden episode was to wonder how a well-fed, well-wined, full-blooded man as Oscar was at 29 could so control himself as to restrict his sexual contacts to once in 42 days.'

Oscar returned to London in early May, his flowing locks shorn and replaced by artificial curls in the style of Nero. Laura Troubridge, who had once been an admirer of Oscar's, confided spitefully to her diary:

> He is grown enormously fat, with a huge face and tight curls all over his head – not at all the aesthetic he used to look. He was very amusing and talked cleverly, but it was all monologue and not conversation. He is vulgar, I think, and lolls about in, I suppose, poetic attitudes with crumpled shirt cuffs turned back over his coat sleeves!

Richard Le Gallienne, an aspiring poet from Birkenhead, paints an even more unflattering portrait of Oscar at this time:

> His amber-coloured hair, naturally straight, was not very long, and was unashamedly curled and massively modelled to his head, somewhat suggesting a wig. His large figure, with his big loose face, grossly jawed with thick, sensuous lips, and a certain fat effeminacy about him, suggested a sort of caricature Dionysius disguised as a rather heavy dandy of the Regency period.

At Oscar's prompting, Constance and Otho were invited to Lady Wilde's salon on 16 May. If Constance was at all taken aback by Oscar's artificial curls and crumpled cuffs, she did not show it. The frequency of their meetings increased dramatically. In May, Otho was writing to Nellie:

> You will think that we must be becoming very intimate with the Wildes, when I tell you that we have been to their house again today, Constance and I . . . Oscar Wilde had a long talk with Constance; it was of art, as usual, and of scenery, he so amused me when he called Switzerland 'that dreadful place, Switzerland, so vulgar with its ugly big mountains, all black and white, like an enormous photograph'.

The next month, Oscar and Lady Wilde were invited for an afternoon at home at Lancaster Gate. There were sixty people there, and Oscar spent the entire time talking to Constance. Otho was sceptical: 'I don't believe that he means anything; that is his way with all girls whom he finds interesting,' he told Nellie. 'Constance told me afterwards that they had not agreed upon a single subject.'

Otho still doubted whether Oscar was in love with Constance. He had observed that 'wherever she went, there followed he, and when he could not approach her then with his eyes he followed her'. Otho admitted there was smoke. But was there any fire? 'If the man were anyone else but Oscar Wilde,' he told Nellie, 'one might conclude that he was in love.' Otho had known Oscar for six years, not well, but sufficiently well perhaps to suspect Oscar of playing at being in love, of going through the romantic motions. He had seen Oscar do it several times before.

Otho thought – and perhaps even hoped – that Oscar found Constance interesting, nothing more. There is an undertow of anxiety in his letters to Nellie. He was very protective of Constance. He had rescued her from their mother's abusive clutches and they had forged an unusually close relationship. Otho was concerned because he knew that behind the facade of a well-educated, intelligent and articulate young woman, Constance was scarred, vulnerable. And Otho could not help but be aware of Oscar's reputation. When he read Oscar's *Poems*, he must, as a classical scholar, have realised that they positively oozed homoerotic sentiments. He must have known how Oscar was pilloried in *Punch*, and how Henry Labouchère, the radical MP and journalist who was destined to play a more insidious role in Oscar's life, had recently called Wilde 'an epicene youth' and 'an effeminate phrasemaker'. And no doubt Otho was aware of some of the ugly rumours about Oscar that had begun in Oxford and still clung to him.

At the end of June, Otho, Constance and Oscar attended a reception for advocates of women's rights where Constance remarked: 'You know everybody says, Mr Wilde, that you do not really mean half of what you say.' Oscar's response was to guffaw with laughter. The courtship was again interrupted by Oscar's return to America in August to supervise the first production of *Vera, or the Nihilists*. The play flopped in New York, running for just a week, and Oscar returned to England in early September. He had asked Constance to read *Vera* which she promised to do. She wrote to Oscar:

> I am afraid you and I disagree in our opinions on art for I hold there is no perfect art without perfect morality, whilst you say they are distinct and separable things, and of course you have your knowledge to combat my ignorance with.

Art and morality. It was a fundamental, unbridgeable chasm between their world views. Constance cleaved to a world ordered by laws and morals, a world in which goodness, decency, justice and virtue prevailed. Oscar was anarchic, questing, questioning. He wanted to push at the boundaries of acceptable art and acceptable morality, eventually embracing and exploring criminality.

But all this lay in the future. For the present, Oscar was intent on courtship. On Wednesday 21 November, Oscar arrived in Dublin and was welcomed like a conquering hero returning to the city of his birth. He was there for three days and very busy. He was to give two lectures – 'Impressions of America' and 'The House Beautiful' – to recite his poems and to take part in a debate with the Fellows of Trinity College. Constance had so arranged things that she too was in Dublin, staying with Mama Mary Atkinson in Ely Place. She had written to Oscar earlier that month saying, 'I told the Atkinsons that you would be here some time soon and they will be very pleased to see you.' On Thursday, Constance and her cousins, Stanhope and Eliza, left a note at Oscar's hotel asking him to drop in that evening which he duly did. Oscar, 'though decidedly extra affected, I suppose partly from nervousness,' Constance told Otho, 'made himself very pleasant.' She dismissed Stanhope's chaffings about romance with Oscar. 'Such stupid nonsense,' she said.

But it was not stupid nonsense. Three days later Oscar and Constance were engaged to be married. 'Prepare yourself for an astounding piece of news!' Constance wrote to Otho. 'I am engaged to Oscar Wilde and perfectly and insanely happy.' It was to be one of the very rare instances of perfect happiness in Constance's life. Oscar and Constance were alone in the drawing room at Ely Place, a situation no doubt deliberately choreographed by Mama Mary Atkinson, who was fully aware of what was about to take place. Constance was playing the piano, the very same piano that her mother had been playing when her father had proposed thirty years earlier.

Otho might well be astounded, but if Constance feigned surprise at Oscar's proposal, she was being disingenuous. Ever since meeting him two and a half years earlier, she had been in love with him and wanted to marry him. She told Otho she had been 'shaking with fright' even before she met Oscar for the very first time, which suggests that she was a little in love with the idea of being in love with the famous Oscar. She had already turned down 'three good proposals', much to the indignation of her Irish aunts.

Constance anticipated some difficulties over the engagement. Otho, she knew, liked Oscar, and 'Grandpapa will, I know, be nice, as he is always so pleased to see Oscar,' she wrote. 'The only one I am afraid of is Aunt Emily.' Otho was instructed to use his charm with Aunt Emily and 'make it all right'. Constance was also concerned about how her mother and stepfather, as well as other relatives, might react to the news: 'I am so dreadfully nervous over my family; they are so cold and practical.' But whatever difficulties there might be, Constance's determination to marry Oscar revealed a steely side to her character: 'I won't stand opposition,' she told Otho, 'so I hope they won't try it.' And remarkably nobody did.

Otho did his work well. Grandpapa Lloyd expressed his approbation of the match. He was still too ill to write to Oscar personally, so Aunt Emily had to be his amanuensis. Five days after the proposal, Oscar received what was, for Aunt Emily, a cordial reply. 'My father,' she wrote, 'desires me to say that he can have no objection to you personally as a husband for Constance. He believes that you and she are well-suited to each other.' Constance's happiness, Aunt Emily continued, was Grandpapa Lloyd's 'first consideration'. Above all, Grandpapa Lloyd wanted to protect his favourite granddaughter from any further abuse or cruelty. In an age where appalling cruelties were not only perpetrated upon women by their husbands, but also tolerated by society, Grandpapa Lloyd wanted a husband who would be a friend and companion for Constance; a husband, who, though he might break the mould of starchy, unbending, domineering Victorian maleness, would prize Constance's gentleness and love her for her vulnerabilities as much as for her strengths. Crucially, Grandpapa Lloyd, Aunt Emily told Oscar, 'has confidence in you that you will treat her kindly'.

Lady Wilde was ecstatic at the news: 'I am intensely pleased at your note of this morning,' she wrote to Oscar. 'You have both been true and constant and a blessing will come on all true feeling.' Speranza had bright visions of the future: 'What endless vistas of speculation open out,' she exclaimed. 'What will you do in life? Where live? I would like you to have a small house in London and live the literary life and teach Constance to correct proofs and eventually go into Parliament.'

Once the engagement had been agreed in principle, there were the financial details to go into. Oscar did not have a penny to his name. He had come back from America with a relatively large amount of cash, but it had all been frittered away in Paris. In fact, he was heavily in debt. He owed a moneylender called Edwin Levy who lived in Hastings at least £1,200, and almost certainly had other debts to his name. To be sure, he was earning good money – 'growing quite rich', he boasted to Lillie Langtry – by travelling the length and breadth of Britain 'civilising the provinces by my remarkable lectures'. But he needed money, a regular, unfluctuating, stable flow of money to enable him to write. 'The best work in literature,' he told an aspiring young writer:

is always done by those who do not depend upon it for their daily bread, and the highest form of literature, poetry, brings no wealth to the singer. For producing your best work also you will require some leisure and freedom from sordid care.

Needless to say, there were those who saw Oscar's marriage as a manoeuvre to earn him a respite him from sordid financial care. After all, his courtship of Charlotte Montefiore, his waverings over Violet Hunt and the rumours of engagements to wealthy women hardly induced his critics to see his marriage to Constance as a love match. At the time she met Oscar, Constance had an income of £250 a year, a generous sum for a young woman. Under the terms of Grandpapa Lloyd's will, she would receive around £800 a year after his death, not exactly a fortune, but a very considerable income and more than sufficient on which to live very comfortably. Additionally, Constance was to receive a dowry of £5,000 from her share of the capital, enough to set up house. Violet Hunt was scathing when she heard of Oscar's engagement to Constance: 'I hear that Oscar's fiancée only has £400 a year instead of £800,' she wrote in her diary. 'I expect to hear of that engagement being broken off.' Violet's venom is understandable. As someone who had 'as nearly as possible escaped the honour of becoming Mrs Wilde' because of her lack of money, she could be forgiven for assuming that Oscar was a fortune-hunter.

But by the standards of his time, Oscar could not be said to have married purely for money. If he had wanted great wealth, he could have found it. He was already famous and had proved himself capable of earning large sums of money from lecturing – and rather smaller ones from writing. He was the companion and confidant of famous and beautiful women. Many women found him irresistibly fascinating. There were richer pickings to be found in England or, for that matter, America.

Nevertheless, money was a natural, normal and important consideration in any marriage. When Oscar and Constance became engaged, the marriage contract had hardly changed since the time of Jane Austen. Women of the middle classes and above were expected to come to the marriage state with some sort of dowry, and if there was an income, then so much the better. In Oscar's play *An Ideal Husband*, Lord Caversham tells his son that marriage 'is not a matter for affection', as 'there is property at stake'. And when, in *The Importance of Being Earnest*, Lady Bracknell discovers that Cecily is wealthy, she suddenly perceives her desirability as a wife for Algernon: 'A hundred and thirty thousand pounds! And in the Funds! Miss Cardew seems to me a most attractive young lady, now that I look at her.' There was love and there was money. And when there was both, happiness, it was generally agreed, was assured. Speranza was matter of fact about Constance's money: 'a very nice, pretty, sensible girl – well connected and well brought up – and a good fortune, about £1,000 a year'.

When Grandpapa Lloyd enquired into Oscar's finances, Oscar was admirably frank. He admitted to his debts and claimed that he had managed to pay off about £300 of them from his lecture fees. Cautious Grandpapa Lloyd was alarmed. 'What causes him some uneasiness,' Aunt Emily wrote to Oscar, 'is yr debts, for tho' the amount is not excessive it would be a considerable burden upon your income for some time to come.' Grandpapa Lloyd wanted to delay the marriage until Oscar had managed to clear another £300 worth of debt. Oscar's reaction verged on the flippant. 'He had an interview in chambers with Mr Hargrove, the family lawyer,' Otho recalled:

> Pressèd as to his ability to pay, Oscar replied that he could hold out no promise 'but I would write you a sonnet, if you think that would be of any help'.

Things had reached an impasse, and Oscar decided to broach the subject of money with Constance. To Oscar's surprise, she refused even to discuss the matter. Aunt Emily sought to explain Constance's behaviour. 'I think it likely that she put you off when you wanted to speak of it because she did not wish to appear to attach too much importance to the question of money,' she wrote, 'and she certainly would not wish to give you up because yr income was small.' Without a trace of irony, Oscar – whose habits of extravagance were already well-developed – set about impressing upon Constance the importance of careful housekeeping and restraint when they were married. Aunt Emily quite agreed. Constance, she said, 'should be made to understand what the income that you will have will enable her to do, and that she will require to practise some economy and self-denial'.

Oscar offered Constance love, companionship and a family of her own in the creation of the Aesthetic House Beautiful. He offered her status as the wife of a poet, a playwright and a man of letters. Oscar also offered her security and safety, commodities which had been in short supply in her life and which looked as if they might be in short supply again. Despite the tranquillity and opulence of Lancaster Gate, where life proceeded in a predictable and well-regulated fashion, Constance craved more. She wanted a home of her own. She felt, she said to Oscar, as if she were a visitor in Lancaster Gate, and not a member of the family. And she knew that her world was about to change in ways over which she had no control. Grandpapa Lloyd was nearly eighty and could not live for ever. His health had taken a turn for the worse just before Constance left for Dublin. Her dearest Otho had recently become engaged, which had come as a surprise to everyone. If – or rather when – Grandpapa Lloyd died, Constance would be alone, forced to live with Aunt Emily, Aunt Mary Napier or with Otho and Nellie. She might even have to contemplate returning to her mother, who had now remarried. It was not a prospect to relish. And she was twenty-six. Not old, but old enough perhaps to worry about being left on the shelf. Faced with a stark choice between dependence and independence, Constance chose to be married to Oscar.

Constance had captured her lion. Now she must tame him.

The marriage cure

LADY BRACKNELL: To speak frankly, I am not in favour of long engagements. They give people the opportunity of finding out each other's character before marriage, which I think is never advisable.

There can be no doubt that when Oscar proposed to Constance he was deeply in love. 'He certainly had been very much in love with her,' Bosie was to write years later. Indeed, Oscar had 'often' told Bosie how 'the marriage was purely a love match'. And there were ample reasons why Oscar had fallen in love with Constance. She was beautiful, she was graceful, she was intelligent. She was well-educated, and she spoke French and Italian fluently, and much of her extensive reading had been undertaken in those languages. She was interested in art and social issues and held quite decided, indeed quite radical, views for a young woman of her time. Adversity and her friendships and travels with remarkable older women – like her 'Mia Madre', Lady Mount-Temple, and Margaret, Ranee of Sarawak – had made Constance wise beyond her years and extended her world view to compass more than the trivialities of fashion and the gossip of girls. The Ranee's brother, Harry de Windt, said that many people would have been surprised if they had realised what 'force and depth of character, what acute power of reasoning and analysis' lay behind Constance's 'placid and beautiful exterior'. She thought deeply and with due consideration, and she could express herself and her opinions with a softness and a tact which were very appealing. She was kind and compassionate and had that rare quality of genuinely being more interested in others than she was in herself – a decided advantage where Oscar was concerned.

Oscar introduced his future wife in glowing terms: 'I'm going to be married to a beautiful young girl called Constance Lloyd,' he wrote to Lillie Langtry, 'a grave, slight, violet-eyed little Artemis, with great coils of heavy brown hair which make her flower-like head droop like a flower, and wonderful ivory hands which draw music from the piano so sweet that the birds stop singing to listen to her.'

Constance exuded a freshness, a purity that appealed to Oscar. His description of her as an 'Artemis', the goddess of chastity, is interesting. Constance was undoubtedly a woman, but not over-womanly. She was certainly beautiful but not in an overtly sexual or sensual way. In a letter to a friend, Oscar described her as 'mystical', a slightly strange epithet to describe his bride-to-be. Oscar's description of her head – 'drooping like a flower' – and her hands of 'ivory' suggest a cool, calm Madonna-like beauty. The heroine of Wilde's poem 'Madonna Mia' remarkably anticipates Constance:

> A lily-girl, not made for this world's pain,
> With brown, soft hair close braided by her ears,
> And longing eyes half veiled by slumberous tears
> Like bluest water seen through mists of rain;
> Pale cheeks whereon no love hath left its stain,
> Red underlip drawn in for fear of love.

The physical similarities between the Madonna Mia of the poem and Constance are extraordinary: Constance's 'flower-like head' and 'her great coils of heavy brown hair' mirror Madonna Mia's 'brown, soft hair close braided by her ears'; as indeed Constance's famous violet eyes mirror Madonna Mia's eyes of 'bluest water'. Emotionally too there are extraordinary coincidences. Like Oscar's poetic Madonna, Constance had experienced, in her short but unhappy life with her mother, more than her fair share of 'this world's pain'. She was certainly 'longing' to fall in love and yet, like Madonna Mia, frightened of what love may bring. But Madonna Mia is not a portrait of Constance. Oscar had almost certainly written this version of the poem before his first meeting with Constance. (In fact, the poem is a reworking of a famous and profoundly homoerotic version written four years earlier called 'Wasted Days' which concerns 'a fair slim boy' with 'hair of gold'.) Was Oscar struck by the similarities between Constance and his Madonna Mia? And did he fall in love with Constance because she was Constance? Or did he fall in love with her narcissistically as the incarnation of the Madonna Mia of his imagination?

André Raffalovich's vicious novel, *A Willing Exile*, published in 1890, is a *roman-à-clef* on the engagement and marriage of Constance and Oscar. Cyprian Broome is a poet and *bon viveur* who meets Daisy Laylham, a simple unspoilt girl who, like Constance, lives with her grandfather. Despite the downright nastiness of Raffalovich's depiction of Wilde – a nastiness born of a friendship gone sour – Raffalovich paints an intriguing portrait of Cyprian/Oscar's attitude to Daisy/Constance at the time of their engagement:

> Impervious as Cyprian was to many things, and conventional as was his acceptance of this world's superficial morality, he could not help being touched by Daisy's sweetness, her kindness to servants, to bores, to all who were weaker or duller than herself.

To his great surprise, Cyprian finds himself drawn irresistibly to Daisy:

> It was not love . . . He had not met a girl before with whom he would have

contemplated marriage; a widow or two, and some married women, older, and of better social position than himself, perhaps, but a girl, never. He had been accustomed to look upon women as the weavers of pretty clothes and of jewels, and as helpers to social success, and as symbols of his progress.

Finally, Cyprian proposes to Daisy as she plays the piano, in the same manner as Oscar proposed to Constance. Raffalovich's source for his jaundiced view of the Wildes' marriage may have been Oscar himself. In 1885, Oscar had reviewed *Tuberose and Meadowsweet*, a volume of poetry by Raffalovich, not failing to pick up the homoerotic resonances. A correspondence was initiated in the pages of the *Pall Mall Gazette* and a friendship ensued. Raffalovich and Oscar were friends from 1886 onwards, until they fell out in the early 1890s, and Oscar almost certainly confided in him.

Raffalovich's view of Oscar's feelings for Constance – as not love, but something approaching, something akin to love; as something more than like and rather less than love – has a certain ring of truth. The love of Oscar for Constance, and of Constance for Oscar, was a strangely arbitrary, ill-considered, precipitate sort of love. Both seemed very ready to fall in love. Oscar had told his mother on the first day he and Constance had met how he was thinking of 'marrying that girl'; and Constance had said she 'can't help liking him' that first day.

By the time Constance and Oscar became engaged, two and a half years after they were first introduced, they hardly knew each other. Oscar had spent an entire year in America, four months in Paris, and then a further month in America. And what time they did spend together was limited and invariably carefully chaperoned. Before Oscar proposed, they had rarely been alone together. No doubt Otho, on their excursions, had allowed the lovers to walk a little ahead together where their conversation would not be overheard; and Speranza, with a great number of knowing winks and pointed allusions, had let them converse comparatively unmolested in her crowed drawing room. But, as for spending any significant amount of time alone together or achieving any real intimacy, that had been more or less impossible. In this respect they were not unusual. Many young couples became engaged and then married with barely an idea of the real nature of their spouse and, once married, were obliged to make the best of it. Love was supposed to be enough.

Even after their engagement, there was virtually no opportunity to get to know each other a little better. When the painter Louise Jopling asked Oscar why he had fallen in love with Constance, he replied tellingly, 'She scarcely ever speaks, and I am always wondering what her thoughts are like.' Between the engagement and the marriage in May 1884, Oscar was constantly travelling the length and breadth of the British Isles on his mission to civilise the provinces and earn some money. He missed Constance desperately. 'It is horrid being so much away from her,' he told Lillie Langtry, 'but we telegraph to each other twice a day, and I rush back suddenly from the uttermost parts of the earth to see her for an hour, and do all the foolish things wise lovers do.'

Constance was equally bereft while Oscar was touring. 'I am with Oscar when he is in town, and I am too miserable to do anything while he is away.'

There was at least one opportunity, though, for Oscar to go through the pre-nuptial ritual of disclosing something of his past to Constance. A letter from Constance to Oscar makes it clear that he had imparted to her some details of his former loves and lovers. The letter revealed the intensity of her love for Oscar and the plenitude of her forgiveness: 'My darling love,' she wrote:

> You take all my strength away. I have no power to do anything but just love you when you are with me . . . I don't think I shall ever be jealous. Certainly I am not jealous now of anyone. I trust in you for the present: I am content to let the past be buried, it does not belong to me: for the future trust and faith will come.

It is unlikely that Constance got anything but a heavily edited version of Oscar's sexual and emotional history. He almost certainly told her of his devotion to Florrie Balcombe and the story of the little gold cross; and of how he had asked Ellen Terry to give Florrie a crown of flowers to wear on the night she made her debut on the London stage so that, unbeknownst to her, she would be wearing a talisman of his unrequited love. Equally, he would have told Constance about his proposal to Charlotte Montefiore, carefully omitting to mention his waspish parting shot about her money and his brains. He would have mentioned his friendship with Violet Hunt and how he had once upon a time fancied himself to be in love with her. There may have been any number of disclosures of innocuous flirtations with the four sisters of Frank Miles at Bingham Rectory – 'all very pretty indeed . . . my heart is torn in sunder with admiration for them all' – and perhaps, for poetic colour, he might have tossed in a few mentions of stolen kisses on moonlit nights.

Oscar would most certainly not have told Constance about his visits to women prostitutes in Oxford, London, America and Paris. Nor would he have told her about his sexual experiences with men. Nor indeed about his love affairs with other men like Frank Miles and his 'Heart's Brother', Rennell Rodd. And he would most certainly not have boasted to Constance – as he did to others – that he had the kiss of Walt Whitman still upon his lips. What Oscar may have tried to imply, and what Constance may have succeeded in inferring from his carefully edited confession, was that he had some degree of sexual experience. Constance was twenty-six, intelligent and had some knowledge and experience of the world. She must have known that Oscar at twenty-nine – 'a very good age to be married', according to Lady Bracknell – was unlikely to be a virgin. But she could take comfort in the fact that Oscar was so ready to tell her all about his past, and that it seemed to have comparatively little in it for him to regret or for her to reproach. Or so she thought.

Constance's letter of plenary forgiveness ended – literally – on an iron note: 'When I have you for my husband, I will hold you fast with chains of love and devotion so that you shall never leave me, or love anyone else.' Had Oscar not believed himself blindly in love, and been so blindly determined to get married to Constance, he might have mused on the comfortableness or otherwise of being held fast with chains of love and run away from his approaching marriage as fast as his legs would carry him.

W.H. Auden described Oscar's marriage to Constance as 'certainly the most immoral and perhaps the only really heartless act of Wilde's life'. Auden argued that Oscar knew himself to be a lover of men but married Constance anyway, coldly calculating the value of her income as well as the value of the social respectability that marriage conferred.

But the truth, as Oscar would later remark, is rarely pure and never simple. Oscar was well aware that he was attracted to men. He had had occasional sexual encounters with men, but rarely, except in the case of Frank Miles, and perhaps Rennell Rodd, had these sexual attractions and sexual encounters coalesced into anything resembling a relationship. Most men who continued to find other men sexually attractive into their twenties and thirties experienced a tremendous struggle with their sexuality, and Oscar was no exception. There were times in his life when he experienced violent, contradictory and disturbing feelings about his sexual and emotional attraction to young men, swinging between feelings of ecstasy and degradation, sexual exultation and remorse. Oscar could invoke the homoerotic glories of Greek pederasty and discuss the joys of sex with 'pretty boys' with Walt Whitman. And then, quite suddenly, he would turn away with abject self-loathing at the grossness of his sexual behaviour. It was perhaps one of these episodes of self-loathing – possibly to do with Frank Miles, or possibly as a result of a casual sexual encounter with a man – which had caused him to seek spiritual guidance from Father Bowden at the Brompton Oratory in April 1878.

Oscar was not alone in struggling with the burden of his sexual attraction to young men. Many men experienced violent feelings of self-loathing and disgust at their sexual urges, and sought to gain mastery over their unacceptable desires. Some chose the path of celibacy, and some chose the solace of the Church – the Catholic Church especially – as Oscar very nearly did. Some attempted, and some even succeeded, in committing suicide, finding the burden of their shameful secret unendurable, like the anonymous 'Case VI' in Havelock Ellis's *Studies in the Psychology of Sex*, for whom 'prayers, struggles, all means used were of no avail . . . Death, even if it meant nothing but a passage into nothingness . . . would be a thousand times preferable' to the living hell of sexual desire for other men.

Many men believed that their homoerotic desires could be neutralised by working up their heterosexual instincts. Fire could be fought by fire. Repeated sex with a woman, they convinced themselves, could instil a habit of normal intercourse. They might even develop a taste for sex with women, which must inevitably bring about the longed-for 'cure'. After Oscar's imprisonment, the Marquis of Queensberry wanted to 'cure' Bosie of his sexual tastes for boys and young men and offered to pay for him to travel to the South Seas where he would 'find plenty of beautiful girls' who were sexually available. Many men tried to 'cure' themselves by forcing themselves to have sex with women in the hope that heterosexuality might blossom. John Addington Symonds wrote in his posthumously published *Memoirs* that what he needed 'was the excitation of the sexual sense for women, and the awakening to their sexual desirableness, combined with the manifold sympathies, half brutal and half tender, which physical congress evokes'. In twelve out of the thirty-five men whose sexual case histories Havelock Ellis published:

> there had been connection with women, in some instances only once or twice, in others during several years, but it was always with an effort or from a sense of duty and anxiety to be normal; they never experienced any pleasure in the act, or sense of satisfaction after it.

Female prostitutes were plentiful and cheap, which made it easy for men to practise 'physical congress' with women. Ellis's 'Case XIII' tried the prostitute 'cure' with little success:

> I sought out a scarlet woman in the streets of —— and went home with her. From something she said to me I knew that I gave her pleasure, and she asked me to come to her again. This I did twice, but without any real pleasure. The whole thing was too sordid and soulless, and the man who decides to take an evil medicine regularly has first to make up his mind that he really needs it.

Oscar had swallowed this 'evil medicine' and visited female prostitutes on a number of occasions that are known about, and perhaps on several more that are not. But these 'animal' encounters were, for Oscar, rarely satisfactory and he famously remarked, after an unappetising visit to a prostitute, that she was 'like cold mutton'.

For those like Oscar who found the prospect of celibacy unappealing and recourse to female prostitutes unappetising, marriage to the right woman seemed to be the only option. For some men, the 'right woman', in practice, meant a woman who resembled a boy as closely as possible. Consciously or unconsciously, they sought out boyish women they could use as a sexual surrogate for the boys or men they really wanted to have sex with. Ellis's 'Case XXV' 'used to dream of finding an exit from his painful situation by cohabitation with some coarse boyish girl'. And Oscar, in an unguarded moment, once exclaimed to Aimée Lowther, the fifteen-year-old daughter of a friend: 'Aimée, Aimée! If only you were a boy, how I would adore you.'

The Austrian sexologist Richard Krafft-Ebing's *Psychopathia Sexualis* includes a case history of a man who had had sex with hundreds of male partners and yet who successfully married a woman, telling how 'the boyish appearance of my wife was of effectual assistance' in stimulating sexual desire. In *Teleny*, the explicitly homoerotic novel which Oscar secretly wrote towards the end of 1890 in conjunction with three other young men, the hero Des Grieux struggles to fight his strong sexual attraction to the pianist René

Teleny. Des Grieux is convinced that he has found a 'means of getting rid of this horrible infatuation' in the person of his mother's new chambermaid, a country wench of sixteen or so, who has:

> the slender lithesomeness of a young boy, and might well have been taken for one, had it not been for the budding, round, and firm breasts, that swelled out her dress.

Des Grieux is prepared to go to any lengths to escape his sodomitical fate: 'Could I but have felt some sensuality towards her, I think I would even have gone so far as to marry her, rather than become a sodomite.' Eventually, in a fit of self-loathing and despair, Des Grieux rapes the chambermaid only to discover that his homoerotic infatuation with Teleny is unimpaired. Significantly, Constance was described as boyish by some observers. Oscar himself described her as 'slight', and Anna, Comtesse de Brémont, who knew Constance well, talked about her 'youthful, almost boyish face with its clear colouring and full, dark eyes'.

Marriage was the main 'cure' offered by doctors to men who were sexually attracted to other men. André Gide consulted an eminent doctor after he had proposed to Madeleine Rondeaux in 1895. Gide was not sure that he would be able to perform sexually in his marriage because of his powerful attraction to young men. The specialist was reassuring: 'You say you love a young lady and yet hesitate to marry her, on account of your other tastes . . . Get married! Marry without fear. And you'll soon see that the rest only exists in your imagination.' He was, the specialist told him, like a hungry man trying to make a meal out of gherkins.

Havelock Ellis warned that 'physicians are often strongly tempted to advise marriage and to promise that the normal heterosexual impulse will appear.' This was dangerous advice, he said: 'There is but too much evidence demonstrating the rashness and folly of those who give such advice, and hold forth such promises, without duly guarded qualification and with no proper examination of the individual case.' No doubt he had in mind the experience of his friend and collaborator John Addington Symonds, with whom Oscar had been in contact since Oxford. In his *Memoirs*, Symonds wrote of his struggle with his sexuality when he realised he was in love with a young man called Alfred Brooke:

> I felt the necessity of growing into a natural man. That is, I think, how the problem presented itself to my innocence. I thought that by honest endeavour I could divert my passions from the burning channel in which they flowed for Alfred Brooke, and lead them gently to follow a normal course toward women.

The twenty-three-year-old Symonds blindly followed the advice of his father and of the eminent physician Sir Spencer Wells, who 'recommended cohabitation with a hired mistress, or, what was better, matrimony' as the only 'cure' for his attraction to young men. Shortly afterwards, Symonds deliberately sought out Catherine North, whom he had met on holiday in Switzerland, as a likely prospect for matrimony. They married, and Symonds fathered four daughters. But, looking back on his life, he described his marriage as the 'great mistake – perhaps the great crime of my life':

> I married without passion or the feeling that this particular woman was the only woman in the world for me. Thus I deceived her practically, if not intentionally or deliberately. And I deceived myself, in so far as her temperament was incapable of sharpening the sexual appetites which in me had hardly any edge where woman was concerned.

Not only was Catherine North incapable of sharpening Symonds's heterosexuality, he discovered that the long-hoped for 'cure' for his sexual attraction to young men failed to materialise. Instead, he 'found, to his disappointment, that the tyranny of the male genital organs on his fancy increased'.

We will probably never know whether or not Symonds passed on to Oscar his experience of marriage as a possible 'cure' for his attraction to young men. Although the two corresponded, most of their letters have been lost. And, even if Symonds had obliquely hinted that marriage offered no cure and little respite from the relentless, compulsive obsession for sex with men, it is doubtful that Oscar would have listened. He was determined to marry Constance. A rumour persists that Oscar visited a doctor before he married. Some have speculated that he wanted to make sure that he was completely cured of the syphilis he was supposed to have contracted from a prostitute at Oxford. There is no evidence that Oscar ever contracted syphilis – at Oxford or elsewhere. But it is possible that this visit to a doctor may have had more to do with Oscar's concerns over his sexual attraction to men and how he might overcome them within marriage to Constance.

Although Oscar was well aware of his attraction to handsome young men, equally he had convinced himself that he could, should and must marry. He had always intended to marry, to do what his mother and what society expected of him, but there were also other obvious – and less obvious – advantages to marriage. Not least, marriage would put an end to the unceasing speculation and sniping about his sexual orientation. 'Bachelors are not fashionable any more,' observes Lord Caversham in *An Ideal Husband*. 'They are a damaged lot. Too much is known about them.'

By marrying, Oscar would be able to draw a line under the uncertainties of the past. He would no longer be the butt of *Punch*'s heavy-handed caricatures of him as poetic, effeminate and languid, with an unhealthy interest in blue china and young men. Marriage provided status and stability – emotional as much as financial – in a jealous, carping and uncertain world. And he was confident that the nuptial couch would provide an appropriate, acceptable and safe outlet for his vigorous sexual energies. Oscar disliked using prostitutes, and there was the constant and recurring dread of contracting a venereal disease – gonorrhoea or, even worse, syphilis. Oscar may have been aware that Frank Miles was suffering from advanced syphilis. The prospect of contracting so fell a disease filled him with terror and may have been an additional impetus to send him rushing towards the bacteriological sanctity and safety of marriage. Not only had Oscar convinced himself that he loved Constance, but he had also told himself that he desired her. She was the one woman who had awoken a strong sexual sense in him.

On 29 May 1884, six months and four days after he had proposed in the drawing room at Ely Place, the impatient lovers, Oscar and Constance, were married by special licence at St James's Church in Paddington. Oscar had taken control of the ceremony, designing his bride's wedding dress and choreographing every last detail. Although it was supposedly a private family wedding, Oscar must have been pleased by the throng of curious onlookers who came to see the wedding of the year. 'There is only this much to be recorded about it,' reported Edmund Yates in the *World*:

> The bride, accompanied by her six pretty bridesmaids, looked charming; that Oscar bore himself with calm dignity; and that all most intimately concerned in the affair seemed thoroughly pleased. A happy little group of *intimes* saw them off at Charing Cross.

Not everybody was so 'thoroughly pleased' by the wedding. Robert Sherard thought it too staged, too showy – more of a publicity stunt than the joining together of two lives. 'No woman,' he observed astutely:

> who was not blindly convinced of the superiority of her bridegroom's taste would have consented to such a masquerade. It may have occurred to some of the onlookers that a union so initiated could not contain the elements of happiness. Where the woman is entirely hypnotised and subjugated her marriage is not often a happy one for her.

It was all too true. Constance was a woman entirely hypnotised, entirely subjugated by her love for Oscar. She entered the marriage grateful for love and blinded by love. Her marriage, like her life, was doomed to unhappiness.

Against nature

'The only way to behave to a woman is to make love to her, if she is pretty, and to someone else, if she is plain.'

On honeymoon in Paris, Oscar wrote a letter to a friend in New York which somehow found its way into the pages of the *New York Times*. In what the newspaper called 'a silly and thoroughly characteristic letter', Oscar declared that 'he has not been disappointed in married life'. Oscar almost certainly wrote the letter within a day or two of his wedding night with Constance, which makes the real meaning of his letter plain. What Oscar really meant by 'married life' was what Marie Stopes was later to call 'married love', or sex in marriage. In the interval between his marriage ceremony and writing to his friend in New York, the only aspect of married life that Oscar had had time to experience was its sexual delights. His letter was evidently an epistolary sigh of relief and betrayed the very real fears he had had that the sexual side of marriage might prove to be in every sense an anti-climax.

Fortunately, the wedding night sex had worked out well, as a delighted Oscar told Robert Sherard the morning after the night before. Sherard had called to congratulate the newly-weds at the Hôtel Wagram on the Rue de Rivoli, where Mr and Mrs Wilde had a suite of rooms on the third floor overlooking the Tuileries Gardens. Sherard had been sceptical about the marriage from the outset, believing Oscar incapable of making any woman happy. Oscar suggested a walk and, leaving Constance behind in the hotel, they strolled towards the Marché St Honoré where, Sherard recalled, Oscar 'stopped and rifled a flower stall of its loveliest blossoms and sent them, with a word of love on his card, to the bride whom he had quitted but a moment before'. What Sherard left out of his published account of this walk was how, as they stood in front of the flower stall, Oscar could not wait to expatiate on the joys of his wedding night sex with Constance and began: 'It's so wonderful when a young virgin . . .' An embarrassed Sherard hurriedly interrupted. 'No, Oscar,' he said. 'You mustn't talk about *that* to me. Ça, c'est sacré.'

Robert Sherard had not always been so easily embarrassed by Oscar's sexual talk. After all, Oscar had told him of his visit to a prostitute in Paris the year before and on another occasion they had had a heated discussion about the language of sex, specifically about the use of the word 'have' in relation to sexual congress between a man and a woman. 'I pointed out to the lord of language,' Sherard recalled:

> that I didn't understand the word 'have' as a description of the sexual act. I said that neither the man nor the woman, though temporarily united, remained other than separate and distinct – each desperately alone, mentally and physically, and that before as well as after the contact it was *solus cum sola*. He didn't agree with me at all. He said that the word 'have' was a perfect description of the possession that the man took of the woman in the sexual act and discoursed about it.

That Oscar felt he had to tell, if not the world, then at least Robert Sherard and his friend in America that the sexual side of his marriage had been an unqualified success betrays a fundamental uncertainty about his sexuality. His public parade of his sexual prowess seems to be a case of protesting too much, of staking a claim to vigorous and normal heterosexuality, rather than an expression of his joy in his spiritual and physical union with Constance. The reality of Oscar's wedding night may have been closer to the experience of John Addington Symonds who wrote to his sister the morning after his wedding night with his bride, Catherine:

> Such a great event as yesterday, however long anticipated, well prepared for, and leading to however thoroughly foreknown a termination, always at last falls suddenly upon one. I felt all through the day that I was acting a part, and this helped me. When men have to do things, there rises up between their self and the deed a screen of unreality. So action is always less essential than contemplation. But after it is done, a sense of inadequacy and incompleteness, proceeding from the contrast between the deed meditated and the deed accomplished, springs up.

Symonds was honest enough to admit to himself and to those close to him that his wedding night sex – the 'foreknown termination' – had been a disappointment, that he felt he had been acting a part, going through the nuptial motions.

Then there was the way Oscar had dwelt on Constance's virginity. Oscar had certainly 'had' – to use his preferred word – Constance on their wedding night, but his particular emphasis on her virginity suggests that the locus of his sexual achievement lay not so much in 'the possession that the man took of the woman' but rather in her deflowering. At a breakfast party where the novelist Vernon Lee was present, Oscar obliquely referred to his deflowering of Constance when he said he loved her because she was 'annulée et tendre', 'tender and surrendered'. This posed a new problem. If Constance had been the incarnation of his Madonna Mia, his Virgin Mary, his Artemis, goddess of chastity, before their marriage, what did she become after her ritualistic deflowering? Once deflowered, no longer chaste, no longer 'a young virgin':

exactly where did her attraction for Oscar lie? It was a paradox, and perhaps one that the greatest master of paradox failed to fully grasp.

If Oscar was protesting too much about the delights of the nuptial couch, Constance was predictably reticent. She wrote to Otho five days after the wedding. 'Of course,' she told Otho, 'I need not tell you that I am very happy, enjoying my liberty enormously.' 'Liberty'. It was a curious word to use. Clearly Constance saw her marriage as a liberation from the correctitude of Aunt Emily and Lancaster Gate, a correctitude that could only become more stifling after the death of Grandpapa Lloyd. It was very much a social and cultural honeymoon. It may have been business as usual for Oscar, but for Constance it presaged the delights of married life with a fashionable young poet and man of letters. There were trips to the Salon, a trip to the theatre to see Sarah Bernhardt in *Macbeth* – 'the most splendid acting I ever saw', Constance told Otho, 'Sarah of course superb, she simply stormed the part' – and dinners to meet Oscar's Parisian friends and acquaintances like 'young Mr Sherard' who has 'a romantic story and a romantic face' and 'the young sculptor Donoghue whom I have seen several times, very handsome Roman face but with Irish blue eyes'. Like Oscar, Constance could appreciate a handsome face. She was flushed with the success of it all. Oscar's friends liked her. Robert Sherard gallantly told her how jealous he was of Oscar, and how he wanted to run him through with his swordstick. Constance's dress caused 'a sensation', and Henrietta Reubell, an American spinster who held a salon – 'frightful, fair, *white*-faced and forty', as Constance described her – wanted her dressmaker to copy it. Constance closed her long, happy letter to Otho: 'Oscar is out,' she wrote, 'so I can give you no message from him.' It was the first of many such absences to come in her married life.

It could never be said that Oscar did not start married life as he meant to go on. Within days of their arrival in Paris, Oscar was out slumming in the bars and brothels of Paris with Robert Sherard and one or two others, leaving Constance to her own devices. They visited what Sherard described as the haunts of the lowest criminals and poorest outcasts of the city, 'the show-places of the Paris Inferno – Père Lunette's, and the Château Rouge, – which everybody who wishes to know the depths of darkness which exist in the City of Light goes to see'. At the Château Rouge, they spent time fraternising with the thieves, with 'the saddest daughters of joy' and the professional beggars who delightedly showed their visitors the tricks by which they feigned their infirmities. Oscar was delighted: 'The criminal classes have always had a wonderful attraction for me,' he exclaimed. Sherard recalled how, 'as a *bonne-bouche*', the landlord of the Château Rouge offered to show them the celebrated 'Salle des Morts' upstairs where the flotsam and jetsam of Paris slept:

> Stretched out in every posture of pain and discomfort, many in the stupor of drink, many displaying foul sores, maimed limbs, or the stigmata of disease, all in filthy and malodorous rags, the sleepers of the Room of the Dead, with their white faces, immobile and sightless, showed indeed like corpses.

Sherard reported that Oscar was horror-struck, his face like one who had looked upon Medusa. But he was later to utilise this sense of horror in his works, in the poem 'The Harlot's House', in passages in *The Picture of Dorian Gray* and, most memorably, in *Teleny*.

The 'Salle des Morts' was, according to Sherard, 'the favourite spectacle of those seeking unhealthy emotions'. And Oscar was certainly in the market for unhealthy emotions. Barely a week after the arrival of the newly-weds in Paris, something happened which heralded the end of the marriage, not that either Oscar or Constance realised its cataclysmic significance at the time. It was a comparatively small thing: Oscar's discovery of a slim volume written in French and published just a fortnight before. The book was *A Rebours*, translatable as *Against Nature* or *Against the Grain*. Its author was an unassuming civil servant called Joris-Karl Huysmans.

The novel tells the story of Duc Jean des Esseintes, a frail, unhappy, nervy young man of thirty, the last in the line of an ancient and distinguished family. Des Esseintes is a neurasthenic, a now-forgotten Victorian word for a person suffering from nervous exhaustion, often believed to be brought about by sexual or masturbatory excess. Des Esseintes is prematurely tired of life and tired of the world and decides to retreat into dreamlike seclusion in a country house where, surrounded by every luxury and an eclectic collection of rare and beautiful jewels, decadent Latin literature and hothouse flowers, he sets out on a voyage of discovery. His quest is to probe, to burrow into the darkest recesses of his soul to try to find the meaning of life. He seeks to cure the malady of the soul through the medium of his senses with hallucinogenic results. As his exploration of the darker recesses of his soul progresses, Des Esseintes becomes increasingly hysterical and increasingly physically weak. Finally, he can take no more and his doctor orders a return to reality and normality. As the book draws to its close, Des Esseintes realises, almost too late, that the only cure, the only salvation for his soul's malady is the pity and the love of God. The novel ends abruptly as this beam of redemptive light shines upon him.

Late in May in Paris, *A Rebours* became a literary sensation, taken up, talked about and argued about over and over again. Whistler praised it, the poet and playwright Arthur Symons called it 'the breviary of decadence', and Paul Valéry called it his 'Bible and bedside book'. Oscar acquired a copy of the book shortly after he arrived in Paris with Constance. Perhaps he started to read it when the weather took a turn for the worse six days after their arrival, when, as Constance told Otho, 'a sudden storm of wind and rain broke over us in the afternoon'. The effect of the book upon Oscar was equally sudden and even more dramatic. He later admitted in the witness box to an inquisitive jury at the Old Bailey that the unnamed 'yellow book' lent to Dorian by Lord Henry Wotton in *The Picture of Dorian Gray* was based on *A Rebours*. In reply to a letter written by Mr E.W. Pratt of Lower Clapton, North London, enquiring where he could buy a copy of Dorian's yellow book, Oscar wrote:

'Dear Sir, The book in *Dorian Gray* is one of the many books I have never written, but it is partly suggested by Huysmans's *A Rebours*, which you will get at any French bookseller's. It is a fantastic variation on Huysmans's over-realistic study of the artistic temperament in our inartistic age.

Oscar's description of the effect of reading *A Rebours* on Dorian Gray is almost certainly autobiographical. Dorian, 'taking up the volume, flung himself into an arm–chair and began to turn over the leaves':

> After a few minutes he became absorbed. It was the strangest book that he had ever read. It seemed to him that in exquisite raiment, and to the delicate sound of flutes, the sins of the world were passing in dumb show before him. Things that he had dimly dreamed of were suddenly made real to him. Things of which he had never dreamed were gradually revealed.

What compelled Oscar's attention about *A Rebours* was its account of 'the sins of the world'. Beneath the jewelled style of Huysmans's writing and the fantastical, grotesque set pieces and flights of imaginative fancy lay a strong homoerotic subtext. The novel tells the story of Des Esseintes's erotic journey towards sexual realisation. Des Esseintes comes from degenerate aristocratic stock whose men, as the decades and centuries have passed, have become 'progressively less manly'. He attends a Jesuit school and then, like most young men of his class and wealth, gives himself up to dissipation:

> In the days when he had belonged to a set of young men-about-town, he had gone to those unconventional supper parties where drunken women loosen their dresses and beat the table with their heads; he had hung around stage doors, had bedded with singers and actresses, had endured, over and above the innate stupidity of the sex, the hysterical vanity common to women of the theatre. Then he had kept mistresses already famed for their depravity . . . and finally, weary to the point of satiety of these hackneyed luxuries, these commonplace caresses, he had sought satisfaction in the gutter, hoping that the contrast would revive his exhausted desires and imagining that the fascinating filthiness of the poor would stimulate his flagging senses.

Bored, disgusted, unsatisfied and increasingly impotent, Des Esseintes shuts himself away, making occasional erotic forays. One day while walking in the Rue de Rivoli – where Oscar and Constance's honeymoon hotel was located, and where he almost certainly read Huysmans's novel – Des Esseintes encounters 'a young scamp of sixteen or so, a peaky-faced, sharp-eyed child, as attractive in his way as any girl'. Des Esseintes takes him to a brothel and offers to pay for the boy to have sex with a prostitute of his choice and is appalled and angry when the Madame of the brothel casually assumes that he is sexually interested in the boy.

Time passes and months, perhaps years, later, Des Esseintes encounters an American circus acrobat tantalisingly, provocatively named Miss Urania, a clear allusion to the emerging new term 'Uranian', signifying love and sex between men. Miss Urania 'has a supple figure, sinewy legs, muscles of steel, and arms of iron', and Des Esseintes is seized with erotic fantasies of sex with her. He imagines a mutual transmutation of gender, where Miss Urania becomes a virtual man, 'as blunt-witted and brutish as a fairground wrestler', for whom he, Des Esseintes, hungers, 'yearning for her just as a chloretic girl will hanker after a clumsy brute whose embrace could squeeze the life out of her'. He pays Miss Urania for sex and is disappointed with the reality when the 'rough, athletic caresses' he at once desired and dreaded fail to materialise.

Finally, one day as Des Esseintes is walking alone, he is accosted by a youth asking him directions. Des Esseintes is struck by the unusual persistence of the youth, by his 'timid and appealing' voice, by his evident poverty, by his cheap, tight-fitting clothes. His face was 'somewhat disconcerting, pale and drawn . . . and lit up by two great liquid eyes, ringed with blue . . . the mouth was small, but spoilt by fleshy lips with a line dividing them in the middle like a cherry'. It was a pick-up:

> They gazed at each other for a moment; then the young man dropped his eyes and came closer, brushing his companion's arm with his own. Des Esseintes slackened his pace, taking thoughtful note of the youth's mincing walk. From this chance encounter there had sprung a mistrustful friendship that somehow lasted several months. Des Esseintes could not think of it now without a shudder; never had he submitted to more delightful or more stringent exploitation, never had he run such risks, yet never had he known such satisfaction mingled with distress. Among the memories that visited him in his solitude, the recollection of this mutual attachment dominated all the rest.

On the morning of 9 June, Oscar was interviewed in his hotel suite by a reporter from the *Morning News*. 'This last book of Huysmans is one of the best I have seen,' he declared. *A Rebours* had struck Oscar with the force of a thunderbolt. The book was a revelation to him, forcing him to recognise that his sexual experiences with men were not, as he had hoped, isolated and unconnected incidents, but were rather markers on the same homoerotic voyage of discovery that Des Esseintes had embarked upon. *A Rebours* resonated not just with Oscar's past, but also with his future. It was a kind of advance autobiography, especially in its shudderingly compelling insights into the dynamics of male homoeroticism.

Reading *A Rebours* was a turning point for Oscar; a moment of startling self-recognition which, coming when it did, just days after the supposed euphoria of his wedding night, pointed up the contrast between the safety, the predictability, the normalness of sex with Constance within marriage, and the sheer danger and unpredictability of sex with young men. Until the point that he read *A Rebours*, Oscar could tell himself that his sexual attraction to men was a passing phase; indeed, a passed phase, now that he was married to his violet-eyed Artemis. He had suppressed that 'thing unworthy' of himself and had taken possession of his bride, legally, physically and sexually. But still it was not enough. The sexual and the emotional intimacy of marriage to Constance still could not quench his sexual hunger for men.

The story of Des Esseintes pointed the way forward for Oscar. The powerful paradoxes in the relationship between Des Esseintes and the youth who picked him up in the street must have struck Oscar forcibly. Some years later he told André Raffalovich how the seduction of Des Esseintes by the young male prostitute particularly thrilled and fascinated him. Even though the young man is clearly a male prostitute who exploits Des Esseintes ruthlessly, Des Esseintes finds such exploitation sweet. Even though he shudders at the risks and dangers of such a liaison, the satisfaction he experiences – inextricably mingled with distress – is incomparable and dominates his erotic memory. Reading *A Rebours* had fired Oscar's sexual imagination and ignited his barely repressed sexual desires. In the years to come *A Rebours* would have its own place in Oscar's erotic memory. Oscar would, just like Des Esseintes, experience a commingling of delight and distress, satisfactions and shudders in his own liaisons with young men.

The marriage of Oscar and Constance was over almost as soon as it had begun. Their love for each other had been consummated and, at least for Oscar, had been found wanting. Even though he had fulfilled his role as suitor, bridegroom, husband and lover, he knew that something essential was absent from the marital equation. He realised that whatever marriage may or may not bring in terms of companionship, stability and security, it had not and would not extinguish his burning desire for sex with young men. Reading *A Rebours* in the rooms he shared with his bride of a few days had opened his eyes to the trajectory of his true sexual nature and inflamed his desires. As he gazed at Constance, as he watched her undress, as he shared a bed with her, as he made love to her, he must have realised that he had made a terrible, terrible mistake. In his search for love, for peace, for normality, he had walked into a trap, the doors of which clanged shut behind him. Paradoxically, Constance had gained her liberty while Oscar had lost his. Ironically, his married state would only magnify and inflame his homoerotic desires. Oscar had made his bed. Now he must lie in it.

An ideal wife

*'What nonsense people talk about happy marriages!' exclaimed
Lord Henry. 'A man can be happy with any woman, as long as he
does not love her.'*

After their four-week honeymoon in Paris and Dieppe, Oscar and Constance
returned to London to start married life in earnest. There was much to do, and
much to take Oscar's mind off the disappointments of married life and distract
him from his real sexual desires. There were decisions to be taken about the
decoration of the House Beautiful in Tite Street, visits to be made and work to
be done. Oscar was still on his mission to civilise the provinces and had to
spend a considerable amount of time travelling.

But marriage had its compensations. When Grandpapa Lloyd died less than
a month after their return from honeymoon, Oscar and Constance were at last
in possession of a more than adequate income. With Oscar's fees from his
lectures and now, increasingly, from his journalism, it seemed they were
assured of a bright future. And it made a pleasant change to be a married man
with a beautiful young wife, respectable, settled and, if not quite beyond
reproach, effectively insulated from the jibes, jeers and insinuations about his
sexual orientation.

Now that she had her 'liberty', Constance was eager to work. She was
young, she was free, and the world seemed full of exciting possibilities. 'I am
thinking of becoming correspondent to some paper, or else of going on the
stage; *qu'en pensez vous?*' she wrote to Otho. 'I want to make some money:
perhaps a novel would be better.' Constance's ambitions were considerably
grander than those Speranza had in mind for her daughter-in-law. She
wanted Constance to learn to correct Oscar's proofs and bask in her
husband's reflected literary glory.

Back in September 1875, Oscar had spent a few days at Clonfin House in
County Longford where a fellow guest, an American, had brought with him a
novelty, a blank album entitled *Mental Photographs, an Album for Confessions of
Tastes, Habits and Convictions*. It was a parlour pastime, probably completed at
teatime or after dinner and then read aloud for the amusement of other guests.
It was a questionnaire, with forty questions designed, as the album's title
suggested, to create a snapshot of a personality. Oscar filled in his

questionnaire and then thought no more about it. But the album survived and his answers are revealing. In reply to the question 'What should be the distinguishing characteristic of a wife?' Oscar had written 'devotion to her husband.' It was more than a throwaway answer. It expressed a profound belief about the role of wives.

Again and again, in his prose and in his plays, the qualities of duty, devotion, self-sacrifice and forgiveness of sins are pointed up as the hallmarks of the ideal wife. These were views inherited from Speranza who, despite her radicalism, had some decidedly old-fashioned opinions on the role of a wife. Speranza believed that wives were there for the benefit of their husbands, not vice versa. Wives, she said, should ask for nothing out of marriage, except 'the divine joy of sacrifice, the ecstatic sense of self-annihilation for true love's sake'. In her essay *Genius and Marriage*, Speranza warned of the dangers of a wife discovering that her husband had feet of clay. She was almost certainly talking of her own marriage to Sir William Wilde, but her words have a curiously prophetic ring about the marriage of Oscar and Constance:

> A woman has a strong tendency to look on a man of genius as a god, and to offer him worship as well as love; but in the fatal intimacy of daily life illusions soon vanish, and she finds that, except in moments of inspiration, his divinity is even weaker than an ordinary mortal, less able to guide or strengthen others; so she resents the knowledge that the idol is only made of clay, and her feelings alternate between contempt and dislike, especially if she is of a passionate, impulsive temperament.

'It is much better to have loved and lost than to have loved and won,' Oscar said to a young friend who had sought his advice about a love affair with a young woman, the course of which was not running smoothly. Oscar was almost certainly talking about his own life and his marriage to Constance. He had loved her and he had won her. And now he had to live with her.

In one respect, though, Oscar found that playing the role of husband was far less irksome than he might have reasonably expected. Even though his real sexual desires lay outside the marriage entirely, even though, like the hero of *Teleny*, he found the joys of married love 'more of a sedative than an aphrodisiac', there was still comfort and convenience to be had in the marriage bed. Whether Oscar was focused on Constance as the object of his sexual desire, or whether, like many other married men in the same predicament, who 'succeeded in accomplishing their object with difficulty, or by means of evoking the images of men on whom their affections were set', Oscar performed his husbandly duties manfully and to good effect. Just four months after her marriage, Constance found herself pregnant. If her hopes of a career were dashed or delayed, she was soon cheerfully reconciled. Cyril Wilde was born in July 1885, and the new parents professed themselves to be delighted. Like many young women who suddenly found themselves wives and mothers,

Constance embraced the role and duties of a devoted mother almost thankfully. In motherhood, at least, there was a clear role for her.

Two days after Cyril's birth, Adrian Hope wrote spitefully to his fiancée, Laura Troubridge: 'Did you see the Wildes have a boy, I rather pity the infant, don't you?' Adrian Hope was a relation of Constance's by marriage and, after the debacle of Oscar's trial and imprisonment, was destined to play an important – if equally spiteful – role in the affairs of the Wilde family. Adrian and Laura belonged to a not-so-select band of doubters and dissenters as to the happiness of Mr and Mrs Wilde. Their animosity was particularly directed at Constance, who was less able and less willing to defend herself than Oscar. Often their dislike was rooted in disappointment. Both Laura Troubridge and Violet Hunt had at one time or another declared themselves to be more than a little in love with Oscar. Constance's dress sense, her shyness and – to some eyes – an apparent stupidity brought forth barbs. 'Mr and Mrs Oscar Wilde to tea,' Laura confided to her diary shortly after the Wildes returned from honeymoon. 'She dressed for the part in limp white muslin, with absolutely *no* bustle, saffron coloured silk swathed about her shoulders, a huge cartwheel Gainsborough hat, white and bright yellow stockings and shoes – she looked too hopeless and we thought her shy and dull. He was amusing of course.' Three months later Adrian Hope met Oscar and Constance at the house of Mrs Napier, Constance's aunt. 'Oscar Wilde and his wife came in while I was there,' he wrote to Laura, 'he dressed quite like anyone else, she in mouse-coloured velvet with a toque to match looking horrid . . . She never opened her lips but seemed in a state of silent sulky adoration.'

The novelist Marie Corelli was scathing about Constance's manner after attending a lecture Constance gave to the Rational Dress Society, a cause especially dear to her heart, as it was to Oscar's: 'Mrs Oscar Wilde is utterly devoid of the correct demeanour that should be observed on the lecture platform; she giggles at her own witticisms, and explodes in a titter of laughter when she says something that she thinks especially smart.' Another acquaintance, Morton Fullerton, found Constance dull: 'Burne-Jones and Oscar Wilde with their respective wives dined here . . . The two women were dull, and the evening slow.' Much of the criticism of Constance was the consequence of her shyness, especially in social situations with people she did not know. As she had written to Oscar during their engagement, she was 'so cold and undemonstrative outwardly', it was easy for people to get the wrong impression.

Even when Constance plucked up her courage and managed to express herself in more intimate social situations, she brought forth ridicule and venom. When Adrian Hope met Oscar by accident, Oscar insisted on taking him home to Tite Street for dinner with Constance where the three of them discussed the virtues – or otherwise – of marriage. Remarkably and radically, Constance thought that trial marriages would be an excellent thing. She 'said during dinner that she thought it should be free to either party to go off at the expiration of the first year', Adrian Hope reported to Laura. Oscar, he said, 'had distinct leanings to a system of Contract for seven years only, to be renewed or not as either party saw fit'. Laura was outraged. She was engaged to be married and clearly could not and would not brook discussion or deviation from the institution of marriage. She called Constance's views 'simply revolting' and wrote to Adrian: 'I dislike Constance Wilde for her remark even more than her opinion on dancing – unless by the by it was a *desperate* attempt at originality. No wonder she has a sulky, dull face if those are the thoughts she has to talk with when she is alone.'

Constance found herself out of her depth. Richard Le Gallienne, the poet and one-time disciple of Oscar, recalled Constance as 'a pretty young woman of the innocent Kate Greenaway type'. It was impossible, Le Gallienne said, 'not to predict suffering for a woman so simple and domestic mated with a mind so searching and so perverse and a character so self-indulgent'. The day-to-day realities of marriage to Oscar were not what Constance had bargained for. She had not anticipated the depth of scrutiny that being the wife of Oscar Wilde attracted, nor had she ever imagined that the venomous criticism which had been heaped on Oscar would now also be directed at her. Arthur Ransome's early biography of Oscar, published in 1912, painted a shrewd portrait of Constance. It almost certainly comes directly from the mouth of Robbie Ross, Oscar's lover, friend and literary executor, who knew her very well:

> She was sentimental, pretty, well-meaning and inefficient. She would have been very happy as the wife of an ornamental minor poet, and it is possible that in marrying Wilde she mistook him for such a character. It must be remembered that she married the author of *Poems* and the lecturer on the aesthetic movement. His development puzzled her, made her feel inadequate, and so increased her inadequacy. She became more a spectacle for Wilde than an influence upon him, and was without the strength that might have prevented the disasters that were to fall through him on herself. She had a passion for leaving things alone, broken only by moments of interference badly timed. She became one of those women whose Christian names their husbands, without malice, preface with the epithets 'poor dear.' Her married life was no less ineffectual than unhappy.

Ada Leverson, the gifted, witty Jewish writer who became the devoted friend of Oscar and Bosie, also recognised this portrait. Although she doesn't mention Oscar or Constance by name, this is clearly a portrait of the Wilde marriage:

> I knew a case of a man of remarkable and brilliant gifts – genius is not too strong an expression – and he fell in love with and married a simple, sweet little woman, not at all clever, who worshipped him. He thought this ideal at first, but his point of view gradually changed. She had, alas! no tact – tact is part of cleverness. She always said the wrong thing, invariably spoilt his

conversation by some irrelevant ineptitude; she worried him with household matters at the wrong moment, and was, in fact, in every way as stupid as the cleverest man could desire. The result was that, though he was deeply attached to her, and felt for her always a sincere affection, he gradually could not stand her society. It became more and more irksome to him. He grew to take interest in other things than his home, and at last they unhappily drifted apart.

Ada Leverson goes on to say that the couple would never have drifted apart if Oscar had 'married a clever woman who would have understood him and not wearied him'. No doubt the 'clever woman' she was thinking of was herself. But both she and Arthur Ransome were wrong in their conviction that a woman who was cleverer than Constance, stronger than Constance would have prevented Oscar's drift. Constance was clever and she was strong, stronger perhaps than anyone could have imagined when the catastrophe broke. It was not Constance, it was her gender. No woman, no matter how clever or how strong, would have been able to stifle Oscar's homoerotic cravings. A different woman might have been able to reach an accommodation, a *modus vivendi* with her husband's sexual desires, allowing him to go off and have sex with men and yet remain a husband and a father. But Constance was not such a woman. She was an idealist. She was blindly devoted to her Oscar. She loved him, she adored him and she was convinced of his genius. 'How passionately I worship and adore you,' she wrote to Oscar when she was pregnant with Cyril.

There was no doubt that Oscar was fond – 'really very fond', he would later say – of Constance: she was the mother of his sons, she was the châtelaine of the House Beautiful, and she had 'some sweet points in her character'. And throughout the marriage she was 'wonderfully loyal' to Oscar. Constance represented certainty, consistency and conformity, qualities that Oscar valued or chose not to value as the mood took him. But marriage and Constance had disappointed Oscar. 'There is one thing infinitely more pathetic than to have lost the woman one is in love with, and that is to have won her and found out how shallow she is,' he remarked. Despite Constance's sterling qualities, the death of the marriage was inevitable. 'She could not understand me,' Oscar wrote later, 'and I was bored to death with the married life.'

'Bored to death.' How long had it taken Oscar to become bored with married life, let alone bored to death? The answer is almost certainly not very long. Oscar was easily bored. '*Ennui* is the enemy!' he said. Though he was fond of Constance, he was bored by her; bored by her frequently expressed sense of conventional morality – 'Women are always on the side of morality, public and private' – so at odds with his own anarchic views; bored and made impatient by her accounts of her unhappy and abusive upbringing. And was Oscar speaking of Constance when he had Lord Henry Wotton tell Dorian Gray that 'the only way a woman can ever reform a man is by boring him so completely that he loses all possible interest in life'?

There was also a darker side to the breakdown of relations with Constance.

Before his marriage Oscar had hoped that regular sex with a woman would curb – indeed cure – his desires for sex with young men. What he had not bargained for was that marriage and the birth of his two sons, Cyril in 1885 and Vyvyan in 1886, would foment a strong physical loathing, a visceral distaste for the bodily trappings of womanhood. It was more complex than simply preferring male bodies to female. It was a sense of disgust, of revulsion, of absolute repugnance for any physical manifestations of female sexuality.

Oscar had married the Madonna Mia of his poetic imagination. With her slender, boyish figure and tremulous, flower-like beauty, Constance was the embodiment of sexual innocence: unsullied, untouched, untainted by any overt manifestation of sexuality. Oscar worshipped her purity, her freshness. But once married, once deflowered, Constance could no longer be the *virga intacta* of his imagination. Her innocence became experience, her purity, a sexual complicity. She became a woman, a creature of flesh and blood, with womanly attributes like breasts and a vagina. She had pubic hair, and every month she menstruated. From the idealised freshness of the flower meadow, she became sentient and sensual, a lover, a mother with breasts that enlarged and a belly that swelled. In his poem 'The Harlot's House', written just after his honeymoon, Oscar put this transition from innocence to experience, from love to lust, into words:

> Then turning to my love I said,
> 'The dead are dancing with the dead,
> the dust is whirling with the dust.'
> But she, she heard the violin,
> And left my side, and entered in;
> Love passed into the house of Lust.

This repugnance for female bodies first manifested itself when Constance was pregnant with Cyril. Frank Harris records a conversation with Oscar about the burgeoning sense of disgust he felt for Constance. 'When I married,' he told Harris:

> my wife was a beautiful girl, white and slim as a lily, with dancing eyes and gay rippling laughter like music. Within a year or so the flower-like grace had all vanished; she became heavy, shapeless, deformed. She dragged herself about the house in uncouth misery with drawn blotched face and hideous body, sick at heart because of our love. It was dreadful. I tried to be kind to her, forced myself to touch and kiss her; but she was sick always and – oh! I cannot recall it, it is all loathsome. I used to wash my mouth and open the window to cleanse my lips in the pure air.

The seeds of Oscar's physical repugnance for women's bodies and women's sexuality were perhaps always there. He had a profound aversion to any physical deformity or pain. 'Ugliness,' he once told Robert Sherard, 'I consider

a kind of malady, and illness and suffering always inspire me with repulsion.'
And Lord Henry Wotton in *Dorian Gray* says:

> I can sympathise with everything, except suffering. I cannot sympathise with
> that. It is too ugly, too horrible, too distressing. There is something terribly
> morbid in the modern sympathy with pain. One should sympathise with the
> colour, the beauty, the joy of life. The less said about life's sores the better.

Pregnancy to Oscar was a deformity, a form of ugliness. When Frank Harris
asked Oscar if he felt no pity for Constance when she was pregnant, he replied
impatiently, 'Pity! Pity has nothing to do with love. How can one desire what
is shapeless, deformed, ugly? Desire is killed by maternity. Passion buried in
conception.'

Oscar was not alone in his distaste for female bodies and female sexuality.
Many men who had sexual desires for other men had strong feelings of
repugnance for the female body, especially the vagina. They were repelled by
the sight and the smell of menstruation. According to André Raffalovich, who
knew Oscar well, 'Many men find the smell of women unpleasant whilst the
sweat of a healthy clean man is exciting and pleasant.' In *Teleny* the hero
describes how a husband 'must love indeed, not to feel an inward sinking
feeling when a few days after the wedding he finds his bride's middle parts
tightly tied up in foul and bloody rags'.

Oscar's misogyny was selective. At an individual level, he liked women
enormously. He liked them socially; he found it easy to be intimate with them,
to be inspired by their beauty or by their intelligence. He could be kind,
incredibly kind, towards women. He wanted their friendship. He wanted –
sometimes – to adore them, at other times to be adored by them. And Oscar
could love women in an idealised, abstract way. But on a collective level,
especially when it came to sex, he was irrationally, almost phobically
misogynistic. Frank Harris tried to talk to Oscar about the sexual desirability
of the opposite sex. 'Don't talk to me of the other sex,' Oscar retorted with
distaste. 'First of all in beauty there is no comparison between a boy and a girl.
Think of the enormous, fat hips which every sculptor has to tone down, and
make lighter, and the great udder breasts which the artist has to make small and
round and firm.' He exhibited this streak of his misogyny to Robert Sherard.
'Oscar had no illusions whatever about female virtue,' Sherard recalled later.
'He considered women as prompted only by sexual urge and devoid of what the
bourgeois call morality.' When Oscar once met Sherard in the Adelphi Hotel
in London, where Sherard was staying with a young woman with whom he had
eloped from Paris and hoped to marry, 'Act dishonourably, Robert,' Oscar told
him. 'Act dishonourably. It's what sooner or later she'll certainly do to you.'

When it came to sex between a man and a woman, Oscar held a curiously
Old Testament view that women set out to ruin men. Women were Eves:
temptresses and sirens; they had eaten of the fruit of the tree of sexual
knowledge, and after they had 'glutted their lust', as Oscar once termed it, they

would bring about the expulsion from Eden. When the weasly Fred Atkins, a blackmailer and male prostitute whom Oscar took to Paris, testified against him in court, he told how Oscar tried to dissuade him from visiting the Moulin Rouge, the haunt, so Oscar said, of women of easy virtue. 'Mr Wilde told me not to go to see those women, as women were the ruin of young fellows,' Atkins told the court. The subject was clearly close to Oscar's heart, and Atkins testified that 'Mr Wilde spoke several times about the same subject, and always to the same effect.'

'A woman's passion is degrading,' Oscar told Frank Harris. 'She is continually tempting you. She wants your desire as a satisfaction for her vanity more than anything else, and her vanity is insatiable if her desire is weak, and so she continually tempts you to excess, and then blames you for the physical satiety and disgust which she herself has created.' This paradox between female sexual desire and male sexual disgust, between lust and satiety, was a theme Oscar developed in his epic poem 'The Sphinx', begun in Paris in 1883 and progressively revised throughout his marriage. Oscar portrays the sphinx as the incarnation of female lust, a monstrous supernatural *femme fatale*, possessed of an amorphous, all-consuming sexuality which tempts, debases and disgusts:

Get hence, you loathsome Mystery! Hideous animal, get hence!
You wake in me each bestial sense, you make me what I would not be.
You make my creed a barren sham, you wake foul dreams of sensual life.

Oscar explores this paradox even more explicitly in *Teleny*. Women tempt men into sex. They gratify men's sexual needs and, in so doing, degrade themselves and their sexual partners, creating a kind of righteous disgust, a virtuous contempt in men. After having sex with Des Grieux's mother in order to clear his debts, the pianist René Teleny is overcome with disgust and remorse as he gazes down at what was immediately previously the object of his passion:

Her thighs were bare, and the thick curly hair that covered her middle parts, as black as jet, was sprinkled over with pearly drops of milky dew.

Such a sight would have awakened an eager, irrepressible desire in Joseph himself, the only chaste Israelite of whom we have ever heard; and yet Teleny, leaning on his elbow, was gazing at her with all the loathsomeness we feel when we look at a kitchen table covered with the offal of the meat, the hashed scraps, the dregs of the wines which have supplied the banquet that has just glutted us.

He looked at her with the scorn which a man has for the woman who has just ministered to his pleasure, and who has degraded herself and him. Moreover, as he felt unjust towards her, he hated her, and not himself.

There is an element of cruelty in Oscar's misogyny, something he perhaps recognised himself when he had Lord Henry Wotton say in *Dorian Gray*: 'I am afraid that women appreciate cruelty, downright cruelty, more than anything else. They have wonderfully primitive instincts. We have emancipated them, but they remain slaves looking for their masters, all the same.'

For Oscar, marriage to the Madonna Mia of his poetic imagination had clearly been a mistake. But in a perverse, paradoxical way, Oscar's marriage had the effect of refocussing his erotic desires towards young men and gave him the impetus and the will to seek them out. In 'Wasted Days', the original version of 'Madonna Mia', the object of Oscar's poetic ardour had been a 'fair slim boy'. It was high time to turn his attention back to boys, to seek again 'the love of the impossible'. It was the first act in an unfolding tragedy.

Playing with fire

'Marriage is a sort of forcing-house. It brings strange sins to fruit, and sometimes strange renunciations.' – Esmé Amarinth in The Green Carnation

When Oscar was touring the provinces six months after his marriage, he wrote a love letter to Constance which combined the poetic and the prosaic:

> Dear and Beloved, Here am I, and you at the Antipodes. O execrable facts, that keep our lips from kissing, though our souls are one.
>
> What can I tell you by letter? Alas! Nothing that I would tell you. The messages of the gods to each other travel not by pen and ink and indeed your bodily presence here would not make you more real: for I feel your fingers in my hair, and your cheek brushing mine. The air is full of the music of your voice, my soul and body seem no longer mine, but mingled in some exquisite ecstasy with yours. I feel incomplete without you. Ever and ever yours.
>
> OSCAR
>
> Here I stay till Sunday.

There is something profoundly unconvincing in this love letter. It seems curiously detached. Written in what Richard Ellmann called Oscar's 'best Olympian', his letter is too studied, too artificial. It is a deliberate artistic composition, rather than a spontaneous outpouring of love and passion.

At about the same time that he was writing this letter of dubious love to Constance, Oscar wrote a much more spontaneous and flirtatious letter to Philip Griffiths, a twenty-year-old young man he had recently met after giving a lecture in Birmingham:

> My dear Philip, I have sent a photo of myself for you to the care of Mr MacKay which I hope you will like and in return for it you are to send me one of yourself which I shall keep as a memory of a charming meeting and golden hours passed together. You have a nature made to love all beautiful things and I hope we shall see each other soon. Your friend OSCAR WILDE

The photograph in question was a standard pre-signed publicity shot. Oscar had added in a different ink 'To Philip Griffiths'. The swapping of photographs was to become a feature of Oscar's affairs with young men. We have no way of knowing the exact circumstances of their meeting, nor exactly how intimate they became. But it was clear that some sort of friendship, some sort of intimacy was established between Oscar and Philip – and established very quickly, as the meeting Oscar refers to almost certainly began and ended in the course of his very brief visit to Birmingham. Presumably Philip had been introduced to Oscar after his lecture, or had introduced himself, perhaps claiming a mutual friend. Oscar, alone in Birmingham and facing the depressing prospect of a solitary evening in his hotel, may well have invited Philip to dinner. They were quickly on Christian name terms, always a badge of Oscar's favour. When Oscar was cross-examined by Edward Carson during his trial on his penchant for calling young men by their Christian names, he replied, 'Yes. I always call by their Christian names people whom I like. People I dislike I call something else.' Exactly what Oscar and Philip did or did not get up to during the 'golden hours' they spent together will never be known.

Oscar's sudden and intimate friendship with Philip Griffiths just six months after his marriage to Constance was the first of many such friendships with handsome and intense young men. Usually he told them, as he had told Philip, that they were possessed of 'a nature made to love all beautiful things', or a variation on the same theme. A stray introduction after a lecture, or a gushing fan letter, would usually elicit an invitation to tea and an encouragement to share confidences. Walt Whitman called these fan letters written by young men, passionately identifying themselves with the homoerotic intensity of his poetry, letters of 'avowal'. Oscar would receive many such letters of avowal and a good number of his responses survive.

Despite his distaste and repugnance for Constance during her pregnancy with Cyril, Oscar probably managed to stay faithful. He might flirt with handsome young men like Philip Griffiths; he might receive and write gushing letters to them; he might even fantasise about having sex with them, but he somehow managed to stay on the right side of marital fidelity. But all this was about to change.

On the morning of 5 November 1885, five months to the day after the birth of Cyril, Oscar received a letter from a young man called Harry Marillier, who was a student at Peterhouse, Cambridge. Oscar had known Harry slightly five years earlier as a fifteen-year-old Bluecoat Boy at Christ's Hospital school in the City of London who had lodged in the same house as Oscar and Frank Miles. Harry Marillier's letter to Oscar was a cautious letter of avowal. He asked if Oscar remembered him from Salisbury Street, told him that he had not forgotten him, that he was a student at Peterhouse, and extended an invitation to Oscar to come to Cambridge and watch a performance of Aeschylus's *Eumenides*. Oscar's reply was equally cautious. He was, he said, 'charmed' to discover that Harry had not forgotten him. 'I have a very vivid remembrance,' he wrote, 'of the bright enthusiastic boy who used to bring me my coffee in Salisbury Street, and am delighted to find he is devoted to the muses, but I suppose you don't flirt with all nine ladies at once? Which of them do you really love?' Oscar extended his own invitation to Harry: 'Whether or not I can come and see you, you must certainly come and see me when you are in town, and we will talk of the poets and drink Keats's health.' There was a cautious and subtle interrogation of Harry's sexual preferences when Oscar asked him to 'write and tell me what things in art you and your friends love best. I do not mean what pictures, but what moods and modulations of art affect you most.'

Harry replied by return of post and, though his letter does not survive, it is clear that his 'moods and modulations' chimed with Oscar's, for two days later they met in London. Oscar only had an hour before he had to catch his train to Newcastle to deliver a lecture at North Shields that evening. But an hour was enough. Both of them realised that there was an intense attraction between them. 'Harry, why did you let me catch my train?' Oscar lamented in a letter written that evening from the Station Hotel in Newcastle. There had been, he went on, 'keen curiosity, wonder, delight' in their meeting. It had been, he said tellingly, 'an hour intensely dramatic and intensely psychological'.

Oscar's use of the word 'psychological' betrays the real nature of the encounter with Harry Marillier. As described earlier, 'psychological' was a contemporary term, almost a euphemism, used by men who had sex with men and by Victorian sexologists alike, to describe the nature of sex and love between men. John Addington Symonds invariably used the word to describe anything pertaining to sex between men. Oscar had started to use 'psychological' at Oxford when discussing love affairs between undergraduates, and would continue using it throughout his life as a word to describe the complex emotional feelings and sexual instincts that impelled men to have sex with other men.

'I find the earth as beautiful as the sky, and the body as beautiful as the soul,' Oscar told Harry and said that, if he were to live again, 'I would like it to be as a flower – no soul but perfectly beautiful.' He added, as an afterthought, 'Perhaps for my sins I shall be made a red geranium!!' Oscar was impatient to see Harry. 'When am I to see you again?' he demanded. 'Write me a long letter to Tite Street and I will get it when I come back. I wish you were here, Harry. But in the vacation you must often come and see me, and we will talk of the poets and forget Piccadilly!! I have never learned anything except from people younger than myself, and you are infinitely young.'

Less than a week later, Oscar was writing to Harry again telling him 'you have the power of making others love you' and asking him to send a photograph of himself. Oscar also mentioned Charles Sayle of New College, Oxford, who had just anonymously published a book of homoerotic poems called *Bertha: A Story of Love*. Sayle had been sent down from Oxford because of a sexual liaison with a young man, probably a fellow undergraduate, and had returned home to Cambridge. 'Do you know him?' Oscar enquired of Harry. 'There is one very lovely sonnet.' Sayle had sent copies of *Bertha* to both Oscar and John Addington Symonds and had inscribed the latter's copy with an effusive dedicatory poem praising Symonds as the leader of the emerging Uranian movement, addressing him reverentially as 'Master'. Sayle's dedicatory poem neatly summed up the philosophy of the Uranians, that, as children of Nature, their sexual instincts were natural:

> There is no Sin, nor any need of cure
> For we are Nature's children, – and she, sure
> It is, is wholly pure and sanctified.

Later, both Oscar and Bosie would describe themselves as 'Nature's stepchildren'. Oscar's copy of *Bertha* is lost, so whether Sayle had inscribed it with an equally effusive dedication is impossible to know. But the mere fact that he sent an overtly homoerotic volume of poems to Oscar suggests that he knew Oscar would be an appreciative reader.

Two days later, Oscar was writing again to Harry. He was in a playful mood:

> What is Harry doing? Is he reading Shelley in a land of moonbeams and mystery? Or rowing in Babylonish garments on the river? Is the world a dung-heap or a flower-garden to him? Poisonous, or perfect, or both?

'Poisonous, or perfect, or both.' This antithesis, and its synthesis, became a mantra for Oscar and was to recur throughout his writing and his letters. He wanted to explore and experience both aspects of the world, the dung-heap and the flower garden. Earth and sky. Heaven and hell. High society and low society. Success and scandal. Fame and infamy. Virtue and vice – especially vice. 'What is your real ambition in life?' Bouncer Ward asked Oscar one evening in Oxford. 'God knows,' said Oscar, serious for a moment. 'I won't be a dried-up Oxford don, anyhow. I'll be a poet, a writer, a dramatist. Somehow or other I'll be famous, and if not famous, I'll be notorious.' Oscar succeeded in realising all these ambitions in the short span of his life.

Just three weeks after their first exchange of letters, Oscar went to Cambridge to spend two or three days with Harry. He almost certainly also saw Oscar Browning, a fellow of King's College and a lover of working-class boys, and may have introduced Harry to him. Oscar was treated royally by Harry and his friends. There was a breakfast where Oscar told one of Harry's friends that 'Nothing is good in moderation. You cannot know the good in anything till you have torn the heart out of it by excess.' This was a very different Oscar from the Oscar who had wanted Constance to practise self-restraint and economy. But Constance's housekeeping and Oscar's appetite – for food and for sex – were two very different things. 'Enough is as bad as a meal,' he said. 'More than enough is as good as a feast.' 'Moderation is a fatal thing,' says Lord Illingworth in *A Woman of No Importance*. 'Nothing succeeds like excess.' Lord Illingworth and Oscar were right. Nothing did succeed like excess, for the time being at least.

It was on this trip to Cambridge that Oscar and Harry almost certainly slept together for the first time. It was probably Oscar's first sexual contact with a man for nearly two years, and it was a memorable experience. On his return to Tite Street, Oscar wrote a blissful letter to Harry:

Does it all seem a dream, Harry? Ah! What is not a dream? To me it is, in a fashion, a memory of music. I remember bright young faces, and grey misty quadrangles, Greek forms passing through Gothic cloisters, life playing among ruins, and, what I love best in the world, Poetry and Paradox dancing together!

There was, according to Oscar, 'only one evil omen – your fire! You are careless about playing with fire, Harry.' Exactly what Oscar meant by this tantalising comment is not certain, but it was clearly intended to resonate with Harry. Maybe the fire in question was love: Harry's love for Oscar and his desire for commitment. Harry had perhaps hinted or even gone so far as to declare his feelings for Oscar. But falling in love was dangerous, not just because sex between men was illegal, but also because long-term relationships no longer formed part of Oscar's plans. 'How much more poetic it is to marry one and love many!' he used to say. By 'love' Oscar meant several things: certainly desire and certainly sex, probably the feelings of excitement and danger of a brief, passionate and illicit affair with a young man, and perhaps feelings of friendship and warmth. There were to be no more marriages, to men or to women.

Oscar wrote a further letter to Harry which would become one of his most memorable and important letters. In it he articulates a new sexual, intellectual and artistic *credo*, a daring manifesto of amorality, which he would stick to, through thick and thin, for the rest of his life. Oscar's letter was a pagan rejection of traditional concepts of love, monogamy and fidelity, and a powerful affirmation of his intention to explore and experience his sexuality. That he was speaking explicitly of sex between men is evident by his use of the phrase *l'amour de l'impossible*, the love of the impossible, another euphemism for love and sex between men. John Addington Symonds used this identical phrase to describe his emotional and sexual feelings for young men. 'You too,' Oscar told Harry, 'have the love of things impossible – *l'amour de l'impossible* (how do men name it?)':

Someday you will find, even as I have found, that there is no such thing as a romantic experience; there are romantic memories, and there is the desire of romance – that is all. Our most fiery moments of ecstasy are merely shadows of what somewhere else we have felt, or of what we long some day to feel. So at least it seems to me.

Walter Pater had written in the famous 'Conclusion' to his *Studies in the History of the Renaissance* that the secret of life was 'not the fruit of experience, but experience itself'. Oscar went one step further. It was not the fruit of experience, nor even the experience itself, but the desire for experience – in particular, the endless, unquenchable desire for sexual experience – that was the secret of life. 'I wanted to eat of the fruit of all the trees in the garden of the world,' he wrote later. It was the scorpion sting of sexual desire that drove him endlessly forwards. There was, of course, the sexual pleasure of the encounter, the orgasmic 'most fiery moment of ecstasy', but this was a subsidiary order of pleasure, a mechanistic pleasure, a pleasure of consumption. True pleasure lay in the simultaneous assuaging and stimulation of desire.

Desire was the beginning and the end of life. Romance and love were transitory emotions, to be anticipated with excitement or recollected in tranquillity. It was an endless, eternal cycle of desire, satiation and desire, a divine and decadent music of the spheres, at once both perfect and poisonous. Oscar recognised and rejoiced in the perverse and paradoxical dualities which his doctrine of desire contained. He told Harry:

> Strangely enough, what comes of all this is a curious mixture of ardour and of indifference. I myself would sacrifice everything for a new experience, and I know there is no such thing as a new experience at all. I think I would more readily die for what I do not believe in than for what I hold to be true. I would go to the stake for a sensation and be a sceptic to the last!

The secret of this doctrine of desire lay in the abandonment of all self-control, a surrender to a mood of endless, eternal and shifting desire. The mystery of moods, he told Harry, was infinitely fascinating. 'To be master of these moods is exquisite, to be mastered by them more exquisite still.' A decade earlier Oscar had articulated this vision of absolute surrender to endless desire in his poem 'Hélas' when he wrote: 'To drift with every passion till my soul/ is a stringed lute on which all winds can play.' Back then, he had rejected such a doctrine, unwilling to sacrifice his 'soul's inheritance' and 'mine ancient wisdom, and austere control' for the pleasure of sex with men. Now he was preparing to abandon all restraint, to surrender and submerge his self and his soul into the great sea of desire and to be washed up on the shore of 'an unknown land full of strange flowers and subtle perfumes, a land of which it is joy of all joys to dream, a land where all things are perfect and poisonous'.

Oscar's intense affair with Harry Marillier continued until January 1886. Only a handful of letters have survived, but Oscar reputedly wrote him 'a suitcase full' of love letters. Harry invited Oscar to spend a night or two at a curiously named house, Ferishtah, near Hampton Court, where Oscar would meet Osman Edwards, a schoolfriend of Harry's, who was now at Oxford. 'Let us live like Spartans,' Oscar replied, 'but let us talk like Athenians.' Two weeks later Oscar invited Harry to Tite Street: 'Come at 12 o'c on Sunday and stay for lunch. So glad to see you dear Harry.' This luncheon was Harry's first introduction to Constance. Quite what she made of the handsome twenty-year-old undergraduate whom Oscar seemed so interested in is not recorded. It may have crossed her mind to wonder whether or not the youthful Harry was an entirely appropriate friend for her thirty-two-year-old husband. She might have thought their sudden intimacy after a five-year gap was a little strange. And, less than a week later, when Oscar insisted on inviting Harry, together with a handsome young Oxonian, Douglas Ainslie, it might well have struck Constance that her husband's fondness for the society of very young men was unusual.

Oscar no doubt managed to set Constance's mind at rest. He would have had an answer – or, much the same thing, a glittering paradox – for everything. In any case, when Oscar invited Harry to lunch, their affair was already waning. Oscar was beginning to get bored. The novelty and the excitement had begun to pall. The sex, once so desired, so anticipated, and so lusted after, was now predictable. Harry's body had yielded up its secrets, and it was time to move on. Harry may have become tedious, or intemperate in his demands for Oscar's attention, so Oscar did what he was to do again and again with his lovers when he wanted to move on: he tried to convert the affair into a friendship. Lovers would be invited to Tite Street, lunched or dined or both, introduced to the shy and charming châtelaine of the House Beautiful, and very soon friendship would fill the place of passion. Oscar would be free to begin his search for a new lover. In this case, he did not have to look too far.

As his affair with Harry was waning, a new erotic interest was waxing in the form of Douglas Ainslie. Ainslie was a twenty-one-year-old undergraduate at Oxford who shared rooms with his Eton schoolfellow, Lord Albert Edward Godolphin Osborne. There is no record of how Oscar and Douglas Ainslie met. Perhaps Ainslie had written a letter of avowal to Oscar. Both he and Osborne were founder members of the Oxford University Dramatic Society, and Ainslie may have written to Oscar to invite him to review their first production, *Twelfth Night*, which opened at the New Theatre on St Valentine's Day. Oscar duly obliged, and when Ainslie invited him to review a second production, he accepted with alacrity. 'Dear Douglas,' he wrote, 'I have lost your note. What is your address, and what day have you asked me for? I really am "impossible" about letters: they vanish from my room.' (Vanishing letters, lost, mislaid – or, more usually, stolen by young blackmailers and male prostitutes – were to be a constant refrain in the years to come.) Oscar's invitation to Ainslie re-used the gist of his earlier invitation to Harry: 'We must have many evenings together,' he told Ainslie, 'and drink yellow wine from green glasses in Keats's honour.' Oscar was also very taken with Ainslie's friend, Lord Osborne: 'I hope you and Osborne are reading hard,' he told Ainslie. 'He is quite charming, with his low musical voice, and his graceful incapacity for a career. He is a little like the moon.' Oscar declared, not for the last time, that 'young Oxonians are very delightful, so Greek and graceful and uneducated. They have profiles but no philosophy.'

With Harry Marillier and then Douglas Ainslie, Oscar's pursuit of desire was only just beginning.

Mad and coloured loves

*'Love is all very well in its way, but friendship is much higher.
Indeed, I know of nothing in the world that is either nobler or
rarer than a devoted friendship.'*

The two years following his wedding were professionally barren for Oscar. He continued to tour the country on his self-appointed mission to civilise the provinces with a new repertoire of lectures on 'Dress', 'The Value of Art in Modern Life' and 'Beauty, Taste and Ugliness in Dress'. It was work and it paid, but it hardly seemed like the realisation of the brilliant promise he had shown at Oxford. He had been on the professional lecturing stump for nearly four years now and it was becoming increasingly obvious to him – and others – that his star was in the descendant. The *Pall Mall Gazette* reported unkindly that 'Oscar's star has been low in the horizon since he cut his hair and became "Benedick the married man"'. The lodestar of lasting literary fame had proved elusive. As a self-styled and self-publicising Professor of Aesthetics, Oscar had mesmerised and scandalised the middle classes in Britain and America, for a while at least. His first volume of poetry had been a financial success, running through five editions in as many months, but had been savaged by the critics. And his play *Vera, or the Nihilists* had opened with fanfares in New York and promptly closed after a week, while *The Duchess of Padua* was languishing unproduced after the American actress Mary Anderson refused to proceed with her planned production.

Despite Constance's income, which should have been perfectly adequate for any normal family to live on quietly but comfortably, money seemed to be in perpetual short supply. Oscar's income was sparse and erratic, and his extravagance meant that finances were a constant problem. He was profligate with money and had absolutely no sense of how to budget. He was contemptuous of those who sought to balance their books and eke out their income. He was determined to deny himself nothing. 'Give me the luxuries,' he used to say, 'and anyone can have the necessaries.' Oscar needed a diversion from the wearisome treadmill of the provincial lecture circuit, and, from early 1886 onwards, he increasingly turned to journalism as a source of income. His work for the *Pall Mall Gazette* consisted of reviews mostly, of books and plays – anything that would bring in a few pounds.

Early in 1886 Oscar even considered taking employment. He applied – unsuccessfully – for the Secretaryship of the newly established Beaumont Trust, an educational charity for the poor. He also considered becoming an Inspector of Schools and wrote to his old tutor and friend, Mahaffy, asking him to use his influence with Lord Spencer, a senior figure in the Liberal government. 'A word from you as to my capabilities would go far towards getting me what I want,' he wrote. It was not just the uncertainties and insecurities of the literary life that pushed him into this uncharacteristic step. There was another, more pressing reason. Constance was pregnant for the second time.

As his affair with Harry Marillier cooled into friendship, Oscar returned to Constance's bed. There would have been a lapse in sexual relations while Constance was pregnant with Cyril: most Victorian doctors did not recommend sexual intercourse for pregnant women, though some thought that sex up to three months before the birth was acceptable. And Oscar and Constance would perhaps have refrained from having sex for some months afterwards to avoid another pregnancy. There are several possible explanations as to why he resumed having sex with her. He may have done it out of a sense of duty, or loyalty. He may have done it to keep Constance's suspicions at bay. He may have done it to get her pregnant again and so avoid having to have sex with her on a regular basis. He may even have done it out of a strange kind of love and affection for her. Despite his strong disgust for the female body and for female sexuality – especially anything to do with pregnancy – Oscar may well have resumed sexual relations with Constance with almost a sense of relief after his entanglement with Harry. However exciting, however compelling the prospect of sex with young men, there were risks and dangers. 'In mad and coloured loves there is much danger,' he wrote. 'There is the danger of losing them no less than the danger of keeping them.' There was a feeling of safety, of predictability, of consistency in sex with Constance. Oscar once said that 'consistency is the last refuge of the unimaginative', and, after the turbulence and excitement of sex with a man, he may have sunk back into the unimaginative repose of married life – for a while at least.

And 'mad and coloured loves' were becoming dangerous for another reason. It was unfortunate to say the least that Oscar's exploration of his sexual desires for men coincided with one of Britain's periodic spasms of public morality. In the early summer of 1885, W.T. Stead, the editor of the *Pall Mall Gazette*, published an exposé of the ease with which depraved men could purchase the sexual services of very young girls. Stead went out and procured a young girl to demonstrate how easily girls could be bought. His series of articles, 'The Maiden Tribute of Modern Babylon', provoked a national moral outrage and forced the caretaker Tory government of Lord Salisbury to hastily enact the Criminal Law Amendment Bill, the long title of which was 'an Act to make further provisions for the Protection of Women and Girls; the suppression of brothels, and other purposes'. The Bill was designed to more effectively suppress brothels, to prevent the procuring of girls for common prostitution, and to suppress what was known as the white slave trade in which young British women and girls were sold into sexual slavery in brothels abroad. The Bill also raised the age of consent for girls to sixteen. It had been thirteen.

Stead was arrested, tried and sent to prison for two months for technically breaking the law by procuring a young girl without the consent of her father. Henry Labouchère, the maverick Liberal MP for Northampton, claimed – several years later – that Stead at this time wrote to him privately, sending him a report about the prevalence of male prostitution in London and other big cities. Labouchère, or Labby as he was known to friends and foes alike, was a former diplomat and now founder and editor of the campaigning weekly magazine *Truth*, which sought to expose corruption, hypocrisy, lax morality and malpractice.

Oscar had been a great admirer of Labouchère. During his tour of the United States in 1882, he had praised Labby as 'the best writer in Europe, a most remarkable gentleman'. Labby was less eager to return the compliment. A review of Oscar's lecture 'Impressions of America' in *Truth* was critical of his profligate and voluptuous use of adjectives. Oscar had, *Truth* reported, used the word 'lovely' forty-three times; 'beautiful' twenty-six times; and 'charming' no less than seventeen times. In an editorial the following day, *Truth* went for Oscar's jugular. The editorial was written by Labby and provocatively described Oscar as an 'epicene youth' and 'an effeminate phrase-maker . . . lecturing to empty benches'.

Labby was so concerned by Stead's report on the prevalence of male prostitution that, during the last stages of the Criminal Law Amendment Bill's passage into law, he tabled an amendment which outlawed sexual acts between men not amounting to sodomy. Sodomy had been illegal in England since the seventh century. But, until the reign of Henry VIII, cases had always been dealt with by the ecclesiastical courts, the usual punishment being death by being buried alive, burning, hanging, or drowning. In 1533, 'the detestable and abominable Vice of Buggery' was codified into secular law and became a felony punishable by death.

In 1885, a conviction for sodomy meant a maximum sentence of life imprisonment. But there was a gap in the law: other sexual acts between men like mutual masturbation and fellatio were not the subject of legislation. Technically, it was perfectly legal for men to have non-penetrative sex with other men, although any sexual expression between men was viewed as utterly perverted. The law required a heavy burden of proof to obtain a conviction of sodomy. There had to be incontrovertible proof of penetration as well as proof of what the law quaintly called 'emission of seed' in the partner's rectum. Unless ejaculation could be proved to have taken place, there was no case to answer.

This had been demonstrated, in spectacular fashion, fifteen years earlier when, in April 1870, Ernest Boulton, known as 'Stella', and Frederick Park, known as 'Fanny', were arrested as they left the Strand Theatre dressed in full drag. The police had been watching them for weeks, and they were charged with conspiracy to commit sodomy with Lord Arthur Clinton, a Member of Parliament and the third son of the powerful Duke of Newcastle, and two other men. Stella and Fanny shared lodgings with Lord Arthur, who had had visiting cards printed for Stella in the name of 'Lady Arthur Clinton'. Before the case came to trial, Lord Arthur conveniently died, apparently of scarlet fever, though suicide is a more likely explanation. The prosecution of Fanny and Stella failed because there was no concrete proof that Lord Arthur, or anyone else, had emitted his seed into their rectums, even though there was very strong evidence to suggest that Fanny and Stella had been regularly sodomised. The police surgeon who examined Stella and Fanny found that both their anuses were dilated to a considerable degree: 'I have never seen anything like it before,' the shocked police surgeon, Mr James Paul, told the court. But anal dilation alone was neither proof of anal penetration nor of emission of seed.

Labby wrote later that the main impetus behind his amendment was a widespread public perception that sex between men was 'on the increase'. Sir Howard Vincent, the first Director of Criminal Investigations at Scotland Yard from 1878 to 1884, had declared that men soliciting sex with other men were 'an increasing scourge'. *The Yokel's Preceptor*, a curious guide to the erotic pleasures and pitfalls of London, described what it perceived as an epidemic of male-to-male sex in the capital:

> The increase of these monsters in the shape of men, commonly designated margeries, poofs, etc., of late years, in the great Metropolis, renders it necessary for the safety of the public that they should be made known . . . Will the reader credit it, but such is nevertheless the fact, that these monsters actually walk the street the same as the whores, looking out for a chance? Yes, the Quadrant, Fleet Street, Holborn, the Strand, etc., are actually thronged with them! Nay, it is not long since, in the neighbourhood of Charing Cross, they posted bills in the windows of several public houses, cautioning the public to 'Beware of Sods!'

Sex between men had from medieval times been seen not just as a sin and a crime – 'the destestable and abominable Vice of Buggery', as the statute of Henry VIII called it – but more particularly as a contagion, a virus which could be spread by sexual contact. Labby and other campaigners for social purity were determined to stamp this contagion out. A year earlier, in 1884, the Dublin Castle Scandal had treated the British public to the unedifying spectacle of a network of sexual contacts between highly placed officials in the British administration in Dublin on the one hand and a ragtag and bobtail assortment of local men on the other.

There were two aspects of the Dublin Castle Scandal that particularly shocked the *amour propre* of politicians, social purity campaigners and the public: the heresy that there should be sexual contact between the classes, and the existence of a social identity, a sub-cultural community, between men of wildly different classes. Both of these factors would work against Oscar when his turn in the dock came. William O'Brien, the Irish Nationalist MP and editor of the *United Ireland* newspaper, which first got wind of the Dublin Castle Scandal, described it as 'a criminal confederacy, which for its extent and atrocity, almost staggered belief. It included men of all ranks, classes, professions, and outlawries, from aristocrats of the highest fashion to outcasts in the most loathsome dens.' These included: Jack Saul, a male prostitute (whose bawdy memoirs, *The Sins of the Cities of the Plain; or the Recollections of a Mary Ann*, Oscar certainly read); one 'Lizzie', Captain of the Royal Dublin Fusiliers; 'The Maid of Athens', or Malcolm Johnstone; and dozens more.

Social purity campaigners were also alarmed by the slow, steady rumblings of medical and legal debate about the rights and wrongs of sex between men. Beginning slowly in Germany in the 1860s, the debate grew in strength. A German lawyer, Karl Heinrich Ulrichs, was the pioneer, producing dozens of books and pamphlets arguing for the legal and social recognition of sex between men. It was Ulrichs, invoking Plato's *Symposium*, who had coined the German term *Uranismus* from the *uranios* or 'heavenly love' of Aphrodite, daughter of Uranus. Translated into English this became 'Uranianism' or 'Uranian love'. Ulrichs fought on two fronts. First, he emphasised the naturalness and normalness of Uranian love. The Urning, he said, was someone who was born with *anima muliebris virili corpore inclusa*, a feminine soul in a male body. If sexuality was inborn, predetermined, a product of nature, Ulrichs argued, then there could be no justification for criminalising sex between men. Ulrichs went further and demanded for Uranians full social and legal equality with heterosexuals as well as the right to marry. Going further still, Ulrichs asserted that Uranian love was of a higher order than *pandemos* or common, heterosexual love.

In Britain, John Addington Symonds's book *A Problem in Greek Ethics* had been privately printed and distributed in 1883. It was subtitled 'An Inquiry into the Phenomenon of Sexual Inversion addressed especially to medical psychologists and jurists' and invoked the glories of Greek *paiderastia*, arguing essentially that what was good for the Greeks was good for the British.

The slow and steady drip, drip, drip of legal, medical and social debate about sex between men alongside a series of high-profile scandals fuelled Labby's perception that the vice was on the increase. His amendment was designed to plug the gaps in the law. Section 11 of the Criminal Law Amendment Act stated that:

Any male person who, in public or private commits or is a party to the commission of, or procures the commission by any male person, of any act of gross indecency with another male person, shall be guilty of a misdemeanour, and being convicted thereof shall be liable at the discretion of the Court to be imprisoned for any term not exceeding two years, with or without hard labour.

The Labouchère Amendment, as it became known, had become law with only one change. Labby had wanted a maximum penalty of seven years with hard labour, but the Home Secretary and the Attorney General had persuaded him to reduce this to two years.

John Addington Symonds was appalled by Section 11. He called it 'a disgrace to legislation, by its vagueness of diction and the obvious incitement to false accusation'. It was the criminalisation of what had previously not been criminal and the catch-all wording of Labby's Amendment that worried Symonds. First of all, there seemed to be little or no burden of proof required. After all, how could anyone prove or disprove what had or had not happened in private? It was a green light for blackmailers, operating singly or in gangs. An allegation of gross indecency would be sufficient to cause a man to be arrested, committed for trial and ruined. Even before Labby's Amendment, men who had sex with men were vulnerable to blackmail; now, the threat of two years' hard labour, with no burden of proof required, signalled an open season for blackmailers. Then there was the element of the Amendment which criminalised anyone who 'is a party to the commission of, or procures the commission of' a sexual act between men. What exactly did this mean? It was, in fact, a conspiracy clause, a catch-all clause that allowed the law to prosecute any man against whom charges of actual gross indecency would not stick, and it was used as such in successive prosecutions under the Amendment right up until 1967.

Labby always thought two years quite insufficient to the crime of gross indecency. It was the legislation under which Oscar was to be tried and convicted a decade later. When Oscar went to bed with Harry Marillier in Cambridge he had, overnight, become a criminal. Later, in *The Picture of Dorian Gray*, Oscar would directly refer to what he considered the real perniciousness of Section 11: by criminalising men's sexual desire for men, the law not only repressed desire, but it also warped and made that desire ugly:

> The only way to get rid of a temptation is to yield to it. Resist it, and your soul grows sick with longing for the things it has forbidden to itself, with desire for what its monstrous laws have made monstrous and unlawful.

At some point during this year of criminalisation, Oscar met the man who was destined to be his devoted friend for the rest of his life. Robert Baldwin Ross was the son of John Ross, a distinguished Canadian politician who had died when Robert – or Robbie or Bobby as he was usually called – was just two. John Ross had expressed a wish that his five children be educated in Europe, a wish that his widow, Eliza, faithfully respected. The family moved to London when Robbie was four, eventually settling in Onslow Gardens.

Robbie had just turned seventeen when he met Oscar but looked much younger. He was not conventionally handsome: slight and slender, with a round, moon-like face, a large intellectual expanse of forehead, a small tilt-turned nose and a rather voluptuous mouth. Oscar said he had 'the face of Puck and the heart of an angel'. And Bosie Douglas, who spent the latter part of his life and energies trying to bring about Robbie's absolute destruction, described him variously as 'a rather pathetic-looking little creature, in appearance something like a kitten' and 'a slender, attractive, impulsive boy'.

The exact circumstances of when, where and how Oscar and Robbie met are unknown. Robbie rarely spoke about his early years, and Oscar never referred to the circumstances of their first meeting. Frank Harris later claimed, however, that Oscar had told him that he had met Robbie in a public lavatory, and that Robbie had importuned him. Certainly Robbie was sexually precocious. Unlike many Victorian young men who struggled painfully with their sexuality for years before coming to terms with it – if they ever did – Robbie seems never to have had any doubts or experienced any disquiet about his sexual orientation. He had spent six years at a prep school in Cobham, Surrey and would have learnt the rudimentary truths about boys and sex there. From the age of twelve, he was educated at home by tutors, and he travelled extensively in Europe, sometimes with his mother, and sometimes with his tutor. By the time he was seventeen, he was intellectually and socially precocious. He had seen far more of the world than most boys of his age and had probably explored and experienced his sexuality on his travels.

It is entirely possible that Oscar and Robbie did meet in a public lavatory. Long after Oscar was dead and Robbie and Bosie had had a bitter falling out, Bosie obtained a deposition from an Inspector West of Scotland Yard, who said he had patrolled the Vine Street area of Piccadilly for fifteen years and 'had known Ross during all those years as an habitual associate of sodomites and male prostitutes'. Robbie may well have started his explorations of the erotic underground of London by hanging around parks and open spaces and loitering in public lavatories. Under the heading of 'Public Necessaries', the Public Health Act of 1875 had laid a duty upon urban authorities to provide an adequate supply of 'urinals, waterclosets, earthclosets, privies, ashpits and other similar conveniences for public accommodation', which led to the construction of both street-level *pissoirs* and more elaborate underground public conveniences in the larger towns and cities. 'Cottages', as they were and are known in Polari, the argot of men who love men, provided an ideal venue for men to meet like-minded men for sex. The technique was simple. Men would stand at urinals masturbating and eventually exposing their erect penises to other interested men. It was crude, but very effective; a fast and efficient means of establishing direct and mutual sexual interest. Often, men would masturbate each other while standing side by side at the urinals until one or both ejaculated. Sometimes they would withdraw to the lockable cubicles and engage in a range of sexual acts, or they might leave together and go to a park or to a house to enjoy sex.

Then as now, 'cottaging' was fraught with dangers: the dangers of discovery, of arrest, of assault. In the 1880s and 1890s, there was an additional danger of falling foul of blackmailers and robbers. In a process called by its perpetrators 'copping for a steamer', young, attractive men would cruise public lavatories, looking for men who were well-dressed and were obviously moneyed. They would make contact, suggest going to a nearby hotel or rooms, have sex and then demand money with menaces. Sometimes, an accomplice would burst in claiming to be the youth's uncle or father and would only be prevented from calling the police by the payment of a large sum of money. Despite these manifest dangers, cottaging was an effective means of finding sexual partners in a city where the sub-culture of men who liked to have sex with boys and men, such as it was, was hidden, difficult to access and was equally vulnerable to blackmail. It was a way, too, for educated middle-class men to make sexual contact with working-class men.

It is perfectly possible, though, that Robbie met Oscar through more conventional avenues. Robbie's older brother, Alec, who had recently graduated from Cambridge and was living the life of a minor man of letters, could easily have met Oscar through London's narrow and incestuous literary and journalistic world. However Robbie and Oscar came to meet, they very quickly became lovers.

Sex with Robbie was probably a very different affair from sex with Frank Miles, Rennell Rodd or Harry Marillier. Although he was just seventeen, Robbie was extremely sexually sophisticated and knew exactly what he wanted out of his sexual encounters. This slender, attractive and impulsive boy was a beacon for men who were attracted to younger men or boys and who often wanted to anally penetrate them. For his part, Robbie was polymorphously perverse. He liked older men to 'play male' to him, taking the receptive role in anal sex, and it is possible that it was with Robbie that Oscar first experienced anal sex. But Robbie also liked sex with younger men and teenage boys, especially from the working classes. Robbie's sexual entanglements with teenage boys would in the years to come pose the gravest threat to him. In 1893 he narrowly escaped prosecution over an ill-advised love affair with a sixteen-year-old schoolboy.

But what was perhaps most important as far as Oscar was concerned was that Robbie had a joyous acceptance of himself as a lover of men. There was no doubt, no self-recrimination, no anguished and prolonged attempts to divert his passions towards women. He was one of the few late-Victorian men who were open with their families about their sexuality, telling his mother and his older brothers when he was nineteen. It was a very courageous and a very foolhardy step to take. Oscar could not help but be dazzled, fascinated and intrigued by a boy who was so sexually knowing, so gloriously accepting of his sexuality.

No letters between Oscar and Robbie survive from this first period of their relationship, but there can be no doubt that Oscar fell violently in love with Robbie, at least for a while. As with all Oscar's love affairs, the intensity of their relationship was short-lived, and neither of them made any attempt at monogamy. Oscar sought sex elsewhere, as did Robbie. But unlike most of Oscar's other relationships, his love affair with Robbie became a deep and abiding friendship, occasionally punctuated by sex. Robbie had a remarkable gift for friendship, especially with literary men. He shared his mother's and his older brother's taste for literature and art. He was well-informed, witty, had remarkable powers of conversation for one so young, and could appreciate and communicate with Oscar in ways that Constance could not.

Bosie Douglas said later that Robbie's gift for friendship was nothing more or less than 'flattery laid on with a trowel':

> He could, when he liked, make himself very agreeable, and he always contrived to convey to the particular person with whom he wished to ingratiate himself that he or she was the object of his profound and respectful admiration. When you had had ten minutes' conversation with him you went away with a pleasing feeling that you were really an important person, and that Ross appreciated it, and would never be likely to forget it.

No doubt there was an element of flattery in Robbie's relationships with literary men, but there was also discrimination, appreciation, understanding and sympathy. Robbie knew the limitations of his own talents but had the gift of recognising and helping to nurture the talents of others. He sensed Oscar's remarkable but, up until that point, latent genius. Their friendship would become a creative partnership which was to last until death.

It is no coincidence that the period of Oscar's greatest work began at about the time he first met Robbie. They were often together, closeted in Oscar's Moorish smoking room in Tite Street, endlessly talking, endlessly laughing and endlessly discussing *l'amour de l'impossible*. As he had done with Harry Marillier and would do with so many others, Oscar introduced Robbie to Constance, who also found him delightful. The following summer, in 1887, Robbie came to stay at Tite Street as a paying guest while Mrs Ross was travelling on the continent. He was attending a crammer's establishment in Covent Garden before going up to Cambridge the following year, and it was felt that his education would suffer if he went abroad with his mother. The arrangement suited Oscar and Robbie perfectly. The first flush of passion between them had long since passed, but there was almost certainly the occasional sexual encounter, after Constance had gone to bed, or when she was away. But the chief glory of their friendship lay in their shared interests in literature, in art and, most importantly in the endlessly fascinating topic of sex.

Poets and lovers

'How much more poetic it is to marry one and love many.'

Oscar always considered himself first and foremost a poet. Although he went on to be a dramatist, the author of at least one novel and the writer of many stories, he invariably described himself as a poet. Poetry was, according to Oscar, the 'highest form of literature', but one which 'brings no wealth to the singer'. Poetry was the medium through which Oscar expressed his most powerful and profound thoughts and emotions, and most of his poems are intensely personal and intensely autobiographical.

In the autumn of 1887, Oscar wrote a poem, 'Un Amant de Nos Jours', which seemed to encapsulate and express his complex feelings about his marriage and the future direction of his sexuality. Writing a poem, let alone publishing it in the *Court and Society Review*, was in itself unusual. Oscar wrote poems only infrequently now. He was frantically busy, 'too busy to lecture', he said. By 1887 he had found the literary success that had eluded him for so long, in that year alone publishing two stories, *The Canterville Ghost* and *Lord Arthur Savile's Crime*, writing numerous reviews and taking on the editorship of a women's magazine, the *Lady's World*, a title which Oscar thought possessed 'a certain taint of vulgarity about it' and which he quickly changed to the *Woman's World*.

The first half of 'Un Amant de Nos Jours', or 'A Lover of Our Time', is a lament and opens with a stark confession of sin:

> The sin was mine; I did not understand;
> So now is music prisoned in her cave,
> Save where some ebbing desultory wave
> Frets with its restless whirls the meagre strand.
> And in the withered hollow of this land
> Hath Summer dug herself so deep a grave,
> That hardly can the silver willow crave
> One little blossom from keen Winter's hand.

The sin of which Oscar speaks is almost certainly a reference to his marriage. The first line of the poem is a confession of guilt over his decision to marry

Constance and its disastrous consequences which he could not have foreseen at the time of his engagement. 'I did not understand,' he writes plaintively of his decision to marry. How could Oscar possibly have understood that the love he felt for Constance at the time he proposed to her was not in fact love, but something akin to love? Fondness, affection, attraction, tenderness. But not love. So Summer has turned to Winter, and now both their lives and their love are diminished, 'withered' and 'meagre', lying 'prisoned' in a cave, buried 'in so deep a grave'.

At one level the poem is a poignant expression of regret and sadness at the unhappiness Oscar has unwittingly brought down on Constance. At another level, it is a powerful lament for the diminishment, the repudiation, the burying, the making invisible of his sexual feelings for men 'save where some ebbing desultory wave', or the occasional love affair, comes to pass. When he wrote the poem, Oscar and Constance had stopped having sex completely. Long after they were both dead, Constance's brother, Otho, told Arthur Ransome, who was writing a biography of Oscar, that there had been 'a virtual divorce' between Oscar and Constance in 1886, by which he meant that sexual relations between them had ceased. The Wildes' second son, Vyvyan, was born early in November 1886 – the exact date remains a mystery as neither parent seems to have been able to remember it when the time came to register Vyvyan's birth.

It has been suggested that the reason for this abrupt cessation of sex between Oscar and Constance was the recrudescence of the syphilis which Oscar is supposed to have contracted at Oxford. But there is no evidence that Oscar ever contracted syphilis, at Oxford or elsewhere; no evidence that he was ever treated for the disease; and no evidence that there was any recrudescence of the disease. In the majority of cases of syphilis, the tertiary stage of the disease is reached within ten years when it begins to affect the internal organs, especially the brain. Oscar's friend, Frank Miles, had to be taken to a lunatic asylum in 1887 when his brain became disordered, and he died there from the effects of advanced syphilis five years later. If Oscar had contracted syphilis at Oxford, there must surely, nearly a decade later, have been some signs of the disease. There were none. Oscar seemed to be enjoying robust good health, apart from a tendency to corpulence, the consequence of over-indulgence in food and wine.

As they had done before the birth of Cyril, Oscar and Constance would naturally have refrained from sex at some point during her pregnancy. But after Vyvyan's birth in November 1886 they never resumed sexual relations. There are a number of possible explanations. Constance had two babies to look after: she would have been exhausted and she may herself not have wished to resume sex, especially if there was any risk of a third pregnancy so soon after Cyril and Vyvyan. Two pregnancies in just over two years was draining, physically, emotionally and financially – and both Constance and Oscar would have been aware that death during childbirth was one of the most common causes of death for women of childbearing age. The most common form of birth control during the nineteenth century was abstinence. It would have been quite unexceptional for a young married couple to practise abstinence – for a while at least – in order to avoid an unwelcome pregnancy. By common consent, two to three years was regarded as the ideal interval between pregnancies. What may for Constance have begun as a period of abstinence became for Oscar a welcome relief from the burden of conjugalities. And even though Constance may have found it strange that they did not resume their sex life, there was little she could do. Oscar would not necessarily have had to explain why he no longer wished to have sex if he did not care to; it was not a subject for discussion between husbands and wives. Sex happened, or it did not. Women of the middle classes were not supposed to have sexual desire, let alone talk about sex. Constance may have shared her anxieties with her closest women friends, or she may have broached the subject with her doctor. It is more likely that she remained silent, wondering why her husband no longer wished to make love to her.

It is unlikely that Oscar followed the example of his friend John Addington Symonds, who one fine spring day in 1869 went for a long walk in 'heavenly hills' outside Bristol with his wife, Catherine. Symonds's purpose was to negotiate an end to the sexual side of their marriage. He told his wife how he had fallen in love with a boy called Norman; how his pent-up sexual frustration was making him ill; and how he would be a better husband and better companion to her once the problem of sex had been resolved. Remarkably, Catherine acceded gracefully. She disliked sex and did not want to have any more children. She was a pragmatist. She agreed to a celibate marriage, having extracted a promise from Symonds that he would indulge in 'nothing base' with Norman, by which she meant anal sex. But Constance was not Catherine. She was a passionate idealist. It is unlikely that she would have agreed to a celibate marriage with Oscar on the grounds that he was in love with a boy.

If the first half of 'Un Amant de Nos Jours' is a lament about the death of the sexual side of his marriage to Constance and the harrowing of his sexual desire for other men, the second half is a triumphant affirmation of homoerotic desire, a brash trumpet blast signalling the coming of the dawn after the long darkness of night:

> But who is this that cometh by the shore?
> (Nay, love, look up and wonder,) who is this
> That cometh with dyed garments from the South?
> It is thy new-found Lord, and he shall kiss
> The yet unravished roses of thy mouth,
> And I will weep and worship, as before.

The 'new-found Lord' dressed in 'dyed garments from the South' is a Christ-like figure, a new Lord of love whose corporeal and spiritual kiss at once sanctions and sanctifies sex between men. There must be no more downcast gazes among men who love men, they must look up and wonder, 'weep and

87

worship', at the coming of this new Lord. More daringly, the love object of this new Lord is clearly a youth, a virginal youth. Oscar employs some highly sexualised imagery to convey the virginity of the youth: the 'roses' of his mouth are as 'yet unravished'. Just as the locus of Oscar's sexual interest in Constance lay in her virginity, and in robbing her of that virginity, so his sexual interest in men turned increasingly towards younger men, youths, boys, especially those without any sexual experience of men, male virgins whom he could deflower. 'Un Amant de Nos Jours' charts the dramatic change that came over Oscar's perception of his sexuality in less than two years – from the young husband and father tentatively exploring his repressed sexuality after the disappointment of marriage, struggling against fear and remorse at his sexual desires and experiences, to the champion not just of the legitimacy – but more importantly, the superiority – of sex between men and boys.

It is perhaps hard to comprehend the importance of poetry to men who loved men at the end of the nineteenth century. Poetry was much, much more than a form of emotional and erotic self-expression. It was the medium in which the erotic, the spiritual and political collided and coalesced. Homoerotic poetry was the *lingua franca* of many men who loved men. They read it, they wrote it, they talked about it and wrote about it; and they used poetry as a badge of, sometimes as a camouflage for, their sexual desires. And those who constituted themselves, or were constituted, the 'leaders of Hellas', as George Ives termed them, those who dedicated their lives to gaining social and political acceptance for men who loved men – Walt Whitman, John Addington Symonds, Edward Carpenter and Oscar Wilde – were all poets who sought to express their sexuality through the medium of their poetry.

Poetry was not just an invocation of homoerotic desire, but also an attempt to define and classify, to order that desire. Like the painter Simeon Solomon's mystic treatise on Uranian love, poetry became a vision of love, a vision of a world where love between men and youths was somehow raised up from its furtive, criminal, despicable status as the *crimen tantum horribile non inter Christianos nominandum*, to a finer, higher plain, to a Higher Philosophy, as Plato had termed love between men and youths in the *Symposium*. When Oscar inscribed a copy of his collection of essays, *Intentions*, for Lord Alfred Douglas, he wrote 'Bosie, from his friend the author . . . In memory of the Higher Philosophy'.

Archetypes of love and lovers were invoked in poetry, usually but not exclusively from classical Greece. Individually and collectively, the body of homoerotic poetry created a taxonomy of homoerotic desire which centred on the classical model of Greek *paiderastia* and celebrated the spiritual and sexual love of an older man for a youth. One of the most distinctive qualities of homoerotic poetry was its embodiment of the yearning quality of homoerotic desire, the eternal striving after love with a youth. Not for nothing was love between men called *l'amour de l'impossible*, the love of the impossible – impossible not only because it was dangerous and illegal, concealed and furtive, but more importantly because of its fleeting, ephemeral nature. Youth was finite. Its very transitoriness made it more rare, more precious, more difficult to capture. And once captured, what then? Uranian love gloried in the thrill of the chase. Once captured, once 'had', to use Oscar's phrase, the glorious chase, the moment of capture, of sexual surrender, could never be replicated. The Uranian lover's erotic doom was an endless cycle, an unrelenting grailquest of desire and satiation which could never result in lasting peace and fulfilment.

Oscar's most important love affairs – and many less important ones – were with young poets. There was Rennell Rodd, with whom he had fallen in love before he married Constance. And there was Richard Gallienne, the first poet Oscar 'loved' after his marriage. Oscar described Gallienne as the incarnation of the Angel Gabriel in Rossetti's painting 'The Annunciation'. Swinburne, rather more clear-sightedly, described him as 'Shelley with a chin', a reference to Gallienne's jutting chin, his most prominent feature. Gallienne's father had taken his seventeen-year-old son to hear Oscar lecture on 'Personal Impressions of America' in Birkenhead in 1883. Young Richard was enraptured by Wilde and determined to follow in his poetic and literary footsteps. In the spring of 1887, Richard Le Gallienne (by now he had added 'Le' to his name, presumably to make it more euphonic, more individual and more poetic) sent Oscar his first, privately printed volume of poems, *My Ladies' Sonnets*, with a pretty letter of avowal.

In his reply, Oscar called Le Gallienne's book 'charming . . . full of much that is dainty and delicate in verse'. 'The whole book,' wrote Oscar, 'is evidently the work of one who is an artist in poetry.' Oscar's eye was caught by Le Gallienne's 'Sonnet to a Young Actor'; sonnets to men, especially to young men, resonated particularly with him: 'I can recognise a whole life in the choice of an adjective,' he told Le Gallienne, extending an invitation to meet. 'When you come to London pray let me have the pleasure of knowing you personally.'

Six months later, Le Gallienne was in London, and he met Oscar for the first time on 6 June. He was an intense young man who had assumed all the visible trappings of the poet and, in imitation of the Oscar of the first period, wore his hair long, 'fanning out', Oscar said, 'into a wonderful halo'. Le Gallienne found Oscar delightful, 'a most charming fellow'. He turned down an invitation for the following afternoon from the publisher John Lane, saying he had 'an opportunity to spend it with Oscar Wilde . . . an opportunity not to be missed'. This afternoon was perhaps the summer day referred to in Le Gallienne's poem 'With Oscar Wilde: A Summer Day In June '88' which opened with the suggestive lines: 'With Oscar Wilde, a summer day/ Passed like a yearning kiss away'. The yearning kiss in question was literal as well as literary. Something more corporeal than poetry had happened that summer afternoon between Oscar and the twenty-two-year-old Le Gallienne. That evening, Oscar inscribed a copy of his *Poems*: 'To Richard Le Gallienne, poet and lover, from Oscar Wilde. A summer day in June '88.' Le Gallienne responded by sending Oscar a copy of his poem, adding 'This copy of verse I have made for my friend Oscar Wilde, as a love-token, and in secret memory of a summer day in June '88'. Poet, lover, love-token, summer afternoons and secret memories were the stuff of illicit love affairs. There can be no doubt that Oscar seduced Richard Le Gallienne that summer afternoon; and no doubt that Richard Le Gallienne was ready and willing to be seduced. Le Gallienne was an ambitious and not especially talented poet and seems to have made a point of forming romantic and sexual friendships with older, more established poets and men of letters. The same month he met and had sex with Oscar, Le Gallienne was also to be found staying with the journalist and poet Gleeson White and his wife in Christchurch, Hampshire, a town which was later to house a small but important colony of Uranian poets and writers.

Oscar's effect on Richard Le Gallienne – and on young men generally – was mesmerising. Le Gallienne wrote to John Lane immediately after their short love affair, in execrable rhyming prose. He was ecstatic:

Oscar Wilde, sweet 'Fancy's child', how can I write of him tonight? of all his dear delightful ways thro' three summer nights and days; suffice it I have never yet more fascinating fellow met, and O! how sweet he was to me is only known to Richard Le G.

Oscar was fascinating, dazzling, powerful. By his sheer brilliance, force of personality, charm and wit, he could dazzle all who met him. Even though Le Gallienne returned to the less than poetic environs of Birkenhead, he and Oscar continued to correspond, conducting a poetic and postal love affair. 'Bother space and time!' Oscar wrote to him. 'They spoil life by allowing such a thing as distance.' 'Yea! Dear Poet,' Le Gallienne wrote in a breathlessly ardent reply. 'The thought that you sometimes recall me is sweet as a kiss and it is blessed to know that but a little while and I shall be with you once more . . . I shall have news to tell you in which I think you will rejoice with your true-lover.' Le Gallienne eventually married and repudiated his short and passionate love affair with Oscar, going so far as to strongly warn Edward Shelley, one of Oscar's lovers, against getting involved with him.

André Raffalovich was another poet-friend of Oscar's. He was the youngest son of a wealthy Russian Jewish family and had been brought up in Paris by a remarkable and formidable Scottish governess, Miss Gribbell, who remained with Raffalovich for nearly seventy years, until her death in 1930 at the age of eighty-nine. Raffalovich's first volume of poetry, *Tuberose and Meadowsweet*, had been published in 1885 and reviewed by Oscar in the *Pall Mall Gazette*. Oscar had scented the unmistakable homoerotic undertones of the poems: 'To say of these poems that they are unhealthy and bring with them the heavy odours of the hothouse is to point out neither their defect not their merit, but their quality merely.' Raffalovich's volume has the distinction of including an early, if not the first, instance of the use of the word 'shame' to denote spiritual and sexual love between men. The word occurs in the poem 'Piers Gaveston', about the murdered lover of Edward II:

The first is Beauty clad in Love's proud weeds,
And Love the second with the badge of grief,
A thorny wreath rose-red, a breast that bleeds.
The third is Sorrow: but men call him Shame.

Later, Bosie was to take the concept of shame and turn it on its head. He wrote a provocative homoerotic sonnet – 'In Praise of Shame' – which proclaimed 'Of all sweet passions Shame is the loveliest.' Bosie's sonnet was to became famous and notorious when Oscar was cross-examined in court on the precise meaning of the word shame. Oscar also used shame as a synonym, a codeword to denote sexual passion between men.

Oscar had become friendly with Raffalovich during 1886. By the end of the year he was referring affectionately in letters to 'Little André'. At the beginning, Oscar was attracted to the twenty-two-year-old Raffalovich. 'You could give me a new thrill,' Oscar told him. 'You have the right measure of romance and cynicism.' Whether anything came of his flirtation with Raffalovich is not known for certain. They were certainly intimate for three or four years, often talking about sex or what Raffalovich termed 'the more dangerous affections'.

Then there was a rupture in their friendship which has never been satisfactorily explained and which may have been the consequence of a lovers' falling out. According to Raffalovich, this happened after an innocent remark by Constance. 'Oscar says he likes you so much,' she told Raffalovich in 1889. 'He says you have such nice improper talks together.' Raffalovich was affronted and appalled. 'Never again did I speak with him without witnesses.' Constance's comment hardly seems a valid reason for so sudden and violent a split. Another version has it that Oscar and a group of friends turned up at Raffalovich's Mayfair house for lunch. When the butler answered the door, Oscar is supposed to have said 'We'd like a table for six, please.' Raffalovich, who was standing in the hallway and heard everything, was deeply insulted.

Whatever the cause of their falling out, the animosity between Oscar and Raffalovich was intense. Oscar used to say of Raffalovich that 'he came to London with the intention of opening a salon, and he has succeeded in opening a saloon' – a quip which he redeployed to good effect in *The Picture of Dorian Gray*. After the rupture, Oscar decided that Raffalovich was ugly – like 'a foetus in a bottle', he said. He used to invoke Raffalovich's name as a symbol of extreme ugliness, and 'As ugly as Raffalovich' became one of his oft-repeated comments. Towards the end of his life, when Raffalovich recorded his memories of Oscar, he confided to a friend that it was an account of 'a dislike, not of a friendship'.

Raffalovich, like many others, would have his revenge on Oscar.

Æolian harps

'This passion for beauty is merely the intensified desire for life.'

From now on Oscar's lovers appeared and disappeared with dizzying and ever-accelerating speed. There were any number of young men who, if not exactly poets, were decidedly poetic, flitting in and out of Oscar's life. Robbie Ross was still very much a favourite of Oscar's. He had gone up to King's College, Cambridge in the autumn of 1888 with a letter of avuncular advice from Oscar telling him to get in touch with Oscar Browning, a fellow of King's: 'You will find him everything that is kind and helpful,' he wrote. Oscar had just been to Stratford for the unveiling of his old friend Lord Ronald Gower's statue of Shakespeare. 'My reception,' he told Robbie, in a decidedly camp aside, 'was semi-royal, and the volunteers played God Save the Queen in my honour.'

Robbie's career at Cambridge came to an abrupt end one evening early in March 1889, when he was violently seized by a gang of half-a-dozen King's undergraduates and unceremoniously ducked in the college fountain. His assailants included one of the sons of the Archbishop of Canterbury, Fred Benson, who was destined to play a minor role in the saga of Oscar and Bosie. Robbie had not been popular with his fellow undergraduates. Unlike the vast majority of his contemporaries, he was not a product of one of the great public schools, particularly Eton, which enjoyed very close links with King's, and his contemporaries found his cosmopolitan sophistication and his literary aspirations bewildering. Robbie had already been proposed for membership of the Savile Club in London and boasted several literary friendships, most notably with Oscar.

Robbie was an outsider, socially – and more importantly – sexually. Although every other undergraduate at King's who had been to a public school must have known about Greek love, if not from direct personal experience, at least from close observation, Robbie was different. He flaunted his sexual difference and sophistication. He bragged about his friendship with Oscar and affected an aggravating air of superiority. The reasons for Robbie's ducking are complex and have never been fully explained. But he had put people's backs up by attacking old Etonians and pitching himself headlong into the uncharted and treacherous waters of college politics. There was strong speculation that Oscar Browning had tacitly sanctioned Robbie's ducking, an accusation

Browning vigorously denied. And Arthur Tilley, a junior lecturer at King's and older brother of John Tilley, one of the six conspirators, was also supposed to have known about and approved of the ducking in advance. But there may have been another, more sinister, reason for the attack. An anonymous margin note in the British Library's copy of the *Autobiography* of Lord Alfred Douglas says that the reason Robbie was ducked 'was for fractions inclining to pederasty'. In other words, Robbie had had a sexual liaison at Cambridge and had been found out and punished.

The effect of the ducking was catastrophic. Robbie was suddenly taken ill with what Oscar Browning called 'a violent brain attack, the result of the outrage preying on his mind'. Robbie had a nervous breakdown, and the college authorities feared that he might even commit suicide. His brother Alec was summoned to take him back to his mother's house in Onslow Square, where he made a slow and painful recovery. Browning, determined to live up to Oscar's encomium of being 'everything that is kind and helpful', was one of Robbie's first visitors after he had recovered and promptly took him to Windsor to stay in his mother's house, where he was introduced to Browning's sister, Mina, her husband, the Reverend Biscoe Wortham, and their two sons, Philip and Oswald. Robbie quickly became firm friends with the Wortham family. It was a fateful friendship, and one that would have terrible repercussions just four years later.

Immediately after spending this fateful weekend at Windsor, Robbie and Browning proceeded to the Isle of Wight where they were to rendezvous with one of Browning's working-class waifs and strays, Matthew Oates, who Robbie dubbed the 'fair sailor'. Oates and Robbie had sex together, and Robbie was smitten, describing him as 'very beautiful and very charming'.

Robbie's illness and recuperation meant that he could spend more time in London with Oscar. He did return briefly to Cambridge in the summer term but contracted measles and was again seriously ill for a time. His first year at Cambridge had been an unmitigated disaster, a disaster which became a catastrophe when Robbie, in a fit of extraordinary courage or extraordinary stupidity, decided to tell his family about his sexual orientation. His mother was deeply distressed, his sister Lizzie deeply hostile. Only his brother Alec took Robbie's part. The upshot of it all was that Robbie would not be returning to Cambridge, and Alec cast around to find him work. In the meantime Robbie became an integral part of the circle of young men who buzzed around Oscar.

Oscar was becoming increasingly confident and increasingly blasé about his sexuality. He had gathered an entourage of attractive and fashionable young men around him, 'his admiring cohort' as they were described at the time. They were sometimes referred to by Oscar, and by others less sympathetic, as his 'disciples'. André Raffalovich called them Oscar's 'sons', while Oscar himself described them as 'the exquisite Æolian harps that play in the breeze of my matchless talk'. Oscar's choice of the word Æolian is significant; the Æolians along with the Dorians and the Ionians constituted the three main tribes of Greece. Oscar's Æolian young men were Greek in the sexual sense of the word. Many of them probably became lovers of Oscar, or, to put it more brutally, had sex with him once, twice or even three or four times, before they were discarded and became captive worshippers at his shrine.

There was, for instance, Robbie's friend, Arthur Clifton, a handsome young solicitor and amateur poet. 'I wish you would send me two or three of your poems,' Oscar wrote. 'You have certainly a delicate ear for music.' Oscar's infatuation with Clifton was short-lived, but their friendship survived. He became a valued friend of the family. Constance was particularly fond of him, and he was of great service to both Oscar and Constance after the tragedy.

In the course of their marriage, Oscar introduced many of his lovers to Constance. It was a strange thing to do, almost as if he sought her approval, as if he wanted to somehow synthesise his lovers into his life at Tite Street with Constance and the children. Several of them, notably Robbie Ross, Arthur Clifton and Graham Robertson, were accepted as family friends. Robbie also became Constance's especial and devoted friend. She had need of friends. She saw less and less of Oscar now. His editorship of the *Woman's World* took up some of his time, though he had very quickly grown bored with his role and hardly bothered to turn up at the office, preferring to work from Tite Street and leave all the administrative details to his able assistant, Arthur Fish.

Oscar was fond of young actors. He wrote an adulatory letter to Henry Dixey, a twenty-six-year-old American dancer and actor, who had taken the title role in a musical play called *Adonis*, which Oscar went to see. 'My dear Adonis,' Oscar wrote. 'I wish you were a wave of the sea, that you might be always dancing. Every movement and gesture that you make is instinct with natural beauty, and expressive of the loveliness of mere life. Some afternoon I will come and sit with you, if you let me, while you are dining.' To Roland Atwood, another young actor of whom he was enamoured, Oscar sent a gift of a necktie: 'I send you your necktie, in which I know you will look Greek and gracious. I don't think it is too dark for you.' Oscar signed himself 'Affectionately yours' and added a romantic postscript: 'Has Gerald Gurney forgiven me yet for talking to no one but you that afternoon? I suppose not. But who else was there for me to talk to?'

Oscar met many of his 'exquisite Æolian harps' after they had written letters of avowal to him. Judging from the handful that have survived, Oscar's replies were invariably graceful: teasingly playful, whimsical, ever so slightly provocative and, above all, encouraging. 'What a pretty name you have! it is worthy of fiction,' Oscar replied to a letter of avowal from a young man called Aubrey Richardson. 'Would you mind if I wrote a book called *The Story of Aubrey Richardson*? I won't but I should like to. There is music in its long syllables, and a memory of romance, and a suggestion of wonder. Names fascinate me terribly. Come and see me some Wednesday.' Such a letter, such an invitation, so beautifully written and so charmingly extended must have been hard to resist, if indeed Aubrey Richardson and the countless other writers of letters of avowal wanted to resist.

There was the twenty-three-year-old Graham Hill, an aspiring poet who wrote to Oscar asking if he might send him some of his poems. Oscar responded immediately. 'Dear Mr Hill,' he wrote. 'Come and have tea on Friday at 5 o'clock if you have nothing to do. So you are a rhymer! We all are when we are young.' Hill sent Oscar his volume of poems, *Under Her Window*, which was dedicated to 'M.L.'. Oscar was 'charmed' with Hill's 'little volume'. 'You certainly have a light touch and a pleasant fancy,' he told him, adding, 'M.L. whoever she is, should feel quite proud at such an artistic offering. Are you very much in love with M.L.? and does M.L. love you? Come and see me some day. Wednesday afternoon usually finds me in.'

Oscar used the same combination of whimsy and charm on W. Graham Robertson, a young writer, artist and stage designer. Tall, willowy and elegant, Robertson was one of the most handsome young men in London. In a prefiguration of Lord Henry Wotton's encounter with Dorian Gray, Oscar met the twenty-year-old Robertson at the studio of a painter, a mutual friend. Their acquaintance took several months to grow into friendship and intimacy. 'What do you allow your friends to call you?' asked Oscar archly, 'W or Graham? I like my friends to call me Oscar.' Robertson sent Oscar some drawings, perhaps to illustrate one of his fairy stories. 'I wish I could draw like you,' Oscar replied, 'for I like lines better than words, and colours more than sentences.' 'However,' Oscar continued:

> I console myself by trying now and then to put 'The Universe' into a sonnet. Some day you must do a design for the sonnet: a young man looking into a strange crystal that mirrors all the world. Poetry should be like a crystal; it should make life more beautiful and less real. I am sorry you are going away, but your narcissus keeps you in my memory.

As usual, Oscar's friendship with Robertson lasted longer than the sexual relationship, but Robertson was proud of having been a favoured lover of Oscar, even boasting of it in later life.

This was not the case with Harry Melvill, a young actor with whom Oscar had a brief fling. They met in the summer of 1888, and there was a pretty exchange of letters. 'What a charming time we had at Abbott's Hill,' Oscar told him. 'I have not enjoyed myself so much for a long time, and I hope that we will see much more of each other, and be often together.' That this friendship, like so many of Oscar's other friendships with young men about town, culminated in sex is borne out by a letter written by Oscar after his release from prison when he was living in Paris. One evening there he encountered Harry Melvill walking along the street in a small party. Oscar greeted him, but Melvill cut him dead and pretended not to see him. It was a bitter humiliation for Oscar, but he retailed the story with characteristic gaiety. He felt, he said, as if he had been cut by a 'Piccadilly renter', slang for male prostitute. 'For people whom one has had to give themselves moral or social airs is childish,' he added on a dignified note. 'I was very much hurt. But have quite recovered.'

By the late 1880s, Oscar seems to have thrown caution to the winds and was readily propositioning good-looking young men for sex, among them Bernard Berenson, an exceptionally handsome young American art historian, recently arrived in London. Berenson turned up at Tite Street with a letter of introduction and was immediately invited to stay. Berenson recalls how Oscar would arrive home late in the afternoon, complaining of exhaustion from yet another luncheon party of rich and fashionable society. Oscar told Berenson that such affairs were 'terrible'. But the rich and fashionable were fascinating to Oscar. 'There is something about them that is irresistibly attractive. They are more alive. They breathe a finer air. They are more free than we are.' Berenson was, in common parlance, something of a prickteaser. He knew of his consummate attractiveness to men, and he enjoyed, exploited and perhaps encouraged their amorous attentions, only to reject any overt sexual advances. Berenson claimed that he had 'a delight in the beauty of the male that can seldom have been surpassed', coupled with 'an unfortunate attractiveness for other men'. On another occasion he was less reticent, boasting that he had made 'homosexuals' mouths water'. Certainly he can hardly have been surprised when he made Oscar's mouth water. Oscar propositioned Berenson in Tite Street only to be met with a polite but firm rebuff. 'You are completely without feeling,' Oscar complained. 'You are made of stone.' But their friendship endured.

Oscar had by now discovered the Crown public house in Charing Cross, a decidedly Bohemian establishment and the nearest thing that London possessed to a bar where men could meet other men for sex. He may have been introduced to the delights of the Crown by Robbie Ross. According to the writer and wit, Max Beerbohm, the Crown was 'a literary tavern full of young nameless poets and cocottes and old men who have been ministers of the Church of England and are no longer. Such a dull, suspect place it is.' The writer Rupert Croft-Cooke described it as a public house full of:

> vociferous young writers and a good many literary charlatans, painters and would-be painters together with male prostitutes and Service men looking for an addition to their miserable wages from one or another of the richer and older men who came there. It was not by any means exclusively a 'queer' pub, but having once gained a reputation for being lively it was used by those who wanted to find a young sailor or an out-of-work stable boy, as well as by artists who may have been scarcely conscious of these activities.

It was almost certainly at the Crown in the winter of 1888 that Oscar met Frederick Althaus. Frederick, or Fred as he liked to be called, was different from the usual run of young men that Oscar mixed with at this time, who were literary, artistic or connected in some way with the theatre. Fred was none of these. He worked as a relatively lowly clerk for a firm of solicitors in the City. Little is known about him except that his father was a German immigrant who taught languages. Fred was not the sort of young man that Oscar could introduce to Constance. He lived with his family in Swiss Cottage and was just twenty when he met Oscar. No letters from Oscar to Fred survive, but there are half-a-dozen letters from Fred to Oscar which document the course of their relationship over six months, a relationship which, like so many of Oscar's other brief but intense love affairs, began well and ended badly. Oscar took a fancy to Fred when they met each other at the Crown. Fred, along with his brother, was a regular there; he called it 'The C–' in his letters to Oscar. On the night they met, Oscar took Fred out, probably for supper, following this up by sending him a ticket for a concert. Fred could not go, as he explained to Oscar:

> I hasten to write and tell you how extremely kind it is of you to send me the concert ticket, pray accept my best thanks for your thoughtfulness. I need hardly say that I should be delighted to use it, but I much regret that I shall not be able to get away from the City. Were it any other day but a Tuesday I might perhaps get free, only Tuesdays and Thursdays are our late days – and I dare not ask – the ticket I return to you with my best thanks!

Fred was at pains to thank Oscar for his generosity at their first meeting. 'I never told you the other evening how much I enjoyed myself and how sincerely I appreciate your kindness to me.' He was poor and blushed at his inability to repay Oscar's hospitality. 'I feel positively ashamed,' he told Oscar:

> of in no way being capable of reciprocating but I can assure you that I hardly know a greater pleasure than being in your society and I am very grateful to you for the kindly interest you seem to take in me. Hoping soon to see you. Believe me yours, F.P. Althaus.

Oscar asked Fred for a photograph of himself, just as he had asked Harry Marillier for one three years earlier, a request which Fred was eager to fulfil. 'I shall as soon as I get them send you a photo of mine an enlarged copy of the one taken in flannels with my German friend – but he of course is not on it,' he told Oscar. The mention of his 'German friend' suggests that Fred had already had at least one relationship with a man, possibly on a visit to see his family in Germany. From his letters, Fred comes across as a rather shy, slightly awkward young man, no more than adequately educated, but determined to better himself. He was idealistic, affectionate and romantic and wanted to meet an older man with whom he could have a conventional courtship and settle down. And he was also slightly neurotic and inclined towards hysteria.

Shortly after their first meeting, Fred replied to a letter from Oscar suggesting a meeting. 'I have heard from Barnes that I can have a room there for two nights,' Fred told Oscar, 'and I feel quite pleased at the idea of going and hope very much that you will join me there after.' Fred signed himself 'Affectionately yours' and added a postscript: 'I do so want you to see my photo.' Whether Barnes was a person, a friend of Fred's, or a reference to Barnes Village, located in a loop of the Thames just south-west of Chelsea, is impossible to know. But the two nights Fred spent there with Oscar were probably when they first had sex.

The next surviving letter from Fred is much more confident. It probably dates from the early spring of 1889, when Fred and Oscar had been seeing each other for two or three months. Oscar would almost certainly have been pursuing a number of other young men, while Fred seems to have set his sights just on Oscar. He refers to a telegram he had sent impulsively. 'Dear Oscar,' he wrote:

> I could not help sending you that telegram, the weather is so heavenly and I thought we must have a couple of days by the sea – of course each goes on his own back *ça va sans dire*. I shall expect an affirmative reply. My photo has come and is *simply splendid*. I wonder what you will hang with it.

This time Fred signed himself off with his 'Best love' to Oscar. But Oscar was clearly losing interest. Fred was beginning to be difficult. Apart from the slight gaucheness of his letter and the rather stiff way he uses hearty phrases like 'simply splendid' and 'each goes on his own back', the fact that Fred was sending impulsive telegrams to Tite Street, demanding that Oscar spend time away with him, and his expectation of 'an affirmative reply' were calculated to make Oscar want to cool things down between them. Fred almost certainly never got his affirmative reply. In his next, rather Pooteresque letter, Fred has taken to telling Oscar where he will be in the hope that he will turn up:

> Dear Oscar, I shall be at the Lyric about 6.30 to 6.45. I can stay there till 7.15. Try and come. What a glorious day. I greatly enjoyed a ride on the top of the 'bus this morning. Ever yours, F.

Fred grew ever more demanding. He wanted more and more of Oscar's time and was continually coming up with plans for them to go away together. 'My dear Oscar,' he wrote in March 1889:

> I have an invitation to go away at Easter but before deciding what I shall do I write to ask you what your plans are? Are you remaining in town or could we perhaps go away together . . . of course I should *much prefer* going with you and of course have as yet given no answer to my friend before consulting you as to your plans for Easter.

The letter makes it clear that they were still seeing each other. 'The other evening was "quite charming",' he tells Oscar, deliberately invoking one of Oscar's favourite and most over-worked phrases:

> When can we meet? I am engaged all of this week but perhaps you will drop in at the office on Sat evening, my brother and I . . . will be at the C— I daresay at 11.30. With much love, Yours as ever. F.

Three months later, in June, Fred is still trying to persuade Oscar to go away with him, this time to Eastbourne. He has already asked Oscar about the trip and is anxiously awaiting Oscar's response, a response which has failed to materialise:

> The afternoon post has come and brought me no letter from you. I wonder what you will decide about Eastbourne, just imagine this gorgeous weather at the seaside lying on the cliffs in flannels – it would be charming. Unless I go with you I shall go away alone as all other people bore me. My parents are going to Croydon and I shall certainly not remain in C. Tomorrow is your At Home – how furious you will be that you ever told me, perhaps I may look in and see you on my way home. At all events let me know by tomorrow afternoon what you decide as I like to know one way or another. 'The Albion' at E is very good; apartments are nice but one gets no food in them. I long to see the lovely blue sea in heavenly sunlight in which I adore basking thinking that it was perhaps generous enough to lend some of its beauty to its admirers. I am gradually getting well again and the cold is showing signs of decreasing.

Fred signed himself with 'Much love', adding a hasty postscript in the light of Oscar's long-awaited reply. Oscar had said he was ill, 'out of sorts', and quite unable to contemplate Eastbourne:

> Your letter just received I am so grieved to hear that you are out of sorts. I should like to take a cab and rush off and see you to try and cheer you up – I am much disappointed that you can't manage Eastbourne . . . Much love

In reality, perhaps, Oscar was perfectly well but desperate to shake off the tenacious Fred. There was more than a hint of menace, of emotional blackmail, in Fred's remarks about Oscar's At Home. 'Perhaps I may look in and see you on my way home' may have sounded innocuous enough, but how would Constance and Oscar's other guests react to the lowly young clerk turning up unannounced and uninvited in their midst and claiming an intimate friendship with Oscar? Fred was entirely correct when he predicted 'How furious you will be that you ever told me.'

Poor Fred Althaus. It was a sad and sordid affair which dragged on for six months. All Fred wanted was for Oscar to fall in love with him and to go off for romantic weekends by 'the beautiful blue sea in heavenly sunlight', locked in a loving embrace. But Oscar was the wrong man for such a quaint and cloying vision of love. Oscar did not love Fred; he had never loved Fred, even if, in the heat of pursuit and in the heat of passion, he had said or suggested that he did. Oscar was attracted by Fred, wanted to have sex with him and, when he had accomplished that, began to lose interest. Certainly he liked Fred, he was touched by Fred's devotion, finding perhaps his old-fashioned romantic views of life and love charming, at least initially. And certainly he treated Fred well enough when they were together, paying for suppers and dinners, buying him expensive gifts and perhaps occasionally making him presents of money. Oscar was generous to a fault with his money but utterly selfish when it came to matters of the heart.

Oscar often confused lust with love. He would often talk about 'loving' a boy, when in truth he meant having sex with him. He had had love affairs with Harry Marillier and Robbie Ross, and with others, but these short, intense relationships were founded upon lust. When Oscar's sexual thirst was slaked, such love affairs quickly faded into affectionate friendship. He had not, as yet, even come close to falling truly in love with anybody, let alone with poor sweet, sad, romantic Fred.

Spiritualised sodomy

'Literature has always anticipated life. It does not copy it, but moulds it to its purpose.'

In the summer of 1889, Oscar startled the literary world with the publication of *The Portrait of Mr W.H.*, an audacious and tantalising work of fiction, which reads like a work of fact. The story takes its title from the mysterious dedication which prefaces Shakespeare's sequence of one hundred and fifty-four sonnets: 'To the onlie begetter of these insuing sonnets Mr W.H. all happinesse and that eternitie promised by our ever-living poet.' The identity of Mr W.H. has puzzled scholars for centuries, and dozens of candidates have been put forward, including the Earl of Southampton, the Earl of Pembroke, and two relations of Shakespeare's: his brother-in-law, William Hart, and his nephew, also called William Hart. One theory even had it that there was no mystery at all about the identity of Mr W.H., claiming that the dedication was a simple printer's error and should have read 'Mr W. Hall happinesse'. In 1766 a scholar called Thomas Tyrwhitt put forward a theory that Mr W.H. was in fact an Elizabethan boy actor, Willie Hughes, a theory based on several clearly signalled puns in the Sonnets, most evident in Sonnet XX, when Shakespeare puns on the surname Hughes in the seventh line: 'A man in Hew, all *Hews* in his controwling'.

The Portrait of Mr W.H. is a fleshing out by Oscar of Tyrwhitt's theory and is presented in the form of a complex story of love unravelled and revealed, a *roman à clef* where the real hero of the story is the spiritual and sexual love that men have for younger men, the love that dare not speak its name. It is the love that Shakespeare has for the boy actor, Willie Hughes; the love that Erskine, one of the protagonists, has for Cyril Graham, the discoverer of Willie Hughes; and the love that the anonymous narrator discovers within himself when he learns about Willie Hughes. The story is a powerful homage to this love which, despite centuries of denial, deceit, death, separation and suicide, triumphantly survives.

Oscar had conceived the story in the autumn of the previous year, after Robbie had decided to leave Cambridge, and the two of them used to spend long hours in Oscar's Moorish study in Tite Street, smoking endless cigarettes and weaving wonderful fantasies about life, love and sex. After the publication of *Mr W.H.*, Oscar wrote to Robbie to thank him for his part in bringing Willie Hughes to life. 'Indeed the story is half yours, and but for you would not have been written.' It was a generous acknowledgement of Robbie's role not just in helping to create Willie Hughes, but also more broadly in stimulating Oscar's creativity. Meeting Robbie, loving Robbie, having sex with Robbie – and with other young men – and absorbing some of Robbie's joyous acceptance of his sexuality had fired Oscar's creativity.

The inherent tensions and contradictions, the paradoxes and the perversities of leading a complicated double life, a life drenched with sexual longings and sexual satiations, being a husband, a father and a dedicated hunter of rare, wonderful and dangerous sex liaisons with young men were the perfect stimulus for Oscar's art. He worked in frenzied bursts of creativity. His output was prolific. Between 1887 and 1889, at the same time as editing the *Woman's World*, he was also turning out a prodigious number of freelance reviews. And in addition to his two long stories, *The Canterville Ghost* and *Lord Arthur Savile's Crime*, Oscar had also published a volume of exquisite fairy tales, *The Happy Prince and Other Tales*, and two major essays: *Pen, Pencil and Poison* and *The Decay of Lying*. And now, seemingly effortlessly, he had produced *The Portrait of Mr W.H.*

For those with eyes to see, for those who could read between the lines, much of Oscar's work seemed to have a strong, all-pervasive homoerotic undertow, flirting with revelation and concealment, affirmation and denial, guise and disguise. As Oscar grew bolder in exploring and embracing his sexuality, this homoerotic strand emerged more strongly. In *Pen, Pencil and Poison*, his admiring biographical essay on Thomas Griffiths Wainewright, the dandy, artist, forger and 'subtle and secret poisoner almost without rival in this or any age', Oscar glorifies Wainewright as an artist and a criminal *par excellence*. The combination of artist and criminal, writer and outlaw fascinated Oscar. It was a mantle he was eager to assume, especially now that the state had decreed with the passing of the Labouchère Amendment that he too was to be a criminal.

In *Pen, Pencil and Poison*, Wainewright was graven in Oscar's own image. Oscar might have been describing himself when he wrote of Wainewright: 'He loves Greek gems, and Persian carpets, and Elizabethan translations . . . and book-bindings, and early editions, and wide-margined proofs.' Just like Oscar, Wainewright was:

> determined to startle the town as a dandy, and his beautiful rings, his antique cameo breast-pin, and his pale lemon-coloured kid gloves were well-known . . . while his rich curly hair, fine eyes, and exquisite white hands gave him the dangerous and delighted distinction of being different from others.

The description might have fitted Oscar perfectly, except that he wore pale lavender-coloured gloves and an antique scarab ring. Like Wainewright, Oscar had rich curly hair – even if the curls were artificially induced – and had fine, luminous eyes and large but wonderfully expressive white hands. Oscar shared

Wainewright's delight in being very distinctly different from the common weal. Rather more worryingly, he also shared Wainewright's delight and fascination with danger. Oscar was already living dangerously; he flirted daily with the thrill of dangerous sex and the fear of discovery. Danger fired him up, gave form and shape to his life, added piquancy and colour, antidoting his great fear of the *taedium vitae*, the boredom, banality and ordinariness of life, its sheer tedium.

And like Wainewright, Oscar was a man who 'sought to be somebody, rather than do something. He recognised that Life itself is an art, and has its modes of style no less than the arts that seek to express it.' Most importantly, Oscar, again like Wainewright, 'had that curious love of green which in individuals is always the sign of a subtle artistic temperament, and in nations is said to denote a laxity, if not a decadence of morals'. This was a coded and deliberate reference to sex between men. There was a widespread belief in late nineteenth-century Europe that one of the distinguishing characteristics of men who loved men was a preference for the colour green. Indeed, men who loved men themselves seemed equally convinced that their preference for green was in some way bound up with their sexuality.

Havelock Ellis's *Sexual Inversion* details several case histories where men who love men claim that they have what Oscar called 'that curious love of green': 'Case VII' 'remarks that he cannot whistle and that his favourite colour is green', and 'Case XII' 'has a special predilection for green: it is the predominant colour in the decorations of his room, and everything green appeals to him. He finds that the love of green . . . is very widespread among his inverted friends.' Ellis himself was convinced that a preference for green was very marked among men who loved men and offered an historical precedent: 'It has also been remarked,' he wrote, 'that inverts exhibit a preference for green garments. In Rome *cinaedi* were for this reason called *galbanati*.' *Cinaedus* meant 'catamite' and *galbanatus* meant 'effeminate wearer of green clothes'. As a classical scholar Oscar would have been well aware of the symbolism of the colour green in ancient Rome. And rather closer in time and space, Oscar knew too that white carnations, artificially dyed green, were worn as badges of sexual preference by men who loved men in Paris. 'The colour green and Hell,' he said 'are both made for thieves and artists.'

And yet *The Portrait of Mr W.H.* was even more audacious in its celebration of the love that dare not speak its name. Oscar was deliberately setting out to shock and undermine the literary and cultural *amour propre* of Victorian England by attempting to prove that Shakespeare, the nation's most venerated poet and playwright, had not just fallen in love but had actually had a sexual relationship with a seventeen-year-old boy actor.

Mr W.H. is a dazzling conjuring trick, telling three intertwined love stories simultaneously: the story of Shakespeare's love for Willie Hughes, the story of Erskine's love for Cyril Graham, and the story of the anonymous narrator's discovery of his love for young men. Cyril Graham is the young man who has decoded the secret of the Sonnets and tells his friend from Eton, Erskine, who is immediately enraptured by the theory that Shakespeare was in emotional and sexual thralldom to a beautiful boy actor 'whose personality for some reason seems to have filled the soul of Shakespeare with terrible joy and no less terrible despair':

> Who was that young man of Shakespeare's day who, without being of noble birth or even of noble nature, was addressed by him in terms of such passionate adoration that we can but wonder at the strange worship, and are almost afraid to turn the key that unlocks the mystery of the poet's heart? Who was he whose physical beauty was such that it became the very corner-stone of Shakespeare's art; the very source of Shakespeare's inspiration; the very incarnation of Shakespeare's dreams?

But, before he can be finally convinced, Erskine tells Cyril that they must find documentary evidence that Willie Hughes did, in fact, exist. Some weeks later, Cyril produces what he claims to be incontrovertible evidence of the existence of Willie Hughes in the form of:

> a full-length portrait of a young man in late sixteenth-century costume, standing by a table with his right hand resting on an open book. He seemed about seventeen years of age, and was of quite extraordinary personal beauty, though evidently somewhat effeminate. Indeed, had it not been for the dress and the closely cropped hair, one would have said that the face, with its dreamy, wistful eyes and its delicate scarlet lips, was the face of a girl.

Was this the face of the boy actor so beloved of Shakespeare, the boy who inspired him with terrible joy and terrible despair? Erskine is convinced that Cyril has discovered the secret of the Sonnets and the secret of Shakespeare's greatest love. There are strong parallels, Erskine realises, with his own feelings for Cyril, who shares many of the elusive and attractive qualities of Willie Hughes. Cyril was 'effeminate', 'very languid in his manner', and 'not a little vain of his good looks'. He was, Erskine says, 'wonderfully handsome':

> People who did not like him, philistines and college tutors, and young men reading for the Church, used to say that he was merely pretty; but there was a great deal more in his face than mere prettiness. I think he was the most splendid creature I ever saw, and nothing could exceed the grace of his movements, the charm of his manner. He fascinated everybody who was worth fascinating, and a great many people who were not. He was often wilful and petulant, and I used to think him dreadfully insincere. It was due, I think, chiefly to his inordinate desire to please.

Erskine has by now completely embraced the theory that Willie Hughes was the object of Shakespeare's passion – that is, until he discovers, quite by chance, that Cyril had the portrait of Willie Hughes forged. Erskine confronts

Cyril, who admits the forgery but then commits suicide, offering his life, as he tells Erskine in his suicide note, 'as a sacrifice to the secret of the Sonnets'. 'It was a foolish, mad letter,' Erskine recalls:

> I remember he ended by saying that he intrusted to me the Willie Hughes theory, and that it was for me to present it to the world, and to unlock the secret of Shakespeare's heart.

Erskine, who has as a result of the forgery lost his belief in Willie Hughes, recounts the strange tale of Cyril Graham and his theory about the identity of Mr W.H. to a young man, little more than a 'boy', who is the anonymous narrator of the story. The narrator is enraptured by the theory. 'I believe in Willie Hughes,' he declares rousingly, and sets out to find the proof that Cyril Graham could not find, becoming obsessed by a vision of the beautiful boy actor, Shakespeare's lover and his inspiration:

> His very name fascinated me. Willie Hughes! Willie Hughes! How musically it sounded! Yes; who else but he could have been the master-mistress of Shakespeare's passion, the lord of his love to whom he was bound in vassalage, the delicate minion of pleasure, the rose of the whole world, the herald of the spring decked in the proud livery of youth, the lovely boy whom it was sweet music to hear, and whose beauty was the very raiment of Shakespeare's heart, as it was the keystone of his dramatic power?

The young narrator tries to conjure up a vision of Willie Hughes in his mind, imagining him 'as some fair-haired English lad whom in one of London's hurrying streets, or on Windsor's green silent meadows, Shakespeare had seen and followed'. As the narrator muses on Willie Hughes, a mysterious osmosis occurs. The more he dwells upon the sexual relationship between Willie Hughes and Shakespeare, upon the 'the mystery of his sin or of the sin, if such it was, of the great poet who had so dearly loved him', the more he realises that his own sexual longings are exactly those of Shakespeare. As he reads and re-reads the Sonnets, it seems to him that he is:

> deciphering the story of a life that had once been mine, unrolling the record of a romance that, without my knowing it, had coloured the very texture of my nature, had dyed it with strange and subtle dyes. Art, as so often happens, had taken the place of personal experience.

Ironically, having once found his true sexual self through the medium of the Sonnets, the narrator loses his faith in the Willie Hughes of the Sonnets. He tells Erskine of this loss of faith. Erskine, however, in a double irony, has rediscovered his own belief in Willie Hughes and determines to commit suicide, just like Cyril Graham, in an attempt to convince the narrator of the truth of the 'cause'. In his suicide note, he writes:

I still believe in Willie Hughes; and by the time you receive this I shall have died by my own hand for Willie Hughes' sake: for his sake, and for the sake of Cyril Graham, whom I drove to his death by my shallow scepticism and ignorant lack of faith. The truth was once revealed to you, and you rejected it. It comes to you now, stained with the blood of two lives – do not turn away from it.

Finally, in a triple irony, the narrator discovers that Erskine has not, in fact, taken his own life but has died rather more pedestrianly of consumption in a hotel in Cannes, bequeathing him the forged portrait of Willie Hughes.

There is a strong element of autobiography in *The Portrait of Mr W.H.* Oscar always boasted that he resembled Shakespeare. When the socialite Margot Tennant first encountered him at a garden party given by Lady Archibald Campbell, Oscar 'was explaining why he thought he resembled Shakespeare; and ended a brilliant monologue by saying he intended to have a bronze medallion struck of his own profile and Shakespeare's'. But for Oscar, there was more to it than mere physical similarity. There were many parallels in their lives. Like Shakespeare, Oscar was a married man with children. Oscar was, of course, also a poet and a playwright. And both of them had fallen in love with seventeen-year-old boys. Falling in love with a boy had filled Shakespeare's soul 'with terrible joy and no less terrible despair', a reflection, perhaps, of the doubts and self-loathing Oscar had experienced in coming to terms with his sexuality. Shakespeare had fallen in love with Willie Hughes, and Oscar had fallen in love with Robbie Ross. Willie Hughes was a 'fair-haired English lad' picked up in one of London's 'hurrying streets', just as Robbie Ross was a fair-haired Scots-Canadian lad, picked up in one of London's hurrying streets or busy cottages. And just as Willie Hughes had been Shakespeare's inspiration, so Oscar's affair with Robbie had helped liberate and realise his artistic potential. Of course Oscar's affair with Robbie had not been filled with anything like the same degree of passion, pain and loss as Shakespeare's affair with Willie Hughes. And Oscar had had love affairs with young men before and after Robbie. That there were strong parallels between Shakespeare's life and his own can hardly have failed to strike a chord with Oscar and, indeed, the readers of *Mr W.H.*

There is also a curious element of autobiographical prefiguration in *The Portrait of Mr W.H.*, a subconscious articulation of Oscar's deepest wishes and desires. Just as Shakespeare had one great life-affirming, life-changing, immortal love affair with a beautiful boy, his ideal boy, so Oscar wanted to scale those impregnable heights of great love and great passion. His search for that ennobling love, for an inspiring love, for a love that could transcend the mundane and enter the sphere of immortality, began at about the time he was writing *The Portrait of Mr W.H.*

At another level, *The Portrait of Mr W.H.* is a barely concealed paean of praise to 'the ambiguity of the sexes', the joys of *paiderastia*, the love of an older man for a youth. Writing *Mr W.H.*, publishing *Mr W.H.* was nothing more and nothing less than a manifesto of *paiderastia*, a closely argued dissertation designed to give cultural and historical legitimacy to sex between men and youths. Oscar wrote, and always intended to publish, an expanded and even more explicit version of the story which explored 'the soul' of what he called 'neo-Platonism' or, put more plainly, the rediscovery of Greek love in the Renaissance and its subsequent dissemination:

> It is only when we realise the influence of neo-Platonism on the Renaissance that we can understand the true meaning of the amatory phrases and words with which friends were wont, at this time, to address each other. There was a kind of mystic transference of the expressions of the physical world to a sphere that was spiritual.

Oscar goes on to explore the historical transmission of this higher, neo-Platonic love, invoking an apostolic succession of great lovers: Michelangelo and Tommaso Cavalieri, Shakespeare and Willie Hughes, Winckelmann and the 'young Roman' who initiated him into the secrets and mysteries of Greek love – an apostolic succession which continues to Cyril Graham, Erskine, the anonymous young narrator and, by the 'kind of mystic transference' associated with Greek love, to the psychologically attuned readers of *Mr W.H.* Just as reading the Sonnets had revealed the secret truth of his sexuality to the narrator, so *The Portrait of Mr W.H.* would reveal to its readers the inner truth of their sexuality. It was an audacious and insidious act of literary insemination.

Oscar would use this argument of a kind of spiritualised sodomy – sanctified by antiquity, tradition, great art and great artists – to justify and defend 'the love that dare not speak its name' many times, invoking Michelangelo and Shakespeare as among its greatest exponents, most memorably during his trials. He was not alone. Many passionate advocates of the social and legal emancipation of men who love men would invoke the argument, almost word for word, on many occasions. John Addington Symonds had already invoked it in his writings on Uranian love, and André Raffalovich would invoke it in his treatise on sex between men, *Uranisme and Unisexualité*, as would Havelock Ellis in *Sexual Inversion*.

At its deepest level, *The Portrait of Mr W.H.* is an essay about sex as religion, about 'the soul, the secret soul' and the 'soul's romance'. It is a parable about sexual revelation and sexual conversion; about sexual faith lost and sexual faith rediscovered; and about sexual martyrdom. All the protagonists experience the revelation of love between men and boys, all experience their conversion to such love, some lose their faith in it, only to rediscover it. Finally, some, like Cyril Graham, die for their sexual faith, martyrs to a cause. Like early Christian martyrs, fired with the ecstatic zeal of the convert, they seek to profess their sexual faith with the mantra 'I believe in Willie Hughes'. They seek to live and, if necessary to die, in the sexual faith. In his suicide note, Erskine speaks of the 'cause'. It was the first time Oscar had linked the politics of sexuality with its pleasures. Soon the word would become capitalised, and 'the Cause' would become the rallying cry of men who loved men, and men who loved boys, to come together to seek social, legal and political reform.

Oscar submitted the story initially to Frank Harris's *Saturday Review*, where an assistant to Harris summarily rejected it. Oscar then turned to the renowned *Blackwood's Magazine*, which agreed to publish the story. The reaction was rather more muted than Oscar had perhaps imagined. There were some severely critical voices, voices which seized upon the pederastic overtones of the story. The *World* commented that Oscar's rapture on 'the golden hair' and the 'tender, flower-like grace' of Willie Hughes, on his 'dreamy, deep-sunken eyes', his 'delicate, mobile limbs, and white, lily hands' was 'unpleasant', 'peculiarly offensive' and 'scarcely what one would have expected' in *Blackwood's*. Oscar was undeterred and determined to press ahead with the expanded, even more explicit version of *Mr W.H.* 'Our English homes will totter to their base when my book appears,' he predicted.

Frank Harris later wrote that *The Portrait of Mr W.H.* 'did Oscar incalculable injury':

It gave his enemies for the first time the very weapon they wanted, and they used it unscrupulously and untiringly with the fierce delight of hatred. Oscar seemed to revel in the storm of conflicting opinions which the paper called forth. He understood better than most men that notoriety is often the forerunner of fame and is always commercially more valuable.

Oscar was well aware of the potential impact of *The Portrait of Mr W.H.* and that inferences about his own sexuality might be drawn from the story. Before he had written, let alone published it, Oscar had outlined the elements of the story to various friends, including Arthur Balfour and H.H. Asquith, respectively Tory and Liberal politicians, who were both destined to become Prime Minister. Both men advised him not to publish, pointing out the danger to his reputation. Oscar refused to listen. To deny the world the truth of Willie Hughes, to deny the wonder of the love, spiritual and sexual, between a man and a youth because of any possible repercussions on himself was a denial of truth revealed, a species of betrayal, a recantation of his sexual faith. Like Cyril Graham, Erskine and the anonymous young narrator, Oscar wanted to live in his sexual faith, to profess and promulgate his sexual faith and, if necessary, to become a martyr to it.

Shadow and song

'My weakness is that I do what I will and get what I want.'

If *The Portrait of Mr W.H.* was a manifesto of Uranian love, it nevertheless signally failed to deal with Uranian lust, preferring instead a series of classical allusions, nudges and winks. Oscar argued that the rediscovery of Greek love in the Renaissance meant that sex, or 'gross bodily appetite', as he preferred to call it, had somehow been subsumed into a higher philosophy, a higher purpose:

> Love had, indeed, entered the olive garden of the new Academe, but he wore the same flame-coloured raiment, and had the same words of passion on his lips.

It was a beautifully written passage which nevertheless was an uneasy compromise. Sexual desire, or what Oscar had once poetically described as 'the quenchless flame, the worm that dieth not', was still in the bud of perfect friendship, even in the sunlit 'olive garden of the new Academe'. However cleverly he argued, however exquisite his phraseology, however carefully he papered over the cracks, everything still boiled down to love and to lust – and how on earth to synthesise the two? It was a tension, a contradiction, a confusion that Oscar had already confronted in his marriage and would confront again in his relationships with young men. He loved Constance, but he lusted after young men. Now, increasingly, he had to try and resolve the tensions between the feelings of love he had experienced with people like Harry Marillier and Robbie Ross, and the powerful lust he had for young men like Fred Althaus. Even on those rare occasions when Oscar had felt love for a young man, it lasted only as long as he felt lust. Oscar's lust rarely lasted longer than a few days, or a few weeks. When his lust withered, his love withered with it.

The contradictions and tensions between love and lust were exemplified in June 1889. At the very same time as he was trying to extricate himself from the cloying 'heavenly sunlight' of his affair with Fred Althaus, Oscar was embarking on another intense love affair, this time with someone rather more couth, rather more socially acceptable. Indeed, Oscar's professions to Fred of being 'out of sorts' were white lies, more to do with finding time to fall in love with Clyde Fitch, a twenty-three-year-old American playwright and aspiring poet. Clyde had met Oscar and Constance the previous summer when he and his mother had been travelling around Europe. They were probably introduced to the Wildes by André Raffalovich, who had entertained them at the home he rented every summer on the Thames at Weybridge.

Clyde was an extraordinarily handsome and engaging young man, 'very aesthetic and romantic looking'. Witty, kind and well-educated, he was, according to his friend Robert Herrick, 'as whimsical as a child, loving, loveable, gay, witty and gracious'. Clyde was 'slight, dark, with black hair brushed back in a wave from his forehead, over which . . . he would pass his hand' when excited or enthusiastic, which he very often was. Like Robbie Ross, Clyde seems to have come to terms with his sexuality at a comparatively early age. But unlike Robbie at Cambridge, Clyde had managed to survive the bullying at university in America unscathed. Clyde was, to use an old-fashioned phrase, rather 'obvious'; not exactly effeminate, but certainly not an overtly rugged specimen of masculinity. He had 'many of the more charming qualities that we used to call feminine, without being effeminate', was how his friend Herrick tactfully phrased it.

Clyde became the target for bullying and abuse at Amherst College as a result of his eccentric taste in clothes and interior design. One of his first tasks when he arrived was to decorate his rooms with a highly unusual and artistic frieze of pink apple blossoms against a Pompeian scene. He was sophisticated, intelligent and very well-dressed, wearing a beautifully tailored bright blue suit, a blue gillyflower in a sea of sombre browns and blacks and loud checks. It was this blue suit which seemed to enrage his fellow students. He received an anonymous note, threatening him with 'dire consequences if he was ever seen again in broad daylight in such a garb'. Clyde showed his professor the anonymous letter. 'Well?' Professor Cowles demanded, handing back the note. 'What would you advise me to do about it?' Clyde asked. Professor Cowles paused and replied: 'What do *you* think you had better do about it?' Clyde thought a moment. 'I don't see why I should let them dictate to me,' he said. 'I think I'll stick it out.' Which is exactly what he did, enduring the bullying 'heroically, silently', until his persecutors seemed to lose interest.

When Oscar and Clyde had first met in the summer of 1888, they were immediately attracted to each other, but there had been no opportunity to take things further. Clyde was travelling with his over-protective and domineering mother, and there was little or no chance to pursue a relationship with Oscar. But there were no such restrictions the next year when Clyde returned to London, alone and ready to fall in love with Oscar. And he did fall in love: deeply, passionately, consumingly. For Clyde, Love with a capital L was paramount. In a letter to a friend, he proclaimed his belief in its power:

I believe myself that the Romance of life which is Love, is the best and most precious thing in it, supreme, most to be desired! That all the colour and music of the world are in it, and its Throne the only one worth reigning on.

Although nearly all their correspondence is lost, most likely destroyed in the aftermath of the scandal that engulfed Oscar, a few fragments survive in the form of some passionate love letters from Clyde to Oscar, written at the height of their love affair in the summer of 1889.

The affair seems to have begun almost immediately after Clyde's arrival in London in May. Clyde was quite ready to commit himself to Oscar, to declare and swear his undying love for him. For his part, Oscar seemed to be holding back. 'What a charming day it has been,' he telegraphed with deliberate understatement to Clyde on 22 June. Two weeks later, Clyde was reading the newly published *Portrait of Mr W.H.* 'You precious maddening man,' he wrote to Oscar, reproaching him for not turning up for a meeting and sending a letter instead. 'Your letters are more than you – because they come and you *don't*.' The story of Willie Hughes had gripped him like a vice, he wrote. He could not stop reading:

> Last night when I came home I flung myself in the best evening clothes and all with my *Blackwood*. 'I will just look at it' I thought. But I could not leave it. I read, unconscious of the uncomfortability of my position and of the fact that one arm and two legs were asleep, fast.
>
> Oh! Oscar!
>
> The story is *great* – and – fine!
>
> *I* believe in Willie Hughes: I don't care if the whole thing is out of your amazing beautiful brain. I don't care for the laughter, I only know I am convinced and I *will*,
>
> I *will* believe in Willie H.

'I *will*, I *will* believe in Willie H.' It was an ecstatic profession of sexual faith, just as Cyril Graham and Erskine and the anonymous young narrator had professed their sexual faith in the story. Clyde's letter was also a declaration of love, a love that overwhelmed him, bewildered him, consumed him. He could not, he told Oscar, find the right word to express his feelings, but it was something close to 'adoration'. 'Invent me a language of love,' he pleaded. '*You* could do it. Bewilderedly, All yours, Clyde.'

The affair continued apace. Constance was herself away for the summer, staying in a rectory in the North York Moors with her friend Emily Thursfield, so Oscar and Clyde were able to meet frequently, and Oscar for once did not have to lie about what he was doing and who he was seeing. Clyde continued to pour out extravagant professions of love. '*Nobody* loves you as *I* do,' he wrote. 'When you are here I dream. When you are away, I awake.' Clyde was prepared to do anything, be anything, sacrifice everything for the sake of his love for Oscar. 'Make me what you will,' he begged, 'only keep me yours forever.' Clyde's abject devotion and his adoration were mingled with a devout belief in Oscar's genius: 'You *are* a great genius,' he told Oscar:

And Oh! such a sweet one. Never was a genius so sweet so adorable. Plod thro' yr history you will find no other. And I – wee I – am allowed to loose the latchet of your shoe . . . Am bidden tie it up – and I do, in a *lover's knot*!

Oscar was flattered by such extravagant praise of his genius and not a little overwhelmed by the intensity of Clyde's feelings for him, feelings which tumbled out over each other in a raging torrent of love:

You are my poetry – my painting – my music – You are my sight – and sound, and touch. Your love is the fragrance of a rose – the sky of a summer – the wing of an angel. The cymbal of a cherubim. You are always with me . . . Time . . . stopped when you left. All, always, in every weather.
    Gloriously, absorbingly Yours Clyde

Clyde's love for Oscar was consuming him, and consuming Oscar. It was hard to be the object of such intense love, hard to live up to the ideal Clyde had constructed, and harder still to match Clyde's seemingly insatiable feelings. Oscar must have felt besieged by the sheer intensity of Clyde's love, which far outweighed his own feelings. Oscar and Clyde were lovers only in the sense that they had sex together, though probably not as often as Clyde would have liked. Oscar liked Clyde. He was fond of him. But he did not love him. With the experience of Fred Althaus's cloying, clinging, suffocating love fresh in his mind, Oscar wanted to keep some emotional distance between himself and Clyde.
    Oscar was not faithful to Clyde. He was rarely faithful to anyone. Apart from the pleasure of variety, infidelity was a useful tool to ward off unwelcome emotional entanglements. In July he met a Cambridge friend of Robbie's, Frederic Wisden, whom he clearly found very attractive. 'Wisden is obviously Willie Hughes in reincarnation,' he told Robbie. 'That is why he is so delightful. He is very honey-coloured and charming.' And a week or so later, when Oscar was in Germany, in connection with his play *The Duchess of Padua*, he wrote to Robbie to say that he was returning by way of Wiesbaden and Ostend, adding: 'Somebody I used to like is at Ostend, and I have promised to stay a day.'
    There were times when Oscar simply failed to turn up and keep his assignations with Clyde, who was immediately cast down into the depths of despair, writing anguished letters of reproachful love to Oscar in the small hours:

It is 3. And you are not coming. I've looked out of the window many, many times. The brown is blurred, quite colourless, and the silver heart is leaden . . . I have not slept. I have only dreamt, and thought. I don't know where I stand, nor why . . . I will only wonder & love. Passionately yrs am I, Clyde.

Clyde's last letter to Oscar was written the night before he was due to set sail for New York. It is a strange, valedictory letter, full of foreboding that his love affair with Oscar would not survive his return to America. It contains a strange parable:

I *am* so glad to come to you tonight – my last night in London. You have dyed all that I have done and am this summer in Angleterre. You have been the sun that has glorified my horizon, and if night came on, and the sun set in a sad splendour, the morning came with its own golden halo and shone sweetly into the thicket where the brown eyed Fawn lay in his grass green bed, with a strangely shaped wound – like this – ❤ – in his side. A hunter in snaring his shadow had wounded his heart. But the Brown eyed Fawn was happy. 'He has my heart, he sang. 'But the *wound*, the wound is mine – and no one can take it from me!'

Clyde is the brown-eyed faun, lying wounded in his green grass bed. Oscar is the hunter, a sexual predator, who, in attempting to snare the faun's shadow, or sexual self, has wounded his heart. But even though he lies bleeding, bereft and left for dead, the faun rejoices in his wound, in his stigmata of love. The sexual imagery of the parable is striking and insistent. The faun has been pierced and penetrated, and bears a heart-shaped wound of love. Oscar has penetrated Clyde, emotionally and physically; and he bears the 'strangely-shaped wound' inflicted by Oscar's anal penetration. And though Clyde's heart is broken, he nevertheless possesses the erotic pleasure of having been penetrated, a pleasure that no one can take away.

Oscar's response to this parable was to write an answering poem, which took up the story of the brown-eyed faun, the hunter and the faun's shadow. The single-sheet manuscript of the untitled poem signed simply 'Oscar' was found, after Clyde's death, carefully folded into a presentation copy of Oscar's *Intentions*, but certainly dates from 1889, as Oscar, always one to recycle, published a slightly amended version of the poem, which he called 'In the Forest', in that year's Christmas number of the *Lady's Pictorial Magazine*. Oscar's poem precisely expresses his confused feelings – not just about Clyde, but about the tensions and contradictions between love and lust:

Out of the mid-wood's twilight,
Into the meadow's dawn,
Ivory-limbed and brown-eyed
Flashes my faun.

He skips through the copses singing,
And his shadow dances along,
And I know not which I should follow,
Shadow or song.

O Hunter snare me his shadow,
O nightingale catch me his strain,
For, moonstruck by madness and music
I seek him in vain.

Clyde is the brown-eyed, ivory-limbed faun who skips and dances through the forest meadows. Oscar is on the horns of a dilemma. He does not know what to follow, the faun's song or his shadow, pure love or impure lust. He can ask the nightingale – the symbol of love – to catch the strain of the faun's song, or the hunter – the symbol of lust – to snare his shadow. In Oscar's fairy story *The Nightingale and the Rose*, the nightingale is the symbol of pure, self-sacrificing love, who deliberately impales herself on a thorn for the sake of love. The shadow is a thing of the night: penumbral, mysterious and elusive. It is the dark side of love, representing sex, lust and desire. The shadow must be hunted, snared, captured by craft and guile.

There is no solution to the dilemma in the poem, just as there was no solution in Oscar's life. Song or shadow? Shadow or song? Love or lust? Lust or love? By the end of the poem, a resolution is as far off as ever, and Oscar, 'moonstruck by madness and music', is doomed to seek in vain. This last line suggests that men who love men or boys are subject to a form of erotic lunacy; literally, a madness of the moon. The moon as arbiter of erotic destiny was to feature in Oscar's play *Salomé*, where a cruel, cold moon presides over and controls the erotic desires and destinies of poor mortals. 'These men are mad,' declares Herodias, mother of Salomé. 'They have looked too long on the moon.' Oscar perhaps knew that in Russia men who had sex with men were known as 'men of the lunar light', a name which suggested that the origins of sexual desire between men lay in the cycles of the moon and that those under the spell of the moon's cold light were incapable of free will. Oscar had most certainly imbibed the idea of lunacy, of moon-induced and moon-controlled madness whilst he was growing up in Ireland. According to Lady Wilde's *Ancient Legends*:

In some parts of Ireland the people, it is said, on first seeing the new moon, fall on their knees and address her in a loud voice with the prayer: 'O moon; leave us well as thou hast found us.'

Oscar frequently referred to the 'magic mirror of the moon' and, after his release from prison, often associated sex with the moon. 'Romance is a profession plied beneath the moon,' he wrote later about sex between men and male prostitutes in Nice. He even began to refer to the penises of boys as 'harvest moons' or 'full moons'.

Clyde Fitch's instincts were right. When he left London for New York in early September 1889, his love affair with Oscar was over. Absence did not make Oscar's heart grow fonder. Out of sight meant out of mind. Besides, Oscar had already met yet another young man, a new ideal boy, in the form of

John Gray, a handsome young poet who was to become the inspiration for one of Oscar's most famous and beguiling creations, Dorian Gray. But Oscar and Clyde were to remain on affectionate terms until just before the scandal broke. Clyde visited London every summer and they continued to meet socially. Constance carried on an intermittent correspondence with Clyde's mother, and Oscar invariably presented Clyde with inscribed copies of his books; in a copy of *The Happy Prince and Other Tales*, Oscar wrote: 'Clyde Fitch from his friend Oscar Wilde. Faëry-Stories for one who lives in Faëry-Land'. It was, in every sense, a just assessment; a reference not just to Clyde's hopelessly romantic, enchanted world view, but also a sly and knowing reference to the slang name for New York's men who had sex with men, the Fairies – among whom Clyde Fitch could now number himself.

In late August 1889, Oscar made the acquaintance of Charles de Sousy Ricketts and Charles Shannon, near neighbours who lived a few minutes' walk away at number 1, The Vale, a cul-de-sac off the Kings Road. Max Beerbohm was later to dub them 'the ladies of the Vale'. Both were talented artists and designers with a keen interest in all aspects of modern literature and art, so keen that they were on the point of launching the first issue of their own journal of contemporary culture, the *Dial*. Ricketts and Shannon sent a copy to Oscar who promptly called at the Vale to thank them. 'It is quite delightful,' he told them. 'But do not bring out a second number, all perfect things should be unique.' Oscar was very taken with his new acquaintances: 'I saw Mr Ricketts on Saturday,' he told his friend, the young artist W. Graham Robertson. 'He seems very cultivated and interesting.' Ricketts and Shannon were cultivated and interesting in every sense. They had met at the City and Guilds Technical Art School in Lambeth when Ricketts was just sixteen and Shannon nineteen. They fell in love, and their relationship was to last the best part of half a century. Ricketts was half-French and had been brought up in France and Switzerland. He was cultured and sophisticated; a fascinating and lively conversationalist with a questioning, probing mind. He was not afraid to disagree with Oscar. 'Oh, nonsense, Oscar,' he would often exclaim during their 'long verbal combats'. Shannon, by contrast, was a clergyman's son from Lincolnshire, handsome in a quintessentially English way, tall, fair and very shy.

Before very long Oscar had christened Shannon 'Marigold' and Ricketts 'Orchid'. They were well-named. Like an orchid, Ricketts was rare, exotic and spectacularly colourful, while Shannon was possessed of all the simple, obvious and straightforward delights of an English country garden flower. Oscar commissioned Ricketts to paint the forged Elizabethan portrait of Willie Hughes for a frontispiece to the expanded version of *Mr W.H.* Ricketts duly obliged and painted a wonderful portrait on 'a decaying piece of oak' and 'framed it in a fragment of worm-eaten moulding, which my friend Shannon pieced together'. Oscar was delighted. 'My dear Ricketts,' he wrote. 'It is not a forgery at all; it is an authentic Clouet of the highest artistic value. It is absurd of you and Shannon to try and take me in!'

115

The flower-like existence of Orchid and Marigold in the Vale was attractive to Oscar. He described it to the artist Will Rothenstein as 'the one house in London where you will never be bored'. Whenever he was at a loose end, or bored by the domesticity of Tite Street, he could walk round to the Vale and be assured of a warm welcome, excellent conversation and interesting company. As men who loved men who had discreetly set up house together, Marigold and Orchid entertained a large circle of writers and artists, many of whom, like Oscar, shared their sexual tastes. It was there, almost certainly, that Oscar met John Gray.

Gray was a young poet and writer who had contributed an article to the *Dial* on the brothers Goncourt and a fairy story, 'The Great Worm'. He was devastatingly handsome. Photographs from the time show an exquisitely dressed young man with a perfect profile, dark blonde hair, full lips and large expressive eyes. He was wonderfully graceful and elegant, charming and intelligent with perfect manners. He looked much younger than his years. He was twenty-three when Oscar first met him, but could easily have passed for seventeen. When the poet Lionel Johnson met him two years later, he thought he had the face of a fifteen-year-old. John Gray retained this quality of youthfulness throughout his twenties, and beyond.

But there was more to John Gray than just being handsome, charming, poetical and exceptionally young-looking. Each and all of these qualities made him desirable, but there was something more. He was quite beautiful; startlingly and arrestingly beautiful. Two years later, when Gray was twenty-five, André Raffalovich's devoted governess, Miss Gribbell, was sitting in her box at the Royal Opera House in Covent Garden:

> Somebody pointed out to her, across the long row of stalls, a seated figure in an opposite box, saying: 'That is the young poet John Gray.' Miss Gribbell looked through her opera glasses and exclaimed: 'What a fascinating man. I never knew that anybody could be so beautiful.'

John Gray was beautiful, coldly and perfectly and poetically beautiful, like porcelain or alabaster. Of all the young men Oscar had met, none was so supremely beautiful as John Gray, none at once so desirable and so seemingly unattainable.

Not long after he met John Gray, Oscar wrote about the suzerainty of beauty:

> And Beauty is a form of Genius – is higher, indeed, than Genius, as it needs no explanation. It is one of the great facts of the world, like sunlight, or springtime, or the reflection in dark waters of that silver shell we call the moon. It cannot be questioned. It has its divine right of sovereignty. It makes princes of those who have it.

John Gray's Beauty was higher than Oscar's Genius. Beauty was made not just to be loved by Genius, but to be worshipped, to be hymned, by Genius. Oscar's meeting with the divine John Gray, Prince of Beauty, was like Shakespeare's meeting with Willie Hughes. Here was the young man, the ideal boy incarnate, who could inspire Oscar's 'passionate adoration', and his 'strange worship'. Oscar fell in love with John Gray at once.

John and Dorian

'There is something tragic about the enormous number of young men there are in England at the present moment who start life with perfect profiles, and end by adopting some useful profession.'

When Oscar met and fell in love with the perfectly beautiful, wonderfully poetic and absurdly boyish-looking John Gray, he thought he had met his ideal boy incarnate. The only problem was that John Gray did not immediately reciprocate. Although he could recognise and respect Oscar's Brobdingnagian intellect, marvel at his conversation, his wit and his humanity, he was not attracted to him. This was a new experience for Oscar, who had spent the years since his marriage having a series of affairs with young men, all of which had ended almost as soon as they had begun – usually when Oscar's beloved started to show dangerous signs of falling in love with him. But John Gray showed no inclination to fall instantly and deeply in love with Oscar. And the more he hesitated, the more he doubted, the more he fired Oscar's passion.

Oscar set about laying amorous siege to John Gray. Oscar was a hard man to resist, even for someone as controlled and controlling as John Gray. And, under the full effulgence of Oscar's professions of immortal, undying love, his flatteries, his generous gifts and his constant attentions, John Gray did eventually consent to become Oscar's officially beloved, several months after they first met. Sex between them did take place but it was sex more as a rite of passage, a rite of possession. For Oscar, sex with John Gray was an act of worship. For John Gray, it was a confirmation of his social and literary status. Oscar became his protector, his patron, his benefactor, poetically and materially.

In fact, the John Gray that Oscar met and fell in love with was a construction, an exquisite fiction, a carefully crafted sonnet of a young man, hewn and marvellously fashioned from very rough clay. John Gray had had no advantages in his life. Everything he was, he had created. He was born in lodgings in Bethnal Green, then as now a poor working-class area of London, the first son of John and Hannah Gray. John Gray senior had moved to London from Scotland and had met and married Hannah Williamson, two years his junior. He was a skilled artisan, a wheelwright and carpenter in the Woolwich Dockyard. The Grays' marriage was not particularly happy. John

Gray senior was dour, probably a drinker; Hannah was strong-minded, intelligent, hard-working and devoted to her children. She was ambitious for them and determined that they would make their way in the world. Money was always short, and in the first years of John's life the family moved around London, from one working-class lodging to another. Eventually, John Gray's father landed the post of Inspector of Stores at the Woolwich Arsenal, a salaried position which brought with it a measure of security. The family now settled in Plumstead, near Greenwich, a couple of rungs up the social ladder.

From a very early age, it was clear that John was an exceptionally gifted boy. As a child, he attended a Wesleyan school, the family being nominally Methodists. Then, at the age of twelve, he won a scholarship to the Roan School in Greenwich, a well-established grammar school. Hannah Gray was delighted by John's success. It was what she had hoped for, planned for. John's time at the Roan School began well and he wrote a prize-winning essay on the subject of cruelty to animals for the Royal Humane Society. But after just a year, John's studies were abruptly terminated. Aged just thirteen, John was set to work in the great workshops of the Woolwich Arsenal as an apprentice metal-turner.

Exactly why John's schooling ended so suddenly remains a mystery. It can hardly have been a simple matter of money. John's school fees of £1 a term were affordable for a respectable working-class family. And an apprentice's wage was so small as to be insignificant to the household budget. Hannah Gray must have been appalled. It was the very opposite of everything she had worked for. That it was John's father's decision to remove him from school is suggested by the deleted lines of an unpublished autobiographical poem: 'My father then commands/That I must learn to use my hands'. It was not a request, not a decision, but a command. Was it possible that John's dour Scottish father had detected dangerous signs of effeteness, of effeminacy in his oldest son's manner, in his behaviour? And had he, in violent reaction, pulled him out of the environment where he was thriving and placed him firmly in a working-class, working-male, overtly masculine environment, to toughen the boy up; to knock any signs of effeminacy out of him; beating, literally and metaphorically, some sense into him? By the age of thirteen, it must have been evident that John was an exceptionally handsome boy, and likely to grow into an extraordinarily handsome young man. Had there been some kind of sexual scandal at the school? And had John been involved? Whatever the reason for his departure from school, John clearly blamed his father and began to hate him with a vengeance. When his father died in 1892, leaving a widow and eleven children, John could not mourn his passing. All he could say was, 'I have lost my father. I am well pleased with the loss.'

John Gray found himself at the age of thirteen in a dirty, noisy metal workshop, part of the vast Woolwich Arsenal, which supplied the British Empire with ordnance and guns. As an apprentice, he was indentured to work long hours for a wage so small that he still had to rely on his parents for his food and lodgings. It was a devastating translation for a sensitive, intelligent boy whose future had seemed assured. Despite the noise, the dirt and the long hours, he somehow managed to educate himself, teaching himself mathematics, Latin, French and German, as well as becoming proficient in drawing and painting. It was a remarkable achievement for a young boy from the working class, and his talent did not go unnoticed. After taking a test, he was promoted to the drawing office, where he started to train as a technical draughtsman. Here, it was warm, dry and quiet. More importantly, the experience had taught John the lesson that hard work and study could produce dividends. At the age of sixteen he sat and passed the competitive entrance examination for a Civil Service Lower Division Clerkship and began work in the Savings Bank Department at the London General Post Office. A year later he was promoted to the Post Office's Confidential Enquiry Branch, a department which dealt with theft or fraud. In his spare time he continued his studies, passing the London University matriculation examination in June 1887 as an independent scholar. In 1888, at the age of twenty-two, he was appointed to a job in the Foreign Office.

In nine long years he had risen from working-class apprentice metal-turner to a position in the Civil Service in one of the great government departments. If his rise through the ranks continued at the same velocity, he could expect great things. Not only had John Gray escaped from his fate as a horny-handed son of toil, but he had also escaped from the strictures of his class. Somehow or other, in addition to working long hours, studying hard, and passing examinations, he had managed to transform himself into a simulacrum of a young man about town: exquisitely dressed, with an accent and manners so perfect as to make him indistinguishable from his contemporaries at the Foreign Office who had been to public school and university. John was a young man of letters, a poet of some ability and a writer of prose with strong literary aspirations. He was also a lover of men.

John Gray's rise was so meteoric that it was almost miraculous – so miraculous that the question has to be asked, was he helped? Had he met an older, wealthier man – or indeed, a series of men – who had helped him on his way, smoothing away the cockney vowels, teaching him the perfect manners that were remarked upon throughout his life, educating his eye, directing his taste, choosing his clothes and generally overseeing the transformation from cockney lad to cultured exquisite? For many young working-class Victorian men, finding a wealthy older man to look after them was highly desirable. It offered them almost the only way out of poverty, a chance to escape the burden of their birthright. John Gray's exceptional looks would have guaranteed any number of wealthy admirers, and he was certainly intelligent enough to allow himself to be courted only by men who showed that they were willing to help him along the way, to smoothe his passage. Even though his wages as a lower-grade civil servant would have been better than any he might have earned in the metal-turning workshop, they would not have been enough to buy him the expensive clothes, the books and the other trappings of a young man about town. There is no firm evidence of such a patron, or indeed, patrons, but John Gray's later career suggests that there was always a wealthy older man who was his protector and his patron. It was a role filled by Oscar for nearly three years until Gray turned to André Raffalovich, whose enormous wealth and endless devotion were then placed at his service.

Some time after their first meeting in the studio of Ricketts and Shannon, Oscar and John Gray were at a dinner party together 'at one of those Soho restaurants that furnish private rooms for supper parties'. According to Frank Liebich, a pianist who wrote a short, unpublished memoir of Oscar, there were five men present. Besides Oscar and John Gray, there was Liebich himself and the poets John Barlas and John Davidson. Barlas, himself a lover of men, had 'hinted, rather vaguely', Liebich recalled, 'of the (alleged) intimacy between Wilde and Gray, so that I was really rather curious about the latter, an extraordinarily good looking youth not much older than myself'. The dinner was not a success, and John Gray made a poor impression on Frank Liebich. 'John Gray and I talked but little,' he remembered. Gray seemed 'bored and tired' and moody. 'I found nothing memorable in his speech nor in his manner,' wrote Liebich, 'which seemed tinged with condescension. I thought him a thoroughly blasé worldling.'

'Bored', 'tired', 'blasé', condescending and worldly. Was this the same John Gray, the poet and writer, whose intelligence, perfect manners and flawless clothes had charmed the ladies of the Vale and captivated Oscar? The truth is that John Gray was all these things. He was, as Oscar once described his fictional counterpart, Dorian Gray, a 'complex multiform creature', capable of multiple and fascinating moods. He could be frivolous or deeply serious; charming or petulant; intelligent, engaging and articulate; or haughty and condescending. He could also be loyal and loving.

Oscar paid John Gray the greatest possible tribute when he immortalised him in his first novel, *The Picture of Dorian Gray*. In August 1889, shortly after his first meeting with John Gray, Oscar had dinner with J.M. Stoddart, the managing editor of the American *Lippincott's Magazine*. It was Stoddart who had brought out Rennell Rodd's *Rose Leaf and Apple Leaf* and who had taken Oscar to meet Walt Whitman at his house in Camden, New Jersey five years earlier. Arthur Conan Doyle was also present at Stoddart's dinner, the purpose of which was to persuade Oscar and Conan Doyle to contribute a story each to *Lippincott's*. Oscar accepted the commission and the result was *The Picture of Dorian Gray*.

There could be no doubt in the minds of Oscar's friends and contemporaries that John Gray was the model for Dorian Gray; that Oscar had fashioned his exquisite amoral hero from the exquisite reality of John Gray. It was an open secret among the confraternity of poets in London: Ernest Dowson told Arthur Moore how 'Dorian' Gray had read 'some very beautiful and obscure versicles in the latest manner of French Symbolism' at a meeting of the Rhymers' Club. Lionel Johnson told Campbell Dodgson that 'I have made great friends with the original of Dorian: one John Gray, a youth . . . with the face of fifteen'. And Arthur Symons recalls meeting Oscar at a private view in the New Gallery. 'As I came downstairs,' Symons wrote:

> I came on Wilde in the midst of his admirers, showing more than ever his gift of versatility. Seeing me he made a gesture, and as I went up he introduced me to John Gray, then in what is called 'the zenith' of his youth . . . I was not aware he was supposed to be the future Dorian Gray of Wilde's novel.

A single letter from John Gray to Oscar survives, in which he signs himself 'Dorian'. And Oscar was in the habit of referring to him as 'Dorian' in conversations with Ada Leverson and others.

Oscar had taken John Gray's surname, changing his Christian name to the suggestive Dorian – a name replete with implicit *paiderastia*. The Dorians were a tribe of ancient Greece, inhabiting the major cities of Sparta, Argos and Corinth. They were famous for their custom of institutionalised *paiderastia*, by which an older man became the lover and the teacher of a youth. The Dorians were generally held responsible for the spread of *paiderastia* throughout ancient Greece. In his privately printed and cautiously circulated *A Problem In Greek Ethics*, John Addington Symonds wrote:

> The Dorians gave the earliest and most marked encouragement to Greek love. Nowhere else, indeed, except among the Dorians, who were an essentially military race, living like an army of occupation in the countries they had seized, herding together in barracks and at public messes, and submitting to martial drill and discipline, do we meet with *paiderastia* developed as an institution.

Oscar began writing his novel in the late autumn of 1889, at the same time as he was laying amorous siege to John Gray, and much of the novel reflects their relationship. Dorian Gray, like John Gray, is a young man of 'extraordinary personal beauty', 'a young Adonis' who 'looks as if he were made out of ivory and rose-leaves', a veritable 'Narcissus'. And like John Gray, Dorian looks much younger than his years. He is 'little more than a lad, although he is really over twenty'. Throughout the original manuscript of the novel, Oscar described Dorian Gray as a 'boy', changing this word to the more neutral 'lad' later, along with dozens of other mutings of the more obvious homoerotic passages. Basil Hallward, an artist in paint, falls in love with Dorian at first sight, just as Oscar, an artist in words, fell in love with John Gray at first sight. At a crush at Lady Brandon's (a thinly disguised portrait of Speranza and her at-homes), Basil suddenly becomes conscious that someone is looking at him:

> I turned half-way round and saw Dorian Gray for the first time. When our eyes met, I felt that I was growing pale. A curious sensation of terror came over me. I knew that I had come face to face with someone whose mere

personality was so fascinating that, if I allowed it to do so, it would absorb my whole nature, my whole soul, my very art itself . . . Something seemed to tell me that I was on the verge of a terrible crisis in my life. I had a strange feeling that Fate had in store for me exquisite joys and exquisite sorrows. I grew afraid, and turned to quit the room.

The 'exquisite joys and exquisite sorrows' that Basil Hallward anticipates from his relationship with Dorian are identical to the 'terrible joy and no less terrible despair' that Shakespeare experienced in his relationship with Willie Hughes.

This was the paradox of *l'amour de l'impossible*, the love of the impossible. For Basil to possess Dorian sexually, to penetrate him anally, just as, perhaps, Oscar had penetrated Clyde Fitch, would be to despoil 'the white purity of his boyhood', to taint and destroy the very purity he worships. In the moral forest of Oscar's fauns, Basil follows the song, not the shadow, and pursues selfless love, not sex. Basil's yearning, aspiring, unrequited love for Dorian is a paradox. It exists merely because it cannot exist. In its realisation lies its destruction.

Dorian Gray, like John Gray, was 'made to be worshipped'. Basil Hallward eventually confesses his feelings to Dorian:

From the moment I met you, your personality had the most extraordinary influence over me. I quite admit that I adored you madly, extravagantly, absurdly. I was jealous of every one to whom you spoke. I wanted to have you all to myself. I was only happy when I was with you. When I was away from you, you were still present in my art.

Basil's only respite is to pour his unquenched and unquenchable love into the portrait he paints of Dorian. It was a work of 'idolatry', Basil tells Dorian. 'There was love in every line, and in every touch there was passion.' Oscar's fictionalised portrait of John Gray is equally a work of idolatry, a hymn of praise, and, like Basil's portrait of Dorian, there is love in every line, and in every touch, passion. And Oscar's portrait of John, just like Basil's portrait of Dorian, betrays 'the secret of his soul', the secret of his sexuality, the only difference being that while Basil seeks to conceal his love, Oscar seeks to proclaim it, wanting those who read *The Picture of Dorian Gray* to understand the true nature of his sexuality.

There are other echoes of Oscar's relationship with John Gray when Basil tells his friend Lord Henry Wotton – another autobiographical aspect of Oscar – of his relationship with Dorian. 'He likes me,' Basil says. 'I know he likes me':

Of course I flatter him dreadfully. I find a strange pleasure in saying things to him that I know I shall be sorry for having said. As a rule, he is charming to me, and we sit in the studio and talk of a thousand things. Now and then, however, he is horribly thoughtless, and seems to take a real delight in giving me pain. Then I feel, Harry, that I have given away my whole soul to some one who treats it as if it were a flower to put in his coat, a bit of decoration to charm his vanity, an ornament for a summer's day.

In her unpublished reminiscences, André Raffalovich's sister, Sophie, commented on a slightly less savoury side of John Gray's character during the early years of his later love affair with André. She claimed that John took André's kindness and generosity too much for granted, that he was 'selfish, over-concerned for his own comfort, inclined to be greedy, and not always polite'. Did Oscar flatter John Gray dreadfully? And was John as a rule charming, but at the same time vain, self-centred, sometimes thoughtless, if not downright cruel? Oscar's greatest act of flattery was to immortalise John Gray as Dorian, to hymn in prose the boyish poet he had fallen in love with.

While Basil follows Dorian's song of love, his friend Lord Henry pursues Dorian's sensual, sexual shadow. One day when Dorian is sitting for Basil in his studio, Lord Henry Wotton arrives and is dazzled by Dorian's perfect beauty, just as Dorian is dazzled by Lord Henry's 'beautiful voice', his worldly wisdom, his sophistication, wit and intelligence:

> Dorian ... could not help liking the tall, graceful young man ... his romantic olive-coloured face and worn expression interested him. There was something in his low, languid voice that was absolutely fascinating. His cool, white, flower-like hands, even, had a curious charm. They moved, as he spoke, like music, and seemed to have a language of their own.

Was this scene a barely disguised fictional counterpart of the scene in the studio of Ricketts and Shannon, when Oscar was dazzled by John Gray's beauty, and John Gray was seduced by Oscar's beautiful voice, his wit and wisdom? Certainly the description of Lord Henry could be a convincing self-portrait of Oscar, who was thirty-five when he met John Gray. Like Lord Henry, Oscar was married. And like Lord Henry, he was tall, six foot tall, with pale olive skin, a low, languid voice that was deservedly famous for being fascinating, and hypnotically expressive hands.

Lord Henry preaches a strange and compelling gospel to Dorian. 'The aim of life is self-development,' he says. By self-development, Lord Henry of course means sexual development, specifically the acknowledgement and acceptance of one's true sexual nature:

> To realise one's nature perfectly – that is what each of us is here for. People are afraid of themselves, nowadays. They have forgotten the highest of all duties, the duty that one owes to one's self . . . their own souls starve, and are naked.

Lord Henry argues that it is society and religion which have conspired to suppress by fear men's true sexual nature:

Courage has gone out of our race. Perhaps we never really had it. The terror of society, which is the basis of morals, the terror of God, which is the secret of religion – these are the two things that govern us . . . the bravest man amongst us is afraid of himself.

Self-denial, sexual denial is a form of emotional and bodily mutilation, a marring of lives which could otherwise be beautiful, perfect and happy. 'We are punished for our refusals,' Lord Henry tells Dorian:

> Every impulse that we strive to strangle broods in the mind, and poisons us. The body sins once, and has done with its sin, for action is a mode of purification. Nothing remains then but the recollection of a pleasure, or the luxury of a regret. The only way to get rid of a temptation is to yield to it. Resist it, and your soul grows sick with longing for the things it has forbidden to itself, with desire for what its monstrous laws have made monstrous and unlawful.

'Desire for what its monstrous laws have made monstrous and unlawful' is a not-so-coded reference to the ancient laws against sodomy and the passing, four years earlier in 1885, of the Labouchère Amendment, which outlawed oral sex and mutual masturbation between men. If men who love men are to realise themselves, are to arrive at their erotic destiny, then morality, law, religion must all be thrown aside. They were prophetic words. Oscar would deliberately cast them all aside in the quest to fulfil his own erotic destiny.

The compelling gospel according to Lord Henry Wotton is also the gospel according to Oscar Wilde. Sexual self-repression is a canker, which eats away the body and the soul. The only true cure is to admit and acknowledge who one is and what one is. It is not enough merely to be a lover of young men, one must proclaim one's love for young men. It was a devastating and daring philosophy, and when Oscar first expounded his gospel to John Gray, he thrilled to its call for erotic revolution. Lord Henry Wotton throws down an erotic gauntlet to Dorian:

> You, Mr Gray, you yourself, with your rose-red youth and your rose-white boyhood, you have had passions that have made you afraid, thoughts that have filled you with terror, day-dreams and sleeping dreams whose mere memory might stain your cheek with shame.

'Stop!' Dorian falters, in a Damascene moment of erotic self-revelation. The nature of these waking and dreaming passions has been revealed to him and revealed to us by the use of the word 'shame' – that resonant Uranian code-word meaning love and sex between men. 'Of all sweet passions,' Bosie was to write after reading *Dorian Gray*, 'Shame is the loveliest.'

Lord Henry Wotton's interest in Dorian is far from avuncular. His powerful speech has disclosed to Dorian his 'life's mystery', has 'revealed him to himself'. It is a kind of forcible coming out, an erotic epiphany. Lord Henry's words have 'touched some secret chord that has never been touched before, but that Dorian feels is now vibrating and throbbing to curious pulses'. The sexual imagery is deliberate and obvious. Lord Henry has touched the 'secret chord' of Dorian's anus, and he experiences a kind of spiritual and penile erection in consequence. Twenty years later, E.M. Forster would experience a similar and equally intense revelation of his true sexual nature on a visit to Edward Carpenter's cottage at Millthorpe, near Sheffield. Carpenter's lover, the working-class George Merrill, 'touched my backside,' wrote Forster:

> The sensation was unusual and I still remember it, as I remember the position of a long-vanished tooth. It was as much psychological as physical. It seemed to go straight through the small of my back into my ideas, without involving my thoughts.

Indeed Oscar takes the metaphor of anal sex and penetration even further in *Dorian Gray*, when Lord Henry considers what he would like his relationship with Dorian to be. It involves a kind of spiritual sodomy:

> To project one's soul into some gracious form, and let it tarry there for a moment; to hear one's own intellectual views echoed back to one with all the added music of passion and youth; to convey one's temperament into another as though it were a subtle fluid or a strange perfume; there was a real joy in that – perhaps the most satisfying joy left to us in an age so limited and vulgar as our own.

Lord Henry wants to ejaculate the very essence of his soul into Dorian's gracious form like 'a subtle fluid', just, perhaps, as Oscar wanted to inseminate John Gray with his own combination of subtle intellect and seminal fluid.

Scarlet threads

'There is no such thing as a moral or an immoral book. Books are well written, or badly written. That is all.'

The Picture of Dorian Gray is an exploration and a celebration of the nature of sexual desire and sexual pleasure between men. With the help of Lord Henry Wotton, Dorian seeks to gather up 'the scarlet threads of life, and to weave them into a pattern; to find his way through the sanguine labyrinth of passion through which he was wandering'. Dorian's purpose is Oscar's purpose, as it is, indeed, the wider purpose of the novel. Oscar had been wandering in a sexual labyrinth and was seeking to somehow 'gather up the scarlet threads', gather up the different, conflicting and confused sexual strands of his life and weave them into a coherent pattern.

Oscar lived in an age when the only intellectual and historical justification for love and sex between men was the tradition of Greek *paiderastia*. But the trouble with Greek love was its emphasis on love rather than on sex. Sex was a conditional, subsidiary part of love. This was not enough for Oscar. He was interested in the shadow, not the song, in the body not the soul, in lust and sex, not love. *Dorian Gray* is an immoral fable; it is Oscar's attempt to explore and legitimise the powerful dynamics of sex and lust between men; to divine a meaning and a pattern; to articulate a new natural philosophy for what were seen as unnatural desires and satisfactions of the flesh.

There was a gap of just a year between *The Portrait of Mr W.H.* and *The Picture of Dorian Gray*, and the two stories represent a radical and dramatic change of attitude on Oscar's part towards love and sex between men. In *Mr W.H.*, Oscar had celebrated love, rather than sex, between men. But in *Dorian Gray*, the reverse is true. The book celebrates the triumph of sex over love, of sensation over spirit, of the body over the soul. The moral battle between love and sex, the body and the soul, between the moral and the morally reprehensible, is fought on a number of fronts.

The neo-Platonic ideal of love so perfectly expounded in *Mr W.H.* is personified by Basil Hallward's pure, spiritual love for Dorian. But it is a love that is effortlessly vanquished when Dorian is seduced – spiritually and sexually – away from Basil by Lord Henry Wotton. The body and the soul of Dorian battle it out for mastery. The body symbolises sex, the soul love. But the struggle between them is unequal. For much of the novel, the soul of Dorian is imprisoned in Basil's portrait, safely locked away in the attic, out of sight and almost out of mind, leaving Dorian's body free to do as he will, safe in the knowledge that his sins have no consequences, other than becoming graven on the face of his portrait.

Like all Oscar's work, *The Picture of Dorian Gray* is immensely and complexly autobiographical, something he acknowledged in a letter to a young admirer:

> I am so glad you like that strange coloured book of mine: it contains much of me in it. Basil Hallward is what I think I am: Lord Henry what the world thinks me: Dorian what I would like to be – in other ages, perhaps.

Much of *The Picture of Dorian Gray* both mirrors and anticipates Oscar's own exploration of his sexuality, a journey which began in doubt, denial and despair, and ended with a confident, triumphal assertion of his sexual self.

Dorian Gray explores and indulges his sexuality to the full and the novel is loaded – almost overloaded – with potent images and invocations of sex between men. Just as Oscar was beginning to become aware of London's hidden Uranian riches, so Dorian experiences an awakening realisation of the vast erotic potential of the city:

> I felt that this grey, monstrous London of ours, with its myriads of people, its splendid sinners, and its sordid sins, as you once said, must have something in store for me.

Dorian is sexually driven, as Oscar was sexually driven. The more sex Dorian has, the more he wants: 'The more he knew, the more he desired to know. He had mad hungers that grew more ravenous as he fed them.' Dorian starts cruising the streets of London, looking for sex:

> As I lounged in the Park, or strolled down Piccadilly, I used to look at every one who passed me, and wonder with a mad curiosity what sort of lives they led. Some of them fascinated me. Others filled me with terror. There was an exquisite poison in the air. I had a passion for sensations.

Dorian is driven by desires over which he has no control, compelled to commit nameless 'psychological' or Uranian sexual sins, a reflection of Oscar's own sexual compulsions which, no matter how hard he had tried to suppress them, forced their way out to the surface:

> There are moments, psychologists tell us, when the passion for sin, or for what the world calls sin, so dominates a nature, that every fibre of the body, as every cell of the brain, seems to be instinct with fearful impulses. Men and women at such moments lose the freedom of their will. They move to their

terrible end as automatons move. Choice is taken from them, and conscience is either killed, or, if it lives at all, lives but to give rebellion its fascination, and disobedience its charm.

Oscar invokes an elaborate battery of gods and saints, emperors and lovers, soldiers and scholars, philosophers and poets from history, from the ancient Greek pantheon of myth to the Renaissance and the Enlightenment. All are there to give corporeal reality to the sexual caresses and excesses of men who love men. Adonis the beautiful and Narcissus the self-loving represent the ideal of the beautiful youth. Saint Sebastian and Antinous, the lover of the Roman Emperor Hadrian, are invoked both as symbols of youthful male beauty and as personifications of self-sacrifice, of martyrdom. Ganymede, another beautiful youth from Greek myth, who was abducted and raped by the god Zeus in the form of an eagle, symbolises anal sex. And the Roman emperors Caligula, Nero and Heliogabalus all represent exploration, experimentation and sexual excess among men who love men. The boy Emperor Heliogabalus stands for the passive pleasures of sodomy. He was obsessed with being anally penetrated by men with enormous phalluses and is supposed to have combed the Roman Empire for such men to pleasure him. Michelangelo, Montaigne, Winckelmann and Shakespeare are all there to emphasise the intellectual traditions of men who love men, while a series of royal favourites, Piers Gaveston, the lover of Edward II, and Robert Carr and Philip Herbert, Earl of Pembroke, both lovers of James I, invoke the royal traditions of sodomy.

Despite his voracious sexual appetite, Dorian's body is unblemished and unblemishable. He has the gift of eternal youth. His love affairs with young men are graphically told when Basil confronts him with a grisly catalogue of unhappy endings. 'Why is your friendship so fateful to young men?' Basil demands:

> There was that wretched boy in the Guards who committed suicide. You were his great friend. There was Sir Henry Ashton, who had to leave England, with a tarnished name. You and he were inseparable. What about Adrian Singleton, and his dreadful end? What about Lord Kent's only son, and his career? I met his father yesterday in St. James's Street. He seemed broken with shame and sorrow. What about the young Duke of Perth? What sort of life had he got now? What gentleman would associate with him? Dorian, Dorian, your reputation is infamous.

The original manuscript was even more explicit. 'Why is it that every young man that you take up seems to come to grief, to go to the bad at once?' It was a highly suggestive passage, and one that would come back to haunt Oscar five years later when he stood in the witness box of the Central Criminal Court at the Old Bailey being cross-examined by one of the most deadly exponents of that art, Edward Carson, his friend from Trinity College, Dublin. Did this passage suggest 'a charge of sodomy?' Carson demanded. 'It describes Dorian Gray as a man of very corrupt influence,' Oscar parried, 'though there is no statement as to the nature of that influence.' It was hardly a convincing denial.

Social ostracism, shame, sorrow, suicide, exile abroad and the other unspecified, dreadful ends of young men were all too sadly familiar to men who had sex with men, and highly suggestive to others. Suicide was a widespread problem. Cyril Graham in *The Portrait of Mr W.H.* committed suicide, and in *Teleny*, the hero Des Grieux contemplates suicide as a way out of the painful dilemma of his sexual attraction to men:

The passion I had tried to stifle, and which was merely smouldering, had burst out with renewed strength, entirely mastering me. That crime could therefore only be overcome by another. In my case suicide was not only allowable, but laudable – nay, heroic.

Robbie Ross had contemplated, perhaps even attempted, suicide, after his ducking in the fountain at King's College, Cambridge, a ducking somehow connected with his sexuality. John Gray would contemplate suicide at a moment of crisis in his life. And John Addington Symonds wrote of the extent of the problem of suicide among men who had sex with men:

I do not think I am far wrong when I maintain that at least half of the suicides of young men are due to this one circumstance. Even in cases where no merciless blackmailer persecutes the Urning, but a connection has existed which lasted satisfactorily on both sides, still in these cases even discovery, or the dread of discovery, leads only too often to suicide.

In *Dorian Gray*, apart from the suicide of 'that wretched boy in the Guards', was the 'dreadful end' of Adrian Singleton, the only son of Lord Kent, also a case of suicide? Was it the same dreadful end as that of Lord Arthur Clinton MP, son of the Duke of Newcastle, who almost certainly committed suicide before he was due to appear in court over the 'Stella' Boulton and 'Fanny' Parke affair? And was Sir Henry Ashton who left England with 'a tarnished name' a thinly disguised reference to Lord Henry Somerset who had fled abroad to exile in Florence a decade earlier in the shadow of a scandal concerning his relationship with a young man, Harry Smith?

Dorian has acquired a reputation for unnatural sex, just as Oscar had acquired a similar reputation. Basil Hallward, the voice of conscience, confronts Dorian over his sexual relationships with young men. As a Uranian in thought – if not in sexual deed – Basil is hardly in a position to object, but he is concerned about rumours of Dorian's nameless depravity, of his sexual vice and violence. 'Then there are other stories,' Basil tells Dorian:

stories that you have been seen creeping at dawn out of dreadful houses and slinking in disguise into the foulest dens in London. Are they true? Can they be true? When I first heard them, I laughed. I hear them now, and they make me shudder.

Dorian had been seen brawling with sailors. Had he been down to the docks, looking for sailors to have sex with? And was the 'foulest dens' a coded reference to public lavatories or 'cottages', or to the male brothels where, for a few shillings, a man could have sex with an off-duty soldier? This is what John Addington Symonds did with an 'old acquaintance of old standing', possibly the poet Roden Noel. This friend, Symonds wrote:

> asked me one day to go with him to a male brothel near the Regent's Park Barracks. I consented out of curiosity. Moved by something stronger than curiosity, I made an assignation with a brawny young soldier for an afternoon to be passed in a private room at the same house.

Dorian's love affair with the young actress, Sibyl Vane, is a thinly fictionalised portrait, a parable, of Oscar's love affair with Constance. Dorian's sexual journey, just like Oscar's, begins in doubt, denial and despair. After Lord Henry Wotton reveals to him the truth of his sexual preference for men, Dorian seeks to deny the truth of the revelation, to master his sexual feelings, to channel them into a more normal, heterosexual course. He falls precipitately in love with Sibyl Vane, an actress who plays the heroines in Shakespearean plays, parts that would have originally been taken by boy actors like Willie Hughes.

Sibyl bears a remarkable physical resemblance to Constance. 'Imagine a girl,' Dorian tells Lord Henry, 'hardly seventeen years of age, with a little flower-like face, a small Greek head with plaited coils of dark-brown hair, eyes that were violet wells of passion.' In a letter to Lillie Langtry written just after their engagement, Oscar described Constance in almost identical terms as 'a beautiful young girl . . . a grave, slight, violet-eyed little Artemis, with great coils of heavy brown hair which make her flower-like head droop'. With the same coiled dark brown hair, the same violet eyes, the same flower-like head and the same 'Greek' quality, Sibyl and Constance are one. And just as Sibyl has her brother James, Constance has a staunchly true defender of her interests in her brother Otho – as well as a mother who has abrogated her duty and responsibility to her daughter.

But Dorian has fallen in love with an illusion, with the Sibyl he sees on the stage bringing Shakespeare's heroines to life. Sibyl is a boy manqué; an actress who in times gone by would have been a boy; and, if only Dorian had the courage to admit it to himself, should, by rights, still be a boy. He declares his love for Sibyl and wants to marry her, but Lord Henry Wotton is not fooled for an instant by this 'sudden mad love'. It is, he realises, 'a psychological phenomenon of no small interest', 'not a simple but rather a complex passion'. 'Psychological' was of course one of Oscar's code-words for love and sex between men. In other words, Dorian's sudden, mad love for Sibyl is a form of denial, a refutation of his true sexual nature. But the illusion is about to be shattered. Sibyl, in love with Dorian, no longer needs to pour her heart and soul into her acting and gives a tawdry, artificial performance as Juliet. Dorian's wonderful illusion of a boy-actor manqué is shattered, and Sibyl appears precisely as she is: a young, sweet girl of seventeen in love with her Prince Charming. The revelation of Sibyl's true being – of her girlhood, her femininity – is what Dorian cannot accept, and his love for her is killed stone dead.

When Dorian tells Sibyl that she is 'shallow and stupid', that she has 'spoiled the romance' of his life, that he does not love her and cannot marry her, Sibyl obligingly kills herself, leaving Dorian free to mourn her – for a day or two – before embarking on a journey of discovery of his true erotic nature. For Oscar, such a melodramatic but undeniably convenient end to his marriage was unthinkable. Oscar was married and must stay married.

Oscar proclaimed that the moral of *Dorian Gray* was that 'All excess, as well as all renunciation, brings its own punishment.' At the end of the novel, Dorian, in a fit of half-remorseful rage, slashes at the ghastly, raddled and corrupt image of himself in Basil's portrait, which magically reverts to its original, pristine and unblemished state. Dorian is found dead, his body slashed as he had slashed the canvas of the portrait. In trying to kill his conscience, Dorian has killed himself, and his corpse now shows all the signs of sin and self-indulgence that his portrait used to bear. It is a moral, but an extremely unconvincing moral. Dorian has led 'a life of mere sensation and pleasure'. His death, following his perfect life, is instantaneous and painless. In this mortal coil, at least, Dorian seemingly pays no price for his self-indulgence and his sins.

The struggle between Dorian Gray's body and his soul has an almost exact counterpart in the real-life struggle John Gray was experiencing between his body and his soul, between the sins of the flesh and the call of the spirit. When Dorian considers becoming a Catholic, it is almost certainly a reference to John Gray's half-hearted conversion to Catholicism, a process which began not long after he met Oscar. In the summer of 1889, John Gray embarked on a course of religious instruction and, on St Valentine's Day 1890, was baptised and conditionally received into the Catholic Church. Like many Catholic converts, John Gray failed to have the transforming experience he had hoped for. 'I went through instruction as blindly and indifferently as ever anyone did,' he wrote later, 'and immediately I began a course of sin compared with which my previous life was innocence.'

John Gray clearly implies that this course of sin was a continuation, an intensification of his previous life of sin. He never revealed exactly what his course of sin consisted of, just as Dorian Gray's sins are only ever adumbrated and never spelt out. But clearly, both Dorian's and John's sins are sexual. Was John Gray's 'course of sin' the inspiration – if inspiration is the right word – for Dorian's course of sin? Oscar began writing *The Picture of Dorian Gray* in the late autumn of 1889, finishing it some time in the late spring of 1890, two and half months or so after John Gray's formal reception into the Catholic Church. Or was it a case of life imitating art? Had Oscar somehow inspired or encouraged John Gray towards a deeper, darker exploration of his sexuality, just as Lord Henry Wotton impels Dorian down the same course?

Lord Henry presents Dorian with a book which Oscar later identified as Huysmans's *A Rebours*. This was of course the book that Oscar had read on his honeymoon and which had, cataclysmically, revealed the truth of his own sexuality to him. The book has the same revelatory effect on Dorian as it had on Oscar:

> The hero, the wonderful young Parisian, in whom the romantic and the scientific temperaments were so strangely blended, became to him a kind of prefiguring type of himself. And, indeed, the whole book seemed to him to contain the story of his own life, written before he had lived it.

Had Oscar, in fact, presented John Gray with a copy of *A Rebours*, and did the book affect him in the same way it had affected Oscar, and had affected Dorian?

Dorian Gray's life of pleasure and sensation was an autobiographical projection of Oscar's own defiant life of pleasure. 'I want to eat of the fruit of all the trees in the garden of the world,' Oscar had told a friend at Oxford. Later, in prison, even though he had regrets, doubts even, Oscar still clung to his creed of pleasure. 'I don't regret for a single moment having lived for pleasure,' he wrote in *De Profundis*. 'I did it to the full, as one should do everything that one does to the full. There was no pleasure I did not experience. I threw the pearl of my soul into a cup of wine.'

Certainly, by the time he came to write *Dorian Gray*, Oscar had developed a profound interest, verging on obsession, in all things sexual, most especially in things sexual between men. At the same time, he also developed an intense preoccupation with the idea of sin. He wanted to probe, explore and celebrate the nature and the mystery of sins and sinners. He wanted to immerse himself in sin, especially in sins of the flesh. If he was to be cast as a sinner, then he would sin, and sin spectacularly. There were, he wrote, 'pleasures subtle and secret, wild joys and wilder sins'. Sin was to be positively sought out because it added an extra dimension to human experience.

Lord Henry Wotton articulates a new, daring and dangerous sexual philosophy for men who love men, 'a New Hedonism', a reaction and an antidote to 'the harsh, uncomely Puritanism' of the age. At its heart this new philosophy of sexual pleasure does not accept, will not accept 'the sacrifice of any mode of passionate experience'. In other words, sex, as much sex, and with as many people as possible, was to be the order of the day. By having as much sex as possible all inhibitions, all doubts, all self-loathing would be overcome. 'The future would be the same as our past,' says Lord Henry, and 'the sin we had done once, and with loathing, we would do many times, and with joy.' The great, abiding and undiscovered secret of life, its salvation, its sacrament, is sex:

Romance lives by repetition, and repetition converts an appetite into an art. Besides, each time that one loves is the only time one has ever loved. Difference of object does not alter singleness of passion. It merely intensifies it. We can have in life but one great experience at best, and the secret of life is to reproduce that experience as often as possible.

Was Lord Henry's new Hedonism, his philosophy of sex as the great sacrament, the great secret of life, the same dangerous philosophy that Oscar had inculcated into John Gray, causing him to embark on his epic course of sin? Did Oscar lead by erotic example, and John Gray follow? Or was it the other way round, with John Gray leading a fascinated Oscar?

Oscar was 'preaching corruption', according to André Raffalovich, who knew Oscar at this time, and who, perhaps more importantly, subsequently became John Gray's lover, patron, protector and confidant. Oscar was fascinated by sexual deviancy. 'He was interested in all sexual perversions,' says Raffalovich:

> He feared them, he was afraid of them for himself. He liked to speak of them . . . He was above all curious, on the prowl, fearful, playing with the idea of danger more than with the evil itself.

Oscar 'prowled around' the sexual labyrinth of London. 'He knew the little anecdotes of all London,' says Raffalovich. 'Great tribades fascinated him as did sodomites who were courageous or in love.'

Dorian's passion for sensation leads him deeper and deeper into the labyrinth, just as Oscar's intellectual and physical exploration of the dark side of London's erotic moon would eventually lead him deeper and deeper into a sexual quagmire. Oscar was, according to André Raffalovich, set on 'the downward path to which he was abandoning himself'. He 'went further and further wrong, and under the sway of vanity and impunity, he ended up living the boldest kind of life and the most dangerous'. Quite how dangerous, Oscar was yet to discover.

Outlawed noblemen

'Not a year passes in England without someone disappearing. Scandals used to lend charm, or at least interest, to a man – now they crush him.'

'It is quite tragic for me to think how completely *Dorian Gray* has been understood on all sides,' Oscar jokingly wrote to Ada Leverson. *Dorian Gray* had been understood, perhaps too well understood, and by too many people, as a novel about love and sex between men. Oscar had set out to write a novel of Uranian love and Uranian lust, a novel that oozed homoeroticism from every pore and from every page. It was a novel of sexual exploration, a novel that took the reader on a journey through a hidden labyrinth of love and sex between men. The love that Basil feels for Dorian, the lust that Lord Henry feels for Dorian, the same lust that Dorian expands and explores and pushes to the very limits, is never named, but ever present. *Dorian Gray* is a triumph of revelation through concealment, of proclamation by insinuating whispers, hints and allusions.

Above all, *Dorian Gray* was a book designed to provoke, to draw attention to itself and to its author, a *roman-à-clef*, a novel with a key – the key being the oblique but nonetheless rousing declaration of Oscar's own allegiance to the love that dare not speak its name. Five years after its publication, *Dorian Gray* was cited in the Marquis of Queensberry's 'Plea of Justification' which charged that in 1890 Oscar wrote and published:

> a certain immoral and obscene work in the form of a narrative entitled 'The Picture of Dorian Gray' which said work was designed and intended by the said Oscar Fingal O'Flahertie Wills Wilde and was understood by the readers thereof to describe the relations intimacies and passions of certain persons of sodomitical and unnatural habits tastes and practices.

'Designed', 'intended' and 'understood' by its readers to be a book about sodomy and those men who practised sodomy. It was a perfectly true and accurate summation of Oscar's motives in writing *Dorian Gray*. The book exceeded all his expectations and became a *succès de scandale*. 'Dangerous' was

135

the word on everybody's lips. Walter Pater described *Dorian Gray* as 'very dangerous', while a delighted Robbie Ross told Oscar:

> Even in the precincts of the Savile, nothing but praise for Dorian Gray, though of course it is said to be very dangerous. I heard a clergyman extolling it – *he* only regretted some of the sentiments of Lord Henry as apt to lead people astray.

Dorian Gray was dangerous because, as Robbie's clergyman at the Savile Club remarked, the novel was 'apt to lead people astray', to arouse those feelings and passions in men best left buried under the weight of Victorian social repression. Sexual feelings between men were sometimes referred to as 'dangerous affections': dangerous for society, and dangerous for the individual who indulged them. 'Oscar once talked to me for several hours about the more dangerous affections,' André Raffalovich said. The subtitle of the *Chameleon*, the explicitly Uranian magazine to which Oscar contributed a set of aphorisms in 1894, and which was to cause him so much trouble at his trial, was 'A Bazaar of Dangerous and Smiling Chances'.

Dorian Gray was dangerous for Oscar personally. The Uranian sexual tastes of Lord Henry Wotton and Dorian were widely interpreted as the sexual tastes of Oscar, and the intense speculation about his sexuality, quelled but never entirely vanquished since his marriage to Constance, flared up again. Pater thought Oscar had gone too far and exposed himself to danger. 'Oscar really is too bold,' he told Frank Harris. 'The forces against him are overwhelming; sooner or later he'll come to grief.' John Addington Symonds agreed that it was bold, but had some reservations. *Dorian Gray* 'is an odd and very audacious production,' he told a friend, 'unwholesome in tone but artistically and psychologically interesting. If the British public will stand this, they can stand anything.'

Some time after the publication of *Dorian Gray*, Oscar was invited to the join the Crabbet Park Club, a rather exclusive literary club run by Wilfred Scawen Blunt, a cousin of Lord Alfred Douglas, and named after his country house where the club met once a year in high summer. Blunt's daughter Judith cruelly described Oscar playing tennis there, as 'a great wobbly blancmange trying to serve underhand'. Before a prospective member's election to the Crabbet Park Club, an existing member was supposed to deliver a eulogy on his behalf. In Oscar's case, George Curzon, the future Lord Curzon and Viceroy of India, rose to deliver the eulogy. But to the surprise and embarrassment of those present, Curzon rounded on Oscar, attacking his sexual reputation and arguing that Oscar would never have been heard of, had it not been for the seduction of strange sins that clung about his name. Curzon, wrote Blunt in his diary, warmed to his theme:

> He had been at Oxford with Wilde and knew all his little weaknesses and did not spare him, playing with astonishing audacity and skill upon his

reputation for sodomy and his treatment of the subject in *Dorian Gray*. Poor
Oscar sat helplessly smiling, a fat mass, in his chair.

Blunt felt sorry for Oscar. 'It hardly seemed fair,' he wrote. Curzon's attack
had been ferocious, much more ferocious than Blunt recorded at the time.
Oscar was nonplussed but, after the initial shock had worn off, 'pulled himself
together as he went on and gradually warmed into an amusing and excellent
speech'. Oscar's speech was a robust and articulate defence of the love between
an older and a younger man, virtually the same rousing speech he was to utter
in his second trial when he was asked to explain what exactly was the love that
dare not speak its name.

Having deliberately, wilfully sailed as close to the wind as he dared in *Dorian
Gray*, Oscar was nevertheless surprised and shocked by the vehemence of the
critical reaction to the book. The reviews of the novel, when it was first
published in the July 1890 issue of *Lippincott's Magazine*, were almost
universally hostile. The book was attacked with what Frank Harris, then editor
of the *Fortnightly Review*, described as 'insane heat and virulent malevolence'.
The *Athenaeum* called the book 'unmanly, sickening, vicious', *Punch* described
Dorian as 'Ganymede-like', while the *Daily Chronicle* – usually a liberal and
forward-thinking newspaper – said 'Dullness and dirt are the chief feature of
Lippincott's this month,' describing *Dorian Gray* as:

> a tale spawned from the leprous literature of the French Décadents – a
> poisonous book, the atmosphere of which is heavy with the mephitic odours
> of moral and spiritual putrefaction – a gloating study of the mental and
> physical corruption of a fresh, fair and golden youth.

'Whether the Treasury or the Vigilance Society will think it worth while to
prosecute Mr Oscar Wilde or Messrs Ward Lock & Co. we do not know,' the
St James's Gazette speculated.

Publicly, Oscar replied to the criticism of *Dorian Gray* in a series of letters
to the newspapers. 'I am quite incapable,' he wrote to the *St James's Gazette*,
'of understanding how any work of art can be criticised from a moral
standpoint':

> The sphere of art and the sphere of ethics are absolutely distinct and
> separate; and it is to the confusion between the two that we owe the
> appearance of Mrs Grundy, that amusing old lady who represents the only
> original form of humour that the middle classes of this country have been
> able to produce.

But despite this bravura public defence of his novel, privately Oscar was
worried. His publishers Ward, Lock and Co, had written to him on 10 July,
barely two weeks after *Dorian Gray*'s publication, to say that *Lippincott's
Magazine* faced a distribution boycott:

We have received an intimation from Messrs. W.H. Smith and Son this morning to the effect that 'your story having been characterised by the press as a filthy one', they are compelled to withdraw 'Lippincott's Magazine' from their bookstalls. We need not say that this is a serious matter for us. If you are in the city during the next day or two we should be glad if you could give us a call.

A distribution boycott by W.H. Smith's was serious enough. But Oscar had other worries, worries serious enough to prompt him to pay a call on Sydney Low, the editor of the *St James's Gazette*, whom he had known slightly at Oxford. Oscar was distinctly worried by calls for his prosecution as the author of *Dorian Gray*, and even more worried by the veiled hints in some newspapers that he shared the sexual tastes of Lord Henry Wotton and Dorian. The visit was a disaster. Low summoned Samuel Jeyes, the author of the *Gazette*'s original review, and a heated discussion ensued. Jeyes was unimpressed by Oscar's by now familiar and unconvincing argument that *Dorian Gray* was a moral parable pointing up the dangers of sexual indulgence. Jeyes challenged Oscar to come clean. Either he was writing about sex between men, or he was not. Which was it? Oscar equivocated. Jeyes pressed his point. 'What is the use of writing of, and hinting at, things that you do not mean?' he demanded. At this point Oscar lost his temper and replied hotly. 'I mean every word I have said, and everything at which I have hinted in *Dorian Gray*.' 'Then,' said Jeyes, 'all I can say is that if you do mean them you are very likely to find yourself at Bow Street one of these days.'

One newspaper went further than either the *Chronicle* or the *St James's Gazette*. The *Scots Observer*, the forerunner of today's *Observer* newspaper, under the editorship of Oscar's supposed friend W.E. Henley, was the most violently critical of *Dorian Gray*: 'Why go grubbing in muck heaps?' Charles Whibley, the paper's reviewer, demanded, accusing *Dorian Gray* of being 'false art'. 'It is false art,' he wrote:

for its interest is medico–legal; it is false to human nature – for its hero is a devil; it is false to morality – for it is not made sufficiently clear that the writer does not prefer a course of unnatural iniquity to a life of cleanliness, health, and sanity.

The phrase 'medico–legal' was a clear reference to the debates about sex between men, and whether sexual activity between men should be cured by the physician or punished by the state. The *Scots Observer* was absolutely clear that punishment by the state was its preferred course:

The story – which deals with matters only fitted for the Criminal Investigation Department or a hearing *in camera* – is discreditable alike to author and editor. Mr Wilde has brains, and art, and style; but if he can write for none but outlawed noblemen and perverted telegraph-boys, the sooner he takes to tailoring (or some other decent trade) the better for his own reputation and the public morals.

'Matters only fitted for the Criminal Investigation Department', 'outlawed noblemen' and 'perverted telegraph boys' were clear references to a celebrated scandal which had unfolded at the same time as Oscar was writing *Dorian Gray*. The *Scots Observer* was making an explicit connection between Oscar and the Cleveland Street Scandal, a scandal which, it was rumoured, involved the highest in the land.

On 15 July 1889, a fifteen-year-old telegraph boy called Charles Swinscow was interviewed by Police Constable Luke Hanks in connection with a series of petty thefts at the Central Telegraph Office. Swinscow was found to have eighteen shillings on his person at the time of the interview, three or four times his weekly wage. PC Hanks asked Swinscow where he had got the money. 'I got it doing some private work away from the office,' Swinscow replied, adding that the work was for 'a gentleman named Hammond' who lived at number 19, Cleveland Street, an ordinary, nondescript street situated between Regent's Park and Oxford Street. PC Hanks repeatedly asked Swinscow what he had done to earn such a sum. 'I will tell you the truth,' Swinscow eventually replied. 'I got the money for going to bed with gentlemen at his house.'

It transpired that Charles Swinscow had been introduced to Hammond and the male brothel at 19, Cleveland Street by a fellow employee of the General Post Office, Henry Newlove. In his statement, Swinscow told how, the previous September, 'I made the acquaintance of a boy named Newlove who was then a Boy Messenger in the Secretary's office and is now a 3rd Class clerk':

Soon after I got to know him he asked me to go into the lavatory at the basement of the old Post Office building – we went into one water closet and shut the door and we behaved indecently together – we did this on other occasions afterwards. In about a week's time Newlove said as near as I can recollect 'Will you come to a house where you'll go to bed with gentlemen, you'll get four shillings each time'.

Swinscow claimed that he was reluctant to go to Cleveland Street but was at last persuaded by Newlove and the promise of the money. Accompanied by Newlove, Swinscow went to Cleveland Street and was introduced to Mr Hammond. 'He said – good evening I'm very glad you've come,' Swinscow recalled in his statement, and detailed his first sexual encounter with one of the Cleveland Street brothel's customers:

I waited a little while and another gentleman came in. Mr Hammond introduced me, saying that this was the gentleman I was to go with that evening. I went into the back parlour, there was a bed there. We both undressed and being quite naked got into the bed. He put his penis between my legs and an emission took place. I was with him about half an hour and then we got up.

Swinscow was not the only telegraph boy that Henry Newlove had recruited in this way for service in the Cleveland Street brothel. George Wright was sixteen when he became friendly with Newlove. Newlove used to speak to him in the lobbies and eventually persuaded him down to the basement toilets. 'On one or two occasions, certainly more than once,' Wright deposed, 'Newlove put his person into me, that is to say my behind, only a little way and something came from him.' Newlove took Wright to Cleveland Street where he was introduced to Hammond. 'Another gentleman came in who I should know again,' Wright said, 'rather a foreign-looking chap':

I went with the latter into a bedroom on the same floor and we both undressed and we got into the bed quite naked. He told me to suck him. I did so. He then had a go between my legs and that was all.

Newlove also persuaded George Wright to find him 'another nice little boy' to take to Cleveland Street. Wright introduced him to seventeen-year-old Charles Thickbroom. Newlove took Thickbroom down to the basement lavatory of the old Post Office building and subsequently recounted to George Wright how he had tried to have anal sex with Thickbroom: 'On one occasion at least,' Newlove told Wright, 'I put my person into his hinderparts. I could not get it in, though I tried and emitted.'

Almost by accident, PC Hanks had uncovered a network of male prostitution involving telegraph boys. Scotland Yard was called in and a warrant for the arrest of Hammond was issued. But when the police arrived at Cleveland Street to apprehend him, they found that he had fled abroad. A warrant for Henry Newlove was also issued and he was successfully arrested and charged with 'the abominable crime of buggery' against George Wright and 'divers other persons'. Newlove was not prepared to carry the entire burden of the scandal, telling the man who arrested him, Chief Inspector Abberline of the Criminal Investigation Department, 'I think it is hard that I should get into trouble while men in high positions are allowed to walk free.' 'What do you mean?' Abberline asked. 'Why,' replied Newlove, 'Lord Arthur Somerset goes regularly to the house in Cleveland Street, so does the Earl of Euston and Colonel Jervois.'

These were names to conjure with. Lord Arthur Somerset, nicknamed 'Podge', was thirty-eight years old, the son of the Duke of Beaufort and the younger brother of Lord Henry Somerset, who had fled to Florence in 1879 to avoid a public scandal over his affair with a young man, Harry Smith. More importantly, Lord Arthur, a cavalry officer, was Assistant Equerry to the Prince of Wales. He was a popular and well-liked man, who was on terms of close friendship with the Prince and other members of the royal family. The

Earl of Euston was the eldest son of the Duke of Grafton and was a man about town with a reputation for womanising.

A watch was immediately placed on the premises at Cleveland Street. Chief Inspector Abberline reported:

> Observation has been kept on the house – 19 Cleveland Street – and a number of men of superior bearing and apparently of good position have been seen to call there accompanied by boys in some instances, and on two occasions by a soldier, but after waiting about in a suspicious manner left without gaining admission. Some of them arrived in separate cabs, and evidently met by appointment at the house for unnatural purposes.

Number 19, Cleveland Street was clearly not just a brothel where men could buy sex with boys, but also a house where they could take their pick-ups, boys or soldiers, perhaps from the streets, perhaps from public lavatories, in order to have sex. Among those seen calling at the house were at least two members of Parliament and Lord Arthur Somerset. On the face of it, there was a strong case for arresting Lord Arthur Somerset. He had been seen calling at the house and, according to Henry Newlove's deposition, not only was he was a frequent visitor at Cleveland Street, but he had also had sex with Newlove several times there.

But a decision to arrest him was delayed. Lord Arthur's social standing merited, it seemed, prolonged and substantial debate in the corridors of power in Whitehall. The Home Secretary, the Director of Public Prosecutions, the Attorney General, the Solicitor General, the Lord Chief Justice and even the Prime Minister, Lord Salisbury, were involved. Lord Arthur was interviewed at his barracks on 7 August about his connections with Cleveland Street. It looked then as if a prosecution was inevitable.

Towards the end of August Lord Arthur quietly went abroad with his servant. He took four months leave of absence from his regiment and conveniently forgot to leave a forwarding address. It all seemed very suspicious. A flurry of letters passed between Whitehall departments, all of which seemed to advocate delay or doing nothing against Lord Arthur, and all of which had his name pasted over. Why? What possible reason could there be for such frenzied and secretive political activity, all designed to delay any arrest or charge against him? Lord Arthur Somerset was on terms of intimacy with the Royal Family. But this cannot adequately explain the extraordinary lengths the government of the day went to avoid any whiff of a scandal involving Lord Arthur. He was an important, even influential, man. But not so important, not so influential as to be above the law. There had to be another explanation.

The reason became clear in September when Arthur Newton, Lord Arthur's solicitor, dropped a bombshell. Significantly, Newton was also acting for Henry Newlove and for George Veck, who was also mixed up in the Cleveland Street affair. Newton quietly let it be known that any prosecution of Lord Arthur would mean that the name of a very important person would be dragged into the scandal, and that this very important person would be exposed as an habitué of 19, Cleveland Street, and as a sodomite. The very important person was none other than Prince Albert Victor, known to his family and friends as Prince Eddy, the eldest son of the Prince of Wales, grandson of Queen Victoria, heir presumptive to the Crown Imperial.

On 16 September 1889, the Honourable Hamilton Cuffe, Assistant Director of Public Prosecutions, gave the game away when he wrote:

> I am *told* that Newton has boasted that if we go on a very distinguished person will be involved (P.A.V.). I don't mean to say that I for one instant credit it – but in such a case as this one never knows what may be said, be concocted or be true.

Lord Arthur Somerset stoutly denied having ever introduced Prince Eddy to Cleveland Street, but significantly did not deny that Prince Eddy was a regular visitor to the premises, only saying obliquely 'Prince Eddy and I must both perform bodily functions which we cannot do for each other.' It was a strange comment. Was Somerset suggesting that the reason he and Prince Eddy visited Cleveland Street was because they both liked to bugger young men, and could hardly bugger each other?

Newlove and Veck were sent for trial. Their case was the last of the day and took less than half an hour. They were both given light sentences, just four months for Newlove and nine months for Veck. Justice, of a sort, had been seen to be done. Hamilton Cuffe called it 'a travesty' and described the sentences handed down to Newlove and Veck as 'ridiculous'. It was a cover-up. Hammond was still at liberty abroad and had received a large sum of money to emigrate to New York, handed to him by the solicitor Newton. Some of the boys involved were offered money to go to Australia and the United States, again by Newton. Lord Arthur Somerset slipped back into England under the impression that the worst was now over. Most importantly Prince Eddy's name had not been mentioned publicly in connection with Cleveland Street.

But this seemingly neat and tidy ending to the scandal was unsustainable. There was still pressure from some quarters in the government, notably from Hamilton Cuffe, to prosecute Lord Arthur Somerset. Throughout September and October there were frenzied communications between the government law officers, the Prime Minister and Sir Francis Knollys and Sir Dighton Probyn, courtiers and fixers to the Prince of Wales. Knollys and Probyn were energetic in trying to quash any chance of a prosecution of Lord Arthur Somerset, calling on Hamilton Cuffe at the Treasury, who wrote an account of the meeting to the Lord Chancellor:

> This afternoon Sir Dighton Probyn and Sir Francis Knollys called here and stated that they were directed by HRH the Prince of Wales to make inquiry as to the rumours about Lord Arthur Somerset, that the matter ought to be

cleared up and that the present state of the case was unjust and cruel to Lord Arthur Somerset.

The Prince of Wales was desperate not to see a prosecution of Lord Arthur Somerset. He knew that if such a prosecution were initiated, Prince Eddy's name would inevitably be dragged in. Probyn and Knollys had their orders. The Prince of Wales had directed them to 'see Lord Salisbury if necessary'. On 17 October, Lord Arthur wrote to a friend:

Just seen Francis K. The Treasury refuses all information at present and so it is likely they will be some time before they can say anything. So K has wired to Lord Salisbury making an appointment for Probyn tomorrow.

The meeting between the Prime Minister and Sir Dighton Probyn took place the next day at King's Cross railway station, where Lord Salisbury was waiting to catch a train to his country seat, Hatfield House. What was actually said is not known, but, later that evening, Lord Arthur fled abroad once again. Was it merely a coincidence, or had he been tipped off that a warrant was about to be issued for his arrest? And if so, by whom? Later, in the House of Commons, Henry Labouchère directly accused Lord Salisbury of tipping off Probyn so that he could warn Lord Arthur to flee.

Even after Lord Arthur's flight abroad, Sir Dighton Probyn, acting for the Prince of Wales, sought to have the charges against Lord Arthur dropped. He wrote directly to Lord Salisbury making it clear that he was acting with the authority of the Prince of Wales: 'I felt that in writing to you I am only doing what the Prince would wish,' Probyn wrote. 'I write now to ask you, to implore of you if it can be managed to have the prosecution stopped':

It can do no good to prosecute him. He has gone and will never show his face in England again. He *dare* never come back to this country. I think it is the most hateful, loathsome story I ever heard, and the most astounding. It is too fearful, but further publicity will only make matters worse.

But a warrant was issued for the arrest of Lord Arthur Somerset, even though it was unlikely that he would ever face a jury in England. And Sir Dighton Probyn and the Prince of Wales were right. Further publicity did make matters worse. Much worse.

On 16 November, the *North London Press* carried the following paragraph:

THE WEST END SCANDALS
NAMES OF SOME OF THE DISTINGUISHED
CRIMINALS WHO HAVE ESCAPED

In an issue of the 28th September we stated that among the number of aristocrats who were mixed up in an indescribably loathsome scandal in

Cleveland Street, Tottenham Court Road, were the heir to a duke and the younger son of a duke. The men to whom we thus referred were the Earl of Euston, eldest son of the Duke of Grafton, and Lord H. Arthur G. Somerset, a younger son of the Duke of Beaufort. The former, we believe, has departed for Peru. The latter, having resigned his commission and his office of assistant Equerry to the Prince of Wales, has gone too.

The paper then went on to accuse the authorities of a conspiracy designed to protect a very important person:

These men have been allowed to leave the country, and thus defeat the ends of justice, because their prosecution would disclose the fact that a far more distinguished and more highly placed personage than themselves was inculpated in these disgusting practices.

The use of the word 'personage' was deliberate and calculated. In the late nineteenth century, the word meant a person of very high rank or importance. So 'a far more distinguished and more highly placed personage' than an earl or the son of a duke pointed directly to a member of the royal family. There had already been rumours about Prince Eddy's involvement in the Cleveland Street affair; now it looked as if the truth was about to come out. But Ernest Parke, the editor of the *North London Press*, had got it wrong. The Earl of Euston had not fled abroad to Peru. Indeed, he had not been abroad for several years. He promptly issued a writ for libel against Parke and the *North London Press*. Parke was determined to fight the charge, and the case came to the Old Bailey on 15 January 1890.

Parke was confident of justifying his story and winning the case. He had, he believed, incontrovertible proof of the Earl of Euston's involvement in the Cleveland Street ménage, in the form of a written statement made by a notorious male prostitute, Jack Saul. This was the very same Jack Saul whose bawdy memoirs, *The Sins of the Cities of the Plain; or the Recollections of a Mary Ann*, were a classic work of Victorian homoerotica, and the same Jack Saul who had been caught up in the 1884 Dublin Castle Scandal, referred to earlier.

In his statement to Inspector Abberline of the Metropolitan Police, taken in August, but seemingly not acted upon, it is clear that Jack Saul had fallen on hard times: 'I am still a professional Mary Ann,' he told Abberline. 'I have lost my character and cannot get otherwise. I occasionally do odd jobs for gay people.' By 'gay people', Jack Saul meant the prostitutes, mostly female, and their pimps, who seemed to form a community of their own in the West End of London.

Jack Saul, it transpired, had known Hammond, the proprietor of 19, Cleveland Street, for just over ten years, 'since the 1st May, 1879', he said. 'We both earned our livings as Sodomites.' It seems as if Saul and Hammond were lovers – certainly Hammond seems to have acted as Saul's pimp. 'I used to give him all the money I earned, often times as much as £8 and £9 a week.' By 1889,

Saul was in his late thirties, and with looks that were starting to fade. Saul resented the fact the Hammond had a ready supply of teenage telegraph boys working for him. 'I complained to Hammond of his allowing boys of good position in the Post Office to be in the house while I had to go and walk the streets for what is in my face, and that is my shame.'

When the libel case went to court, Jack Saul was the star witness for the defence. It was while walking the streets looking for punters, Saul said, that he first met the Earl of Euston, 'a tall, fine-looking man with a fair moustache'. 'I picked him up just as I might have picked any other gentleman up,' Saul told the court. 'Where did you meet this person?' Parke's counsel, Frank Lockwood, asked. 'In Piccadilly, between Albany Courtyard and Sackville Street,' Saul replied. 'He laughed at me and I winked at him. He turned sharp into Sackville Street.' Jack Saul followed him and their encounter followed the classic pattern of such street cruising:

> The Duke, as we called him, came near me, and asked me where I was going. I said 'Home' and he said 'What sort is your place?' 'Very comfortable', I replied. He said, 'Is it very quiet there?' I said yes it was, and then we took a hansom cab there. We got out by the Middlesex Hospital, and I took the gentleman to 19 Cleveland Street, letting him in with my latchkey.

Saul took Lord Euston into the 'back parlour or reception room', the same room in which Charles Swinscow and George Wright subsequently entertained their gentleman clients, and Hammond 'came and knocked and asked if we wanted any champagne or drinks of any sort, which he was in the habit of doing'. The sexual encounter between Jack Saul and Lord Euston was peremptory, little more than masturbation. Lord Euston was not, according to Jack Saul, 'an actual Sodomite. He likes to play with you and then "spend" on your belly.' The Earl's parting words to Jack Saul were, 'Be sure, if you see me, don't speak to me in the street.'

Lord Euston's version of events was naturally very different. One evening around midnight in May or June 1888 a man had come up to him and handed him a card printed with the address of 19, Cleveland Street and with the words '*Poses Plastiques*' handwritten at the top. *Poses Plastiques* was a euphemism for live displays of nudity, where women, singly or in pairs, would display their naked bodies in a variety of erotic postures. Sometimes, these events went further than mere display, involving live sex acts and prostitution. Having kept the card on his chimneypiece for a week or so, Lord Euston, 'prompted', as his counsel Sir Charles Russell put it, 'by prurient curiosity which did him no credit', took a hansom carriage to Cleveland Street where Hammond answered the door:

> I rang the bell and the door was opened by a man of medium height, clean shaven except for a dark moustache, and with hair that was getting thin on top. He took me into the first room on the right of the passage. He asked me

145

for a sovereign, which I gave him, and then I asked him where these *pose plastiques* were going to take place. He said 'there's nothing of that sort here', and then stated the real character of the house. I asked him what he meant by saying such a thing as that to me, and told him if he did not let me out I should knock him down.

The case came down to who was to be believed: the Earl of Euston, an upright member of the aristocracy without a trace of obvious vice about him, or Jack Saul, a self-confessed male prostitute, obviously effeminate, who had lived a life of vice and dishonesty. In his summing-up, Mr Justice Hawkins said of Jack Saul that he could not imagine 'a more melancholy or a more loathsome object'. The jury was out for just forty minutes and returned a verdict of 'Guilty of libel without justification'. Parke was sentenced to twelve months imprisonment without hard labour.

By a strange irony, many of those involved in the political and legal aspects of the Cleveland Street affair and in the prosecution of Ernest Parke were to reappear five years later when Oscar stood in the dock. Hamilton Cuffe, by 1895, had been promoted to Director of Public Prosecutions. Charles Gill, who held a watching brief for Lord Arthur Somerset during Ernest Parke's trial, prosecuted Oscar in his first criminal trial at the Old Bailey. And Frank Lockwood, who defended Parke, became Sir Frank Lockwood, and by 1895 was a senior Liberal politician in Lord Rosebery's government. Lockwood prosecuted Oscar with terrible ferocity. Herbert Henry Asquith, junior defence counsel for Parke, was another senior Liberal politician and by 1895 had risen to become Home Secretary; he would eventually become Prime Minister. All these men experienced at first hand the complex conspiracy of the Cleveland Street Scandal. Five years later, they would all be involved, in one way or another, in what some would claim as another conspiracy, another cover-up.

Even before the publication of *Dorian Gray*, Oscar's name had been mooted in connection with the Cleveland Street Scandal. At the time of the scandal, Henley, the *Scots Observer*'s editor, had asked his reporter Charles Whibley what was the nature 'of this dreadful scandal about Mr Oscar Wilde?' There is no evidence that Oscar ever visited 19, Cleveland Street, but then again, there is no evidence that he did not. He had certainly read and enjoyed Jack Saul's *Recollections of a Mary Ann*, and it is quite possible that the two men had met. Now, whether he liked it or not, Oscar's name was inextricably entwined with the most appalling scandal. His novel had been categorised as 'a filthy one', and was widely regarded as being in some way connected with the events of Cleveland Street.

Apples of Sodom

'In the study hall, in the classroom – nay at very prayers – I have known masturbation carried on. Such was the daily regime, and yet the powers that be never made an attempt to check the mischief. Of its existence they could not have been unaware, for soiled bed clothes and torn trousers' pockets, apart from the pimpled foreheads and emaciated appearance of the boys, told their sad tale.' – 'A Schoolboy' in Reynolds's News, *May 1895*

The Picture of Dorian Gray was the most explicit novel about love and sex between men that had ever been published – at least by a respectable publisher. There had been works of pornography like *The Sins of the Cities of the Plain*, but these had never had the mass audience reached by *Dorian Gray*. The novel was a rallying cry for men who loved men, a Uranian clarion call to arms, a sexually political manifesto, 'designed', 'intended' and 'understood', as Lord Queensberry's 'Plea of Justification' had it, to be a novel about sodomy and sodomites.

Max Beerbohm, not himself a lover of men, but someone who was fascinated by Uranian love, wrote a poem, 'Ballade de la vie joyeuse', in praise of *Dorian Gray*, as well as composing a witty mock examination paper with knowing questions like:

What about the young Duke of Perth? What sort of life had he at this period? Give the name of any gentleman who would associate with him. Is any one, besides Dorian, credited with a *moue*? Write down as accurately as possible Lord Henry's terrible panegyric on youth.

And Lionel Johnson, a precocious young poet at New College, Oxford, also wrote a poem in Latin, 'In honour of Dorian and his creator'. Johnson's poem left no doubt about the novel's locus of interest for him and for the other young men who surrounded Oscar. 'Bless you, Oscar,' the poem went, 'for honouring me with this book for friendship's sake. Casting in the Roman tongue praises that befit Dorian, I thank you':

This lovely rose of youth blossoms among roses, until death comes abruptly.

147

Behold the man! Behold the God! If only my soul could take his part.

He avidly loves strange loves and, fierce with beauty, he plucks strange flowers.

The more sinister his spirit, the more radiant his face, lying – but how splendidly!

Here are apples of Sodom, here are the very hearts of vices, and tender sins.

In heaven and hell be glory of glories to you who perceive so much.

Lionel Johnson was a comparatively new recruit to Oscar's circle of disciples. Oscar had sought his acquaintance in February 1890, on the very day that John Gray was being received into the Roman Catholic Church. Oscar was in Oxford, ostensibly to watch a production of Browning's *Stafford* with Henry Irving in the title role, and to see Walter Pater, though the physical charms of Oxford's undergraduates may have been a much stronger draw.

Walter Pater and Lionel Johnson had become very close the previous year, when Johnson went to visit Pater at the house in London he shared with his sisters. 'I lunched with Pater, dined with Pater, smoked with Pater, went to Mass with Pater and fell in love with Pater,' Johnson had written to his friend, Campbell Dodgson, also a lover of men. Pater had told Oscar about his new young friend and shown him some of Johnson's poems, including one which was dedicated to Johnson's schoolfellow, Lord Alfred Douglas. It oozed homoeroticism, and in the last three lines contained a rather clumsily buried reference to bending over for anal sex:

> Their eyes on fire, their bright limbs flushed,
> They dominate the night with love:
> While stars burn and flash above,
> These kindle through the dark such flame,
> As is not seen, and hath no name:
> Can night bear more?
> Can nature bend
> In benediction without end,
> Over this love of friend for friend?

Oscar was eager to meet Lionel Johnson. His first attempt to call on him was unsuccessful: Johnson was either not in, or he was still asleep, as he kept notoriously irregular hours. Oscar left a note. 'Dear Mr Johnson,' he wrote. 'I called to see you as I wanted so much to know you as well as I know your poems. Are you really invisible?' The next day, Oscar essayed another call on Johnson. This time he was successful. Johnson wrote to a friend about his first encounter with Oscar:

On Saturday at mid-day, lying half asleep in bed, reading Green, I was roused by a pathetic and unexpected note from Oscar: he plaintively besought me to get up and see him. Which I did: and I found him as delightful as Green is not. He discoursed, with infinite flippancy, on everyone: lauded the *Dial*, laughed at Pater, and consumed all my cigarettes. I am in love with him.

Lionel Johnson's head was easily turned by the magnetic force of Oscar's charm. Equally, Oscar found much to attract him in Lionel Johnson. He was very short, just over five feet, and looked extremely young, 'more like the head boy of a Preparatory School' than a twenty-three-year-old Oxford undergraduate. Johnson looked so absurdly child-like that Oscar once quipped about him going out and hailing the first passing perambulator. The lesbian poets Katherine Bradley and Edith Cooper, who published their collaborative work under the name 'Michael Field', described Johnson in their journal as:

> a learned snowdrop (his friends say he is so old he has become a child again). He is quite young, quite pale, drooping under book-lore, with curved lids, nearly as fine as Keats's *Hyperion*.

Oscar and Johnson parted after this first meeting determined to see each other again. 'I hope you will let me know when you are in town,' Oscar wrote immediately after his return to London:

> I like your poetry – the little I have seen of it – so much, that I want to know the poet as well. It was very good of you getting up to see me. I was determined to meet you before I left Oxford.

Oscar and Johnson probably became lovers at some point in 1890, and Johnson was duly inducted into Oscar's circle of young admirers. John Gray was, of course, still Oscar's officially beloved, but for a while, at least, Johnson played the role of Oscar's 'new boy'.

During their affair, Oscar must have asked Johnson about Lord Alfred Douglas, the dedicatee of his poem, and made pertinent enquiries about the exact nature of 'the love of friend for friend' in Johnson's poem and whether the kindled, nameless 'flame' of their passion was the 'the love that dare not speak its name'. It was Lionel Johnson who, in the spring of 1891, loaned his copy of *Dorian Gray* to his schoolfriend and fellow Oxford undergraduate, Bosie Douglas. Years later, Bosie wrote about the 'intoxicating' impact the novel had on him:

> About Dorian Gray. I read it at Magdalen about 2 or 3 months before I first met Oscar. Curiously enough I don't remember hearing much about it from other undergraduates except Lionel Johnson. It had a terrific effect on me. I read it about 14 times running. For years it produced the same effect every time I read it.

Reading *Dorian Gray* made Bosie impatient to meet its author. Three months later, in June 1891, Lionel Johnson called on Bosie at his mother's house in Cadogan Square and took him the short distance to Tite Street to meet Oscar, where the three of them sat and drank tea in Oscar's little writing-room facing the street on the ground floor.

Lord Alfred Douglas, known universally as Bosie, was three years younger than Lionel Johnson. As a child, his devoted mother Sybil had called him by the West Country vernacular for 'little boy', Boysie, and the name had stuck. Bosie was the third son of John Sholto Douglas, the ninth Marquis of Queensberry, and his wife, Sybil Montgomery. Queensberry was a short, vigorous man who lived for hunting, gambling and women. He had been educated at a naval training school in Portsmouth and entered the Royal Navy as a midshipman at the age of fourteen. For the next five years he had travelled extensively, getting into a good many scrapes and fights along the way. When he was nineteen, Queensberry, or 'Q' as he was sometimes known, resigned his naval commission and decided to enter Magdalene College, Cambridge. It was a strange decision. Queensberry, as his grandson later wrote, was entirely void of intellectual and artistic qualities. He was, moreover, 'inordinately proud of having achieved ignorance concerning them'. But he may have felt that a university degree would be of help when he came into his majority and took possession of a large fortune of £78,000 and estates in Scotland of some 30,000 acres. The following year, tragedy struck when Q's beloved younger brother Lord Francis Douglas was killed, along with three other climbers, during their descent of the Matterhorn, after becoming the first party to reach the summit. Queensberry was devastated and rushed off to Switzerland to try and find his brother's body. It was a futile quest. 'I have not been able to find a trace of darling Francy's body,' he told his family, 'I am convinced it is useless to search further, and that his dear body is resting beyond the power of mortal man to reach him.'

Queensberry left Cambridge without a degree, declaring that he had never known a degree 'to be worth twopence to anybody'. He promptly got married, at the age of twenty-one, to Sybil Montgomery, the daughter of Alfred Montgomery, a Commissioner of the Inland Revenue, who was rumoured to be a natural son of the elder brother of the Duke of Wellington. The Montgomerys were extremely well-connected socially – Alfred Montgomery was a particular friend of the Prince of Wales, and Fanny, his wife, was a friend of the then Prime Minister, Benjamin Disraeli. The Montgomerys' two daughters had been brought up in an atmosphere of cultured ease. Sybil was extremely well-educated and widely read. Her winters had been spent in Florence, and she spoke Italian and French fluently. According to Gertrude, one of her future sisters-in-law, she was extraordinarily beautiful with 'delicate features and creamy complexion, pretty turquoise-blue eyes and her lovely mouth, small as a rose bud and quite as bewitching'. The other sister-in-law, Florrie, was not convinced about the suitability of the match. Her brother, she thought, had fallen in love with Sybil's 'beautiful face', and not with Sybil herself. It was a prescient observation.

Queensberry and his bride were mismatched from the very start. Almost immediately after their marriage, the couple went to live at Kinmount, the vast family estate near Dumfries. Kinmount was a large Georgian pile, an imposing neo-classical house built in forbidding grey sandstone mined in Cumbria, a great stone palace, designed to impress rather than to be comfortable or beautiful. In the long chill of a Scottish winter the house was draughty and uncomfortable, and there was little to occupy Sybil, who was already missing the civilised and sociable life she had led as a young woman, as well as the mild winters in Florence. Queensberry used to get up at dawn and spend the best part of the day hunting, while his wife lay in bed reading novels. There was not much in the way of society in the vicinity, and what society there was Queensberry deliberately eschewed, choosing instead to mix with an ill-assorted gang of professional bruisers and sportsmen. Sybil spent her time with her children and in running the house. It was obvious that the marriage was in trouble. Fanny Montgomery visited the couple in June 1867 and wrote to Disraeli that Queensberry possessed 'good abilities and good principles' but was 'suffering from the overwhelming weight of high rank and nothing to do'.

Alfred Bruce Douglas was born in Worcestershire where, in 1869, in one of those fits of impulsiveness which were increasingly to dominate his life, Queensberry had bought a house so that he could take on the Mastership of the Worcestershire Hounds. From the very beginning, Alfred was his mother's darling and remained his mother's darling throughout her long life. 'After Bosie's birth, virtually no one else mattered to her,' her grandson wrote later. Perhaps it was something to do with his exceptional, breathtaking beauty, a beauty which reflected her own. Like Sybil, Bosie was fair-haired and blue-eyed, with a peaches-and-cream complexion. But there was a special quality to Bosie's beauty, a pure, dreamy, poetic, spiritual kind of beauty which enthralled his mother, and most of those around him.

Sybil's devotion to Bosie was further intensified by the fact that, as a very small boy, Bosie had to wear leg-irons to straighten his legs. Queensberry, alone in the family, was unaffected by Bosie's beauty and disgusted by his physical deformity, feelings which he recalled at the height of his feud with his son and Oscar: 'When he was a child swathed in irons to hold him together it used to make me sick to look at him and think he could be called my son.' Bosie's deformity was quickly corrected and he became a healthy active child and a fine athlete.

When he was ten, he and his older brother, Francis, Viscount Drumlanrig, were sent away to school, to Lambrook, near Windsor, then one of the most fashionable preparatory schools, patronised by the aristocracy and by royalty – two of Queen Victoria's grandsons were pupils there. But a year later, Lambrook was rocked by a scandal, almost certainly a sexual scandal. Bosie called it 'a row' and throughout his adult life steadfastly refused to speak about it, suggesting that his time there had scarred him in some way, though it is impossible to know whether he was involved in, or a victim of, the scandal. From Lambrook, Bosie was sent to Wixenford, where he seems to have been quite happy, though he was regarded by his headmaster as a very spoilt boy. While he was at Wixenford, Bosie became 'passionately fond' of an American boy called Edward Shepherd who left to go to Eton. Bosie desperately wanted to follow Shepherd to Eton, and begged his mother to arrange this. But Queensberry was having none of it. He saw the whole scheme as 'a plot', concocted by Bosie and Sybil, a conspiracy against his authority. Bosie, he said, must go to Winchester instead. Bosie was thirteen, very nearly fourteen, when he arrived at Winchester at the start of the Christmas term, 1884.

Like every Victorian public school, Winchester was a den of intense sexual activity between boys – usually, but not always, between older boys and younger boys. The problem of sex between boys in boarding schools, invariably referred to as 'immorality', was well known, having been discussed as early as the 1830s in the *Quarterly Journal of Education*. John Addington Symonds wrote how he was 'filled with disgust and loathing' at the appalling 'moral state' of Harrow where he found himself a pupil at the age of thirteen, and where Bosie's brother, Francis, had also been sent to be schooled:

> Every boy of good looks had a female name, and was recognised either as a public prostitute or as some bigger fellow's 'bitch'. Bitch was the word in common usage to indicate a boy who yielded his person to a lover. The talk in the dormitories and studies was incredibly obscene. Here and there one could not avoid seeing acts of onanism, mutual masturbation, the sports of naked boys in bed together. There was no refinement, no sentiment, no passion; nothing but animal lust in these occurrences.

Symonds recalled two boys in particular whose behaviour was disgusting:

> Barber annoyed and amused me. He was like a good-natured longimanous ape, gibbering on his perch and playing ostentatiously with a prodigiously developed phallus . . . Cookson was a red-faced strumpet, with flabby cheeks and sensual mouth – *the notissima fossa*, the most infamous trench, of our house.

A similar situation prevailed at Winchester. Sex between boys there was rife. The school was 'a sink of iniquity', Bosie wrote. 'I remember thinking that my parents must be quite mad to send me to such an awful place . . . My first eighteen months there were pretty much of a nightmare.' But he gradually adapted to his surroundings:

> However, after the first shock I got used to the conditions, adapted myself to the standard of morality – or rather immorality – and enjoyed the whole thing immensely.

Boys who did not have sex with other boys were the exception rather than the rule at Winchester. Bosie estimated that 'at least ninety per cent' of his contemporaries there had sex with other boys. The remaining ten per cent were doomed to celibacy by circumstance rather than by choice. After Oscar was sent to prison, Bosie wrote that from his 'own personal experience' of public school:

> The practice of Greek love is so general that it is only those who are physically unattractive that are reduced to living without love.

A near contemporary of Bosie's at Winchester was Trelawny Backhouse, who was a little more forthcoming about sexual activity between boys at the school in his unpublished autobiography, written in Peking in 1943:

> Six years at Winchester College were little other than a carnival of unbridled lust . . . I do not vouch for the statistics but fancy that between 1886 and 1892 I enjoyed carnal intimacy with at least thirty (perhaps more) boys, ascendant and descendant.

Those boys caught in the act of having sex were, according to Backhouse, punished either by beatings or by expulsion, depending on the severity of the offence:

> In my time perhaps a score of boys were expelled for 'pedicatio' and for 'coitus inter crura' offences (apart from actual penetration) for both of which corporal chastisement was deemed over-light.

Mutual masturbation was, it seems, frowned upon at Winchester, and it was an offence punishable by beating, but not by expulsion. '*Pedicatio*' or anal sex, or even 'coitus inter crura' – intercrural sex, where ejaculation was achieved between the thighs or between the buttocks – was invariably a matter for expulsion. Backhouse alleges that Bosie practised *pedicatio* or *coitus inter crura* with him at Winchester:

> Bozie, as he was commonly called (a corruption for Boyzie), would probably not thank me for recalling numerous love episodes at Winchester in which he was usually the ascendant and I the pathic, although positions were sometimes reversed.

'Pathic' is an archaic seventeenth-century word for the passive partner in anal sex or in inter-crural sex. Although Trelawny Backhouse's memoirs are not always accurate or, indeed, true, his accounts of his schooldays at Winchester and of his subsequent involvement in the Oscar Wilde scandal have the ring of authenticity. Sodomy was much less common in public schools than either mutual masturbation or fellatio, but it was not unheard of. Jack Saul, in his *Recollections of a Mary-Ann*, claims that he was multiply sodomised during his first night at the boarding school he had been sent to in Colchester.

And, according to the account of one Fred Jones, a soldier in the Foot Guards, who recounted his life story to Jack Saul:

> Young fellows are quite as much after us as older men. I have often been fucked by young gentlemen of sixteen or seventeen, and at Windsor lots of the Eton boys come after us.

After Oscar's trial and conviction, progressive newspapers like *Reynolds's News* were starting to campaign for a clean-up of 'the great public schools of England':

> It is a fact, atrocious to all acquainted with the subject, that at certain educational establishments of the highest class the morality of the students is past praying for; innocent lads, with the purity and refinement of home life in their hearts, become tainted with the traditional vices of these schools and colleges before they have been many months within their walls.

W.T. Stead, in the *Review of Reviews*, pointed up the hypocrisy of punishing men like Oscar Wilde and Alfred Taylor, his co-defendant, for sexual crimes with men when the very same crimes were perpetrated every day in the great public schools:

> If all persons guilty of Oscar Wilde's offences were to be clapped in gaol, there would be a very surprising exodus from Eton and Harrow, Rugby and Winchester, to Pentonville and Holloway . . . But meanwhile public school boys are allowed to indulge with impunity in practices which, when they leave school, would consign them to hard labour.

Reynolds's News and the other newspapers which made similar calls for a clean-up were missing the point. They believed in a theory of sexual contamination, a theory that still has its adherents today. They argued that the prevalence of sex between men was the consequence of boy-to-boy sexual experiences between the sons of the upper classes who populated the great public schools and the great universities of England. By cleaning up the public schools, by extirpating every vestige of 'immorality', the vice of sodomy could not flourish and therefore would not exist. They were wrong.

The assumption was that sex between men was a vice of *luxuria*, a vice that sprang up spontaneously among the rich, the privileged, the effete, who spread it, almost as a communicable disease, outwards into the commonality of the population. Male prostitutes from the working classes, they argued, only existed to service degenerate men from the upper classes. This view of male prostitution was articulated by Henry Labouchère, when he railed against the evils of male prostitution in the House of Commons in the wake of the Cleveland Street Scandal:

In the streets, in the music halls, you have these wretched creatures openly
pursuing their avocation. They are known to the police, yet the police do
nothing to stop this sort of thing . . . these poor and wretched creatures live
to minister to the vices of those in a superior station.

But sex between boys had nothing to do with class or social status. Same-sex
relationships existed at every level of society, from the highest to the lowest.
They were as likely to manifest themselves in the schools, reformatories,
workhouses and orphanages of the poor, as in the great public schools of
England. An acquaintance of Jack Saul's, a male prostitute called George
Brown, given to blackmailing his clients, said to him one day 'Did you ever
hear that I was four years in the Reformatory at Red Hill? That was where I
first had a prick up my arse.'

From an early age, Bosie was capable of inspiring great love in others. In his
Autobiography, he says that he had several friendships at school 'which were
neither pure nor innocent', including two which seemed to be especially
intense. One such was with Lucas D'Oyly Carte, the son of impresario Richard
D'Oyly Carte. Lucas was a year younger than Bosie, and they seem to have had
a tortured love affair which lasted throughout their time together at
Winchester, up until, and perhaps even beyond, the time when Bosie met
Oscar. Lucas followed Bosie to Magdalen College in 1891, and wrote many
emotional letters to him, with phrases such as 'Bosie, I love you more now than
I ever have before. I never did really love you before but I do now.' Some of
these letters were later stolen from Bosie and used to blackmail him.

At Winchester, Bosie also had an intense friendship with the pallidly
beautiful Lionel Johnson. Johnson was sexually active at Winchester, where his
smallness and delicate build cast him, as one biographer tactfully put it, for the
role of Giton, the beautiful youth lusted after by Encolpius and Ascyltos in *The
Satyricon* of Petronius and whom they wish to sodomise. When Bosie arrived
at Winchester, he and Johnson, who was three years older, seem to have
become lovers. According to Robbie Ross, Johnson was a 'bedfellow of
Douglas at Winchester', and Bosie himself later boasted that he had had sex
with Johnson. But these bald accounts gloss over what seems to have been, for
Johnson at least, a passionate love affair. Johnson's poem dedicated to Bosie –
the poem which Pater showed to Oscar – exudes erotic love, a love which he
seems never to have lost or, indeed, recovered from. Bosie's feelings for Lionel
Johnson can only be guessed at. He seems to have liked him, but was
emphatically not in love with him. Their friendship continued beyond
Winchester to Oxford, and on to their lives in London as poets.

Bosie Douglas, Lucas D'Oyly Carte and Lionel Johnson were different from
the majority of public school boys who indulged in sex with other boys, but
when they left school, or university, made the transition to sex with women.
Bosie, Lionel and Lucas did not. 'I left Winchester,' Bosie wrote forty years
later, 'neither better nor worse than my contemporaries – that is to say a
finished young blackguard, ripe for any kind of wickedness.' Bosie arrived at

155

Oxford a decided and determined lover of his own sex. He went to Magdalen College which was, according to Bosie's nephew, the epicentre, 'the Temple of Eros', for the then extremely fashionable 'cult of boy-love'. Bosie was soon 'the unquestioned leader' of a rich and influential set of young undergraduates who flouted convention and had love affairs with good-looking freshmen.

Bosie's sexuality was not fluid, but fixed, fixated in fact, on boys and young men. He saw himself as 'a frank and natural pagan'; a child of Hellas, a pre-Christian for whom the sins of the flesh were not sins at all. Bosie convinced himself that, in the firmament of 'pagan ethics', sex was virtuous and life-affirming, and sexual abstinence pernicious and life-denying. Bosie was convinced that Uranian love was not just an alternative to sex with women but was actually superior, a higher form of love, 'the higher philosophy' as he and Oscar and others termed it. Later, Bosie told his mother that when he arrived at Oxford in 1889 his sexual orientation was decided, that he was already 'quite certain of the truth'. Bosie was determined not merely to pursue his sexual truth. More dangerously, he wanted to be its prophet.

Wild and terrible music

'I have never sowed wild oats: I have planted a few orchids.'

Bosie was twenty when Oscar first met him. He was devastatingly, radiantly attractive. 'His was a peculiarly English type of youthful beauty,' Bosie's nephew wrote, 'an exquisite pink and white complexion, golden hair, cornflower blue eyes and a slim elegant figure.' Bernard Shaw said Bosie was 'gifted, or cursed' with a beauty that inspired 'passionate admiration in men and women indiscriminately. Poets wrote sonnets praising his beauty, as Shakespeare has praised Mr W.H.'s.'

Apart from his arresting physical beauty, Bosie had other qualities which were bound to attract Oscar. He was a lord, and Oscar, a mild snob, had always been attracted by the aristocracy. Bosie was also a poet of some talent, and Oscar had always loved poets, especially if they were handsome young poets. And Bosie was one of those so very delightful young Oxford undergraduates Oscar found so irresistible. But, unlike the majority of young Oxonians whom Oscar considered to have 'profiles, but no philosophy', Bosie had both; he was highly intelligent, well-educated and his view of the world exactly chimed with Oscar's. Both thought of themselves as pagans, and both were passionate about what they called 'the higher philosophy', about Uranian love and Uranian sex.

Bosie's first, momentous meeting with Oscar took place on a summer's day in June 1891. Bosie had invited Lionel Johnson to lunch at his mother's London house at 18, Cadogan Place. Afterwards, Johnson took Bosie the short cab ride to Tite Street to take tea with Oscar. Bosie had wanted to meet Oscar ever since he had first read *Dorian Gray*, and he must have persuaded, perhaps even cajoled, Johnson into arranging the introduction.

As with most people meeting Oscar for the first time, Bosie's first impressions were unfavourable. He must have been struck by Oscar's size and commanding physical presence. The lesbian poets 'Michael Field' compared Oscar to an overfed herbivore, describing him as 'grass-gorged':

> There is no charm in his elephantine body, tightly stuffed into his clothes –
> no charm in his great face and head of unselect Bohemian cast – save the
> urbanity he can adopt or the intelligence with which he can vitalise his
> ponderousness.

The actress Elizabeth Robins thought Oscar had been stuffed with spices and caviar: 'Poke him and he would bleed absinthe and clotted truffles,' she noted. And the French writer Marcel Schwob confided his first impressions of Oscar to his journal, describing him as:

> A big man, with a large pasty face, red cheeks, an ironic eye, bad and protrusive teeth, a vicious childlike mouth with lips soft with milk ready to suck some more. While he ate – and he ate little – he never stopped smoking opium-tainted Egyptian cigarettes.

Max Beerbohm sketched Oscar wonderfully in a few words: 'Luxury – gold-tipped matches – hair curled – Assyrian – . . . not soigné . . . cat-like tread – heavy shoulders – enormous dowager – . . . jollity overdone – But real ability.' It was this real ability of Oscar's, his supreme intelligence and the sublimity of his conversation, which turned those put off by his unprepossessing physical presence into ardent disciples. Bosie once tried to capture the 'remarkable and arresting' essence of Oscar's conversation:

> Without any apparent effort he exercised a sort of enchantment which transmuted the ordinary things of life and invested them with strangeness and glamour. The popular idea of him as a man who fired off epigrams at intervals and was continually being amusing is quite inadequate to explain his charm and fascination. He had a way of looking at life, and a point of view which were magical in their effect.

The first meeting between Oscar and Bosie went well. 'We had tea in his little writing-room facing the street on the ground floor,' Bosie later recalled, 'and before I left, Oscar took me upstairs to the drawing-room and introduced me to his wife.' Tea in Oscar's study was rather formal, little more than 'just the ordinary interchange of courtesies', Bosie said. 'Wilde was very agreeable and talked a great deal, I was very much impressed.' But it seems scarcely credible that Oscar, Lionel Johnson and Bosie, all of them avowed Uranians, all of them poets, did not talk about the higher philosophy, as well as the baser passions.

Oscar was most certainly attracted to Bosie at that first meeting. 'Oscar took a violent fancy – it is no exaggeration to describe it as an infatuation – to me at sight,' Bosie wrote in a more revealing version of his love affair with Oscar. Bosie did not, could not, reciprocate. But he felt 'flattered that a man as distinguished as he was should pay me so much attention and attach so much importance as he apparently did, to all my views and preferences and whims'. They parted, but only after Oscar had made him promise to lunch with him or dine with him soon, which he did a few days later at the Lyric Club. Oscar brought along a copy of the newly published large-paper edition of *Dorian Gray* and presented it to Bosie, inscribing it 'Alfred Douglas from his friend who wrote this book. July 91.'

Oscar wasted no time in propositioning Bosie. 'From the second time he saw me (when he gave me a copy of *Dorian Gray* which I took back with me to Oxford), he made "overtures" to me.' But Oscar was not remotely Bosie's type. With the exception of Lionel Johnson, Bosie had never been to bed with anyone older than himself. All his sexual instincts were, he said later, 'for youth and beauty and softness'; in other words, for boys. Nevertheless, Oscar was unfazed by Bosie's refusal to go to bed with him. The more often Bosie refused, the more persistent Oscar's 'overtures' became. Oscar was infatuated:

> He 'made up to me' in every possible way. He was continually asking me to dine or lunch with him, and sending me letters, notes and telegrams. He flattered me, gave me presents, and made much of me in every way. He gave me copies of all his books, with inscriptions in them. He wrote a sonnet to me, and gave it to me at dinner one night in a restaurant.

At one of those early lunches or dinners Oscar inscribed a copy of his collection of essays, *Intentions*, with the words 'Bosie, from his friend the author . . . In memory of the Higher Philosophy'. They talked endlessly about love and about sex, mostly about sex, as Bosie was fascinated by and fascinating on the subject. He talked obsessively about boys and about buggery. It was 'the one topic round which your talk invariably centred', Oscar later told him. Oscar found Bosie's conversation 'fascinating, terribly fascinating'. Despite his air of boyish purity, his almost angelic beauty and his poetic sensitivity, Bosie was very sexually experienced. He had a voracious sexual appetite and had already begun to explore the darker side of the Uranian moon. In addition to his sexual encounters at Winchester, Bosie had already started having sex with working-class boys and male prostitutes, boys he picked up on the streets or met while out slumming in pubs and music halls. He was wildly promiscuous, seemingly addicted to sex, to dangerous sex, with dangerous young men. As Oscar later told him, 'The gutter and the things that live in it had begun to fascinate you.'

What Constance thought of Lord Alfred Douglas when she first met him that summer afternoon in June is not recorded. She would have been charming and gracious, as she always was when she met Oscar's friends, if a little shy at first. 'I was always on the best of terms with Mrs Wilde,' Bosie wrote. 'I liked her and she liked me. She told me, about a year after I first met her, that she liked me better than any of Oscar's other friends.' There was no reason for Constance not to like Bosie. He was delightful, charming, handsome, aristocratic and poetic. Constance had, by this time, met a good many of Oscar's young men, some of them his lovers, some not, who formed his circle of 'disciples'. She had made friends with several of them: with Robbie Ross and Arthur Clifton, with Richard Le Gallienne and Clyde Fitch. She was used to the strange sight of her husband standing at the centre of an adoring circle of young men who all shared, to a greater or a lesser extent, a certain quality.

As the young men in Oscar's life flitted in and out of favour, flitted in and out of Tite Street, lunching or dining or smoking cigarettes with Oscar in his Moroccan smoking room, Constance (rather like Daisy Broome, the wife of the poet Cyprian Broome, in André Raffalovich's thinly disguised fictional portrait of the Wildes' marriage, *The Willing Exile*) may have felt slightly bewildered by the parade of young men:

> Cyprian was, or seemed to be, intimate with countless young or youngish men; they were all curiously alike. Their voices, the cut of their clothes, the curl of their hair, the brims of their hats, the parties they went to: Daisy could not see much difference between them. Her house was full of them – at lunch time, at tea time, at dinner time, they sometimes came to suppers, and they sometimes called on Cyprian at twelve o'clock in the morning. Affectation characterised all these men, and the same sort of affectation. They were all gushers, professional gushers ... Married (some were married) or unmarried, they gushed alike, only some were ruder than others, and some were duller than others. Some were gentlemen, and some were not; but they might all have been more robust. Some were permanent friends; they did not come frequently one season, and not the next, but they remained devoted. Others brought friends, very similar to themselves, inseparable duplicates, with whom they quarrelled in due course.

Raffalovich was well-placed to observe the comings and goings at Tite Street, having been at the centre of Oscar's circle for five years. His description is cruel but accurate, especially his depiction of Daisy/Constance's response to the small army of young men who traipsed in and out of Tite Street monopolising most of Oscar's time.

Although to all outward appearances Oscar and Constance were a happily married couple with two beautiful children, there were barely concealed strains and tensions in the marriage. Constance, in particular, was unfulfilled and unhappy. 'Honesty compels me to say,' Bosie wrote later:

> that Oscar during the time I knew him was not very kind to his wife ... At the time when I first met him he was still fond of her, but he was often impatient with her, and sometimes snubbed her, and he resented, and showed that he resented, the attitude of slight disapproval she often adopted towards him.

And if Constance was suffering from one of her periodic bouts of depression resulting from the unhappiness of her childhood and tried to talk to Oscar about it, he could be brutally uninterested. She told her brother and his wife how Oscar was 'quite unsympathetic if she referred to the past', saying he was 'bored with people who go back to their childhood for their tragedies'.

Oscar was often out, and Constance was left alone with just the children and the servants for company. She was lonely and she felt neglected. However much she tried to hide it, her unhappiness was obvious, at least to Speranza, who wrote several letters to Oscar, while he was in Paris in the autumn of 1891, urging him to pay her more attention. 'Constance was here last evening,' she wrote. 'She is so nice always to me. I am very fond of her. *Do* come home. She is very lonely, and mourns for you.' And a few days later, Speranza was again emphasising how lonely Constance was:

> I would like you home. I want to see my poet son and Constance would like you back. She is very lonely. Finish your dramas *now* and come back to us, though London is very dull and dark and wet and cold and foggy.

The state of affairs between Oscar and Constance is reflected in *Dorian Gray*, where the misogyny of Lord Henry Wotton is the misogyny of Oscar Wilde. The novel oozes a dislike, a contempt, for women and their feelings, and, significantly, it is Lord Henry Wotton, the only married man in the trinity of the novel's leading characters, who is far and away the most misogynistic. Oscar's misogyny, like Lord Henry Wotton's, was selective, targeted not so much at women, but at wives, and specifically at Constance. It was a brittle, witty misogyny almost certainly born out of Oscar's feelings of frustration and irritation at being incarcerated in a marriage he no longer wished to be in. According to Charles Ricketts, 'Oscar always said that women would be wonderful if they had not been taught to speak.'

In *Dorian Gray*, women, more particularly wives, are presented as bovine, stupid and dull. 'No woman is a genius,' Lord Henry tells Dorian. 'Women are a decorative sex. They never have anything to say, but they say it charmingly.' For both Oscar and Lord Henry, marriage is both a farce and a form of bondage. Though slaves themselves, women somehow fetter men, clinging on to them like leeches long after love has died. 'Always!' says Lord Henry. 'That is a dreadful word. It makes me shudder when I hear it. Women are so fond of using it. They spoil every romance by trying to make it last forever.' If Dorian had married Sibyl Vane, he would have been 'wretched', Lord Henry tells him:

> Of course you would have treated her kindly. One can always be kind to people about whom one cares nothing. But she would have soon found out that you were absolutely indifferent to her.

There are echoes of Oscar and Constance in Lord Henry's words. When Oscar proposed to Constance, Grandpapa Lloyd approved the match, telling Oscar that he had every 'confidence in you that you will treat her kindly'. Oscar had always treated Constance kindly. But it was a passionless kindness, born out of emotional and sexual indifference.

Lord Henry's married life is based on a series of deceptions and lies. 'The one charm of marriage,' he says, 'is that it makes a life of deception absolutely necessary.' Likewise, a life of deception was absolutely necessary to Oscar. Without a cascade of lies, untruths and half-truths, it would have been impossible for Oscar to lead the life he wanted to lead; impossible for him to fall in and out of love with a series of young men; impossible to have sex with all the young men he wanted to have sex with. Friendships, infatuations and love affairs with young men constitute the true reality and the true satisfaction of Lord Henry Wotton and Oscar. But there was no question of any change to the status quo between Lord Henry and Lady Wotton, or between Oscar and Constance. 'The only way a woman can ever reform a man,' Lord Henry remarks, 'is by boring him so completely that he loses all possible interest in life.'

Constance had not succeeded in reforming Oscar, but she had succeeded in boring him. He was 'bored to death with the married life', bored with domesticity, bored with Constance, and bored, revolted and repulsed by sex with Constance, by the very idea of sex with Constance. Five years earlier, when they had ceased to have sex, Constance had, perhaps, harboured hopes of a resumption of sexual relations. If so, she had been disappointed. As far as Oscar was concerned, the sexual side of their marriage was well and truly over. Any physical contact was disgusting to him. In Tite Street they slept apart, and Oscar was not prepared to share a bedroom with Constance under any circumstances. When the Wildes were invited to stay in the country house in Berkshire of their wealthy friends the Walter Palmers, Mrs Walter Palmer was surprised at what she considered Oscar's impertinence when he telegraphed his conditional acceptance of the invitation 'if you will give us two rooms, one for Mrs Wilde and one for me'. It was not mere impertinence, but the act of a man who was completely and utterly incapable of any physical or emotional intimacy with his wife. The long, slow death of Oscar's love, his neglect, his absences, had a devastating effect. Photographs of Constance taken in the garden of the Walter Palmers' house show her looking frumpy, older, worn out and unhappy. When Louise Jopling showed Constance a photograph of her playfully making up to Oscar, all she could reply was a weary, wondering and compassionate 'Poor Oscar!'

Did Constance know about Oscar? Did she suspect that he was having a series of love affairs with young men, some of whom she had met, had welcomed into her home? It seems inconceivable that she had no suspicions about Oscar's 'friendships' with young men; no suspicions about his not coming home until the early hours, if at all; no suspicions about the flurry of telegrams and hand-delivered notes sent to and received from young men; no suspicions about the whispers and the rumours of sexual unorthodoxy that swirled around him, or about the barely concealed homoeroticism which seemed to saturate *Mr W.H.* and *Dorian Gray*. Paradoxically, the answer is yes and no. Constance almost certainly had some inklings, some doubts, a general uneasiness about the life that Oscar led. But what she knew and what she chose to allow herself to know were two very different things. There is a strange penumbral landscape where truths can exist and not exist, where they can be at once buried in the shadowlands of the mind, and yet illuminated by the light of rationality. Constance must have known or at the very least suspected that something was wrong with her marriage. But she chose not to confront this knowledge, preferring instead to gloss over any problems, explain away the inexplicable, and swallow, uncomplainingly, the unpalatable.

Constance was by nature kind, yielding and generous. 'There's nothing in the world like the devotion of a married woman,' says Cecil Graham in *Lady Windermere's Fan*. 'It's a thing no married man knows anything about.' Constance would grant plenary forgiveness for sins she knew nothing about and wished to know nothing about. Love for Constance meant something altogether different from Oscar's conception of love. Her love was quieter and more tranquil than Oscar's. She believed in love enduring, in love forgiving and, at the last blast of the trumpet, in love triumphant. Having promised at the time of their engagement to hold Oscar 'fast with chains of love and devotion', Constance was herself now bound by those same chains. She would never, could never, leave Oscar, nor ever love anyone else. She was bound by love and blinded by love. But it would not be long before the scales would fall from her eyes.

Oscar's relentless pursuit of Bosie was interrupted by Bosie's return to Oxford in the autumn of 1891, and by his own visit to Paris. It was Oscar's third extended visit to the City of Light. On his first visit he had been a literary young Turk, the poet and Professor of Aesthetics who had taken America by storm and was now determined to storm the literary Bastilles of Paris. His second visit had been very different. Then he was an enraptured bridegroom on honeymoon in the City of Love with his beautiful young wife. Now, on his third visit, Oscar returned as a conquering hero, a writer at the height of his powers whose output was prodigious: he was an acclaimed essayist, a penetrating critic, a writer of exquisite fairy stories and arresting short stories, as well the author of a daring homoerotic novel which had so shocked and outraged Britain's bourgeoisie. Not only that, Oscar had written a play, provisionally entitled *A Good Woman*, which was shortly to go into production, and he had signalled his intention, while in Paris, of writing a play in French.

That play was *Salomé*, a short and intensely symbolic version of the biblical story of Salome, who danced the dance of the seven veils for her stepfather Herod in return for the severed head of John the Baptist. In the late nineteenth century, the story of Salome had captured the imagination of French poets, writers and painters, and Salome had become the incarnation of decadence: mysterious, alluring, erotic, a symbol of the spectacular collision of love and death. Mallarmé had written a poem about Salome, and Gustave Moreau had painted two famous pictures of her, depicting her dance of the seven veils and the moment when she is presented with John the Baptist's severed head. Both of these paintings were bought and obsessed over by Des Esseintes, the hero of J.K. Huysmans's novel *A Rebours*, the novel which had so fascinated Oscar when he read it on his honeymoon in Paris seven years earlier. In *A Rebours*, Salomé is 'the symbolic incarnation of undying lust, the Goddess of immortal Hysteria, the accursed Beauty ... the monstrous Beast, indifferent, irresponsible, insensible, poisoning'.

Oscar had been minded to write about Salome for some time, initially in the form of a story, then in a narrative poem. According to the young Guatemalan diplomat and writer, Enrique Gomez Carillo, whom Oscar befriended on this trip to Paris, Oscar was 'obsessed by the spirit of Salome'. Never a day went by, said Gomez Carillo, 'when he didn't speak to me of Salome':

Sometimes women passing in the street made him dream of the princess of Israel. He used to stand for hours in main streets, looking at jewellers' windows and imagining the perfect jewellery of his idol's body.

At lunch one day with a group of young French writers, he extemporised so brilliantly on the story of Salome that his audience was spellbound. Returning home to his rooms in the Boulevard des Capucines late that afternoon, Oscar saw a blank notebook lying on the table, and the simple fact that it was there inspired him to begin to write down – in French – what he had just been relating. 'If the blank book had not been there on the table I should never have dreamed of doing it,' he told Vincent O'Sullivan several years later. 'I should not have sent out to buy one.'

Oscar wrote and wrote in a kind of reverie, induced, perhaps, by the 'opium-tainted cigarettes' which Marcel Schwob claimed Oscar smoked in Paris. When he looked at the clock, it was gone ten. He had been writing for hours and needed to eat. So he walked to the nearby Grand Café where a gypsy orchestra was playing. Oscar called over Rigo, the orchestra leader, and said:

'I am writing a play about a woman dancing with her bare feet in the blood of a man she has craved for and slain. I want you to play something in harmony with my thoughts.' And Rigo played such wild and terrible music that those who were there ceased their talk and looked at each other with blanched faces. Then I went back and finished *Salomé*.

In Oscar's *Salomé*, the cold and chaste moon is the cruel and heartless arbiter of fate presiding over the action of the play, inspiring madness, lust, suicide and murder. Oscar's Salomé is every bit as cruel as the Salomé of Huysmans. Lust, the lust of a man for a woman, and, more markedly, the lust of a woman for a man, pervades, poisons and destroys every relationship in the play save one. To gratify his lust for Salomé's mother, Herodias, Herod has imprisoned and executed her husband – his own brother, Philip. Now he lusts after Salomé, while Salomé lusts after Herod's prisoner, Jokanaan – John the Baptist. Only the Uranian love of the young Page of Herodias for the Captain of the Guard, the Young Syrian, is perfect and pure and remains unsullied by the cyclic carnival of lust played out in Herod's palace.

Oscar's *Salomé* portrays female sexuality as predatory, degrading and often fatal. Herodias is manipulative, incestuous and extremely promiscuous. She lies, Jokanaan declares, in a 'bed of abominations'. When Salomé attempts to seduce Jokanaan, the pure and beautiful ivory-white prophet, he curses her in the name of her mother's iniquities. 'Daughter of adultery . . . Daughter of an incestuous mother,' Jokanaan brands her, 'Daughter of Babylon', 'Daughter of Sodom', 'wanton', 'harlot'. The more Jokanaan repudiates her sexual advances, the more Salomé is determined to possess him. 'I am amorous of thy body,' says Salomé to Jokanaan. 'Let me touch thy body.' Like a mantra she repeats hypnotically, 'I will kiss thy mouth, Jokanaan. I will kiss thy mouth.' Salomé's obsessive desire for Jokanaan is matched and ratcheted up by his absolute revulsion for her. Underpinning this axis of lust and revulsion is the fact that Jokanaan is, like Oscar, only attracted to his own sex. Salomé desires him because she knows he can never desire a woman.

Cross-examined during the celebrated trial for criminal libel in 1918 of the eccentric MP Noel Pemberton-Billing, Bosie testified that before he wrote *Salomé*, Oscar had been reading *Psychopathia Sexualis*, Richard Krafft-Ebing's monumental study of the whole gamut of sexual deviation. The characters of Salomé and her mother, Herodias, are clearly informed by Krafft-Ebing's chapter on sexual hyperaesthesia, or the 'abnormal predominance of sexual sensations with mighty and frequent demands for sexual gratification', and in particular by his 'Case VII': an account of a woman plagued by lust and the desire for coitus from the age of thirteen. Salomé's unslakable lust for Jokanaan mirrors Case VII's unslakable lust for a man who refuses to respond to it because he is a lover of men. 'The latest turn which her sex life has taken is rather peculiar,' Krafft-Ebing wrote of 'Case VII':

> She is devoting all her affection, her means and her devotion to a man who, being a homosexual, has never had the taste for sexual intercourse with woman. The circumstance that it is men he loves provokes, she reports, an indescribable excitement in her, because she knows that she will have to forego any sexual intercourse with him.

After Jokanaan is executed and his head delivered on a silver charger, Salomé taunts the dead prophet. 'Thou wouldst not suffer me to kiss thy mouth, Jokanaan,' she says. 'Well, I will kiss it now. I will bite it with my teeth as one bites a ripe fruit.' Salomé does kiss Jokanaan's mouth. 'There is a bitter taste on thy lips,' she says. 'Was it the taste of blood . . . ? But perchance it is the taste of love . . . They say that love hath a bitter taste.' And then a moonbeam lights up Salomé on stage as Herod gives orders for her to be killed, crushed beneath the shields of the soldiers.

Written in a reverie, *Salomé* expresses and reveals the extent of Oscar's subconscious fear and loathing of the articulate flesh of female sexuality. Salomé is the vampiric, emasculating incarnation of the ancient Hebrew *beth shenayim*, or 'toothed place', the *vagina dentata*, the dangerous, castrating, consuming vagina. Throughout the play there are images of beheading, biting, piercing, severing and tearing. Oscar told Gomez Carillo that he wanted his Salomé to be cruel and to be shameless. 'Her lust must be an abyss,' he said, 'her corruptness, an ocean.' Krafft-Ebing's Case VII not only helps to explain the nature of Salomé's obsessive love for a man she knows she can never arouse, but it also sheds some light on Jokanaan's sense of utter disgust at the sexual desires of Salomé and Herodias. Jokanaan, like Oscar, is a lover of men and a prophet of divine love who is, prophetically, incarcerated and martyred because he dared to preach a new form of love.

Apart from Oscar's obsession with Salome, there was plenty to occupy his mind, and his eye. Oscar met old friends and made new ones, with young poets and writers like Marcel Schwob, Pierre Louÿs and André Gide. Pierre Louÿs was in his very early twenties, a poet and writer who was attracted by Wilde's wit, intelligence and status as the most interesting and exciting writer in Britain. And part of the attraction was Oscar's sexuality, which he positively flaunted in Paris. Louÿs was ostensibly a vigorous heterosexual, but he nonetheless harboured a degree of sexual interest in men. He was not remotely sexually attracted to Oscar, but he was drawn to the aura of sexual unorthodoxy that swirled about him like a mist.

'Paris is a city that pleases me greatly,' Oscar told a reporter from the *Écho de Paris* as he lay stretched out on a divan smoking Egyptian cigarettes. 'While in London one hides everything, in Paris one reveals everything . . . the lowest dive interests me as much as the most elegant café.' It was a telling comment. In London, Oscar had to hide his sexual liaisons from Constance and from society. In Paris, where sex between men was legal under the Code Napoléon, Oscar could afford to be much more relaxed, to reveal – if not quite everything – then a good deal more about his sexual desires than he ever dared to in London.

For his part, Oscar liked Pierre Louÿs, he found him interesting and attractive, and inscribed a copy of his collection of fairy stories *A House of Pomegranates* to Louÿs in terms that were extravagantly erotic:

> To the young man who adores beauty
> To the young man whom Beauty adores
> To the young man I adore

It was through his friendship with Oscar that Pierre Louÿs was finally able to explore his sexual feelings for men when he visited London the following year.

André Gide was a friend of Pierre. He persuaded Louÿs to arrange a dinner where he could meet the fascinating Oscar Wilde, and at their first encounter on 29 November Gide was mesmerised. 'There were four of us,' Gide recalled, 'but Wilde was the only one who talked':

> Wilde did not converse: he narrated. Throughout almost the whole of the meal he did not stop narrating. He narrated gently, slowly; his very voice was wonderful.

André Gide was twenty-two, a tubercular, neurotic, sexually repressed young man who was finding it difficult to acknowledge, let alone come to terms with, his sexual preferences for boys. He had been expelled from school at the age of eight after having been caught masturbating, and had experimented sexually with the young son of a servant. Meeting Oscar was revelatory and unsettling. For three weeks Oscar became the Lord Henry Wotton to André's Dorian Gray, a harbinger of sexual truth and sexual liberation. In his engagement book for 11 and 12 December, Gide scrawled the words 'Wilde, Wilde' across the pages, and, in an ecstatic letter to his friend Paul Valéry, he wrote: 'Oh how extraordinary, extraordinary he is.' Gide said he felt like 'someone who is stunned, who no longer reads, no longer writes, neither sleeps, eats nor thinks'.

Oscar's feelings for Gide are not recorded, although he later said, 'I love André personally very deeply.' There is no evidence that the two of them had a love affair or even had sex, and, indeed, it is hard to imagine Oscar and Gide – 'the egoist without an ego', as Oscar dubbed him – in bed together, though the beardless Gide had a certain boyish charm, and Oscar was already becoming less particular about his sexual partners. But Gide was obsessed. Meeting Oscar had affected him profoundly, and his friends were convinced he had fallen in love. 'Gide est amoureux d'Oscar Wilde', 'Gide is in love with Oscar Wilde,' Jules Renard confided to his journal, and Marcel Schwob thought the same. Less than a week after meeting Oscar, Gide wrote:

> Wilde is piously setting about killing what remained of my soul, because he says that in order to know the essence of something, one has to suppress it. He wants me to deplore my soul. The effort to destroy it is to be the measure of it. Everything is made up only of its emptiness.

By his soul, Gide really meant his conscience. Oscar's vivid gospel of scarlet sins and sexual liberation shook and shocked André, who was tortured by homoerotic desires which he sought to quell by means of his Protestant faith and by a rigorous, puritanical asceticism consisting of sleeping on bare boards, rising at dawn, ice-cold baths, scripture study and prolonged prayer. Just eleven months earlier, he had proposed marriage to his cousin and childhood soulmate, Madeleine Rondeaux, with whom he would eventually have a *marriage blanc*, a sexless marriage. But spiritual exercise and bodily scourging were no match for Oscar's seductive evangel. Oscar made André confront his sexual self, spiritually and perhaps even physically.

But after Oscar had returned to London, André ripped out the pages of his journal which covered the three weeks or so he had spent almost continuously in Oscar's company. Whatever had happened was not to be bequeathed to posterity. On New Year's Day 1892, Gide opened his new diary with the declaration that:

> Wilde, I believe, did me nothing but harm. In his company I lost the habit of thinking. I had more varied emotions, but had forgotten how to bring order into them.

If Oscar could have read André's words, he might have smiled and wondered exactly which of André's 'varied emotions' he had brought into play during their brief and intense friendship: love or lust, or perhaps even both? They would meet again, but in the meantime Oscar barely gave André a backward thought. He had other things, and another young man, on his mind.

Strange green flowers

'One should always be in love. That is the reason one should never marry.'

Just minutes before the curtain went up at the St James's Theatre on a chilly evening in late February 1892, a dozen or so young men filed into the stalls, each wearing a vivid green carnation in his buttonhole. It was the premiere of *Lady Windermere's Fan*, Oscar's first society comedy, and expectations were high. As the young men took their seats, the audience craned their necks to see what was going on. Who were they? And why did they all sport a green carnation? There was, after all, no such flower known to nature.

Oscar had planned to cause a stir at the premiere of his play and succeeded in causing a sensation. He had stage-managed the dramatic appearance of the green carnation down to the last detail. The day before, Oscar had told Graham Robertson to go to Goodyear's the florist in the Royal Arcade and order a green carnation to wear for the performance. Robertson was puzzled. 'A *green* carnation?' he repeated. 'I know there's no such thing,' said Oscar, 'but they arrange them somehow at that shop; dye them I suppose. I want a good many men to wear them tomorrow – it will annoy the public.' Robertson was still bewildered: 'But why annoy the public?' he asked. 'It likes to be annoyed,' replied Oscar:

> A young man on the stage will wear a green carnation; people will stare at it and wonder. Then they will look round the house and see here and there more and more specks of mystic green. 'This must be some secret symbol,' they will say: 'What on earth can it mean?'

'And what does it mean?' Robertson asked. 'Nothing whatever,' said Oscar. 'But that is just what nobody will guess.'

Oscar later claimed that the mystic green carnation was his own idea. 'I invented that magnificent flower,' he said. In fact, he had merely borrowed the idea from the Parisian Uranians who had in the summer of 1891 begun a craze for wearing carnations, artificially dyed green, as a badge, a secret symbol, of their sexual preferences. Just a few years earlier, in Paris, green cravats had been the rage among men who loved men. Now it was green carnations. As

169

Oscar had predicted, the audience was suitably annoyed, especially as all the young men wearing the curious green carnations shared, or seemed to share, a certain quality that today might be described as camp. Many of them 'were wearing make-up, or seemed to be', according to André Raffalovich, who added that, 'There is a way of styling one's hair and of swaying one's hips which goes with the artificial bistre, lipstick etc.'

The *coup de grâce* of the evening was Oscar's appearance on stage after the performance. The 'unspeakable animal', as Henry James called him, had responded to curtain calls by appearing with a 'metallic blue carnation' in his buttonhole and a lighted cigarette in his fingers. 'Ladies and Gentlemen,' Oscar said, as the applause for the author died away:

I have enjoyed this evening *immensely*. The actors have given us a *charming* rendering of a *delightful* play, and your appreciation has been *most* intelligent. I congratulate you on the *great* success of your performance, which persuades me that you think *almost* as highly of the play as I do myself.

Oscar's short speech infuriated Henry James, who thought it predictably 'impudent'. A large proportion of the audience, including several theatre critics, thought the same. They considered it to be in bad taste, and downright cocky. The cigarette, in particular, struck them as the very height of bad manners. Etiquette dictated that gentlemen should never smoke in the presence of ladies. 'People of birth and breeding don't do such things,' the critic Clement Scott expostulated. The *Daily Telegraph* reported in shocked tones how Oscar had 'addressed from the stage a public audience, mostly composed of ladies, pressing between his daintily-gloved fingers a still burning and half-smoked cigarette'. *Punch* produced a cartoon of Oscar delivering his speech captioned, 'Quite too-too puffickly precious!! Being Lady Windy-mère's Fan-cy Portrait of the new dramatic author, Shakespeare Sheridan Oscar Puff, Esq.' In the cartoon Oscar adopts a languid pose leaning on a column and holding an open fan while a cigarette dangles from his mouth. Three entwined smoke rings hover above his head, each containing a single word: 'Puff!!! Puff!! Puff!'. 'Puff' had multiple meanings: it could mean a vainglorious and self-serving speech, as well as an insolent braggart. It was also a relatively new slang term for an effeminate man. *Punch*'s cartoon was a two-edged sword. On the surface, it was a reprobation of Oscar's arrogance, his cockiness, his tireless and, to some, tiresome self-promotion. At the same time it was a not-so-coded reference to his sexuality.

Others were well aware that the sudden efflorescence of the green carnation, far from meaning 'nothing whatever' as Oscar had maintained, actually had a very clear meaning. Just twelve days later, at the first performance of John Gray's translation of Théodore de Banville's play *Le Baiser*, *The Kiss*, the green carnation made another equally dramatic appearance. The *Star* reported the presence of 'Mr Oscar Wilde and a suite of young gentlemen, all wearing the vivid dyed carnation, which has superseded the lily and the sunflower'. The

Lady's Pictorial denounced the wearing of the green carnation as 'unmanly'. Even Oscar's former lover, Richard Le Gallienne – 'Shelley with a chin' – attacked the appearance of 'these strange green flowers that spring from daisy roots and seem to bear a sting'. When Oscar heard of Le Gallienne's attack, he shrugged it off, declaring that Le Gallienne's betrayal was the natural consequence of his debt of gratitude. Le Gallienne was now happily married and anxious to distance himself from Oscar's increasing notoriety.

There was one place where the appearance of the green carnation was welcomed: in the monthly magazine the *Artist and Journal of Home Culture*, edited for the past four years by Charles Kains Jackson, a London solicitor, poet and lover of boys. Under the editorship of Kains Jackson, the *Artist* developed a subtle Uranian flavour with 'a thin scarlet thread' of homoerotic material woven into 'the homespun' of its usual contributions. The *Artist* gave instructions to its Uranian readership on how to make their own:

> The green carnation to which we have referred is a white carnation, dyed by plunging the stem in an aqueous solution of the aniline dye called malachite green. The dye ascends the petals by capillary attraction, and at the end of twelve hours they are well tinged. A longer immersion deepens the tint.

The audience on that memorable first night of *Lady Windermere's Fan* constituted an emotional and sexual autobiography for Oscar. There were lovers past, present and even future seated in the auditorium. Constance was there, of course, though the ever-mindful Speranza had written to Oscar expressly to remind him of the attentions due to his wife: 'Do try to be *present yourself at the first performance* – it would be right and proper and Constance would like it. Do not leave her all alone.' Arthur Clifton, an old friend of Oscar's and one of the disciples, was duly drafted in to escort Constance to the theatre and to sit with her and her aunt, Mrs William Napier, in a private box.

Almost two years earlier, in July 1890, Oscar had been commissioned to write a play by the actor manager George Alexander but did not start writing *Lady Windermere's Fan* until the summer of 1891, the summer he met Bosie. It was his first comedy, and his first play to find popular and commercial success. Like so much of Oscar's work, the four society comedies are strongly autobiographical and teasingly revealing of the truths of Oscar's sexual life and sexual identity. *Lady Windermere's Fan* explores the tensions between sex and morality, between love and lust, between appearance and reality, and between truth and lies.

The play tells the story of Lady Windermere's imagined discovery of her husband's secret sexual life – of his affair with an older, quite shameless woman, Mrs Erlynne, who appears to have some kind of hold over him. There is more than a hint of blackmail in the relationship between Lord Windermere and his mistress, as his wife discovers when she finds he has been paying Mrs Erlynne very large sums of money. A secret life, illicit love affairs and the stench of blackmail were all part and parcel of Oscar's life. There are recognisable elements of Constance in the character of Lady Windermere, who is young,

171

beautiful and rather stern. Like Constance, she is governed by a set of moral precepts, 'hard and fast rules', which she will not and cannot bend: 'You think I am a Puritan, I suppose?' Lady Windermere asks Lord Darlington, who is hopelessly in love with her. 'Well, I have something of the Puritan in me. I was brought up like that. I am glad of it.' Constance, too, had something of the puritan in her, a puritanism based on a strong and enduring sense of a moral universe that increasingly irked Oscar and rankled with what he called his antinomianism. The Antinomians were a sixteenth-century sect of dissenters who believed they were God's chosen people, the elect, predestined for salvation, and consequently they were not bound by conventional moral laws. 'Morality does not help me,' he wrote in *De Profundis*. 'I am a born antinomian. I am one of those who are made for exceptions, not for laws.'

The dramatic crisis in *Lady Windermere's Fan* is precipitated by Lord Windermere's insistence that his wife should receive his mistress at their home. This determination reflects Oscar's habit of introducing his youthful lovers to Constance, of entertaining them at Tite Street, and, on occasions, having sex with them there. This had happened with Robbie Ross when he was a paying guest. Oscar had probably wanted it to happen with André Raffalovich in the early days of their acquaintance, when he had sent a note to André inviting him to call at Tite Street, saying, rather pointedly, 'Constance will be away.' And there had almost certainly been other occasions when Oscar had had sex in Tite Street, and in the course of the next three years there would be more.

Oscar was well aware of the effect his secret life was having on Constance and writes about it with an almost uncanny autobiographical frankness in *Lady Windermere's Fan*, when Lord Darlington tells Lady Windermere about what her life will be if she remains with her husband:

> You would feel that he was lying to you every moment of the day. You would feel that the look in his eyes was false, his voice false, his touch false, his passion false. He would come to you when he was weary of others; you would have to comfort him. He would come to you when he was devoted to others; you would have to charm him. You would have to be to him the mask of his real life, the cloak to hide his secret.

It was all true. It was all just. Oscar's life with Constance was predicated on a falsehood, a lie. Behind the facade of his marriage, behind the facade of the House Beautiful, Constance was 'the mask of his real life', 'the cloak to hide his secret'. When the poet W.B. Yeats spent Christmas with Oscar at Tite Street, he remembered thinking 'that the perfect harmony of his life there, with his beautiful wife and two young children, suggested some deliberate artistic composition'.

And yet, as Lord Darlington's speech suggests, Oscar's relationship with Constance was not entirely deliberately exploitative, not completely calculatedly cynical. There was an emotional dynamic between them, a hidden, unbreakable bond, which would endure even beyond the catastrophe which would engulf them. 'He would come to you when he was weary of all others,' Lord Darlington tells Lady Windermere, 'you would have to comfort him.' It was true of Oscar and Constance. Oscar did have days of bleakness and depression; days when his work was going badly; when his love affairs were becoming difficult or tiresome, or unravelling into a complex, often dangerous, nightmare. Then, he would seek Constance out, taking refuge in her comfort and her love. Some time before he wrote *Lady Windermere's Fan*, Oscar began but never finished a play entitled – significantly – *A Wife's Tragedy* in which the main protagonist, Gerald Lovel, a poet rather like Oscar, tries to explain to an uncomprehending friend the secret of why his marriage endures. 'Life is a wide stormy sea,' says Gerald. 'My wife is my harbour of refuge.'

There were other speeches in *Lady Windermere's Fan* which may have held particular resonances for some of the audience there that first night. 'I am told there is hardly a husband in London who does not waste his life over *some* shameful passion,' says Lady Windermere. As she heard these words, it may have occurred to Constance to wonder whether Oscar was one of those London husbands wasting his life over some shameful passion. A 'shameful passion' invokes the Uranian code-word, shame, meaning the love that dare not speak its name. It would have been understood by many of those wearing the green carnation in their buttonhole that night, especially by Bosie Douglas who attended the premiere and is supposed to have shared Oscar's box.

Six months later, Bosie would write his famous poem 'Two Loves', which encapsulated the Uranian resonances of 'shame'. The poem interrogates a 'Sweet youth' wreathed in moon-flowers:

> Tell me why, sad and sighing, thou dost rove
> These pleasant realms? I pray thee, speak me sooth
> What is thy name? He said 'My name is Love.'
> Then straight the first did turn himself to me
> And cried: 'He lieth, for his name is Shame,
> But I am Love, and I was wont to be
> Alone in this fair garden, till he came
> Unasked by night; I am true Love, I fill
> The hearts of boy and girl with mutual flame,
> Then sighing, said the other: 'Have thy will,
> I am the love that dare not speak its name.'

Oscar and Bosie had kept in touch in the six months since their first meeting. They had written to each other, though none of these letters now survive the bonfire that Bosie later made of them. And Oscar had been to Oxford at least once to press his sexual suit. At that stage, Bosie was still not sexually attracted to Oscar. He was much more interested in handsome young men, the younger the better and the rougher the better. As he was writing *Lady Windermere's Fan*, Oscar was almost certainly thinking of Bosie and his obsession with boys and buggery when he has the Duchess of Berwick exclaim:

173

Boys are so wicked. My boy is excessively immoral. You wouldn't believe at
what hours he comes home. And he's only left Oxford a few months – I really
don't know what they teach them there.

Loyal, loving Robbie Ross was there that night, no doubt dutifully wearing
his green carnation. He had brought along his friend More Adey, who was
destined to play a part in Oscar's unfolding drama. John Gray was there,
though where he sat, and with whom, is not known. If Bosie, as some accounts
claim, was sharing Oscar's box, Gray would have been decidedly put out at
being usurped by a younger, stunningly handsome poet. It may have been this
event which sowed some of the seeds of the bitter falling out which took place
later that year between Gray and Oscar, and which took Gray to the brink of
suicide. There were newer friends at the premiere too: Reggie Turner, a young
friend from Oxford, and Sydney Barraclough, a twenty-year-old actor that
Oscar had taken rather a violent fancy to. He was seated in the dress circle next
to a tall and attractive young man, carefully dressed – perhaps a little too
carefully dressed – in evening clothes, and also wearing a green carnation.

His name was Edward Shelley, and he, too, had his part to play in the
evening's proceedings. After Constance had been sent home on her own, Oscar
entertained his friends to supper. Later, he and Edward Shelley went up to
Oscar's suite in the Albemarle Hotel, where they drank whisky and sodas
before Oscar led Edward Shelley into the bedroom, undressed him and took
him into his bed.

Oscar had met Shelley in the autumn of 1891, when Shelley was seventeen
and working as a clerk in the Vigo Street shop of the publishing partnership of
Elkin Matthews and John Lane. Edward Shelley has been described as
'distinguished-looking', tall and attractive in a classical, rather masculine way,
with a square jaw, clear blue eyes and brown hair. He had 'an intellectual face,'
Oscar said later. 'I wouldn't call him good-looking.' Like John Gray, Shelley
came from a large working-class family. His father was a blacksmith in
resolutely working-class Fulham. And, like John Gray, he had left school at the
age of thirteen and was making his way in life on his wits alone. Shelley had
advantages: he was intelligent, he was personable, and he had taught himself to
speak and to dress properly. Neighbours remembered how he used to leave
home for work each day dressed in a frock coat.

At the age of sixteen, Edward Shelley had landed on his feet with a junior
clerkship earning fifteen shillings a week at Elkin Matthews and John Lane,
who published for the most part poetry and *belles lettres*. It was a publishing
partnership fraught with mistrust and misunderstandings, a partnership that
would shortly dissolve acrimoniously. Elkin Matthews and John Lane
published some of Oscar's work and at the time Oscar met Edward Shelley
were preparing to reprint his *Poems*. Lane's relationship with his teenage clerk
was a little out of the ordinary, to say the least. He seems to have entered into
some sort of compact with Shelley with the aim of keeping tabs on his business
partner, Elkin Matthews. Lane worked in the Railway Clearing House at

Euston, and his main contribution to the partnership was searching out promising new writers. He did not trust Matthews and needed to know what he was getting up to while his back was turned. Lane and Shelley held regular meetings, their 'Once-a Weeks', Shelley called them, and Shelley wrote almost daily reports to Lane on the doings and the sayings of 'M', as he called Elkin Matthews. Some of these letters have survived and are interesting not so much for what they reveal about the partnership of Matthews and Lane – most of the letters consisted of trivial gossip: 'M was in such an ill-temper' and 'M was irritable for the remainder of the day' are typical comments – but for their insights into Edward Shelley's troubled personality.

Shelley had taken to his surveillance of Matthews with disturbing gusto, secretly copying letters that 'M' received and sending them to Lane, silently sneaking up on 'M' to find him 'with his coat off, & in his shirt sleeves, *examining your parcels!*' Shelley's letters to Lane became positively conspiratorial. 'I should like to have a few minutes conversation with you,' he wrote to Lane in December 1890:

> nothing very important but I have some information, that can be used to advantage. If I see you, before I can receive a reply, make some sign to me, by which I shall know where to meet you. If you cannot do that with safety, please shut the door if I am to meet you at the coffee-house but leave the door open (as you come in) if you cannot meet me.

Spying, surveillance and secret signals in the unlikely surroundings of a small publishing house had clearly fired the imagination of Shelley, to an obsessive, almost worrying degree.

There is a suggestion, no more than a suggestion, that John Lane was sexually interested in, and perhaps even sexually involved with, Shelley, which might help to explain why John Lane destroyed the vast majority of his letters from Shelley, and why he was at such pains at the time of Oscar's trial to vigorously refute the suggestion that it was he who had introduced Shelley to Oscar. Trelawny Backhouse claims that Aubrey Beardsley gave him a caricature entitled 'A Physical Impossibility' which showed:

> a fat, squatty little Lane of the large paunch endeavouring vainly to insert a flaccid, inert organ into the 'proctodaeum' of his office boy, named Shelley.

It was inevitable that Oscar and Edward Shelley would meet sooner or later. Oscar was visiting Vigo Street fairly often in connection with the publication of his *Poems* and would exchange a word or two with the pleasant, attractive young man who was tying up parcels of books. 'He seemed to take notice of me,' Shelley said. 'He generally stopped and spoke to me for a few moments.' One day, as he was leaving, Oscar invited Edward Shelley to dinner at the Albemarle Hotel, where he had a suite of rooms. Something had gone wrong with the drains at Tite Street, and with a true Victorian dread of anything remotely connected with raw sewage, the family had fled: Constance and Vyvyan to Lady Mount-Temple's, Cyril to Mrs William Napier's, and Oscar, conveniently alone, to the Albemarle Hotel.

Oscar's dinner with Edward Shelley took place a few days before the premiere of *Lady Windermere's Fan*. The evening went well. 'We dined together in a public room,' Shelley testified later. 'Mr Wilde was very kind and attentive, and pressed me to drink. I had champagne with dinner.' Edward Shelley was literary-minded, and cherished ambitions of a literary career. He had, he said, read a good deal of 'the lighter forms of literature, dramatic and poetic,' and he had 'written a few things', some poems and some stories, none of which were ever published and none of which have survived. Oscar charmed and enchanted Shelley and drew out of him his literary ambitions. Will Rothenstein, who had met Oscar in Paris only a few weeks earlier, recalled how Oscar encouraged and inspired people younger than himself. 'I had met no one who made me so aware of the possibilities latent in myself,' says Rothenstein:

> He had a quality of sympathy and understanding which was more than mere flattery, and he seemed to see better than anyone else just what was one's aim; or rather he made one believe that what was latent perhaps in one's nature had actually been achieved.

According to the statement he made three years later to the Marquis of Queensberry's solicitors, Shelley said that Oscar had flattered him outrageously, told him he was clever and talented and offered to help him on his way. After dinner, Oscar invited Shelley up to his suite to drink whisky and sodas and to smoke cigarettes. Then, when Oscar said, 'Will you come into my bedroom?' Shelley agreed. Once in the bedroom, 'Mr. Wilde kissed me. He also put his arms round me,' he said. 'I felt insulted, degraded, and objected vigorously.' Shelley said Oscar started to touch his private parts, and it was at this point that he fell into a state resembling 'stupor' and woke to found himself unwittingly and unwillingly in Oscar's bed. André Raffalovich confirmed Shelley's version, writing with righteous indignation that the 'flattered, inebriated, terrified' Shelley 'fainted under the ignominious kiss of the poet whom he admired above all'. When he testified in court, Shelley would give a slightly different version. Deeming the actual words Shelley used unfit for publication at the time, the newspapers reported that Oscar had 'placed his hand on the private parts of the witness and sought to put his, the witness's, hand in the same indelicate position as regards Wilde's own person'.

Edward Shelley claimed he was traumatised by his sexual experience with Oscar, that he had been 'entrapped', as he later put it, into having sex against his will. Oscar, he claimed, had taken advantage of him, of his admiration, to seduce him. If this was the case, why did he return the very next night to have dinner and to again go to bed with Oscar? When he was asked why, he could only reply 'I was weak of course.'

Shelley's account of his 'seduction' by Oscar was made three years after the event. It deliberately presented Oscar in an extremely unfavourable light as a man who set out to seduce him, who turned his head with dinner and drinks and literary talk, before manipulating him, drunk with champagne and whisky and sodas, into bed. In the three years that had elapsed since his affair with Oscar had petered out, Shelley had suffered a series of reversals of fortune; he had lost his job, suffered a severe nervous breakdown and had been arrested. He had also become a fervent Christian. When he gave his evidence against Oscar in court, it was evident that he was still labouring under some sort of mental illness. As he gave his testimony, he had what Oscar's counsel, Sir Edward Clarke, called 'a peculiar sort of exaltation in and for himself', suggesting that he might be 'the victim of delusions'.

Edward Shelley was not however deluded about the sexual substance of his allegations against Oscar. They had certainly had sex, and, indeed, had sex more often than Shelley claimed. But the nature and the course of the relationship was almost certainly very different to the bald account of seduction he presented to the court. There is a question mark over whether Oscar was the first man to have sex with Shelley. Under cross-examination, Shelley equivocated and seemed to suggest that he was not entirely innocent when it came to sex between men. Speaking about the first night he had sex with Oscar, Shelley said 'I was entrapped . . . he took advantage of me, of my admiration, and of – I won't say my innocence – I don't know what to call it.'

'I won't say my innocence.' Edward Shelley could not swear to his sexual innocence under oath. Had he had sex with other men before he slept with Oscar? Quite possibly. It is hard to cast Shelley in the role of the outraged virgin he later constructed for himself. There was, for instance, the ugly rumour doing the rounds about John Lane's sexual interest in his junior clerk. And Shelley used to go to work dressed in a frock coat and wore evening clothes to the premiere of *Lady Windermere's Fan*. It would have been extremely hard for a working-class boy earning just fifteen shillings a week to afford evening dress. Was Edward Shelley following the time-honoured route of many working-class youths and taking advantage of the protection, the financial favours of an older, wealthier man?

At its height, Oscar's affair with Edward Shelley lasted from February to May 1892, and there is plenty of evidence to suggest that he enjoyed his status as Oscar's newest boy enormously. The day after the premiere of *Lady Windermere's Fan*, after they had had sex for the third time, Shelley sent a gushing, rather gauche, letter to Oscar. 'What a triumph was yours last night!' he wrote:

> The play is the best I have seen on the stage, with such beauty of form and wit that it adds a new phase of pleasure to existence. Could Lady Blessington live anew the conversations would make her jealous. George Meredith might have signed it. How miserably poor everything else seems beside it! Except, of course, your books – but then your books are part of yourself.

177

Oscar presented Shelley with copies of his books, inscribing a copy of *Dorian Gray*: 'To Edward Shelley, poet and friend, from Oscar Wilde, poet and friend.' Oscar took Edward Shelley up. They went to restaurants together, to Kettner's and to the Café Royal, and to the Lyric Club. Oscar took him to the Earl's Court Exhibition, and they went several times to the theatre together. Shelley was one among the 'suite of young men wearing the vivid dyed carnation' at the premiere of John Gray's translation of *The Kiss*. Shelley was also taken to Tite Street on at least two occasions, where he dined with Oscar and Constance. Oscar and Shelley spent several nights together at the Albemarle Hotel, and, up to the time Oscar was arrested, Edward Shelley always acknowledged Oscar's kindness to him. 'I have longed to see you all through the week,' he wrote to Oscar:

> I have much to tell you. Do not think me forgetful in not coming before, because I shall never forget your kindness to me and am conscious that I can never sufficiently express my thankfulness to you.

Shelley's favours were not confined to Oscar. He had sex with several of Oscar's disciples, almost certainly with Bosie and with John Gray, both of whom he had been introduced to at the premiere of *Lady Windermere's Fan*. Later that year, Gray wrote to his new friend, Pierre Louÿs, in terms which proclaimed his erotic interest in Shelley: 'I saw Edward Shelley two or three days ago. His eyelashes are still very long, almost those of a poet.' Louÿs had met both John Gray and Edward Shelley when he came to London in June. Gray and Louÿs quickly got into the habit of writing rather arch and suggestive letters to each other, and it seems likely that they had discussed Shelley's obvious erotic attractions. Although Pierre Louÿs is usually regarded as a red-blooded heterosexual, there seems to be some evidence that he experimented sexually with men, perhaps even with Edward Shelley.

Edward Shelley was never going to be anything more to Oscar than a pleasing and attractive young man, a pleasant companion and desirable bed partner. There were times when Oscar must have felt that the relationship was a re-run of his affair with Fred Althaus, from which he had managed to extricate himself only with great difficulty. As Oscar's interest in Fred had started to wane, Fred had become neurotic and bombarded him with letters. Now with Shelley history was repeating itself. As Oscar's interest started to wane, Shelley became increasingly demanding, increasingly neurotic. Oscar was still kind, offering him money to buy books, money to pay for a tutor. But he could not offer him what he needed most: love, affection and attention. Shelley lost his job at Vigo Street. He said he had left because of the 'intolerable' situation he found himself in when his fellow clerks called him names like 'Mrs Wilde' and 'Miss Oscar'. But it later emerged that John Lane had paid him off because of his association with Oscar. Shelley subsequently described John Lane to Oscar as 'that viper'. Lane, he said, 'had hurt me too much. I despise him, but I cannot forget.'

Oscar the Aesthete
parodied in *Punch*

Oscar and
friend, *c.*1877

Frank Miles – 'a very pleasant, handsome young fellow'

Oscar the Poet as featured in *Society*, 1882

Constance at the
time of her marriage

Neronian Oscar in 1885

Oscar in 1883

Robbie Ross - 'a slender, impulsive, attractive boy'

Henry Labouchère

John Gray

A weekend party: Oscar, Constance
and Mrs Walter Palmer

André Raffalovich

Oscar *c.*1890

(*Above and right*) Bosie

Oscar and Bosie in Norfolk,
August 1892

Oscar and Bosie in Oxford, Spring 1893

Bosie and a friend

'Stella' Boulton and 'Fanny' Park

Stella, Fanny and Lord Arthur Clinton

Things went from bad to worse. Shelley's father somehow found out about his son's friendship with Oscar and temporarily threw him out of the house: 'I have had a very horrible interview with my father and been told to leave the house,' Shelley told Oscar. 'I am on the verge of despair. I am sick and tired, body and soul, of my harsh existence.' Shelley started to experience mental problems. 'I am most anxious to see you,' he told Oscar. 'I would have called on you this evening but I am suffering from nervousness, the result of insomnia, and am obliged to remain at home.' In another, later letter, he wrote, 'I am afraid sometimes I am not very sane. I feel so nervous and ill.'

Certainly, Shelley's behaviour became increasingly erratic. He started sending Oscar letters in which he announced that he had become a devout Christian. 'I am determined to live a Christian life,' he wrote, 'and I accept poverty as part of my religion.' 'Shelley was in the habit of writing me many morbid, very morbid letters which I tore up,' Oscar said later. 'In them he said he was a great sinner and anxious to be in closer touch with religion.' Eventually Shelley assaulted his father and was arrested and taken into custody, sending for Oscar to bail him out.

Edward Shelley's story was tragic. When he testified in court, it was clear that he attributed his downfall, the problems with his father, his mental instability and all his other woes to his seduction, to what he called his 'entrapment', by Oscar. Certainly, at the time he appeared to believe what he said, even though it emerged that he was being paid handsomely by the Marquis of Queensberry, and then by the Crown, to testify against Oscar. André Raffalovich, who had met Shelley at the premiere of *Lady Windermere's Fan*, and who got to know him through John Gray, called him 'a foolish young man' whose head had been turned by Oscar. It was a just assessment. Shelley was a foolish, impressionable and altogether sad young man. Oscar had picked him up and charmed him into bed, just as he had already picked up and charmed many other young men into bed. It was not the premeditated, calculated act of corruption presented at Oscar's trials, but nor was it a marriage of two true minds, a love affair of equals.

Edward Shelley was undoubtedly damaged by his love affair with Oscar. And Oscar was damaged by Shelley. His brief and inconsequential affair with Shelley would be presented to the court and the public as an act of calculating and unspeakable corruption of an innocent youth, seemingly the only innocent among a ragtag and bobtail pack of ruffians, rent boys and blackmailers. It did Oscar incalculable harm in court. Later, after he came out of prison, Oscar expressed his regret over some of his love affairs and the consequences they had for the boys concerned. 'I used to be utterly reckless of young lives,' he told Reggie Turner:

I used to take up a boy, love him 'passionately' and then grow bored with him, and often take no notice of him. That is what I regret in my past life.

Oscar was, perhaps, thinking about Edward Shelley.

Hyacinth and Narcissus

'In this world there are only two tragedies. One is not getting what one wants, and the other is getting it. The last is much the worse, the last is a real tragedy.'

In the late spring of 1892, much to his consternation, Bosie Douglas found himself the victim of blackmail. He turned for help to his older brother Francis, Viscount Drumlanrig, who wrote 'a very pathetic letter' to Oscar, appealing for his help. Drumlanrig's letter spoke of the 'terrible trouble' Bosie was in. It was not an exaggeration. Bosie was facing disaster and he was frightened – frightened to death.

The Labouchère Amendment of 1885 had quickly been dubbed 'The Blackmailer's Charter', and ever since its passage into law an increasing number of men had fallen prey to blackmail. Blackmailers, working singly or in pairs, were quick to cash in on the changes in the law. Blackmail became endemic. In his *Recollections*, Jack Saul recounts a conversation he had with a young blackmailer called Yonny Wilson, a very handsome youth of sixteen or thereabouts, 'very fair and pretty; with chestnut hair, dark blue eyes, and a set of pearly teeth which, combined with the rosy colour of his cheeks, makes him an almost irresistible bait to old gentlemen – or for that matter to young ones too – who are addicted to the pederastic vice'. Yonny Wilson explained to Saul that he had a tried and tested method of extorting money from men. He would never have sex with the men who picked him up:

Do you think, Jack, I ever let those old fellows have me? No fear, I know a game worth two of that. You see, I never bring them home with me, and in fact always affect the innocent – don't know where to go to; am living with my father and mother at Greenwich or some out-of-the-way part of London, and only came to the West-End to look about and see the shops and swells, etc. If a gentleman is very pressing I never consent to anything unless he asks me to accompany him to his house or chambers. Once got home with him, I say, 'Now, sir, what present are you going to make me?'

'Stop a bit, my boy, till we see how you please me,' or something very like that is the answer I generally get.

'No; I'll have it now, or I'll raise the house, you old sod. Do you think I'm a greenhorn? I want a fiver. Don't I know too well that little boys only get five or ten shillings after it's all over? but that won't do for me, so shell out at once, or I'll raise the house, and a pretty scandal it will be!'

That frightens them at once, so I almost always get at least five pounds, and sometimes more, as I take care to write and borrow as much as I can afterwards. There's nothing like bleeding one of these old fellows; and young ones are better still – they are so easily frightened.

Men who had sex with other men had to learn very quickly how to live with the blackmailers, or perish – literally, in some cases – at their hands. Those unfortunates unable to extricate themselves from the net of especially vicious and determined blackmailers would often be driven to insanity or suicide. John Addington Symonds gave a sobering account of how easy it was for a man to fall 'into the hands of some pretty fellow' and have sex with him only to discover that he had slept with a blackmailer. 'At that point,' says Symonds, 'the subtlest methods of blackmailing begin to be employed':

The miserable persecuted wretch, placed between the alternative of paying money down or of becoming socially impossible, losing a valued position, seeing dishonour bursting upon himself and family, pays, and still the more he pays, the greedier becomes the vampire who sucks his life-blood, until at last there lies nothing else before him except total financial ruin or disgrace. Who will be astonished if the nerves of an individual in this position are not equal to the horrid strain?

Finally, says Symonds, 'the nerves give way altogether; mental alienation sets in; at last the wretch finds in a madhouse that repose which life would not afford him.' Others, he says, 'terminate their unendurable situation by the desperate act of suicide'.

The relationships between the blackmailers and the blackmailed were not, however, always clear-cut. Often, blackmailers and blackmailed enjoyed a symbiotic relationship, feeding off each other. For many Uranians, blackmail was neither more nor less sinister than prostitution, an extension to a codified system of risk and reward, of pleasure and payment. Blackmailers and male prostitutes were both called 'renters', a term which has survived to the present day in 'rent boy', meaning a male prostitute. There were degrees of blackmail. In a climate of extreme hostility and growing hysteria about sex between men, any relationships between men were likely to be tainted with an element of blackmail. At what point did extracting money turn into extorting money? Was there any real difference between the common or garden blackmailers, who demanded money with menaces, and young men like, for example, Edward Shelley, who wrote morbid letters seeking to extract money from Oscar using phrases like 'God forgive the past. Do your best for me now'?

Oscar understood and accepted blackmail as a natural consequence of his sexual choices. He was fascinated by male prostitutes. He knew and liked many boys who were notorious blackmailers and continued to like them even when they tried to blackmail him. And they, in turn, liked Oscar. He admired and applauded what he called 'their infamous war against life'. When Robert Cliburn told Oscar how he had blackmailed the Earl of Euston, who had figured prominently in the Cleveland Street Scandal, Oscar declared that Cliburn's determination, his avarice and his tenacity entitled him to the Victoria Cross.

Oscar was also fond of the weasly Fred Atkins, who was one of his favourite bed partners. Fred Atkins, alias Denny, and on high days and holy days, St Denis, was by turns a bookie's clerk, a not very successful music hall artiste, a part-time female impersonator, a male prostitute and one half of a notorious and very successful blackmailing duet. With his partner, James Burton, known throughout London's underworld as 'Uncle' Burton, Fred Atkins would go out and pick up likely-looking gentlemen at the Empire Promenade, at the back of the circle at the Alhambra, or even in a public lavatory, and take them back to his lodgings. Once they were naked, and usually after sex, Burton would burst in and, claiming to be Fred's uncle, take a high moral tone over the outrage committed on his nephew. The upshot was that the hapless punter would pay up handsomely, glad to escape without the police being called. But things did not always work out like that.

Once, when Fred had picked up a gentleman from Birmingham, taken him back to his lodgings in Tachbrook Street, Pimlico and done the business, the Birmingham gentleman refused to be intimidated by the arrival of Uncle Burton. He was not an average punter. He demanded the return of his gold watch and chain, which Fred had pocketed, and there was a scene which was interrupted by the arrival of the landlady. Finding a middle-aged man and a youth semi-naked on a bed, and another man shouting at them, the landlady sent for the police. By the time Police Constables 396A and 500A from Rochester Row Police Station arrived, Fred and the Birmingham gentleman were fully dressed. It had all been a storm in a teacup, they said, an argument over a game of cards. Everything was now resolved. All the Birmingham gentleman wanted was his watch and chain and he would be on his way. But the two police constables marched Fred, Uncle Burton and the Birmingham gentleman round to Rochester Row police station where statements were taken – statements that would reappear during Oscar's trials.

There were severe penalties against blackmail, ranging from seven years to life imprisonment. And there were occasional prosecutions. Robert Cliburn was convicted of blackmail at Lewes Assizes in 1890 but somehow evaded serving a prison sentence. Seven years later, he was prosecuted again, and it was stated in court that he had been receiving through a solicitor an annuity of £100 a year from a gentleman he had been blackmailing. But few victims of blackmail were willing to risk being prosecuted for gross indecency or sodomy by going to the police and revealing all. There were suspicions that in some large cities throughout the country, the police not only tolerated blackmailers, but actively encouraged them for the information they yielded about more prominent citizens. Uncle Burton himself was alleged to be a police informer.

Little is known about Bosie's brush with blackmailers at Oxford. There were two of them, at least, as Drumlanrig had written to Oscar of the 'people' who were blackmailing his brother. Even less is known about what exactly the blackmailers had on Bosie, except that it was serious enough for Bosie's father, the Marquis of Queensberry, to speak of his son's 'infamous conduct at Oxford' and to describe the whole affair as 'a horrible story'. Was it a foolish love letter to a boy dashed off in an unguarded moment, all but forgotten until a badly written copy on cheap paper arrived in the post one morning with a demand for money in return for the original? Letters were a favoured weapon of the blackmailer. A passionate, indiscreet love letter addressed to another man or a youth was the equivalent of hard currency. Or was it the threatened testimony of 'some pretty fellow' Bosie had picked up and slept with? Bosie had been wildly promiscuous in Oxford and had slept not just with undergraduates, but with servants, grooms and assorted other youths. Or it may have been something worse – much worse.

Bosie was in a state of panic and despair. His mother could see that he was in trouble and begged him to confide in her, but he did not dare. The only person he could turn to was Oscar. He added his appeals to those of Drumlanrig and wrote to Oscar himself – 'a most pathetic and charming letter', Oscar called it – begging him to help. Oscar, he knew, must have come across blackmail before, and had even, perhaps, been a victim. Bosie had read *Dorian Gray* no less than fourteen times and can hardly have failed to pick up on its scattered references to blackmail. During their several lunches and dinners, they may have talked about it, and Oscar could have recounted the experiences of any number of his friends like Frank Miles and Lord Ronald Gower. Oscar Browning, too, had had problems with several of his working-class protégés and may have told Oscar about his difficulties.

Oscar rose to the occasion. He went to Oxford to see Bosie and to try and find a way out of the mess. On his return, he consulted his friend George Lewis, the wily London society solicitor who was well-versed in extricating his clients – including the Prince of Wales – from difficult situations. 'Oh, he knows everything about us, and forgives us all,' Oscar once airily said of Lewis. An arrangement was made with the blackmailers to pay them £100 in full and final settlement. Oscar was to stump up the cash, and Edwin Levy, a strange character from Oscar's past, part money-lender, part private detective, was engaged to make the actual payment. Whatever it was that Bosie was being blackmailed over, both Lewis and Levy were shocked. Oscar said later that it was because of the sordid details of the blackmail that he began to lose George Lewis's esteem and friendship. 'When I was deprived of his advice and help and regard,' Oscar wrote, 'I was deprived of the one great safeguard of my life.' Levy was so shocked, Oscar recalled, that he went to great pains to urge Oscar to have nothing more to do with Bosie:

Edwin Levy at the very beginning of our friendship, seeing your manner of

putting me forward to bear the brunt, and annoyance, and expense even of
that unfortunate Oxford mishap of yours, if we must so term it, in reference
to which his advice and help had been sought, warned me for the space of a
whole hour against knowing you.

But there was another, quite different, more potent and more enduring
consequence of the 'unfortunate Oxford mishap'. Oscar and Bosie, quite
suddenly and quite unexpectedly, fell deeply and passionately in love.

Bosie was grateful, eternally grateful, to Oscar for saving him from the
clutches of the blackmailers. And Oscar, though he grumbled later about the
expense and annoyance, was thrilled to have saved Bosie from such a
predicament. It was as if Oscar had saved Bosie's life, and now, rescued and
rescuer, they were bound together, their destinies entwined, as if 'the Fates,'
Oscar wrote later, 'were weaving into one scarlet pattern the threads of our
divided lives.' As he got to know Oscar, Bosie's initial physical repugnance was
replaced by a fascination for his genius, for the subtleties of his mind, for the
enchantment of his conversation and for the generosity of his spirit. Bosie once
said that Oscar 'quickened' him, that he brought him to spiritual life, and
nurtured that life. Oscar, he said, fed his 'soul with honey of sweet bitter
thoughts', and transported him 'out of this tedious world into a fairy land of
fancy, conceit, paradox and beauty by the power of a golden speech'. 'I was
fascinated by Wilde,' Bosie said later. 'I really . . . *adored* him and was "crazy"
about him.'

For most of his life, Oscar had been searching for his one great life-
affirming, life-changing, immortal love affair with a beautiful boy, his ideal
boy, with whom he could scale the impregnable heights of great love and great
passion. He found it in Bosie. Bosie was not only beautiful and boyish, he was
brilliant, charming, aristocratic and poetic. Oscar was beguiled by both his
vices and his virtues. Bosie was, he said later, a 'wilful, fascinating, irritating,
destructive, delightful personality'. He was a force of nature, a glorious, guilt-
free sexual pagan, with a capacity to live life as intensely and as vividly as
Oscar.

Oscar felt that he had come face to face with his erotic and emotional
destiny. Bosie was the prophesied and prefigured 'new-found Lord' dressed in
'dyed garments from the South' from Oscar's poem 'Un Amant de Nos Jours'.
He was Willie Hughes, who had so inspired and inflamed Shakespeare. And he
was the extraordinarily beautiful Dorian Gray, the 'young Adonis', the
'veritable Narcissus', who looked as if he 'were made out of ivory and rose-
leaves'. Bosie was to Oscar what Dorian Gray had been to Basil Hallward, 'the
visible incarnation of that unseen ideal, whose memory haunts us artists, like
an exquisite dream'.

Bosie was the ideal boy, the realised incarnation of sexual and spiritual
desire. He was the *puer eternus*, the boy who would never grow old, the boy who
could never grow up. If he was frustratingly childish in many ways, he was also
appealingly childlike. His petulance, his selfishness, his wild and reckless

enthusiasms, as much as his sense of honour and his passion for life, were those of an adolescent boy. Bosie himself regarded himself as little more than a boy when he met Oscar and said his love affair with him belonged to his 'boyhood'.

When he fell in love with Bosie, Oscar's grailquest was over. Long after the tragedy broke, when Oscar had been released from prison, he was asked by Reggie Turner how he could justify his return to the man who had destroyed him. Oscar's answer was a proclamation of love. 'Say that I love him,' Oscar told Turner:

> that he is a poet, and that, after all, whatever my life may have been ethically, it has always been romantic – and Bosie is my romance. My romance is a tragedy of course, but it is none the less a romance – and he loves me very dearly, more than he loves or can love anyone else, and without him my life was dreary.

The love of Oscar and Bosie was consummated in the early hours of a June morning at Tite Street. Constance was away, and Oscar and Bosie had been out on the town: dinner at the Savoy, a play, and then supper at the Lyric Club. They had both been drinking. 'I was filled up with drinks by the time I got back to his house at almost two o'clock in the morning,' Bosie remembered. There were more drinks and more conversation. 'After about two hours discussion he induced me to stay the night in a spare bedroom,' Bosie told Frank Harris, in a remarkably candid letter written in 1925. 'In the end he succeeded in doing what he had wanted to do ever since the first moment he saw me.' The sex was predictable, according to Bosie, but with one important difference:

> Wilde treated me as an older boy treats a younger one at school, and he added what was new to me and was not (as far as I know) known or practised among my contemporaries: he 'sucked' me.

Shortly after his first night with Bosie, Oscar wrote ecstatically to Robbie Ross from the Royal Palace Hotel in Kensington. 'My dearest Bobbie,' he wrote:

> Bosie has insisted on stopping here for sandwiches. He is quite like a narcissus – so white and gold. I will come either Wednesday or Thursday night to your rooms. Send me a line. Bosie is so tired: he lies like a hyacinth on the sofa, and I worship him.

The letter is a coded reference to oral sex: Bosie 'so white and gold' lies naked on the sofa, his penis erect, 'like a hyacinth' and Oscar 'worships' him – 'worship' being a euphemism for fellatio. To worship a boy is not only to adore him emotionally, but also to adore him sexually, to gratify him, by sucking his penis. Oscar was fond – very fond – of oral sex, and there are many testimonies to this fondness for 'performing certain operations with his mouth', as one of the witnesses against him tactfully termed it. Laurence Housman, the brother of the poet, spoke of Oscar's predilection for what he called '*pollution labiale*', while Bosie's father, the Marquis of Queensberry, was rather more to the point, when he said of Oscar, 'That man is a cock sucker.' André Raffalovich was also direct, asserting that Oscar 'practised penis-sucking and paid delivery boys to let themselves be worshipped in this fashion'. Sucking cocks gave him 'inspiration', Oscar said. He told George Ives on several occasions, no doubt with his tongue in his cheek, that 'Love is a sacrament that should be taken kneeling.'

Oral sex was, then as now, perhaps the most common sexual activity between men. Robert Sherard, who in later life regarded himself as something of an authority on sex between men, said that from his 'most distasteful observance of the practices of homosexuals', oral sex – or what he rather quaintly called 'buccal onanism' – was the most frequent method of sexual satisfaction. Raffalovich observed that among some sexual inverts, including Oscar, 'penis-sucking' had 'become a habit and a mania, a sexual and cerebral need which he requires to become aroused'. Indeed, some men offered cock-sucking as an inducement to 'soldiers and common men' to have sex with them. 'After they have made sure of his sanitary condition,' says Raffalovich:

> they may well practise oral coitus on him – out of a desire to seduce, out of vanity, or to give him a new pleasure, a pleasure which cheap or very cheap women have not given, or would not give him. Oral coitus is one of the inducements of the unisexual in the presence of a heterosexual; and more than one heterosexual has let himself be convinced.

According to Raffalovich, men who loved men could be divided into two camps. There were sexual inverts like Oscar, he said, who were addicted to cock-sucking and other unsavoury sexual practices, and then there were sexual inverts like himself, who were 'sensual, without being debauched'. These latter, he said:

> may very well forego oral coitus: many inverts do not find it worthy of their love; many also find it lacks natural and spontaneous sensuality.

Bosie may have admitted that Oscar 'sucked' him, but he was adamant on one point: there was never any question of anal sex. 'It is hateful to me now to speak or write of such things,' he told Harris, 'but I must be explicit: sodomy never took place between us, nor was it thought or dreamt of.' Indeed, Bosie always denied that he had indulged in anal sex at any time in his life, either at Winchester, at Oxford, or at any time afterwards. He even told Harris that he was prepared to submit himself to a medical examination to prove that he had never indulged in sodomy:

If I had ever allowed anyone (either Wilde or any other single person) to treat
me in that way, surely a medical examination would reveal the fact.

But by sodomy, Bosie more properly meant being sodomised, being anally
penetrated. Presumably the kind of medical examination Bosie had in mind
was the same kind performed on 'Stella' Boulton and 'Fanny' Parke by the
police surgeon who found that their anuses were so dilated, so slack, that he
had 'never seen anything like it'. In Bosie's case such a test, taken a quarter of
a century later might, or might not prove whether he had ever been anally
penetrated. What it could not prove, as Bosie must have known, was whether
or not he had sodomised another man, whether or not, as Trelawny Backhouse
alleges, he had been the 'ascendant' to Backhouse's 'pathic'.

For Bosie, as for many men, there was a huge distinction between the act of
anally penetrating another man and the act of being anally penetrated. It was
far more acceptable to sodomise another man, or even better, a beardless,
androgynous boy, than to allow oneself to be sodomised. To penetrate is
essentially, integrally male. But to be penetrated is essentially female. One
affirms masculinity, the other undermines it. Few men were willing to own up
to a taste for being the passive partner in anal sex. John 'Soddington' Symonds
bravely said that he 'did not shrink from passive *pedicatio*', or sodomy, but
added that, thankfully, it had never been demanded of him. Of the thirty-eight
men whose life stories and sexual histories are included in Havelock Ellis's
Sexual Inversion, sixteen men said they enjoyed active sodomy, while only five
admitted enjoying being sodomised. The books did not balance.

Bosie's reticence on the subject of sodomy is not surprising. When, in the
1920s, he was writing about his sexual experiences, he had renounced his
sexual past and become a devout Catholic, and any suggestion of sodomy was
anathema to him. He had fallen out with Robbie Ross many years earlier, and
had publicly and persistently denounced him as a sodomite and a bugger. To
now admit to having engaged in what he regarded as the vice and the cardinal
sin of buggery was impossible.

Anal sex was almost as taboo among the men who practised it as it was
among those who condemned it. Campaigners for reform of the laws on sex
between men persistently underplayed the incidence of anal sex because it was
such a taboo subject, likely to disgust and alienate legislators and the general
public alike. The penalty for gross indecency was a maximum of two years,
with hard labour. But the maximum penalty for sodomy was life
imprisonment. Anal sex was a stumbling block standing in the way of reform.
According to Symonds, it was 'a vulgar error' to assume that sodomy was the
desire and pursuit of all men who had sex with men, or, indeed, that anal sex
had a deleterious effect on the health of those who practised it:

It is the common belief that one, and only one, unmentionable act is what the
lovers seek as the source of their unnatural gratification, and that this
produces spinal disease, epilepsy, consumption, dropsy, and the like.

187

Nothing can be more mistaken, as the scientifically reported cases of avowed and adult sinners amply demonstrate. Neither do they invariably or even usually prefer the *aversa Venus;* nor, when this happens, do they exhibit peculiar signs of suffering in health.

André Raffalovich was also at pains to emphasise the rareness of sodomy. 'Anal intercourse (active or passive) is not the end of their sexuality and the satisfaction of their sexual instinct; rather this is a deviation, just as anal intercourse is a deviation for heterosexuals.' Raffalovich went further, and argued that men who loved men would cheerfully support changes in the law which permitted activities like mutual masturbation and fellatio between consenting adults, while continuing to treat sodomy as a crime.

For Oscar and Bosie, sex was never the most important component of their relationship. Once, after Oscar's release from prison, when they were discussing the sexual side of their relationship, Oscar said, 'Oh, it was so little that, and then only by accident, essentially it was always a reaching up toward the ideal, and in the end it became utterly ideal.' Bosie told his mother that nobody could ever love him as 'faithfully, loyally, devotedly, unselfishly and purely as Oscar loves me'. Their love, he said, was 'perfect love, more spiritual than sensual, a truly Platonic love, the love of an artist for a beautiful mind and a beautiful body'.

Bosie was right. It was an ideal and idealised love: poetic, pure and perfect. But the perfect love of Oscar and Bosie had foundations of perfect, and more generalised, lust. As they played out the drama of their great love, both Oscar and Bosie were having as much sex as they could with boys and young men. They were addicted to sex. Sex, frequent sex, with as many people as possible, drove them. After all, Oscar declared, sex was 'all a question for physiology', a biological function, a bodily need. 'Sins of the flesh are nothing,' he said. 'They are maladies for physicians to cure, if they should be cured.' To find the sex they craved, Oscar and Bosie hunted singly and as a pair. They would find lovers for each other, and they were happy to share lovers. Sexual fidelity was unimportant. What mattered was spiritual fidelity. 'Those who are faithful know only the trivial side of love,' declared Lord Henry Wotton. 'It is the faithless who know love's tragedies.'

Love or lust? Lust or love? And how on earth to synthesise the two? It was a tension, a contradiction, a conundrum which had vexed Oscar for most of his adult life. Now, in a single, brilliant and inspired stroke, Oscar and Bosie had cut through the Gordian Knot of Victorian morality's thorniest problem. Love and lust were not, they realised, contradictory. They were complementary. Why choose one or the other, when you could have both? Indeed, it was impossible to choose one or the other, when they were indissolubly linked. Love and lust were like the sun and the moon, light and shadow. One could not exist without the other. They were part of the great wheel of life, part of the perfect harmony of the spheres.

Gay, gilt and gracious

'Be careful to choose your enemies well. Friends don't much matter. But the choice of enemies is very important.'

The summer of 1892 seemed to go on for ever and ever. For Oscar and Bosie, it was a gilded, golden time, a honeymoon. They had fallen deeply and passionately in love and wanted to spend every moment together. Oscar presented Bosie with a copy of his *Poems*, recently reprinted by Elkin Matthews and John Lane. Inside he wrote 'From Oscar to the Gilt-mailed Boy at Oxford, in the heart of June.' It was a bad pun. From being the blackmailed boy, Bosie had become the golden, gilt-mailed lover of Oscar. Oscar would always think of Bosie as shrouded in an alliterative golden haze. He was 'the gilt and graceful boy', 'the gay, gilt and gracious lad', possessed of a 'slim gilt soul' and 'gilt silk hair'.

Early in July, Oscar announced to Constance that he was going to the fashionable spa town of Bad Homburg, near Frankfurt, to take the cure. This was only partly true. His real reason for going was that Bosie was already there, holidaying with his grandfather, Alfred Montgomery. Oscar also wanted to live down the fiasco surrounding the production of *Salomé*, which had been due to open later that month. Oscar had persuaded the divine Sarah Bernhardt to take the title role in *Salomé*, but, after three weeks of rehearsals, Edward Pigott, Examiner of Plays in the Lord Chamberlain's Office, announced that he would not be granting *Salomé* a licence for performance. Officially, the reason given was that the play depicted Biblical characters, but a letter Pigott wrote privately to a friend makes it clear that it was the play's seething sexual content which lost it its licence. Pigott called *Salomé* 'a miracle of impudence':

> Salomé's love turns to fury because John will not let her kiss him *in the mouth* – and in the last scene, where she brings in his head – if you please – on a 'charger' – *she does* kiss his mouth, in a paroxysm of sexual despair. The piece is written in French – half Biblical, half pornographic – by Oscar Wilde himself. Imagine the average British public's reception of it.

Oscar was incensed by the refusal of the licence. 'I shall leave England and settle in France, where I will take out letters of naturalisation,' he announced, rather hot-headedly. 'I will not consent to call myself a citizen of a country that shows such narrowness of artistic judgement.' Oscar's threat roused the poet William Watson to write a mock lament in the *Spectator*:

> And wilt thou, Oscar, from us flee,
> And must we, henceforth, wholly sever?
> Shall thy laborious *jeux d'esprit*
> Sadden our lives no more for ever?

'There is not enough fire in William Watson's poetry to boil a tea-kettle,' was Oscar's sharp retort. Max Beerbohm was never in much doubt about whether Oscar would leave England. He wrote to Reggie Turner in July 1892:

> I do not exactly know which course Oscar will take: but inasmuch as French naturalisation entails a period of service in the French army, I fancy that his house in Tite Street will not be in the hands of an agent.

In Bad Homburg, Bosie introduced Oscar to his grandfather, with disastrous results. Montgomery immediately took a 'violent and invincible' dislike to Wilde and 'declined to meet him again'. The urbane and worldly-wise Montgomery had good reasons for his antipathy towards Oscar. He must have known about Oscar's reputation for unorthodox sexual tastes and realised that his interest in Bosie was more than literary. Montgomery's dislike of Oscar may well have been because of his own sexual tastes. There were rumours that he, too, preferred the company of young men. Perhaps the discreet Montgomery feared that Oscar might compromise him.

Oscar wrote to Constance with a highly coloured account of the rigorously healthy life he was leading. 'Oscar is at Homburg under a *régime*,' Constance told her brother Otho, 'getting up at 7.30, going to bed at 10.30, smoking hardly any cigarettes, and being massaged, and of course drinking waters. I only wish I was there to see it.'

After his return to England, Oscar took Constance and the boys on holiday to what the theatre critic Clement Scott had dubbed 'Poppyland', the stretch of the Norfolk coast from Sheringham to Mundesley which was renowned for its beauty and the purity of its air. The Wildes rented Grove Farm, in the village of Felbrigg, near Cromer, for August and September. It was to be both a family holiday and an opportunity for Oscar to work on his new play, *A Woman of No Importance*. But the pleasures of domesticity soon palled. Oscar invited Edward Shelley to come and spend a week at Grove Farm. On impulse, he sent Shelley a telegram at the end of August asking him to visit, and posted £3 for his fare. Oscar's motive in inviting Shelley was entirely selfish. Shelley would provide a welcome sexual outlet. But Shelley declined. He had his hands full with John Gray, who he had met at the première of *Lady Windermere's Fan*. Gray and Shelley were having some sort of relationship. John Gray's sudden interest in Edward Shelley might have been a response to Oscar's obsessive affair with Bosie. To be displaced, effortlessly, by Bosie after nearly three years as Oscar's officially beloved was humiliating. More humiliating still was the ease with which Oscar had simply forgotten about him, letting him slither out of his life with barely a backward glance.

In early September Bosie arrived for a three-week stay. It was a happy, carefree time. Oscar and Bosie played golf almost every day. 'Oscar had a pony cart,' Bosie remembered, 'which he used to drive himself, to the great danger of traffic as he had not much idea of driving!' Oscar, Constance and Bosie spent a week together before Constance and the children left to go and visit Lady Mount-Temple at Babbacombe Cliff, near Torquay. After she left, Bosie was unwell for a couple of days, and Constance was concerned enough to write a solicitous note to Oscar. 'I am so sorry about Lord Alfred Douglas, and I wish I were at Cromer to look after him. If you think I could do any good, do telegraph for me.'

Oscar's second society comedy, *A Woman of No Importance*, was conceived and largely written at Grove Farm, and then polished and revised towards the end of the year. Oscar again weaves autobiographical strands into the play. The story revolves around a rather bland and colourless young man called Gerald Arbuthnot, based perhaps on Edward Shelley, who is 'an underpaid clerk in a small provincial bank in a third-rate English town', living with his widowed mother. Gerald has been asked by the brilliant epigrammatist and provocatively amoral dandy, Lord Illingworth, to become his secretary, an offer which seemingly has more to do with Gerald's personal charms than with his secretarial skills. Again and again, Lord Illingworth says he has taken 'a great fancy' to Gerald, telling him 'It is because I like you so much that I want to have you with me.'

Oscar told the actor-manager who played Lord Illingworth, Herbert Beerbohm Tree, 'He is certainly not natural. He is a figure of art. Indeed, if you can bear the truth, he is MYSELF.' Indeed, Tree played Lord Illingworth as if he were Oscar, affecting Oscar's voice, his intonations and his mannerisms. 'Ah, every day dear Herbert becomes *de plus en plus Oscarisé*,' Oscar remarked during rehearsals. 'It is a wonderful case of Nature imitating Art.'

In a deleted passage from an earlier draft of the play, the amoral Mrs Allonby teases Lord Illingworth about his interest in Gerald. 'How you delight in your disciples!' she says. 'What is their charm?' To which Lord Illingworth replies, 'It is always pleasant to have a slave to whisper in one's ear that, after all, one is immortal. But young Arbuthnot is not a disciple . . . as yet. He is simply one of the most delightful young men I have ever met.' 'Disciples' was a word often used by Oscar, and by others, to describe the young men who hovered around him, and it seems clear here that the transition from 'delightful young man' to 'disciple' was a sexual rite of passage.

The erotic sub-plot of *A Woman of No Importance* was wittily and pithily summed up by Lytton Strachey when he went to a revival in 1907. Writing to Duncan Grant, Strachey described the play as 'the queerest mixture'. It was rather amusing, he said, 'as it was a complete mass of epigrams, with occasional whiffs of grotesque melodrama and drivelling sentiment':

> A wicked Lord, staying in a country house, has made up his mind to bugger one of the other guests – a handsome young man of twenty. The handsome young man is delighted; when his mother enters, sees his Lordship and recognises him as having copulated with her twenty years before, the result of which was – the handsome young man. She appeals to Lord Tree not to bugger his own son. He replies that that is an additional reason for doing it (oh! he's a *very* wicked Lord!).

Lord Illingworth articulates many of Oscar's own beliefs and attitudes. 'It is perfectly monstrous the way people go about nowadays saying things against one behind one's back that are absolutely and entirely true,' declares Lord Illingworth, a reference to the increasing gossip about Oscar's unorthodox sexual tastes. Sex and sexual desire are for Lord Illingworth, as they were for Oscar, paramount. 'Nothing is serious except passion,' he says. 'There is no secret of life':

> Life's aim, if it has one, is simply to be always looking for temptations. There are not nearly enough of them. I sometimes pass a whole day without coming across a single one. It is quite dreadful. It makes one so nervous about the future.

For the time being, at least, Oscar was assured of plenty of temptations.

The worldly, witty and amoral Mrs Allonby, who seems to have divined the true nature of Lord Illingworth's interest in Gerald, was probably based on the writer and wit Ada Leverson, whom Oscar had met a few months earlier and with whom he had instantly formed a close bond. Ada Leverson was fascinated by men who loved men, and Oscar was completely candid with her about his love life. She met and befriended several of Oscar's lovers, including Bosie, and was happy to allow Oscar to bring his lovers to dinner at her house.

There are other autobiographical inferences to be drawn from *A Woman of No Importance*. The triangular relationship between a young man, his mother and a dandy closely resembles the triangular situation of Bosie, Lady Queensberry and Oscar. Both Mrs Arbuthnot and Sybil Queensberry are women with a handsome twenty-something son. Both are alone in the world: Mrs Arbuthnot because Lord Illingworth would not marry her when she was pregnant, Sybil because of Queensberry's drunken, brutish behaviour and womanising. Both are extremely protective of their sons, and both have deep anxieties about their son's relationship with an older, dazzling, dandiacal man of the world who wishes to take him away for purposes they suspect are improper.

It is unclear exactly when Sybil Queensberry was first introduced to Oscar. Certainly, by the early autumn of 1892, social relations between the Wildes and

Sybil were firmly established. Oscar and Constance visited Sybil at Cadogan Place and stayed with her at her house, 'The Hut', near Ascot. Sybil and Constance seem to have become quite close. Constance 'frequently came to my mother's house', recalled Bosie, 'and was present at a dance which my mother gave during the first year of my acquaintance with her husband'.

But behind the veneer of superficial friendliness with the Wildes, Sybil was deeply uneasy about her son's friendship with Oscar. It was not just the disparity in age, nor the evident gulf between Oscar's worldly experience and Bosie's apparent innocence. There was something else. Sybil sensed that their relationship transgressed the normal boundaries of male friendship, that there was a concealed sexual dynamic between them. Her father, Alfred Montgomery, must have communicated his absolute dislike of Oscar, and had, perhaps, hinted at his suspicions about the sexual nature of the friendship.

Sybil wrote to Herbert Warren, President of Magdalen, Bosie's Oxford college, asking his opinion. What kind of man was Oscar Wilde, she wanted to know. And was she right to be worried? Warren's reply was soothing. Oscar Wilde, he said, was a man of enormous talents and great integrity. Bosie was fortunate to have him as a friend. Warren's letter failed to assuage Sybil's anxieties, but there was little that she could do. Bosie would brook no interference in his affairs. So, for the time being, Sybil was content to play a cautious, waiting game, appearing to accept the friendship, while anxiously watching and hoping that it would burn itself out.

Privately, she sought to enlist Oscar to her cause, to make him collude with her in helping to resolve what she called Bosie's problems. Her purpose was twofold: by alerting Oscar to Bosie's defects of personality, she hoped to persuade him that his relationship with Bosie would be fraught with difficulties. At the same time, she wanted Oscar to subtly change his role from that of a lover to a sort of surrogate parent. Knowing, as she did, Bosie's absolute dislike of parental interference, Sybil maybe hoped that the relationship would then end in bitterness and recrimination. Before long, Sybil started writing to Oscar, sending him:

> endless little notes, marked 'Private' on the envelope, begging me not to ask you so often to dinner, and not to give you any money, each note ending with an earnest postscript *'On no account let Alfred know I have written to you'*.

Oscar recalled in *De Profundis* how he had 'two long interviews' with Sybil, one in the summer, and another in the autumn, of 1892. 'She told me of your chief faults, your vanity, and your being, as she termed it, *'all wrong about money'*. 'I asked her why she did not speak directly to you herself,' Oscar wrote. 'On both occasions she gave the same answer: "I am afraid to: he gets so angry when he is spoken to".'

Oscar was puzzled by this reference to Bosie's anger. 'The first time, I knew you so slightly that I did not understand what she meant,' Oscar told Bosie. 'The second time, I knew you so well that I understood perfectly.' Oscar is referring to a trip he took with Bosie early in November 1892. Bosie had been ill, felled by an attack of jaundice, and they had decided to go to recuperate at the Royal Hotel in Bournemouth. It was there they had the first of their many rows, and Oscar experienced, for the first time, one of Bosie's sudden and terrible bursts of uncontrollable rage. Sybil told Oscar how Bosie was 'the one of my children who has inherited the fatal Douglas temperament'. It was something Bosie, too, recognised in himself when he told his mother, 'I have in my blood the love of a scene and a tragedy.' In *De Profundis*, Oscar reflected on:

> those incessant scenes that seemed to be almost physically necessary to you, and which in your mind and body grew distorted and you became a thing as terrible to look at as to listen to: that dreadful mania you inherit from your father, the mania for writing revolting and loathsome letters: your entire lack of any control over your emotions as displayed in your long resentful moods of sullen silence, no less than in the sudden fits of almost epileptic rage.

But to the lovestruck Oscar in these early days, Bosie's rages, his tantrums were an expression of the depth of his passion, a potent measure of his love. And, after the terrible storms of rage, would come Bosie's childlike tears of repentance, which would always melt what Bosie described as Oscar's 'loyal, kind and forgiving' heart.

Despite Bosie's manifold imperfections, despite his petulant tantrums and his frightening rages, despite his recklessness, his vanity and his spendthrift habits, Sybil loved Bosie with more passion and more devotion than she did any of her other children. This meant that Sybil and Oscar, like Mrs Arbuthnot and Lord Illingworth, were rivals for Bosie's love. Sybil became increasingly concerned about what she euphemistically referred to as Oscar's 'eccentricities and peculiar views of morality'. She was convinced that Oscar, as she said later, was acting 'the part of a Lord Henry Wotton', corrupting Bosie morally, and seducing him sexually. Oscar was, Sybil told Bosie, 'the murderer of your soul'. For his part, Oscar always regretted his collusion with Sybil. His love for Bosie had become compromised and tainted by his strangely mistrustful friendship with Sybil. When Lord Illingworth says, 'People's mothers bore me to death', Oscar may have been thinking about Sybil and her influence over Bosie.

Sybil's concerns were almost certainly shared by Bosie's father, Lord Queensberry. Queensberry had met Oscar ten years earlier and had had a desultory conversation with him. He knew Oscar by sight and was alarmed when, one day during the summer of 1892, he saw his son and Oscar together in a hansom cab. Bosie, he said later, 'looked unhappy'. In the deposition he made justifying his public accusation of Oscar as a sodomite, Queensberry said that he had 'part-read' *Dorian Gray* – read enough to realise that it was 'a sodomitically-inclined novel'. He did not consider, he said, that Oscar was in any way 'a desirable companion' for his son.

Bosie had always had an equivocal relationship with his father, loving him and at the same time loathing him. 'All through my childhood and youth,' Bosie wrote later:

> the shadow of my father lay over me, for though I loved him, and had indeed a quite absurd admiration for his supposed heroic qualities, I could not be blind to his infamous treatment of my mother.

During much of Bosie's childhood Queensberry and Sybil had lived apart. In 1886, Sybil and the children had the Hut near Ascot, which 'at a pinch would hold quite twenty-five people'. That year, during Ascot Week, Queensberry had arrived without notice in the company of some of his sporting friends and his mistress, demanding to stay for the duration of the race meeting. Sybil was obliged to put off her own guests at the last minute and leave the Hut with her children. She was humiliated, and the following year succeeded in divorcing Queensberry on the grounds of adultery and cruelty. Queensberry did not bother to contest the case and the decree was granted in less than a quarter of an hour.

Whatever depths of resentment Bosie may have felt towards his father over the treatment of his mother, at least on the surface father and son managed to maintain a friendly and respectful relationship. Queensberry stumped up a more than generous allowance for Bosie when he went to Oxford and they maintained regular contact.

When Queensberry spotted Bosie and Oscar in the hansom cab in that summer of 1892, he decided to tackle Bosie on the subject. 'My father suddenly one day spoke to me about it,' Bosie remembered, 'and told me that Wilde was not a fit man to associate with.' Queensberry broached the subject with surprising tact. He was not 'unkind or offensive,' Bosie said. 'He light-heartedly told me that I must give up knowing Wilde, and seemed to think that this would be enough.' It was not enough. Not nearly enough. Bosie wrote what he described as a 'perfectly respectful and affectionate letter' telling his father that he had no intention of giving up his friend, 'begging' him not to interfere. Queensberry tried again, this time by a letter, and Bosie parried. And there matters appeared to rest. The exchange left 'some strained feelings' between Bosie and Queensberry, as Sir Edward Clarke, Oscar's barrister, later termed it, but it was a coolness rather than an outright rift.

When Oscar and Bosie returned from Bournemouth in November, they were lunching in the Café Royal one day when Lord Queensberry walked into the principal dining room. Oscar suggested to Bosie that this was a good opportunity to speak to his father and repair matters between them. So Bosie got up, shook hands with Queensberry and, after a few minutes' conversation, brought him over to Oscar's table. The three of them had lunch together. It went splendidly. Oscar turned the full force of his charm on Queensberry, and Bosie was equally charming, conciliatory and filial. Bosie was obliged to leave at about 2.30, leaving Oscar and his father chatting. In the course of conversation it emerged that they were both going to be in Torquay later that month. Oscar was going to be at Babbacombe Cliff with Constance and the boys, and Queensberry was to give a lecture, probably on the subject of Atheism. Would Oscar like to come to one of his lectures, Queensberry asked. Oscar said he would be delighted, and that he hoped to see Lord Queensberry at Babbacombe Cliff. In the event, Queensberry never went to Torquay. But he wrote a friendly note to Oscar there, saying he was sorry that they would not be meeting after all.

Whatever his faults of personality, and despite his reputation as a brute and a boor, Queensberry appears to have behaved in an exemplary fashion during these early months of the relationship between Oscar and Bosie. He was concerned, as indeed any Victorian father would be concerned, about his son's friendship with a man who had a reputation for sexual unorthodoxy and who had recently published a novel which had drawn fierce criticism for its aura of sodomy. He was concerned that Bosie might be corrupted, morally and sexually, by such a man, and he was sensitive enough to try and 'light-heartedly' suggest that Bosie should draw away from Oscar's friendship. But after lunching with Oscar, Queensberry's fears were allayed. He had been seduced by Oscar's qualities and charms and was ready to admit that he may have misjudged him and that the world was in error about him.

A family crisis had, it seemed, been averted. Oscar could travel down to Torquay and Bosie could return to Oxford secure in the knowledge that Queensberry's disapprobation of their friendship had been surmounted, charmed away. It was too good to last.

Prophets and priests

'How can you have the flower of romance without a brotherhood of soul?'

In November 1892, Bosie acquired a new toy in the form of the Oxford magazine the *Spirit Lamp*, one of Oxford's many ephemeral magazines produced by undergraduates for undergraduates. Its original subtitle, under the editorship of Sandys Wason, was *An Oxford Magazine Without News*. Bosie contributed an essay under Wason's editorship and was surprised and gratified when Wason approached him and offered to sell him the title. As the owner of the *Spirit Lamp* Bosie automatically became its editor, a task he took to with enthusiasm. He had had plenty of experience. At Winchester he had co-founded and edited the *Pentagram*, the first of five magazines he was destined to edit, and, as he later admitted ruefully, 'the only one that ever showed a profit'.

Bosie was determined to transform the *Spirit Lamp* from a slightly gauche undergraduate magazine into what its new subtitle ambitiously proclaimed as 'An Aesthetic, Literary and Critical Magazine'. Bosie worked extremely hard to produce his first edition, which appeared in early December and included a sonnet by Oscar entitled 'The New Remorse'. Oscar had presented Bosie with the sonnet a year earlier during their courtship. Bosie was flattered and believed that Oscar had written it specially for him as a love token. In fact, Oscar had published the poem four years earlier as 'Un Amant de Nos Jours'. But its distinctly Uranian tone clearly signposted the *Spirit Lamp*'s future direction.

For the next four issues, the contents of the *Spirit Lamp* became still more Uranian. There were contributions from notable lovers of men and lovers of boys. John Addington Symonds contributed, as did Charles Kains Jackson, editor of the Uranian-inclined *Artist and Journal of Home Culture*. Kains Jackson contributed three 'Impressions' to the March 1893 number of the *Spirit Lamp*, one of which rather daringly seemed to invoke the joys of oral sex:

> rapt I gaze upon
> > Those glowing limbs, those lips which take
> Love's rose-pink and vermilion.

Robbie Ross contributed. Max Beerbohm, the much younger half-brother of the actor-manager Herbert Beerbohm Tree who was appearing as Lord Illingworth in *A Woman of No Importance*, contributed an essay, 'The Incomparable Beauty of Modern Dress'. Bosie also managed to persuade Lord Henry Somerset, who was living in exile in Florence after fleeing England in the wake of his scandalous love affair with a young man, to contribute a poem in Italian, 'T'Amo', 'I Love You'. The work of the editor himself was much in evidence, especially in the March 1893 number which even carried a short apology from Bosie about the number of his own poems he had published. In the May 1893 number, Bosie published his 'Sicilian Love Song' which could hardly have proclaimed his sexual preferences more explicitly:

> His lips are sweet and red;
>> Where starlight and moonlight mingle
> We will make our bridal bed,
>> Down in the cool dark dingle,
> When the long day is dead.

Material had been submitted for publication that was too explicit even for Bosie to publish. In the *Spirit Lamp*'s 'Answers to Correspondents' column in May, Bosie responded to A.R. Bayley, 'A.R.B. – I like your story very much, but I dare not publish it.'

The *Spirit Lamp* attracted plaudits from its Uranian-inclined readers, and brickbats from others. The first issue of the rival Oxford magazine, the *Ephemeral*, called the *Spirit Lamp* an 'unholy, decadent academy'. But Oscar was vastly excited by the very idea of the *Spirit Lamp*. He immediately commissioned Will Rothenstein, the young artist he had met in Paris the previous year, to do a portrait in pencil of Bosie in flannels lying back in an armchair, to be entitled 'The Editor of *The Spirit Lamp* at Work'. And in a spirit of high good humour, Oscar wrote to Bosie at Salisbury after his poem had appeared in the magazine, complaining that he had never received a copy and teasingly demanding a fee. 'I never got the *Spirit Lamp*, nor even a cheque!' he wrote. 'My charge for the sonnet is £300. Who on earth *is* the editor? He must be rented. I hear he is hiding at Salisbury.'

The *Spirit Lamp* advertised itself as a magazine for 'all who are interested in modern life and the new culture'. The 'new culture' was code for the new Uranian culture which Bosie, Oscar and many others wanted to see established. Kains Jackson called it 'the New Chivalry', while Oscar and Grant Allen named it 'the New Hedonism'. It was a literary, a poetic and a political moment, a movement where Culture, Chivalry and Hedonism were fermented together in the heady, revolutionary brew of a new sexual order. It aspired to make *l'amour de l'impossible*, the love of the impossible, possible; to translate the higher philosophy into articulate social and political flesh. It was a strange and powerful combination of passion and politics which used any and all tools at its disposal, invoking the glory that was Greece, deploying Malthusian arguments about over-population and sexological arguments that men who loved men were born and not made, and presenting medical arguments that sexual inversion was a biological fact, not a criminal choice. The primary aim was reform of the laws against gross indecency and sodomy, followed by a wish to win a wider social acceptance for men who loved men.

Oscar had incautiously argued in favour of the new culture in his work. Both *Mr W.H* and *Dorian Gray* had contained powerful passages hymning the glories of Greece and their revival in the Renaissance. In *Dorian Gray*, he had explicitly argued against the Labouchère Amendment when he wrote how 'monstrous laws' made the love of men for men 'monstrous and unlawful'. And his essay 'The Soul of Man Under Socialism', published in 1891, can be read as a clarion call for the sexual freedom of the individual. The essay is not so much about socialism as a hymn to 'the new Individualism, for whose service Socialism, whether it wills or not, is working'. And, as Oscar unambiguously declares, 'the new Individualism is the new Hellenism'. Not only does Oscar invoke ancient Greece, he also proclaims the innate right of all to live without moral restraint, and the sovereignty of nature in deciding what is sexually right and sexually wrong. 'Pleasure is Nature's test, her sign of approval,' he wrote. 'When man is happy, he is in harmony with himself and his environment.'

When Oscar and Bosie first met, they were both already convinced of the rightness of the 'new culture', and both were intellectual activists for it. But the alchemy of love brought about a surprising political reaction. Merged emotionally and sexually, Oscar and Bosie were to merge politically. Their attitudes to their sexuality and to the 'new culture' became radicalised and intensified. They jointly underwent a process of 'coming out', of con-textualising their situation politically and socially, and both started to see themselves as advocates working for what they and many others referred to simply as 'the Cause'. Both of them knew and accepted that there were risks and dangers inherent in becoming political activists, just as both of them knew that there were risks and dangers of exposure, violence, blackmail and imprisonment inherent in having sex with boys and young men.

Bosie wrote to Charles Kains Jackson about the 'new culture', extolling Oscar's leading role in it. 'Perhaps nobody knows as I do what he has done for the "new culture",' wrote Bosie:

> the people he has pulled out of the fire and 'seen through' things not only with money, but by sticking to them when other people wouldn't speak to them. He is the most chivalrous friend in the world, he is the only man I know who would have the courage to put his arm on the shoulder of an ex-convict and walk down Piccadilly with him, and combine with that the wit and personality to carry it off so well that nobody would mind.

In June 1892, the month that Oscar and Bosie first had sex together, Oscar met George Ives, who was to play an important role in further developing

Oscar and Bosie's political awareness. Ives was the illegitimate son of an army colonel who had been brought up by his paternal grandmother, whom he always referred to as Mother in his – literally – voluminous diaries. Ives's diaries number one hundred and twenty-two thick volumes containing about eight million words. Much of the text of the diaries is indecipherable. Oscar once 'dived' into Ives's diaries and 'struggled with the bad handwriting'. The diaries are unreadable in another sense too. Ives wrote page after page in an exalted, half-ecstatic, ranting Old Testament style of thees and thous, prophesying bright visions of a Uranian future, alternating with terrible and Mosaic diatribes on the hypocrisy of society – the whole liberally soused with maudlin passages of misery and self-pity.

Oscar picked Ives up at an Author's Club dinner on the evening of 30 June. His interest in Ives was initially sexual. Ives recorded the event in his diary. 'Our meeting was quite droll and romantic,' he wrote, 'and would be pronounced far-fetched in a play but such meetings are not new to me or to him.' According to Ives, Oscar:

> looked at me with his sleepy eyes and said What are *you* doing here? I replied I was attending the literary dinner. But, he answered – tho' I forget the words used it is so long ago – What are *you* doing here among the bald and the bearded?

Oscar invited Ives to come on with him to the Lyric Club. If he found Ives attractive when he picked him up, it seems that by the end of the evening he had thought better of it. Perhaps it was Ives's moustache that put him off. Oscar had never got over his abhorrence of facial hair. A year later, though, he did kiss Ives 'passionately' on the lips, but by that time Ives, 'having obtained permission from Mother', had shaved off his 'anti-Hellenistic' moustache. After Oscar's trial and imprisonment, Ives spent several pages of his diary fantasising about how different Oscar's life might have been had he fallen in love with him, Ives, instead of with Bosie. Ives was amiable, attractive and likeable. He was moneyed and leisured, a poet and a penal reformer. But he was also depressive, highly secretive and obsessed with the 'new culture', with 'the Cause', as he called it. What physical attractions he possessed were outweighed, at least for Oscar, by his obsessive secrecy and, at times, dreary and repetitive conversation. Oscar was frequently exasperated by George Ives. Once, after Ives had particularly irritated him, Oscar suggested – not entirely in jest – that he should 'establish a Pagan Monastery, possibly on some small rocky island in the Mediterranean'.

In the autumn of 1893, a year or so after meeting Oscar, George Ives set up a secret society to promote 'the Cause'. His diary for October recorded that he was 'moving very rapidly now at last but I am prepared, it is well', and that his 'time has been so full of plotting and planning'. Ives was still busy with his secret society in December, writing that he was 'all creativity, laying plans and plots for the great movement of the future'. Ives named his secret society the

Order of Chaeronea, after the battle of the same name where the male lovers of the Theban Band were slaughtered in 338 BC. Ives started to date his correspondence from 338 BC, this being year one of 'the Faith'. The 'Rules of Purpose' stated that the Order of Chaeronea was 'A Religion, A Theory of Life, and Ideal of Duty', although its purpose was primarily political. 'We demand justice for all manner of people who are wronged and oppressed by individuals or multitudes or the laws,' the Order's Rules of Purpose stated. Members of the Order were 'Brothers of the Faith', although it seems there were some lesbian members who were 'Sisters of the Faith'. The 'Service of Initiation' for the Order still survives. It was 'revised in the Year of the Faith, 2237' – or more prosaically 1899 – and it contains 'The vow that shall make you one of our number':

> That you will never vex or persecute lovers.
> That all real love shall be to you as sanctuary.
> That all heart-love, legal and illegal, wise and unwise, happy and disastrous, shall yet be consecrate for that love's Holy Presence dwelt there.

> Dost thou so promise?

It is impossible to know exactly how many men and women did so promise and were recruited to Ives's Order of Chaeronea, but at its peak 'the Elect' numbered perhaps two or three hundred. No membership lists survive, and the members referred to each other by initials, if at all. And as in the best-organised radical political groups, new members were recruited by just two existing members in a cell structure. Ives impressed on new members the vital need for secrecy in his best Old Testament prose. 'Thou knowest the two who received thee in the Order. Thou dost not need to know any others. Thou art forbidden to mention who belongs to anybody outside it.'

The Order of Chaeronea was, according to Ives, emphatically not to be used as a forum for men to meet other men for sex. Sex 'is forbidden On Duty, and the Order is most ascetic', Ives wrote. 'Yet we condemn not any sensuality, so long as it is passionate. All flames are pure.'

It is almost certain that Oscar was an early recruit to the Order of Chaeronea. 'Oscar Wilde's influence will be considerable I think,' Ives confided to his diary on 26 October, when he was in the process of establishing the Order. Two of Oscar's sayings are quoted, reverentially, in the 'Thoughts' which preceded the solemn vow members were expected to swear to, suggesting that Oscar was a potent and profound source of inspiration to the Order. The first was Oscar's ambiguous 'Love is a sacrament that should be taken kneeling', the second, a line from his play *Salomé*, 'The mystery of love is greater than the mystery of death.'

Bosie almost certainly became a member of the Order of Chaeronea as well. As one of the most passionate and outspoken advocates of the Cause it is inconceivable that he would not have joined. Bosie met Ives for the first time at

201

a luncheon party at which Oscar and the young poet Theodore Wratislaw were also present. Ives was on the point of launching the Order and this luncheon may well have been to recruit Bosie and Wratislaw. Ives was suitably bewitched by Bosie. 'He was very beautiful, I was indeed fascinated by him,' Ives confided to his diary. 'I have an idea that we shall influence one another greatly.'

In his diaries, Ives frequently makes reference to Oscar's belief that love, specifically sex, was the only true form of democracy. 'Love is the only democratic thing,' Ives quotes Oscar as saying, and later adds 'Oscar, you were right there; Love is the only democratic thing. The only bond which really binds the brotherhood of man.' The 'democracy of Uranianism' was both idealistic and pragmatic. John Addington Symonds, 'our dear brother of the Faith' as Ives called him, firmly believed that love and sex between men could and would undermine the rigid class system that prevailed. A lord sleeping with a labourer meant that both could break free from the 'cataract-blinded' destiny of their class. Symonds put his principles into practice by having long and intense affairs with a Swiss peasant and a Venetian gondolier, as well as hundreds of sexual encounters with working men. 'The blending of Social Strata in masculine love seems to me one of its most pronounced, and socially hopeful features,' Symonds wrote to Edward Carpenter. 'Where it appears, it abolishes class distinctions.'

Edward Carpenter agreed. Carpenter, who was from a wealthy middle-class background, had studied at Cambridge to become a minister in the Church of England but had renounced this for a new calling as a poet, socialist and sexual prophet. Carpenter established himself in a cottage at Millthorpe, just outside Sheffield, where he grew his own vegetables, made his own sandals and lived perfectly happily with a young man he had encountered one day pushing a cart through a blizzard. George Merrill's nickname was 'Georgette' and he became Carpenter's devoted companion. Both Symonds and Carpenter were influenced by Walt Whitman's vision of 'adhesiveness' between men, of 'the high towering love of comrades' which was somehow separate from and more noble than the love between men and women. Whitman envisioned a bright world of democracy and equality, a spiritual commonwealth of conceptual cities and states built and cemented together 'by the love of comrades, by the manly love of comrades'.

In the early 1890s, Carpenter began work on an epic prose poem *Towards Democracy*, an ecstatic meditation on the journey that men and women must undertake to reach the millennium of true democracy. This goal, like Oscar's socialism, seems to hinge on the freedom and the flowering of sexual expression:

> I conceive of a millennium of earth – a millennium not of riches, nor of mechanical facilities, nor of intellectual facilities, not absolutely of immunity from disease, nor absolutely of immunity from pain; but a time when men and women all over the earth shall ascend and enter into relation with their bodies – shall attain freedom and joy.

Carpenter's own sexual and democratic inclinations emerge from *Towards Democracy* when he writes of 'entering the chamber' of a young male prostitute, dwelling on the image of the 'thick-thighed hot coarse-fleshed young bricklayer with the strap around his waist'. Carpenter imagines himself as erotic putty in the hands of working men:

> I will be the ground underfoot and the common clay. The ploughman shall turn me up with his plough-share among the roots of the twitch in the sweet-smelling furrow. The potter shall mould me, running his finger along my whirling edge (we will be faithful to one another, he and I). The bricklayer shall lay me: he shall tap me into place with the handle of his trowel.

There was a widespread belief among Uranians that sex and love between men of the working class were innate, natural and spontaneous, free from guilt and free from notions of vice and sin. In E.M. Forster's novel *Maurice*, the handsome young gamekeeper Alec Scudder is the incarnation of a joyous, spontaneous and natural homoeroticism, in sharp contrast to Clive Durham and Maurice Hall, both of them angst-ridden middle-class lovers of men who seek to escape their sexual destiny through marriage and medical hypnosis respectively. According to 'Q', an anonymous correspondent of Havelock Ellis:

> Among the working masses of England and Scotland 'comradeship' is well marked, though not very conscious of itself. Friends often kiss each other, though this habit seems to vary a great deal in different sections and coteries. Men commonly sleep together, whether comrades or not, and so easily get familiar. Occasionally, but not so very often, this relation delays for a time, or even indefinitely, actual marriage, and in some cases is highly passionate and romantic.

Another anonymous correspondent told Ellis how it was a fact, 'patent to all observers, that simple folk not infrequently display no greater disgust for the abnormalities of sexual appetite than they do for its normal manifestations'. He went on to tell Ellis 'of many cases in which men of the lower class were flattered and pleased by the attentions of men of the higher class' and gave, as proof positive, the testimony of a friend who had successfully propositioned many working class men:

> He had made advances to upward of one hundred men in the course of the last fourteen years, and that he has only once met with a refusal (in which case the man later on offered himself spontaneously) and only once with an attempt to extort money.

Oscar also believed that sex between men was natural and endemic among the working class. 'What is called the vice of the upper classes is really the pastime of the working classes,' he proclaimed.

Behind all the talk of comradeship, of democracy, of adhesiveness lay some uncomfortable truths. Whatever the sexual relations between the classes, they were rarely accompanied by any lasting emotional interactions. Working-class men and boys were fair game. They were there, Oscar declared, to serve genius. They made good bed partners, but rarely became long-term lovers, unless they had, like John Gray and Edward Shelley, achieved for themselves a simulacrum of middle-class identity which gave them an entrée to the realm of the emotions as well as the realm of the erotic. Edward Carpenter's affair with George Merrill, and the fictional affair between the middle-class Maurice Hall and the working-class Alec Scudder in *Maurice*, were the exception rather than the rule.

Many middle- and upper-class men were sexually attracted to working-class men and boys. They saw them as 'rough trade', whose fascination lay in their dangerous masculinity, in their feral maleness, a maleness untrammelled and unfettered by any civilising or effeminising influences. 'Manliness has become quite effeminate,' Oscar remarked in a deleted aphorism from 'Phrases and Philosophies for the Use of the Young', which he contributed to the Uranian magazine the *Chameleon* in 1894. Whatever philosophical or social virtues effeminacy might hold for Uranians, it was clear that when it came to sex, many Uranians craved what they saw as the unpredictable, unknowable, untameable, often violent and sometimes criminal masculinity of rough trade. Rough trade was, Oscar said, 'all body and no soul'. That many bits of rough trade were predominantly heterosexual merely underlined their true masculinity and added spice to the frisson of danger. The attractions Alec Scudder held for Maurice were magnified by the fact that he was bisexual, equally at home, equally sexually competent with both women and men.

Unlike John Addington Symonds, who demanded sex from his working-class contacts as 'a pledge of comradeship', Oscar never deluded himself that his relations with rough trade consisted of anything more than sensual and sexual excitement. He had a pure and perfect idealised love with Bosie, and he wanted an equally impure and erotic love with rough street boys, the rougher, the dirtier, the more dangerous the better. 'I deliberately went to the depths in the search for new sensations,' Oscar said. It was different, exciting, exotic and, most of all, addictive. Hunting rough trade and having sex with rough trade was 'like feasting with panthers', Oscar said. 'The danger was half the excitement.' He was straying into a parallel sexual universe, an 'imperfect world of coarse uncompleted passions, of appetite without distinction, desire without limit, and formless greed'; a world populated by male prostitutes, blackmailers and criminals who were 'the brightest of gilded snakes'. 'Their poison,' he said, 'was part of their perfection.'

Oscar had a name for this coarse, formless world of unbridled lust. He called it 'the mire': a dark, dirty morass, an erotic swamp peopled by the rough denizens of the demimonde. The mire both repelled and fascinated him. Oscar had sought to tread and chart its dark untrodden paths and had often fallen, 'sprawling in the mire'. Bespattered and besmirched, he had tried to extricate himself, to escape, only to find himself sucked back into its gelatinous embrace. Oscar believed that the mire was his fate, his destiny. 'His Doom' he called it, always with a capital D. In prison, he recalled this sense of impending, inexorable Doom that seemed to drive him and draw him ever closer to destruction. In all his relations with Bosie he discerned 'not Destiny, merely, but Doom: Doom that walks always swiftly, because she goes to the shedding of blood'. Oscar sought to enter the mire and consume it, knowing that he was, in turn, to be consumed by it. He was impelled by what Freud was later to christen the death drive: the ultimate paradox where life is experienced at its greatest intensity in the pursuit of danger, destruction and death. Oscar said he had been snared by the Greek goddess of retribution:

> Nemesis has caught me in her net: to struggle is foolish. Why is it that one runs to one's ruin? Why has destruction such a fascination? Why, when one stands on a pinnacle, must one throw oneself down? No one knows, but things are so.

And yet, paradoxically, Oscar also recognised that for him a curious salvation lay in the mire. Just as Dorian Gray had visited the lowest dens of the East End to 'cure the soul by means of the senses', so Oscar, in the rabid sexual abandonment of the mire, in the abnegation of self, of status, of reason and of morality, found a sense of ease and freedom, of escape. 'Only in the mire can I know peace,' he admitted later. In the many *petit morts*, or little deaths, of the mire, Oscar searched for and found the poetic azure of oblivion, knowing full well that sooner or later, *le grand mort*, the great death would call him.

By November 1892, Oscar had both embraced the Cause and embarked upon his exploration of the mire. Dangerous politics and dangerous sex were an explosive combination. The outcome would prove fatal.

For love or money

'What a fuss people make about fidelity! Why, even in love it is purely a question for physiology. It has nothing to do with our own will. Young men want to be faithful, and are not: old men want to be faithless, and cannot: that is all one can say.'

At the end of November 1892, Oscar and Constance rented Babbacombe Cliff, Lady Mount-Temple's pre-Raphaelite fantasy of a house near Torquay. They planned to spend the winter there, to get away from the London fogs which, according to Oscar, were getting worse every year. Oscar also needed, he said, peace and quiet in which to work. More importantly, for a while at least, he needed to get away from the erotic distractions and temptations of London. But, pleasant as Torquay was in the late autumn, Oscar quickly became bored. 'Are there beautiful people in London?' he asked Robbie Ross plaintively:

> Here there are none; everyone is so unfinished. When are you coming down? I am lazy and languid and doing no work. I need stirring up.

The ever-faithful Robbie did go down and spend a few days at Babbacombe. Oscar also invited the young actor Sydney Barraclough, who, against the wishes of the actor manager Herbert Beerbohm Tree, Oscar wanted to play the part of Gerald in the forthcoming production of *A Woman of No Importance*. Oscar's interest in Sydney clearly extended beyond the merely dramatic. 'You are my ideal Gerald, as you are my ideal friend,' he wrote to Sydney from Babbacombe. 'I want you down here: it is a lovely place, and you need rest and quiet and I need you too.'

Despite his dalliance with Sydney, Oscar was missing Bosie desperately. They wrote to each other constantly, Oscar sending passionate love letters, of which only a handful survive. In early January, Bosie sent Oscar an exquisite sonnet he had written, 'In Sarum Close', which neatly expresses and explains the strange amalgam of pure love and unbridled lust in their relationship. In the sonnet, Bosie writes how he is exhausted and disenchanted with sex merely for sex's sake, how he is 'Tired of passion and the love that brings Satiety's unrest'. The sonnet asks Oscar to share the joys and sorrows of love:

> But thou, my love, my flower, my jewel, set
> In a fair setting, help me, or I die,
> To bear Love's burden; for that load to share
> Is sweet and pleasant, but if lonely I
> Must love unloved, 'tis pain; shine we, my fair,
> Two neighbour jewels in Love's coronet.

Oscar and Bosie were those 'two neighbour jewels' in Love's coronet, who could love each other deeply and passionately and yet share 'Love's burden'. In practice, sharing the burden of love meant not just sharing the compulsion to have sex with as many young men and boys as possible, it also meant, at its most prosaic and literal, sharing the young men and boys themselves – sometimes at the same time.

Although Oscar would later slightingly refer to this sonnet of Bosie's as a poem 'of the undergraduate school of verse', at the time he was rhapsodic and wrote in reply what was destined to become one of his most famous and controversial letters, signing it with his 'undying love':

> My Own Boy, Your sonnet is quite lovely, and it is a marvel that those red rose-leaf lips of yours should have been made no less for music of song than for madness of kisses. Your slim gilt soul walks between passion and poetry. I know Hyacinthus, whom Apollo loved so madly, was you in Greek days.

When Bosie received this letter from Oscar, he stuffed it in the pocket of the suit he was wearing and promptly forgot all about it.

Oscar was finding his time at Babbacombe Cliff irksome. He was spending more time than he was accustomed to with Constance and the children, and such unrelieved domesticity bored him to death. In January 1893, he decided to return to foggy London alone for a couple of weeks. Rehearsals for *A Woman of No Importance* were about to get under way, and his play *Salomé* was about to be published. Or that was what he told Constance. In reality he was desperate for some mental and sexual stimulation. He could see Robbie. He could see Bosie, and he could call on his new friend, Alfred Taylor, for tea and beauties of an entirely novel and beguiling kind.

Alfred Waterhouse Somerset Taylor was thirty years old when he met Oscar in the autumn of 1892. He was a good-looking man: tall, dark and clean-shaven, running a little to fat, but with a good-natured face and a beaming smile. He had been born a gentleman, the son of a wealthy cocoa manufacturer, and had been sent to Marlborough, from where he had been expelled after a few terms, after being caught, quite literally, with his pants down in the school lavatories with a much younger boy. When he came of age in 1883, he inherited a fortune of £45,000 and ran through it in eight years. At the time he met Oscar, he had rooms above a disused bakehouse in Little College Street, Westminster, which he rented for £3 a month, and he was living on the last remnants of his fortune, spending £40 or £50 a week, a huge amount of money, on boys. Within a year, he would be bankrupt.

Taylor had never struggled with his sexual identity. He was a happy, rather camp, well-adjusted, feather-pated lover of young men. Later, when he was asked in court by Sir Frank Lockwood, 'Was it not repugnant to your Public School idea, this habit of sleeping with men?' Taylor bravely stood his ground. 'Not to me,' he replied. 'Where there is no harm done I can see nothing repugnant in it.' He loved gossiping, parties, dressing up in drag – 'for a lark' – and singing sentimental songs at the piano. Taylor had a particular friend, a 'husband', in the person of Charles Spurrier Mason, a twenty-five-year-old male prostitute, with whom he went through a mock marriage service in 1893. Taylor wore drag and the couple exchanged rings and entertained friends to a wedding breakfast afterwards. Pierre Louÿs excitedly reported the event to André Gide – 'a marriage – a real marriage – between two of them, with an exchange of rings and so on'. But Oscar was cynical. 'I hope marriage has not made you too serious?' he quipped to Charlie Mason. 'It has never had that effect on me!'

There were always boys and young men at Little College Street. Taylor's landlady, Mrs Grant, deposed that there was a steady stream of male visitors. She used to overhear conversations. Taylor would call his guests by their Christian names – 'Charlie, dear' and 'Dear boy'. To them he was Alf or Alfie. Alfred Taylor like his boys rough, but he was not at all fussy. His great talent in life was his ability to pick boys up. His easy manners, his charm and his genuinely sympathetic nature were invaluable assets. He had some favoured hunting grounds: the Alhambra and the Empire, the notorious bar at the St James's Restaurant and the skating rink in Knightsbridge, where he would fall into conversation with likely-looking lads, especially those who were unemployed or who seemed to be at a loose end. He was a mother hen, always ready to listen to the problems of the boys he met, always ready to give them a bed for the night, the week or the month, and always ready with the gift of a few shillings, or a loan of a pound or two, and some sound advice. Since he had moved to Little College Street, Taylor had effectively been procuring boys for his friends. It was partly social, partly business. More often than not, a satisfied 'friend' might bung him a fiver, or take him out for dinner, as a thank you for introducing him to a boy. But the money was always secondary for Taylor. He liked bringing people together, it gave him pleasure. If there was a little money as a result, to help stretch his tight budget, well, that was a bonus.

Oscar was introduced to Alfred Taylor by Maurice Schwabe. There are conflicting accounts of how Oscar met Schwabe. Some say it was Bosie who introduced them, others that it was Robbie Ross. Schwabe had been at the first night of *Lady Windermere's Fan* and had struck up a friendship with Oscar. Like Taylor, Schwabe inclined towards plumpness and, according to one of the bits of rough trade he had slept with, was 'a very girlish boy'. He was a 'fat talkative queen with glasses and a pronounced giggle', recalled a bar keeper in Tangier who knew him in 1910. Schwabe took Oscar to one of Taylor's celebrated afternoon tea parties in Little College Street, a first-floor front with permanently shuttered and heavily draped windows, artificially lit with lanterns and heavily scented with pastilles. Taylor's landlady particularly noticed his fancy bed-linen. His pillowcases, she said, were expensively and elaborately decorated with lace. Oscar liked Alfred Taylor. Most people did. He was entirely without malice or guile. Above all, he was trusted by everyone he knew; by the boys he procured and by the gentleman he supplied with boys. He was discreet and he was on everybody's side.

Taylor and Schwabe shared a penchant for butch young trade. Within a few days of meeting Oscar, Alfred Taylor picked up a man called Edward Harrington in the house of a friend, a schoolmaster called Court. Taylor invited Harrington back to Little College Street, where he stayed for two nights, sharing Taylor's bed, the only bed in his suite of rooms. 'What was the attraction about Harrington?' Sir Frank Lockwood demanded during Oscar's second trial. 'I don't know what his attraction was,' Taylor answered evasively. Harrington's attraction was, in fact, primarily sexual. He was in his mid-twenties, tall, well-built and extremely attractive in a butch way. Taylor and Schwabe took him out to dinner and then introduced him to Oscar. The meeting was not a success. Harrington was far too masculine, far too manly for Oscar, who only wanted boyish young men.

A few days later, towards the end of September 1892, in the bar at the Gaiety Theatre, Taylor picked up another young man who he thought might appeal to Oscar. Sidney Mavor was twenty and was hardly rough trade. He was slim and rather feminine with a slight cast in his eye. His friends called him 'Jenny', and he had ambitions of going on the stage. He was the son of a veterinary surgeon and lived with his widowed mother in genteel penury in South Kensington. He worked in the City, in a small firm manufacturing and supplying lamp-wicks. According to Jenny Mavor, Taylor was 'very civil and friendly'. He asked Jenny to come home with him, and they had sex together, even though the rather feminine Jenny was not really Taylor's type. 'Bread and bread' – as opposed to bread and butter, or even, in the case of working-class boys, bread and dripping – was a slang phrase used to describe sexual incompatibility between two men like Alf Taylor and Jenny Mavor who both preferred rough, butch men and boys. But Taylor certainly was not too fussy, and Jenny clearly did not mind if he did.

Jenny was invited back for tea parties. On 2 October, Taylor said to him, 'I know a man in an influential position who could be of great use to you. He likes young men when they're modest and nice in appearance. I'll introduce you.' The man in the influential position was of course Oscar. 'It was arranged that we should dine at Kettner's Restaurant the next evening,' Jenny testified later. 'I called for Taylor, who said, "I'm glad you've made yourself pretty. Mr Wilde likes nice clean boys." '

Dinner in a private room at Kettner's was a great success. Oscar liked Jenny and, turning to Taylor at the evening's end, proclaimed regally, 'Our little lad has pleasing manners. We must see more of him.' It's likely that Oscar saw everything that Jenny had to offer that very night. They had sex together 'in

Oscar's room at the Albemarle Hotel,' Jenny said later. And a few days later he was surprised to receive a parcel at his home in South Kensington containing a silver cigarette case. It was inscribed inside: 'Sidney from O. W. October 1892'. 'It was quite a surprise to me!' Jenny said.

Jenny Mavor's silver cigarette case had cost £4 11s 6d. It was an expensive gift and the first of many silver cigarette cases which Oscar presented to his lovers. 'I have a great fancy for giving cigarette cases,' Oscar testified during his trial. He had given, he said, seven or eight of them to young men in 1892 and 1893. But Oscar was being economical with the truth. Many more than that were presented to his sexual partners, though some of the recipients were not as lucky as Jenny Mavor and received cigarette cases costing only £1. Bosie's, of course, as was his due, was made of solid gold. When Oscar was arrested and taken to Bow Street Police Station, a search of his pockets revealed writs for the non-payment of bills for silver cigarette cases.

During Oscar's trial, the *Evening News* commented with particular disgust on how the trial had left the realms of literature and 'penetrated the dim-lit perfumed rooms where the poet of the beautiful joined with valets and grooms in the bond of silver cigarette cases'. Cigarette cases were the sterling symbol of an erotic compact. There were strong links between smoking cigarettes and sucking cocks. 'A cigarette is the perfect type of a perfect pleasure,' Lord Henry Wotton had pronounced in *Dorian Gray*. 'It is exquisite and it leaves one unsatisfied.' And what was true for smoking cigarettes was also true for cock-sucking. It was exquisite and left one unsatisfied, hungry for more. When Pierre Louÿs wrote to André Gide about the elegant customs and manners of Oscar and his disciples, he was charmed by the way 'X', a young man to whom he had just been introduced, offered him a cigarette. 'Instead of simply offering it as we do,' Louÿs wrote, 'he began by lighting it himself and not handing it over until after he had taken the first drag. Isn't that exquisite?' Louÿs overlooked, or pretended to overlook, the homoerotic symbolism of the gesture. 'They know how to envelop everything in poetry,' he said.

A few weeks after he met Jenny Mavor, on 18 November, Oscar and Bosie called by invitation at Little College Street for tea and to be introduced to Taylor and Schwabe's newest find: sixteen-year-old Fred Atkins. He was 'pale-eyed and pimply-faced', a precocious and knowing cockney lad with lively and engaging manners. Maurice Schwabe had picked up Fred Atkins at the roller skating rink in Knightsbridge, blithely unaware that he was already a hardened young criminal, an experienced rent boy and an accomplished blackmailer. Schwabe found him delightful, as did Taylor. Both of them were sure Oscar and Bosie would like him too. They did. The five of them – Oscar, Bosie, Taylor, Schwabe and Atkins – went out to dinner that evening to the Florence restaurant in Rupert Street, where they had dinner in a private room. Oscar's behaviour at dinner was, according to Atkins, most unusual. 'Mr Wilde kissed the waiter,' he testified in court. And Oscar, he said, kept making indecent gestures towards him with his tongue, and continually stroked his thighs. Fred and Oscar did not however sleep together that night. Fred went off to have sex with someone else, either Bosie or Schwabe. Oscar would have to wait his turn.

But before the party broke up, Oscar invited Fred to lunch the next day at the Café Royal, where he asked Fred if he would like to accompany him to Paris for a few days as his 'secretary'. Fred was thrilled. He had never been abroad before. Maurice Schwabe was to follow on, a day or two later. On 21 November, Oscar and Fred took the 2.45pm Club train for Paris and arrived that evening. They stayed at 29, Boulevard de Capucines, the small private hotel run with absolute discretion by Madame Goly where Oscar had stayed two or three times before. They had a small suite on the third floor, with two inter-connecting bedrooms. They lunched the next day at the Café Julien, after which Oscar asked Fred to copy half a page of manuscript for him. Fred was happy to oblige, and the task took him all of ten minutes. Then the pair of them went to Pascal's, the hairdressing shop under the Grand Hotel, where Fred decided on a whim to have his hair curled. Oscar tried, not very hard, to dissuade him. A sumptuous dinner followed. Oscar was tired out, so he went back to the hotel while Fred went out to the Moulin Rouge with the money Oscar had given him, and a lecture about the dangers of consorting with loose women he would find there ringing in his ears. Oscar told him, Fred said, 'not to go to see those women, as women were the ruin of young fellows'. Fred returned to the hotel in the early hours. Oscar heard him come in and came into Fred's room. 'Shall I come into bed with you?' said Oscar and offered to suck him off, or as Fred phrased it, 'perform certain operations with his mouth'.

Maurice Schwabe arrived the next day and Fred was surprised to walk into Oscar's room on the morning of 23 November and find the pair of them in bed together. Schwabe was as far from being Oscar's type as Oscar was from being Schwabe's type, but neither of them seems to have minded about this. Oscar had learned to take his pleasures where and when he could. If it was Fred Atkins one night and Maurice Schwabe the next, so be it. There was no harm done. It was all very light-hearted, pleasant and pleasurable, a happy Parisian jaunt. Oscar enjoyed being with boys like Fred Atkins. He liked to treat them, to show them something of the world, to buy them presents and to experience their excitement and their gratification. It was Fred's birthday on 24 November and a special lunch was called for, at which Oscar presented him with a silver cigarette case. There had been no time between meeting Fred and taking him to Paris to have it inscribed.

Surprisingly, Fred never tried to blackmail Oscar. He seemed to be genuinely fond of him. Unlike many recipients of Oscar's silver cigarette cases who sold them immediately, Fred kept the one Oscar had given him, and they continued to meet and have sex regularly. Two days after their return to London, Oscar wrote to Fred at his lodgings in Pimlico and asked him to come and see him at Tite Street, where he was, he said, ill in bed. Oscar had been alerted, almost certainly by Alfred Taylor, to Fred's blackmailing activities and, for once, was on his guard. He asked Fred to give him back the letter he had just written to him, making him promise never to reveal anything about their trip to Paris. That small matter resolved, they proceeded to have sex.

When Oscar rushed back to London from Babbacombe at the end of January 1893, it was almost certainly in response to a telegram from Bosie in Salisbury, who had arranged a pleasant surprise for him in the person of Alfred Wood. Wood was an unemployed clerk, or so he claimed. It is more likely that he was well on the way to becoming a professional 'renter'. In January 1893, Wood was homeless and was sharing Alf Taylor's bed at Little College Street. Bosie had met Wood at one of Taylor's tea parties in early January, and they had had sex several times. According to Wood, Bosie telegraphed him and told him to meet Oscar at the Café Royal. Bosie wanted Oscar to share 'Love's burden', to sleep with Wood. What neither Bosie nor Oscar knew was that in Wood's case the cost of 'Love's burden' would prove to be extremely high.

Oscar arrived at the Café Royal first. Wood turned up, as arranged, at nine o'clock in the evening, and was directed to where Oscar was sitting. 'Are you Alfred Wood?' asked Oscar. 'Yes,' Wood replied. Oscar ordered drinks. He liked what he saw. Wood was attractive, very attractive. He was seventeen – not twenty-three as Oscar later tried to claim – a thickset blonde, with a nice face, working-class, fairly presentable and very sexually willing. Oscar whisked Wood off to supper at the Florence. Oscar ordered champagne, and the meal was, according to Wood, 'one of the best to be got'. The private room was convenient, enabling Oscar, so Wood claimed, to 'put his hand inside my trousers beneath the table at dinner and compel me to do the same to him'.

After supper, in the early hours of the morning, Oscar and Wood went back to Tite Street for sex. Oscar let himself in with a latchkey and they tiptoed upstairs to Oscar's bedroom where they had some hock and seltzer. The sex was very successful. After the usual 'kissing &c', Oscar, according to Wood's account, placed his 'person' between Wood's legs, pushing it back and forth until he ejaculated. Oscar gave him £2 in cash that first night, having cashed a cheque at the restaurant so that he could pay Wood for his services. Wood went to Tite Street the next day where the same thing happened. The liaisons continued every day for a week or more. Oscar would write or telegraph to Wood at Little College Street and arrange to meet him, usually between 10pm and midnight at the corner of Tite Street. In court, Wood testified that Oscar had eventually sodomised him. 'It was a long time, however, before I would allow him to actually do the act of sodomy,' Wood said. After the first night, Wood's rates went up. Now Oscar was giving him '£3 or £4 at a time'. Oscar also gave Woods a gunmetal watch on a silver chain. But Woods was contemptuous of this cheap present and sold it for a few shillings. Oscar had also promised to take him away somewhere and to buy him more jewellery. But, as Woods deposed aggrievedly, he 'did not fulfil his promises'. The now daily sexual contact between Oscar and Woods only ceased because Oscar had to return to Babbacombe Cliff. Constance was about to go to Florence, leaving Cyril at Babbacombe.

Oscar's place with Wood was taken by Bosie, who had returned to London for a few days. Wood said that he stayed 'several times' with Bosie at chambers in Jermyn Street, possibly those of Maurice Schwabe. 'Familiarities', as Wood termed them, similar to those which he had engaged in with Oscar, took place on these occasions. But he did not say whether these familiarities included sodomy. Early in February, Bosie was in Oxford and summoned Wood – probably by telegram – to come and see him. Bosie was staying at the Mitre Hotel, and the two of them dined together that evening in the hotel. Wood may not have been presentable enough to sit in the hotel's dining room with a lord, so Bosie lent him one of his suits. Afterwards, they spent the night together in the Mitre and had sex.

The next morning Bosie departed for Salisbury, to his mother's house, and Wood was to return to London. Bosie had paid him for his pleasures and given him a suit, possibly the suit he had lent Wood the previous evening. Oscar's 'madness of kisses' letter was still in the pocket. To make matters worse, before he left, Wood helped himself to a handful of other letters from the new scarlet morocco box Oscar had presented to Bosie – the perfect receptacle, Oscar had assured him, for compromising letters. The letters were from Oscar, Lucas D'Oyly Carte and others, and were indeed compromising. Wood knew that they were worth their weight in gold.

Bosie had been sent down from Oxford for the Hilary, or spring, term, having failed an examination. The *Spirit Lamp* had been taking up all his time and energy, and he needed a private tutor to help him catch up. Lionel Johnson suggested a friend of his, a fellow Uranian, Campbell Dodgson. The plan was for Dodgson to join Bosie at his mother's house in Salisbury, where, Dodgson assumed, they would be able to work undisturbed. He was wrong. 'Bosie's whims have led me dancing on devious ways, many and strange, since Saturday last, and more improbable things have befallen me in these few days than usually brighten my sombre and cowlike existence in as many months,' a slightly dazed Dodgson reported to Johnson. Bosie arrived at his mother's house in Salisbury, 'a flutter of telegrams about him and dishevelled locks', and promptly plunged himself into correspondence about the *Spirit Lamp*.

At lunch the next day, Bosie informed Dodgson 'that we were going to Torquay that afternoon to stay with Oscar Wilde!' Dodgson's account perfectly captures the disorganised, hectic, almost hysterical style in which Bosie conducted his life:

> Our departure was dramatic; Bosie was as usual in a whirl: he had no boots, no money, no cigarettes, and had omitted to send many telegrams of the first importance. Then, with a minimum of minutes in which to catch our train, we were required to overload a small pony chaise with a vast amount of trunks, while I was charged with a fox terrier and a scarlet morocco dispatch box, a gorgeous and beautiful gift from Oscar. After hurried farewells to the ladies, we started on a wild career, Bosie driving. I expected only to drag my shattered limbs to the Salisbury Infirmary, but we arrived whole at the station. When we had been gone an hour or so it occurred to Bosie that he never told Oscar we were coming, so a vast telegram was dispatched from Exeter.

Bosie's stay at Babbacombe was a happy and carefree interlude. There were the children to play with, drives to be taken along the coast, conversation and laughter. Bosie recalls going with Oscar into a hotel in Torquay one morning for breakfast and being told by the waiter that there was some nice fish. 'If you knew the breeding habits of fish you would scarcely call them *nice*,' said Oscar. They spent the rest of the day in a happy cloud of endless absurdities and cheerful nonsense. 'Babbacombe Cliff has become a kind of college or school,' Oscar told Lady Mount-Temple:

for Cyril studies French in the nursery, and I write my new play in Wonderland and in the drawing-room Lord Alfred Douglas – one of Lady Queensberry's sons – studies Plato with his tutor for his degree at Oxford in June. He and his tutor are staying with me for a few days, so I am not lonely in the evenings.

As the self-styled Headmaster of Babbacombe School, Oscar told Dodgson that he really thought he had 'succeeded in combining the advantages of a public school with those of a private lunatic asylum'. Oscar also composed a set of school rules:

Babbacombe School

Headmaster – Mr Oscar Wilde
Second Master – Mr Campbell Dodgson
Boys – Lord Alfred Douglas

Rules.
Tea for masters and boys at 9.30 a.m.
Breakfast at 10.30.
Work. 11.30-12.30.
At 12.30 Sherry and biscuits for headmaster and boys (the second master objects to this).
12.40-1.30. Work.
1.30. Lunch.
2.30-4.30. Compulsory hide-and-seek for headmaster.
5. Tea for headmaster and second master, brandy and sodas (not to exceed seven) for boys.
6-7. Work.
7.30. Dinner, with compulsory champagne.
8.30-12. Écarté, limited to five-guinea points.
12-1.30. Compulsory reading in bed. Any boy found disobeying this rule will be immediately woken up.

Campbell Dodgson's account of the visit to Babbacombe was rather more revealing:

Our life is lazy and luxurious: our moral principles lax. We argue for hours in favour of different interpretations of Platonism. Oscar implores me, with outspread arms and tears in his eyes, to let my soul alone and cultivate my body for six weeks. Bosie is beautiful and fascinating but quite wicked . . . Oscar sits in the most artistic of all the rooms, called 'Wonderland', and meditates on his next play. I think him perfectly delightful, with the fullest conviction that his morals are detestable. He professes to have discovered that mine are as bad. His command of language is extraordinary, so at least it seems to me who am inarticulate, and worship Irishmen who are not. I am going back on Saturday. I shall probably leave what remains of my religion and my morals behind me.

Such insouciance could not last. One evening Bosie lost his temper and there was a hideous scene. There was no reason for the scene; if there ever was, it was forgotten, dwarfed by the emotional explosion it had precipitated. Bosie became contorted by rage, his face livid, snarling obscenities and invective at Oscar. The next morning, Bosie flounced out, leaving Oscar feeling aggrieved and angry. The scene had been so terrible that Oscar was fully determined to end their love affair:

When you left my house at Torquay I had determined never to speak to you again, or to allow you under any circumstances to be with me, so revolting had been the scene you had made the night before your departure. You wrote and telegraphed from Bristol to beg me to forgive you and meet you.

Bosie's extreme penitence, his pathetic entreaties softened Oscar. They met, most probably in Salisbury, and Oscar forgave him. It was the start of a pattern of behaviour of idyllically happy times followed by ugly and terrifying scenes. This in turn resulted in Bosie's tearful pleas for forgiveness and Oscar's granting of plenary absolution.

After this reconciliation they parted. Bosie was to spend a few days more in Salisbury and then join Oscar in London, at the Savoy Hotel, where Oscar had taken rooms at Bosie's special request. But the events at Babbacombe were still preying on Oscar's mind. From the Savoy, Oscar wrote to Bosie 'with a heart of lead' begging him not to make any more scenes:

Dearest of all Boys – Your letter was delightful – red and yellow wine to me – but I am sad and out of sorts – Bosie – you must not make scenes with me – they kill me – they wreck the loveliness of life – I cannot see *you*, so Greek and gracious, distorted by passion; I cannot listen to *your* curved lips saying hideous things to me – don't do it – you break my heart – I'd sooner be rented all day, than have you bitter, unjust and horrid – horrid.

'I'd sooner be rented all day.' It was a strangely prophetic comment. Less than a month later, both Bosie and Oscar found themselves being blackmailed. The renter was none other than Alfred Wood.

215

Feasting with panthers

'Moderation is a fatal thing. Enough is as bad as a meal. More than enough is as good as a feast.'

Oscar arrived at the Savoy at the beginning of March 1893, with Bosie following a few days later. There was, of course, absolutely no necessity for Oscar to stay there. He could easily have returned to Tite Street, or to the suite of rooms he had been renting since the autumn in St James's Place, where he could work undisturbed, or so he said. The Savoy Hotel was the most modern and the most opulent hotel in London, fully lit by electricity and with more bathrooms than any other establishment. The legendary Auguste Escoffier was the *maître de cuisine*. It was Bosie who had been so determined to stay at the Savoy, a determination which may have been the root cause of the hideous scene he made just before flouncing out of Babbacombe. Whatever the cause, the price of reconciliation was, it seemed, a lengthy stay at the hotel. Oscar wrote later how Bosie had 'begged' him to take him there. 'That was indeed a visit fatal to me,' Oscar later reflected.

They stayed until the end of the month, running up an enormous bill. When he was made bankrupt, Oscar owed the Savoy the enormous sum of £63 7s 10d for 'food and drink' consumed there. In a deleted scene in his last play, *The Importance of Being Earnest*, bailiffs call on Algernon to arrest him and incarcerate him in Holloway Prison for an unpaid bill for food and drink run up at the Savoy. 'I really am not going to be imprisoned in the suburbs for having dined in the West End,' says Algernon. 'It is perfectly ridiculous.' The unpaid bill in question is £762 14s 2d. 'How grossly materialistic!' says Miss Prism disapprovingly. 'There can be little good in any young man who eats so much, and so often.'

Oscar and Bosie's stay at the Savoy was certainly grossly materialistic. In *De Profundis*, Oscar recalled the expensive and exquisite luxury of their dinners there: 'the clear turtle soup – the luscious ortolans wrapped in their crinkled Sicilian vine leaves' and 'the heavy amber-coloured, indeed almost amber-scented champagne'. Food and sex became inextricably intertwined. Oscar and Bosie had an insatiable appetite for both, an unquenchable desire to consume, to gorge, to gourmandise. Oscar likened his sexual tastes to food and drink, to the difference between white wine and red wine. 'Suppose I like a food that is poison to other people, and yet quickens me,' he demanded of Frank Harris. 'How dare they punish me for eating of it?' And Bosie wrote a poem about this time, 'A Port in the Aegean', addressed to a boy. Bosie yearned, he wrote, to know 'the honey of thy sugar lips' which was 'food to my starved eyes'. Oscar and Bosie entertained rough trade at a succession of lunches, dinners and suppers, where the best wine and the best champagne flowed, nearly always a prelude to sex. They called boys who were willing to suck their cocks 'gourmets', and they saw themselves as connoisseurs of this rare and delectable cuisine.

Oscar and Bosie's arrival at the Savoy marked the beginning of a two-year binge of intense and unremitting sexual activity with dozens of boys and young men; an endless cycle of pursuit and capture, of desire and satiation. 'I am sorry to say that Oscar drinks more than he ought,' Max Beerbohm told Reggie Turner. 'He has deteriorated very much in appearance, his cheeks being quite a dark purple and fat to a fault. I think he will die of apoplexy.' Oscar and Bosie became intoxicated not only by the copious amounts of alcohol they were consuming every day, but also by the thrill of the chase and the excitement of transgression. The more risks they took, the more they wanted to take. 'It was like feasting with panthers,' Oscar said. 'The danger was half the excitement.'

On the same day that Oscar was checking into the Savoy, Alfred Taylor found himself yet again in the bar of the St James's Restaurant, a place he regularly liked to trawl. His friend and former lover, Edward Harrington, was already there, chatting to a pair of fresh-faced, rosy-cheeked likely lads with thick dark hair slicked down. They could have been country boys. They were reasonably smartly dressed, but Alfred Taylor could sense that they were down on their luck. He noticed the fraying cuffs, the greying linen, the crumpled jackets and creased trousers, and the shoes literally down at heel. Taylor guessed that they were sixteen or seventeen, or thereabouts. Harrington called Taylor over and introduced him to the young men.

It turned out that Charles and William Parker were brothers. Charlie, the younger of the two, had been valet to a gentleman, and William had been a groom. Now both were unemployed and out of cash and were knocking around London in search of a place. They had met Edward Harrington a couple of weeks before and had been staying with him. Harrington had been sleeping with both of them, but Taylor's arrival was in many ways a blessing. The Parkers had been scrounging off Harrington and he had taken, and paid for, his pleasures. Now Harrington was ready to move on.

Alfred Taylor was all smiles. The rosy-cheeked Parkers were a pair of extremely well set-up boys, butch but not too butch, just the right age, and thankfully neither of them wore a moustache. They clearly enjoyed having sex with men. They were also flat broke. It was not going to be difficult at all to persuade them to meet and sleep with various gentlemen of his acquaintance in return for a little cash. Taylor stood everyone another round of drinks, and the conversation turned to sex: 'I can't understand sensible men wasting their money on painted trash like that,' he said contemptuously, referring to the female prostitutes who frequented Piccadilly Circus. 'Many do, though. But there are a few who know better.' 'Now you,' he said with a knowing look at Charlie and William, 'you could get money in a certain way easily enough, if you cared to.' Charlie made what he described as 'a coarse reply' to the effect that he was agreeable 'if any old gentleman with money took a fancy to me'. 'I was agreeable,' Charlie later explained. 'I was terribly hard up.' Taylor laughed and said that 'Men far cleverer, richer and better than you prefer things of that kind.'

That night, Charlie and William went off with Taylor to Little College Street, where they would spend the best part of a month, taking turns to share Taylor's bed. Charlie claimed that during the first week or so, they rarely went out and that Taylor repeatedly committed sodomy with him, calling him by such endearments as 'Darling' and 'My little wife', while William alleged that 'indecencies' took place with Taylor several times.

On 10 March, Alfred Taylor told the Parker brothers that they had all been invited out to dinner by Oscar. Ostensibly it was to celebrate Taylor's birthday two days earlier, but it was also an ideal opportunity for Oscar to meet Charlie and William. They went to Kettner's, not the Solferino, as Charlie later mistakenly claimed in court, and were shown into a private room with a piano and red-shaded candles on the table. Oscar was a few minutes late and arrived full of charming apologies. He sat next to Charlie and was clearly enamoured of him from the outset. According to William, Oscar 'paid all his attention to my brother'. As the meal progressed and the champagne flowed, sex and food commingled. Oscar 'often fed my brother off his own fork or out of his own spoon', said William, adding that Charlie even accepted a preserved cherry from Oscar's own mouth. 'My brother took it into his, and this trick was repeated three or four times.' It was quite clear to everybody that Oscar wanted Charlie to take more than just a preserved cherry into his mouth.

During the course of dinner, Charlie told Oscar that he had ambitions, like so many of the boys Oscar had met, to go on the stage and asked Oscar if there was any way he could help him. For his part, Oscar seemed genuinely interested in the Parkers. 'He showed curiosity about my family and affairs,' said Charlie, 'and I told him my father was a horse dealer.' At the end of dinner Oscar turned to Charlie and proclaimed: 'This is the boy for me!' and asked him if he would come back to the Savoy. 'Yes,' said Charlie. They left Kettner's and hailed a hansom cab. 'Your brother is lucky!' Alfred Taylor remarked to William. 'Oscar does not care what he pays if he fancies a chap.'

When they got to the Savoy they went straight to Oscar's room on the third floor, Room 362, which had a connecting door to Bosie's room, 361. Oscar ordered iced champagne which they drank before Oscar locked the door of the sitting room and took Charlie into the bedroom. They undressed completely and got into bed. 'I was there about two hours,' Charlie testified:

I was asked by Wilde to imagine that I was a woman and that he was my lover. I had to keep up this illusion. I used to sit on his knees and he used to play with my privates as a man might amuse himself with a girl.

Oscar asked Charlie to 'toss him off'. He also sucked Charlie's cock and wanted Charlie to suck him off in turn, to be a 'gourmet'. 'He suggested two or three times that I would permit him to insert "it" in my mouth,' said Charlie. 'But I never allowed that.' The next morning Oscar gave Charlie £2 and told him to come back to the Savoy in a week's time at 11 o'clock in the evening. This was probably the occasion when Oscar presented him with a silver cigarette case, which had cost £1. 'I don't suppose boys are any different to girls in taking presents from them that are fond of them,' Charlie later remarked philosophically in court.

Charlie was emphatic that he and Oscar had had anal sex that first night at the Savoy. At Oscar's second trial, his defence counsel, Sir Edward Clarke, interrogated Charlie. 'You say positively that Mr. Wilde committed sodomy with you at the Savoy?' he asked. 'Yes,' answered Charlie, without any equivocation. In his deposition to Lord Queensberry's solicitors, Charlie had gone no further than indicating that Oscar had only performed 'certain operations with his mouth' – or oral sex. His revelations in court caused a considerable stir. By alleging that Oscar had sodomised him, Charlie was laying Oscar open to new and terrible charges. Sodomy carried a penalty of between ten years and life in prison.

There was strong circumstantial evidence that anal sex had taken place in Oscar's bed, if not with Charlie, then with other boys. Jane Cotta was a chambermaid at the Savoy who remembered Oscar arriving at the hotel on 2 March. She could fix the date, she said, because Oscar arrived on the same day as the third floor re-opened to guests after its spring cleaning. Just after eight o'clock in the morning, on or around 9 March, Oscar rang the bell in his room to summon the chambermaid. Jane Cotta knocked on the door of Room 362 and entered. Oscar was already up but not dressed. He wanted, he said, a fire lit in the room. Jane Cotta left to get wood and coal, but not before she noticed, to her surprise, that there was a boy asleep in the large double bed. Jane Cotta told Lord Queensberry's solicitors that the boy was 'a common boy, rough-looking', aged, as far as she could tell, about fourteen. Later in court, she thought the boy might have been sixteen, eighteen or even nineteen and had 'close-cropped hair and a sallow complexion'. A few minutes later she returned to light the fire. The boy was still asleep in bed.

Later that day, as Jane Cotta was making Oscar's bed, she noticed that the bed sheets 'were stained in a peculiar way'. They were, she told Lord Queensberry's solicitors, in a most 'disgusting' state. She was quite specific about the nature of the stains on the sheets: there was vaseline, there was semen, and there was 'soil', by which she meant human excrement. Oscar's night-shirt, she said, was also stained in the same way.

Jane Cotta pointed out the stains to another chambermaid, Alice Saunders, and went to seek the advice of Mrs Perkins, the Savoy's housekeeper. 'How disgusting!' was Mrs Perkins's first reaction. She advised Jane Cotta not to discuss the matter with any other members of staff. After all, she said, Mr Wilde was sure to have some explanation for the presence of the boy in his bed, and it could all be perfectly innocent. As for the sheets, Mrs Perkins gave directions on how the sheets should be treated to remove the staining. The advice was timely. For this was not the only incidence of staining and soiling on Oscar's sheets, which were, according to Jane Cotta, continually stained in the same way – and often to a much worse degree.

At Oscar's trials, similar evidence was produced from a quite different source. Mrs Mary Applegate was the housekeeper at 28, Osnaburgh Street, a rooming house where Fred Atkins and 'Uncle' Burton had lived for almost two years. Mrs Applegate claimed that Oscar had, to her knowledge, twice visited Fred Atkins there, staying about two hours on each occasion. 'One of the housemaids came to me and complained of the state of the sheets on the bed in which Atkins slept after Mr. Wilde's first visit,' said Mrs Applegate. 'The sheets were stained in a peculiar way.'

Mr Justice Charles, the judge who presided over Oscar's second trial, summarised the evidence of the stained sheets. 'I do not wish to enlarge upon this most unpleasant part of this most unpleasant case,' he told the jury:

> but it is necessary for me to remind you as discreetly as I can that, according to the evidence of Mary Applegate, the housekeeper at Osnaburgh Street, where Atkins used to lodge, the housemaid objected to making the bed on several occasions after Wilde and Atkins had been in the bedroom together. There were, she affirmed, indications on the sheets that conduct of the grossest kind had been indulged in. I think it my duty to remind you that there may be an innocent explanation of these stains, though the evidence of Jane Cotta certainly affords a kind of corroboration of these charges.

The 'innocent explanation' put forward by Sir Edward Clarke, Oscar's defence counsel, was that Oscar had been suffering from diarrhoea, and it was this which caused the staining to the sheets, rather than what one contemporary account of the trials described as the consequences of 'the sodomistic act' which 'has much the same effect as an enema inserted up the rectum. There is an almost immediate discharge, though not, of course, to the extent produced by the enema operation.' When he was confronted about the evidence of the soiled bed-linen at the Savoy in court, Oscar stoutly maintained that the evidence of the housemaids was 'untrue'. 'You deny that the bed-linen was marked in that way described,' Sir Frank Lockwood demanded. 'I do not examine bed-linen when I arise,' Oscar retorted grandly. 'I am not a housemaid.'

Whether the boy that Jane Cotta saw in Oscar's bed was Charlie Parker is impossible to say. The dates more or less fit, but there was a succession of boys going in and out of Oscar's suite. The 'Plea of Justification' filed by the Marquis of Queensberry before his trial for criminally libelling Oscar alleged that Oscar committed 'sodomy and other acts of gross indecency and immorality' with boys on five dates during his stay at the Savoy. Only one boy is named: Charles Parker, who is alleged to have had sex with Oscar on the night of 14 March, as well as 'on divers dates' during March 1893. Oscar's other bed partners at the Savoy, on 7, 9, 20 and 21 March, were 'boys unknown', though Alfred Wood was almost certainly one of them. He testified that Oscar and Bosie summoned him to the Savoy by telegram.

Jane Cotta was not the only employee of the Savoy to find a boy in Oscar's bed. Antonio Migge, who described himself rather grandly as a 'Professor of Massage', detailed what he saw when he walked into Oscar's room one morning to give him his customary massage. 'It was in March, 1893,' he said, 'from the 16th to the 20th of the month':

> On going to the room – I entered after knocking – I saw someone in bed. At first I thought it was a young lady, as I saw only the head, but afterwards I saw it was a young man. It was someone about sixteen to eighteen years of age.

Oscar was dressing himself when Migge came in. He airily told Migge that he felt much better that morning, that he was very busy and would not, after all, have the massage.

Emile Becker, a waiter at the Savoy, claimed that he saw at least five different young men in Oscar's sitting room on different occasions. He served them whisky and sodas, and on one occasion, he brought up a supper of 'chicken and salad for two' for Oscar and a boy, almost certainly Charlie, paying his second visit to the Savoy. The bill for this supper was sixteen shillings, prompting Mr Justice Wills to comment during Oscar's third trial, 'I know nothing about the Savoy but I must say that in my view "Chicken and salad for two. 16s." is very high! I am afraid I shall never have supper there myself.'

The neurotic Edward Shelley was almost certainly another of the five boys seen by Emile Becker. Shelley visited Oscar twice at the Savoy. He had received a letter from Oscar inviting him to 'come and smoke a cigarette' with him. Shelley turned up at the Savoy one morning at about 11am and found Bosie with Oscar. A week or so later, Shelley went again, and this time Oscar was alone. They had tea in Oscar's sitting room and a quarrel took place. In his testimony to the court, Shelley did not give any reasons for the quarrel, but it is not hard to guess that Oscar had attempted to kiss him or fondle him. Shelley said that he told Oscar 'not to be a beast' and that Oscar, by way of expiation, replied 'I am so fond of you, Edward.'

The Marquis of Queensberry also alleged that Oscar committed 'indecencies' with one Herbert Tankard, a hotel pageboy whose pet name was 'Chips'. Herbert Tankard was either thirteen or fourteen when Oscar and Bosie arrived at the Savoy. He told Queensberry's solicitors that he was often in Oscar and Bosie's rooms, delivering and receiving messages. He was clearly something of a favourite with Oscar, who used to greet him with the words 'Hello! Here's my Herbert.' On at least one occasion, Oscar bent down to kiss his Herbert, which startled the boy enormously. Oscar and Bosie were popular among the Savoy pageboys mainly because of their large tips. They invariably tipped them half-a-crown, a huge tip to a pageboy. Both Herbert Tankard and Jane Cotta had heard about these tips and about the kisses that Oscar was in the habit of bestowing on the pageboys. Jane Cotta deposed that she overheard one of the pageboys telling another that Mr Wilde 'is always kissing me' and adding 'but he always tips me 2/6'.

During his stay at the Savoy, Oscar was throwing caution to the winds. He brought back at least five boys to his room and allowed at least two of them to be seen in his bed by hotel staff. His bed sheets were often stained with a mixture of vaseline, semen and excrement. The circumstantial evidence alone was compelling. But what was the truth of the matter? Had Oscar dragged boys back, had sex with them, sodomised them? Did he do this with sublime, blind indifference to who might see these boys in his room and to what Trelawny Backhouse called 'ocular and horrible proofs of a most painstaking *pedicatio*' staining the sheets? Or was he, as his defence counsel claimed, innocent of all charges? The stains on the sheets, said Sir Edward Clarke, could be explained away by repeated attacks of diarrhoea. Besides which, he argued, if Oscar was really guilty of such terrible crimes, why had he been so unconcerned about entertaining boys at the Savoy, and why had he taken so little trouble to conceal the stained sheets in his room? True guilt presupposed cunning, deception and concealment.

There is a curious absence from the trial records and the witness depositions. Bosie is rarely mentioned, and then only in passing. And yet he spent almost as much time at the Savoy as Oscar. Where was Bosie, for example, on the night of Alfred Taylor's birthday dinner at Kettner's, the evening when Oscar first met the Parker brothers? Although Bosie's room adjoined Oscar's, none of the hotel staff who gave evidence at Oscar's trial mentioned seeing Bosie in his room or in Oscar's room. There were good reasons why Bosie's name did not figure prominently. Both Oscar and Bosie's father, the Marquis of Queensberry, were determined to keep Bosie's name out of the scandal as far as they possibly could, and both believed that they were acting out of love for Bosie.

Exactly what went on at the Savoy will never be known, but there is strong evidence that Bosie, as well as Oscar, indulged in 'sodomy and other acts of gross indecency and immorality' with the five boys, including Charlie Parker, named in Queensberry's 'Plea of Justification', and perhaps with several others not named. Like the 'two neighbour jewels in Love's coronet' of Bosie's poem, Oscar and Bosie had adjoining rooms at the Savoy and were ideally placed to share what they poetically termed 'Love's burden'. Hunting singly, or as a pair, they found and brought boys back to Savoy where they both had sex with them, either *à trois*, or sequentially, or both. In an early draft of the statement made to Queensberry's solicitors by Charlie Parker, he recounts how, six weeks or so after his first visit to the Savoy with Oscar, he was invited to call on Oscar at the Albemarle Hotel. Lord Alfred Douglas, Charlie said, was in Oscar's room, and on that occasion *both* men had behaved indecently with him.

Bosie would have wanted to sodomise the boys at the Savoy. He was invariably the penetrator in anal sex; he had a pathological horror of being penetrated. Oscar may have been flexible, perhaps taking both roles, that of penetrator and penetrated. Being sodomised may have been what he was referring to when he spoke to Frank Harris of the 'sting of sexual pleasure'. Significantly, it was Oscar's night-shirt which, according to Jane Cotta, had been stained with a mixture of vaseline, semen and excrement, suggesting that the discharge had come from Oscar's rectum. For an older man to allow himself to be penetrated by a younger one, let alone to enjoy it, may have seemed perverse – if not unthinkable – to some of Oscar's contemporaries, but would hardly shock, or even surprise today. 'What the paradox was to me in the sphere of thought,' Oscar said, 'perversity became to me in the sphere of passion.'

Oscar enjoyed irrumination, or cock-sucking, and there was no reason why he should not have equally enjoyed being sodomised. In the same way, there is no reason why some of the boys and young men he had sex with should not have preferred to penetrate, rather than be penetrated. Some of them, certainly, also enjoyed sex with women and may, or may not, have preferred to be the penetrator in anal sex. The weasly Fred Atkins seems to have hankered after women. Edward Shelley was deeply confused about his sexuality and eventually married. William Allen, one of a gang who blackmailed Oscar and with whom Oscar may have slept, was already married. Ironically, if Oscar had been sodomised by any of the boys he slept with, Sir Edward Clarke's defence that it was diarrhoea that caused the staining on the sheets may have contained a germ of truth.

While he was in prison, Oscar dropped dark hints that at least some of the charges against him were in fact committed by Bosie. In *De Profundis*, Oscar wrote that 'the sins of another were being placed to my account. Had I so chosen, I could on either trial have saved myself at his expense, not from shame indeed, but from imprisonment.' Oscar alleged that the Marquis of Queensberry and his solicitors 'carefully coached' the witnesses who were produced to testify against Oscar 'not in reticences merely, but in assertions, in the absolute transference deliberate, plotted and rehearsed, of the actions and doings of someone else on to me'.

While he was out on bail between his second and third trial, Oscar told Frank Harris that Jane Cotta's evidence was wrong. 'It was not me they spoke about at the Savoy Hotel,' he told Harris. 'It was ——. I was never bold enough. I went to see —— in the morning in his room.' Harris asked Oscar why on earth Sir Edward Clarke had not brought this out at the trial. 'He wanted to,' replied Oscar. 'But I would not let him. I told him he must not. I must be true to my friend. I could not let him.'

Harris's version is backed up by Bosie's account of the affair. After giving in to Oscar's entreaties for him to go abroad just before the first trial, Bosie went to Calais, from where he telegraphed Sir Edward Clarke, 'giving him certain information which I implored him to use, although it was compromising to myself, and again offering to give evidence'. Bosie's offer was peremptorily refused:

In reply I got a 'stern rebuke' from Wilde's solicitors, who informed me that my telegram was 'most improper,' and that Sir Edward Clarke had been greatly upset by receiving it. I was solemnly adjured not to attempt any further interference, 'which can only have the effect of rendering Sir Edward's task still harder than it is already'.

Sir Edward Clarke was quite right to turn down Bosie's offer to take the blame for one of the alleged incidents at the Savoy. He was trying to defend Oscar by pretending that nothing improper had ever taken place there. If Bosie was prepared to admit that it was he, and not Oscar, who had sodomised at least one of the boys at the Savoy, it would undermine the entire foundation of Oscar's defence.

Oscar's belief that he could have saved himself, had he so chosen, by naming Bosie as the culprit is only partly true. It may well have been the case that it was Bosie, and not Oscar, who had sodomised Charlie Parker, or that it was in Bosie's bed, and not Oscar's, that Jane Cotta saw the sleeping, sallow-skinned boy. But to prove that Oscar was innocent of one charge did not and could not exculpate him from the morass of other allegations. Oscar himself admitted that he 'was not in prison as an innocent man'. After he came out of prison 'nothing irritated him more than to meet – as he occasionally did – admirers who refused to believe that he was addicted to the vices for which he was condemned,' said Bosie. 'This used to infuriate him.'

Oscar and Bosie left the Savoy at the end of March. Bosie's father claimed that they had been asked to leave the hotel because of a sexual scandal – 'a stinking scandal' – Queensberry termed it. In his deposition to his solicitors, Queensberry said that he had been told by 'a Lady' that Oscar and Bosie had been refused rooms at the Savoy because of their scandalous behaviour there during their stay in March 1893. Queensberry said that he was so concerned about the allegations that he went to see the manager of the Savoy, who denied the story, as well he might. The Savoy could not afford to have the faintest whiff of scandal clinging to its name. Better to deny the story altogether, than risk its promulgation.

The Savoy came up again a year later, when Queensberry confronted Oscar in Tite Street. 'You were both kicked out of the Savoy Hotel at a moment's notice for your disgusting conduct,' he said. 'That is a lie,' retorted Oscar. But was it? Certainly, Oscar and Bosie never stayed at the Savoy again, although they continued to dine there. But their presence, it seemed, was unwelcome. Once when Frank Harris was dining at the Savoy, he thought he saw Oscar and Bosie leaving the dining room. 'Isn't that Mr. Oscar Wilde?' he asked the head waiter, Cesari. 'Yes,' said Cesari, 'and Lord Alfred Douglas. We wish they would not come here; it does us a lot of harm.' 'How do you mean?' asked Harris sharply. 'Some people don't like them,' answered Cesari.

As Oscar and Bosie started to work their way through the best and the worst of London's rent boys, as well as having sex with a variety of other young men who crossed their path, they were living Oscar's gospel of sexual self-realisation to the full. According to Bosie, Oscar preached that it was the duty of every man to 'live his own life to the utmost', to 'be always seeking for new sensations', and to have what he called 'the courage' to commit 'what are called sins'. They certainly did not lack courage or daring. Thoughts of prosecution, of punishment and disgrace were far away. They were invulnerable and invincible, fearless warriors fighting for a Cause they believed sacred. Sex, they convinced themselves, was not so much a pleasure, as a duty, almost a sacrament. But even as they took their pleasures, gastronomic and sexual, the storm clouds were ominously gathering.

The madness of kisses

'The criminal classes are so close to us that even the policemen can see them. They are so far away from us that only the poet can understand them.'

Oscar's prolonged absence from Tite Street was causing Constance acute unhappiness. She could perhaps understand his taking rooms at St James's Place so that he could work undisturbed by the endless interruptions of family life, and from where he could conveniently attend rehearsals for *A Woman of No Importance*. But she could hardly overlook the fact that her husband was living with a young man in an expensive suite of rooms at the Savoy and rarely – if ever – spent time with her and the children.

Pierre Louÿs visited Oscar at the Savoy several times during March 1893 and was an embarrassed witness when Constance turned up in Oscar's suite one morning, ostensibly to bring him his post from Tite Street. Neither she nor Louÿs could have failed to notice that the bed looked as if it had been slept in by two people. Constance tried to persuade, to plead with Oscar to come home. There were, Louÿs noted, tears in her eyes and tears trickling down her cheek when Oscar loftily explained that he could not return home: it was so long since he had been at Tite Street, he said, that he had quite forgotten the number of the house. Constance tried bravely to smile despite her distress, but it was a bad joke, and a cruel one. Pierre Louÿs was shocked and disgusted by Oscar's insensitivity, by his downright cruelty. He told Henri de Régnier what he had seen and de Régnier quickly spread the word throughout literary Paris. Edmond de Goncourt confided to his diary for 30 April what de Régnier said when Oscar's name came up in conversation.

'Ah! You don't know? After all, he doesn't attempt to conceal it. Yes, he admits to being a pederast. He told me once that he has been married three times in his life: once to a woman and twice to men! After the success of his play in London, he left his wife and three children and moved into a hotel where he lived conjugally with a young British lord'.

It is hardly credible that Constance was unaware that her husband was cohabiting with Bosie at the Savoy. Whatever comforting half-truths about

Oscar's fondness for young men she had forced herself to swallow in the past, she could hardly obliterate the evidence of her own eyes: the bed in which clearly two people had slept. Constance was powerless to do anything. She must have considered separation from Oscar, and perhaps even thought about divorce. In the months that followed, London was awash with gossip that Constance was going to divorce Oscar. The gossip reached the ears of Queensberry. 'I now hear on good authority, but this may be false, that his wife is petitioning to divorce him for sodomy and other crimes,' he wrote to Bosie. 'Is this true or do you not know of it?'

But it is unlikely that Constance seriously considered divorcing Oscar. She knew if she cited Oscar's love affair with Bosie, or his sexual relations with other men, Oscar would be ruined and probably imprisoned. And Constance knew only too well that divorced women, however innocent, however wronged, still faced shame and social ostracism, as did the children of divorced parents. Besides which, Constance still loved Oscar, and the thought of taking any steps which might harm him was anathema to her. Constance decided that she would wait, wait for this particular infatuation with Bosie to burn itself out. After all, Oscar had had passionate friendships with young men before, and in every case the passion had cooled, the infatuation had faded into friendship. Oscar would, she felt sure, come back to her.

Oscar had more pressing worries than the unhappiness of his wife. Both he and Bosie were being blackmailed, this time by Alfred Wood. Wood had stolen a bundle of letters after he had sex with Bosie in Oxford at the Mitre Hotel. One of Oscar's letters, the 'madness of kisses' letter, was found by Wood in the suit which Bosie had given him to make him look respectable enough to dine at the Mitre. The others were filched from the splendid scarlet morocco writing case which ironically Oscar had given to Bosie to keep his compromising letters in.

Seventeen-year-old Alfred Wood had been a clerk, but he was unemployed when he first met Oscar and Bosie through Alfred Taylor. By the time he stole Bosie's bundle of letters, he was well on the way to becoming a professional renter, a boy who sold his body for money and who was not averse to a little blackmail to supplement his income. Through Taylor, who knew and liked most of the boys on the game, Wood had met two of the most notorious and accomplished professional renters then working in London: Robert Cliburn and William Allen. Cliburn boasted that he had rented the Earl of Euston, who had figured so prominently in the Cleveland Street Scandal, and he had already served a prison sentence for blackmail. Cliburn and Allen recognised that the young, fair-haired and attractive Wood might be very useful to them. They cultivated him and told him how easy it was to make a little extra money from the gentlemen he slept with. All he had to do was to keep his eyes sharp open and pocket any letters he saw lying around. It was easy money, they said, and they would do all the dirty work.

Wood was persuaded, and his first theft of letters was from Bosie in Oxford. Shortly after the theft, Wood showed his cache of compromising letters to

Cliburn and Allen. There were four letters from Oscar in all, and Cliburn and Allen read them all before pocketing Oscar's 'madness of kisses' letter. 'This one's quite hot enough,' said Allen. Wood later claimed in court that Allen had 'stolen' the letter from him. It was half true. Cliburn and Allen were wily and experienced renters in their mid-twenties. Alfred Wood was young, inexperienced and not particularly cunning. He stood no chance against Cliburn and Allen. But he kept the other three letters from Oscar, as well as those from Lucas D'Oyly Carte to Bosie, and decided to try and use them to make a little money on his own account.

At some point in March, Wood told Alfred Taylor that he had some letters and wanted money for their return. He was in trouble, serious trouble, and wanted to go to America. He needed the money, he explained, 'to get away from a certain class of person' – by which he meant Cliburn and Allen. Wood was naive but not stupid. He realised that Cliburn and Allen were dangerous and that he was being drawn ever deeper into their net, that he was being used by them as bait to entrap vulnerable men with a taste for teenage boys, or 'chickens'.

Taylor was distraught. It was he who had introduced Wood to Oscar and Bosie, and now they were being blackmailed by him. He went to see them and it was agreed that Oscar should approach his friend and solicitor Sir George Lewis, who had so ably dealt with matters when Bosie was being blackmailed a year earlier. It was the second time Oscar had asked Lewis to help him resolve a case of blackmail, and this time he himself was involved. It was a humiliating experience, and Oscar sensed Lewis's air of disapproval. Nevertheless, the business-like Lewis immediately despatched a stern solicitor's letter to Wood at his lodgings in Langham Street which produced little effect. Anguished entreaties from Alfred Taylor and a sheaf of telegrams finally induced Wood to go to Taylor's rooms at Little College one afternoon towards the end of March where he found Oscar. According to Wood, Oscar was kind and friendly and shook hands with him. Wood appeared to be suitably chastened. 'I suppose you think very badly of me,' he said to Oscar, handing him the three letters which Oscar read straight away. The 'madness of kisses' letter was not among them. 'I don't consider these letters of any importance,' said Oscar. Wood repeated the story he had told Taylor about needing to get away from Cliburn and Allen. 'I'm very much afraid of staying in London,' he said, 'as Allen and other men are threatening me.' Oscar gave Wood £30, two £10 notes and two £5 notes, and apologised that it was not very much. He promised to send Wood a further £5 the following day and arranged to take him for a farewell lunch at the Florence, where they had oysters and champagne and said their goodbyes. When Wood sailed for New York on the S.S. *Servia* in mid-April, Oscar must have heaved a huge sigh of relief.

With Wood safely somewhere in mid-Atlantic, Oscar could give his full attention to the rehearsals for *A Woman of No Importance*, which was due to open in a week's time at the Haymarket Theatre. Oscar had attended rehearsals assiduously, much to the disgruntlement of Herbert Beerbohm Tree, who resented what he saw as Oscar's patronising manner and endless interference in the production. Tree later told Oscar's younger son, Vyvyan, that Oscar was an 'infernal nuisance' during rehearsals, continually interrupting the proceedings with minor objections and impractical suggestions. As the first night drew near, Tree came across Oscar looking through the playscript and asked him what he was doing. 'I am making some slight changes in the text,' replied Oscar. 'But after all, who am I to tamper with a masterpiece?'

Despite Oscar's interference and his tamperings – perhaps even because of them – *A Woman of No Importance* was a great success. Oscar boasted that he had had to turn away 'royalties and bigwigs', such was the pressure for tickets for the premiere. 'The first night was very brilliant in its audience,' Max Beerbohm told Reggie Turner:

> Balfour and Chamberlain and all the politicians were there. When little Oscar came on to make his bow there was a slight mingling of hoots and hisses, though he looked very sweet in a new white waistcoat and a large bunch of little lilies in his coat. The notices are better than I had expected: the piece is sure of a long, of a very long run, despite all that the critics may say in its favour.

That evening Oscar attended a supper given by Blanche Roosevelt, who had invited the celebrated palmist Cheiro to read the hands of her guests. Cheiro sat behind a curtain so that he was unable to identify whose palms he was reading. Oscar, always hugely superstitious, was one of those who was eager to find out what fate held in store. Cheiro later recalled that Oscar's hands struck him as rather fat, and he had no idea that they belonged to one of the most talked-about men in London. His reading was starkly accurate:

> I pointed this case out as an example where the left had promised the most unusual destiny of brilliancy and uninterrupted success, which was completely broken and ruined at a certain date in the right. Almost forgetting myself for a moment, I summed up all by saying, 'the left hand is the hand of a king, but the right that of a king who will send himself into exile.'

Oscar was deeply struck by Cheiro's reading. 'At what date?' he asked rather quietly. 'A few years from now,' Cheiro answered, 'between your forty-first and forty-second year.' Oscar left the party abruptly.

There was fresh trouble the very next morning. Beerbohm Tree was handed a letter written in large, rather ungainly clerkly handwriting on the cheapest writing paper. At the top of the letter was written 'Kindly give this letter to Mr Oscar Wilde and oblige yours', followed by a set of initials. Written out beneath this message was a copy of Oscar's 'madness of kisses' letter to Bosie. Tree, who must have been aware of Oscar's predilections for young men, handed this strange epistle to him. When he read this copy of his love letter to Bosie, Oscar was bewildered, shocked and sick with anxiety. After paying

Alfred Wood to disappear to New York, Oscar had hoped that he had extricated himself from a squalid but not too serious blackmailing incident. Now he realised that the blackmail was not resolved. Far from it. But who was blackmailing him? Had Alfred Wood changed his mind about New York and returned to London to haunt him? Or had someone else got hold of his letter to Bosie? Tree wanted to know what it all meant. He thought – rightly – that the letter spelt trouble.

Oscar was not kept in suspense about the identity of the blackmailer for long. A day or so later, as he left the theatre by the stage door, Robert Cliburn approached him and introduced himself. He told Oscar that he wanted to speak to him about a letter in the possession of a friend of his. Oscar had to think on his feet. He decided to bluff it out. 'I told him that I was rehearsing and could not be bothered, and that really I did not care tuppence about it,' Oscar remembered. Cliburn departed but Oscar knew that he would be back before too long. There were anxious and anguished discussions between Oscar and Bosie. What to do? Pay up and hope for the best? Or pay up and pay again and again and again? They decided on a bold strategy. The letter was decidedly homoerotic in sentiment but not explicitly obscene. Oscar had couched his feelings of love in purple, poetic prose, sprinkled with fine classical allusions to Apollo and Hyacinthus. Why not pretend it was a kind of prose poem, written as a draft and sent to Bosie in his capacity as editor of the *Spirit Lamp*? Better still, get Pierre Louÿs to translate it into French verse and publish it as soon as possible. As an expression of his feelings for Bosie the letter was lethal; but as a published prose poem, it was, well, poetic. Nobody had ever been blackmailed over a poem, especially a published poem.

The plan was speedily put into operation. Pierre Louÿs was happy to translate the letter into French, though he was probably not privy to the real reason why he was doing it. Louÿs's translation appeared in the May issue of the *Spirit Lamp* under the heading 'A letter written in prose poetry by Mr Oscar Wilde to a friend and translated into rhymed poetry by a poet of no importance'. The whole operation had been accomplished in less than a fortnight. Now Oscar was ready for the next encounter with the blackmailers. This time it was Allen who called at Tite Street. Calling on Oscar at home was designed to put the frighteners on him.

Two years later, in court, Oscar recalled the events of that April evening. It was about a quarter to eight and Oscar was about to have dinner. 'I was told by my servant that a Mr Allen wished to see me on particular business, and I went down to the hall.'

'I suppose you have come about my beautiful letter to Lord Alfred Douglas,' Oscar told Allen. 'If you had not been so foolish as to send a copy to Mr Beerbohm Tree, I would gladly have paid you a very large sum of money for the letter as I consider it to be a work of art.'

'A very curious construction could be put on that letter,' Allen replied.

'Art is rarely intelligible to the criminal classes,' Oscar parried.

'A man has offered me sixty pounds for it,' Allen said.

'If you take my advice,' said Oscar, 'you will go to that man and sell my letter to him for sixty pounds. I myself have never received so large a sum for any prose work of that very small length.'

Allen was taken aback at Oscar's bravura. 'This man is out of town,' he said weakly.

'He is sure to come back,' Oscar replied smartly. When he reiterated that he 'would not pay one penny' to get his letter back. Allen started to plead poverty, telling Oscar that 'he hadn't a single penny.'

'He had been on many occasions trying to find me in order to talk about this matter,' Oscar recalled. 'I said that I couldn't guarantee his cab expenses, but that I would gladly give him half a sovereign.'

Allen took the money and went away, but not before Oscar had told him that the letter in question was a prose poem that 'will shortly be published in sonnet form in some delightful magazine'.

'I will send you a copy,' he told Allen as a parting shot.

About five minutes later, Oscar's servant came to him in the library and told him that another man wanted to see him. This time it was Cliburn.

'I really cannot be bothered any more about this letter,' Oscar told him. 'I don't care tuppence for it.' Much to his surprise, Cliburn pulled the original letter out of his pocket.

'Allen has asked me to give it back to you,' said Cliburn.

'Why?' Oscar said. 'Why does he give me back this letter?'

'Well, he says that you were kind to him and there is no use trying to rent you as you only laugh at us.'

Oscar noticed that the letter was extremely soiled. 'I think it quite unpardonable that better care was not taken of an original manuscript of mine,' Oscar said, giving Cliburn half a sovereign. 'I am afraid you are leading a wonderfully wicked life.'

'There is good and bad in every one of us, Mr Wilde,' said Cliburn.

'You are a born philosopher,' Oscar replied.

The version of that evening's events given to the court by Oscar was a wittily embroidered version of the more menacing and nerve-wracking reality. Oscar confessed to Frank Harris that he was in fact 'empty with fear' during these exchanges. This was not quite the end of the affair however. There was another copy of Oscar's 'madness of kisses' letter still in circulation, a copy which, in due course, would find its way into the hands of Queensberry. Nor did Oscar's entanglement with Robert Cliburn end. In fact, the two became friends, and maybe even lovers. Cliburn was noted for his good looks. George Ives, who refers to Cliburn several times in his diary, reported that Oscar once asked Cliburn, the 'notorious boy scoundrel', what his feelings were for his victims. 'What I want to know,' Oscar asked Cliburn, 'is did you ever love any boy for his own sake?' 'No, Oscar, I can't say that I ever did,' he replied. Towards the end of 1893, Ives recorded in his diary that Oscar, with 'his strong love of nature study', had said he 'would much enjoy witnessing a meeting between the bold scheming enchanting panther and the cold disciplined Hellenist'. Oscar clearly wanted to

231

watch Cliburn and Ives having sex. Years later Ives amplified his diary entry. 'I suppose this means that OW would have liked to have witnessed a meeting between me and one Robert Cliburn – a beautiful but very dangerous youth.'

Despite the blackmail, Oscar was growing increasingly heedless, increasingly reckless and increasingly passionate about his sexual preferences. 'Vague whispers, all the more awful, perhaps, for their very vagueness, passed from masculine lips about the horror of his inner life,' wrote the *New York Herald*. 'The whispers did not reach the blazonment of print, they did not pollute the ears of the innocent. None the less, they caused Oscar Wilde to be shunned by those whose taboo is a stigma and a reproach.' Oscar's flaunting of his lovers, and his radical political views on reform of the laws on sex between men, were beginning to alarm and alienate some of those closest to him. According to Robert Sherard, there were 'evil rumours' doing the rounds about Oscar and 'renunciations by mutual friends began to occur, distressing me greatly'.

Frank Harris recorded how he came across Oscar in the Café Royal one day, enthroned between two working-class boys of 'vulgar appearance'. Harris was perhaps describing the Parker brothers. 'They looked like grooms,' Harris wrote. One of the boys struck Harris as depraved, the other was nice-looking in a fresh boyish way, 'with rosy cheeks, hair plastered down in a love-lock on his forehead, and low cunning eyes'. To Harris's astonishment, Oscar was talking about the Olympic Games, talking brilliantly, says Harris, and telling how in ancient Greece:

> the youths wrestled and were scraped with strigulae and threw the discus and ran races and won the myrtle-wreath. His impassioned eloquence brought the sun-bathed palaestra before one with a magic of representment. Suddenly the younger of the boys asked: 'Did you sy they was niked?' 'Of course,' Oscar replied, 'nude, clothed only in sunshine and beauty.' 'Oh, my,' giggled the lad in his unspeakable Cockney way.

Harris 'could not stand it' and left. At about this time, the publisher John Lane and the poet Richard Le Gallienne jointly warned Edward Shelley to keep away from Oscar, and the journalist John Boon recalled how a number of 'very unpleasant stories' about Oscar 'began to be freely circulated in the West End of London'. Boon took the unusual step of warning at least three young men that their friendship with Oscar placed them in 'a dangerous situation'. Boon and Oscar were members of the same club, and one day Boon seized 'a favourable opportunity' of telling Oscar that he should be 'glad if he ceased his visits altogether'. Oscar made no reply but was never seen in the club again. 'By this time,' Boon recalled, 'I think he must have been aware that his life was attracting a great deal of grave criticism.' 'Poor Oscar!' Max Beerbohm told Robbie Ross, after spying Oscar from a cab 'walking with Bosie and some other members of the Extreme Left'. Oscar, said Beerbohm, 'looked like one whose soul has swooned in sin and revived vulgar. How fearful it is for a poet to go to bed and find himself infamous.'

232

'The Extreme Left' was an apt description for those Uranians, like Oscar and Bosie, who were passionately, fiercely committed to the Cause. For Oscar and Bosie, the personal had become the political. To believe in the Cause was not enough. They needed to realise their erotic selves, to proclaim their sexual orientation to the world. 'Nothing is serious except passion,' Wilde wrote in *A Woman of No Importance*. The choice was perfectly clear: promiscuity or puritanism. 'The real enemy of modern life, of everything that makes life lovely and joyous and coloured for us,' wrote Oscar, 'is Puritanism, and the Puritan spirit.' Only those with the courage and vision to sin promiscuously, to squander, to spill their sexual seed have any hope of self-realisation. 'The wildest profligate who spills his life in folly,' Oscar wrote, 'has a better, saner, finer philosophy of life than the Puritan has. He, at any rate, knows that the aim of life is the pleasure of living, and does in some way realise himself, be himself.'

Part of the air of corruption that seemed to swirl around Oscar may have had something to do with the publication of the anonymous and highly sexually explicit novel *Teleny, or The Reverse of the Medal*. It was published in a limited edition of two hundred copies at some point during 1893 by Leonard Smithers, who Oscar once called 'the most learned erotomaniac in Europe'. Smithers issued a 'Prospectus' announcing the forthcoming publication of the novel at the prohibitively expensive price of five guineas a copy:

This work is, undoubtedly, the most powerful and cleverly written erotic Romance which has appeared in the English language during recent years. Its author – a man of great imagination – has conceived a thrilling story, based to some extent on the subject treated by an eminent *littérateur* who died a few months ago – i.e. on the Urning, or man-loving-man. It is a most extraordinary story of passion; and, while dealing with scenes which surpass in freedom the wildest licence, the culture of its author's style adds an additional piquancy and spice to the narration. The subject was treated in a veiled manner in an article in a largely-circulated London daily paper, which demonstrated the subtle influence of music and the musicians in connection with perverted sexuality. It is a book which will certainly rank as the chief of its class, and it may truthfully be said to make a new departure in English amatory literature.

The Prospectus gave rise to considerable speculation among London's wealthier Uranians about the identities of the two men mentioned in connection with the novel. The 'eminent *littérateur*' could be none other than John Addington Symonds, and there were whispers that the 'man of great imagination' who had written what promised to be the most audacious book on love and sex between men was none other than Oscar.

What little is known about the authorship of *Teleny* comes from just one man: Charles Hirsch, a French citizen who had opened a shop in 1889 – the *Librairie Française* in London's West End – specialising in French books.

Among his first and best customers was Oscar who, in addition to purchasing the more usual French publications, also asked Hirsch to order a number of what he called 'Socratic' works. Hirsch was happy to oblige, and supplied Oscar with explicitly homoerotic works in both French and English, including *Monsieur Venus* by 'Rachilde' and Jack Saul's *Recollections of a Mary Ann*. According to Hirsch, Oscar rarely came to his shop alone:

> He was usually accompanied by distinguished young men who seemed to be writers or artists. They showed him a familiar deference. In a word he seemed the Master surrounded by his pupils.

Towards the end of 1890, Oscar turned up at the *Librairie Française* with a wrapped and carefully sealed package and asked Hirsch if he would be kind enough to keep it for him. 'A friend of mine will call for this manuscript and will show you my card,' he told Hirsch. A few days later, one of the young men Hirsch had previously seen in Oscar's company called at the shop, showed him Oscar's card, and took the package away. Some days later, this young man returned the package to Hirsch and informed him that another young man would call for it shortly. In all, three young men called for and returned the package. On the last occasion, Hirsch noticed that it had been badly wrapped and left unsealed. He could not resist investigating. Gingerly untying the strings, he unwrapped a manuscript entitled *Teleny*, written in several different hands with numerous crossings-out, emendations and additions. 'It was evident to me,' Hirsch recalled many years later, 'that several writers of unequal merit had collaborated on this anonymous but profoundly interesting work.'

John Gray and Robbie Ross may well have been two of the three young men who had a hand in writing *Teleny*. But Hirsch was convinced that Oscar's was the dominant voice. When he read the manuscript, Hirsch noted that some of the furnishings and decorative details of René Teleny's rooms were remarkably similar to those Hirsch had noticed in Oscar's house in Tite Street where he had had occasion to call and deliver books. 'I can easily see why, with his wife, children and servants, he could not leave this compromising, and extra-licentious manuscript at home,' Hirsch wrote.

Teleny tells the story of the love affair between Camille Des Grieux and René Teleny. Like many men, Des Grieux – whose initials curiously echo those of Dorian Gray – has 'always struggled against the inclinations of my own nature' and has made several, abortive attempts to love women. When he finally confronts the fact that he is attracted to other men, Des Grieux is disgusted and revolted. He is on the point of suicide when he is rescued, spiritually and sexually, by the darkly handsome pianist René Teleny to whom Des Grieux is irresistibly drawn by the magical power of his music. In his treatise on sex between men, *Uranisme et Unisexualité*, André Raffalovich suggested that the word 'musical' had a special sense for men who loved men, that to be 'musical' not only signified the special affinity for music experienced by men who loved men, but also functioned as a code-word indicating their sexual orientation. Certainly, by the beginning of the twentieth century, 'being musical' was in comparatively common usage in England as a badge of sexual orientation.

Sex with Teleny is not only profound, potent and rapturous, it is also revelatory. The morning after the night before, Des Grieux wakes up; his shame and self-loathing at his unnatural desires are banished, replaced by pride and exultation:

> Far from being ashamed of my crime, I felt that I should like to proclaim it to the world. For the first time in my life I understood that lovers could be so foolish as to entwine their initials together. I felt like carving his name on the bark of trees, that the birds seeing it might twitter it from morn till eventide; that the breeze might lisp it to the rustling leaves of the forest. I wished to write it on the shingle of the beach, that the ocean itself might know of my love for him, and murmur it everlasting.

Teleny has received short shrift from biographers and critics. It has often been described – unfairly – as crude and coarse. In its detailed and powerful descriptions of sex between Des Grieux and Teleny, the book is certainly extremely explicit, but it is at the same time poetic, passionate and quite beautiful, and certainly not unworthy of Oscar's hand. Unlike much Victorian pornography, the central theme of *Teleny* is rapture: rapture at the discovery of the erotic self and rapture at erotic fulfillment. *Teleny* is as much about love as about sex. From shame to rapture, Des Grieux's erotic odyssey follows that made by Oscar and by many of his friends and contemporaries. The story ends unhappily when Teleny commits suicide, and Des Grieux is caught up in the ensuing scandal. Des Grieux's final words have an ominously prophetic ring:

> Then, Heaven having revealed my iniquity, the earth rose against me; for if Society does not ask you to be intrinsically good, it asks you to make a goodly show of morality, and, above all, to avoid scandals.

The proposed publication of *Teleny* may have contributed to John Gray's final rupture with Oscar. In March 1893, John Gray was the first of Oscar's close friends to abruptly terminate their friendship. He wrote to Pierre Louÿs, 'About the falling out with Oscar. I say it to you only and it is absolute. It will suffice that I recount its origins when I see you in London.' Gray had become increasingly unhappy about his friendship with Oscar. It was more than jealousy at Bosie's unassailable position of primacy in Oscar's affections, though Gray would have had to be a saint not to feel slightly jealous at being ousted as Oscar's officially beloved. Oscar was making waves, drawing unwelcome attention to himself and to his friends, including Gray.

Swirling rumours were solidifying into specific allegations. Oscar had left his wife, and had taken up with Lord Alfred Douglas. Oscar had been thrown out of the Savoy after an incident with a boy. Oscar had been seen in the Café

Royal with two obvious renters. Max Beerbohm wrote – not altogether in jest – that, had Oscar lived in the days of Socrates, he, too, would have been impeached on charges of 'corrupting the youth'. Indeed, Beerbohm wrote, 'the harm that Mr. Wilde has done within a certain radius is incalculable'. Beerbohm thought John Gray was 'one of the corrupt', certainly corrupted and perhaps corrupting, or on the verge of becoming corrupting. Oscar was not only 'preaching corruption', said André Raffalovich, he was also practising it, by seducing vulnerable young men, turning their heads, riding roughshod over their feelings and emotions.

Gray, now a Catholic convert, no longer wanted to be part of what he saw as this web of corruption, blackmail and prostitution surrounding Oscar and Bosie. Nor did he wish to be identified with the Cause, to be seen as part of a crusading, proselytising movement which, as far as he was concerned, could only damage his reputation and his career. If Oscar was indeed the chief author of *Teleny*, and Gray one of the three young men who had helped to write the novel, then the prospect of its publication would have appalled and enraged him. It would be a reminder as well as a constant reproach of a period in his life he now preferred to forget.

In any case, Gray could afford to take the moral high ground. He was no longer dependent on Oscar's goodwill, his literary connections or his financial assistance. For several months now, André Raffalovich had been assiduously courting him, offering him not only his patronage but also his single-minded devotion. Oscar had been prepared to pay John Lane to publish Gray's first volume of verse, *Silverpoints*, but at the very last minute, Raffalovich stepped in instead. Gray's new-found reticence about his sexual orientation was reflected in his choice of poems for the book. He decided not to include some of his more openly homoerotic poems. The book was an exquisite and expensive flop. Writing in the Uranian-inclining magazine *The Artist and Journal of Home Culture*, Theodore Wratislaw said that Gray was 'a young man with a promising career behind him'. Wratislaw may have been making a rather acid reference to Gray's physical attractions and what was seen as his successful exploitation of these assets. When Ada Leverson saw 'the tiniest rivulet of text meandering through the very largest meadow of margin' in *Silverpoints*, she suggested to Oscar that he should 'publish a book *all* margin; full of beautiful unwritten thoughts'.

Pierre Louÿs was not long behind John Gray in terminating his friendship with Oscar and was rather more forthcoming about his reasons. Bosie was the problem. Louÿs disliked Bosie and the more he saw of Bosie, the more he disliked him. The visit Louÿs made to London in the spring of 1893 confirmed all his doubts. Louÿs wrote to his brother Georges three days after the premiere of *A Woman of No Importance* to say that 'Oscar Wilde has been charming on my behalf, I have lunched with him almost every day. But I should have been glad if he had provided different company.' In Paris, three weeks later, Louÿs called on Oscar at the Hôtel des Deux-Mondes. There was a terrible scene. Louÿs began by accusing Oscar of cruelty to Constance and other 'frightful things' concerning Bosie. Oscar responded by telling Louÿs that he should not believe every piece of tittle-tattle he heard, that it was not fair and that, in any case, he did not recognise Louÿs's right to judge him. Louÿs told Oscar that he had said what he had come to say, that he was not going to stay a moment longer and that Oscar would have to choose between his friendship and his 'fatal connection' with Bosie. Needless to say, Oscar chose Bosie. 'I wanted to have a friend,' was Oscar's parting comment to Louÿs. 'From now on I will only have lovers.'

It was an appropriate comment, given the circumstances. After the trauma of being blackmailed, first by Alfred Wood and then by Cliburn and Allen, Oscar was spending a wild few days in Paris with Bosie, Trelawny Backhouse, then a young Oxford undergraduate, and an actor, probably Harry Barford. Everyone seemed to be sleeping with everyone else. Oscar and Trelawny Backhouse were enjoying a lively sexual relationship. 'Sexual relations were frequently commemorated between us,' Trelawny recalled, although Oscar admitted to him that he preferred sleeping with rough trade 'because their passion was all body and no soul'. Their sexual relationship was destined not to last; Oscar began by eulogising Trelawny's 'pomegranate lips' and his 'alluring pedicandial presentment' but ended by telling the bewildered undergraduate, 'My poor Trelawny, you are simply banal. I am sorry for you, because you are so ugly!'

And – as if to symbolise Oscar's 'better, saner, finer philosophy of life' – it was on this trip to Paris that he underwent, according to Trelawny Backhouse, 'a mock marriage in the Hotel Bristol with a catamite in female attire from the gutter and the results of their union were concrete and visible (as formerly at the Savoy Hotel) on the drapery of the nuptial couch'.

Brazen candour

'Really, if the lower orders don't set us a good example, what is the use of them?'

Bosie and Oscar returned from their brief trip to Paris in May 1893, Bosie to Oxford and Oscar to London. Bosie did almost no work during this summer term, instead preferring to continue to concentrate his efforts on the *Spirit Lamp*. But the lovers saw a great deal of each other. Bosie was often in town, and Oscar visited Oxford almost every weekend, going up on Saturday morning and returning on Monday.

Oscar's presence in his alma mater did not escape the satirical attentions of the editors of the *Ephemeral* who published a scathing article on a playwright they called 'Ossian Savage', 'a man of coarse habit of body and of coarse habits of mind'. The *Ephemeral* also ran a 'missing word competition' for their readers:

> To – –
> He often writes of things with brazen candour
> *Non inter Christianos nominanda.*

This doggerel was a clear reference to sodomy and its conventional Latin appellation, the *crimen tantum horribile*, the crime so horrible that it was 'not named among Christians'. And the unnamed addressee of the doggerel was clearly Oscar. But when Bosie invited the editors of the *Ephemeral* to meet Oscar, they were quickly charmed out of their antipathy towards him.

Oxford had other attractions for Oscar, in the person of sixteen-year-old Walter Grainger. Grainger was employed as a servant in the house where Bosie shared rooms with his friend Lord Encombe, known as 'Jane', at 34, High Street. Grainger was, according to Oscar, 'a peculiarly plain boy', 'unfortunately very ugly' – so ugly that Oscar said he pitied him for it. Ugly or not, Oscar had sex with Grainger on many occasions. Bosie had probably already had sex with him and passed him on to Oscar. When Grainger gave his statement two years later to Queensberry's solicitors, he said that, on the Sunday morning of Oscar's first visit to 34, High Street, he had gone into Oscar's room to wake him, and Oscar had kissed him. The next morning,

Grainger again went in to wake Oscar. On this occasion, he claimed, Oscar started to caress him, unbuttoning his trousers and playing with his 'private parts'. Afterwards Oscar gave the boy ten shillings. Oscar returned to Oxford the next weekend, and Grainger again came into his room to wake him up on the Sunday morning. This time, Oscar pulled Grainger's trousers and undergarments down and persuaded the boy to lie down on his back on the bed. According to Grainger, Oscar 'placed his penis between my legs and satisfied himself'.

Sex with Grainger was now a fixture almost every weekend. But, disturbingly, in an effort to ensure Grainger's silence, Oscar threatened him, telling him that if he told anyone about what had happened, he would be in 'very serious trouble'. Oscar was being cautious. He did not want the boy blabbing to his friends or family about what had gone on. By now both he and Bosie had had enough experience of being blackmailed to last them a lifetime. It was not that Oscar coerced Grainger into having sex. Although he was not a renter, or a male prostitute, Grainger was clearly willing to gratify the whims of gentlemen, especially if it meant a large tip. But it was probably not the first time – or the last time – that Oscar warned boys he had sex with that they would get into serious trouble if they breathed a word about it.

In June, Bosie suddenly left Oxford. He had not taken his degree. There were rumours that he had been asked to leave on account of an unsavoury scandal involving a local boy and blackmail. But no evidence has yet come to light to suggest that this was indeed the case. Like his father before him, Bosie may have decided that a degree would be of limited use to him in the literary life that seemed to be beckoning. 'I really don't care twopence about having a degree,' he said, eerily using the self-same words his father had uttered when he left Oxford without a degree thirty years earlier. Bosie's first impulse was to telegraph to Oscar in London, begging him to come to Oxford. Oscar did so at once. Bosie announced that he did not like 'under the circumstances' to return home to his mother's house. Instead, he wanted to go to Goring-on-Thames to spend a few quiet days with Oscar.

They arrived in Goring on 12 June and took two bedrooms and a sitting room at the Miller of Mansfield Hotel. Bosie liked Goring and, during the week of their stay, they saw a large and attractive house, rather misleadingly called the Cottage, which was available to rent. Bosie persuaded Oscar to take it, not that Oscar needed much persuasion, whatever he said later. Within a week, they were in possession of the Cottage. It was their first home together. They would live the literary life in this idyllic corner of England. Oscar would write his next play, and Bosie, in between writing poetry, would translate Oscar's *Salomé* into English. For recreation, there were the gardens, and there was the river. They would spend the perfect English summer there, perfectly happy. There was even room for Constance and the boys.

In a fit of optimism, Oscar took the Cottage for twelve months. At two hundred guineas a year it was expensive. Apart from the rent, the house needed staffing: a butler, a pair of parlourmaids, a cook and a scullerymaid were the minimum complement needed. With food and drink and other expenses, the costs for the three months that Oscar and Bosie actually spent at the Cottage amounted to a staggering £1,340. The rent and the servants' wages were the least of it. By far the largest proportion was spent on costly food and drink, especially drink.

On about 20 June, just a week after their arrival in Goring, the 'peculiarly plain' Walter Grainger received a telegram from Oscar telling him to come to the Cottage at one o'clock the next day. Grainger was given the rather grand title of 'under-butler'. His official duties were to assist the butler, one Harold Kimberley, who had formerly been in the service of the Marquis of Queensberry. Unofficially, Grainger was there for Oscar to have sex with. Two or three nights after his arrival at the Cottage, Oscar went into the boy's bedroom, woke him up and told him to come into his bedroom quickly and quietly. This was easily accomplished, as Grainger had been given the room next to Oscar's, no doubt to facilitate such night-time manoeuvres. Oscar 'acted as before to me', Grainger deposed, 'except that he worked me up with his hand and then made me spend with his mouth'. The same thing happened almost every other night: Oscar would have inter-crural sex with Grainger and suck him off.

According to Grainger, Oscar continued to threaten him. He said in his deposition to Queensberry's solicitors that Oscar told him that he would be in serious trouble, that he would go to gaol, if anyone found out what was going on. He was, he said, 'frightened' by Oscar's threats of dire consequences. If Grainger was telling the truth, Oscar's threats reflect little credit upon him, and today would be condemned as a classic stratagem of sexual abuse. But was Grainger telling the truth? The statement he made sounds plausible. Yet it is possible that his account of the threats made by Oscar was fabricated. Grainger's statement was taken down by Queensberry's solicitors, who were gathering evidence to use against Oscar. Did they 'prompt' Grainger to record these threats of dire consequences? If it was a prompt, why was Grainger the only one of the witnesses persuaded to speak of threats? And, if it was true, why was nothing made of such threats during the trials?

It was not long before the secret of Oscar's night-time trysts with Walter Grainger was out. One night, when Grainger was lying naked in Oscar's bed, and Oscar was out of the room, Harold Kimberley, the butler, looked into the room. Kimberley said nothing, but saw everything. Soon, the other servants would get to know what was going on between Oscar and the young under-butler.

Oscar was trying to write his next play, but life was so pleasant he found it hard to concentrate. Oscar and Bosie's life together was idyllic. Towards the end of his life, Bosie lamented that 'the *fun* of being with Oscar', the sheer, shimmering joy of being in his company, had been overshadowed by the catastrophe which engulfed them. It was not, Bosie said, 'his epigrams or more studied humour' which created this aura of joy, 'but his continuous light-heartedness and love of laughter. Everyone felt gay and carefree in his company . . . he bubbled all the time with frivolous, happy humour.'

'I have done no work here,' Oscar wrote to Charles Ricketts from Goring. 'The river gods have lured me to devote myself to a Canadian canoe, in which I paddle about. It is curved like a flower.' And Oscar told a young man called Stuart that his interest was divided between paddling a canoe and planning a comedy, and he was 'finding that life in meadow and stream is far more complex than life is in streets and salons'. The summer was warm, and Oscar and Bosie were in the habit of stripping off in the garden and turning the garden hose on each other to cool down. On one occasion, the vicar called and, finding his way to the garden, discovered Oscar, enveloped in a bath towel. The vicar was not amused. 'You've no idea the sort of face he pulled,' Oscar told Frank Harris. 'I am delighted to see you,' Oscar told the vicar, pointing to Bosie lying naked on the grass. 'You have come just in time to enjoy a perfectly Greek scene.' The vicar gasped, went very red and fled to the accompaniment of gales of laughter. The vicar was not slow to disseminate the 'perfectly Greek scene' he had stumbled across at the Cottage.

Constance paid four extremely short visits to Goring in the course of the summer. Her husband had taken a large house for a year where he and a young man had effectively set up home together. She must have felt affronted. It was galling for her to visit a house where she felt like a guest. But the boys needed to see their father, and Constance still hoped that she would, in the long run, prevail in Oscar's affections.

Gertrude Simmonds – a young woman who had been very recently employed by Constance as governess to Cyril and Vyvyan – accompanied Constance and the boys to Goring. It was not long before she was let into the secret of Walter Grainger's night-time peregrinations into Oscar's bed. One of the parlourmaids, Alice Saunders, told her about it first. Alice Saunders had heard it from Harold Kimberley, and it was not very long before the three of them were discussing the matter in hushed tones. Gertrude Simmonds recalled that she thought it very 'peculiar'. She started to notice other small things. Early in July, the family went to see the fireworks display at the Henley Regatta. It was during the fireworks, Gertrude Simmonds said, that she heard Mr Wilde's voice behind her and turned round. Oscar was speaking to George Hughes, the boy he employed to look after the boats. 'Much to my surprise,' she recalled, 'Mr Wilde had hold of his arm and was patting his shoulder familiarly. I was very much surprised.'

The unusual goings on at the Cottage were common knowledge below stairs and the subject of village gossip. According to the proprietor of the Miller of Mansfield, there was gossip in the village about Oscar. Some villagers had said that they would like to 'punch him'. Constance must have sensed an atmosphere: strange looks of commingled pity and contempt from her servants, and simmering, if inexplicable, hostility from the villagers. It was no wonder that she disliked spending time at Goring, and left the boys there under the care of Gertrude Simmonds.

Like any couple living together for the first time, Oscar and Bosie had their share of rows and reconciliations. But one row in particular stood out. A group of Bosie's friends from Oxford had come to spend a weekend at the Cottage. 'The morning of the day they went away,' Oscar recalled in *De Profundis*, 'you made a scene so dreadful, so distressing that I told you we must part':

> I remember quite well, as we stood on the level croquet-ground with the pretty lawn all round us, pointing out to you that we were spoiling each other's lives, that you were absolutely ruining mine and that I evidently was not making you really happy, and that an irrevocable parting, a complete separation was the one wise philosophic thing to do.

Oscar gave no clue as to the cause of the row. It may have had something to do with Bosie's Oxford friends. Oscar may have flirted with one or more of them a little too decidedly, arousing Bosie's ire. Nether Oscar nor Bosie were in the least bit jealous of each other's sexual adventures. That was merely 'trade'. But a handsome and articulate undergraduate from Oxford posed a significant emotional threat. Whatever the cause of the row, Bosie left 'sullenly' after lunch, leaving behind one of his 'most offensive letters' with the butler, to be handed to Oscar after his departure. But before three days had elapsed, Bosie was telegraphing Oscar begging to be forgiven and to be allowed to return. Oscar relented and it was perhaps to mark this reconciliation that, as a present for Bosie, he extravagantly ordered – but never paid for – 'four wire baskets filled with flowers' from the Royal Berkshire Floral Establishment in Reading. Everything was as it had been before, or almost so.

While Oscar was busy with Walter Grainger, Bosie was having his own sexual adventures. Earlier in the year he had met Robbie Ross, and some sort of relationship ensued, sexual as well as emotional. 'Ross was by way of being devoted to me in those days,' Bosie recalled in his *Autobiography*:

> If I had followed his example and kept the letters he wrote to me, I could have showed that he professed devotion and admiration for me in as extravagant terms as those used by Oscar.

Devotion and admiration. Bosie was easy to admire, easy to fall in love with, and easy to become devoted to. Many of those in Oscar's circle, like George Ives and Reggie Turner, fell head over heels in love with the young and impossibly beautiful aristocrat and poet, who combined a boyish sense of freshness and purity with a compelling lust for life and sex. Many years later, Robbie wrote to his friend and amanuensis, Christopher Millard, about his relationship with a young man called Freddie Smith. 'Freddie is the one friend besides Oscar and Douglas for whom I have made sacrifices.' By bracketing Bosie's name with those of Oscar and Freddie Smith, his avowed lovers for whom he had also made sacrifices, Robbie implies that his relationship with Bosie was one of the most important in his life.

Robbie was a 'slender, attractive, impulsive boy' when they first met, Bosie recalled. As he did with Oscar, Bosie was happy to share his sexual conquests with Robbie, and vice versa. They were the best of friends, sometimes lovers and, until force of circumstance caused them to part in the autumn of 1893, spent a great deal of time together. Robbie was a frequent and welcome guest at Sybil Queensberry's house in Cadogan Place. In a letter to his older brother, Percy, written in October 1893, Bosie described Robbie as 'one of my greatest friends and one of the best fellows that ever lived'.

Despite the erotic complexities of country living and the lure of the river gods, Oscar did manage to sketch out the scenario and some of the dialogue for what was to be his third society comedy, *An Ideal Husband*. Like all his work, the play is heavily autobiographical. Oscar told his friends Marigold and Orchid – Charles Shannon and Charles Ricketts – that the play 'contains a great deal of the real Oscar'.

The plot revolves around forty-year-old Sir Robert Chiltern, Under-Secretary for Foreign Affairs and rising star in the Liberal government, tipped for Cabinet rank. Sir Robert's wife Gertrude – quite probably named after the Wildes' governess, Gertrude Simmonds – is 'a woman of grave, Greek beauty', possessed of a faultless, if unbending, sense of moral rectitude. Significantly, 'grave' was also the epithet Oscar applied to Constance during their engagement, and Constance's grave beauty was also allied to a strong sense of what is right, a belief in what Constance herself described as 'perfect morality'.

The play opens with a brilliant evening reception for the cream of London society at Sir Robert's mansion in Grosvenor Square, which is marked by the unexpected arrival of the fascinating Mrs Cheveley, elegant, orchid-like, with red hair, pale skin and grey-green eyes. She has come to blackmail Sir Robert. Many years ago, as a young, ambitious but penniless politician, Sir Robert leaked the government's secret plans to invest in the Suez Canal to a mysterious Austrian financier, Baron Arnheim, enabling the Baron to make a large fortune from buying and selling the shares. Sir Robert was rewarded handsomely with a large sum of money and advice on how to invest it. In time Sir Robert became a wealthy man and married a wealthy woman.

The Baron has since died, but the fascinating Mrs Cheveley is in possession of the letter Sir Robert Chiltern wrote to him about the Suez Canal shares, a letter Sir Robert thought had been destroyed. Mrs Cheveley's mission is clear. Unless Sir Robert publicly commits the British government to back the fraudulent Argentine Canal Company scheme, Mrs Cheveley will make sure that his incriminating letter reaches the newspapers. 'Suppose when I leave this house,' she tells him, 'I drive down to some newspaper office, and give them this scandal and the proof of it!':

> Think of their loathsome joy, of the delight they would have in dragging you down, of the mud and mire they would plunge you in. Think of the hypocrite with his greasy smile penning his leading article, and arranging the foulness of the public placard.

'Yours is a very nasty scandal,' Mrs Cheveley tells Sir Robert. 'You couldn't survive it.' Oscar's evocation of the miring of Sir Robert Chiltern in scandal accurately reflected what he knew might have happened to him, had an incriminating letter – his 'madness of kisses' letter – been made public. Oscar's recent experiences of blackmail – first by Alfred Wood, and then by Allen and Cliburn – are reflected in the fictional blackmail of Sir Robert Chiltern. And like Chiltern, Oscar's blackmailers did not merely hold in their hands the power to destroy his career and his reputation, they could also destroy his marriage.

In both Oscar's life and in Sir Robert's life, the blackmailer is sexually attractive, charming and delightful – as well as decidedly dangerous. Oscar recognised, in his life and in his fictions, that there is an essential bond of commonality between blackmailer and victim. Mrs Cheveley says of Sir Robert: 'He and I are closer than friends. We are enemies linked together. The same sin binds us.' The same sin, sex between men, bound Oscar and Bosie and their blackmailers together. Blackmail is 'the game of life as we all have to play it sooner or later', Mrs Cheveley tells Sir Robert. Oscar had already played the game, and won. Eventually, with luck and the help of his good friend Lord Goring, Sir Robert Chiltern too wins the game. In a morally ambiguous ending, the incriminating letter is tricked away from Mrs Cheveley, and Sir Robert and his reputation do not merely survive, but prosper. Sir Robert is offered a seat in the Cabinet, ironically because of his perceived 'high character, high moral tone, high principles'.

But it is not the blackmail, nor even its happy resolution, which gives *An Ideal Husband* its force and vigour. The power of the play lies in its interrogation of what is truly moral and truly immoral, especially when it comes to sex and marriage. There are many parallels between the situations of Sir Robert and Lady Chiltern and Oscar and Constance. Like Oscar, Sir Robert has committed a terrible sin and hides a terrible secret from his wife and the world. That Oscar's sins are plural and sexual, as opposed to Sir Robert's single, financial sin, makes little difference. Sir Robert speaks of his single sin as if it were, in fact, plural and sexual. He describes his sin as 'my secret and my shame', evoking the Uranian meaning of shame as love and sex between men, and defends his conduct to his greatest friend, Lord Goring, in terms that Oscar might have used to defend the courage of his sexual convictions: 'Do you really think that it is weakness that yields to temptation?' Sir Robert demands of Lord Goring:

> I tell you that there are terrible temptations that it requires strength, strength and courage, to yield to. To stake all one's life on a single moment, to risk everything on one throw, whether the stake be power or pleasure, I care not – there is no weakness in that. There is a horrible, a terrible courage. I had that courage.

Sir Robert's strength and courage in yielding to temptation are counterpointed by his wife's inflexible and overwhelming sense of moral certainty. Gertrude Chiltern as 'pitiless in her perfection', 'cold and stern and without mercy'. When Mrs Cheveley, who happens to have been at school with Gertrude Chiltern, reads one of her letters she exclaims: 'The ten commandments in every stroke of the pen, and the moral law all over the page.'

Much of the drama of *An Ideal Husband* is pivoted on Sir Robert's reluctance to disclose his terrible secret and his wife's accidental discovery of that secret. Gertrude Chiltern confronts her husband and demands to know if there is any truth in the aspersions cast by Mrs Cheveley – 'any secret dishonour or disgrace', any 'act of shame' or any 'horrible secrets' in his life. If there were, then the inevitable consequence would be that their lives would 'drift apart', that they would become 'entirely separate'.

Oscar had any number of horrible secrets and numerous acts of Uranian shame in his life. Although Constance may not have come right out and asked him about his relationships with young men, especially his relationship with Bosie, she knew that she had lost her husband to a man. Had Oscar and Constance drifted apart? Were they leading almost separate lives? Certainly, the couple had seen very little of each other during 1893. Constance had been in Florence for the early part of the year. When she returned, Oscar was ensconced at the Savoy with Bosie, and then in his rooms at St James's Place or at the Albemarle Hotel, before taking the Cottage at Goring. Oscar did spend some time at Tite Street, but it must have been measured in days, rather than weeks. And Constance's four brief visits to Goring with the children suggest that she and Oscar were in effect separated, spending time together for the sake of the children.

Although Sir Robert and Oscar are far from ideal husbands, the play ends with a heart-felt plea for forgiveness, for understanding. 'Women are not meant to judge us, but to forgive us when we need forgiveness,' Lord Goring tells Lady Chiltern. The unconditional, unequal love of a woman for her husband holds within itself the power of redemption. It was as if Oscar was asking Constance for her forgiveness and for her understanding. Sooner or later, he knew he would have to seek redemption in the love of his wife. And Constance would not fail him.

A pugilist of unsound mind

'The basis of every scandal is an absolutely immoral certainty.'

Though much of *An Ideal Husband* appears to refer to Oscar himself, Oscar rather more sensationally may have been alluding to a real Liberal politician. The character of Sir Robert Chiltern, a rising Liberal politician and Under-Secretary of State for Foreign Affairs, may have been based on Archibald Philip Primrose, fifth Earl of Rosebery, who had just been appointed Foreign Secretary for the second time when Oscar was writing the play.

Like the forty-year-old Sir Robert Chiltern, the forty-six-year-old Lord Rosebery belonged to the younger, coming generation of Liberal politicians who were waiting for the passing of Gladstone to realise their ambitions. Rosebery was a rising star of the Liberal Party and had already been talked about as a future Prime Minister, just as Sir Robert had been told by Lord Caversham that 'we shall have you Prime Minister, some day'. Oscar wrote a particularly detailed description of Sir Robert Chiltern as 'a man of forty, but looking somewhat younger' who was 'clean-shaven, with finely-cut features, dark-haired and dark-eyed'. Oscar's description of Sir Robert chimes remarkably with contemporary portraits of Rosebery. Like Sir Robert, Rosebery was a man in early middle age, and he was unusually clean-shaven in an era of whiskers, moustaches and beards. Rosebery's features were also fine-cut, and his hair was dark. Only their eyes differed: while Sir Robert's were dark, Rosebery's were a piercing blue. Sir Robert was possessed of 'a nervous temperament, with a tired look'; there was, Oscar wrote, 'nervousness in the nostrils, and in the pale, thin, pointed hands'. Rosebery suffered from chronic exhaustion and was renowned for his nervous temperament, which often manifested itself in prolonged bouts of insomnia so severe that doctors feared for his sanity, if not his life.

Many of the traits of character ascribed by Oscar to Sir Robert could equally well have been attributed to Rosebery. Sir Robert was, Oscar wrote:

A personality of mark. Not popular – few personalities are. But intensely

246

admired by the few, and deeply respected by the many. The note of his manner is that of perfect distinction, with a slight touch of pride.

Rosebery was also a personality of mark, intensely admired by his supporters, and widely respected both inside and outside the Liberal Party. Queen Victoria particularly admired him as Foreign Secretary and regarded him as a safe pair of hands to succeed Gladstone when he stepped down as Prime Minister in 1894. But Rosebery was also seen as proud, aloof and disdainful. Throughout his political career he had been torn between ambition and ennui, between his sense of duty and his dilettantism. As a peer of the realm and a man of almost immeasurable wealth, Rosebery never had to face the judgement of the electorate or the harsh realities of earning a living. Oscar was perhaps thinking of the dualities and contradictions in the personality of Lord Rosebery when he described how Sir Robert Chiltern's 'firmly-chiselled mouth and chin contrast strikingly with the romantic expression in the deep-set eyes':

> The variance is suggestive of an almost complete separation of passion and intellect, as though thought and emotion were each isolated in its own sphere through some violence of will-power.

Many of those who knew Rosebery as a colleague, as a politician and even as a friend, sensed the paradoxes in the man. Lord Acton, the celebrated historian and grandee of the Liberal Party, warned Sir George Murray, Rosebery's private secretary when he became Prime Minister in March 1894, to be on his guard against what he called Rosebery's 'peculiarities', by which he meant the 'undisciplined temper and the strong self-consciousness' which lurked under 'the excessively agreeable surface':

> What one can hardly exaggerate is his exceeding sensitiveness, combined with a secretiveness, that easily makes him suspicious. For he does not easily think very well of people, and his likings are not predominant. One has to be careful not to be duped by his cordiality, for he can be both very obstinate and very hard.

Sensitive, secretive, suspicious. Did Rosebery, like Sir Robert Chiltern, have a 'secret' and a 'shame'? And did Rosebery, like Sir Robert, possess the same strength and the same 'horrible, terrible courage' to yield to temptations, to stake his all 'on a single moment, to risk everything on one throw, whether the stake be power or pleasure'? The gambling metaphors in Sir Robert's famous speech are entirely appropriate. Rosebery was noted for his lifelong love of horseracing as both an owner and a punter. He is supposed to have said that he had three great ambitions in life: to win the Derby, marry an heiress and become Prime Minister. He achieved all three. Rosebery did indeed have a secret, a shameful secret. And it was a secret of which Oscar was only too well aware, a secret with which he could sympathise only too well. Lord Rosebery,

Foreign Secretary and future Prime Minister, had a secret lover who was none other than Bosie's older brother, Francis, Viscount Drumlanrig.

Drumlanrig was twenty-four when he met Rosebery, a tall, dark-haired and dashingly handsome young man. He struck many people as shy on first acquaintance, but charmingly so. He was universally liked by all those who met him, 'an excellent, amiable young man' radiating 'brightness and good temper'. According to Trelawny Backhouse, he was 'cultured, charming and generous to friend and foe'. Sir Edward Hamilton, a senior civil servant and close friend of Rosebery's, confided to his diary that 'there was something very winning' about Drumlanrig, 'he was much liked by everybody'. The Liberal MP Arthur Ellis summed up Drumlanrig's special qualities when he wrote that he was 'the most loveable youth I ever met'.

Rosebery and Drumlanrig's love affair had begun in 1892, not long after Bosie and Oscar had fallen in love after the attempted blackmail of Bosie in Oxford. Drumlanrig was Lord Queensberry's oldest son and was educated at Harrow, where, according to John Addington Symonds, 'every boy of good looks had a female name, and was recognised either as a public prostitute or as some bigger fellow's "bitch".'

After school, Drumlanrig had taken a commission in the Coldstream Guards and was, in 1892, living with his grandfather, Alfred Montgomery, at his house in Hertford Street, less than five minutes' walk from Lord Rosebery's 'little bandbox' of a house at 2, Berkeley Square. There was a family connection between Rosebery and the Montgomerys. Rosebery's sister Constance was married to Drumlanrig's great-uncle, and the two families would have been on visiting terms. Drumlanrig was Alfred Montgomery's favourite grandchild. According to Bosie, Montgomery was 'devoted' to Drumlanrig and was no doubt anxious to use his political and social contacts to further his grandson's career.

It was probably Montgomery who introduced Drumlanrig to Rosebery in the spring of 1892 with a view to opening up a political career for his grandson. The two men took an immediate liking to each other, and Rosebery, exactly like Lord Illingworth with Gerald Arbuthnot in Oscar's *A Woman of No Importance*, invited Drumlanrig to become his private secretary. Indeed, it is possible, perhaps even likely, that the idea of a wealthy aristocrat with political ambitions inviting a young and handsome man to become his private secretary – with all the ambiguities that surrounded such an invitation – was based on Rosebery's invitation to Drumlanrig. Oscar wrote *A Woman of No Importance* in the summer and early autumn of 1892 and would have known about Drumlanrig's appointment, certainly from Bosie, and perhaps even from Drumlanrig himself. Though no letters survive, there is evidence that Oscar was well acquainted with Drumlanrig, and that they corresponded and met frequently at Sybil Queensberry's family gatherings at the Hut and in Cadogan Square, and on other, less formal occasions.

Exactly how and when the secret sexual relationship between Rosebery and Drumlanrig began is impossible to know. Rosebery, like Lord Illingworth and

Sir Robert Chiltern, and, indeed, like Oscar himself, was ostensibly heterosexual. He had married Hannah de Rothschild, heiress to a fabulous fortune, in 1878, and they appear to have been very happily married up until Hannah's early death in 1890. Trelawny Backhouse's unpublished memoirs contain a wealth of detail about Rosebery's sexuality and the course of his love affair with Drumlanrig. According to Backhouse, Rosebery told him that it was some months after the death of his wife when he experienced a sudden and intense Damascene conversion to the desirability of sex with men. While he was staying near Naples, Rosebery told Backhouse, he visited the famous Blue Grotto in Capri and:

> became attracted, 'à l'instar de Tibère', to an Italian 'ephebus' who was disporting himself in utter nakedness at that historical post sacred to love and lust. He then for the first time revelled in the beauty of the masculine posterior which was to become his dominant passion, perhaps not even yielding place to his bookloving propensities which were literally his second nature.

Backhouse, who claims to have had sex with both Rosebery and Drumlanrig, as well as with Oscar and Bosie, says that Rosebery was an expert in the art of anal intercourse:

> Like the Arabs and the Ottomans (today called Turks) Lord Rosebery was fortunate in his ability to perform a lingering and protracted copulation equally agreeable to both parties; it was his custom to prolong the action of sex for some twenty minutes if not more, retaining his large, thickset organ stationary and fixed in the patient's rectum.

By the early 1890s, rumours about Lord Rosebery's sexual preferences were beginning to seep out. Rosebery was notoriously secretive about his private life and insisted on opening all his own letters. Lewis 'Loulou' Harcourt, son and private secretary to Sir William Harcourt, Rosebery's great rival to inherit Gladstone's crown, wrote in his diary that he was not in the least surprised by this, 'considering some of the things which, to my knowledge, some of them must contain'. But Rosebery seemed to have some sort of protection. The disgruntled actor, Charles Brookfield, who was to help the Marquis of Queensberry find damning evidence of Oscar's sexual relationships with young men, was warned off when he tried to find incriminating material about other men who loved men, especially Rosebery. In the 1940s, the actor Seymour Hicks, who knew Oscar, Brookfield and the Metropolitan Commissioner of Police of the time, told Harford Montgomery Hyde that:

> Brookfield's zeal in the pursuit of homosexuals was so great that he continued his enquiries into the activities of others much more highly-placed

than Wilde, with the result that he was sent for by the Commissioner of Police and warned in his own interest that if he persisted in what he was doing, his dead body might be found floating in the Thames one morning, face downwards.

In *The Intersexes*, his study of sex between men, written in the late 1890s after Rosebery had retired to spend much of his time in Italy, but not published until 1908, the pseudonymous 'Xavier Mayne' makes a not-so-coded reference to Lord Rosebery's sexual interests:

> One eminent personage in British political life, who once reached the highest honours in a career that has appeared to be taken up or thrown by with curious capriciousness or hesitancy, is a constant absentee in his beautiful home in Southern Europe, whence only gentle rumours of his racial homosexuality reach his birth-land.

After Rosebery's death in May 1929, George Ives confided to his diary that Rosebery was:

> said by almost everybody to have been a homosexual. I was told by a deputy coroner, that one of the chiefs of the CID, Dr McNaughton, told him that the Hyde Park Police had orders never to arrest Lord R. on the principle that, too big a fish often breaks the line.

Although some of the wilder claims in the memoirs of Trelawny Backhouse are dubious, he appears to have been extremely and convincingly well-informed about the course of the tragic love affair between Rosebery and Drumlanrig. Backhouse first met Drumlanrig at a small '*soirée*' of a distinctly Uranian character at Rosebery's house in the autumn of 1892 where the guests included 'the very eccentric' Professor Ray Lankaster and the famous John Addington Symonds – 'homosexual to the finger tips', as Backhouse described him. Ray Lankaster was an eminent biologist and zoologist and was also a Uranian: he was arrested and subsequently acquitted over sexual offences concerning young men in 1895. And John Addington Symonds was certainly in London up until September 1892. It was to be his last visit to the city. He died the following year.

Backhouse and Drumlanrig fell naturally into conversation. Backhouse had been at Winchester with Bosie and, by his own admission, had been Bosie's catamite on many occasions. 'Lord Douglas', as Backhouse calls Drumlanrig, appeared to be very curious about Backhouse's sexual experiences with Bosie:

> Lord Douglas took me aside and asked me many pointed questions regarding my Winchester days and my intimacies with his brother. I neither dissembled nor cloaked the facts and Douglas listened with interest.

It appeared that Drumlanrig's interest in Trelawny Backhouse was distinctly sexual, as Backhouse made clear:

> He was extremely and ideally handsome, an Adonis or a Ganymede of charming manners and a pleasing habit (like Bozie) of blushing if anyone's 'propos' became 'risqués'! Douglas begged me to dine with him in town after the Oxford term . . . my intimacy with Douglas rapidly developed: we had tastes in common and allowed them to expand to the fullest amplitude.

Those 'tastes in common' were, of course, anal sex, and allowing them 'to expand to the fullest amplitude' was Backhouse's rather witty admission that he and Drumlanrig had sex on at least one occasion.

At first, the love affair between Rosebery and Drumlanrig attracted little or no attention. There was some surprise in political circles that Rosebery should have appointed a charming and engaging young guardsman without any apparent political acumen or talent as his private secretary, but this soon passed. And, as it happened, Drumlanrig was rather good as Rosebery's private secretary. He was universally liked and his engaging personal qualities smoothed his political passage. There was, however, one large fly in the ointment in the squat and ungainly form of Drumlanrig's father, the Marquis of Queensberry. Queensberry was surprised when Drumlanrig resigned his commission in the Coldstream Guards to take up a career in politics, and not a little annoyed that his son and heir had chosen to ally himself with the Liberal Party, which represented the antithesis of every political belief Queensberry held.

In the spring of 1893, less than a year after his appointment as Rosebery's private secretary, Drumlanrig was offered a peerage so that he could sit in the House of Lords in a junior ministerial role, as Lord-in-Waiting to the Queen. It was Rosebery's gift to his lover and it was Drumlanrig's first step on the political ladder. But before he could accept the peerage, Drumlanrig felt that he had to consult his father, who had lost his right to sit in the House of Lords as a Scots Peer when he refused to swear the oath of allegiance to Queen Victoria. In his unpublished memorandum of the events surrounding Drumlanrig's peerage, Rosebery recorded the outcome of Drumlanrig's meeting with his father. Drumlanrig, he wrote, had gone to consult his father in Brighton where he was living in a hotel. Queenberry's reactions were, to say the least, mixed. He wrote directly to Rosebery saying that he had no intention of allowing his personal feelings to stand in the way of his son's political career, but that the offer of a peerage to his son brought back bitter memories of his own thwarted political career. Rosebery was unconvinced that Queensberry had given his full and free consent and so Drumlanrig was despatched to Brighton again to clarify his father's views. This second visit was successful. Drumlanrig told Rosebery that he had his father's full consent. The peerage was granted and Rosebery gave the matter no further thought.

But shortly after Drumlanrig's elevation to the peerage as Baron Kelhead had been announced, Queensberry started writing abusive letters to Rosebery, to Queen Victoria and to the Prime Minister, Gladstone. On 5 June 1893, Sir Algernon West, Gladstone's private secretary, confided to his diary that Lady Queensberry had told him that:

> Lord Queensberry was for the moment furious, as he himself had not a seat in the Lords as a representative peer and had written a very offensive letter to Mr Gladstone. I promised Lady Queensberry that a soothing answer should be sent.

But Queensberry could not be so easily soothed and continued to despatch offensive and abusive letters. Two weeks later, on 20 June, one of his letters to Gladstone was read out at a Cabinet meeting. Rosebery advised that the letter should be ignored. Queensberry's accusations were, he said, the ravings of a madman. Queensberry believed that Drumlanrig's peerage was a plot, deliberately designed to humiliate him by allowing his own son and heir a seat in the House of Lords. The prime author of the plot was Alfred Montgomery, his former father-in-law, who had, in Queensberry's eyes, been fomenting plots and intrigues against him for years, poisoning his children's minds against their father. After he received a letter in which Queensberry excoriated the role of 'that arch pimp Alfred Montgomery' in securing Drumlanrig's peerage. Rosebery realised too late that he had become caught up in the terrible feud between Queensberry and his former wife and her family. Despite having given his full consent to Drumlanrig's peerage, Queensberry had brooded over it and had soon begun to regard it as a calculated insult – an insult to which Rosebery must have been a full party. For his part, Rosebery concluded that Queensberry was insane, that he was suffering from a form of persecution mania.

Rosebery's estimate of Queensberry's mental state was entirely just. The 'Scarlet Marquis', as Oscar dubbed him, was becoming increasingly mentally unstable. Queensberry's diseased hatred of his wife and her family had been growing since his divorce from Sybil six years earlier. He was on distant terms with his children. He provided them with an allowance but rarely saw them. His life was very unsettled. He lived in a series of hotels and was more or less excluded from polite society because of his scandalous treatment of his wife. Typically, Queensberry claimed that it was he who had chosen to exclude himself from society. 'I have quite given up going out in what is called *English Society*,' he told his friend Moreton Frewen in 1889. 'They don't understand me and I don't care much about them.' Although Queensberry was still, by any standard, a wealthy man, mismanagement meant that the revenues from his estate had dwindled dramatically over the years and he had been forced to sell off parcels of land. He also lost money when the City of Glasgow Bank spectacularly crashed in 1878. Gambling, hunting, horse racing and boxing were his main occupations, and drinking and womanising his recreations. Oscar painted an unappetising portrait of Queensberry as 'drunken, déclassé and half-witted' with a stableman's gait and dress, bowed legs, twitching hands, a hanging lower lip and a bestial grin.

Queensberry's life had gone badly wrong. The bright promise of a life as a great landowner, rich, respected and secure in the bosom of his loving family, had given way to a feckless, deeply unsatisfying existence. He was unwilling, unable to accept that he was the author of his own misfortunes and sought to lay the blame on others. There was his wife who had turned his children against him, set his sons against their father. Then there was his father-in-law, the loathsome Alfred Montgomery, literate, sophisticated, effete – and quite possibly effeminate, Queensberry thought – who had encouraged his daughter to defy her husband and was now acting *in loco parentis* with his eldest son. Queensberry desperately wanted to restore relations between himself and his children, but his methods were brutal, blunt and entirely wasted. By attacking Sybil and Alfred Montgomery, he merely pushed his children further away. And when they did see him, they were embarrassed by their uncouth, unconventional father whose long, glowering silences they found so disconcerting. And when Queensberry did speak, it was invariably to bluntly disagree, to argue, to lambaste and to humiliate.

Queensberry's acute sensitivity on the subject of Drumlanrig's peerage was inflamed dramatically by the scandalous rumours which started to circulate in the summer of 1893. It was whispered that Drumlanrig was Lord Rosebery's catamite, and that he owed his peerage not so much to his political acumen, as to his abilities to accommodate Rosebery's 'large, thickset organ' in his rectum. The author of this rumour was 'Loulou' Harcourt, who was desperate to see his father succeed Gladstone. 'Any possibility there may have been of a peaceful development of the argument over the succession,' wrote Rosebery's biographer, Robert Rhodes James, 'was bedevilled by the intrigues of Harcourt's charming, popular, but unscrupulous son, Loulou':

> Having set his heart upon his father becoming Prime Minister, Loulou began the task of undermining Rosebery's position with a cold ruthlessness which was to poison the Liberal Party for the next decade.

Loulou was well placed to know Rosebery's secrets. He himself was known to be a lover of men, and, according to Trelawny Backhouse, his love of men was 'the paramount influence of his life'. Backhouse also claimed that at one time Loulou had unsuccessfully set his cap at Rosebery. It was Loulou's jealousy of Drumlanrig, coupled with his political ambitions for his father, that caused him to deliberately set out to try and destroy Rosebery. Loulou spread his poison assiduously. 'Many scandalous anonymous letters reached Douglas and, I believe, Lord Rosebery himself,' Trelawny Backhouse recalled, 'including a cartoon inscribed "The New Tiberius" which was unblushingly obscene.' Backhouse says that it was Loulou himself who informed Queensberry that there was a sexual relationship between his son and Lord Rosebery.

In the summer of 1893, the tone of Queensberry's letters changed dramatically. There was still the same ranting about 'insults', coupled with references to Rosebery's Jewish connections. Rosebery was not Jewish, but his wife Hannah was, and this was enough to bring out Queensberry's virulent anti-Semitism: he frequently referred to 'Jew pimps' and 'this dirty Jewry business'. But now there were also references to Rosebery's 'bad influence' on Drumlanrig. As yet, Queensberry had no absolute proof that his son was having a sexual relationship with the Foreign Secretary. But he became increasingly agitated and disgusted at the thought of his eldest son being sodomised by an older man. That Rosebery had somehow corrupted Drumlanrig into becoming his catamite went without saying. That the effeminate Alfred Montgomery had somehow connived at Rosebery's corruption of his son also went without saying. The idea that a son of his could ever consent to, let alone enjoy, such vile, disgusting and degrading sexual practices simply did not occur to him. Rosebery must have beguiled Drumlanrig with the gift of a peerage: he had bought his son's sexual complaisance. Queensberry felt that he had to do something. He had no choice. Although he was estranged from his son, he knew that it was his duty as a father to intervene to save him. It would be better for Drumlanrig to be dead than to be so sexually shamed, so sexually dishonoured. Queensberry's reaction may seem extreme, but it was unexceptional by the standards of the time. Sodomy was considered by many to be a worse crime than murder.

In early August, Queensberry discovered that Rosebery was to visit Bad Homburg where Bosie and Oscar had spent some time the year before. He determined to go there and confront the corrupter of his son in person. According to Rosebery's memorandum of events, he started to receive letters from Queensberry boasting of his boxing prowess and containing not-so-veiled threats of violence. Just before leaving England for Germany, Rosebery was in receipt of a letter in which Queensberry announced that he intended to take the first opportunity of publicly assaulting him. Two days later, Queensberry sent a telegram to Rosebery: 'Too hot to come today – would strongly recommend a skipping rope.' Queensberry was referring to Rosebery's slight podginess. Using a skipping rope would help Rosebery get in shape for his forthcoming pugilistic encounter.

On 11 August, in Bad Homburg, Rosebery received another letter from Queensberry, this time from Nice, addressed to 'Cher Fat Boy' and consisting of two barely decipherable pages. in which Rosebery was variously described as a 'snob', a 'prig', the 'greatest liar in the world' and a 'Jew pimp'. Significantly, Rosebery did not add that in the same letter Queensberry had also called him a 'Jew nancy boy' and made several references to foreskins. Queensberry's letter was an incoherent rant about how Rosebery had made bad blood between himself and his son, about the 'peerage business' and about his father-in-law 'Alfredo Montgomerino' – whom Queensberry called 'a pimp of the first water and quite fitted by nature to run in double harness with yourself'. The literal thrust of Queensberry's letter was that he was going to fight Rosebery:

I have a punching ball here on which I am having inscribed in black letters 'The Jew Pimp'. I shall daily punch it to keep my hand in, until we meet once more.

Eight days later, on Saturday 19 August, Rosebery was taking his usual morning stroll when a friend rushed up to tell him that he had seen Lord Queensberry in the Kurpark gardens. Rosebery decided to consult Sir George Lewis, the society solicitor, who happened to be in Bad Homburg. It was Lewis who had so successfully resolved Bosie's blackmail in Oxford the previous spring, and to whom Oscar had turned when faced with Alfred Wood's blackmailing threat a few months earlier. The cautious Lewis begged Rosebery to go straight back to his rooms in order to avoid any possibility of a meeting with the lunatic Queensberry. In the meantime, Lewis said, he would go to the Chief of Police and see what could be done to restrain Queensberry. A council of war was held in Rosebery's rooms between Rosebery, his friend Ronald Munro Ferguson, Sir George Lewis, the Chief of Police and the Duke of Cambridge. The Duke was brother to the Prince of Wales, who was also in Bad Homburg. It was decided that a confrontation between Her Majesty's Foreign Secretary and the mad Marquis of Queensberry must be avoided at all costs. For the rest of the day Queensberry stalked Bad Homburg telling anyone who would listen of the dreadful thrashing he was going to give that bloody pimp and bloody bugger Rosebery.

The Chief of Police called on Queensberry at 9 am the next morning and asked for his word of honour that he would not assault or in any other way insult Lord Rosebery. Queensberry reluctantly agreed. To make assurance doubly sure, the Chief of Police had arranged for some discreet surveillance. Rosebery later recorded how Queensberry had changed his lodgings twice before noon and how he spent the afternoon bragging to all and sundry about an infallible system he had devised of winning at roulette in Monte Carlo. Late that evening Queensberry managed to have a few minutes conversation with the Prince of Wales. He was not going to cause any trouble, he told the Prince, and was leaving for Monte Carlo in the morning. But everything he had said about Rosebery was true. Rosebery was a liar, a damned liar.

Queensberry kept his word and left Bad Homburg the next morning. The Chief Commissioner of Police wrote to inform Rosebery that:

The Marquis of Queensberry, in consequence of the entertainment I had with him, found it advisable to part this morning with the 7 o'clock train for Paris.

Rosebery himself wrote dryly to the Queen that: 'It is a material and unpleasant addition to the labours of Your Majesty's service to be pursued by a pugilist of unsound mind.'

Bad Homburg had been a humiliation for Queensberry. He had gone there to thrash Rosebery to within an inch of his life. He had failed signally. The Prince of Wales, no less, had intervened to protect 'that bloody pimp and bloody bugger', and Queensberry had quite literally been railroaded out of town. He slunk back to England, frustrated and furious, muttering threats and imprecations against Rosebery. Whichever way he looked at it, Bad Homburg had been a fiasco. He had been made a laughing stock. What he needed, he decided, was proof: proof that Rosebery was a sodomite and proof that he had bribed and corrupted his son into becoming his catamite. Proof would wipe the smug smile off Rosebery's face, and he, the devoted and dutiful father, would be vindicated. Proof. And how to get it? That was the problem which exercised Queensberry's mind as he journeyed back to England.

Rosebery, behind his air of imperturbability, was more than a little shaken by the episode. His decision to record in detail the events leading up to the confrontation at Bad Homburg reflected his concern. There was one phrase in particular in Queensberry's ranting, incoherent letter which nagged at him. 'God help the country say I,' Queensberry had written, 'if ever such as yourself come to guide her destinies, if she is in *trouble*.' 'To guide the country's destinies?' What exactly did Queensberry mean? It must be a reference to Rosebery eventually becoming Prime Minister. Was it an insult, one of many insults heaped upon him, or, more sinisterly, did it constitute a threat? Only Queensberry knew. It was unsettling and it was troubling. Rosebery must have felt that he had not heard the last of this disturbed and disturbing pugilist.

A schoolboy with wonderful eyes

'Little boys should be obscene and not heard.'

Rumours of the narrowly avoided confrontation between Lord Rosebery and Lord Queensberry must have percolated back to Oscar and Bosie at Goring. They would have been mortified and amused in equal measure. But Bad Homburg was a long way away, and they had more pressing concerns. The Cottage at Goring-on-Thames was not proving to be quite the Arcadian idyll that Oscar and Bosie had anticipated. They were beginning to get on each other's nerves badly. Neither of them was constitutionally suited to unrelieved domesticity. Oscar had been bored, bored to death, by marriage to Constance. But by contrast, marriage to Bosie was far too tumultuous and unpredictable. Enforced domesticity bred contempt, frustration and irritation with each other. In the confines of the Cottage, Bosie's charming capriciousness had turned into sullen moodiness or sudden emotional squalls, and Oscar's good-humoured tolerance had been strained almost to breaking point.

By July, Oscar and Bosie were spending almost as much time apart as they were together. Both of them paid several visits to London. Apart from the dubious charms of the pitiably ugly, but nevertheless sexually available, Walter Grainger, and the perhaps untasted charms of George Hughes, the boat boy, there was no feasting with panthers to be had in Goring. London was where they had to be if they wanted to meet and have sex with the young men and the rough trade they so desired.

Oscar and Bosie were together in London on 16 August for the last performance of *A Woman of No Importance*. Robbie Ross was with them, as were Max Beerbohm and Aubrey Beardsley. As Beerbohm delicately put it, Oscar, Bosie and Robbie wore 'rich clusters of vine leaves' in their hair. In other words, they were all extremely drunk and inclining towards the disorderly. Beerbohm was not amused. 'Nor have I ever seen Oscar so fatuous,' he told Reggie Turner:

He called Mrs Beere 'Juno-like' and Kemble 'Olympian quite' and waved his cigarette round and round his head. Of course I would rather see Oscar free

257

than sober, but still, suddenly meeting him . . . I felt quite repelled.

Beerbohm's reference to Oscar being 'free' was telling, suggesting that, in his opinion at least, Oscar was running dangerous risks.

Behind such scenes of revelry, tensions were running high. The fuse was lit at the end of August when Bosie presented Oscar with his translation of *Salomé*. Bosie had been working at it, more off than on, for three or four months. But Oscar was decidedly unimpressed by Bosie's work and, unusually for him, extremely tactless in how he expressed his opinions. There was a series of 'scenes', Oscar recalled in *De Profundis*, 'the occasion of them being my pointing out the schoolboy faults of your attempted translation of *Salomé*. The translation Bosie had produced, Oscar told him, 'was as unworthy of you, as an ordinary Oxonian, as it was of the work it sought to render'. His comments were deliberately hurtful and cutting, designed to put Bosie in his place, to remind him that Oscar was the intellectual sorcerer, and Bosie very much his apprentice.

Bosie was furious. Although he admired Oscar's work enormously, he also had an extremely high opinion of his own talents, and always considered himself to be a great poet. 'I suspected that I was a great poet when I was twenty-three,' Bosie wrote later, 'and as the years went by my suspicion became a conviction.' Bosie flounced out of the Cottage, sending a series of violent and vituperative letters to Oscar, in which he announced that he was under 'no intellectual obligation of any kind' to him. In Bosie's statement, Oscar recognised a fundamental truth. It was, he thought, 'the one really true thing' Bosie had written 'in the whole course of our friendship'. Oscar realised that there was an unbridgeable gulf of understanding, of culture, of intellect between them. They had tried a form of Uranian marriage and it had failed dismally. 'Ultimately,' Oscar wrote:

> the bond of all companionship, whether in marriage or in friendship, is conversation, and conversation must have a common basis, and between two people of widely different culture the only common basis possible is the lowest level.

Bosie was, Oscar convinced himself, 'trivial in thought and action', charmingly so. Bosie's endless talk of boys and buggery, no less than the fascination of their exploration of their shared and forbidden sexuality, had begun to pall:

> The froth and folly of our life grew often very wearisome to me: it was only in the mire that we met: and fascinating, terribly fascinating though the one topic around which your talk invariably centred was, still at the end it became quite monotonous to me. I was often bored to death by it.

Oscar's version of this crisis in his relationship with Bosie was written while he was in Reading Gaol and is tinted and tainted by the bitter and painful experiences of incarceration. Oscar was right: Bosie was indeed obsessed by what he called 'the eternal quest for beauty', by which he meant boys and sex. Yet Oscar had been equally obsessed. It was their life, their passion, their addiction. They were predators in the murky undergrowth of Victorian sexuality. They could not have stopped, even if they had wanted to. The endless cycle of sexual desire and sexual satiation had by now become 'a malady, or a madness, or both'. There was no escape, no cure.

Oscar decided that he would join Constance and the boys in Dinard, in Brittany, for a fortnight. Bosie wanted to come too. 'You were extremely angry at me for not taking you with me,' Oscar recalled. There were more arguments, more scenes culminating in a series of unpleasant telegrams sent to the country house where Oscar was staying. This time Oscar was more tactful, telling Bosie that he ought to spend at least a week or two with his family. 'But in reality,' Oscar wrote, 'I could not under any circumstances have let you be with me.' Oscar realised that after twelve weeks in each other's company:

> I required rest and freedom from the terrible strain of your companionship.
> It was necessary for me to be a little by myself. It was intellectually necessary.

Oscar travelled to France determined to end a relationship which seemed to be going so catastrophically awry. The trip to Dinard was 'a good opportunity for ending the fatal friendship that had sprung up between us, and ending it without bitterness'.

Bosie meanwhile was staying at the house of his uncle, George Finch, in Burley-on-the-Hill in Rutland. 'I have just finished translating Oscar Wilde's *Salomé*,' he told Charles Kains Jackson. 'It is to be published in October.' In his reply, Kains Jackson made some slighting allusion to Oscar. Bosie sprang vigorously to Oscar's defence. 'The general philistine attacks him quite enough without any assistance from the elect,' he reprimanded Kains Jackson, reminding him that Oscar 'is the most chivalrous friend in the world'.

Bosie was lonely. He was missing Oscar, blithely unaware of the most unchivalrous thoughts that were running through the mind of his most chivalrous friend. 'I am bored to death and very unhappy and unloved!' he told Kains Jackson. 'I am surrounded here by what is popularly known as "a bevy of fair girls" which fills me with misery. I am also very seedy.' To console himself, Bosie wrote two Uranian sonnets.

The first of these sonnets concerned a boy in a straw hat. As he explained to Kains Jackson:

> What I said about the 'Straw Hat' . . . was quite deliberate. I was trying to get the *modern* sentiment into it. It was a bit of realism. Really I think a straw hat had all the feeling of a modern Oxford boy in it, it's my idea of a boy of that sort that he should always have a straw hat on.

Bosie's sonnet – which is now lost – may well have been a piece of poetic realism and was perhaps inspired by an encounter with an unknown and unnamed boy in London a fortnight earlier. On 18 August, two days after his drunken evening with Oscar, Robbie, Beerbohm and Beardsley, Bosie had ordered a straw hat from his hatters, James Lock and Company in St James's Street. The company's ledgers record simply that Bosie purchased a 'Straw Hat, No Band (for Friend)'. Giving straw hats to boys was a potentially dangerous pastime. The following summer, Oscar would buy a straw hat, this time with a band of red and blue, for Alfonso Conway, a boy Oscar and Bosie picked up on the seafront at Worthing. Conway and his straw hat would come back to haunt Oscar during his trials.

Bosie's second Uranian sonnet concerned the exquisitely desirable lips of a boy:

> and I saw thee
> In thy white tunic gowned from neck to knee,
> And knew the honey of thy sugar lips.

'I was so fascinated by the expression "sugar lips" used of a boy in one of Burton's translations,' Bosie told Kains Jackson, 'that I wrote a sonnet on purpose to bring it in. I haven't named it yet, I can't think of a good name. Something Eastern I think it ought to be.' Bosie was referring to Sir Richard Burton, the extraordinary explorer, traveller and scholar who had translated much Eastern poetry and who had made an extensive study of sex between men in India, North Africa and the Near East. Sugar lips were for kissing – and also for cock-sucking. Later, Bosie would use the same expression to describe the allure of a fourteen-year-old Algerian boy. 'I am held fast,' he told Robbie Ross, 'by the lassoo of desire to a sugar-lipped lad,' with whom he had had sex 'once, sometimes twice for the past ten days.'

Two weeks in Brittany with Constance and the boys rapidly brought Oscar to his senses. Much as he was fond, 'really very fond' of Constance, and deeply as he loved his sons, he realised that he could never again attempt a simulacrum of normal family life. Besides which, he started to miss Bosie desperately. Even though he sometimes fancied himself weary and exhausted by the 'froth and folly' of Bosie's sexual obsessions, the sudden and complete absence of Bosie's 'fascinating, terribly fascinating' talk about boys and sex was unnerving and unsettling. And Oscar knew that for all his faults – his greed, his selfishness, his self-indulgence – Bosie really loved him. 'No matter what you wrote or did, you were absolutely and entirely devoted to me.'

On his return to London, Oscar allowed himself to be persuaded by Robbie Ross, Bosie's new best friend, that he had, perhaps, behaved unjustly towards Bosie in the matter of the *Salomé* translation. He decided to repent and relent. 'It was represented to me,' Oscar wrote in *De Profundis*:

> that you would be much hurt, perhaps almost humiliated at having your work sent back to you like a schoolboy's exercise; that I was expecting far too

much intellectually from you . . . I knew quite well that no translation, unless one done by a poet, could render the colour and cadence of my work in any adequate measure: devotion seemed to me, seems to me still, a wonderful thing, not to be lightly thrown away: so I took the translation and you back.

A pattern of behaviour was beginning to emerge. A period of simmering tension would erupt in a terrible scene, or series of scenes. Bosie would flounce out, sending Oscar vituperative telegrams and letters. Oscar would decide that the friendship must end. As they both cooled off, each realised that they could not live without the other. Bosie was penitent, Oscar magnanimous. Reconciliation and joy unconfined – at least until the next flashpoint.

There were still problems about the *Salomé* translation, exacerbated when Oscar unwisely told Bosie that he was considering asking Aubrey Beardsley to translate the play, as well as illustrate it, though, in the event, Oscar stuck with Bosie's rendering. Robbie Ross had introduced Beardsley to Oscar that spring, after Beardsley had been commissioned to do an illustration inspired by the recently published French edition of *Salomé* to accompany an article on Beardsley's work for the new art magazine, the *Studio*. Beardsley's illustration was suggestively entitled 'The Climax' and depicts an orgasmic Salomé in transports of erotic delight as she kisses the decapitated head of Jokanaan, symbolically levitating herself into the air under the impetus of her expressed lust. Oscar was delighted with Beardsley's acute and sexually knowing interpretation of his play and presented the artist with a copy of *Salomé* inscribed:

> March '93, for Aubrey: for the only artist who, besides myself, knows what the dance of the seven veils is, and can see that invisible dance.

Oscar's enthusiasm for the work of his new friend resulted in Beardsley being commissioned by John Lane to illustrate the English version of *Salomé*.

Aubrey Beardsley was just twenty-two when he first met Oscar and was on the threshold of a spectacular and extremely short-lived career. He was a striking young man. Oscar called him 'the most monstrous of orchids'. He was very tall and very thin, with very elongated, graceful hands and a long, equine face. Like his art, the consumptive Beardsley was a study in black and white, the extreme pallor of his skin contrasting sharply with his shock of black hair. He was artistically and intellectually precocious, with a sharp wit and a profound interest in all matters sexual, an interest which was reflected in his frequently priapic drawings. 'Absinthe,' Oscar remarked when lunching one day with Beardsley and Frank Harris:

> is to all other drinks what Aubrey's drawings are to other pictures; it stands alone; it is like nothing else; it shimmers like southern twilight in opalescent colouring; it has about it the seduction of strange sins. It is stronger than any other spirit and brings out the subconscious self in man. It is just like your drawings, Aubrey; it gets on one's nerves and is cruel. Baudelaire called his

poems *Fleurs du Mal*, I shall call your drawings *Fleurs du Péché* – flowers of sin.

Like Max Beerbohm and Will Rothenstein, Aubrey Beardsley was drawn to Oscar by the magnetic force of his personality. Although not lovers of men or boys themselves, Beerbohm, Rothenstein and Beardsley were fascinated by what Beerbohm once described as 'certain forms of crime', and they enjoyed their status as privileged observers of Oscar's circle. They were non-combatants who made a breathless, excited audience to the vivid Uranian comings and goings, complications, scandals, squalls and scenes, a vocal Greek chorus watching Oscar's tragedy unfold.

Oscar's friendship with Aubrey Beardsley began well but quickly degenerated in the course of the first six months. This was almost certainly Oscar's fault. He was curiously attracted to Beardsley who, though hardly conventionally good-looking, was young and interesting and seemingly sexually ambiguous. Beardsley may have sent out conflicting signals about his sexual preferences. 'Yes, yes, I look like a sodomite,' he once told Arthur Symons. 'But, no, I am not one.' It seems almost certain that, at some point in 1893, Oscar propositioned Beardsley for sex. Oscar was in the habit of propositioning young men. He had suggested sex to Bernard Berenson in Tite Street, pulled an alarmed Will Rothenstein on to his knee during a drunken carriage ride in Paris, and tried it on with many others. Like Havelock Ellis's anonymous correspondent in *Sexual Inversion* who had 'made advances to upward of one hundred men in the course of the last fourteen years, and only once met with a refusal', Oscar had discovered that even the most determinedly heterosexual young men were willing to experiment more often than might reasonably be supposed. Robert Sherard was convinced that Oscar had made 'advances on Beardsley, who took offence thereat and afterwards restricted his relations with Oscar to purely business transactions'.

The mutual admiration Oscar and Aubrey felt for each other quickly turned to animosity. In consequence of Oscar's sexual overtures, Beardsley manifested an increasing hostility towards Oscar and towards any discussion of sex between men. At an after-theatre supper in the Savoy with Beardsley and others, Oscar started to discourse about his favourite topic: boys and sex. On this occasion, he was going into unusual detail, seemingly about the practice of anilingus, or rimming. Beardsley told Trelawny Backhouse how Oscar had:

> boasted of having had five love affairs and resultant copulations with telegraph and district messenger boys in one night. 'I kissed them each one of them in every part of their bodies,' asserted Oscar: 'they were all dirty and appealed to me for just that reason.'

Beardsley was shocked and rather disgusted. To know that Oscar was a sodomite was one thing, to be forced to listen to the goriest of gory details was quite another. Oscar's braggadocios about five sexual connections in one night, and his taste for anilingus, were perhaps more than Beardsley could stomach. 'I don't mind his morals,' Beardsley said, 'but his lamentable repetitions bore me to death and give me nausea like an emetic.' Trelawny Backhouse's rather unhelpful response to Beardsley's sense of disgust was to quote a line from a sonnet by Paul Verlaine: *'Sales sont tes parties secrètes, mais je les aime.'* 'Unclean your private parts but dear to me!'

Beardsley cruelly satirised Oscar in four of his drawings for *Salomé*, most obviously in 'The Woman in the Moon', originally entitled 'The Man in the Moon'. The face of the woman in the moon is clearly that of Oscar, sporting a green carnation and presiding over the action of his play as the pagan moon coldly presides over the fates of Salomé and Jokanaan. Oscar would not have thanked Beardsley for the comparison with the woman in the moon, whom Herod describes as 'like a mad woman, a mad woman who is seeking everywhere for lovers', who 'reels through the clouds like a drunken woman'. Drunken, reeling and sexually insatiable might be an accurate portrait of Oscar when he had, more often than not now, 'vine leaves in his hair', but it was not kind.

Oscar bridled when he saw Beardsley's drawings, describing them as 'like the naughty scribbles a precocious schoolboy makes in the margins of his copybooks'. The publisher, John Lane, was also very anxious lest Beardsley manage to slip any obscene imagery into his drawings. According to Trelawny Backhouse, Lane:

> used to inspect with absurd minuteness (magnifying glass in hand) each and every sketch, searching for hidden suggestiveness, finding it sometimes where none whatsoever was dreamed of by the artist.

Like absinthe, Beardsley's drawings were cruel and had begun to get on Oscar's nerves. Relations between *Salomé*'s author, translator, illustrator and publisher became increasingly strained. 'I can tell you I had a warm time of it between Lane and Oscar and Co,' Beardsley told Robbie Ross:

> For one week the number of telegraph and messenger boys who came to the door was simply scandalous . . . I have withdrawn three of the illustrations and supplied their places with three new ones, simply beautiful and quite irrelevant.

Beardsley went on to describe Oscar and Bosie as 'really very dreadful people'.

Oscar's account in *De Profundis* of the events of the autumn of 1893 is very sketchy, deliberately so. There was another scandal from which Oscar, Bosie and Robbie Ross only escaped by the skin of their teeth. 'There have been very great and intimate scandals,' Max Beerbohm breathlessly told Reggie Turner:

> A schoolboy with wonderful eyes, Bosie, Bobbie, a furious father, George Lewis, a Headmaster (who is now blackmailing Bobbie), St John Wotner, Calais, Dover, Oscar Browning, Oscar, Dover, Calais, intercepted letters,

private detectives, Calais, Dover and returned cigarette cases were some of the ingredients of this dreadful episode.

The origins of the scandal went back five years, to 1888, when Robbie was recovering from the nervous breakdown he suffered after being ducked in the fountain at King's College, Cambridge. Oscar Browning, a friend of Oscar's and fellow of King's, had taken Robbie to spend a recuperative weekend at the Beehive, the house of his elderly mother in Windsor.

The Windsor weekend was certainly recuperative, if not in any conventional sense. At the Beehive, Robbie met Browning's sister, Mina, and her husband, the Reverend Biscoe Hale Wortham, and their two sons, Philip, then fourteen, and Oswald, always called Toddy, who was a year or so younger. The friendship blossomed, and Robbie kept in close touch with the Worthams, staying with them 'frequently' in England and in Bruges, where Biscoe Wortham had taken over a boarding school for English boys called 'Laurence's', re-christening it rather more grandly 'The English College'. Philip and Toddy also used to visit Robbie in London, sometimes staying a night or two in Mrs Ross's house in Onslow Square, or in Robbie's rooms in Kensington Church Street. Robbie's most recent visit to Bruges had been over Easter 1893, when he stayed about a week with the Worthams. Naturally, he spent time with Philip and Toddy, but on this visit he also met and befriended another boy – 'a nice-looking, well-mannered, rather attractive boy a little over sixteen, of no particular strength of character' was how Biscoe Wortham described him.

The boy in question was probably Claude Dansey, the son of a retired Lieutenant-Colonel in the Life Guards. Wortham later confessed to his brother-in-law Oscar Browning that, at the time, he had thought 'there was something suspicious' in the sudden friendship between Robbie and Claude but decided to say and do nothing, as Robbie was a trusted family friend. Robbie and Claude started to correspond, writing to each other regularly. None of their letters survive, but it seems that Robbie was in love with Claude. He told Max Beerbohm that the boy was 'the desire of his soul'. Nor is it known quite how often they met between Easter and October, when the scandal broke. The Danseys may have had a house in London, so it is entirely possible that Claude and Robbie had ample opportunities to meet during the summer holidays.

At the beginning of October, Robbie and Claude met and had sex together, most probably at Robbie's rooms in Kensington. Perhaps unwisely, Robbie wrote to Bosie and mentioned the fact that Claude was spending the night with him on his way back to school in Bruges. 'The letter contained the word "Boy",' Oscar Browning gleefully recounted to Frank Harris many years later. At the very sight of the word, Browning said, Bosie rushed round to Robbie's and, finding Claude Dansey there, swept him up:

On Saturday the boy slept with Douglas, on Sunday he slept with Oscar. On

Monday he slept with a woman at Douglas's expense. On Tuesday he returned to Bruges three days late.

Claude's absence had not gone unnoticed. His late return had caused great anxiety at the English College. When he finally turned up in Bruges, with no adequate explanation, Biscoe Wortham confronted him and demanded to know where he had been and what he had been doing. Eventually Claude confessed that he had stayed with Robbie and while there, as Wortham indignantly recounted to Oscar Browning:

> formed the acquaintance of a young man, a friend of Mr Ross's, with whom he afterwards stayed at the Albemarle, and with whom he admits (the boy I mean) that he behaved in an indecent manner.

Max Beerbohm backs up this account. 'The schoolboy Helen', he told Reggie Turner, was:

> stolen from Bobbie by Bosie and kept at the Albemarle Hotel: how well I remember passing this place one night with Bobbie and his looking sadly at the lighted windows and wondering to me behind which of the red curtains lay the desire of his soul.

In Bruges, Wortham kept 'a pretty sharp lookout' on Dansey's letters over the next few days and intercepted one he had written to Robbie which, as Wortham told Oscar Browning, 'left absolutely no doubt of the relations which existed between them'. A horrible suspicion now struck Biscoe and Mina Wortham. Had Robbie also behaved indecently with their sons, Philip and Toddy? After talking to his older son, Biscoe sent a copy of his son's statement – 'in its naked hideousness' – to Oscar Browning. Robbie had had sex with Philip on his first visit to Mrs Browning's house in Windsor, and then on two subsequent occasions. 'I was in his room alone with him early one morning, before breakfast,' Philip confessed:

> I was in my night shirt. He was in his pyjamas: he put me on the bed. He had me between the legs. He placed his **** between my legs. He did it on three occasions. When I was staying in London with him on a second occasion. The 3rd time was in his rooms at Church St. It was when I was reading with Mr Edwards. I went to London and spent the night there from Windsor.

'You will be as much horrified as we are, I doubt not,' Wortham told Browning. But Browning did not appear to be unduly horrified. Throughout the tense days of October, Browning was in the eye of the storm, the trusted confidant of both Mina and Biscoe Wortham, and the devoted friend of Robbie Ross. Browning kept closely in touch with Robbie, keeping him informed of developments in Bruges.

In the light of Philip's confession, the Worthams were also worried about Robbie's relations with their second son, Toddy. 'I am miserable about poor Toddy,' Mina confided to Browning:

> Of course, I have no idea what his relations are with Mr Ross. Up to the last few days I looked upon Mr Ross as Toddy's valued friend and I wrote to Mr Ross last summer and told him how much I valued his friendship for the two boys.

A few days later Mina wrote again to her brother in a state of great relief. Nothing improper had occurred between Toddy and Mr Ross. He had answered all his father's questions entirely to their satisfaction. But Toddy had not been telling the whole truth. He had certainly written to Robbie, and probably had sex with him, but as Robbie's close friend More Adey told Oscar Browning, all Toddy's letters to Robbie had been safely burnt and there was now no evidence to connect them.

Claude Dansey's father, Colonel Dansey, arrived in Bruges on 12 October. After further interrogation of Claude, Biscoe Wortham was in a position to give Oscar Browning more details:

> Ross is simply one of a gang of the most absolutely brutal ruffians who spend their time in seducing and prostituting boys and all the time presenting a decent appearance to the world. Two other persons besides himself are implicated in the business.

Those two other persons were Bosie and Oscar. Bosie's name had been blurted out by Claude to his father and Biscoe Wortham, but had he also blurted out Oscar's name? Almost certainly not. Perhaps Claude's encounter with Oscar was extremely brief, and restricted to sexual, rather than social, intercourse. And Oscar may have been introduced to Claude as just 'Oscar', with no mention of his surname.

Biscoe Wortham told Oscar Browning that his and Colonel Dansey's first concern was to retrieve any letters from Claude in the possession of Robbie and Bosie, together with any letters from Philip. Oscar Browning duly told Robbie, who in turn told Bosie. Robbie, Bosie and Oscar were in a state of extreme consternation. And none of them could be sure exactly how much the outraged fathers knew. Not one, but two, outraged fathers posed a serious threat. They knew that this time they were not dealing with renters, however dangerous and experienced. Professional blackmailers were not interested in seeing their victims arrested and imprisoned. But outraged fathers generally did want to see the seducers of their sons arrested, tried, punished and shamed. If Max Beerbohm's breathless account of the scandal was correct, private detectives had already been engaged. Were they searching for more evidence to corroborate Claude's account – with a view to instituting criminal proceedings? Or were they employed simply to ensure that the scandal was quietly and effectively suppressed? Robbie, Bosie and Oscar must have spent many agitated hours going over and over their options.

They decided on a bold strategy, not without risk. Oscar Browning had told them that Biscoe Wortham and Colonel Dansey's main concern was to retrieve the compromising letters their sons had written. Robbie and Bosie decided to go to Bruges and see what could be settled. They arrived in Ostend on 15 October, taking rooms in the Grand Hôtel du Phare, before travelling on to nearby Bruges and sending a note to Wortham requesting a meeting. 'Biscoe was surprised last evening by a note from Mr. Ross asking for an interview at the Hôtel de Flandre – with him was Lord Alfred Douglas, one of his accomplices,' Mina told Oscar Browning. The day after, Robbie reported back to Oscar Browning on their 'very unsatisfactory' meeting with Wortham:

> He refuses to tell me what he proposes doing. He says he possesses documentary evidence but what he intends doing with this (if it exists) he will not say. He also speaks of 'coming to terms' but does not state what those terms are beyond the fact that I have certain letters from the boy Dansey which I must hand over.

On the same day, Bosie wrote to his brother, Lord Percy Douglas, whom he always called 'Turts'. 'It is frightfully dull here,' he wrote. 'Not a soul in the place, and the casino and every place is shut up.' The purpose of Bosie's letter was to explain to his brother why he had come out to Ostend, 'in a fearful hurry', and was not in fact at Datchet, as he had said he would be. 'What has really happened,' wrote Bosie:

> is that Ross, one of my greatest friends, has got into a scrape connected with some people out here, and I have come with him to see him through it. He is one of my greatest friends and is also one of the best fellows that ever lived, and I could not possibly refuse to come out with him. Although he did not ask me to come I saw that he wanted somebody to keep him company etcet. Of course this involves me in nothing, and the thing is sure to come all right as it is not really at all his fault. I cannot explain the affair, so please don't ask any questions.

Bosie's representation of himself as the disinterested friend, offering to travel to dreary Ostend so that he could lend his support to Robbie, is a masterpiece of protesting too much. To be sure, Bosie had only had sex with Claude Dansey, whereas Robbie was accused of seducing both Claude and Philip Wortham, and quite probably Toddy as well. 'Please don't let Mamma get in a fuss,' Bosie concluded. 'There is really nothing to be excited about, but I have quite determined to stay with Ross till the thing is settled.'

Ross and Bosie returned to London in due course and, on 19 October, at the height of the crisis, George Ives held an intimate Uranian dinner, where Oscar and Bosie were the only guests. Bosie was, according to Ives, 'decidedly ruffled, and so lost some of his fascination'. The Dansey crisis was the main topic of conversation. Ives, as usual, occupied the moral high ground: 'I felt bound to take a certain line but now I've done my best and must leave matters to take their chance.' Ives amplified these comments later. 'PS: I believe that I had warned Lord A. more than once that he was indulging in homosexuality to a reckless and high dangerous degree. For tho' I had no objection to the thing itself, we were all afraid that he would get arrested any day.'

Despite the apparent stalemate at the first meeting in Bruges with Biscoe Wortham, clearly there was some room for negotiation. There was some furious diplomatic activity. 'The fact is that there are some letters in the possession of Mr Ross and Lord Alfred Douglas which must be had,' Mina wrote to Oscar Browning:

> If they would give them up, nothing would be done. Do you think you could get them? Sooner or later Biscoe thinks they will be in the hands of the police, and then of course these compromising letters would be public property.

Oscar Browning agreed to try and broker a deal to secure the return of any compromising letters from Claude and Philip, in exchange for Robbie's letters to them. Robbie also got his close friend, the good-natured More Adey, involved in negotiations. And both sides, as Max Beerbohm indicated in his telegraphic summary of the scandal, may have consulted their solicitors: St John Wotner acting for the outraged fathers; and Sir George Lewis for Robbie, Bosie and, possibly, Oscar. Finally some sort of settlement was agreed on, which involved the return of each side's letters.

But there was a sticking point in the form of Colonel Dansey, who did not want to see the seducers of his son escape scot-free. 'Col. D— has been like many "military" men by no means easy to manage,' Biscoe Wortham told Oscar Browning. 'His great desire was to punish the culprits, and it was not until the very last moment that he was convinced that he could not punish them, without involving his own son.' Sir George Lewis supposedly told Colonel Dansey that, if Robbie and Bosie were to be prosecuted, 'they will doubtless get two years but your son will get six months'.

'At length I am thankful to say we have got to the end of this dreadful case,' Biscoe Wortham told Oscar Browning on 25 October:

> The letters have been returned on both sides, and now one feels relieved of a nightmare . . . It has been a *horrible case,* & the details, which I have, and am the only one who knows except the chief actors in the business are beyond everything abominable. We may be thankful that it has ended quietly, but it has been a near thing.

It had been an uncomfortably close shave. Had Colonel Dansey followed his first instinct, Robbie, Bosie and, had his name emerged, perhaps even Oscar might have found themselves having to flee abroad rather than face trial and imprisonment at home.

On a gilded barge

'I don't think England should be represented abroad by an unmarried man . . . it might lead to complications.'

Colonel Dansey's decision, taken very reluctantly, not to prosecute Robbie and Bosie was not quite the end of the Bruges affair. There were repercussions. Towards the end of October, Robbie wrote to Bosie from Davos in Switzerland where he was in exile in consequence of the scandal at Bruges. 'I am not allowed to live in London for two years,' he told Bosie. As 'the purse strings' were in the hands of his family, 'and a stoppage is threatened, I have to submit'. More Adey had successfully managed to conceal the worst of the scandal from his family, Robbie said:

> but the worthy Rev Mr Squeers wrote a full and particular account of how things were to my brother. It was news to him, as [Adey] had hitherto concealed everything, but the trouble with the noisy military gentleman. My elder brother here gets letters about the disgrace of the family, the social outcast, the son and brother unfit for society of any kind, from people at home. I am sure you will be amused to hear this.

Wackford Squeers was the corrupt and bullying headmaster of Dotheboys Hall in Charles Dickens's *Nicholas Nickleby*. The 'worthy Rev Mr Squeers' had to be a reference to the Reverend Biscoe Wortham, who clearly had taken it upon himself to inform Robbie's older brother, Alec – and presumably their mother, Mrs Ross – of all the sordid details of the Bruges affair. It is clear from Robbie's letter that Colonel Dansey – 'the noisy military gentleman' – had already been in some kind of contact with Robbie's family. Was Robbie's sojourn in Switzerland the result of a decision taken by his family, or was it part of the settlement of the scandal? Had Biscoe Wortham and Colonel Dansey demanded that Robbie leave London and live in exile abroad for a time as some kind of punishment? This may have been what Max Beerbohm meant when he told Reggie Turner that Biscoe Wortham was now 'blackmailing' Ross.

Rumours of Bosie's part in the suppressed scandal were beginning to seep out. Will Rothenstein told Max Beerbohm that Bosie had been 'going in for the wildest folly in London, and, I imagine, will shortly have to take a tour round the world, or something of the kind'. George Ives, who was dazzled by Bosie and more than a little in love with him, continued to fret over his troubles. On 28 October, three days after the affair had been finally resolved, Ives confided to his diary that he had 'a long chat with O.W. about private matters'. These private matters principally concerned Bosie, whom Ives with his mania for secrecy referred to simply as 'X', only inserting Bosie's name into the manuscript in parenthesis many years later as 'Lord A.D. afterwards a traitor':

> Was up very late last night, partly working out an attempt to save poor dear X from the effects of a course of the wildest foolishness, if I can – in truth I have pondered many hours on this point having no small regard for X but as things point now, unless some happy change takes place, I see very little hope, but I have done my best from public and private reasons.

Ives was quite specific. He wanted to save Bosie from the 'effects', or consequences, of a course of 'wildest foolishness', not from the 'wildest foolishness' itself. It was too late to turn back the clock. Bosie's liaison with Claude Dansey had already happened. But what were the effects or consequences that Ives was referring to? It may only be speculation, but was Bosie under some kind of injunction to go abroad? If Colonel Dansey and Biscoe Wortham had demanded that Robbie go into exile, were they equally insistent that Bosie should go too? And had Bosie refused, threatening to stay and face whatever consequences his non-compliance might bring?

Eleven days later, Oscar was writing a carefully phrased letter to Bosie's mother, expressing his fears for Bosie's health and for his future. Bosie, Oscar wrote, 'is sleepless, nervous, and rather hysterical':

> He does absolutely nothing, and is quite astray in life, and may, unless you or Drumlanrig do something, come to grief of some kind. His life seems to me aimless, unhappy and absurd.

Oscar urged Sybil to send Bosie abroad. 'Why not try and make arrangements of some kind for him to go abroad for four or five months, to the Cromers in Egypt if that could be managed?' Oscar told Sybil that he liked to think of himself as Bosie's greatest friend:

> so I write to you quite frankly to ask you to send him abroad to better surroundings. It would save him, I feel sure. At present his life seems to be tragic and pathetic in its foolish aimlessness.

Oscar concluded by begging Sybil not to let Bosie know anything about his letter. But, in fact, Bosie knew all about it. Oscar states quite clearly in *De Profundis* that he wrote to Sybil with Bosie's 'knowledge and concurrence'.

Was a six-month sojourn in Egypt the solution that Oscar, George Ives and Bosie had hammered out together to get Bosie out of London until the vengeful instincts of the outraged fathers had subsided? Robbie was certainly convinced that Bosie's hurriedly arranged trip to Egypt was in consequence of the Bruges affair. 'Douglas went to Egypt to avoid the consequences of a scandal which he had caused entirely himself,' Robbie told Frank Harris many years later, adding bitterly that 'he left others to face the consequences of it.' Robbie was being very unfair. Bosie had indeed slept with Claude Dansey, but only after Robbie had slept with him, and Bosie had never had sex with Philip Wortham. Bosie's chief culpability lay in the fact that he had caused Claude's late return to Bruges – a late return which led to the scandal being exposed.

Sybil Queensberry agreed with Oscar that Bosie should leave the country. She even followed Oscar's prompt that he should go and stay with Lord and Lady Cromer in Cairo. Lady Cromer had been a close friend of Sybil's since they were children. Lord Cromer was a recently created peer who was the British Agent and Consul-General in Egypt. Egypt was theoretically an outpost of the Ottoman Empire, enjoying independent dominion status and governed by a Khedive or 'ruler'. But in reality, it was a client state of the British Empire. As recently as 1882, Britain had intervened militarily to reinstate Khedive Tawfik, who was sympathetic to British interests, and who had been overthrown by Egyptian nationalists. Lord Cromer was the ruler of Egypt in all but name and was the most powerful man in the country.

Matters were fixed up with almost indecent haste. Bosie was to depart for Cairo on 31 November, just three weeks after Oscar proposed it, and only five weeks after the settlement of the Bruges affair. It is possible that Sybil was fully aware why Bosie needed to leave the country. Rumblings of discontent from Colonel Dansey and Biscoe Wortham may have reached her. And by now Bosie's older brother, Percy, might have had a clearer understanding of how matters had stood in Bruges and told their mother.

If Oscar's letter to Sybil was written with Bosie's full knowledge and concurrence, then Cairo must have been Bosie's choice. A sojourn at the Agency in Cairo as the guest of the British ruler of Egypt, with all the vice-regal privilege and consequence that entailed, would require no sacrifice of comfort, and might conceivably be amusing. There was also the prospect that Bosie might be found a post as an attaché in the diplomatic service, providing him with a career fit for an aristocrat, a gentleman and a poet.

More importantly, Egypt had other attractions which were perhaps more to Bosie's taste. 'I understand that the population of Alexandria is an interesting one,' George Ives confided to his diary. Like Ives, Bosie could not have been unaware that sex with boys was widely available in Egypt, as it was elsewhere in North Africa and the Middle East, and he would no doubt have heard Uranian travellers' tales about the sexual delights to be had there. Bosie had certainly read Richard Burton's translation of Eastern poetry, and may well have been familiar with Burton's famous 'Terminal Essay' appended to his 1885 translation of *The Thousand and One Nights*, which defined 'the Sotadic Zone', a geographical band taking in the broadly equatorial regions of the world where, Burton claimed, pederasty and sodomy are 'popular and endemic, held at the worst to be a mere peccadillo'. Egypt was at the heart of the Sotadic Zone and was, according to Burton, the 'classical region of all abominations'. Burton quoted from various authorities as to the prevalence and popularity of sodomy in Egypt and gleefully retailed how, in the 1860s, 'the highdried and highly respectable' Dutch Consul-General for the Netherlands had been rebuked by the Khedive of Egypt after criticising the prevalence of sodomy in Egypt. The Consul-General 'was solemnly advised' by Khedive Said Pasha 'to make the experiment, active and passive, before offering his opinion upon the subject'.

Just before he left, Bosie wrote to Charles Kains Jackson, a solicitor as well as the editor of the *Artist and Journal of Home Culture*. Bosie was seeking Kains Jackson's help for a man called Burnand who shared a house with the novelist Roy Horniman, the brother of a former boyfriend of Oscar's. 'I want to ask if you cannot do anything for this poor man Burnand who is now waiting his trial for an assault on a boy,' Bosie wrote:

I saw a most piteous letter from him today which almost made me cry. Surely for the sake of the cause something can be done for this poor man who seems quite friendless and penniless. As far as I can make out, there is not a *bad* case against him, and if the thing was properly managed I feel sure he could get off. Do try and do something, my heart bleeds for the poor chap.

Although Bosie's commitment to 'the Cause' was evidently as strong and as passionate as ever, his empathy with Burnand may have been intensified by the irony of their relative situations. Both had had sex with boys. But while Burnand faced trial, imprisonment and public shame, Bosie was escaping to Cairo, scot-free.

Bosie was not in the best of spirits on the eve of his departure. 'I am very unhappy about other things,' he confessed to Kains Jackson. One of the chief causes of Bosie's unhappiness was his deteriorating relationship with Oscar. Things had not been going well. Towards the end of November, just days before Bosie's planned departure to Cairo, there had been yet another series of scenes 'culminating,' according to Oscar, 'in one more than usually revolting when you came one Monday evening to my rooms accompanied by two of your friends'. The rooms in question were at 10, St James's Place. Quite what happened is impossible to know, but Oscar's pointed reference to Bosie's two friends may suggest that Bosie had turned up with two extremely unsuitable boys, expecting a *ménage à quatre* with Oscar. For Oscar, still nervous, still recovering from the anxiety of the Bruges affair, the boys may have been too young, too rough, or too obviously criminal – or indeed, a combination of all three – for him to want to risk a sexual encounter.

The next day Oscar fled abroad to Paris, having given his servant a false address for fear of Bosie's following him or finding him. 'I remember that afternoon,' he recalled in *De Profundis*, 'as I was in the railway-carriage whirling up to Paris, thinking what an impossible, terrible, utterly wrong state my life had got in to from the intellectual or ethical point of view.'

Oscar was probably right. From any conventional ethical or moral standpoint, his life was in a 'wrong state'. His relationship with Bosie was legally wrong, utterly impossible. But from a sexual and from an emotional standpoint, their relationship made perfect sense. At some level, Oscar could still experience a sense of guilt and disgust at the lived experience of his sexuality, a guilt and disgust paradoxically intensified by his compulsive, ever-strengthening desire for more sex, with more boys. There were times when Oscar was cast down by the weariness of the treadmill of desire and satiation, by the ever-present, raging thirst of lust: slaked, but never quenched, by sex. But these storms of self-loathing were just that: storms. They were over almost as soon as they began. Afterwards, the sun would shine, and Oscar would feel the warm rays of his love for Bosie, and Bosie's love for him, beating down.

'The usual telegrams of entreaty and remorse followed,' Oscar recalled. 'I disregarded them.' Bosie finally played his trump card. Unless Oscar agreed to meet him, he would refuse to go to Egypt. Oscar capitulated. By refusing to go to Egypt, Bosie might be placing himself in danger. Besides which, an angry, remorseful, importuning Bosie in London would have been infinitely more difficult to manage than a Bosie in Cairo, distracted by venerable antiquities and readily available boys. Oscar and Bosie met, probably in France, on the first leg of Bosie's journey to Cairo. 'Under the influence of great emotion, which even you cannot have forgotten,' Oscar wrote, 'I forgave the past, though I said nothing about the future.'

Bosie continued on to Cairo and Oscar returned to London. Gertrude Simmonds later claimed that she had seen and read a letter from Bosie, written from on board ship en route to Cairo, in which he several times addressed Oscar as 'darling' and said that he had 'found a very nice boy on the way' that would have 'suited' Oscar very well.

Oscar did not share Bosie's high spirits. In *De Profundis* he recalled that, on the day after their reconciliation, he sat in his rooms in St James's Place:

> sadly and seriously trying to make up my mind you really were what you seemed to be, so full of terrible defects, so utterly ruinous both to yourself and to others, so fatal a one to know even or to be with.

Oscar's negative thoughts about Bosie never lasted for very long. In fact he loved Bosie as much for his 'terrible defects' as for his finer points. He was fascinated by Bosie's wilful, mercurial moods, by his sexual paganism and by his determination to get what he wanted at almost any cost. But Oscar also knew that his love affair with Bosie was 'ruinous' and 'fatal'. He loved Bosie, he once said, 'with a sense of tragedy and ruin' and made a deliberate choice to embrace the inevitable tragedy and ruin that knowing Bosie would bring. In his poem 'Panthea', Oscar had written, 'One fiery-coloured moment: one great love; and lo! we die'. Bosie was Oscar's fiery-coloured moment, his one great love.

Less than three weeks later he was writing joyously to Bosie in Cairo:

> I am happy in the knowledge that . . . our love has passed the shadow and
> night of estrangement and sorrow and come out rose-crowned as of old. Let
> us be infinitely dear to each other, as indeed we always have been.

Bosie felt the same. His love for Oscar never wavered, never faltered, never
flickered for an instant, even though Oscar often doubted and often repudiated
his love for Bosie. Bosie knew that his love for Oscar was ennobling and
unselfish, that it represented the very best of him.

On the night before his departure for Cairo, Sybil had had a searing and
painful conversation with Bosie on the subject of his relationship with Oscar.
She poured out her long-suppressed feelings that Oscar had acted the part of
the corrupt and corrupting Lord Henry Wotton to Bosie's Dorian Gray and
was 'ruining his soul'. Sybil even confessed that she 'would almost like to
murder' Oscar. Bosie answered her charges in a series of impassioned letters
written from Cairo. He told Sybil that he didn't believe he had a soul before he
met Oscar, that it was Oscar, and only Oscar, who had opened up and
illuminated the moral universe:

> He has taught me everything I know that is worth knowing, he has taught me
> to judge of things by their essential points, to know what is fine from what is
> low and vulgar.

Underpinning Sybil's charges of corruption lay her conviction that Oscar had
seduced Bosie and initiated him into the mysteries of Uranian love. Bosie
vigorously refuted this:

> I should also like to tell you, that I did *not* imbibe those ideas from Oscar
> Wilde and that he did *not* put them into my head and encourage them. I had
> formed them in my own mind and was quite certain of their truth *two years*
> before I had ever seen him or even heard of him.

'I am passionately fond of him,' Bosie told Sybil:

> There is nothing I would not do for him, and if he dies before I do I shall not
> care to live any longer. The thought of such a thing makes everything black
> before my eyes. Surely there is nothing but what is fine and beautiful in such
> a love as that of two people for one another.

Their love was on an epic, heroic scale. When Oscar's life comes to be written,
Bosie told Sybil, their love for each other would be 'remembered and written
about as one of the most beautiful things in the world, as beautiful as the love
of Shakespeare and the unknown Mr W.H. or that of Plato and Socrates'.

Sybil was unconvinced by Bosie's protestations and decided to write to

Oscar, begging him to leave her son alone and to promise not to meet him abroad. She may have hinted at her belief that Oscar had sexually corrupted Bosie and specifically reproached him for having introduced Bosie to Robbie Ross, and so entangling Bosie in the Bruges incident. Oscar was affronted and wrote a frank reply which left Sybil in little doubt of Bosie's Uranian proclivities and the endless trouble they had got him into:

> I went as far as I could possibly go, I told her that the origin of our friendship was you in your undergraduate days at Oxford coming to beg me to help you in very serious trouble of a very particular character. I told her that your life had been continually in the same manner troubled. The reason of your going to Belgium you had placed to the fault of your companion in that journey . . . I replaced the fault on the right shoulders, on yours.

Oscar told Sybil that he had no intention of meeting Bosie abroad, or anywhere else, and that he hoped she would try and keep Bosie in Egypt for at least two or three years. Oscar had decided that he needed a rest from Bosie. He needed to work, to finish *An Ideal Husband*, and to write other plays.

Despite the success of his plays, money was in desperately short supply. The costs of the three-month stay at Goring had been enormous. And afterwards, in London, Oscar and Bosie had continued in the same extravagant lifestyle. In *De Profundis*, Oscar described their daily routine:

> At twelve o'clock you drove up, and stayed smoking cigarettes and chatting till 1.30, when I had to take you out to luncheon at the Café Royal or the Berkeley. Luncheon with its liqueurs lasted usually till 3.30. For an hour you retired to White's. At tea-time you appeared again, and stayed till it was time to dress for dinner. You dined with me either at the Savoy or at Tite Street. We did not separate as a rule till after midnight as supper at Willis's had to wind up the entrancing day.

After his trials and conviction, Oscar would also have the further humiliation of being declared bankrupt. He was obliged to attend bankruptcy hearings where he had to account, in minute detail, for his previous expenditure. It was then that Oscar worked out that his expenses for an ordinary day in London with Bosie, 'for luncheon, dinner, supper, amusements, hansoms and the rest of it ranged from £12 to £20, and the week's expenses were naturally in proportion and ranged from £80 to £130.' In 1893, a pound was worth £60 in today's money, which means that Oscar was spending a staggering £5,000 to £8,000 a week. Creditors were pressing. Gertrude Simmonds, the governess to Cyril and Vyvyan, recalled how 'things were not so prosperous' in October 1893, 'the butcher even refusing to send a joint until the account was settled, Oscar himself driving round in a hansom and settling up'.

But with Bosie in Egypt, there were distractions in Oscar's life. Though Oscar claimed he had taken his rooms at 10, St James's Place so that he could 'work undisturbed', they were equally convenient for entertaining a stream of young male visitors. According to Thomas Price, head waiter at St James's Place, Oscar 'had a great number of callers', some of them 'young boys'. They included some old friends, like Charlie Parker and Fred Atkins, and some new friends, among them Ernest Scarfe, whom Alfred Taylor had picked up at the roller skating rink in Knightsbridge, notorious as a place where older gentlemen could pick up younger men.

Scarfe was twenty-one and unemployed, and spent almost every afternoon at the rink. One evening, Taylor took Scarfe round to meet Oscar at St James's Place. The three of them chatted for a couple of hours and drank whisky and soda. As Scarfe was leaving, Oscar invited him to call again soon. In his statement to Queensberry's solicitors, Scarfe recounted how he returned for tea a day or so later. Oscar, he said, made flattering remarks, stroked his hair and tried to caress him. Scarfe claimed that he would have none of it and gave Oscar no encouragement. On the next occasion Scarfe came to tea, Oscar tried to fondle Scarfe's penis through his trouser fly-buttons. 'I would not allow him,' Scarfe deposed, 'although he tried to undo the buttons.' Thomas Price remembered Scarfe's visits to Oscar very clearly. 'I remember him because he was rather impudent,' said Price. Scarfe was not telling the truth, the whole truth and nothing but the truth in his statement. In the weeks between making his statement and the date of Oscar's trial, he changed his story, alleging that Oscar had committed both sodomy and acts of gross indecency with him.

There were other young men in Oscar's life, including an unidentified 'Frank' who had recently returned from a trip to Spain. 'You must tell me about your trip to Spain,' Oscar wrote. 'Your letter from there charmed me. *No*: you must tell me all about yourself. You are much more interesting to me than even Spain is.' And Oscar was still responding positively to letters of avowal from young men. Ralph Payne wrote to Oscar in February 1894 praising *Dorian Gray*. 'I am so glad you like that strange coloured book of mine,' Oscar wrote in reply. 'Will you come and see me?' he asked:

I am writing a play, and go to St James's Place, number *10,* where I have rooms, every day at 11.30. Come on Tuesday about 12.30, will you? But perhaps you are busy? Still, we can meet, surely, some day. Your handwriting fascinates me, your praise charms me.

Later that month Oscar wrote to Philip Houghton, an artist, whose letter of avowal had 'deeply moved' him. 'Write to me about yourself,' Oscar wrote 'tell me about your life and loves and all that keeps you wondering.'

In Cairo, Bosie was blissfully unaware of the state of dudgeon that Oscar had worked himself up into. 'I am enjoying this place very much,' he told Sybil. There was much to enjoy. Shortly after his arrival, he went to have tea with Wilfred Blunt, who described him as 'a pretty, interesting boy, very shy and youthful'. Bosie was also spotted one day at a race meeting by a young journalist called Robert Hichens. As the Consul-General's party arrived, the cry went up 'Here comes Cromer!' and Hichens pushed his way to the front where he saw an open carriage in which Lord Cromer, resplendent in a white top hat, was seated. 'By his side,' Hichens recalled, 'sat a young man, indeed almost a boy, fair, aristocratic, even poetic looking I thought.'

Reggie Turner, whom Bosie had met eighteen months earlier at the premiere of *Lady Windermere's Fan*, was also in Egypt. Turner was a fellow Uranian with an especial attraction to boys, whom Oscar later christened 'the boy-snatcher of Clement's Inn'. Turner was a great friend of Max Beerbohm's and of Bosie's, and it may well have been Turner's presence there which swayed Bosie to choose Egypt. Turner was staying on his half-brother's *dahabeeyah*, the arabic word for gilded barge, which was 'the last word in comfort and luxury', Bosie recalled. Reggie was attracted to the youthful-looking Bosie, and was moved to write his one and only sonnet to him which began, rather leadenly: 'More fair than any flower is thy face,/Thy limbs from all comparison are free.'

It was through Turner that Bosie made the acquaintance of Robert Hichens and the young novelist E.F. Benson – or Fred, as Bosie called him. Bosie and Reggie were openly and avowedly Uranian; Hichens and Benson were also Uranians, but rather less reconciled to their sexual urges. Throughout his life, Fred Benson struggled between his Uranian inclinations and what he saw as the 'filthy' and 'bestial' activities of sex, though perhaps in his youth he was rather more relaxed about the idea of love and sex between men. The four young men decided to take a trip up the Nile on a post boat.

Despite the poverty of his poetical imagination, Reggie Turner was a hugely gifted and witty conversationalist, as indeed was Bosie. Bosie, Reggie, Fred and Bob – as the four Uranian young men now called each other – sailed leisurely up the Nile and talked endlessly and well about the subject closest to their hearts: boys and sex. Bosie took the lead. He was, after all, a widely experienced authority on the subject. As a proud and proselytising Uranian, as well as someone incapable of reticence or discretion, Bosie talked at length and with passion of his love for Oscar, of their sexual explorations and adventures together, and of the primacy of the Cause. Robert Hichens listened greedily, and may have even taken notes in the privacy of his cabin, notes he would use for a novel, a *roman à clef*, in which the real lives of Oscar and Bosie would be masqueraded as the fictitious lives of Esmé Amarinth and Lord Reggie Hastings. Nine months later, the child of Robert Hichens's imagination, *The Green Carnation*, sprang into life fully formed, amazing and dazzling London. It was, Bosie reflected later, 'a piece of perfidy' which was to do Oscar and Bosie incalculable harm.

The Scarlet Marquis

'A typical Englishman, always dull and usually violent.'

The exact circumstances of Bosie's departure from Cairo are unclear. He left abruptly in early February 1894, to take up a post in Constantinople as honorary attaché to Lord Currie, the British Ambassador to Turkey. Strings had been pulled by Bosie's mother and grandfather to procure the post for him. But he may have left Cairo under a cloud. According to Robbie Ross, Bosie was 'hurled out of the official residence in consequence of the way in which he carried on in Cairo'. Bosie had almost certainly had sex with some willing Egyptian boys, just as he would almost exactly a year later with the willing boys of Algiers. Oscar later made a disparaging reference in *De Profundis* to Bosie and 'the fleshpots of Egypt', which suggests that he either knew or suspected a good deal of what had gone on. And Bosie had another sexual encounter while he was in Cairo: many years later, he told his nephew that he had had 'a romantic meeting' with Lord Kitchener, who was then forty-four years old.

Bosie decided to break his journey to Constantinople at Athens to spend a fortnight with Fred Benson, who was working for the British Archaeological Society. It was probably during his stay there that Bosie heard the news that Lord Currie had withdrawn his offer of the post of honorary attaché. Rumours of Bosie's 'carryings on' in Cairo may have reached him. Or James Rennell Rodd, Oscar's 'true poet and false friend', now a diplomat in Constantinople, may have dripped some poison into Currie's ears about Bosie's sexual preferences.

But the post in Constantinople was the last thing on Bosie's mind. He was becoming increasingly agitated about Oscar. He had not received any letters from him for several weeks now, not since the end of December, and he was bewildered, hurt and upset by the stony silence. Bosie had written a poem in Cairo – 'The Sphinx' – the last lines of which seem to express his fears and anxieties over his relationship with Oscar:

> I know that on the sand
> Crouches a thing of stone that in some wise
> Broods on my heart; and from the darkening land
> Creeps fear and to my soul in whispers speaks.

Bosie began to brood, to worry – rightly as it turned out – that Oscar was falling out of love with him, that he had, perhaps, already fallen out of love. He had written several letters to Oscar and despatched a swathe of telegrams, none of which had elicited a reply. After writing to tell Bosie that their love was 'rose-crowned as of old', Oscar appears to have changed his mind about the relationship yet again, unilaterally deciding to end the affair without telling Bosie.

From Athens, Bosie wrote in great distress to Sybil, begging her to get in touch with Oscar and persuade him to write to him. Oscar was surprised to hear from her. 'I confess I was absolutely astounded at her letter,' Oscar recalled in *De Profundis*:

> I could not understand how, after what she had written to me in December, and what I in answer had written to her, she could in any way try to repair or renew my unfortunate friendship with you.

Oscar wrote a frigid reply to Sybil to the effect that Bosie's best interests would be served by his remaining abroad. Thereafter, Bosie's telegraphic entreaties accelerated, and, when no letter came from Oscar, he turned to Constance for help. 'Finally you actually telegraphed to my wife begging her to use her influence with me to get me to write to you,' Oscar recalled:

> Our friendship had always been a source of distress to her: not merely because she had never liked you personally, but because she saw how your continual companionship altered me, and not for the better: still, just as she had always been most gracious and hospitable to you, so she could not bear the idea of my being in any way unkind – for so it seemed to her – to any of my friends.

Oscar's account in *De Profundis* is revealing. Behind her hospitable and gracious facade, Constance quite clearly loathed and hated Bosie; she was jealous of him and of his relationship with Oscar – a relationship which had long been 'a source of distress' to her. At Constance's request, Oscar did get in touch with Bosie. He sent a telegram to him in Athens, and every word he wrote was seared into his memory: 'I said that time healed every wound but that for many months to come I would neither write to you nor see you.'

Bosie was devastated by Oscar's telegram. He started back for Paris immediately, sending 'passionate telegrams' to Oscar pleading with him to meet him there, adding credence to the hypothesis that Bosie was under some sort of injunction to remain abroad. On the face of it, there was no reason to prevent Bosie from returning to London and laying amorous siege to Oscar at St James's Place, at Tite Street or at any one of their favourite haunts. Oscar declined to meet Bosie in Paris. Bosie begged and beseeched. Finally he despatched an eleven-page telegram to Oscar in Tite Street which contained 'a threat of suicide, and one not thinly-veiled'. Oscar agreed to meet. 'When I arrived in Paris,' he wrote:

your tears, breaking out again and again all through the evening, and falling over your cheeks like rain as we sat, at dinner first at Voisin's, at supper at Paillard's afterwards: the unfeigned joy you evinced at seeing me, holding my hand whenever you could, as though you were a gentle and penitent child: your contrition, so simple and sincere, at the moment: made me consent to renew our friendship.

It was an epic reconciliation for an epic love affair. The passion and intensity of Bosie's love for him, a love he was ready to sanctify by the sacrifice of his life, must have left Oscar shaken and humbled. Oscar had written about suicide as the ultimate sacrifice, the ultimate expression of love. In *The Portrait of Mr W.H.*, Cyril Graham commits suicide to demonstrate his faith and belief in the love between Shakespeare and Willie Hughes, and in Uranian love generally. And in Oscar's story 'The Nightingale and the Rose', the nightingale ritually sacrifices herself to the ideal of a decidedly masculine, 'flame-coloured' Uranian love by slowly impaling herself on the thorn of a rose bush. 'Love is wiser than Philosophy, though he is wise, and mightier than Power, though he is mighty,' the Nightingale declares.

That the love affair of Shakespeare and Willie Hughes might be spurious, and the beneficiary of the Nightingale's sacrifice unworthy, is not the point. To believe in love so powerfully, so passionately was an act of almost religious faith. George Ives wrote of Oscar that 'love to him was always a sacrifice, a sacrament, a religious rite'. The flames of Bosie's love may have consumed both himself and Oscar, but they also purified and sanctified their love. If Bosie was prepared to offer the ultimate sacrifice, then Oscar could hardly fail to reciprocate. He had passed a lifetime seeking for, and never quite finding, true love. Bosie's readiness and willingness to sacrifice his young and beautiful life at the altar of love was a revelation to Oscar. Never before had he encountered such intense flames of passion and knew that he might never do so again. Oscar and Bosie's reconciliation in Paris was arguably one of the great turning points in their relationship, the moment when they shed the skin of their previous passion to reveal a greater, deeper, more potent love for each other. In the course of their love affair they had feasted with panthers, fought with blackmailers and gambled with the danger of exposure, arrest, and imprisonment. Now they were both playing for the highest stakes.

With their love truly 'rose-crowned', Oscar and Bosie decided to return to London, arriving in early March. Bosie's relationship with his father had continued to be difficult and problematic. Queensberry disapproved of almost every aspect of his life: of his leaving Oxford without a degree, of his fecklessness and extravagance, and most of all of his friendship with Oscar. Indeed, he had urged Bosie, on more than one occasion, to end his intimacy. Only days after their return to London, Oscar and Bosie were lunching together at the Café Royal when Queensberry entered and they invited him to join them.

It was eerily reminiscent of the occasion eighteen months earlier when they had met Queensberry by chance, also the Café Royal, and invited him to lunch. Then, as now, the luncheon went off very well, and Bosie left Oscar and his father chatting amiably. Oscar even boasted that he 'completely got round' Queensberry and that they were great friends. With this happy state of affairs continuing, Bosie decided to pay a visit to Oxford, where he saw Max Beerbohm. 'Dear Bosie is with us,' Beerbohm told Reggie Turner. 'Is it you who have made him so amusing? Never in the summer did he make me laugh much, but now he is nearly brilliant.'

But disaster struck just days later when Oscar and Bosie had the bad luck to be spotted in each other's company by Queensberry. In a statement to his solicitors, Queensberry told how he happened to be standing near a window in Carter's Hotel when he noticed a hansom cab draw up outside the Albemarle Club which was just next to Carter's. Oscar and Bosie were in the cab, and Queensberry watched with horrified fascination as Oscar 'caressed' his son in what he considered to be 'an effeminate and indecent fashion'.

Queensberry was 'exceedingly distressed' and decided to write immediately to both of them and demand that they terminate their friendship. Signing himself 'Your disgusted so-called father', Queensberry wrote on 1 April to take Bosie to task about his intimacy with 'this man Wilde':

> It must either cease or I will disown you and stop all money supplies. I am not going to try and analyse this intimacy, and I make no charge; but to my mind to pose as a thing is as bad as to be it. With my own eyes I saw you both in the most loathsome and disgusting relationship as expressed by your manner and expression. Never in my experience have I ever seen such a sight as that in your horrible features.

Queensberry told Bosie that everyone was gossiping and speculating about his relationship with Oscar. 'No wonder people are talking as they are,' he wrote. 'Also I now hear on good authority, but this may be false, that his wife is petitioning to divorce him for sodomy and other crimes. Is this true, or do you know of it?' Queensberry closed his letter by stating that, if it was true that Oscar and Bosie were lovers, he would be quite justified in shooting Oscar on sight.

The letter Queensberry sent to Oscar two days later was slightly more temperate. 'Sir,' he wrote:

> I would request of you that you will close this acquaintance with my son Alfred. I make no accusations neither do I wish to characterise what your relationships are in this friendship. You must be aware that you are doing my son a great deal of harm and that any amount of people are talking about it. I myself saw you a short time ago with him in a hansom cab on terms of familiarity that actually made my blood curdle.

Bosie's response to his father's letter was calculated to enrage him. He sent a

281

telegram to Queensberry which read simply: 'What a funny little man you are.' Bosie proudly described his telegram as 'My celebrated telegram'. But it was, as Oscar later and more accurately remarked, 'a telegram of which the commonest street-boy would have been ashamed'. Queensberry was duly enraged. 'You impertinent young jackanapes,' he wrote to Bosie. 'I request that you will not send such messages to me by telegraph. If you send me any more such telegrams, or come with any impertinence, I will give you the thrashing you deserve.' Queensberry closed his letter with a clear threat:

> If I catch you again with that man I will make a public scandal in a way you little dream of; it is already a suppressed one. I prefer an open one, and at any rate I shall not be blamed for allowing such a state of things to go on.

Bosie followed up his telegram with a solicitor's letter in which he announced that he was relinquishing any claim to financial support from his father and that he declined to hold any more communication with him. He also demanded 'some withdrawal of your grave and unwarrantable insinuations'.

It had taken less than five days for a state of war to be declared between Bosie and his father. Queensberry could hardly be blamed for rising to the bait. It was barely six months since the debacle at Bad Homburg, where his plan of 'thrashing' Lord Rosebery over his rumoured sexual relationship with his eldest son, Drumlanrig, had been thwarted after the personal intervention of the Prince of Wales. Queensberry had been sent away, his tail between his legs. To add insult to injury, Rosebery – 'that bloody bugger' and 'Jew nancy boy' – had, three weeks earlier, on 3 March, become Prime Minister after Gladstone's resignation. 'God help the country say I if ever such as yourself come to guide her destinies,' Queensberry had told Rosebery the previous summer.' Now Queensberry's worst fears had come to pass. Rosebery was indeed guiding the country's destinies.

Queensberry was motivated by a complex blend of paternal instincts and gross personal insecurities. In attempting to 'save' his sons from sodomy, a fate regarded by most Victorians as worse than death, Queensberry was doing what any dutiful father would have done. His threats to thrash Rosebery and to shoot Oscar would have been seen as entirely laudable. At the same time, Queensberry must have felt a deep sense of shame that two of his sons were apparently being sodomised by older, powerful men. To have one sodomitical son might be regarded as a misfortune, to have two looked like heredity. Queensberry must have asked himself whether the blood of his sons was somehow tainted. He repeatedly referred to Bosie's birth as a 'crime', a crime against nature. 'I cried over you the bitterest tears a man ever shed,' he told Bosie, 'that I had brought such a creature into the world, and unwittingly had committed such a crime.' Queensberry could and did point an accusing finger at his wife's family, the Montgomerys, especially 'Alfredo Montgomerino', the 'Jew pimp' and general n'er do well. 'There is madness on your mother's side,' he told Bosie. But there must have been times when Queensberry asked himself whether or not it was the tainted blood of the Douglases, his blood, which had produced so unnatural a brood.

Even worse, Queensberry's confidence in his own sexual normalcy and prowess had recently taken a severe battering. Six months earlier, on 7 November 1893, he had suddenly married Miss Ethel Weedon, a young woman he appears to have met while he was on holiday in Eastbourne. No one from either the bride's or the groom's family was invited to the wedding, and it was left to Tom Gill, Queensberry's valet, to act as one of the two witnesses. Whatever Queensberry's motives for this precipitate marriage, the wedding night was a disaster. Within days, Ethel Weedon had left Queensberry and petitioned for an annulment, on the grounds of 'malformation of the parts of generation' and 'frigidity and impotency'. Queensberry was furious and humiliated. His young wife's allegations, coupled with the rumours about his two sodomitical sons, goaded him into a fury. He was determined to make a public scandal.

Having enraged his father to the point of apoplexy, Bosie left London in the second week of April to spend two months in Florence. He may have thought that discretion was the better part of valour, and that some time away from his father might allow things to cool off. He may also still have been worried that his premature return to London might arouse the wrath of the outraged fathers, Colonel Dansey and the Reverend Biscoe Wortham. Bosie also hoped that Florence might yield up some of its youthful sexual treasures. 'I wish you would write and tell me anything you know about Florence, as I have never been there before and am going by myself,' he wrote insouciantly to Charles Kains Jackson. 'I mean of course anything you know with regard to the eternal quest for beauty to which I am bound.' 'Beauty' was of course a euphemism for sex with young men, and was a term very much in vogue in Oscar's circle. Oscar had described Shakespeare's passion for Willie Hughes by saying that he was 'the slave of beauty'. George Ives had spoken of the 'Beauty-Spirit', confiding longingly to his diary how he wanted 'to get a glimpse of the beauty side of life – so long as it does not harm the Cause'. Florence had always had a reputation for tolerance when it came to sex between men, and was popular with English Uranians. Bosie also got in touch with his friend Lord Henry Somerset, who had contributed a Uranian poem in Italian to Bosie's magazine, the *Spirit Lamp*, and who was at the centre of a small expatriate Uranian community there.

Once Bosie had left for Italy, Oscar began to miss him. 'The gay, gilt and gracious lad has gone away,' Oscar wrote to him, complaining that he was short of money. 'I am in the purple valleys of despair, and no gold coins dropping down from heaven to gladden me.' There were titbits of news about trade:

> I had a frantic telegram from Edward Shelley, of all people! asking me to see him. When he came he was of course in trouble for money. As he betrayed me grossly, I, of course, gave him money and was kind to him. I find that forgiving one's enemies is a most curious morbid pleasure; perhaps I should check it.

Oscar might also have told Bosie about an argument he had had with his former lover, Clyde Fitch. One gloomy, wet afternoon Oscar spotted Fitch walking along the street and offered him a lift in his cab. Taking his courage in both hands, Fitch started to remonstrate with Oscar regarding the 'ugly rumours', presumably about his relationship with Bosie and Lord Queensberry's ire, which were swirling round London. Despite Oscar's airy dismissals and evident wish to change the subject, Fitch persisted. 'Stop to let this man out!' an exasperated Oscar called to the driver. 'I invited him for a drive, but he is not a gentleman!'

Oscar joined Bosie in Florence in early May, and the lovers spent a month together, both of them bound on 'the eternal quest for beauty'. Oscar certainly met Lord Henry Somerset, who was clearly not one to hold a grudge. Five years earlier, in a review in the *Pall Mall Gazette*, Oscar had scathingly dismissed his volume of poetry, *Songs of Adieu*, with the words: 'He has nothing to say and says it.' André Gide was also in Florence. 'Who did I meet here?' Gide wrote to his mother. 'Oscar Wilde!! He looks older and ugly, but he is still an extraordinary storyteller.'

If either Oscar or Bosie had thought that their absence from London might calm Queensberry down, they were sadly mistaken. The scandalous, sodomitical activities of his two sons continued to prey on Queensberry's mind. He was obsessed with 'saving' his sons, at any cost. When Oscar returned from Florence, he received several vile letters from Queensberry, none of which survive. Judging by his usual epistolary style, they would have been long and incoherent rants, threatening exposure, thrashings or even death. In at least one of these letters, Queensberry brought in Lord Rosebery's name, as well as the names of other 'exalted personages', almost certainly accusing them of being sodomites. Oscar was unsure what to do. Should he dignify Queensberry's disgusting invective with a reply? Or should he do nothing and hope that the screaming 'Scarlet Marquis' would quickly tire of the game and slink away? More importantly, Queensberry's allegations posed a serious risk. If Queensberry was intent on 'a public scandal', how long would it be before he was bruiting his allegations abroad? How long before they reached the ears of Constance or came to the attention of Scotland Yard? Oscar and Bosie were still debating what on earth to do when matters came abruptly to a head.

On the afternoon of 30 June, at approximately four o'clock, Queensberry turned up at Tite Street unannounced. He was accompanied by a friend, 'a burly friend'. Queensberry and his burly friend were shown into the library on the ground floor. Oscar was upstairs, changing. He was in the highest of high spirits, about to depart to spend an idyllic weekend with a young man in the country, and a carriage laden with bags was waiting outside. 'I am off to the country till Monday,' he had told George Ives that morning. 'I have said I am going to Cambridge to see you, but I am really going to see the young Domitian, who has taken to poetry.' It is not hard to guess the type of young man Oscar was planning to visit. The Roman Emperor Domitian was famous for his sexual vigour and for having sold himself as a male prostitute when he was young and poor.

When his servant told him that Lord Queensberry and another gentleman were waiting in the library, Oscar was surprised, and not a little taken aback. He immediately went into the library where Queensberry was standing by the window:

'Sit down!' said Queensberry curtly.

'I do not allow you to talk like that to me in my house or anyone to talk like that to me in my house or anywhere else,' Oscar replied. 'I suppose you have come to apologise for the statement you made about my wife and myself in letters you wrote to your son,' he added. 'I could have you up any day I chose for criminal libel for writing such a letter.'

'The letter was privileged, as it was written to my son,' retorted Queensberry.

'How dare you say such things to me about your son and me?' Oscar demanded.

'You were both kicked out of the Savoy Hotel at a moment's notice for your disgusting conduct,' said Queensberry. 'You have taken furnished rooms for him in Piccadilly.'

'Somebody has been telling you an absurd set of lies about your son and me,' said Oscar reasonably. 'I haven't done anything of the kind.'

But Queensberry was not in the mood to be reasoned with. He knew what he knew, he said, and he had evidence.

'I hear you were thoroughly well blackmailed last year for a disgusting sodomitic letter that you wrote to my son,' he said.

'The letter was a beautiful letter, and I never write except for publication,' replied Oscar. 'Lord Queensberry,' he continued. 'Do you seriously accuse your son and me of sodomy?'

'I don't say you are it,' Queensberry growled. 'But you look it and you pose as it, which is just as bad. If I catch you and my son together in any public restaurant, I will thrash you!'

Oscar was by now thoroughly riled. 'I don't know what the Queensberry rules are, but the Oscar Wilde rule is to shoot on sight!' Oscar declared, telling Queensberry to leave his house at once.

Queensberry was still muttering about disgusting scandals and sodomitic letters.

'You have to go,' repeated Oscar firmly. 'I will not have in my house a brute like you.'

'I won't stay longer than I can help, I don't want to get the reputation you've got!' Queensberry sneered as he and his burly friend shuffled out into the hall.

'This,' Oscar told his servant, 'is the Marquis of Queensberry, the most infamous brute in London. You are never to allow him to enter my house again. Should he attempt to come in, you must send for the police.'

Oscar's courtroom account of the scene at Tite Street was an edited version. The actual encounter was much nastier, and there was a much stronger streak of barely suppressed violence and threat. Oscar later wrote how he remembered Queensberry:

> waving his small hands in the air in an epileptic fury . . . uttering every foul word his foul mind could think of, and screaming the loathsome threats he afterwards with such cunning carried out.

After the initial shock of Queensberry's unexpected incursion into Tite Street had worn off, Oscar and Bosie paused to take stock. They were confronted with the disturbing fact that Queensberry knew rather more about their lives than he ought to. He knew that they had both stayed at the Savoy, and he knew something about the existence of Oscar's rooms at St James's Place. Most significantly, Queensberry knew that Oscar had been 'thoroughly well blackmailed last year for a disgusting sodomitic letter that you wrote to my son'. This was alarming. Queensberry's information was exact. Oscar had been twice blackmailed the previous year over his 'madness of kisses' letter to Bosie. How had Queensberry found this out? Though Oscar and Bosie never did find out, the culprit may have been Oscar's old friend, the solicitor, Sir George Lewis, who had successfully extricated Bosie from the Oxford blackmailing incident in the spring of 1892, and who had intervened when Alfred Wood tried to blackmail Oscar over the 'madness of kisses' letter. Queensberry had retained Lewis to act for him in annulment proceedings instituted by Ethel Weedon.

What to do about the mad, screaming Marquis was the topic of much discussion between Oscar, Bosie and other intimate friends like Robbie Ross and George Ives. Doing nothing was no longer an option. Queensberry was bandying about accusations of sodomy, which were very serious. He had to be effectively gagged before the accusations became common currency and, crucially, before they reached the ears of Scotland Yard. It was agreed that legal advice, and even perhaps legal remedy, should be sought. After all, the good offices of Sir George Lewis had resolved Bosie's Oxford blackmail, and helped to resolve Alfred Wood's attempted blackmail. And Bosie and Oscar knew that Lewis had been involved behind the scenes in trying to settle the stand-off in Bad Homburg between Queensberry and Rosebery. It was worth a try. A stiff solicitor's letter, with a strong threat of legal action, might just be enough to scare Queensberry away.

It was to Sir George Lewis that Oscar now turned. Bosie was very anxious that Oscar should sue his father for criminal libel. 'I am not and never have been ashamed of the fact that I urged Oscar from the very first to take proceedings,' Bosie wrote many years later. 'I told him he should go for my father at once.' Oscar wrote to Lewis in the first days of July about the possibility of instituting proceedings against Queensberry. Lewis sent a curt and businesslike reply to say that he was acting for Lord Queensberry:

> Under these circumstances you will see that it is impossible for me to offer

any opinion about any proceedings you intend to take against him. Although I cannot act against him, I should not act against you.

On Robbie Ross's advice, Oscar now consulted the firm of C.O. Humphreys, Son and Kershaw.

Bosie's family were beginning to be alarmed. Queensberry had caused the family quite enough trouble and involved them in quite enough scandal without the further spectacle of a prosecution in the open courts for criminal libel over an alleged sexual relationship between his youngest son and a famous playwright. There was also Drumlanrig and his career to think of. For a junior government minister in the House of Lords, and a close and trusted friend and ally of the Prime Minister, any scandal involving his father could be ruinous to his career. The family made strenuous efforts to calm things down on either side. Alfred Montgomery wrote a cautious, civil letter to Queensberry, suggesting that they should meet to discuss the Oscar and Bosie situation. 'I do not see why I should come dancing attendance on you,' Queensberry replied pugnaciously. 'Your daughter is the person who is supporting my son to defy me. This hideous scandal has been going on for years':

I have made out a case against Oscar Wilde and have to his face accused him of it. If I was quite certain of the thing I would shoot the fellow on sight, but I can only accuse him of posing. It now lies in the hands of the two whether they will further defy me. Your daughter appears now to be encouraging them, although she can hardly intend this. I don't believe Wilde will now dare defy me. He plainly showed the white feather the other day when I talked to him – damned cur and coward of the Rosebery type.

Sybil Queensberry asked Bosie's cousin, George Wyndham – 'plausible George Wyndham', as Oscar dubbed him – to dissuade Oscar from launching legal proceedings. Wyndham's intervention was successful. (Wyndham's other piece of advice, that he should 'gradually drop' Bosie, was treated by Oscar with the contempt it deserved.) Oscar settled for a solicitor's letter demanding a retraction and an apology. Yet even this was too much for Sybil. She wrote a personal note to Oscar begging him not to send a solicitor's letter.

Oscar and Bosie disregarded Sybil's entreaties and the solicitor's letter was sent on 11 July. 'My Lord Marquis,' the letter ran:

We have been consulted by Mr Oscar Wilde with respect to certain letters written by your Lordship in which letters you have most foully and infamously libelled him as also your own son Lord Alfred Douglas. In those letters your Lordship has mentioned exalted personages and Mr Oscar Wilde not being desirous of wounding their feelings by a publication of your letters has instructed us to give you the opportunity of retracting your assertions and insinuations, in writing, with an apology for having made them.

Queensberry's reply was short and to the point. 'I have received your letter with considerable astonishment,' he wrote. 'I shall certainly not tender to Mr. Oscar Wilde any apology for letters I have written to my son.' Queensberry said that he was at a complete loss to understand the allusion to exalted personages. 'With Mr Wilde's horrible reputation,' he concluded, 'I can afford to publish any private letters I have written to my son, and you are quite at liberty to take any steps you please.'

According to the statement he made to his solicitors before his trial for criminal libel, Queensberry was determined to confront Oscar and Bosie in public:

> I now made up my mind to have a public row with them, if I met them together. I went about all the cafés they usually frequented hoping to find them but I was not fortunate enough to do so. I told the manager at the Berkeley, Willis's Rooms and the Café Royal what I intended to do.

Bosie was incandescent with rage and dashed off an impetuous note. 'As you return my letters unopened, I am obliged to write on a postcard':

> I write to inform you that I treat your absurd threats with absolute indifference. Ever since your exhibition at OW's house, I have made a point of appearing with him at many public restaurants such as the Berkeley, Willis's Rooms, the Café Royal etc., and I shall continue to go to any of these places whenever I choose and with whom I choose. I am of age and my own master.

Bosie informed his father that Oscar could prosecute him and have him sent to prison for his 'outrageous libels'. He concluded with a threat. If Queensberry attempted to assault either himself or Oscar:

> I shall try to defend myself with a loaded revolver which I always carry; and if I shoot you, or if he shoots you, we should be completely justified as we should be acting in self-defence against a violent and dangerous rough, and I think if you were dead not many people would miss you.

Bosie was extremely proud of this letter and boasted to Oscar that he could beat his father 'at his own trade'. But he was also deadly serious. He did indeed go about with a loaded gun, which once accidentally went off in the Berkeley and shattered a window. It was lucky that neither he or Oscar, nor indeed anyone else, was injured or killed.

Bosie's threat further inflamed the situation. Queensberry's response was to pay a personal visit to Oscar's solicitors on 18 July and inform them that unless Bosie stopped carrying a loaded revolver, he would personally inform the police of the fact.

Later the same day, Queensberry wrote a letter to the solicitors repeating his threat:

If I am to be openly defied by Mr Oscar Wilde and my son by further scandals in public places, I shall have no other resort but to do as I have threatened and give information at Scotland Yard as to what has happened.

The wording was ambiguous, perhaps deliberately so. By 'further scandals in public places' did he simply mean Bosie's carrying a revolver? Or was his threat altogether broader? Queensberry's letter could be construed as a shot across Oscar and Bosie's bows. If they continued to flaunt their friendship in public, Queensberry would give what information he had to Scotland Yard. It was a credible threat. Queensberry already knew about the 'madness of kisses' blackmail and was actively trying to find out more, interrogating Sybil as to whether Bosie had ever stayed at the Savoy.

For Oscar and Bosie, Queensberry was something between a nuisance and 'a maniac'. Neither of them believed that he would really carry out his threat to make a public scandal. They knew he was violent, foul-mouthed and obsessive, but they also knew that over time he tended to lose interest in his vendettas. In spite of all the dramas of July 1894, they still hoped that Queensberry would get bored, go away and leave them alone. But Oscar and Bosie made the mistake of under-estimating their enemy and the extent of his malice and his cunning. It would prove to be a fatal mistake.

The boys on the beach

'When you really want love, you will find it waiting for you.'

The summer of 1894 saw Oscar and Bosie more committed to each other than ever. Paradoxically, the threatening shadow of the Scarlet Marquis seemed to magnify the intensity of their love. Adversity shaped and honed it, defining and giving value to their Uranian passion. Oscar's letters to Bosie are gentler, more tender and more true than his earlier more flamboyant and self-consciously 'poetic' love letters. Bosie was his 'own dear boy', his 'own dearest boy' and his 'dear, wonderful boy'. 'I want to see you,' he told Bosie in July, at the height of the Queensberry crisis:

> It is really absurd. *I can't live without you*. You are so dear, so wonderful. I think of you all day long, and miss your grace, your boyish beauty, the bright sword-play of your wit, the delicate fancy of your genius, so surprising always in its sudden swallow-flights towards north or south, towards sun or moon – and above all, you yourself.

Two or three weeks later Oscar was writing again to tell Bosie how much he loved him. 'You are more to me than any one of them has any idea,' he wrote. 'You are the atmosphere of beauty through which I see life; you are the incarnation of all lovely things.'

Both Oscar and Bosie saw a great deal of George Ives during the summer. Ives had recently moved into the Albany, the exclusive bachelor apartments in Piccadilly, and Oscar and Bosie were in the habit of dropping in for afternoon tea and long discussions about the Cause. Ives's transcendent vision of Uranian love as a love apart, a love superior and a love persecuted appealed to them both at this moment of crisis. As a result of Queensberry's attack they felt themselves to be emblematic of all vexed and persecuted lovers. And their fight for the freedom to love each other was emblematic of the struggle of all men who loved men. It was a noble cause, a call to arms. They were crusaders, not just in a political sense, but in a spiritual, almost mystical sense. They were what Oscar and George Ives, among others, called 'the Elect', the chosen Uranian few, predestined for salvation – and perhaps even for martyrdom.

Ives was by turns dazzled and bewildered by Oscar and Bosie. 'Their ideals

290

are so different from mine,' he confided to his diary. Obsessed with secrecy and with his work for the Cause, Ives was a prude and a puritan. He alternately struggled with and submitted to what he called 'the beauty side of life', enjoying sex and then feeling guilty after taking his pleasure. Oscar and Bosie's joyous erotic paganism, searching for and seizing sexual pleasure as often as they could, was the antithesis of Ives's anguished idealism. Oscar was, Ives thought, as 'brilliant as a shining jewel', but 'he either cannot or will not, give the key to his philosophy. Until I get it, I can't understand him.'

George Ives's interest in Bosie was altogether more earthy. Like many of Oscar's circle, Ives was violently attracted to Bosie, and more than a little in love with him. The previous autumn, just before Bosie's departure for Egypt, Ives had been kept awake by erotic thoughts about him. 'Was awake till past 3 and am not sleeping so well as usual lately,' he confided to his diary. 'I attribute this to the influence of A.D. about whom I am spinning a friendly web.' He thought Bosie 'bright as Apollo' but was not blind to his faults. Ives recognised that Bosie had 'a difficult character, swayed by passion, shaken by impulse'. He wanted Bosie to 'change his life', to pause 'to reflect on himself, to conquer himself and obtain freedom'. If Bosie could be reformed, a bright future lay before them. But if not, there could be nothing between them for 'the Cause must not be injured by an individual however charming'.

George Ives never did succeed in reforming Bosie, but he did manage a snatched night of passion with him in the summer of 1894. Ives recorded in his diary how 'B', as he called Bosie, 'the original of Dorian Gray and a bigger scoundrel', had come to tea at the Albany. Afterwards, Bosie took Ives to his mother's house in Cadogan Place, where Ives played the piano and was introduced to Bosie's older brother, Drumlanrig. They dined together at the Café Royal, and Ives's diary coyly records how Bosie 'is staying here tonight'. Ives was rather less coy about that single sexual encounter with Bosie in an addendum to his diary entry made a quarter of a century later: 'That miserable traitor actually stayed one night and slept with me!' he wrote. It is clear that Bosie wanted a threesome. 'He pressed me to ask —— in,' wrote Ives, adding with unconscious wit, 'but I declined as I thought it wouldn't do in the Albany.'

As a defiant Queensberry continued to stalk them, Oscar and Bosie increasingly turned to the occult: to a series of fortune tellers, clairvoyants and palm readers. Oscar had been weaned on the myths and legends of Ireland and had always been very superstitious. 'I love superstitions,' he wrote in January 1894. 'They are the colour element of thought and imagination.' When the actor-manager George Alexander asked him if he really believed in palmists, Oscar replied, 'Always . . . when they prophesy nice things.' Oscar and Bosie wanted to read the runes of their lives, to find out what the future held in store. But they were not in search of the truth. Rather they were seeking comfort and reassurance, and they found it, in large measure, in the person of Mrs Robinson, 'the Sibyl of Mortimer Street', as Oscar dubbed her. Mrs Robinson was a fashionable palm reader who numbered several MPs and society ladies among her clientele. Oscar seems to have first visited her in July, at the height of the Queensberry crisis. Mrs Robinson was suitably reassuring, as Oscar told Bosie:

> The only thing that consoles me is what the Sibyl of Mortimer Street (whom mortals term Mrs Robinson) said to me. If I could disbelieve her I would, but I can't, and I know that early in January you and I will go away together for a long voyage, and that your lovely life goes always hand in hand with mine.

Mrs Robinson's prophesy was correct. Oscar and Bosie did go away together in early January the following year, to Algiers.

Not long after his first reading, Oscar felt that he needed to pay another visit to the Sibyl. 'I have been deeply impressed by what you told me. It has made me very happy,' he wrote to Mrs Robinson in the first week of August, 'but the thing is so serious that I must see you again.' The so serious 'thing' that Oscar was referring to must have been the troubles he and Bosie were having with Queensberry. 'Your father is on the rampage again,' Oscar told Bosie, '– been to the Café Royal to enquire for us, with threats etc.':

> I think now it would have been better for me to have had him bound over to keep the peace, but what a scandal! Still, it is intolerable to be dogged by a maniac.

Still they trusted to Fate. Bosie had consulted another, unnamed sibyl who had prophesied a bright future. He had written to tell Oscar the glad tidings. 'Your new Sibyl is really wonderful,' Oscar replied. 'It is most extraordinary. I must meet her.'

Oscar and Bosie's sudden interest in divining the future reflected their passionate commitment to the Cause. Some Uranians – like Edward Carpenter and George Ives – believed that many of their kind were gifted with special, mystical powers and that sodomy was, quite literally, a magical act. Edward Carpenter had studied the 'curious and interesting' worldwide phenomenon of 'the connection of the Uranian temperament with prophetic gifts and divination' and had come to the firm conclusion that Uranians in many cultures and civilisations, from the most primitive to the most sophisticated, were 'prophets or priests', 'wizards or witches'. George Ives wrote about the Uranian 'spiritual sight' and mused upon why it is 'full and strong in some, and in many so absent or undemanding – but I love those best to whom it is given, they are of the higher life'. Ives believed he was possessed of the spiritual sight. 'Only in the darkness, amidst solitude, do I feel to, somehow, come to my real Life. I seem to be in touch, then, with wonderful things and with mystic Powers.'

As the Uranian Cause was finding its first, faint and tremulous voice in the early 1890s, it also sought to divine its spirit, to articulate its mystical philosophy. The commonwealth of shared sexual experience was not enough, not nearly enough, to launch an ideological battle against a virulently hostile world. Uranianism needed something more, something which could bind together the diverse strands of the movement, and the even more diverse individuals within it. And so the idea of a sexual and psychic solidarity, of a shared Uranian spirituality, was born.

Just before midnight on the night of 27 July, Oscar and Bosie attended a Uranian 'thought-reading' at the flat of George Ives in the Albany. The invited 'thought-reader' was 'C.D.', or Campbell Dodgson, a friend of Lionel Johnson's, and the same Campbell Dodgson who had gone to stay with Oscar at Babbacombe Cliff as Bosie's tutor two years earlier. Dodgson was, according to Ives:

> positively prophetic in his power of thought-reading. He has an occult or magnetic power which surpasses anything I have yet seen, and would have been burnt as a sorcerer in the bad old times.

But for Oscar and Bosie, there was little occult comfort to be garnered that evening. When they walked into the flat, Ives records, 'difficulties arose':

> 'C' was very nervous and for mystic reasons, would not come farther than the outer door. I think he must have known by instinct and his gift that 'O' who came in and 'B' were very cross – I have never seen 'O' so ruffled and knew there must be something *wrong*. ('C' says yes, but it is nothing very serious, I have no doubt he is right).

Dodgson was wrong about the nature of what was ruffling the feathers of Oscar and Bosie and making them so cross. It was not trivial. It was deadly serious.

Oscar was so deeply impressed with Mrs Robinson that he not only recommended her to two of his friends, but also persuaded Constance to go to her for a reading. Like her husband, Constance was deeply superstitious and had, in 1888, become a member of the fashionable Order of the Golden Dawn, a heady blend of Kabbalism, Buddhism, Theosophy and Freemasonry, whose members sought enlightenment and wisdom through occult ceremonies. Constance was seeking comfort and reassurance about the future. She was probably unaware of the threat Queensberry posed to her husband and her family in the summer of 1894. But she was only too well aware that Bosie was back in Oscar's life, and their attachment seemed stronger than ever.

Oscar was desperately strapped for cash that summer. 'I am overdrawn £41 at the bank,' he told Bosie. 'It really is intolerable the want of money. I have not a penny. I can't stand it any longer, but don't know what to do.' It was shortage of money which forced Oscar and Constance to economise on their summer plans by taking a house, the Haven, on the Esplanade in Worthing for the long summer vacation. Property was plentiful and very cheap in Worthing that year. The previous summer there had been a serious outbreak of typhoid fever in the town, after the fresh water supply had become contaminated with sewage.

In sharp contrast to the luxurious house at Goring that Oscar and Bosie had taken the previous year, the Haven was rather modest. 'The house, I hear, is small,' Oscar told Bosie before he left London, 'and I have no writing room.' Bosie was invited to come and stay at the Haven. 'When you come to Worthing, of course all things will be done for your honour and joy,' he wrote. But a day or so later, Oscar was earnestly trying to dissuade Bosie from coming to stay. 'Dearest Bosie,' Oscar wrote from the Haven. 'I have just come in from luncheon':

> A horrid ugly Swiss governess has, I find, been looking after Cyril and Vyvyan for a year. She is quite impossible. Also, children at meals are tedious. Also, you, the gilt and graceful boy, would be bored. Don't come here. I will come to you.

Oscar was trying to be tactful. Constance must have made it clear that she had no wish to receive Bosie in Worthing. But Bosie was not to be put off. He came and stayed on three occasions during August and September. In a letter to Robbie Ross, he admitted that his presence there had been a source of friction. 'I had great fun,' he told Robbie, 'though the last few days the strain of being a bone of contention between Oscar and Mrs Oscar began to make itself felt.' Though he later repudiated this statement, pretending it was a joke, Bosie admitted that relations between Oscar and Constance were at this time 'distinctly strained'. Oscar's joke about just discovering that a governess had been looking after Cyril and Vyvyan for a year, though clearly an exaggeration, does suggest that he had little interest and took little part in domestic arrangements. Certainly the couple seemed bent on spending as little time as possible with each other and appeared to be living almost separate lives, coming together for the sake of the children.

Constance spent August in Worthing, making at least one and possibly more trips to London on her own in the course of the month. She returned to London with the boys in early September, leaving Oscar in sole possession. She had found consolation for the neglect of her husband in a passionate friendship with a younger man. Arthur Humphreys was twenty-eight, a bookseller and publisher who worked for Hatchard's in Piccadilly. He was bringing out a small edition of Oscar's aphorisms, *Oscariana*, chosen by Constance, and this is presumably how they came to meet. Arthur was married, seemingly happily. He and his wife Eleanor had one child, a daughter. Quite when Constance and Arthur realised that they had feelings for each other is not known, but a letter she wrote to him in early June seems to mark a significant turning point in her feelings. 'I feel as tho' I must write you one line to emphatically repeat my remark that you are an ideal husband, indeed I think you are not far short of being an ideal man!'

Constance's note of 'one line' extended to eight pages and includes an account, a justification, of how and why her feelings for Arthur came into existence. It seems that she was attracted to him at first sight. 'I liked you and was interested in you, and I saw that you were good, and it is rarely that I come across a man that has that written in his face.' Constance made it clear to Arthur that she was attracted to him. 'I stepped past the limits perhaps of good taste in the wish to be your friend and to have you for my friend,' she wrote. Arthur was easy to talk to, a good and sympathetic listener. Constance opened up to him, revealing, as she had done to Oscar, the sadness and bitterness she still felt about her unhappy childhood at the hands of her mother. 'I spoke to you very openly about myself,' she told Arthur, 'and I confess that I should not like you to repeat what I said about my childhood: I am afraid it was wrong to speak as bitterly as I did.'

Constance knew that there could never be a physical dimension to her love affair with Arthur, a fact she was ready to acknowledge. 'Your marriage,' she told him, 'was made for the sake of good, was the result your character, and so was ideal.' Constance concluded her letter by saying 'I speak of you in terms of high praise to every-one,' and adding 'but it is unnecessary to give reasons for so doing.' This is only one of two surviving letters which Constance wrote to Arthur. There is a gap of almost three months between the two. That dozens of letters were written and received during those three months, and that their relationship grew in intensity over the summer, is clear from Constance's second letter of 11 August when she wrote to 'My Darling Arthur' to 'tell you how much I love you, and how dear and delightful you have been to me to-day':

> I *have* been happy, and I *do* love you dear Arthur. Nothing in my life has ever made me so happy as this love of yours to me has done . . . I love you just because you ARE, and because you have come into my life to fill it with love and make it rich.

She signed herself 'Your always devotedly loving Constance' and added:

> I shall try and give you this; and if I can't I shall post it. I shall come up on Thursday, so let me have a letter when I arrive PLEASE.

Oscar was not blind to his wife's infatuation with Arthur Humphreys, and he could see the parallels and ironies of their situations as a husband and wife each in love with somebody else. In August 1894, while he was in Worthing and while Constance was going up to London to exchange furtive *billets doux* with Arthur, Oscar sketched out to George Alexander a scenario for a play, reputedly to be called *Constance*. As he explained to Alexander, the play concerned a husband and a wife: a man – like Oscar – 'of rank and fashion' married to a woman very like Constance, 'a simple sweet country girl – a lady – but simple and ignorant of fashionable life'. Eventually, 'he gets bored with her', just as Oscar had been 'bored to death' by Constance.

The husband 'invites down a lot of fashionable *fin-de-siècle* women and men' who are 'horrid to the wife, they think her dowdy and dull', just as Oscar's friends had thought Constance dowdy and dull. The husband lectures the wife on how to behave. She must not, he enjoins, be 'prudish', nor must she mind if anyone, especially the dashing Gerald Lovel, flirts with her. Constance, as Oscar knew only too well, was inclined to be prudish, with her views on 'perfect morality'.

The husband makes love to 'Lady X', one of the fashionable *fin-de-siècle* guests, in the darkened drawing room, unaware that his wife is in the room and hears and sees everything. Oscar, of course, had made love to – and had sex with – dozens of young men in Tite Street, including Bosie. It is entirely possible, indeed probable, that Constance either knew or had very strong suspicions about what Oscar got up to. When Lady X's husband beats violently on the door of the drawing room, demanding admittance and threatening to plunge the family into scandal (just as Lord Queensberry had violently beaten on the doors of Tite Street, threatening to plunge the Wildes into scandal), it is the wife who saves the day by telling Lord X that they had all been engaged in 'an absurd experiment in thought-reading'. The wife then falls in love with Gerald Lovel, and too late the chastened husband begs forgiveness. The wife tells her husband she cannot forgive him, and, besides which, Gerald Lovel is the father of her unborn child. The husband promptly kills himself.

Oscar thought the scenario 'extremely strong'. 'I want the sheer passion of love to dominate everything,' he told Alexander. Love was to dominate the play, and the suicide of the husband was the proper due paid to true love, 'leaving love its tragedy, and so making it a still greater passion'. Although Oscar most certainly did not envisage committing suicide so that the sheer flame of love could burn even more brightly between Constance and Arthur Humphreys, it is significant that he believed suicide and tragedy were part of the power and passion of love. Oscar had by now begun to recognise that his love for Bosie was tragic, doomed and therefore all the more passionate. 'I love him as I always did,' he said later, 'with a sense of tragedy and ruin.'

During August, there was some more disturbing news from London. Oscar read in the newspapers of a police raid on the basement of a house in the West End of London in which Alfred Taylor and Charlie Parker were caught up:

Eighteen men were taken into custody by the police in a midnight raid in Fitzroy Street on Sunday, August 12, 1894, two of them being men in feminine clothing. Amongst them were Charles Parker, 19, of no occupation, 72, Regent Street, Chelsea; Alfred Taylor, 32, of no occupation, of 7, Camera Square, Chelsea; John Watson Preston, 34, general dealer, 46, Fitzroy Street, W., the proprietor of the raided premises; and Arthur Marling, 26, of 8, Crawford Street. The last named was described as a female impersonator, and was charged with being an idle and disorderly person. He appeared in court dressed in a fantastic female garb of black and gold.

The house was being used as an unofficial club for drag queens, renters and their punters. The police testified how they had seen two of the arrested men,

Preston and Marling, in a hansom cab, dressed as women, with men in ordinary clothes sitting on their laps. The police had apparently been watching the premises in Fitzroy Street for some time and claimed that most of the men they had arrested were 'known' to them. This was alarming. Were the police beginning to systematically keep tabs on the Uranian demimonde? Only the previous year, in August 1893, Alfred Taylor's landlady had allowed a police sergeant to secretly search his rooms.

The Fitzroy Street raid prompted Max Beerbohm to joke to Reggie Turner, 'Oscar has at length been arrested for certain kinds of crime. He was taken in the Café Royal (lower room). Bosie escaped, being an excellent runner, but Oscar was less nimble.' Alfred Taylor's 'husband', Charles Spurrier Mason, appealed to Oscar for help. 'I was very sorry to read in the paper about poor Alfred Taylor. It is a dreadful piece of luck,' Oscar replied. He appeared not to be unduly concerned about Alfred Taylor. 'Do tell me all about Alfred?' he wrote again a day or so later. 'Was he angry or amused? When I come back to town do come and dine. What fun our dinners were in the old days!' Alfred Taylor and Charlie Parker were given unconditional discharges for lack of evidence, though the magistrate did comment that he had received a number of letters indicating that most of the arrested men were of 'the vilest possible character'. Alfred Taylor immediately went back to his previous happy, chattering, rather vacuous life as everybody's friend and resumed his profession of part-time procurer. Charlie Parker reacted rather differently. Six weeks after his discharge, on 3 October, he enlisted for the Royal Artillery. His military records curiously note that his eyebrows met and that he had scars on the palms of both hands.

Meanwhile, in Worthing, the weather during the first half of August was terrible. The wind blew and the rain poured down. But there were at least some pleasant diversions. On 13 August a Councillor Smith drew the problem of men's nude or 'indecent' bathing to the attention of a Borough Council committee and asked if some kind of awning could be erected to screen off the beach at the east end of the Parade – practically in front of the Haven – where the men were joyously disporting themselves, weather permitting. Oscar and Bosie would have enjoyed such a perfectly Greek scene and may even have taken part in it.

On 20 August, Oscar and Bosie picked up two boys on the beach at Worthing: Stephen and Alfonso. Oscar and Bosie were in the habit of going out sailing most afternoons, and that day Oscar and Bosie had spotted Alfonso Conway and a younger boy dressed in flannels 'helping the two boatmen to drag down our boat which was high-beached' to the shoreline. 'Shall we ask them whether they would like to have a sail?' Oscar apparently said to Bosie, who said 'Yes.' The two boys 'seemed very delighted' and went sailing and swimming with Oscar and Bosie nearly every day afterwards. A third boy, Percy, also seems to have become part of Oscar and Bosie's circle in Worthing. Percy may have been a holidaymaker, as Oscar refers to his departure from Worthing, but Alfonso and Stephen were residents.

There can be no doubt from Oscar's letter to Bosie that their relationship with the boys was sexual:

> Percy left the day after you did. He spoke much of you. Alfonso is still in favour. He is my only companion, along with Stephen. Alfonso always alludes to you as 'the Lord', which however gives you, I think, a Biblical Hebraic dignity that gracious Greek boys should *not* have. He also says, from time to time, 'Percy was the Lord's favourite', which makes me think of Percy as the infant Samuel – an inaccurate reminiscence, as Percy was Hellenic.

Though Oscar later claimed that Alfonso was 'a youth of about eighteen', he was in fact only fifteen. He lived with his widowed mother who kept a lodging house in Worthing. That summer she had just one lodger, and the family had very little money. Alfonso told Oscar that he wanted to go to sea as an apprentice in a merchant ship, but that his mother was reluctant to let him go. To help make ends meet, Alfonso had sold newspapers and stationery from a kiosk on the pier, but at the time he met Oscar and Bosie he was unemployed – a 'loafer', as Edward Carson later sarcastically described him; Oscar, rather more charitably, said he was leading 'a happy, idle life'.

Oscar was certainly very taken with Alfonso. The morning after they met, the four of them, Oscar, Bosie, Alfonso and Stephen, went fishing off Lancing in the boat. On their return to Worthing, they all had lunch at the Marine Hotel. In the ensuing days, Alfonso later said, he was 'nearly always with' Oscar and Bosie. He was introduced to Oscar's sons, Cyril and Vyvyan, and seems to have become especially friendly with Cyril, even attending a children's tea party at the Haven.

A few days after they met, Oscar suggested to Alfonso that they should go on an evening walk. They met at nine o'clock at night at the East Parade and walked along the coast road towards Lancing. According to Alfonso's statement, Oscar suddenly 'took hold' of him, unbuttoned his trousers, and masturbated him until he 'spent'. 'He did not ask me to do anything,' Alfonso said. The same thing happened a night or two later. Alfonso also had dinner at the Haven on two or three occasions. Each time after dinner, he recalled, Oscar 'took me to his bedroom and we both undressed and got into bed'. These dinners must have taken place in September, after Constance and the boys had returned to London, as it is scarcely credible that Oscar would risk taking Alfonso to bed while Constance was in the house.

Towards the end of September, Oscar took Alfonso to stay in a hotel. It was to be a great treat. 'I promised him that before I left Worthing I would take him somewhere, to some place to which he wished to go, as a reward for his being a pleasant companion to myself and my children,' Oscar said. 'He chose Portsmouth, as he was anxious to go to sea, but I told him that was too far. So we went to Brighton.' Oscar bought Alfonso a suit of blue serge, a pair of flannels and a new straw hat, trimmed with a red and blue ribbon. He bought the clothes for Alfonso, he said, 'in order that he shouldn't be ashamed, as he told me he was, of his shabby and ordinary clothes'. Oscar's generosity was also tinged with self-interest. It would have been almost impossible for Oscar to take Alfonso in his ordinary clothes to a hotel without raising eyebrows and suspicions.

They booked into the Albion Hotel. Oscar took a pair of rooms with a folding green baize door between them. They had tea in the hotel and then went out to a restaurant to dine. That night, Oscar was careful to lock the outer doors of both rooms before he and Alfonso got into bed. 'He acted as before,' Alfonso said, only this time, 'he used his mouth'. In all they spent two hours together in Oscar's bed. The next day, Oscar presented Alfonso with a cigarette case inscribed 'Alfonso from his friend Oscar Wilde', a signed photograph, a walking stick and a book, William Clark Russell's *The Wreck of the Grosvenor*.

Oscar's expedition to Brighton with Alfonso Conway marked the end of the summer of 1894, his last summer of freedom. As the nights began inexorably to draw in, new problems and new challenges were to assail him.

The arsenic flower

'It is perfectly monstrous the way people go about nowadays saying things against one behind one's back that are absolutely and entirely true.'

On his journey up the Nile early in 1894, in the company of Reggie Turner and Fred Benson, Bosie had struck up a warm friendship with Robert Hichens. Hichens was a good listener, perhaps too good a listener. As Bosie extolled the genius of Oscar and the joys of his 'eternal quest for beauty' to his three companions and fellow Uranians, Hichens listened greedily. Previously, he had been able to admire Oscar only from afar. He had heard him lecture in the Victoria Rooms in Clifton in October 1884 and seen him several times since at a distance, most memorably at a premiere at the Independent Theatre in May 1892, when Oscar had appeared 'immaculately dressed, and wearing in his buttonhole a large carnation dyed a violent green' followed by 'five ultra-smart youths, all decorated with similar green carnations'.

In the spring of 1894, Bosie fulfilled his promise to introduce Hichens to Oscar. They met over lunch at the Café Royal and, like Bosie, Oscar took an immediate liking to him. 'I thought him rather pleasant,' he told Frank Harris. There was no question of sexual attraction. Hichens was 30 when they met and was, as Oscar later wittily commented, 'unrelieved by any flashes of physical beauty'. Though Hichens later sought to distance himself from Oscar and his circle, claiming in 1948 that he had only ever met him on three occasions, he was clearly on intimate terms with Oscar and Bosie. Oscar said that he 'saw a good deal' of Hichens in the spring and summer of 1894. Hichens was a Uranian, albeit a reluctant one. He had been dazzled by Bosie's beauty, and now he was dazzled by Oscar's genius and the unorthodox sexual gospel he preached. He became Oscar's newest disciple. But Hichens was also a journalist who aspired to be a novelist. When he met Bosie in Egypt, and then Oscar in London, he realised that he had found the theme for his first book, *The Green Carnation*.

The Green Carnation was published anonymously on 15 September 1894. It was the publishing sensation of the year and went through four editions in as many months. The short, sharp novel was a brilliantly witty portrait of Oscar and Bosie. Although it purported to be a work of fiction, everyone knew that it was based on fact. The book was not so much a skit or a satire on Oscar and Bosie as a documentary – and a rather dangerous documentary at that. Frank Harris said 'it was a sort of photograph of Oscar', and Trelawny Backhouse called it 'an undisguised portrait'.

The novel opens with its 'hero', Lord Reggie Hastings, carefully pinning a green carnation on to his evening coat. Lord Reggie is an extremely unflattering, if not downright unpleasant, portrait of Bosie as a consummately vain, selfish and egotistical young man who is supremely conscious of his startling beauty. 'It is so interesting to be wonderful,' Lord Reggie tells himself:

> to be young, with pale gilt hair and blue eyes, and a face in which the shadows of fleeting expressions come and go, and a mouth like the mouth of Narcissus.

Setting out for the evening in a cab, he spies an elderly gentleman with a red face and small side-whiskers who stares at him and sniffs ostentatiously:

> 'What a pity my poor father is so plain,' Reggie said to himself with a quiet smile. Only that morning he had received a long and vehement diatribe from his parent, showering abuse upon him, and exhorting him to lead a more reputable life. He had replied by wire – 'What a funny little man you are – Reggie.' The funny little man had evidently received his message.

Lord Reggie's wire to his father uses the exact wording that Bosie had used in his telegram to Queensberry, the first devastating salvo in the terrible feud with his father. That Robert Hichens not only knew about the telegram, but could reproduce its exact wording and the exact context in which it was sent, was proof enough that he was privy to Bosie and Oscar's most private affairs.

It soon becomes clear that, behind his beauty and his intelligence, Lord Reggie is a sodomite. He looks like 'a young Greek god' and is 'one of the most utterly vicious young men of the day', a young man who 'worshipped the abnormal with all the passion of his impure and subtle youth'. Lord Reggie has a penchant for slumming it with rough trade. 'There are moments,' he says, 'when I desire squalor, sinister, mean surroundings, dreariness and misery':

> The great unwashed mood is upon me. Then I go out from luxury. The mind has its West End and its Whitechapel. The thoughts sit in the Park sometimes, but sometimes they go slumming. They enter narrow courts and rookeries. They rest in unimaginable dens seeking contrast, and they like the ruffians whom they meet there, and they hate the notion of policemen keeping order.

The plot of *The Green Carnation* – in so far as it has one – concerns the courtship of Lord Reggie Hastings and Lady Locke. Lady Locke is 'a fresh-looking woman of about twenty-eight, with the sort of face that is generally called sensible, calm observant eyes, and a steady and simple manner'. She is the widow of a colonial administrator and has a delightful young son, Tommy. Emily Locke epitomises all the qualities of prime English womanhood: purity, universal rightmindedness and a fortune in excess of twenty thousand pounds a year.

Lady Locke and Lord Reggie are brought together by Mrs Windsor, 'a very pretty woman of the preserved type, with young cheeks and a middle-aged mouth' – almost certainly a portrait of Ada Leverson, Oscar and Bosie's devoted friend and devout Uranian sympathiser. Lady Locke is fascinated by Lord Reggie's androgynous beauty and Lord Reggie is fascinated by Lady Locke's money. It is impossible to know whether or not Lord Reggie's determination to marry for money mirrored a similar determination on the part of Bosie to marry an heiress. With no funds from his father, it is entirely conceivable that Bosie had declared his intention of finding a rich woman to support him. Indeed, seven years later, Bosie carried the scheme into practice when he set sail for the United States in search of an heiress, writing that he had had three firm offers, one of whom had 'quite £20,000 a year'.

Lord Reggie's greatest friend and influence is Esmé Amarinth, an undisguised portrait of Oscar. He is a 'tall and largely built man, with a closely shaved, clever face, and rather rippling brown hair' with 'a gently elaborate voice', whose conversation is a cascade of witty epigrams and beguiling paradoxes. 'I was born epigrammatic and my dying remark will be a paradox,' says Esmé – prophetically. 'How splendid to die with a paradox upon one's lips!' Like his counterpart in real life, Esmé Amarinth articulates a dazzling gospel of sin and sinning, where all virtues are vices, and all vices virtuous. His gospel, like Oscar's, proclaims that to sin is to be healthy and natural. Virtue, or the conscious repression of the urge to sin, is unnatural and shameful. 'Prolonged purity wrinkles the mind as much as prolonged impurity wrinkles the face,' he says. 'Nature forces us to choose whether we will spoil our faces with our sins, or our minds with our virtues.'

Esmé's concept of sin – like Oscar's – is entirely sexual. What society calls sin, Uranians call love. He makes an impassioned speech about the persecution of Uranians. 'There are only a few people in this world,' Esmé declares:

> who dare to defy the grotesque code of rules that has been drawn up by that fashionable mother, Nature, and they defy in secret, with the door locked and the key in their pockets. And what is life to them? They can always hear the footsteps of the detective in the street outside.

It could so easily have been – and perhaps it even was – a speech by Oscar. And the phrase 'the footsteps of the detective' evokes the increasingly hostile social and legal environment for Uranians in England, a hostility which was already palpable. When, in November 1894, Oscar attended the premiere of *John-a-Dreams*, a play by Haddon Chambers, at the Haymarket Theatre, he experienced this growing hostility first-hand. 'The bows and salutations of the lower orders who thronged the stalls were so cold that I felt it my duty to sit in the Royal Box,' he told Bosie. 'How strange to live in a land where the worship of beauty and the passion of love are considered infamous.'

Esmé – like Oscar – is the 'inventor' of the green carnation. He describes it as 'the arsenic flower of an exquisite life' and first wore it 'because it blended so well with absinthe'. Lady Locke is bewildered and confused by the appearance of so many green carnations adorning the lapels of young men at the opera. 'All the men who wore them looked the same,' she tells Mrs Windsor:

> They had the same walk, or rather waggle, the same coyly conscious expression, the same wavy motion of the head. When they spoke to each other, they called each other by Christian names. Is it a badge of some club or some society, and is Mr. Amarinth their high priest? They all spoke to him, and seemed to revolve round him like satellites around the sun.

Intrigued, Lady Locke decides to quiz Lord Reggie about the significance of the green carnation. He tells her that those who wear the green carnation are 'followers of the higher philosophy'. 'The higher philosophy! What is that?' asks Lady Locke. Lord Reggie replies with a rousing declaration about needing courage to love as a Uranian:

> The philosophy to be afraid of nothing, to dare to live as one wishes to live, not as the middle-classes wish one to live; to have the courage of one's desires, instead of only the cowardice of other people's.

Believing that he can either ignore or overcome the marital sexual expectations of Lady Locke – 'the one awkwardness that walked in the train of matrimony' – Lord Reggie has almost made up his mind to ask Lady Locke to marry him, and Lady Locke has almost made up her mind to accept his proposal, when she overhears Lord Reggie promising her nine-year-old son a green carnation. 'Do you love this carnation, Tommy, as I love it?' Lord Reggie asks the boy:

> Do you worship its wonderful green? It is like some exquisite painted creature with dyed hair and brilliant eyes. It has the supreme merit of being perfectly unnatural. To be unnatural is often to be great. To be natural is generally to be stupid. To-morrow I will give you a carnation, Tommy, and you shall wear it at church.

It is a symbolic act of seduction and corruption and Lady Locke is horrified. It is possible that the planned seduction of Tommy Locke was based on Bosie's hoped-for seduction of Cyril Wilde, Oscar's oldest son, who was also nine years old. A few months later, in Algiers, Bosie was waxing lyrical about Cyril's beauty to André Gide. 'He will be for me,' he told a shocked Gide.

In the light of Lord Reggie's designs on Tommy, Esmé Amarinth's lengthy panegyrics on youth and its joys take on a much more sinister face. 'How exquisite rose-coloured youth is,' says Esmé Amarinth as a troop of choirboys is ranged in front of him:

> There is nothing in the world worth having except youth, youth with its perfect sins, sins with the dew upon them like red roses – youth with its purple passions and its wild and wonderful tears. The world worships youth . . . Let us sin while we may, for the time will come when we shall be able to sin no more. Why, why do the young neglect their passionate pulsating opportunities?

Esmé's comments go much further than merely celebrating the joys of youthfulness: they appear to stray dangerously towards suggesting that youth in general – and choirboys in particular – are ripe for the sexual plucking. Horrified, Lady Locke turns down Lord Reggie's proposal of marriage, much to his chagrin and to Esmé's relief, who fears that marriage to Lady Locke might alter his protégé. 'The refining influence of a really good woman is as corrosive as an acid,' he remarks.

The Green Carnation was a *succès de scandale*. There was intense speculation about the identity of the author. The names of the novelist Marie Corelli and the poet Alfred Austin were put forward as candidates. So many people believed that Oscar himself had written it, as yet another exercise in self-advertisement, that he was obliged to deny these rumours. 'Kindly allow me to contradict, in the most emphatic manner, the suggestion, made in your issue of Thursday last, and since then copied into many other newspapers, that I am the author of *The Green Carnation*,' he wrote from Worthing to the *Pall Mall Gazette*:

> I invented that magnificent flower. But with the middle-class and mediocre book that usurps its strangely beautiful name I have, I need hardly say, nothing whatsoever to do. The flower is a work of art. The book is not.

Oscar's tone of frigid *hauteur* was the best response he could muster under the circumstances. To rail against the caricatures of himself and Bosie would be to dignify them with his attention and make it appear as if he and Bosie could not take a joke. But Oscar and Bosie spent many anguished hours wondering who in their circle had – Judas-like – so grossly betrayed them. The chief suspect was Ada Leverson, 'the Sphinx of Modern Life', as Oscar had christened her, who had written skits and satires for *Punch*. They must have voiced their suspicions abroad. 'I am not surprised that our Worthing friends think anything so witty as the "Green Carnation" must have been written by you,' Max Beerbohm wrote to Ada. 'What agitated discussions Bosie and Osis must have had over the authorship of that book. I wonder if they have thought of Hichens at all?'

When it finally emerged that Robert Hichens had indeed written the novel, Oscar and Bosie were obliged to send a witty telegram of retraction to the Sphinx: 'Esmé and Reggie are delighted to find that their Sphinx is not a minx after all . . . Reggie goes up to town tonight – Cadogan Place. He proposes to call on the dear and rarely treacherous Sphinx tomorrow.' But behind the wit, both Oscar and Bosie were flustered and made uncomfortable by the appearance of *The Green Carnation*. Hichens had behaved ignobly, Oscar said. His description of Hichens as not so much a Judas as 'a doubting disciple' was a penetrating insight. The ugly and unflattering portrait of Uranian love contained in the novel speaks volumes about Hichens's own sexual equivocations and self-loathing.

The damage to Oscar and Bosie's reputations was real and significant. '*The Green Carnation* ruined Oscar Wilde's character with the general public,' said Frank Harris. 'On all sides the book was referred to as confirming the worst suspicions.' The novel's barely disguised portrait of them as proselytising, politicised sodomites was damaging and dangerous enough, but the portrayal of Bosie as a predatory pederast, intent on marrying Lady Locke not just for her fortune but also for her nine-year-old son, was an appalling indictment. It was no wonder the publisher, William Heinemann, had taken the precaution of having the manuscript read for libel by Sir George Lewis, fearing that he might be sued for libel by Oscar or Bosie, or both.

But the real damage of *The Green Carnation* was its promulgation of the existence of a Uranian subculture infecting and corrupting the body social. It was, as André Raffalovich termed it, the 'invisible city of Sodom', the enemy within, not just secret, unknown and unknowable, but highly contagious, a virus that spread by stealth, undermining and destroying all that was healthy, all that was sacred. Although the Victorians were utterly repelled by any sexual acts between men, they were more repelled, more fearful of any manifestation of social organisation between men who loved men. It was these fears of a spreading social and sexual contagion in the wake of scandals like the Dublin Castle and the Boulton and Parke affairs which had prompted Henry Labouchère to introduce his new legislation in 1885 criminalising not just sex between men but anything that even vaguely hinted at 'conspiracy' between men who loved men. The phrasing of Labby's law was so loose that even social contact between Uranians was potentially criminal.

The Green Carnation stirred up a hornet's nest of fear and loathing. Privately, Oscar told Robert Sherard that the book had 'really raised the hue and cry', and Bosie admitted later that 'the book did me a lot of harm'. Nevertheless, when Trelawny Backhouse and Robbie Ross tried to warn Oscar of the dangers he faced in the hostile climate generated by *The Green Carnation*, he dismissed them, saying, 'The Treasury will always give me twenty-four hours notice to leave the country, just as they did in Lord Henry Somerset's case.'

There were other unpleasant consequences resulting from the novel's publication. *The Green Carnation* had, according to Bosie, further inflamed the anger of Queensberry, who was now furious on all fronts: furious at the description of himself as 'an elderly gentleman with a red face and small side-whiskers'; furious at the washing of the family's dirty linen in public; and furious that his son's relationship with Oscar was now so publicly known to be sodomitical. Queensberry felt that he had been publicly humiliated and that the question on everybody's lips was 'What is his father about, and why does he not interfere?'

At the beginning of October, Bosie paid a surprise visit to Oscar in Worthing, turning up at the Haven late one Sunday. 'You suddenly appeared,' Oscar recalled in *De Profundis*:

> bringing with you a companion whom you actually proposed should stay in my house. I (you must admit now quite properly) absolutely declined. I entertained you, of course; I had no option in the matter: but elsewhere and not in my own home.

Bosie's 'companion' was quite clearly a renter. He must have been very rough, very dangerous or very young for Oscar to refuse to allow Bosie to spend the night with him at the Haven. After all, Constance and the boys were no longer in residence, and Oscar had twice or three times entertained Alfonso Conway to dinner and sex. 'The next day, a Monday,' Oscar recalled, 'your companion returned to the duties of his profession and you stayed with me.'

A Monday morning in October in Worthing. Bosie was 'bored'. The long days of summer were over, and now Worthing seemed dull and deserted. Any semblance of domesticity between Oscar and Bosie invariably spelled disaster. Much as they genuinely loved each other, any time they spent together undiverted by friends and amusements, or undiluted by 'the eternal quest for beauty', by their compulsive pursuit of boys, created friction. Bosie insisted on being taken to Brighton. They arrived there on 4 October and booked into the Hotel Metropole, where Bosie was immediately struck down with 'that dreadful low fever that is foolishly called the influenza'. As he recalled in *De Profundis*, Oscar nursed Bosie devotedly, waiting on him and tending him 'with every luxury of fruit, flowers, presents, books and the like', as well as with 'affection, tenderness and love'.

After four days, Bosie recovered, and, since their hotel bill was already £9, Oscar decided to take cheaper rooms in Brighton where he would have sufficient peace and quiet to finish off the play he was working on. No sooner were they installed in the lodgings than Oscar too went down with influenza. After the devotion he had shown in nursing Bosie, he quite reasonably expected Bosie to reciprocate. He was to be bitterly disappointed. Bosie announced that he had to go to London – on business, he said – but that he would return the same day. 'In London you meet a friend,' Oscar recalled in *De Profundis*, 'and do not come back to Brighton till late the next day.' For those two days, Bosie left Oscar 'entirely alone without care, without attendance, without anything'.

On the Saturday evening, Oscar begged Bosie to come back a little earlier than usual and sit with him. Bosie agreed with an 'irritable voice and ungracious manner'. Oscar waited till eleven o'clock. Still Bosie did not appear. 'I then left a note for you in your room just reminding you of the promise you had made me, and how you had kept it,' wrote Oscar. It was hardly tactful. Oscar must have known by now that Bosie could brook no criticism. It brought out the very worst in him. 'At three in the morning, unable to sleep,' Oscar continued, 'and tortured with thirst, I made my way, in the dark and cold, down to the sitting room in the hopes of finding some water there. I found *you*':

> You fell on me with every hideous word an intemperate mood, an undisciplined and untutored nature could suggest. By the terrible alchemy of egotism you converted your remorse into rage. You accused me of selfishness in expecting you to be with me when I was ill; of standing between you and your amusements; of trying to deprive you of your pleasures.

It transpired that Bosie had come back to the lodgings at midnight and, finding Oscar's note waiting for him, had fallen into an angry brooding rage. He told Oscar he had come back simply to change out of his dress clothes before going out again in the hope that 'new pleasures were waiting'. Those new pleasures were sexual. Bosie had hoped to go out and find a boy, but Oscar's note of recrimination had effectively doused his mood of sexual expectation.

The row continued the next morning when there was another nasty scene – 'with renewed emphasis and more violent assertion' – in Oscar's bedroom. 'I told you at length to leave,' Oscar recalled:

> You pretended to do so, but when I lifted up my head from the pillow in which I had buried it, you were still there, and with brutality of laughter and hysteria of rage you moved suddenly towards me. A sense of horror came over me, for what exact reason I could not make out; but I got out of my bed at once, and bare-footed and just as I was, made my way down the two flights of stairs to the sitting room.

Bosie left the lodgings that morning, having silently helped himself to some of Oscar's money. Three days later, on the morning of his birthday, Oscar received a particularly foul letter in which Bosie congratulated him on his prudence in leaping out of his sickbed when he did. 'It was an ugly moment for you,' Bosie wrote, 'uglier than you imagine.' He savagely and sneeringly concluded his letter. 'When you are not on your pedestal you are not interesting. The next time you are ill I will go away at once.'

Oscar's melodramatic account of this event in *De Profundis* strongly suggests that Bosie was on the point of attacking him, either with the revolver he had bought to try and frighten Queensberry, or with 'a common dinner knife that by chance was lying on the table between us'. It was an ugly row, but it was not the first they had had, nor would it be the last. Max Beerbohm gleefully told Ada Leverson that Oscar and Bosie had had 'a very serious quarrel' and 'Oscar does not answer Bosie's telegrams'.

Despite the row, Oscar managed to complete the play he had been working on for George Alexander. *The Importance of Being Earnest* was Oscar's fourth society comedy, and it was to be his last and greatest play. Oscar wrote *Earnest* extremely quickly out of a desperate need for money. 'I am so pressed for money,' he told Alexander, 'that I don't know what to do.' He managed to extract £150 from Alexander for an option on the play and seems to have started work the moment he arrived in Worthing, hindered – or perhaps even helped – by the well-meaning efforts of Arthur, his butler. 'My play is really very funny: I am quite delighted with it,' Oscar told Bosie. 'But it is not shaped yet. It lies in Sibylline leaves about the room, and Arthur has twice made a chaos of it by "tidying up". The result, however, was rather dramatic.'

Both Bosie and Robbie Ross claimed to have had a hand in helping Oscar create what has become his most enduring and characteristic work of art. Bosie told his friend Marie Stopes that he was 'in and out of his study' all the time Oscar was writing *Earnest*, that 'they talked and laughed about it' and a number of the jokes were his. Robbie Ross said that, when he spent two months lodging with the Wildes in Tite Street in 1887, he had written down many of Oscar's bon-mots and epigrams. 'To tell you *a great secret* which I ought not to do,' Ross told their mutual friend Adela Schuster shortly after Oscar's death, 'I gave him my notes and he used a great deal of them for one of his later plays which was written in a great hurry against time as he wanted money.'

Unlike Oscar's three previous society comedies, *The Importance of Being Earnest* does not explore moral themes like adultery, illegitimacy and corruption. Nevertheless, Oscar was adamant that the play did indeed have a philosophy, which he expounded in an interview he gave to Robbie Ross for the *St James's Gazette*. It was 'that we should treat all the trivial things of life seriously, and all the serious things of life with sincere and studied triviality'. *Earnest* is both a comedy of manners and a comedy of errors, where accident and design conspire to simultaneously mislead and yet safely guide its quartet of young men and women to a prosperous – if not a happy – ending. The action of the play spins on the merry-go-round of courtship and marriage where birth, breeding, rank and wealth count for more than honesty, affection, love and honour.

The women of the play – Gwendolen, Cecily, Lady Bracknell and Miss Prism – emerge particularly badly and reflect Oscar's dislike of women and his fundamental distrust of their motives, especially in matters of love and marriage. 'Women are the ruin of young fellows,' Oscar told the weasly Fred Atkins more than once, and he counselled his friend, Robert Sherard, to 'act dishonourably' over an affair of the heart. 'Act dishonourably. It is what sooner or later she'll certainly do to you!' Oscar portrays the women in *Earnest* as selfish, scheming, manipulative, jealous and grasping. All are seeking husbands, either for themselves or, in the case of the Gorgon-like Lady

Bracknell, for her daughter. And all of them, to a greater or a lesser degree, pretend to be something or somebody they are not: Gwendolen Fairfax pretends to be a girl with 'a simple, unspoiled nature' though she is, like her mother, Lady Bracknell, extremely knowing and very calculating. Cecily Cardew pretends – to herself at least – that she is engaged to be married, even though the engagement is entirely the product of her imagination. Lady Bracknell pretends to be the epitome of the blue-blooded, thoroughbred *grande dame*, even though she was a penniless nobody when she married into the aristocracy. And the prim, prudish Miss Prism poses as Egeria, the wise teacher, though she is far from wise and has distinctly unvirginal ambitions towards Canon Chasuble.

The two young 'heroes' of the play emerge with not much more honour. Jack Worthing is a wealthy foundling, and his 'best friend', Algernon Moncrieff, is an idle young man about town. Both are seeking a wife. Without a family of his own, without any pedigree, Jack wants to marry the aristocratic Gwendolen, while the feckless Algy, without a penny of his own, wants to marry Jack's ward, the extremely rich Cecily. Algy is particularly cynical about marriage. 'If I ever get married,' he declares, 'I'll certainly try to forget the fact.' When Jack tells him that he has come up to town expressly to propose to Gwendolen, Algy's response is cynical in the extreme. 'I thought you had come up for pleasure?' he says. 'I call that business.'

Both Jack and Algy lead double lives. In his country house where he lives with his ward, Cecily, Jack is forced to adopt 'a very high moral tone on all subjects'. But since a high moral tone 'can hardly be said to conduce very much to either one's health or one's happiness', he pays frequent visits to his flat in London, in the Albany, where, Dr Jekyll-like, he assumes the mantle of wicked Ernest Worthing. Algy also has a double life, escaping to the country to visit an imaginary and invaluable permanent invalid called Bunbury. Bunburying is Algy's means of escape, his way of evading his social duties and family responsibilities. Algernon has Bunburyed all over the country and recommends the device to Jack. 'Nothing will induce me to part with Bunbury,' he says:

> If you ever get married, which seems to me extremely problematic, you will be very glad to know Bunbury. A man who marries without knowing Bunbury has a very tedious time of it.

That Bunbury is in some way a codeword for the love that dare not speak its name is signalled when Algy informs Lady Bracknell that his friend has 'exploded'. 'Exploded!' Lady Bracknell exclaims:

> Was he the victim of a revolutionary outrage? I was not aware that Mr Bunbury was interested in social legislation. If so, he is well punished for his morbidity.

309

'Social legislation' was a euphemism for the movement to change the laws governing sex between men, and 'morbidity' was a word frequently used perjoratively to characterise sex between men in terms of disease, decay and death. The extraordinary Uranian writer and poet John Moray Stuart-Young, who claimed to have had an affair with Oscar, and who even went so far as to forge letters from him, published a volume of poetry entitled *An Urning's Love. (Being a Poetic Study of Morbidity)*. And when, nine months later, Oscar wrote from prison to petition for a reduction in his sentence, he described himself as 'the sure prey of morbid passions, and obscene fancies'.

Oscar was almost certainly drawing on his own considerable experience of Bunburying. He had spent the best part of ten years leading a double life, inventing excuses to get away from Constance and the children and spend time with young men of his own kind. 'I am off to the country till Monday,' he had told George Ives in June, in a clear act of Bunburying. 'I have said I am going to Cambridge to see you, but I am really going to see the young Domitian'. According to Aleister Crowley, there was an even more specific circumstance behind the concept of Bunburying. In 1913, Crowley wrote to a friend, Bruce Lockhart, who was an official at the British Embassy in Moscow. 'I was going to tell you a story which very few people know,' he wrote, taking great care not to mention Oscar by name. 'That is the inner history of the catastrophe that overtook the gentleman in whom Russia is so interested':

> The story is called 'Danger of Bunburying'. Bunbury is a portmanteau word [of] Banbury and Sunbury. The author in question hastily getting into the train at Banbury found the carriage already occupied by a schoolboy who was returning from a public school not far away. They got into conversation and subsequently met by appointment at Sunbury. Hence the word Bunbury and its meaning. For our author began a series of frequent and unexplained absences.

Jack and Algy, Gwendolen and Cecily inhabit an inverted, topsy-turvy, through-the-looking-glass world where nothing is what it seems, where right becomes wrong, where truth becomes lies and where the serious becomes trivial, and the trivial serious. The immoral universe of *Earnest* was the same immoral universe which Oscar had inhabited for so long, the same immoral universe in which he had successfully lived a double life, and where, adopting Algy's advice, he had tried very hard to forget the fact that he was married. Much of the fabric of the play is stitched together from Oscar's experience as a Uranian. Indeed, it is only truly explicable when understood in these terms.

Just like Oscar and Bosie, Algy and Jack, the play itself has a secret Uranian life, comprehensible only to those with eyes to see, to the initiated, to the elect. 'I hope some of the faithful, and all the elect, will buy copies,' Oscar told Robbie five years later, when *Earnest* was about to be published for the first time. The very title of the play is a Uranian pun, inspired in part by a volume of Uranian poetry, *Love In Earnest*, published in 1892 by a schoolmaster called

John Gambril Nicholson, which recounted his obsessional love for a boy, probably one of his pupils. 'One name can make my pulses bound/No peer it owns, nor parallel,' ran his poem, 'Of Boys' Names', each verse concluding triumphantly: 'Tis Ernest sets my heart a-flame.' Nicholson's poems were noticed by the great and the good of the Uranian community. 'Have you read a volume of sonnets called "Love in Earnest"?' John Addington Symonds asked a friend. 'It is written by a School-master in love with a boy called Ernest.' Among less literary Uranians, 'earnest' – a corruption of the French *Uraniste* – enjoyed a short vogue as a coded signifier of Uranian inclinations. 'Is he earnest?' had the same meaning, at about the same time, as the question 'Is he musical?' No wonder then, that the name 'Ernest', as Gwendolen remarks, 'produces vibrations'. It was meant to.

The play is littered with references to Oscar's Uranian life and Uranian friends. Jack Worthing takes his name from the town where Oscar spent the summer and met Alfonso Conway. In the earliest version of the play, the cynical Algy was originally called Lord Alfred Rufford, a name too similar to Bosie's name to be coincidence. And, like the reckless Bosie, who took innumerable risks in his eternal quest for beauty, Algy was always getting into 'scrapes'. 'I love scrapes,' says Algy. 'They are the only things that are never serious.' Oscar also makes a not-so-veiled reference to Bosie's continuing feud with Queensberry when Jack says 'I don't know a single chap at the club who speaks to his father,' and Algy replies feelingly, 'Yes! Fathers are certainly not popular just at present.'

Jack Worthing's double life is revealed by an affectionate inscription in a cigarette case, just as Oscar's double life would be revealed in court six months later by not one but several affectionate and highly indiscreet inscriptions in several cigarette cases. There is a nod to George Ives, or rather to his rooms in the Albany: Ives lived in E.4 the Albany, which Oscar used as the exact address of Jack Worthing's chambers in an early draft of the play. In the course of the summer Bosie had introduced Oscar to his handsome schoolfriend from Winchester, John Bloxam, who was now an Oxford undergraduate and fervent fellow Uranian. Bloxam makes an appearance in *Earnest* in drag as Lady Bloxham, the lessee of Jack's house in Belgrave Square and 'a lady considerably advanced in years'. 'Ah,' remarks Lady Bracknell. 'Nowadays that is no guarantee of respectability.' And Oscar could not resist slipping in a sly denunciation of the recently published *The Green Carnation*. 'This treatise, "The Green Carnation", as I see it is called, seems to be a book about the culture of exotics,' says Lady Bracknell. 'It seems a morbid and middle-class affair.'

John Bloxam may also have been the inspiration for the character of Jack Worthing. In his diary, George Ives refers to Bloxam as 'Jack Bloxam', describing him as 'a most sweet and interesting dual character'. Ives does not explain the nature of Jack Bloxam's interesting dual character, but it was clearly worthy of note. Was Jack Bloxam's 'dual character' the inspiration behind Jack Worthing's double life as Uncle Jack of the 'high moral tone' in the country, and as the wicked, irresponsible Ernest in town, running up impossibly high debts at the Savoy, and constantly getting into 'the most dreadful scrapes'?

Among Oscar and Bosie's less salubrious friends, Charlie Parker turns up in the original four-act version of the play as one half of the firm of writ-serving solicitors, Parker and Gribsby. Gribsby arrives at Jack's country house to arrest the fictitious Ernest Worthing and take him to Holloway Prison for debts run up for food and drink at the Savoy. At the time he was writing *Earnest*, Oscar still had a large unpaid bill from the Savoy for food and drink he and Bosie had consumed during their lengthy stay there in March 1893, which combined gluttonous luxury with an orgy of sex. The scene is one of the funniest and one of the most resonant – in Uranian terms – of the play. 'I really am not going to be imprisoned in the suburbs for having dined in the West End,' says an indignant Algy. 'There can be little good in any young man who eats so much, and so often,' tut-tuts Miss Prism. Throughout the play, eating and drinking become sexualised metaphors for the Uranian consumption of 'trade'. Phallic cucumbers are swallowed with 'reckless extravagance' and dripping muffins consumed with decorous care to avoid spillage on the cuffs.

The Importance of Being Earnest opened on 14 February 1895, and attracted glowing notices. To describe the play as 'farce', said Oscar's contemporary, the critic William Archer, would be 'far too gross and commonplace a word to apply to such an iridescent filament of fantasy'. It was, he said, 'a *rondo capriccioso*, in which the artist's fingers run with crisp irresponsibility up and down the keyboard of life'. *Earnest* was a strange paradox. Written quickly with the aim of generating some much-needed cash, aided by Robbie's Boswell-like jottings of his master's epigrams from a long-forgotten summer, and abetted by Bosie's not inconsiderable wit, the play represented the apogee of Oscar's career as a dramatist. And yet curiously it contained the very seeds which led to Oscar's destruction. Uncontrolled appetites, double lives, unpopular fathers, impure truths, shameful debts, scrapes, scandals, Scotland Yard, Holloway Prison, and indiscreetly inscribed cigarette cases given to young men all ominously prefigured Oscar's own future: in Canon Chasuble's prescient words, the 'bitter trials' to come.

Love's sacrifice

'A kiss may ruin a human life.'

At approximately 3.30 on the afternoon of Thursday 18 October, a shot rang out from the direction of a turnip field belonging to Halsey Cross Farm in the village of Over Stowey, near Bridgwater, in Somerset. The sound of gunfire was not, in itself, unusual. A party of five gentlemen and half-a-dozen gamekeepers and beaters had set out that morning from nearby Quantock Lodge for a day's shooting, as they had done every morning for nearly a fortnight, and spluttering volleys of shots had been booming and echoing across the countryside all day. The weather was fine and bright. Lunch had been 'partaken of out of doors in picnic fashion', and the shooting had been excellent with 'a goodly number of pheasants and partridges killed'. Afterwards, everyone was agreed that it had been a perfect day's sport – up until the moment when that single shot rang out in the field of turnips.

There was something about this shot that was different and alarming. It was a single report and not part of a more usual volley of shots. And there was something about the sound of the shot that was odd. It was, according to Mr William Elton, one of the gentlemen in the shooting party, 'a very deadened report', as if it had been somehow muffled. Furthermore, the shot 'seemed to be about 100 yards off', and it sounded as if it had come from *behind* the shooting party, from the turnip field they had just tramped through.

Whether by coincidence, or whether from an unconscious sense that something was wrong, Webber, the head gamekeeper, almost immediately asked 'Where can his Lordship be?' The Lordship in question was Bosie's beloved older brother, Francis, Viscount Drumlanrig, who had spent the last fortnight as the guest of Mr Edward Stanley MP at his home, Quantock Lodge. 'I hope he hasn't shot himself,' was William Elton's response – made, as he ruefully admitted later, 'half in jest'. 'Oh no,' Webber replied. 'We won't think that.'

But Drumlanrig was nowhere to be seen. As far as anyone could remember, Drumlanrig had been with them only minutes before. He had, it appeared, told one of the beaters that he was going back to look for a partridge he had winged. Webber started blowing his whistle and shouting out loudly for him. Ominously, there was no answer. Gerald Ellis, another member of the shooting

313

party, was beginning to get worried. 'I will walk along beside the hedge,' he called out, 'and see if I can find him.' In the company of another man, Ellis crossed into the turnip field, and it was not long before they found Drumlanrig:

> lying in the hedge, apparently dead, from injuries sustained in the head, seemingly from the accidental discharge of his double-barrelled gun, the right-hand barrel being found empty.

They could see that Drumlanrig's 'head was very much sprinkled with blood, as also was the collar. There was a wound in the forehead.' Nothing could be done and the police were sent for.

Five days later an inquest was held at Quantock Lodge. Various speculations about the cause of the tragedy were put forward to the Coroner by the members of the shooting party. Most were agreed in thinking that it had been a terrible accident. Drumlanrig's gun had gone off accidentally, they said, as he was crossing a stile and his attention was distracted by the appearance of the carriage holding a party of the ladies from Quantock Lodge. On the face of it, it was a very plausible explanation. Clambering over a stile while carrying a loaded gun was tricky at the best of times. If Drumlanrig had slipped or lost his footing, even for a split-second, the gun could have accidentally gone off. But there was one insurmountable problem with this theory: when the gun went off, Drumlanrig was nowhere near a stile, let alone climbing one.

The medical evidence, too, seemed to strongly militate against an accident. 'On my arrival I found that life was extinct,' Mr Alfred Egerton Smith, the doctor who had attended the scene, told the Coroner:

> On examining him I found that the charge had entered his mouth fracturing the lower jaw on the right side. Some of the shot passed out between the nose and eyes on the right hand side. The charge had entered and passed through the roof of the mouth on the left hand side. The base of the skull must have been completely shattered. The lower lip was slightly blue as if by powder. The roof of the mouth was so lacerated that it was impossible to say whether it was discoloured by powder or not. I did not notice that the moustache was singed.

The Coroner then asked Dr Smith the crucial question. 'Do you consider from what you saw that the mouth of the deceased was open or shut?' 'I should say it was open,' Dr Smith replied emphatically. Drumlanrig's mouth was open when the shot was fired, and it seems probable that the barrel of the shotgun was inserted into his mouth. This would account for the strangely 'deadened' sound of the shot which those who heard it testified to. Drumlanrig's death no longer looked like an accident, but much more strongly like suicide. Yet despite this evidence, the inquest returned a verdict of 'Accidental Death'. As the Member of Parliament for Bridgwater and a man of considerable influence and importance locally, Edward Stanley would have done his best to avoid any whiff of scandal. The suicide of one of his guests was a major scandal, and Stanley would have exerted the utmost pressure to ensure that a less socially embarrassing verdict of 'Accidental Death' was returned.

But why on earth should a young man like Drumlanrig choose to end his life? It was incomprehensible. He was widely liked and already making a good career in politics as a junior minister in the House of Lords under the aegis of his friend and patron, Lord Rosebery. And with Rosebery now Prime Minister, there was every chance that promotion would follow. Everyone who was at Quantock Lodge agreed that Drumlanrig had seemed to be in the best of spirits during the previous fortnight. He had every reason to be. Exactly a month earlier, on 18 September, Drumlanrig had become engaged to be married to Alexandra Ellis, the third daughter of Major-General Arthur Ellis, equerry to the Prince of Wales.

Alix, as she preferred to be called, was the niece of Edward Stanley, and Drumlanrig had been invited to Quantock Lodge to get to know Alix's family better, including her brother, Gerald Ellis, who subsequently found Drumlanrig's body. When the news of Drumlanrig's engagement got out there had been some audible murmurs of surprise among those who were privy to Drumlanrig's sexual preferences. Harry Foley, a friend of both Drumlanrig and Rosebery, called Drumlanrig's engagement 'terrible news', and Lewis 'Loulou' Harcourt, the son of Lord Rosebery's great political rival, Sir William Harcourt, was incredulous at the news. 'Drumlanrig is going to marry General Ellis's daughter,' he confided to his diary. 'It makes the institution of marriage ridiculous.'

On the day of his engagement, Drumlanrig had written a letter announcing the fact to Lord Rosebery and telling him of his intention of going north to Dumfriesshire to see his father, the Marquis of Queensberry:

> What the result of the interview will be I don't know, and I feel it is not exactly an auspicious moment! However, that cannot be helped and of course I know in any case that I shall have to look forward to considerable difficulties.

Drumlanrig does not elaborate on the nature of the 'considerable difficulties' he would have to face, or explain why it was an inauspicious moment to tell Queensberry about his impending marriage. Queensberry did not feel especially well-disposed towards marriage as an institution. His first wife had divorced him acrimoniously, and now his second wife was about to have the marriage annulled on the grounds of Queensberry's 'frigidity and impotence'.

The biggest difficulty between father and son was Queensberry's determined and highly embarrassing campaign to bring an end to Drumlanrig's relationship with Lord Rosebery. After the fiasco in Bad Homburg the previous summer, when Queensberry had stalked the Kaiser Friedrich Promenade hoping to find Rosebery and thrash him, father and son had barely been speaking. Queensberry had left Bad Homburg, at the request of the Prince of Wales, determined to find proof of the sexual relationship between Rosebery and his son. He had obtained his proof in the course of the summer of 1894, at least according to Trelawny Backhouse, who records in his unpublished memoirs how, 'by setting private detectives to work', Queensberry had obtained 'very damaging evidence of a carnal bout after a supper party at Bourne End on the River Thames' between Drumlanrig and Lord Rosebery. 'Apparently,' Backhouse continued:

> the evidence upon which he relied was that of two maid servants at the inn and the concrete proofs afforded by the condition of the drapery of the bed on which the two lovers had passed the night.

The 'concrete proofs' of sheets, stained in the same way as those on Oscar's bed at the Savoy with a mixture of semen, excrement and vaseline, were what Queensberry had been hoping and praying for since the previous summer. He was convinced that he now had the upper hand. According to Backhouse's version of events:

> Queensberry wrote to the Prime Minister threatening exposure in a letter to the republican owner of *Truth*, Mr. Henry Labouchère, Lord Rosebery's inveterate enemy, unless he resigned office and severed relations with Drumlanrig.

For Lord Rosebery to resign as Prime Minister under threat of blackmail by Queensberry was unthinkable. If Trelawny Backhouse's account of the affair is correct, Drumlanrig must have been desperately manoeuvring to try and save Rosebery's career and find a way out of a seeming impossible situation. His proposal of marriage to Alix Ellis may have been his best hope of averting scandal. Once safely married to a woman of impeccable pedigree, and with a promise to sever his relations with Rosebery, Drumlanrig may have believed that he had done enough to quell his father's wrath and allow Rosebery to retain office.

This may have been the purpose of Drumlanrig's proposed visit to Queensberry in Dumfriesshire in late September. Whether the meeting ever took place, and, if it did, what was said between father and son, will never be known. After Drumlanrig's death, Queensberry told his hated and despised ex-father-in-law, Alfred Montgomery, that he 'had not met or spoken frankly' with his eldest son 'for more than a year and a half'. Perhaps Queensberry refused to see Drumlanrig, and they communicated instead by letter, or perhaps they did in fact meet – a meeting which Queensberry, in the tumult of guilt and self-recrimination after his son's death, chose not to reveal to Alfred Montgomery. Either way, if it had been Drumlanrig's purpose to seek some sort of accommodation with his father, he was to be disappointed. Queensberry's hatred of Rosebery, the 'Jew nancy boy' and 'bloody bugger', was implacable. It had been Queensberry's greatest fear that Rosebery would one day become Prime Minister, and now that Rosebery was indeed guiding his country's destiny, Queensberry could invoke – along with his rabid anti-Semitism and his phobic hatred of sodomites – a spurious and twisted patriotism as grounds for demanding Rosebery's political suicide.

It must have become clear to Drumlanrig that his forthcoming marriage to Alix Ellis was not going to be enough to save his patron, his friend and his lover from scandal and oblivion. There was only one option left to him. To save Rosebery from political suicide, Drumlanrig decided that he must himself commit suicide and make it look like an accident. It was, as Trelawny Backhouse commented, 'a noble sacrifice on the altar of his chief's fame'.

Drumlanrig's cousin, the poet Wilfred Scawen Blunt, heard the news in Tunis. It was, Blunt wrote in his diary, 'an appalling tragedy'. 'Terence', Blunt's companion on the trip to Tunis:

who knows him better than I do, thinks that things may have gone wrong in regard to his intended marriage. He asked him last summer abt it, he seemed doubtful then whether it wd ever really take place. I have heard too that he had scruples about marriage, seeing what madness there is in his family.

Although Blunt clearly suspected that something had 'gone wrong' in Drumlanrig's life, something that had to do with his marriage to Alix Ellis, he was still unwilling to accept that Drumlanrig had taken his own life. 'It seems unlikely it could have been suicide,' he wrote. But other members of the Queensberry clan were convinced that Drumlanrig had taken his own life. Francis Douglas, later the 11th Marquis of Queensberry, and Bosie's nephew, told Oscar and Bosie's biographer, Harford Montgomery Hyde, that he was 'positive that his uncle Drumlanrig had taken his own life in the shadow of a suppressed scandal', and, towards the end of his life, Bosie told Sheila Colman, the woman who eventually became his literary executrix, that Drumlanrig had indeed committed suicide and that 'a scandal lay behind it'.

Speculation about Drumlanrig's death was rife. Oscar wrote in *De Profundis* that Drumlanrig's death was 'stained with a darker suggestion'. Sir Edward Hamilton, a very senior civil servant and friend and confidante of Rosebery, recorded Drumlanrig's death the day after it happened. 'There is no reason to suppose that it was anything but an act of carelessness; though people are already jumping to other conclusions,' Hamilton wrote in his diary. 'Curiously enough, his grandfather met with a similar fate.'

Hamilton's observation was an understatement. It was not a similar fate, it was an identical fate. On 6 August 1858, Archibald Douglas, 7th Marquis of Queensberry, had left the family home at Kinmount to go shooting. At about 3.30 in the afternoon, the last in a series of shots was heard from the woods by men working in the grounds. At 4pm, Archibald's body was discovered 'prostrate on the earth and covered with blood'. Archibald had been shot through the chest by his own gun. As with Drumlanrig, there were mutterings about suicide, but it was never to be proved. Had Drumlanrig meticulously and grotesquely re-enacted the death of his grandfather, convinced that there was a good chance that his death would be seen as an unfortunate shooting accident?

Lord Rosebery was grief-stricken. He more than anyone seemed unwilling to countenance the possibility that Drumlanrig's death was anything but accidental. But Sir George Murray, Rosebery's private secretary, was not so sure. Three days after Drumlanrig's death, Murray met with his cousin, H.J. Mordaunt, who had been a guest at Quantock Lodge and a member of the ill-fated shooting party. Murray quizzed his cousin about the day's events and wrote to Rosebery with a detailed account and an accompanying map which made it clear that Drumlanrig's death could have no other explanation than suicide. 'Dear Lord Rosebery,' Murray wrote. 'I have been able to arrive at some comprehension of what took place. But the newspaper accounts of the inquest are not intelligible without a commentary of some kind':

The guns had beaten through the turnip field A in the direction shown by the arrow; when they got to the end of it they turned off to their left in the direction of the second arrow, crossed over into field B and formed up in line along the fence preparatory to beating that field in the other direction.

D, instead of going with them, stopped at the hedge at the bottom of Field A to look for a running bird of his. While there, it is thought, he must have been attracted by a carriage in the road beyond; for he went through a gap in the hedge and proceeded some way (about 25 yards) into the grass field.

He was last seen alive at the point I have marked in red X, and he was found at the place marked O, close up to the hedge, and about halfway between the gap he crossed by and another gap at the pond where the two fences join.

It is very difficult to account for his going up to the hedge at the point where he was found. The hedge was barely passable there; but there was nothing that could be called a gap; and it was by no means the natural place to choose if he wanted to rejoin the guns as soon as possible.

To add to the mystery he was shot *through the mouth* upwards, a circumstance almost impossible to produce by accident.

On the other hand the hypothesis of suicide is almost equally improbable for want of motive. He seems to have been in his usual spirits all through the week; and no reason is known why he should have been otherwise. The whole thing is to my mind quite inexplicable; but Mordaunt told me that his own opinion, which was shared by the Doctor, and the two other guns (Elton and Fortescue) is that it was suicide.

Publicly, at the inquest into Drumlanrig's death at Quantock Lodge, these 'other guns' had testified to the likelihood of an accident. Privately, they were convinced it was suicide.

318

Queensberry was beside himself with grief, anger and hatred. He wrote a typically foul and ranting letter to Alfred Montgomery in which he blamed 'the Snob Queers like Rosebery' and the 'whole lot' of the Montgomery family for Drumlanrig's death. 'I smell a Tragedy behind all this and have already *got Wind* of a more *startling one*,' he wrote, without explaining what he meant. But, if Trelawny Backhouse, Bosie, More Adey and several others are to be believed, Queensberry had by this time already uncovered more damaging evidence of sodomy in the Liberal Party, which he would put to good use six months later. According to Backhouse, Bosie and others, the government's vigorous prosecution of Oscar in April and May 1895 was driven entirely by the fear that Queensberry would make public the sexual secrets he knew about Lord Rosebery and about other senior members of his government.

More immediately, Drumlanrig's suicide brought about a reconciliation between Oscar and Bosie. After Bosie had flounced out of their lodgings in Brighton and sent an especially foul letter, Oscar said he felt as if he had been 'polluted' by his love affair with Bosie. It was a friendship which 'had soiled and shamed my life irretrievably'. He was, he recalled in *De Profundis*, determined to bring about a formal end to the friendship:

> I settled with myself to go back to London on the Friday, and see Sir George Lewis personally and request him to write to your father to state that I had determined never under any circumstances to allow you to enter my house, to sit at my board, to talk to me, walk with me, or anywhere and at any time to be my companion at all.

Whether Oscar would have abided by his decision to end his love affair with Bosie is a moot point. However badly they had quarrelled in the past, abject contrition on Bosie's part and plenary forgiveness on Oscar's had invariably brought about a reconciliation. On the morning of Friday 19 October, the very day he had arranged to go to London to see Sir George Lewis, Oscar opened the newspaper and read of Drumlanrig's death. All thoughts of separation were forgotten. Oscar could only think of Bosie's sorrow and his grief. 'I telegraphed at once to you my deepest sympathy,' Oscar recalled, 'and in the letter that followed invited you to come to my house as soon as you were able':

> You came at once to me very sweetly and very simply, in your suit of woe, and with your eyes dim with tears. You sought consolation and help as a child might seek it . . . Your grief, which was real, seemed to me to bring you nearer to me than you had ever been. The flowers you took from me to put on your brother's grave were to be a symbol not merely of the beauty of life, but of the beauty that in all lives lies dormant and may be brought to light.

Oscar and Bosie must have been aware of Drumlanrig's relationship with Rosebery. For Bosie, Drumlanrig would always be his 'dear saint' and 'true knight', a martyr, slain before his time to appease his father and the forces of reaction. Oscar's flowers, symbolic of 'the beauty that in all lives lies dormant', were perhaps a reference to 'beauty' in the Uranian sense, the eternal sexual grailquest. Drumlanrig's sexuality had lain hidden and secret and had never been 'brought to light', never freely expressed. If his suicide proved anything, it proved the nobility and supremacy of love in the face of mindless prejudice. Yet again, Uranian love and Uranian persecution had conspired together to produce tragic consequences in the lives of Oscar and Bosie. And yet again, adversity had brought them closer together.

Now they worked together on a new literary project. In the course of the summer, Bosie had introduced Oscar to his handsome friend, John Bloxam. Bloxam was a Uranian, and equally as dedicated to the Cause as Bosie and Oscar. He was determined to follow in Bosie's footsteps with the *Spirit Lamp* and start up a new magazine of Uranian culture – the *Chameleon* – to which he wanted Oscar and Bosie to contribute. Oscar produced a set of witty but subversive sayings, collectively entitled 'Phrases and Philosophies for the Use of the Young', which contained some overtly sexual aphorisms like 'Wickedness is a myth invented by good people to account for the curious attractiveness of others' and – in a clear reference to prostitution – 'If the poor only had profiles there would be no difficulty in solving the problem of poverty.'

Bosie contributed two daringly political Uranian poems, both set in Arcadian nocturnal dreamscapes where beautiful but sad phantasmagorical youths walk abroad and proclaim the bittersweet joys of Uranian love. The first, 'In Praise of Shame', is a paean to the joys of Uranian sex. 'I am Shame,' cries one wanton phantom:

'That walks with Love, I am most wise to turn
Cold lips and limbs to fire; therefore discern
And see my loveliness, and praise my name'.

Whereupon the dreamer awakes and duly decides that 'Of all sweet passions, Shame is the loveliest.'

Although many years later Bosie unconvincingly tried to argue that 'Two Loves', the second of his two poems in the *Chameleon*, had 'nothing on earth to do with the vice which was the subject of Wilde's trials', the poem is emphatically Uranian, a dialogue where two beautiful youths symbolise the contrast between the joyous, fair and blooming love of boy and girl, and the pallid, moonlit, ineffably sad love between boy and boy. 'I am the Love that dare not speak its name,' says the 'sad and sighing' personification of Uranian love. The message is clear. Uranian love languishes in a dimly-lit prison because the world cannot countenance it. Less than six months after the publication of 'Two Loves', Oscar would stand in the witness box of the Central Criminal Court at the Old Bailey, bravely and brilliantly extemporising on the nature and nobility of 'the Love that dare not speak its name'.

Oscar's and Bosie's involvement in the *Chameleon* was rather more extensive than either would later admit. From a letter Bloxam wrote to Charles Kains Jackson on 19 November, it seems clear that Oscar was more a partner in the enterprise than merely a contributor. A few days earlier Bloxam had called on George Ives at the Albany, where, he said, he had 'the good luck to meet Oscar':

> We discussed the paper fully, and the name. After a good deal of discussion we decided to change the first title yet again (from the Parrot Tulip). I think we have fixed on a very good one for which Ives must have the credit – 'The Chameleon'. I think it is excellent.

The subtitle of the *Chameleon* was 'A Bazaar of Dangerous and Smiling Chances', a line from Robert Louis Stevenson, but highly suggestive of the eye contact used by men in dangerous street pick-ups – what Xavier Mayne and others called the 'gaze' – 'the mysterious *Anblick* of the Uranian fraternity, that psychic-sexual interrogation, that signal and challenge, everywhere current and understood among Uranians'.

Apart from Oscar's subversive but essentially cheerful aphorisms, and one or two other neutral contributions, the mood of the *Chameleon* was unrelievedly bleak and sombre. The rapture of easeful death and the savage joy of martyrdom pervaded the atmosphere of the magazine. There was an intensely poetic prose meditation by John Gambril Nicholson called 'The Shadow of the End', about the death of a beloved boy, and an anonymous story, 'The Priest and The Acolyte', about the love affair between a twenty-eight-year-old priest and his fourteen-year-old acolyte who, when their relationship is discovered, form a suicide pact.

Ada Leverson thought she detected the hand of John Gray in the story. '"The Priest and the Acolyte" is not by Dorian,' Oscar told her in early December, after the *Chameleon* was published, 'though you were right in discerning by internal evidence that the author has a profile. He is an undergraduate of strange beauty.' The story was in fact written by Bloxam, who was subsequently to follow his fictional hero's footsteps into the priesthood. 'The Priest and the Acolyte' made for grim but explicit reading. There was not a shadow of a doubt that the story concerned the sexual relationship between a man and a boy. Shockingly, the story portrayed the boy not as the seduced and traumatised victim of an older man, but as a full and willing partner. Perhaps more shockingly still, the story was unblinkingly partisan in its insistence that the love between the man and the boy was divinely ordained: 'There is no sin for which I should feel shame,' says the Priest:

> God gave me my love for him, and He gave him also his love for me. Who is there that shall withstand God and the love that is His gift?

Oscar thought the story 'too direct'. 'There is no nuance,' he told Ada, 'it profanes a little by revelation: God and other artists are always a little obscure. Still, it has interesting qualities, and is at moments poisonous: which is something.'

There were others who found the *Chameleon* poisonous, and not in the pleasing sense that Oscar meant. Jerome K. Jerome, the celebrated author of *Three Men in a Boat*, thought the *Chameleon* was 'certainly a case for the police'. 'The publication appears to be nothing more nor less than an advocacy for indulgence in the cravings of an unnatural disease,' he thundered in an editorial in his newspaper *To-day* on 29 December. The *Chameleon* was bound to absolutely corrupt and ruin any boys and young men attracted to members of their own sex:

> That young men are here and there cursed with these unnatural cravings, no one acquainted with our public school life can deny. It is for such to wrestle with the devil within them; and many a long and agonised struggle is fought, unseen and unknown, within the heart of a young man. A publication of this kind, falling into his hands before the victory is complete, would, unless the poor fellow were of an exceptionally strong nature, utterly ruin him for all eternity.

The *Chameleon*, Jerome declared, 'is an insult to the animal creation', 'an outrage on literature', 'unbridled licence' and 'garbage and offal'.

It was not long before a copy of the magazine found its way into Queensberry's hands. 'I have now in my possession, a copy of a most odious work, suppressed on account of its utter filth,' Queensberry told his daughter-in-law, Minnie. It contained, he said:

> two so-called poems, if filthy gibberish strung together can be called poetry, by Alfred, and signed with his name, and headed 'In Praise of Shame' and 'Two Loves', the last ending up with the words – 'I am the love that dare not breathe its name', meaning sodomy.

Queensberry also mistakenly thought that 'The Priest and the Acolyte' was by Oscar. The *Chameleon* was further proof, if proof were needed, of what Queensberry thought of as 'the unnatural and hideous love' practised and promulgated by Oscar and Bosie.

Queensberry had brought about an end to Drumlanrig's relationship with Lord Rosebery, though at the impossibly high cost of his son and heir's life. Mad with grief and remorse, and filled with a seething hatred of 'Snob queers' and 'Jew nancy boys', Queensberry was now determined to bring to an end his youngest son's infatuation with Oscar. He had declared war on sodomy and sodomites, and he would not rest until he had destroyed Oscar – 'this hideous monster' – Sodom's chief architect and apologist.

Passionate fauns

'You do not feel the beauty of a nation till you have slept with one of them.' – John Addington Symonds

Eighteen ninety-five was 'the year of the Faith 2233', according to George Ives's calendrical reckoning, which started with the Battle of Chaeronea in 338 BC, when the male lovers of the Theban Band were slaughtered. Oscar celebrated the new year in style with a brilliant dinner party at the Continental for his closest young Uranian friends, including George Ives, Jack Bloxam and quite possibly Bosie. Ives was, as usual, dazzled by the glittering company he found himself in. 'After going among that set it is hard to mix in ordinary society,' he confided to his diary that night, 'for they have a charm which is rare and wonderful.' But Ives was also worried about his friends, who seemed hell-bent on pleasure and laughter. 'I wish they were less extravagant and more real,' he wrote, 'so gifted and so nice, and yet here is this terrible world waiting for the word of truth to set it free.' Ives had the uncomfortable sense that something was wrong, that something was going to happen. 'I see the storm of battle ahead,' he wrote presciently.

The year looked set to be an *annus mirabilis* for Oscar. His play *An Ideal Husband* opened to generally laudatory notices on 3 January, and *The Importance of Being Earnest* was already in rehearsal and due to open in February. Oscar would then have the remarkable distinction of two plays running simultaneously in the West End. Quite apart from the prestige, the revenue from these two 'roaring successes', as Henry James called them, would bring to an end the money worries that had plagued Oscar for months.

Oscar installed himself at the Albemarle Hotel at the beginning of January. It was convenient for the theatre and, even more importantly, convenient for entertaining boys. The neurotic Edward Shelley was among those who – 'in a moment of weakness', he said – visited Oscar there. There were other, more dangerous and altogether more exciting visitors, as Ada Leverson found on a visit she made to Oscar at the Albemarle shortly after the premiere of *An Ideal Husband*. 'I saw a knife lying on a table in Oscar's rooms,' she recalled years later. 'I asked him who left it there. "Oh, some careless young murderer," he said.'

With the prospect of unlimited showers of gold falling from the theatrical

323

skies, Oscar was in confident and expansive mood. He and Bosie had not forgotten the consoling prophecy made the previous summer by Mrs Robinson, 'the Sibyl of Mortimer Street', that early in January they would go away together for 'a long voyage'. They decided to fulfil the Sibyl's prophecy, settling on the French colony of Algiers. 'Yes. I fly to Algiers with Bosie tomorrow,' Oscar told Ada Leverson on 14 January. 'I begged him to let me stay to rehearse, but so beautiful is his nature that he declined at once.' Bosie's appetite for North Africa had been whetted by his short exile in Cairo the previous winter. The climate in winter was delightful, and the brilliant light and warm zephyrs were a tempting alternative to the unrelieved greyness, damp and chill of London. But the real attraction of Algiers for Oscar and Bosie was the fabled beauty of its boys and their ready availability. Algiers was also in Richard Burton's 'Sotadic Zone', where pederasty and sodomy were 'popular and endemic'. Oscar had long been aware of the Uranian attractions on offer in Algiers, already a favourite destination for French Uranians. Dorian Gray once owned a 'little white walled-in house at Algiers' where he and Lord Henry Wotton 'had more than once spent the winter'. And there were references in *Teleny* to the 'new pleasures Algiers could afford'.

Oscar and Bosie arrived in the city of Algiers on 17 January and spent ten days there at the Hôtel de l'Europe. Oscar was enchanted by what he found. 'There is a great deal of beauty here,' he wrote to Robbie, saying he found the boys from the Kabyle tribe 'quite lovely':

> At first we had some difficulty in procuring a proper civilised guide. But now it is all right, and Bosie and I have taken to haschish: it is quite exquisite: three puffs of smoke and then peace and love. Bosie wakes up at night and cries like a baby for the best haschish.

The city of Algiers and its surrounding countryside were for Oscar a new Uranian Arcadia, 'full of villages peopled by fauns' where, he told Robbie, 'we were followed by lovely brown things from forest to forest'. There were beautiful boys wherever they turned, seemingly all of them smiling sexual invitation. 'Several shepherds fluted on reeds for us,' Oscar wrote, in what was probably an oblique reference to oral sex. 'The beggars here have profiles,' he added glibly, 'so the problem of poverty is easily solved.' Neither Oscar nor Bosie had any sense that their pursuit of boys was wrong, or that paying them for sex might be exploitative. They were used to paying renters for sex in London. As far as they were concerned, Algiers was no different to London, other than that the supply of boys seemed unending and that, for Bosie in particular, boys – some as young as thirteen or fourteen – were readily available. After a week or so in Algiers, they decided to make an excursion to the small and attractive walled city of Blidah, about thirty miles away, which the French had turned into a winter resort. They were to stay at the Grand Hôtel de l'Orient where, by coincidence, André Gide was also staying.

Gide was severely depressed. 'I have the feeling that I am going through a very important *crisis*, and I don't understand anything about it at all,' he had written to his mother four days before Oscar and Bosie's arrival. It was 'a decisive crisis', Gide wrote, 'and one from which I shall emerge fully grown'. Gide's crisis was a crisis of sexual denial. He desired sex with boys but was disgusted by what he considered to be his unnatural lusts, writing how he felt 'ashamed' of himself, how he wanted to 'disown' and 'repudiate' himself.

Gide was on the point of leaving the Grand Hôtel de l'Orient to return to Algiers when he saw the names of Oscar and Bosie chalked up on the board listing the guests in the hotel. His first instinct was akin to panic. He wanted to flee Blidah, to leave without seeing or talking to them. Oscar was, he told his mother, 'that terrible man, the most dangerous product of modern civilisation'. After his initial panic subsided however, Gide went into an agony of indecision. Oscar might have already seen dear André's name on the visitor's board and would feel insulted that he had left without bothering to say hello. To flee seemed feeble, but to stay might be dangerous. He could not make up his mind what to do. As the minutes ticked by, André realised that the decision had been made for him: he had missed his train. He would stay and face whatever it was that he so feared and yet was so fascinated by. André may well have sensed that the resolution of the 'decisive crisis' was in some way bound up with Oscar. He was right. This chance encounter with Oscar and Bosie in Blidah would profoundly affect the rest of his life.

Oscar was alone when he turned up in the hotel and seemed almost put out at finding André there. It was barely six months since they had met each other in Florence, but André thought Oscar had changed since that last encounter. There was 'less softness in his look, something raucous in his laughter and something frenzied in his joy', André observed. 'He seemed both more sure of pleasing and less ambitious to succeed in doing so; he was bolder, stronger, bigger.' Bolder, stronger, bigger. In the warm Sotadic Algerian sun, Oscar was all three. He had, he told André, followed the sun to Algiers and found a kind of pagan Paradise. He wanted to worship and 'adore' this exotic, erotic sun, under whose bold, unblinking gaze so many Uranian pleasures seemed to pulsate.

Oscar and André were joined by Bosie after dinner. A tour of Blidah's nightlife was proposed, to which André reluctantly agreed. A guide was hired – a 'vile procurer', André recalls – and Oscar announced that he wanted to see some young Arabs 'as beautiful as bronze statues'. No sooner were they in the street than Bosie took André affectionately by the arm. 'All these guides are idiotic,' he said:

It's no good explaining – they will always take you to cafés which are full of women. I hope you are like me. I have a horror of women. I only like boys. As you are coming with us this evening, I think it's better to say so at once.

André could not speak. He was shocked and stupefied – not so much by Bosie's bold and unashamed declaration of his sexual preferences, but by the clarity with which he had pierced the murky overlay of guilt and self-loathing which concealed André's own Uranian desires. André was alternately repulsed and fascinated by Bosie, just as he was repulsed and fascinated by Oscar, and repulsed and fascinated by the idea of sex with a boy. The evening went badly. Their guide took them to a low dive where a brawl immediately broke out between some Spaniards and some Arabs. When knives were pulled, and the first blood was spilt, Oscar, Bosie and André thought it prudent to return to their hotel. 'On the whole,' André recorded, the evening had been 'a rather dismal affair'.

Early the next morning, André quietly left the hotel and caught the train to Algiers, with an overwhelming sense of relief at having avoided being drawn into the erotic entanglements with local boys which Oscar and Bosie so clearly sought. André's relief may have been tinged by disappointment. He had tasted the guilty joys of Uranian passion only twice: once with Ali, a young Arab boy who had joyously seduced him a year earlier in the sand dunes outside Sousse in Tunisia, and once with a handsome young Italian oarsman whom he had hired to take him out for a moonlit row on Lake Como. Both encounters had left him confused about his sexuality, a confusion compounded by an affair he had in the Algerian oasis of Biskra with a beautiful sixteen-year-old girl prostitute, Mériem, who was destined to become the muse of Pierre Louÿs.

André's encounter with Oscar and Bosie did not end with his flight from Blidah. A few days later, Oscar was back in Algiers and, late one afternoon, André came across him sitting in a bar at a table strewn with papers. Bosie was not there. 'I have a friend in London who looks after my correspondence for me,' Oscar told André. 'He keeps back all the boring letters – business letters, tradesmen's bills and so on – and only forwards the serious letters – the love letters.' Oscar was especially delighted by a letter from a poorly educated young acrobat. 'It's the first time he has written to me,' he laughed, 'so he doesn't like to spell properly.'

At this point a clearly furious Bosie walked in and, brushing past André as if he did not recognise him, stood over Oscar and:

in a hissing, withering, savage voice, rapped out a few sentences of which I understood not a single word, then turning on his heels, went out.

Oscar turned very pale. 'He does nothing but make scenes like that,' Oscar told André after a long pause. 'He's terrible. Isn't he terrible?' But behind Oscar's words, André astutely discerned Oscar's profound 'admiration' for Bosie. Oscar had, André recalled, 'a kind of lover's infatuated pleasure in being mastered'. Bosie's personality, thought André, seemed much stronger and more marked than Oscar's. It was 'overweening':

a sort of fatality swept him along; at times he seemed almost irresponsible; and he never attempted to resist himself, he would not put up with anyone or anything resisting him either.

After the scene with Oscar, Bosie returned to Blidah where he had unfinished business with a young boy called Ali who worked as a *caouadji*, a boy making and serving coffee in a café. Bosie was obsessed with Ali who was, according to André, only 'twelve or thirteen', though Bosie said he was in fact fourteen. Bosie was determined to 'elope' with him to the desert oasis of Biskra, after hearing André's glowing descriptions of the place. 'But,' André wrote, 'to run away with an Arab is not such an easy thing as he had thought at first; he had to get the parents' consent, sign papers at the Arab office, at the police station, etc.' There was enough bureaucracy to keep Bosie busy in Blidah for several days.

While Bosie had his hands full in Blidah, Oscar suggested to André that they go to a Moorish café where they could listen to wonderful music. They took a carriage, which dropped them off at the edge of a labyrinth of small streets and alleyways. Oscar had procured the services of a guide, who led them to a dark steep alley where the café was located. Oscar was already an habitué of the café, but, at first, André was puzzled as to why Oscar had dragged him there. There seemed to be nothing special about the place; a few elderly Arab men sitting cross-legged and smoking kief, and a young *caouadji* half-hidden in the darkness brewing ginger tea. 'Lulled by the strange torpor of the place, I was just sinking into a state of semi-somnolence,' André recalled, 'when in the half-open doorway, there suddenly appeared a marvellous youth.' The boy hesitated at the door, seemingly unsure whether to enter, until Oscar beckoned him over to join them. The boy's name was Mohammed, Oscar said, and he was one of Bosie's lovers. André was dazzled by Mohammed's beauty, by his large, languorous black eyes, by his flawless olive skin and by his wonderfully slender and graceful body. Gide was also attracted by Mohammed's youth. In the original French of his memoir of this night, André dwelt lovingly on Mohammed's *'corps enfantin'*, on his 'childlike body'.

Mohammed took out a reed flute from his waistcoat and began to play exquisitely. Within a few minutes the young *caouadji* came to sit beside him, accompanying him on a *darbouka*, a kind of drum:

> The song of the flute flowed on through an extraordinary stillness, a limpid steady stream of water, and you forgot the time and the place, and who you were and all the troubles of this world. We sat on, without stirring, for what seemed to me to be infinite ages.

The spell was broken by Oscar. *'Venez,'* he said, rising from the table and propelling André towards the door. Outside, Oscar stopped abruptly. 'Dear,' he whispered into André's ear, 'would you like the little musician?' André's heart was beating uncontrollably. He felt as if he was going to choke. With 'a dreadful effort of courage', he croaked out 'Yes'. It was an epiphany, the moment when André's 'important crisis' was decisively resolved. By accepting and acknowledging his sexual desires, André emerged from his crisis of sexual denial 'fully grown'. In the space of a moment in a dark and foul-smelling alleyway in Algiers, André had been reborn a Uranian. And he had Oscar to thank for it.

Oscar muttered a few words to their guide and then took André off to drink cocktails at the Hôtel de l'Oasis. After an hour or so Oscar escorted a nervous André to a dingy hotel in a run-down part of the city. As soon as they crossed the threshold, 'two enormous policemen' appeared. André was terrified, thinking they were going to be arrested. 'Oh no, dear, on the contrary,' Oscar told him:

> It proves the hotel is a safe place. They come here to protect foreigners. I know them quite well. They're excellent fellows and very fond of my cigarettes. They quite understand.

Oscar was right to be cautious. He had already had one potentially fatal encounter with an Arab boy. The young Arab, Oscar told Laurence Housman later, had 'planned to trap him for robbery and possible murder'. But after Oscar had had sex with him, he was, apparently, 'ready to lay down his life for him'.

They went up to the second floor where Oscar had a key to a suite of two adjoining rooms. The guide appeared, followed by the two boys. Oscar sent André and Mohammed into the further room, while he went in the other room with the *darbouka* player for a night of passion. The sex with Mohammed was electrifying. André was in 'transports of delight at holding in my bare arms that perfect, wild little body, so dark, so ardent, so lascivious'. André had five orgasms with Mohammed that night, and several more after the boy left. It was the most profound and potent sexual experience of his life. 'Since then, whenever I have sought pleasure, it is the memory of that night that I have pursued,' Gide wrote a quarter of a century later.

Early the next morning, on 31 January, Oscar left Algiers to return to London. Bosie was still in Blidah, waiting to start his journey to Biskra with Ali. As Ali only spoke Arabic, Bosie suggested to André that he should travel to Biskra with them to relieve the tedium of the two-day journey. André was eager to see Bosie again. Although he considered that Bosie was 'blackened', 'ruined' and 'devoured by an unhealthy thirst for infamy', André admitted to his mother that Bosie nevertheless maintained an air of 'ambiguous distinction'. André was fascinated by the flagrancy and intensity with which Bosie flaunted his sexuality, even if he was embarrassed by the way his conversation continually returned 'with disgusting obstinacy' to boys and sex. He was, André wrote, almost wistfully, a man 'who seeks shame and finds it'. Bosie was a joyfully unapologetic sexual predator who knew what he wanted and who was ready to go to almost any lengths to get it. Despite his protestations to the contrary, André secretly admired Bosie's single-minded devotion to sex. Besides which, there was an erotic bond of sorts between them. After all, André had slept with Bosie's boy, Mohammed, and he may have thought there might be a chance of sex with Ali. In any case, the boy who could cause Bosie to take such infinite pains must be worth seeing.

André arranged to meet Bosie and Ali at Sétif, half-way to Biskra. He was unprepared for the magnificent sight of Ali stepping out of the railway carriage. Before him stood 'a young prince' dressed in dazzling silks:

> How stately his bearing, how proud his glance! What masterful smiles he bestowed on the hotel servants as they bowed before him! How quickly he had understood that, however humble he had been the day before, it was now for him to enter a room first, to sit down first ... Douglas had found his master and however elegantly dressed he was himself, he looked like an attendant, awaiting the orders of his sumptuously apparelled servant.

André has often been accused – most vociferously by Bosie himself – of inventing the sexual escapades of Oscar and Bosie in Algiers. 'I have been trying to read your book,' Bosie wrote to André in 1929 after he had read his account of their time in Algiers, 'but frankly I find it ugly, squalid and boring.' Bosie claimed that André's version of events was 'a mass of lies and misrepresentations' about Algiers, 'a clumsy fabrication of lies founded on a small substratum of truth'. 'Gide is a shit!' Bosie told Harford Montgomery Hyde in 1931. 'Like a person who has an abscess on his bottom and continuously displays it to the world.' But the truth of André's account of Bosie and the boy Ali in Biskra is borne out by a letter marked 'PRIVATE' which Bosie wrote to Robbie Ross on 11 February. 'My dear Bobbie,' he began:

> Oscar will have told you that I am held fast by the lassoo of desire to a sugar-lipped lad. He is of extraordinary personal beauty, and is aged fourteen.

'In fact, between me and you,' Bosie somewhat ambiguously added, 'his sugar has not yet been wiped by the nurse from milk' – presumably suggesting that Ali had not yet sucked Bosie. 'I constantly compare my boy to a gazelle,' a delighted Bosie went on, describing how he and Ali had had 'a fearful scene' the other day, carried on through an interpreter:

> My boy, Ali, insisted upon wearing an old pair of trousers, I having just, at vast expense, bought him two new pairs. Words followed (through the interpreter, who speaks moderate French), and finally I told him that I had seen another boy named Achmet who was far more like a gazelle than he was; I said he was so like a gazelle that *on dirait une vraie gazelle*, and that he was in constant danger of being shot in mistake for one. This completely overcame my boy who lay on his bed and wept for two hours, the interpreter saying: *Il dit que puisque vous avez fait venir ici un autre garçon qui ressemble une gazelle, c'est mieux qu'il retourne à Blidah à ses parents, parce que ici il est comme orphelin, n'ayant ni père ni mère, mais vous seulement, et cet. et cet.* All this quite seriously.

'Finally,' wrote Bosie, 'we made it up and had each other, as we have done every single day since I brought him from Blidah ten days ago (sometimes twice).' The interpreter was Athman, the fifteen-year-old boy André had met the previous year in Biskra.

Bosie was delighted with Biskra. He was especially fascinated by 'the street of the courtesans' which he found quite extraordinary:

> They sit at their doors and call to the passers-by. There are among them two male courtesans (of course there are heaps of other amateurs, but these are real professionals). One of them is astounding, he is exactly like a Greek slave of the late Roman Empire. Yesterday as I passed he was sitting in his doorway crowned with a wreath of narcissus, and he called to me to come in the house . . . He is about nineteen, just Oscar's style.

Tempted as he was by the beautiful courtesan, Bosie passed up the opportunity to sleep with him. 'I am far too occupied with Ali to look at anyone else,' he told Robbie, 'and Ali has sworn to stab me if I have any other boy.' Ali was not so insistent about fidelity when it came to his own pleasures. He wanted to have as much sex, with as many people, as he could and started an affair with a local boy. Bosie could just about tolerate this, but when Ali went to bed with Mériem, the beautiful young prostitute from the Oulad Nail tribe whom André had slept with the previous year, Bosie lost his temper. 'Boys, yes boys, as much as he likes,' he told André. 'But I will not stand for his going with women!'

Despite the alarums and excursions in his relationship with Ali, Bosie was enjoying his stay in Biskra enormously. 'I am really having a splendid time,' he told Robbie. But Bosie's idyll was brought to an abrupt end on 15 February when he received a telegram from his older brother, Percy. Queensberry was back on the rampage. Bosie was needed in London. The charms of the gazelle-like Ali were forgotten and the boy, once so fêted, was summarily cast aside. Bosie rushed back to London. George Ives had been right. The storm of battle did indeed lie ahead.

Hideous words

'If your sins find you out, why worry! It is when they find you in that trouble begins.'

Oscar's departure from Algiers on 31 January was rather abrupt. He had been there for just a fortnight, hardly the 'long voyage' that the Sibyl of Mortimer Street had prophesied. The row with Bosie had not helped matters. With Bosie in Blidah trying to organise taking Ali to Biskra, Oscar was left alone in Algiers with only the less-than-scintillating André for company, and London may have seemed a tempting alternative. The premiere of *The Importance of Being Earnest* was another consideration. Oscar had of course planned to return in time for the first performance on St Valentine's Day. But with nothing to keep him in Algiers now, apart from the readily available sex, he may well have decided to return and give full rein to his predilection for meddling in the productions of his plays.

There was, perhaps, another, more compelling reason for his early return. Oscar may well have contracted a sexually transmitted disease in Algiers, probably gonorrhoea, and he would have wanted to get treatment for the infection as quickly as possible. If he had indeed contracted gonorrhoea, the symptoms would have quickly begun to manifest themselves. Urethral discomfort and discharge usually occur within five days of infection, and often within two. Early treatment was essential. On his return to London, Oscar consulted Dr Lanphier Vernon Jones, rather than his usual physician, Dr Charles de Lacy Lacy of Grosvenor Street. Dr Vernon Jones was an acknowledged expert in the treatment of gonorrhoea, who was to publish, in 1902, *Gonorrhoeal Arthritis*, a well-regarded treatise on one of the complications arising from untreated or partially treated gonorrhoea. As his unpaid bill attests, Oscar remained under the care of Vernon Jones for three months, until his trial began.

Before the introduction of antibiotics, gonorrhoea was a notoriously difficult infection to deal with, and treatment involved poisoning the patient with noxious substances like mercury, zinc, aluminium and turpentine, purging and starving them, or making them heartily sick on 'monstrous doses' of derivatives of Cubebs and Copaiba pepper. The treatment had to be endured for weeks if not months and was considered even by doctors to be disgusting and sickening, nauseating and repulsive. Stephen Yeldham, Surgeon to the London Homeopathic Hospital, described in sickening detail the 'disgusting hodgepodge' of Cubebs and Copaiba that men were obliged to swallow several times a day:

> Let a man take a turn at this for a week, and, if he has not the stomach of a
> dog, and the constitution of a horse, tell you at the end of it how he feels, and
> if you have not a heart of stone, you will pity him.

The treatment for gonorrhoea was almost worse than the disease itself, and it was not uncommon for those infected with it to be prescribed strong opiates for the pain and discomfort of the treatment.

Rather than go home to Tite Street, Oscar installed himself at the Avondale Hotel in Piccadilly, a 'loathsome' place he said. He would have much preferred to stay at the Albemarle Hotel but could not, as he had failed to settle an outstanding bill. On the surface, at least, he appeared to be in good spirits and had acquired a new young friend. 'You were kind enough to say I might bring someone to dinner tonight,' Oscar wrote to Ada Leverson in early February. 'I have selected a young man, tall as a young palm tree (I mean tall as two young palm trees).' The young man's name was Tom, 'a very rare name in an age of Algies and Berties', wrote Oscar. 'I met him on Tuesday, so he is quite an old friend.' Tom Kennion was nineteen and a student at Oxford University when he met Oscar, and, unlike so many of Oscar's other boys, was from a good family, his father being an army Colonel.

A few days before the opening night of *The Importance of Being Earnest*, Oscar was told about a plot by Lord Queensberry to wreck the performance. Algy Bourke, Bosie's cousin and the owner of White's Club and Willis's restaurant, had got wind of Queensberry's intentions and wrote urgently (and with scant regard to his spelling) to warn Sybil Queensberry:

> What I wanted however to tell you was that Q has obtained a seat at St. James
> Theatre tonight for the 1st night of OW's play. It is his present intention to
> go there and make a public scandle. Cant you get Bosie to go and see his
> Father and dissuade him from this. It would be most detrimental to the boy.

With Bosie still in Biskra with Ali and André Gide, Sybil turned to Bosie's elder brother Percy, Lord Douglas of Hawick, who lost no time in communicating the plot to Oscar.

Ever since the death of his eldest son, Drumlanrig, in October 1894, Queensberry had been in Scotland, grieving for him, and cursing and raging against the sodomitical conspiracy that had already robbed him of one son and looked as if it would almost certainly rob him of another. When he returned to London towards the end of January, he discovered that Bosie and Oscar were together in Algiers. Queensberry had been threatening a public scandal for months: now he was going to have one. He wanted to goad Oscar into action, into an act of violence or into some sort of legal action, or both. But he needed a platform from which he could make the scandal public. If he were arrested and charged with assault or breach of the peace, then he could justify his actions from the dock.

The premiere of *The Importance of Being Earnest*, when the great and the good and the fashionable of London society would be assembled together, would be the perfect occasion to air 'this hideous scandal of Oscar Wilde', Queensberry thought. With luck, he might get himself arrested for breach of the peace, or even criminal libel. There would be plenty of witnesses. The plan was simple: he would go to the theatre and wait until the end of the performance when Oscar appeared on stage to take an author's call. During Oscar's speech, Queensberry intended to stand up like an Old Testament prophet and denounce Oscar to the glittering assembly as a disgusting and dangerous sodomite. For good measure, he would hurl a bouquet of rotting vegetables on to the stage as an expression of his contempt. A group of Queensberry's sporting friends took a box for the performance. They were there to give him support, to barrack Oscar, and to applaud when Queensberry's rotting bouquet landed on stage, preferably on Oscar himself.

St Valentine's Day 1895 saw the worst snowstorm in London that anyone could remember. It was a 'dark, sinister winter's night', Ada Leverson recalled thirty years later. 'A black, bitter, threatening wind blew the drifting snow', causing chaos among the crowds of hansom cabs and carriages which were bringing the glittering first night audience to the St James's Theatre. Despite the appalling weather, Little King Street was thronged with crowds who had come to gawp at the gorgeously dressed ladies and gentlemen. Many were what Ada Leverson called 'Wilde fanatics' – young men mostly, with a sprinkling of women – who stood in the bitter wind waiting to catch a glimpse of Oscar as his carriage drew up outside the theatre. He was dressed that night, Ada Leverson recalled, 'with elaborate dandyism and a sort of florid sobriety' in a black coat with a velvet collar and a white waistcoat, from which, in an echo of the Prince Regent, a bunch of seals on a black moiré ribbon dangled.

Inside, the theatre was 'the very breath of success', Ada wrote. The atmosphere was perfumed, metaphorically and literally. Oscar had decreed that 'the lily of the valley was to be the flower of the evening as a souvenir of an absent friend'. Nearly all the women wore sprays of lily of the valley, and large numbers of elegant young men sported buttonholes of the flower. It was a charming tribute to Bosie. Amid the heady sea of lilies of the valley, 'a single green carnation bloomed savagely' in Oscar's buttonhole. It was a defiant gesture. Oscar was in the highest spirits. He was 'beaming with euphoria', Ada said, firing off an endless series of epigrams and witty one-liners. Aubrey Beardsley, who was there with his sister Mabel, was the target of Oscar's wit. 'What a contrast the two are,' he told Ada Leverson, 'Mabel like a daisy, Aubrey like the most monstrous of orchids.' 'Don't sit on the same chair as Aubrey,' he told Ada. 'It's not compromising.'

Amidst the noise, the congestion and the crowds, the discreet cordon of police around the entrances to the theatre was barely noticeable. The police were there at the request of Oscar and George Alexander, who had acted quickly to foil Queensberry's plot. The theatre's business manager had written to Queensberry and told him that his ticket had been issued in error and enclosing a refund. To make assurance doubly sure, Scotland Yard had been alerted. 'I had all Scotland Yard – twenty police – to guard the theatre,' Oscar told Bosie. Despite these precautions, Oscar was nervous. He was diffident about taking an author's call. 'I don't think I shall take a call tonight,' he told a member of the cast. 'You see, I took one only last month at the Haymarket, and one feels so much like a *German band.*' Wit was the best antidote to fear.

As it happened, the plans to exclude Queensberry were successful, and Oscar made light of the matter in reply to a frantic telegram from Bosie in Biskra. 'Yes: the Scarlet Marquis made a plot to address the audience on the first night of my play!' he wrote. 'Algy Bourke revealed it and he was not allowed to enter.' Queensberry had turned up outside the theatre, clutching his bouquet of rotting turnips, and tried and failed to gain entry. A prize-fighter accompanied him. 'He prowled about for three hours,' Oscar wrote, and 'then left chattering like a monstrous ape.' The frustrated Queensberry had left his 'grotesque bouquet' with a message for Oscar at the box office. 'This of course makes his conduct idiotic,' Oscar wrote, and 'robs it of dignity'.

Despite this air of amused detachment at Queensberry's antics, Oscar was worried – worried enough to return to his solicitors to discuss the possibility of prosecuting Queensberry and getting some sort of restraining order against him. In order to make a case to the courts, Charles Humphreys needed evidence in the form of affidavits of Queensberry's behaviour at the St James's Theatre that night. But the evidence was deliberately withheld. 'Upon investigating the case,' Humphreys wrote to Oscar:

> we have met with every obstruction from Mr George Alexander the Manager and his staff at the Theatre who declined to give us any statements or to render any assistance to you in your desire to prosecute Lord Queensberry and without whose evidence and assistance we cannot advise you to venture upon a prosecution. You personally would of course be unable to give evidence of that which occurred behind your back as to which you have no personal knowledge beyond the information of others who apprised you of the insulting threats and conduct of his Lordship.

George Alexander was not about to become embroiled, however obliquely, in a legal battle between Oscar and Queensberry, especially as he was well aware that it was Oscar's love affair with Bosie that was the root cause of the quarrel. There was, however, a small crumb of comfort from the solicitors. 'Such a persistent persecutor as Lord Queensberry will probably give you another opportunity sooner or later of seeking the protection of the Law in which event we shall be happy to render you every assistance in our power of bringing him to Justice and thus secure your future Peace at his hands.' The solicitors were quite right, and the chance would come sooner, much sooner, than anyone expected.

Percy Douglas tried to pour oil on troubled waters. He visited his father at Carter's Hotel two or three days after the incident at the St James's Theatre, and put it to him that his increasingly noisy persecution of Oscar and Bosie was itself creating a scandal and exposing the family to ridicule. Predictably, Percy's attempts at diplomacy were doomed to failure and only enraged his father more. Queensberry heartily disliked both Percy and his wife, Minnie. He wrote to Minnie after Percy's visit:

> I may say that as Percy came here and quarrelled with me and had the audacity and impertinence to bring accusations against me of being the cause of this hideous scandal about his brother so that I am obliged to bring out more evidence about Alfred's character, and to speak about something that I knew about. I have kept secret until now, entirely to myself but I will do it no longer after this wretched accusation.

Queensberry went on to relate the details of Bosie's blackmail at Oxford in 1892, for which Drumlanrig had sought Oscar's assistance. The affair had been settled for £100, with the help of Oscar's solicitor and friend, George Lewis. According to Queensberry, it was George Lewis, in a professional and personal betrayal of Oscar, who had told him the whole sordid story. Percy refused to believe that either Oscar or Bosie could have been involved in anything quite so sordid. The story had to be a figment of Queensberry's diseased imagination. Try as hard as he might, Queensberry could not convince Percy that he was telling the truth. 'You must be all mad,' Queensberry ranted:

> If you choose to make inquiries, you will find the whole town has been reeking with this hideous scandal of Oscar Wilde for the last three years, and it is only in the last year that I have taken any action in the matter. If I were to shoot this hideous monster in the street, I should be perfectly justified, for he has almost ruined my so-called son.

Meanwhile, Bosie had come rushing back to London from Algiers as soon as he heard about his father's attempt to ruin the first night of *Earnest*. 'I am greatly touched by your rushing over Europe,' Oscar wrote. 'For my own part I had determined that you should know nothing.' Oscar's reluctance to inform Bosie of the events in London resulted partly from a natural desire not to worry him, but mostly from the fact that he knew that Bosie would fly off the handle and would almost certainly make matters very much worse by writing one of his impetuous and insulting letters to his father. All in all, it would be better for Oscar to try and deal with the situation as calmly as he could.

Bosie arrived back in London on or around 20 February, turning up at the Avondale Hotel in combative mood, just as Oscar had feared he would. He wanted to know every last detail of what had been going on. Oscar had wanted to get some sort of restraining order, but Bosie saw his father's behaviour as a golden opportunity to put him behind bars. 'You thought simply of how to get your father into prison,' Oscar told Bosie later:

> To see him 'in the dock', as you used to say: that was your one idea. The phrase became one of the many *scies* of your daily conversation. One heard it at every meal.

As ever, sex was never very far from Bosie's mind, and it was not long before he picked up a boy and brought him back to the hotel, expecting to stay there with him for a few days. 'A.D. brought to my hotel a companion of his own,' Oscar recalled from prison two years afterwards:

> one whose age, appearance, public and private profession, rendered him the most unsuitable companion possible for me in the terribly serious position in which I was placed. On my remonstrating with him, and asking him to let his companion return to his home, he made a violent scene, and preferring the society of his companion to mine retired at once to another hotel, where I subsequently had to pay the bill for them both, I need hardly say.

Oscar's comments were written in a letter from Reading Goal to More Adey and were constrained by the fact that all prisoners' letters were read. But reading between the lines, it was clear that Bosie's 'companion' was very young, very rough and almost certainly a 'renter'. For Oscar to be seen to be associating in any way with such a boy could be highly compromising. Belatedly he was exercising a degree of caution. But from his new hotel, Bosie began to 'bombard' Oscar with a series of more than usually 'revolting letters', none of which have survived but which probably accused Oscar of moral cowardice in worrying about what people might think.

At about five o'clock in the afternoon on Thursday 28 February, two or three days after Bosie's 'violent scene', Oscar drove to his club, the Albemarle. It was the first time he had been there since his return from Algiers. As he walked in, he was greeted by the hall porter, Sydney Wright, who knew both Oscar and Constance by sight. Oscar greeted Wright and asked him to give him a blank cheque. 'Lord Queensberry desired me, sir, to hand this card to you, when you came into the club,' Wright replied, perhaps a little hesitantly, handing Oscar a small, unsealed envelope.

Six days earlier, Queensberry had marched into the Albemarle and asked Sydney Wright where Oscar might be found. When Wright told him that Oscar was not there and had not been there for some time, Queensberry produced a printed calling card and furiously scrawled five words on it in ink. 'Give this card to Oscar Wilde,' he growled and stalked out. Queensberry's handwriting was so appalling that Wright had difficulty in deciphering the scrawl. After puzzling over it, he thought the words Queensberry had written were: 'For Oscar Wilde ponce and somdomite.' In his rage, Queensberry had misspelt sodomite. Wright was unsure what to do after Queensberry had left. Clearly, His Lordship's message to Mr Wilde was a terrible insult. He turned it over and wrote on the back the time and date. He placed the card in an envelope and kept it on his desk until such time as Mr Wilde showed up at the club. There seemed little more he could do.

Because of Queensberry's handwriting, it took Oscar a few seconds to absorb the full import of the message. His heart must have missed a beat. This was the final insult, the public slap across the face. Oscar believed that he had no alternative now but to act. By writing the card and allowing Sydney Wright – and anyone else who happened to examine the contents of the unsealed envelope – to read what he had written, Queensberry had libelled Oscar by accusing him of a vice many considered worse than murder. According to Mr Justice Wills, who presided over Oscar's last trial, 'The action of Lord Queensberry was one which no gentleman would have taken and left Wilde no alternative but to prosecute or to be branded publicly as a man who could not deny a foul charge.'

Oscar drove back to his hotel only to find yet another 'loathsome letter' from Bosie waiting for him. Oscar immediately dashed off a note in pencil to Robbie Ross. 'Dearest Bobbie,' he wrote:

Since I saw you something has happened. Bosie's father has left a card at my club with hideous words on it. I don't see anything now but a criminal prosecution. My whole life seems ruined by this man. The tower of ivory is assailed by the foul thing. On the sand is my life spilt. I don't know what to do. If you could come here at 11.30 please do so tonight. I mar your life by trespassing on your love and kindness. I have asked Bosie to come tomorrow.

Oscar sent the note by hand to Robbie, who noted that he received it at exactly 6.40pm, less than two hours after Oscar had first read Queensberry's hideous words. Significantly, it was Robbie, rather than Bosie, that Oscar wanted to see. He needed wise counsel and thought that Robbie would be more impartial than Bosie, who was wildly irrational on the subject of his father.

Oscar had another letter to write that evening. Constance must be told. He pencilled a note to her and had it sent by messenger to Tite Street. 'Dear Constance,' he wrote. 'I am coming to see you at nine o'clock. Please be in – it is important.' There is no record of what passed between Oscar and Constance at this meeting, but Oscar must have told her about Queensberry's card with hideous words and that a criminal prosecution now seemed inevitable. He would have warned her that the trial was likely to be sensational and that she must prepare herself and their children for an orgy of publicity in the newspapers.

Constance may have been devastated by the news, but she can hardly have been surprised. She and her husband had been leading separate lives for almost two years, and for most of that time Oscar had lived away in hotels and suites of rented rooms. They did spend time together as a family in the school holidays, and Oscar had not entirely absented himself from Tite Street, making visits and spending occasional nights there. But, for most of the time, Constance was kept in the dark about Oscar's movements and often did not have an address where she could write to him. She had not been aware that Oscar had gone to Algiers, and, towards the end of January, she had been obliged to write to Robbie to ask him to ask Oscar to send her some money as she was £5 overdrawn at the bank. Their marriage was a work of fiction, a *modus vivendi*, designed to maintain a facade of respectability and normality.

Constance must have had her suspicions about the nature of Oscar's close friendships with young men. But there is very strong evidence to suggest that they were more than mere suspicions. It seems that she was fully aware of at least one – and perhaps several – of his relationships. In 1897, long after the trials were over, when Oscar was in prison, Constance seriously considered divorcing him on the grounds of sodomy and gross indecency with boys and young men. But Oscar was convinced that he could successfully defend himself against any petition for divorce because of what he called Constance's 'condonation'. 'My only chance of resisting a divorce was the fact of *condonation* by my wife,' he told Robbie. By italicising the word, it is clear that Oscar was using condonation in its legal and technical sense, rather than in its more general sense.

In late-nineteenth century divorce law, 'condonation' was a strictly technical term and meant 'forgiveness with a condition'. According to Napoleon Argles, author of *How to Obtain a Divorce*, published in 1895, the law on condonation was clear and unambiguous: 'If the petitioner has condoned, that is, has conditionally forgiven the adultery complained of, the petition shall be dismissed.' And, according to Napoleon Argles, to constitute condonation, there must be:

1. Full knowledge of all prior offences.
2. Forgiveness conditional upon avoidance for the future of a matrimonial offence.
3. Voluntary conjugal cohabitation following upon such forgiveness.

Oscar evidently believed that he could use Constance's condonation to defend himself against any divorce petition she might bring based on his sexual infidelities with young men. But he quickly realised that her condonation did not meet all the strict requirements of the law. 'I now learn that no condonation is of any value where more than one offence may be charged,' he told Robbie. 'My wife has simply to say that she condoned X, but knew nothing of Y, and would not hear of condoning Z.' The full extent of Oscar's revelations to Constance about his love affairs with young men, and the plenitude of her condonation, her forgiveness of his Uranian sins, will never be known. But it does appear that Oscar had confessed to, and received absolution for, at least one affair with a young man.

Now Constance was being forced to ask herself some uncomfortable questions, to delve into subjects which hitherto had been best left alone. Why was Lord Queensberry doing this? Was it because Oscar and Bosie were lovers? And what evidence did he have for his allegations? After his promises to reform, to resist, had Oscar crawled back to his sodomitical vices? When Constance put direct questions to him, Oscar may have admitted to some sort of idealised love affair with Bosie. But he would have kept silent about his other lovers, about the short and intense affairs, the chance encounters and the feastings with renters who had figured so prominently in his sexual life. These revelations were yet to come.

Oscar's visit to Tite Street was not prolonged. Afterwards he paid a brief call on Charles Ricketts round the corner at the Vale. Ricketts sensed that something was wrong. Oscar's conversation seemed forced and stilted. But one comment of Oscar's struck him forcibly: 'I live in a world of puppets, who do not understand, and yet would play with the strings,' Oscar said musingly. His observation betrayed a strange fatalism, a sense of predestination. He was perhaps recalling the words of the palmist Cheiro, who had told him two years earlier that his 'most unusual destiny of brilliancy and uninterrupted success' would be 'completely broken and ruined'. Oscar left the Vale and met Charles Shannon hastening home along the King's Road in the thick fog. They stopped outside a shop where sausage rolls and pork pies were piled up in the window and garishly lit by gaslight. Oscar looked 'tired and preoccupied', Shannon thought. 'What curious things people will eat!' Oscar said suddenly. 'I suppose they must be hungry.' With that, Oscar hailed a passing cab and returned to Piccadilly to meet Robbie.

Long after the trials, Oscar would blame Bosie, Bosie would blame Robbie, and Robbie would blame Bosie for the decision to enter into the disastrous prosecution of Queensberry. In truth, all three were more or less equally responsible. Robbie and Oscar sat up in the Avondale Hotel until the early hours of the morning talking over what to do. Though he later denied it, Robbie was convinced that Queensberry had to be stopped and that a prosecution for criminal libel was the only course open to Oscar. Oscar was not so sure. At one particularly low point, he seriously considered fleeing to Paris where he would at least be safe and where he could think clearly. But there was the question of the hotel bill of £148. With no money to pay the bill, the hotel would not have allowed him to take his luggage. When Bosie arrived the next morning and saw Queensberry's card, he fell into a fury. He was adamant that his father must be prosecuted, that he must be sent to prison for the insult he had offered to Oscar. Egged on by Bosie, white with anger and indignation, and supported by Robbie, equally determined that prosecution was the only course, Oscar agreed to go and see Charles Humphreys immediately. That Queensberry's insult was more or less true, and its publication justifiable in law, seemed to have occurred only to Robbie. When he suggested that it might be sensible to inform Charles Humphreys and Percy Douglas that Queensberry's allegations were substantially true, neither Oscar nor Bosie would hear of it.

Oscar wrote later that he had been more or less driven into the action against

Queensberry against his better judgement. 'Blindly I staggered as an ox into the shambles,' he wrote. Oscar was certainly in no fit state to stand up to Bosie. 'My judgement forsook me,' he said. 'My will-power completely failed me.' Since first reading Queensberry's card with hideous words, Oscar had not stopped thinking about it and not stopped talking about it – painfully with Constance, and exhaustively and exhaustingly with Robbie. He had been drinking heavily and had barely slept. Physical, mental and emotional prostration were bound to affect the clarity of his judgement. A further clouding factor could have been the narcotic effects of any drugs he was taking to relieve the discomfort of the gonorrhoea he may have contracted in Algiers.

And so the three of them – Oscar, Bosie and Robbie – drove to Holborn on the Friday morning to see Charles Humphreys, who listened gravely to what Oscar had to say and carefully examined Queensberry's card with its hideous words. With evidence such as this, he told Oscar, it would be possible to mount a prosecution against Lord Queensberry for criminal libel. But, before he could proceed, he needed to ask a very important question. Could Oscar swear on his solemn oath that there was absolutely no truth in the libel? Oscar assured him that there was not. It was the first of many lies that Oscar and Bosie would tell to solicitors and barristers. 'What is loathsome to me,' Oscar told Bosie later:

> is the memory of interminable visits paid by me to the solicitor Humphreys in your company, when in the ghastly glare of a bleak room you and I would sit with serious faces telling serious lies to a bald man, till I really groaned and yawned with *ennui*.

There was only one other question to be resolved: money. When Oscar told Humphreys that he had no money to pay for the prosecution, Bosie interposed at once with an offer of financial support. 'You said that your own family would be only too delighted to pay all the necessary costs,' Oscar later reminded Bosie:

> that your father had been an incubus to them all: that they had often discussed the possibility of getting him put into a lunatic asylum so as to keep him out of the way: that he was a daily source of annoyance and distress to your mother and to everyone else: that if I would only come forward to have him shut up I would be regarded by the family as their champion and their benefactor: and that your mother's rich relations themselves would look on it as a real delight to pay all costs and expenses.

Humphreys consented to this arrangement, and Oscar found himself hurried to the police court to swear out a warrant for Queensberry's arrest. 'If you are innocent,' Humphreys had assured Oscar, 'you should succeed.' But Oscar knew only too well that he was not innocent. He realised with a sudden shudder that he had unwittingly walked into what Queensberry boasted of as his 'booby-trap'.

Raking Piccadilly

'One should never make one's début with a scandal. One should reserve that to lend an interest to one's maturer years.'

On the morning of Saturday 2 March, just two days after Oscar had received the 'card with hideous words', two detectives arrived at Carter's Hotel to arrest Queensberry. Although there was very little danger that the event would pass unnoticed by the newspapers, Bosie was not taking any chances. He drafted a hasty press release about his father's arrest and sent it to James Nicol Dunn, editor of the *Morning Post*. 'Dear Mr Dunn,' he wrote. 'Is this any use to you?':

> The Marquis of Queensberry was arrested on a warrant this morning at nine o'clock at Carter's Hotel, Albemarle Street by Inspector Greet and Detective-Sergeant George Shaddock. The warrant was issued in consequence of information sworn in connection with the alleged publication on the 18th Feby last by the Marquis of Queensberry of a defamatory libel on Mr Oscar Wilde. The Marquis of Queensberry who was in bed when the detectives called was taken to Vine Street Police Station. He will be brought up today at Marlborough Street.

Detectives Greet and Shaddock were taken up to Queensberry's room and knocked on the door. 'Are you the Marquis of Queensberry?' Greet asked him as he entered the room.

'I am,' growled Queensberry.

'I am a Police Officer and hold a warrant signed by R.M. Newton Esq. of Marlborough Street Police Court for your arrest,' said Greet, proceeding to read the warrant aloud to Queensberry.

'Yes,' said Queensberry. 'I have been trying to find Mr Oscar Wilde for eight or ten days – this thing has been going on for over two years.'

Queensberry dressed quickly and was taken to Vine Street Police Station where he was formally charged with 'publishing a certain defamatory libel of and concerning one Oscar Wilde, at Albemarle Street, on February 18, 1895, at the Parish of St. George'. Queensberry made no formal reply to the charge, but asked to be allowed to send for his solicitor, Sir George Lewis.

Shortly afterwards, Queensberry – described as 'fifty years of age, no

341

occupation' – appeared before the sitting magistrate, Mr R.M. Newton, at Marlborough Street Police Court. A group of Queensberry's sporting friends had gathered and were present in court. Charles Humphreys was there with Oscar. A beaming Bosie sat in the public gallery, delighted at finally seeing his father in the dock. The hearing was short and to the point. Humphreys opened the case for the prosecution, laying great stress on the normality and respectability of Oscar's family life. Mr Oscar Wilde, he said, was a married man living on the most affectionate terms with his wife and family of two sons. Humphreys briefly outlined the history of Queensberry's 'most cruel persecution' of Oscar, which had culminated in Lord Queensberry leaving his card for Oscar scrawled with 'epithets of the foulest nature' at the Albemarle Club.

Humphreys called Sydney Wright, hall porter at the Albemarle, to give evidence. Wright testified that the words on Queensberry's card, 'For Oscar Wilde ponce and somdomite', were 'written in my presence'. At this point, Queensberry interposed loudly and claimed that the words he had written were 'posing as sodomite'. Whether Queensberry had written 'ponce and somdomite' or 'posing as somdomite' is a moot point. When Queensberry called on Oscar at Tite Street six months earlier, he had accused Oscar of posing as a sodomite, and he had told Bosie that 'to pose as a thing is to be as bad as to be it'. But the word on the card does look suspiciously like 'ponce'. Between leaving his card at the Albemarle and his arrest, Queensberry had had nearly a fortnight to think about what he had written and to discuss it with Sir George Lewis. To accuse Oscar of 'posing' as a sodomite was a much more defensible position than calling him a ponce and sodomite. Ponce was and is a slang word with a range of meanings, all of them offensive. A ponce was akin to a pimp, not just a man who lived off the earnings of prostitutes, but also a procurer and supplier of young flesh for the purposes of prostitution. Ponce was also a slang term for an obvious, effeminate man, who might also be involved in prostitution. To justify the original wording of his libel, Queensberry would have to prove that Oscar was an habitual associate of prostitutes, that he had lived off their immoral earnings and that he had procured boys to act as prostitutes.

After Detective-Inspector Greet had given a perfunctory account of his arrest of Lord Queensberry, Sir George Lewis rose to speak. 'I venture to say that when the circumstances of this case are more fully known, you will find that Lord Queensberry acted as he did under feelings of great indignation and –'. 'I cannot go into that now,' the magistrate, Mr Newton, snapped, adjourning the case for a week's time. Bail was set at £1,500, and a smiling Queensberry left the court with his friends.

Seeing the ape-like Queensberry squirming and writhing in the dock boosted Oscar's confidence that by prosecuting him he was doing the right thing. His initial hesitations and reluctances were forgotten. Humphreys had assured him that he would win the case. For months, Queensberry had been persecuting Oscar consistently, and now had libelled him foully. Here was an opportunity to bring Queensberry's persecution to an end and silence his foul mouth. Bosie and Robbie were both agreed that prosecution was the only course. Besides which, there were distinct dramatic possibilities in the prosecution. If Oscar won – and there seemed little doubt that he would – he would be the hero of the hour, the David who had taken on Goliath, the slayer of the dragon Queensberry. 'Temporarily exalted' was how Robbie Ross described Oscar's state of mind at this time. It was, Robbie wrote, 'an unfortunate condition which induced him to think that his personality would triumph over scandal and the forces of law'.

If Oscar felt any pique at seeing his former friend Lewis in court acting now for his deadliest enemy, he did not show it. It was Lewis who felt decidedly uncomfortable and not a little shamefaced. Six months earlier he had promised Oscar that he would never act against him. Now he was not only appearing in court for Queensberry, he had also grossly betrayed Oscar's trust by revealing to Queensberry the details of Bosie's Oxford blackmail, as well as telling him about Alfred Wood's attempted blackmail of Oscar over his 'madness of kisses' letter. But immediately after the police court hearing at Marlborough Street, Lewis returned his brief to Queensberry. He would no longer act for him.

Queensberry was due to appear again at Marlborough Street in a week's time and needed to find another solicitor urgently. It was Saturday and the only solicitor's offices he found open that afternoon were those of Messrs Day and Russell. Queensberry saw Charles Russell who, after hearing his account of his feud with Oscar and the reasons that lay behind it, agreed to act for him. That night, back at Carter's Hotel, Queensberry held a press conference about his arrest. He had been drinking and was, as a reporter from the *New York Herald* tactfully put it, in 'a somewhat nervous and excited condition'. Queensberry was defiantly open about why he was persecuting Oscar. 'I sent that card to Wilde,' he told the *Herald* reporter, 'to bring matters to a head':

> For the past two years I have been hunting for him in order that I might have an opportunity of assaulting him in consequence of what I believe to be well founded rumours in connection with persons in whom I am interested. I wished to assault him so that he should be forced to bring an action against me and thus give me an opportunity of stating what I believe to be the truth about the matter. I am delighted at the result of my action in leaving that card, and I feel much easier in my mind now.

Oscar's friends were shocked when they heard about Queensberry's arrest. 'Poor, poor Oscar!' Max Beerbohm wrote sorrowfully from Chicago to Reggie Turner:

> How sad it is. I cannot bear to think of all that must have happened – the whisperings and the hastenings hither and thither – before he could have been seduced into Marlborough Street. I suppose he was exasperated too much not to take action. I am sorry he has not got George Lewis, wonder if

Bosie has returned, what evidence will be brought in for the defence – and so forth.

Beerbohm was right to wonder what evidence Queensberry might bring forth in his defence. Oscar, Bosie and Robbie had gone ahead with the prosecution in the conviction that they could win a resounding victory. Queensberry was charged with the offence of 'defamatory libel', part of Lord Campbell's Libel Act of 1843. As far as Oscar, Bosie and Robbie were concerned, the case against Queensberry was already proved. He had admitted to writing 'epithets of the foulest nature' on the card, admitted to leaving it at the Albemarle Club for Oscar and admitted that both these actions were undertaken deliberately. It was an open and shut case. Without a shadow of a doubt Queensberry had defamed and libelled Oscar. The only question now was what his sentence would be. Under the provisions of the Libel Act, defamatory libel carried a maximum sentence of one year's imprisonment. But, if it could be proved that the accused knew the libel to be false, the statutory maximum penalty was two years' imprisonment. Oscar, Bosie and Robbie were confident that Queensberry would be found guilty and sentenced to two years in prison – or forced to flee abroad to escape incarceration. Either way, there would be jubilation.

To defend himself, Queensberry had to justify the libel. He had to prove that what he had written was true and that it had been published and promulgated for the public good. Oscar, Bosie and Robbie must have known that Queensberry would seek to justify his libel, but they gambled that such evidence he might be able to come up with in court would pale into insignificance when set against the enormity of the insult. There would of course be a literary side to the case: old chestnuts about *Mr W.H.* and *Dorian Gray* would be rehashed and reheated and served up in court. But these were pitiful doings. Oscar had confronted and confounded his critics before and could do so again.

The only real danger would be if Queensberry had solid evidence that Oscar had habitually associated with sodomites or that he had indeed had sodomitical sexual relations with men. And where could Queensberry possibly find that sort of evidence? The very murkiness of the penumbral realm of sex between men in London was Oscar's best defence. Few who moved in that shadowy world betrayed its secrets to outsiders, and few outsiders could ever penetrate its beguiling veils. Ironically, it was the oppressive weight of society's 'monstrous laws' against men who loved men that was the best guarantee of Oscar's secrecy and safety. Oscar was supremely confident that no one would dare to come forward and admit to having had sex with him – for if they did, they would be opening themselves up to prosecution.

It was true that there had been two or three rather unfortunate incidents of blackmail. But it was unlikely that anyone other than the blackmailer and the blackmailed would know about them – and blackmailers were hardly likely to come forward and testify in court to their crimes. Sir George Lewis, of course, knew about the blackmail. Seeing him in court representing Queensberry caused Oscar some momentary pangs of unease. But surely Sir George Lewis would be bound by professional vows of secrecy, if not by ties of ancient friendship. Besides which, Oscar had been clever. He had persuaded Pierre Louÿs to translate the 'madness of kisses' letter into a prose poem in French for publication in the *Spirit Lamp*.

With less than a week until his next appearance at Marlborough Street Police Court, it was imperative that Queensberry find a barrister to represent him in the proceedings. Charles Russell, on the advice of his illustrious father, Lord Russell of Killowen, the recently appointed Lord Chief Justice of England, approached a brilliant Irishman, Edward Carson, a Member of Parliament and Queen's Counsel at both the English and the Irish Bar. Carson hesitated. The case was an extremely unsavoury one, involving a father and a son, and seemingly based on hearsay and gossip. And apart from that, he knew Oscar personally. They had met and played together as small boys. In the summer of 1859, when Oscar was four years old, the Wilde family had been on holiday at Dungarven in County Waterford. The children had been looked after by a fifteen-year-old girl who also looked after Edward Carson. And when Oscar went up to Trinity College, Dublin in 1871, Carson had been a fellow student. They were friends, good friends, at Trinity, he said. At the time of the trials, Oscar told Bosie that Ned Carson 'used to walk about with him' at Trinity 'with his arms around his neck'. Carson always vehemently denied that there was anything more between himself and Oscar than mere acquaintance, claiming that he had always disapproved of Oscar's flippancy.

Their paths had crossed once more a few years before Oscar's trial. Carson was walking towards the House of Commons when a fine carriage pulled up beside him and a stout, elaborately dressed, effeminate-looking man with a huge white buttonhole in his overcoat jumped out. 'Hullo, Ned Carson, how are you?' said Oscar. 'Fancy you being a Tory and Arthur Balfour's right-hand man. You're coming along, Ned. Come and dine with me one day in Tite Street.' Oscar never did follow up his invitation and fix a date for Ned Carson to dine. Had he done so, things might have turned out very differently, as Carson made a point of never accepting briefs involving friends or people from whom he had received hospitality.

Carson initially rejected the brief. Though Oscar was not quite a friend, he was not exactly a stranger. They had known each other at Trinity, and Oscar was, when all was said and done, an Irishman, a Dubliner like himself. But Russell was undeterred. A day or so later he went back to Carson and apparently showed him some convincing evidence that Oscar had indeed had sex with young men. When Carson discovered Oscar had not merely posed as a sodomite, but was a practising sodomite, 'deep moral indignation boiled up inside him', as his friend and biographer, Edward Marjoribanks, wrote. When Oscar heard that Carson was representing Queensberry and would be cross-examining him in court, his only response was to say, 'No doubt he will perform his task with all the added bitterness of an old friend.'

Queensberry was shrewd enough to know he would have to be able to justify the libel or face imprisonment. He knew that he would have to present convincing evidence to the court that the libel was true and that its publication was for the public good. If Trelawny Backhouse is to be believed, Queensberry had already employed the services of private detectives in the summer of 1894 to search out proof of Drumlanrig's love affair with the Prime Minister, Lord Rosebery. The detectives had found their proof at a hotel in Bourne End on the River Thames, where two maid servants said they had seen 'concrete proofs' of sodomy on the sheets of a bed which Drumlanrig and Rosebery had shared. Queensberry almost certainly used the same detectives to find damaging proof of Oscar's sexual relationships with Bosie and with other young men. In a letter to Minnie, the wife of his son, Percy, written on the same day he left the card for Oscar at the Albemarle, Queensberry had urged Percy to 'go and speak to Cook the detective' who 'knows more about him (O.W.) than I do'.

Queensberry was already in possession of at least one major piece of evidence against Oscar: a copy of his 'madness of kisses' letter to Bosie. 'Some Gentle Criticisms of British Justice', published shortly after Oscar's conviction in 1895, was a pamphlet containing detailed and swingeing criticisms of the corruption and cant surrounding Oscar's trials. Its author, 'I. Playfair' – the *nom de plume* of James H. Wilson – alleged that Queensberry bought the 'madness of kisses' letter from a blackmailing solicitor he calls 'Macpelah', whose real name was Bernard Abrahams.

But such evidence against Oscar as Queensberry possessed was deemed insufficient by Charles Russell, who urged him to secure the services of the formidable Inspector Littlechild, a former Chief Detective-Inspector of Scotland Yard, and Frederick Kearley, a retired Detective-Inspector. Queensberry is said to have given Littlechild and Kearley £500, the equivalent of £30,000 in today's money, to secure sufficient evidence against Oscar to justify his libel. Russell was keen to enter the fray himself and poured his considerable energies into tracking down witnesses.

Their initial investigations were not promising. Rumours of Oscar's sexual habits abounded, but hard evidence was in short supply, until Russell mentioned the case to Charles Brookfield. Brookfield was an actor and playwright who was currently appearing in *An Ideal Husband*, playing the role of Lord Goring's servant, Phipps. Brookfield hated Oscar and was only too ready to dig for dirt. According to Frank Harris, Brookfield 'constituted himself private prosecutor in this case and raked Piccadilly to find witnesses against Oscar Wilde'. Although Oscar is said to have once snubbed Brookfield for wearing the wrong kind of suit, Brookfield's hatred of Oscar was out of all proportion to the slight. 'With Brookfield alas! Wilde became a monomania,' wrote Vincent O'Sullivan, who knew both men. 'There came a time when he could not keep Wilde out of his talk. I can only guess at the cause of this obsession.' Brookfield was driven by an irrational, visceral loathing of any manifestation of love and sex between men that would today be called homophobia.

Brookfield's irrational fear and loathing of sodomy was extreme but hardly unusual. His views were shared by Queensberry, by Edward Carson and by Charles Russell – and by the vast majority of Victorian men who found the idea of sex between men utterly repugnant. It was a crime: a crime against nature, a crime against God, and a crime against the laws of the land. There was little comprehension of the arguments put forward by George Ives and other adherents of the Cause that their sexuality was prescribed by nature, rather than chosen by themselves. 'Nature was in this matter a stepmother to each of us,' Oscar had said of his and Bosie's sexuality. In the eyes of the Victorians, there was only one thing worse than a sodomite, and that was a proselytising sodomite. Sex between men was a contagion, and Oscar was at the very heart of the darkness. He was high priest and prophet, physically corrupting young men into sodomy and preaching a diseased intellectual gospel. Destroying Oscar would not destroy sodomy at a stroke. But it would bring to an abrupt halt what many saw as the creeping contagion of his gospel of unnatural love.

'I. Playfair' alleges that an unholy alliance – the corrupt, blackmailing solicitor Bernard Abrahams, Charles Brookfield and Queensberry's detectives, Littlechild and Kearley – now scoured the West End in search of witnesses. Abrahams probably supplied the names of Allen and Cliburn himself, from whom he had acquired his copy of Oscar's 'madness of kisses' letter. Littlechild ran Cliburn and Allen to ground in Broadstairs. According to the journalist John Boon, it was 'a fine old Irish Commissionaire', employed at one of the theatres where Oscar's plays were being performed, who unwttingly helped uncover crucial evidence. In answer to Brookfield's amiable questions, the commissionaire happily gave details of Oscar's friends who called for him at the theatre. One name was crucial: Alfred Taylor.

It was a comparatively easy matter for two former Scotland Yard detectives to track down Alfred Taylor. They found out his previous addresses at 13, Little College Street in Westminster and 3, Chapel Street in Belgravia, where Taylor had lived until December 1893. Mrs Sophia Gray, the landlady at Chapel Street, was very helpful. Taylor had left the house owing her money. When Kearley turned up with Charles Russell, Mrs Gray was only too willing to hand over a 'hatbox full of papers' which Taylor had carelessly left behind. The hatbox was a veritable goldmine of information. There were several letters from Oscar, and various telegrams from him, making and breaking appointments with Taylor. 'Obliged to see Tree at five o'clock so don't come to Savoy,' Oscar had telegraphed to Taylor. 'Let me know at once about Fred. – OSCAR.' Who was 'Fred'?, Littlechild and Kearley asked themselves. There were also documents concerning a number of young men: letters from 'Jenny' Mavor, and two cheques, one for 30 shillings and one for £2 – made out to him.

Kearley and Littlechild were also intrigued by a letter from Charles Spurrier Mason, Alfred Taylor's 'husband', dated November 1891. 'My dear Alfred,' Mason had written:

Soon as you can afford to let me have some money, I shall be pleased and

347

obliged. I would not ask you if I could get any myself, you know. Business is not so easy as one would think. There is a lot of trouble attached to it. I have not met anyone yet. Come home soon dear and let us go out sometimes together.

It was signed 'With much love, Charlie'. It did not take Littlechild and Kearley too long to work out that the 'business' in question was prostitution. There were other names and addresses in Taylor's hat box too. Before long, Queensberry and Russell had a list of names: Alfred Taylor, 'Jenny' Mavor, William Allen, Robert Cliburn, Alfred Wood, Fred Atkins and the Parker brothers, William and Charles. Charles Parker had joined the Royal Artillery. Littlechild and Russell tracked him down, and he was interviewed in barracks in Dover by Russell.

Russell and Littlechild alternately cajoled and terrorised the boys they found into making statements. Their methods were crude but effective. According to 'I. Playfair', one of Oscar's young renters, a boy he names 'Hades', was interviewed by Russell while Littlechild waited in the adjoining room. 'Hades' was told that if he did not make a statement incriminating Oscar, then he would be prosecuted. George Ives asserted that the boys were 'terrified into giving evidence: they were even locked up and kept on bread and water'. 'Such is justice,' Ives sighed into his diary, 'when the sex taboos are made to come to the assistance of private malice.' Bosie wrote how one of Oscar's friends from the Uranian underworld, 'a blackmailer and professional pederast', came 'to forewarn Mr Wilde against what was going on'. The man told Bosie how:

Mr Bernard Abrahams came up to me and asked if I was willing to go to —'s office to denounce Mr Wilde under oath. 'I don't see why I should,' I replied. 'I have never had any dealings with Mr Wilde in my life.' 'Oh, that doesn't matter,' said Abrahams.

As the days wore on, the net was widened. Littlechild and Kearley visited every hotel and every house where Oscar was known to have lived. They went to the Savoy, to the Albemarle Hotel, to St James's Place, to Goring and to Worthing. They interviewed everyone they could find, for the most part servants. There were hefty cash inducements on offer to loosen reluctant tongues. These tireless investigations yielded up the names of Walter Grainger and Alfonso Conway. They also came up with Edward Shelley's name, possibly through the malign offices of the publisher, John Lane.

Constance was taking it all very badly. 'We are very worried just now,' she wrote to the novelist Marie Belloc Lowndes, turning down an invitation. Two nights before he was due to return to Marlborough Street Police Court for the adjourned hearing, Oscar, Constance and Bosie appeared in public together. True to Oscar's belief that 'in matters of grave importance, style, not sincerity, is the vital thing', the three of them had dinner together in a restaurant, before taking a box at the St James's Theatre for a performance of *Earnest*. Oscar was making a public statement. If his wife found nothing objectionable in his friendship with Lord Alfred Douglas, how on earth could anyone else? Constance smiled bravely, but found the whole experience excruciating. She was 'very much agitated', Bosie recalled afterwards, 'and when I said good-night to her at the door of the theatre she had tears in her eyes'.

Oscar made an ostentatious arrival at Marlborough Street Police Court on Saturday 9 March. The *Evening News* reported that 'Oscar Wilde drove up in a carriage and pair, a magnificent turn-out with coachman and cockaded footman, accompanied by Lord Alfred Douglas.' Oscar himself was also magnificently turned out in a long blue overcoat with velvet collar and cuffs and a large white flower in his button hole. He was still sublimely confident that he was going to win. As yet he had no idea of the scale of the success of Queensberry's investigations, and no idea of the dangerous fruits they had yielded. To those of his friends who advised caution, or even flight, Oscar was airily dismissive. 'Have no fear,' he quipped with unconscious irony. 'The working classes are with me – to a boy.'

Vexed and persecuted lovers

'A short primer, When to Lie and How, if brought out in an attractive and not too expensive a form, would no doubt command a large sale, and would prove of real practical service to many earnest and deep-thinking people.'

On the morning of Tuesday 19 February, Lord Rosebery, the Prime Minister, called an emergency Cabinet meeting to announce that he had made his mind up to resign. Reading a prepared statement, Rosebery said that following a debate in the House of Commons the day before where he had been attacked by members of his own party, he did not feel he had the full support of the Party and would therefore leave office. 'God knows I never sought my present office and would have done anything consistently with honour to avoid it, and I renounce it to say the least without regret,' he told his Cabinet colleagues, who listened in shocked silence. 'The whole thing came upon us like a thunderbolt, no one having the slightest idea that he would contemplate such an amazing *coup de tête*,' wrote Lord Kimberley, the Foreign Secretary.

Rosebery's bombshell was delivered the morning after Queensberry had left his card scrawled with 'hideous words' for Oscar at the Albemarle Club. Were these two events connected? To Oscar and those in his circle who, in the course of Oscar's trials, came to believe that he was caught up in a political conspiracy, the answer was a resounding yes. When Queensberry threw down the gauntlet to Oscar by leaving his card at the Albemarle Club, had he also thrown down a similar gauntlet for Rosebery? Had he written to Rosebery demanding his resignation, threatening, as he had done the previous summer, to expose Rosebery as a sodomite to his enemy Henry Labouchère? And was this why, like a thunderbolt out of the blue, Rosebery had summoned the Cabinet and announced his intention to resign?

'Loulou' Harcourt, son of Rosebery's great rival, Sir William Harcourt, and himself a leading Liberal, suspected that that there was more to Rosebery's resignation than met the eye. 'George Murray says R is in no better mood today than he was yesterday,' Loulou wrote in his diary on 20

February, the day after Rosebery's shock announcement:

> He says this outburst has been brewing up for a long time and that the recent debate was not the *causa causarus*.

Loulou even considered it 'possible' that Rosebery might 'commit suicide'. Two days later, however, Rosebery was prevailed upon to withdraw his resignation. It was clear to his friends and his enemies that the Prime Minister was labouring under an intolerable burden of stress and unhappiness. From the day he announced his resignation at Cabinet, Rosebery started to experience the symptoms of a sudden and extreme physical and mental breakdown. Officially, he was suffering from severe influenza, which somehow mutated into prolonged 'insomnia'. He could barely sleep, rarely managing more than an hour or two a night. Rosebery felt he was caught up in a waking nightmare. 'I cannot forget 1895,' he wrote later:

> To lie night after night, staring wide awake, hopeless of sleep, tormented in nerves, and to realise all that was going on, at which I was present, so to speak, like a disembodied spirit, to watch one's own corpse as it were, day after day, is an experience which no sane man with a conscience would repeat.

Rosebery's symptoms, as recorded by his friends, by his doctors, and not least by himself, portray a man in absolute mental torture, suffering from a combination of grief at Drumlanrig's death, and terror of exposure and public shame at Queensberry's hands. Rosebery complained to his friends of loneliness and of depression. He spoke about marrying again and said he was 'frightened' by it. He also spoke, more than once, about suicide, telling Lord Kimberley how 'for the first time in his life he understood why people committed suicide'. Significantly, Rosebery had experienced similar symptoms of nervous illness once before, in 1893 when Queensberry had bombarded him with abusive letters about Drumlanrig.

On 25 February, Rosebery's doctor, Sir William Broadbent, was shocked to discover that the Prime Minister's pulse was barely perceptible. Rosebery's illness was caused by 'long-continued derangement of the digestive organs', he thought. It was 'the most obstinate and puzzling case he had ever come across'. Two days later, on 27 February, Loulou Harcourt recorded in his diary that George Murray 'thinks Rosebery's illness is more mental than physical'. Rosebery's health continued to deteriorate. By 13 March, Sir William was convinced that if the downward spiral continued 'there must be fatal termination'. Rosebery might die.

There were some who were convinced that Rosebery's declining health was in some way related to Oscar's prosecution of Queensberry. Four days before Sir William's dire predictions, there had been a development in the libel case which may have precipitated the sudden, significant deterioration in

351

Rosebery's health. At the reconvened hearing at Marlborough Street Police Court on 9 March, Charles Humphreys had first alluded to the series of abusive and offensive letters which Queensberry had sent to Bosie and to his father-in-law, Alfred Montgomery. Though he wanted to introduce the letters as evidence, he did not want them read aloud in open court, the reason being, Humphreys said:

> with reference to one particular letter the names of exalted persons are used and I don't think it would be right to them that their names should be called into question in matters of this description.

The key 'exalted person' was Lord Rosebery. In a letter written to Montgomery on 6 July 1894, not long after he had turned up at Tite Street with a prize-fighter, Queensberry had said that Oscar had 'plainly showed the white feather the other day when I tackled him – damned cur and coward of the Rosebery type'. Though Queensberry's comments could not be construed as a direct accusation of sodomy, they were still extremely damaging. By bracketing Oscar and Rosebery together as two of a 'type', Queensberry's implication was clear. Oscar Wilde and Lord Rosebery were both sodomites. The press were quick to catch the whiff of scandal. Who were the unnamed 'exalted persons', and were they in some way implicated in the sodomitical scandal that seemed to be unfolding before them? When the magistrate asked Humphreys and Carson to discuss the admissibility of Queensberry's letters in a private room, 'a buzz of conversation filled the court'. 'What was the reason for the retirement?' the reporter from the London *Evening News* demanded. 'Was the case to be nipped in the bud in the interest of "exalted personages" once or twice so distantly referred to?'

Meanwhile, Oscar and Bosie were prepared to go abroad. After the hearing at Marlborough Street on 9 March, Bosie declared that he and Oscar must both spend a week in Monte Carlo. 'At a time when I should have been in London taking wise counsel, and calmly considering the hideous trap in which I had allowed myself to be caught,' Oscar said later:

> You insisted on my taking you to Monte Carlo, of all revolting places on God's earth, that all day, and all night as well, you might gamble as long as the Casino remained open. As for me – baccarat having no charms for me – I was left alone outside to myself.

Bosie refused to discuss 'even for five minutes' the court case hanging over Oscar. 'The slightest allusion to the ordeal awaiting me was regarded as a bore,' Oscar told Bosie in *De Profundis*. 'A new brand of champagne that was recommended to us had more interest for you.'

In view of Queensberry's energetic search for witnesses, Oscar and Bosie's trip to Monte Carlo appears to be decidedly quixotic. On 11 March, the day before he and Oscar were due to depart for Monte Carlo, Bosie wrote to his brother Percy, 'I saw Humphreys today. He says everything is splendid and we are going to walk over.' But in truth everything was not quite so splendid as it might appear. Clouds were starting to bank up ominously on the horizon. On his own admission, Bosie knew by 9 March that Queensberry was trying to beguile and blackmail boys into making statements about Oscar's sexual activities. Was the trip to Monte Carlo designed to take Oscar's mind off the forthcoming trial, a distraction to stop him wavering?

Oscar's short-lived surge of optimism and confidence was slowly beginning to bleed away. He was alarmed at news of Queensberry's determined search for witnesses among the Uranian demimonde. Though Oscar still clung to the belief that no one he had actually had sex with would dare make any admission for fear of incriminating himself, that still left those who could be bullied or bribed into swearing a false statement. He was beginning to feel unnerved by what he sensed as a widespread hostility towards him, made manifest when he and Bosie were asked to leave a hotel in Monte Carlo after the other guests complained about their presence.

After his return to London, Oscar went to discuss the case with his barrister, Sir Edward Clarke QC MP. Sir Edward Clarke was one of the most highly regarded barristers of his time. A former Solicitor General, he was famous for fearlessly cross-examining the Prince of Wales in the celebrated Baccarat gaming case. When Humphreys first took Oscar to meet him, Clarke had said, 'I can only accept this brief, Mr Wilde, if you can assure me on your honour as an English gentleman that there is not and never has been any foundation for the charges that are made against you.' Oscar gave his solemn assurance that Queensberry's charges were 'absolutely false and groundless.' It was a bald lie, but then again, Oscar was not an English gentleman. He was an Irish gentleman which, as he had once famously said, 'is quite another thing'.

Money, or rather the lack of it, was becoming an increasing problem. Humphreys and Clarke were demanding something on account towards their fees. 'Can you do me a very great favour?' Oscar wrote in desperation to Ada Leverson's husband, Ernest:

> Can you advance me £500 for my legal expenses, in this tedious and dreadful trial? Lord Douglas of Hawick, the eldest son has promised to pay half my costs, and Lady Queensberry has promised to pay 'any amount required', but Lord Douglas is in Devonshire and Lady Queensberry in Florence, and the money is required by my lawyer at once.

Leverson stumped up the cash and a grateful Oscar wrote a graceful letter of thanks.

On Monday 25 March, with barely a week to go before the trial proper of Queensberry was due to begin at the Old Bailey, Oscar and Bosie paid a most satisfactory visit to Mrs Robinson, the Sibyl of Mortimer Street. 'We have been to the Sibyl Robinson,' Oscar joyously telegraphed to Ada Leverson. 'She prophesied complete triumph and was most wonderful.' Fate, it seemed, was on their side and Oscar's confidence that he would win once again surged.

As Oscar was visiting the Sibyl of Mortimer Street, a Grand Jury was being sworn in at the Old Bailey to consider whether the evidence was sufficient to warrant proceeding with the prosecution. If the Grand Jury were convinced that there was a case to answer, they would return a 'True bill' and the case would proceed to court. The Grand Jury looked at the evidence for Oscar's prosecution of Queensberry: the statements of Oscar, Queensberry and Sydney Wright, the card with hideous words itself, and the series of letters Queensberry had written to Bosie and to Alfred Montgomery, including the letter of 6 July with its references to Rosebery. The foreman of the Grand Jury was Paul Villars, a French journalist resident in London, who wrote for *Le Figaro* and the *Journal de débats*. Although the deliberations of a Grand Jury were supposed to be secret, when Villars saw the name of the British Prime Minister twinned with that of Oscar Wilde, he knew he had an explosive story on his hands. Inevitably, the story began to seep out, and it was widely reported throughout Europe and the United States that Lord Rosebery was in some way mixed up in the Oscar Wilde affair. There were endless rumours about the Prime Minister's health and about his imminent resignation. In the nine days between the convening of the Grand Jury and the start of Queensberry's trial for libel, rumours of Rosebery's involvement were everywhere and had reached fever pitch. In the event, these rumours would do Oscar nothing but harm.

On the same day that they visited the Sibyl of Mortimer Street, Oscar and Bosie went to the Café Royal, where Oscar had arranged to meet Frank Harris at 3pm. Sir Edward Clarke had advised Oscar that he would need to defend *Mr W.H.* and *Dorian Gray* against charges that they in some way expressed and advocated unnatural vice. They were the weakest point of a strong case, and Oscar would need to mount a robust defence, preferably producing expert witnesses who could testify to this. Oscar wanted to ask Harris whether he would agree to stand up in court in his position as editor of the *Saturday Review* and say he did not consider *Dorian Gray* to be in any way immoral. Harris had been lunching with George Bernard Shaw, and Oscar's forthcoming appearance in court had inevitably taken centre stage in their conversation. Both were in sombre mood when Oscar arrived with Bosie. A day or so earlier, Harris had taken it upon himself to discover what he could about the case and what evidence, if any, Queensberry had collected to justify his libel. Harris was well-connected and had spoken to several 'people of importance', including a senior figure in the Office of the Director of Public Prosecutions. His investigations yielded appalling results. Most people were convinced that Oscar was not merely posing as a sodomite, but that he was actually guilty of sodomy. There was, so Harris discovered, a substantial body of evidence already stacked against him.

Oscar sat down in high good humour and gracefully explained his mission. He did not get the answer he had been expecting. 'For God's sake, man, put everything on that plane out of your head,' Harris expostulated. 'I know what evidence they have got':

Two young 'panthers'

The Chameleon, 1894

The Marquis of
Queensberry

QUEENSBERRY, MARQUESS OF. (Douglas.)

JOHN SHOLTO DOUGLAS, 8th Marquess, and a Baronet: *b.* July 20th, 1844; *s.* 1858; ed. at Magdalene Coll., Camb.; formerly Lieut. R.N., and Lieut.-Col. 1st Dumfriesshire Rifle Vol.; was a Representative Peer for Scotland 1874-80; is a D.L. of Dumfriesshire: *m.* 1866, Sibyl, dau. of Alfred Montgomery, Esq. [see Montgomery, Bart.]. and has issue.

Arms.—Quarterly: 1st and 4th argent, a human heart gules, ensigned with an imperial crown or, on a chief azure, three mullets of the field, *Douglas*: 2nd and 3rd azure, a bend between six cross crosslets fitchee or, *Mars*: the whole within a bordure or, charged with a double tressure of Scotland. *Crest.*—A human heart gules, ensigned with an imperial crown, and between two wings displayed or. *Supporters.*—Two pegasi argent, wings, tails, manes, and hoofs, or.

Seats,—Kinmount House, near Annan, co. Dumfries; Glen Stuart, Dumfriesshire, N.B. *Clubs,*—Turf, Hurlingham.

SONS LIVING.

FRANCIS ARCHIBALD (*Viscount Drumlanrig*), *b.* Feb. 3rd, 1867; ed. at Roy. Mil. Coll., Sandhurst; is Lieut. 2nd Batn. Coldstream Guards.

Lord Percy, *b.* 1868; is Lieut. 3rd Batn. King's Own Scottish Borderers.
Lord Alfred Bruce, *b.* 1870.   Lord Sholto George, *b.* 1872.

DAUGHTER LIVING.

Lady Edith Gertrude, *b.* 1874.

BROTHERS LIVING.

Rev. Lord Archibald Edward, *b.* 1850; is in Holy Orders of Church of Rome. *Residence,*—Wellington Street, Annan, N.B.

Lord James Edward Sholto, *b.* 1855; was Lieut. West Kent Militia 1875-6; *m.* 1888, Martha Lucy, widow of — Hennessy, Esq. *Residence,*—16, Kensington Court, W. *Club,*—Boodle's.

SISTERS LIVING.

Lady Gertrude, *b.* 1842: *m.* 1882, Mr. Thomas-Stock. *Residence,*—Maryland, Dumfries, N.B.
Lady Florence Caroline, *b.* 1855 (twin): *m.* 1875, Sir Alexander Beaumont Churchill Dixie, 11th Bart. *Residence,*—The Fishery, Windsor.

AUNT LIVING. (*Daughter of 6th Marquess*).

Lady Georgina, *b.* 1819. *Residence,*—68, South Eaton Place, S.W.

'a card with hideous words'

'Bitter Bit: The arrest of Oscar'

'Oscar in prison'

Alfred Taylor

Edward Shelley

Fred Atkins, alias 'Denny'

Alfred Wood

Charlie Parker

William Parker

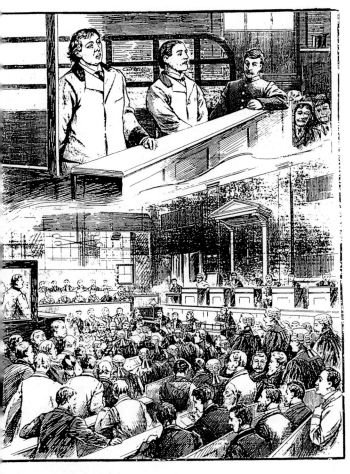

'Scene at the
Old Bailey'

Oscar's cell at
Reading Gaol

Robbie Ross and
Reggie Turner

Oscar and Bosie in Naples

Uranian photograph
belonging to Oscar

Uranian photograph belonging to Oscar

Constance two years
before her death

Oscar in Rome

You don't realise what is going to happen to you. It is not going to be a matter of clever talk about your books. They are going to bring up a string of witnesses that will put art and literature out of the question.

Harris urged Oscar to go abroad immediately with Constance and leave the whole legal boxing ring, with its gloves and ropes, its sponges and pails, to Queensberry. Harris appealed to Shaw, who said he agreed that the case was certain to go against Oscar. Oscar was visibly shaken. It was as if Harris and Shaw had thrown a bucket of cold water over him. Throughout the conversation Bosie had sat in what Shaw described as 'a haughty indignant silence'. Now he stood up, his face white and distorted with rage. 'Such advice shows you are no friend of Oscar's,' he hissed. To Shaw and Harris's astonishment, Oscar got up to leave. 'It is not friendly of you, Frank,' he said. 'It really is not friendly.'

Thirty years later, Bosie recalled that afternoon in the Café Royal in a letter to Frank Harris. Bosie freely admitted to Harris that he had, with a great deal of persuasion and cajoling, screwed Oscar to the 'sticking place': he had got him to the psychological point where he was convinced that a prosecution of Queensberry was both inevitable and necessary. Bosie was frightened that Harris and Shaw would 'argue Wilde out of the state of mind I had got him into'. He was, he said, 'terribly afraid that Oscar would weaken and throw up the sponge'.

As it turned out, Frank Harris's predictions were uncannily correct, and his and Bernard Shaw's advice to Oscar to throw up the case and go abroad at once was entirely sound and rational. What they did not know and could not understand was the curious configuration of the love between Oscar and Bosie, a love born in danger and a love which thrived on adversity. Now, as their love faced its greatest danger, its greatest threat from Queensberry, it blossomed anew.

Persuading Oscar to prosecute his father may have been a question of psychological manipulation for Bosie, but for Oscar it had become both an expression of his love for Bosie and an article of his Uranian faith. The epic love affair between Oscar and Bosie had been on the wane for some months before the trials began. Oscar had several times sought to end their relationship, and Bosie later recalled that he was 'beginning to get a little tired' of Oscar:

We had had several acrimonious quarrels. In the ordinary course of events my infatuation for him would have worn out, and obviously his for me was a very much less enduring and tremendous affair than he himself imagined it to be.

Paradoxically, 'the emotion of the great crisis fanned the waning fires of our devotion to each other,' Bosie wrote.

And just as Oscar's love for Bosie was an epic love, so his battle with the man who sought to destroy that love had assumed epic proportions. In the quasi-liturgical language of the 'Rules of Purpose' of the Order of Chaeronea, Oscar and Bosie were 'vexed and persecuted lovers'. The Order demanded 'justice for all manner of people who are wronged and oppressed by individuals or multitudes or the laws'. Oscar and Bosie were Uranians wronged and oppressed by both an individual and by the laws of their land. It was his duty, Oscar considered, to stand up for his love for Bosie, to stand up for the love that dare not speak its name. It would be a battle between love and hate, between the nobility of Uranian love and the seething foulness of those who sought to deny, to destroy that love. It was a battle that Oscar was convinced he could and must win.

Three days before the trial, on 30 March, Queensberry filed his 'Plea of Justification'. It made grim reading. Predictably, *Dorian Gray* was singled out as a book 'designed', 'intended' and 'understood' to describe 'the relations intimacies and passions of certain persons of sodomitical and unnatural tastes habits and practices'. More surprising was the inclusion of the *Chameleon*, Jack Bloxam's 'Bazaar of Dangerous and Smiling Chances', to which Oscar had contributed his 'Phrases and Philosophies for the Use of the Young'. The *Chameleon* was described as containing 'divers obscene matters and things relating to the practices and passions of persons of sodomitical and unnatural habits and tastes'. Queensberry's Plea alleged that Oscar 'joined in procuring the publication' of the *Chameleon*, an allegation which happened to be true.

But the real shock of Queensberry's Plea lay in its allegations that Oscar 'did solicit and incite' a baker's dozen of named individuals and 'boys unknown' to commit 'sodomy and other acts of gross indecency and immorality'. There were dates, places and nine names: Edward Shelley, Jenny Mavor, Fred Atkins, Maurice Schwabe, Alfred Wood, Charles Parker, Ernest Scarfe, Walter Grainger and Alfonso Conway. As if this was not enough, Oscar was also alleged to have taken 'indecent liberties' with Herbert Tankard, the pageboy from the Savoy.

Oscar and Bosie read Queensberry's Plea with a mounting sense of horror. The literary side of the case was neither here nor there. It was the list of names of boys Oscar had had sex with which frightened him. He had underestimated Queensberry, underestimated his cunning, his resolve and his resourcefulness in hunting down boys to use as evidence against him. With a sinking feeling, it must have dawned on Oscar that losing the libel case was now the least of his problems. If Queensberry could persuade any one of the boys to give evidence, Oscar knew that he would face a criminal prosecution. Alarmingly, Queensberry's Plea alleged not only gross indecency and immorality, but also that Oscar had 'solicited and incited' boys to commit sodomy in every one of the thirteen counts. In other words, Oscar had attempted sodomy with every one of the named and unnamed boys. Whether or not he succeeded was deliberately left unclear, a ploy designed, said Oscar's barrister, Sir Edward Clarke, to ensure that the boys did not incriminate themselves as partners in Oscar's crimes. Attempted sodomy and actual sodomy: the difference was academic. The mere fact that he was alleged to have solicited and incited sodomy with thirteen boys was damning enough. With sodomy carrying a maximum penalty of life imprisonment, Oscar knew that, if charged with and convicted of these allegations, then he would almost certainly die in prison.

Oscar and Bosie went through Queensberry's Plea with Charles Humphreys and Sir Edward Clarke line by line, allegation by allegation. They could do nothing but sit in Clarke's chambers telling serious lies with serious faces and hope that they would be believed. Queensberry's allegations were delusions, figments of the Scarlet Marquis's imagination. But there was, they conceded, a kernel of truth in them. Oscar had met the boys named, had befriended them, entertained them and helped them on occasion with money. Oscar also decided to come clean about the attempted blackmail, first by Alfred Wood, and then by William Allen and Robert Cliburn, over his 'madness of kisses' letter to Bosie.

However bizarre it may have seemed that a renowned playwright had met and befriended boys and young men less than half his age and from wholly different backgrounds to his own, Humphreys and Clarke failed to smell a rat and were somehow or other convinced that Oscar was telling the truth. Here was the faintest glimmer of light. If Oscar could convince Clarke and Humphreys, then he could perhaps convince Ned Carson, the judge and the jury.

These fleeting moments of optimism alternated with more prolonged periods of pessimism. In the days before his trial, Oscar visited Cheiro the palm-reader. He wanted to know if the breach in his line of destiny that Cheiro had seen at Blanche Roosevelt's party two years earlier was still there. 'I told him it was,' Cheiro recalled, adding on a more hopeful note that Oscar's powerful trajectory of success could surely not now be broken. Oscar was unconvinced. 'He was very, very quiet, but in a far-off way,' wrote Cheiro. 'My good friend,' Oscar told him, 'you know well Fate does not keep road-menders on her highways.'

Oscar told Max Beerbohm's friend Reggie Turner that Queensberry's Plea had been 'a knock-down blow'. He knew that any discussion of Queensberry's allegations in open court would be catastrophic. And yet despite the knowledge that he faced certain ruin, disgrace and, most likely, imprisonment, Oscar went to meet his destiny in the Central Criminal Court at the Old Bailey. He went 'bravely, wondrously bravely,' Reggie wrote, 'but with death in his heart'.

Fighting with panthers

*'The truth is rarely pure and never simple. Modern life would be
very tedious if it were either, and modern literature a complete
impossibility!'*

'All trials,' Oscar declared, 'are trials for one's life.' Though technically the
prosecutor, Oscar must have known only too well that he was in reality the
defendant in the case. It was his life and his loves that would be on trial. And
it was his life, 'that tiger life', the life he had lived so fully and so thrillingly,
that was to be exchanged for a life in prison. He had feasted with panthers, and
now, he told Ada Leverson, he was going to 'fight with panthers'. The outcome
of the contest was a foregone conclusion, and Oscar bravely set off from Tite
Street on the morning of Wednesday 3 April with 'death in his heart', knowing
that in a day or two he would almost certainly be behind bars, awaiting trial for
gross indecency and perhaps for sodomy. He would be convicted and would
spend years, probably the rest of his life, as a convict.

The strain of the last weeks was beginning to take its toll. Oscar looked tired.
Like Lord Rosebery, he had not been sleeping at all well. In the last fortnight
he had bought no less than a dozen sleeping draughts from Alsop and Quiller,
the chemists. But on what he saw as his day of judgement, the day that Nemesis
would finally catch up with him, Oscar was outwardly calm and self-assured.
He had made a most elaborate toilette that morning and his hair was perfectly
waved. He was dressed immaculately in a long dark Chesterfield coat and an
impossibly tall silk top hat. But today there was no buttonhole of lilies of the
valley, no savagely blooming green carnation in his coat. A carriage and pair
with a coachman and two footmen in livery had been hired from William
Bramley's stables in Sloane Square to convey Oscar and the equally elaborately
dressed Bosie to the Old Bailey. Oscar stopped the carriage outside a shop in
St James's Street. He wanted, he explained, to buy 'a gayer tie'.

The small courtroom was badly ventilated and was already full to capacity
when Queensberry arrived alone. He spoke to no one as he pushed through the
crowded courtroom and stood hesitantly in front of the dock, unsure of exactly
where he should go. He wore a hunting stock instead of a tie and looked more
like a bookmaker's tout than a peer of the realm, with his drooping lower lip,
red mutton-chop whiskers and short legs. Just before half-past ten, Oscar and

Bosie arrived and squeezed their way to the front of the court. Someone joked about the 'The Importance of Being Early', and there was a ripple of laughter through the courtroom.

By a quirk of the system for selecting jurors, nine of the twelve jurymen were from the neighbouring parishes of Clapton and Stoke Newington in north-east London, once villages, but by 1895 dominated by newly built streets of terraced houses for the newly constituted lower middle classes. There was a butcher, a bootmaker, a bank messenger and a stockbroker – in those days a more lowly profession – and eight jurors who styled themselves 'gentleman' but who were in truth shopkeepers, tradesmen or clerks. It was, reported the *Star*, 'a commonplace-looking jury', a stolid, solid jury of lower middle-class men brimful of Victorian values of morality, continence and respectability. They must have regarded Oscar as a bizarre creature far removed from their own world.

Sir Edward Clarke, looking, recalled Frank Harris, exactly like 'a nonconformist parson of the old days', began the proceedings with a suave and soothing opening speech in which he outlined the events leading up to the case. The impression he sought to convey was that Oscar had been forced – more in sorrow than in anger – into seeking legal remedy when all other avenues to halt Queensberry's persecution had failed. Oscar was, he said, a distinguished author with a brilliant career who, in 1891, was introduced to Lord Alfred Douglas by a mutual friend. They became friends, and their families had become friends. Oscar had 'again and again' been the guest of Lady Queensberry, and Bosie had been 'the accepted and welcome guest' of Oscar and Constance in Tite Street and elsewhere. Oscar had even tried on at least two occasions to heal the 'strained feelings' between Bosie and his father, with little or no success. There was loud laughter in court when Clarke came to describe Queensberry's abortive attempt to disrupt the first night of *Earnest* with 'a large bouquet of vegetables', and even louder laughter when Clarke, by a slip of the tongue, substituted the name of Lord Rosebery for that of Lord Queensberry.

Clarke skilfully glossed over the allegations of gross indecency and attempted sodomy with a sly dig at the probity of any witnesses who might be produced. He would not trouble the jury, he said, with a blow-by-blow refutation of the sexual allegations:

> It is for those who have taken the very grave responsibility of putting into the plea those allegations to satisfy you if they can, by credible witnesses whose evidence you will consider worthy of consideration and entitled to belief that these charges are true.

Clarke went into some detail about the attempted blackmail of Oscar, first by Alfred Wood and then by Allen and Cliburn, over his extravagantly worded 'madness of kisses' letter to Bosie. This was one of Oscar's weakest points. It was not only the wording of the letter that was incriminating, it was the fact that Oscar had been prepared to pay money to retrieve it. Clarke attempted to draw the sting by making a joke. Though 'the words of that letter appear extravagant to those who are in the habit of writing commercial correspondence', Clarke said to the jury, provoking laughter in court, it was in fact 'a sort of prose sonnet', something of which Oscar 'was and is in *no* way ashamed'.

Clarke turned next to the literary part of the case. It was alleged that Oscar had 'joined in procuring the publication' of the *Chameleon* which contained material relating to 'the practices and pastimes of persons of sodomitical and unnatural habits and tastes'. Such allegations were ludicrous, Clarke maintained. Oscar played no part in procuring the publication of the *Chameleon*. When he was asked to contribute to the magazine, he was good enough to send a selection of leftover epigrams, 'Phrases and Philosophies for the Use of the Young'. Though Queensberry's Plea of Justification had described these 'epigrammatic statements' as 'immoral', Clarke would be 'amazed' if his learned friend, Edward Carson, appearing for Lord Queensberry, could find anything morally reprehensible in any of them. Indeed, when Oscar saw a copy of the *Chameleon* and read 'The Priest and the Acolyte', he thought it a 'disgrace to literature' and wrote immediately and indignantly to the editor to insist that the magazine be withdrawn from circulation.

As for *The Picture of Dorian Gray*, Clarke ridiculed the allegations in Queensberry's Plea. It was an extraordinary way of proceeding to attack a man on the basis of a novel which had been openly available 'upon the bookstalls, and at bookshops and in libraries' for five years. 'I have read the book for the purpose of this case and with care to see upon what my learned friend can build,' Clarke told the jury. With a flourish he held a copy of *Dorian Gray* aloft for the jury to see:

Here is the thing with Mr Oscar Wilde's name upon the title page and I shall be surprised if my learned friend can point to any passage within those covers which does more than describe as a novelist may or a dramatist may – nay, must – describe the passions and the vices of life if he desires to produce any work of art.

It was an accomplished opening speech which presented Oscar as a loving father, a devoted friend, and an accomplished writer and artist reluctantly driven to the recourse of law.

Oscar, 'ponderous and fleshy, his face a dusky red', as the *Star* reported, took the stand, and Clarke led him gently through a recapitulation of the events leading up to Queensberry's card with hideous words. Oscar's performance was assured and impressive. He answered the questions Clarke put to him fluently and confidently, and with flashes of wit. The jury appeared to be warming to him. Meanwhile Carson was biding his time, listening intently to Clarke's opening speech and his examination of Oscar. He was still undecided about what his first question to Oscar would be. According to his friend and biographer, Edward Marjoribanks, Carson always considered that the first question put in cross-examination was the crucial moment in any case. Oscar unwittingly solved Carson's problem for him, when in answer to a question from Sir Edward Clarke about his age, Oscar confidently replied, 'I am thirty-nine years of age.'

It was a small lie, a lie born out of Oscar's vanity, but nevertheless a lie that Carson would ruthlessly exploit. The well-prepared Carson had a copy of Oscar's birth certificate in front of him, and it may have been that he had heard of Oscar's propensity to knock a year or two off his real age. Carson rose to begin his cross-examination. He was extremely tall and thin, with a slight stoop. On this morning, he was suffering from a bad cold, which had given his voice a slightly rasping quality.

'You stated at the commencement of your examination that you were thirty-nine years of age. I think you are over forty. Isn't that so?' said Carson matter-of-factly. Oscar was immediately flustered.

'I don't think so. I think I am either thirty-nine or forty – forty at my next birthday,' Oscar floundered. 'If you have my certificate there, that settles the matter.'

'You were born, I believe, upon the 16th October 1854?' Carson continued. 'Did you wish to *pose* as being young?'

'No.'

'This makes you more than forty?'

'Yes,' said Oscar. 'I have no intention of posing for a younger man at all. I try to be correct in the date.'

Carson had done his work well. He had demonstrated to the jury that Oscar had lied under oath. And if Oscar was prepared to lie about small things, then surely he would be prepared to lie about bigger things. If Oscar could 'pose' as being younger than he really was, could he not also pose as a sodomite? Not only that, Oscar had been detected in vanity, a vice unlikely to endear itself to the upstanding burghers of Clapton and Stoke Newington.

Carson's cross-examination of Oscar was to last a day and half, and must go down as one of the most bruising encounters in English legal history. Unlike Sir Edward Clarke's courtly, gentle questions, Carson's cross-examination was tantamount to an interrogation. Carson was fast on his feet, moving with lightning speed from one topic to another and back again, ambushing Oscar who found himself ill-prepared for such an encounter. Carson began with the literary part of the case. His technique of cross-examination was simple but devastating. He would take a damning position about the work in question and invite Oscar to agree with him. Carson's questions came short and fast and repetitive, like the staccato fire from a machine-gun. Had he read Bosie's poems? Did he approve of them? Were they 'improper'? Was 'The Priest and the Acolyte' improper? Was it 'wrong'? Was it 'immoral'? Was it 'blasphemous'? Was it 'scandalous'? Was it 'sodomitical'? Had Oscar publicly disavowed it? If not, why not? Did Oscar agree with his own 'Phrases and

Philosophies'? Were they moral or immoral? Were they true? Were they safe? Were they likely to lead to immorality in young men?

Oscar was caught between the devil and the deep blue sea. If he agreed with Carson's extreme and damning analyses, then he damned himself. If he disagreed, he unleashed another burst of Carson's machine-gun fire. If he hesitated for a second, paused to collect his thoughts or frame his reply, Carson leapt in demanding an immediate answer. A yes or a no? Did he agree or disagree? Was it or was it not the case? Oscar's attempts to explain, to expound and to qualify his answers were ruthlessly mown down by Carson's deadly volleys. The cumulative effect was devastating. Oscar was being exposed as a liar and an equivocator, as a vain man of nebulous morality, a man who, if he did not directly condone the sodomitical in literature, equally would not or could not condemn it.

Oscar did his best but was visibly flustered by Carson's onslaught. Giving evidence was fatiguing, and Oscar was already tired out with insomnia and worry. What was more, he was deprived of his accustomed endless supply of gold-tipped cigarettes and their gently narcotising effect. Smoking for Oscar was a necessary adjunct to talking, and he was used to the smoke of his cigarettes wreathing and curling around him in fantastic arabesques, just as his conversation wove its own complex rhythms and intricate patterns. Oscar was the most accomplished and sought-after conversationalist of his day, but this interrogation by Carson gave him no time to beguile and enchant, to charm and hypnotise the jurymen, though he did, at least, manage to amuse them with some memorable epigrams.

Just before the court adjourned for lunch, Carson turned his attention to *Dorian Gray* and read aloud extracts from a letter of 19 July 1890 which Oscar wrote to the *Scots Observer*. 'Each man sees his own sin in Dorian Gray,' Oscar had written. 'What Dorian Gray's sins are, no one knows. He who finds them has brought them.'

'Then you left it open to be inferred, I take it,' said Carson, 'that the sins of Dorian Gray, some of them, may have been sodomy?'

'That is according to the temper of each one who reads the book; he who has found the sin has brought it,' Oscar replied.

'Then, I take it that some people upon reading the book, at all events, might reasonably think that it did deal with sodomy?' Carson persisted.

'Some people might think so.'

Oscar was faltering. 'Whether it would be reasonable or not—' Carson wheeled about and tried another line of attack.

When *Dorian Gray* came out in book form: had it been modified and purged a good deal?

'No.'

'In contrast with the original book?'

'No.'

'Did you say "not at all"?'

'No,' said Oscar. 'I say there were additions made in one or two – in one case,

362

certainly. It had been pointed out to me, not by any newspaper criticism or anything, but by the only critic of this century I set high, Mr Walter Pater. He had pointed out to me that a certain passage was liable to misconstruction.'

'In what respect?' Carson demanded.

'In every respect.'

'In what respect?' Carson snapped.

'In the respect that it would convey the impression that the sin of Dorian Gray was sodomy,' Oscar wretchedly conceded.

Carson had finally wrung it out of him. Dorian Gray's sin was sodomitical. The court rose for lunch. Carson had cross-examined Oscar to deadly effect. He had drawn first blood in less than three quarters of an hour.

The afternoon session was, if anything, worse. Carson reopened his cross-examination with a fresh volley of questions about *Dorian Gray*, determinedly focusing on Basil Hallward's confession of his love for Dorian. Carson read out a lengthy passage, laying particular emphasis on the part where Basil says to Dorian, 'I quite admit that I *adored* you madly, extravagantly, absurdly. I was jealous of everyone to whom you spoke.'

Were the feelings between these two men natural and moral? Had Oscar ever known these feelings towards a younger man? Never?

'Have you ever adored a young man, some twenty-one years younger than yourself, madly?' Carson demanded.

'No, not madly,' Oscar replied. 'Not madly.'

'Well, adored him?'

'I have loved one friend in my life,' said Oscar seriously.

Carson refused to let the question go. Had Oscar ever 'adored' a young man?

'I prefer "loved", that is higher.'

'"Adored", sir?'

'And I say "loved" – it is greater.'

'Never mind going higher,' Carson snarled. 'Keep down to the level of your own words.'

Oscar was stung into a rebuke. 'Keep your own words to yourself. Leave me mine,' he snapped. 'Don't put words to me I haven't said.'

But Carson refused to be deflected. 'I want an answer to this simple question,' he declared. 'Have you ever felt that feeling of adoring madly a beautiful male person many years younger than yourself?'

'I have never given adoration to anyone except myself,' Oscar declared, provoking loud laughter in court.

Carson did not smile. He turned to the subject of the 'yellow book' that Lord Henry Wotton gave to Dorian and which had exerted such a strange and compelling influence over Dorian's life. Had Oscar a particular novel in mind at the time he wrote *Dorian Gray*? Oscar admitted that he had *A Rebours* by Huysmans in his mind. Somehow or other, Carson already knew that Dorian's 'yellow book' was *A Rebours*. He had a copy of it in court with him and had read it thoroughly. Was it an immoral book? Did it deal with undisguised sodomy? Was it a sodomitical book? Was it a book depicting sodomy? Oscar equivocated, Carson persisted, even offering to read a sodomitical passage until he was overruled by the judge, Mr Justice Collins.

Oscar's declaration that he had in the course of his life 'loved one friend' was significant. Though he would vigorously deny all the sexual allegations against him, telling lie after lie after bald lie, his love for Bosie was sacred. It was the tower of ivory that could not be besmirched or sullied by lies, falsehoods and half-truths. When Carson turned to cross-examine him about the 'madness of kisses' letter, once again Oscar rousingly and unambiguously declared his love for Bosie. 'I have expressed, and feel great and, I hope, undying love for him as I say I do. He is the greatest friend I have.'

Oscar had rallied after lunch but he was oddly unprepared for Carson's next great onslaught. Carson turned to the sorry saga of the 'madness of kisses' letter and Alfred Wood's attempts to blackmail Oscar over this and other letters. Oscar was forced to endure a long cross-examination as to how he first met Wood and what occurred between them that first night. Why did Oscar invite Wood to dine with him at the Florence that first evening? Had he taken Wood to Tite Street? Had he ever taken Wood to Tite Street? Did Oscar swear to that? Did Wood go with Oscar to Tite Street? Did Oscar ever engage in any immoral practices with Wood? Had he ever opened his trousers? Put his hand upon his person? Ever put his own person between the legs of Wood?

Then Carson began to ruthlessly reconstruct the sequence of events surrounding the attempted blackmail of Oscar first by Wood and then by William Allen and Robert Cliburn.

Did Oscar consider that Wood was trying to levy blackmail?

'Yes,' said Oscar, 'and I was determined to face him on the subject.'

'You thought he was going to levy blackmail and you determined to face it?' Carson reiterated.

'Yes.'

'And the way you faced it was by giving him sixteen pounds to go to America?' Carson made no attempt to keep the sarcasm out of his voice. Did Oscar call Wood by his Christian name? And did Wood call Oscar by his Christian name? 'Did you think it a curious thing that a man with whom you were on such intimate terms as to call him "Alfred" should try to levy blackmail?' Carson demanded witheringly.

Carson turned from the unappetising subject of Oscar's dealings with blackmailers to his relationship with Edward Shelley, his publisher's 'office boy', as Carson called him, and in particular to Oscar's seduction of Shelley in the Albemarle Hotel. Had Oscar asked 'this lad' to dine with him at the Albemarle Hotel? Was it to be 'an intellectual treat'?

'Well, for him, yes,' Oscar replied, provoking laughter in court.

The deadly volley of questions continued. Was Oscar alone with Shelley in his sitting room in the Albemarle Hotel? Was there a bedroom leading off? Did they smoke cigarettes? Did he give Shelley whisky and sodas? Did Oscar embrace Shelley in the sitting-room? Did he kiss him? Did he put his hand on Shelley's person? Did he take him into the bedroom? Did they take off their clothes? Did they sleep together all night? Did Oscar take his person in his hand? Oscar could bear it no more.

'My Lord,' he protested to the judge, 'is it not sufficient for me to give an entire denial without being exposed to the ignominy of detail after detail of an imaginary thing going on?' Mr Justice Collins agreed, but as far as the jurymen were concerned the damage was done.

Carson's pace never slowed for a second. He turned abruptly to Oscar's relationship with Alfonso Conway. 'Did you become intimate with a young lad named Conway?' he demanded. Was it true that Conway sold newspapers on the pier at Worthing? Had Oscar arranged to meet Conway one evening at about nine o'clock? Did they walk towards Lancing? Was the road lonely? Did Oscar kiss him on the road? Did he put his hands inside his trousers? Were there familiarities of any kind? Did Oscar give him money? Oscar gave a decided negative to all Carson's questions. Now with a flourish Carson produced a cigarette case, a book and a photograph of Oscar, all of which were inscribed with the words 'Alfonso Conway from his friend Oscar Wilde'. These, together with a silver-topped walking stick, were all gifts from Oscar to Alfonso. There were further questions which led to damaging revelations. Had Oscar bought a straw hat and a suit of clothes for Alfonso? Did he take the boy to stay in a hotel in Brighton? 'You dressed him up to bring him to Brighton?' Carson sneered. 'In order that he might look more like an equal?'

When the court rose for the day, Oscar left the witness box feeling bruised and battered by Carson's mauling. Though he had rallied himself after lunch and fought Carson bravely, there was no disguising from himself or from anyone else that Carson's blows were hitting home. It was not just a question of searching out real or imagined sodomitical incidents and intent in his work, though that was damaging enough. Carson's persistent interrogation was laying bare unsavoury and decidedly suspect facts about his life. It was clear to the jury that Oscar had been blackmailed over letters he had written to Bosie. He had paid Alfred Wood, a youth he barely knew, an enormous sum of money to retrieve these letters. And it was clear, too, that he had had some sort of murky encounters and exchanges with at least two other professional blackmailers.

More damaging still, Carson had shown that Oscar had had questionable friendships with two young men. And, though the jury might just have been able to swallow Oscar's version of the innocent literary friendship that existed between the celebrated writer and the publisher's office boy, it was well nigh impossible for them to understand what species of friendship – other than sodomitical – could exist between an unemployed teenage newspaper vendor plucked from the beach at Worthing and the author of *The Importance of Being Earnest*. Oscar's denials of any impropriety had been vehement and frequent. But whether these protestations would be sufficient to convince the sceptical burghers of Clapton and Stoke Newington was anybody's guess.

So very ugly

'I often betray myself with a kiss.'

That evening the rumour got about that Oscar had fled abroad, that he had panicked after his first day in the witness box and caught the boat train to Ostend. In fact, Oscar and Bosie had spent a wretched evening closeted in the Holborn Viaduct Hotel with Humphreys and Clarke, engaged in a depressing post-mortem on the day's proceedings. Oscar and Bosie had been invited to the Leversons' that night for what was intended to be a celebratory dinner, but they were obliged to cry off. 'Pray excuse us from dining tonight as we have a lot of very important business to do,' they told her in a joint telegram. 'Everything is very satisfactory,' they added, in a dismal attempt at optimism. It was a long way from the 'complete triumph' prophesied by the Sibyl Robinson just a week earlier.

Oscar's interview with Humphreys and Clarke must have been painful for all concerned. The questions Carson had asked Oscar about his sexual relations with Alfred Wood, Edward Shelley and Alfonso Conway had been so very detailed and so very precise that it was obvious that Queensberry's defence team had managed to interview the boys concerned and take statements. Oscar could no longer claim that the allegations of sodomy and gross indecency outlined in Queensberry's Plea of Justification were groundless and absurd. It was perhaps during this conference that Oscar asked Clarke if there were any limits on the questions Carson could put to him.

'Can they examine me about anything and everything they choose?' he asked Clarke, and went on to inquire whether 'they' could question him about an incident which had so far not been mentioned at all.

'Certainly,' rejoined the advocate. 'What is it that is in your mind?'

'Well,' said Oscar, 'some time ago I was turned out of the Albemarle Hotel in the middle of the night and a boy was with me. It might be awkward if they found out about that!'

By now it must have been patently obvious to all concerned that Oscar had been less than frank about his friendships with young men.

The question was how to proceed. Should they continue with the prosecution? If they did, Oscar would face another gruelling cross-examination by Carson. More damaging revelations might emerge. Oscar would lose the case and face almost certain arrest and prosecution himself. Alternatively, Oscar could gracefully withdraw from the case. This would mean that he would lose the case by default and be forced to pay Queensberry's costs. He would face shame and opprobrium. But with luck that might be all. The evidence for the defence which Carson had presented so far was extremely damaging. But there had not – as yet – been any conclusive proof that Oscar was a practising sodomite. There was a chance – a good chance – that matters would be allowed to rest. Oscar would live quietly abroad, the details of the affair would fade, and he would perhaps in time be able to rehabilitate himself as a man of letters.

Exactly how and by whom it was decided to continue with the prosecution is not recorded. Bosie was still determined to see his father imprisoned and no doubt vehemently urged Oscar to continue with the case. Clarke and Humphreys probably advised Oscar to withdraw before he did himself irreparable damage. Oscar hesitated and wavered and in the end sided with Bosie. He would fight on. Fate could not be cheated. 'Nemesis has caught me in her net,' he wrote later. 'To struggle is foolish.'

The atmosphere in the Old Bailey on the morning of Thursday 4 April was electric as Oscar stepped into the witness box. He seemed more subdued and a little ill at ease and 'did not look so fresh or so bright as on the previous day'. He knew he faced another furious onslaught from Carson. Carson took up his cross-examination by asking Oscar about his friendship with Alfred Taylor. Who was this Alfred Taylor and what kind of a person was he? How did he live? Was it true that he never opened his curtains? That his rooms were always artificially lit? That they were always strongly perfumed? And was it true that Taylor kept a lady's costume, a lady's fancy dress, in his rooms? Had Oscar ever seen him wearing such a costume?

The jurymen appeared to be shocked, as Carson had intended them to be shocked, by these revelations about Taylor's manner of living. Highly perfumed and dimly lit rooms, endless tea parties for young men, and a lady's costume in a place where no ladies lived were all highly suspicious, highly sodomitical. It was clear to the jury that Oscar was intimate with the unusual Alfred Taylor, and that made him guilty by association. There was more. In a damaging exchange, Carson managed to extract an admission from Oscar that Taylor had introduced several young men to him.

'How many young men did he introduce to you?' Carson demanded.

'You can hardly ask me to remember,' Oscar replied.

'In or about,' snapped Carson.

'Do you mean people mentioned in the indictment?' Oscar said evasively.

'No,' said Carson with growing impatience. 'Young men with whom you afterwards became intimate?'

'I should think six – seven – eight,' Oscar reluctantly replied.

'Six, seven, or eight?'

'Yes, I have constantly met young men.'

'No, no, that you became intimate with?'

367

Here Sir Edward Clarke interrupted to try and head off Carson. 'Became friendly with, you mean?' he said helpfully.

'Became friendly with, I think, is the better word – that I became friendly with. I think about five,' Oscar conceded.

It was a damning admission. 'Intimate' or 'friendly' – it did not much matter – Taylor had introduced Oscar to five young men. More damning still was Oscar's further admission that he had given money and presents to all five. Carson now turned to one of these young men, Charles Parker. Oscar had met Charlie Parker when he entertained Alfred Taylor and the Parker brothers to dinner at Kettner's. On that evening Oscar had fed Charles Parker with preserved cherries from his own mouth, driven back with him to the Savoy, given him iced champagne and taken him to bed. The next morning he had given him money.

Carson dwelt at length on Charlie Parker. There were rich pickings to be had from Oscar's relationship with an unemployed gentleman's valet. Oscar's answers were guarded and, at times, appeared to the jury to be downright evasive, damagingly evasive.

'How old was Parker?' Carson asked, knowing full well that he was seventeen when he met Oscar.

'I don't keep a census,' replied Oscar evasively.

'I am not asking you about a census.'

'I don't know what his age was.'

'What about was his age?'

'I should say about twenty; he was young. That was one of his attractions, the attractions of youth.'

And with this, Oscar was hoist with his own petard. Not only did it look as if he had something to hide, but his needless comments on Charlie Parker's youthful attractions in particular, and the attractions of youth in general, took on a decidedly sinister complexion.

Carson wanted to know more about the nature of the friendship between Oscar and Charlie Parker. 'What I would like to ask you is this,' he said. 'What was there between you and this young man of this class?'

'Well, I will tell you, Mr Carson,' said Oscar with a dangerous lack of caution. 'I delight in the society of people much younger than myself. I like those who may be called idle and careless. I recognise no social distinctions at all of any kind, and to me youth – the mere fact of youth – is so wonderful that I would sooner talk to a young man for half an hour than even be, well, cross-examined in court.'

Despite the titter of amusement that rippled through the court at his poor joke, Oscar's paean to the joys of youth – and youths – was damaging. Just as damaging were his views on social distinctions, which struck the jury as something akin to anarchism. Carson was quick to follow up his advantage.

'Then, do I understand that even a young boy that you would pick up in the street would be a pleasing companion to you?' enquired Carson innocently.

'Oh, I would talk to a street Arab if he talked to me, with pleasure,' said Oscar guilelessly.

'And take him into your rooms?'

'If he interested me.'

Oscar had blindly stumbled into yet another trap. He had admitted that he would happily 'pick up' a young street boy and take him to his rooms. Picking up young street boys could, to the jurymen, mean only one thing: prostitution.

Carson interrogated Oscar in turn about his relationships with Fred Atkins, Ernest Scarfe and 'Jenny' Mavor. The account of Oscar's trip to Paris with Fred Atkins, a bookmaker's tout and aspiring music hall artiste, plainly surprised the jury, particularly Oscar's explanation that he had taken Atkins to Paris as a favour to 'a very great friend of mine'. The friend in question was Maurice Schwabe, and, to the great surprise of many of those present, his name was never spoken aloud in court. His name had been written down on a piece of paper and passed to the judge the previous day, and Schwabe was subsequently always referred to as 'that gentleman whose name you handed up'. Why Schwabe alone merited such discretion and confidentiality was a mystery. There could be only one explanation. Maurice Schwabe was a nephew by marriage of Sir Frank Lockwood, the Solicitor General in Lord Rosebery's Liberal government, and heavy political pressure had clearly been brought to bear to keep Schwabe's name out of the proceedings.

Oscar had been in the witness box for almost an hour and a half and was already exhausted when, at around noon, Carson turned to Oscar's relationship with Walter Grainger, the servant in Bosie's lodgings in Oxford. Carson began asking Oscar about his visits to Bosie at Oxford and his encounters with Walter Grainger there. It was to be the climax of the trial.

'Were you on familiar terms with Grainger?' Carson began, deliberately stressing the word 'familiar'.

'What do you mean by "familiar terms"?' retorted Oscar.

'I mean to say did you have him to dine with you or anything of that kind?' said Carson.

'Never in my life.' Oscar was emphatic.

'What?'

'No! It is really trying to ask me such a question,' Oscar was becoming extremely exasperated by Carson's refusal to accept his answers at face value, as Carson fully intended that he should. 'No, of course not. He waited on me at table; he did not dine with me.'

'I thought he might have sat down. You drew no distinction,' said Carson snidely.

'Do you think in the case of Lord Alfred Douglas and Lord Encombe's room that would have happened with the servant?'

'You told me yourself –'

'It is a different thing,' Oscar interrupted. He was now thoroughly irritated. 'If it is people's duty to serve, it is their duty to serve; if it is their pleasure to dine, it is their pleasure to dine and their privilege.'

'You say not?'

'Certainly not.'

'Did you ever kiss him?' Carson slipped the question in like a rapier, and Oscar answered before he realised the full import of what he said.

'Oh no, never in my life; he was a peculiarly plain boy – '

'He was what?' Carson leapt on Oscar's answer. Oscar was visibly flustered. He knew he had made a terrible mistake and had allowed himself to be ambushed by Carson. He tried desperately and without success to explain away his remark. For the first time in the trial Oscar was almost incoherent.

'I said I thought him unfortunately – his appearance was so very unfortunately – very ugly – I mean – I pitied him for it.'

'Very ugly?' repeated Carson grimly.

'Yes,' faltered Oscar.

'Do you say that in support of your statement that you never kissed him?'

'No, I don't; it is like asking me if I kissed a doorpost; it is childish.' But Carson was not to be deflected.

'Didn't you give me as the reason that you never kissed him that he was too ugly?

'No,' said Oscar warmly. 'I did not say that.' Carson repeated his question. He knew this was the deciding moment of the trial.

'Why did you mention his ugliness?'

'No, I said the question seemed to me like –' Oscar had lost his thread and had to begin again. 'Your asking me whether I ever had him to dinner, and then whether I had kissed him – seemed to me merely an intentional insult on your part, which I have being going through the whole of this morning.'

'Because he was ugly?' Carson rapped out.

'No.'

'Why did you mention the ugliness?' Carson demanded. 'I have to ask these questions.'

Oscar tried, in vain, to evade answering Carson's question.

'I say it is ridiculous to imagine that any such thing could possibly have occurred under any circumstances,' he said.

'Why did you mention the ugliness?' It had become a battle of wills between them, and Carson was determined that Oscar would answer.

'For that reason. If you asked me if I had ever kissed a doorpost, I should say, "No! Ridiculous! I shouldn't like to kiss a doorpost." Am I to be cross-examined on why I shouldn't like to kiss a doorpost? The questions are grotesque.'

'Why did you mention the boy's ugliness?' Carson rasped.

'I mentioned it perhaps because you stung me by an insolent question,' said Oscar, trying to deflect Carson's focused fire.

'Because I stung you by an insolent question?' Carson's tone was undisguisedly sarcastic.

'Yes,' said Oscar. 'You stung me by an insolent question; you make me irritable.'

'Did you say the boy was ugly because I stung you by an insolent question?'

'Pardon me, you sting me, insult me and try to unnerve me in every way,' blustered Oscar. 'At times one says things flippantly when one should speak more seriously. I admit that, I admit it – I cannot help it. That is what you are doing to me.'

Oscar was – for once – telling the truth. He really could not help it. He had been stung, insulted, unnerved and made irritable by the relentless cross-examination, just as Carson had intended him to be. Thoroughly exasperated and thoroughly irritated, Oscar had incriminated himself. He had as good as admitted that he would have kissed Walter Grainger had he not been so ugly. It was now obvious to the jury that Oscar was not merely posing as a sodomite, he was a sodomite. Oscar had lost the case. He knew it and everyone present in the court knew it. Montague Crackanthorpe, a solicitor who was present in court that day, told his wife that he had never witnessed 'anything so horrible' as Carson's cross-examination. Oscar, he said, 'was like a tortured, hunted animal':

> His whole demeanour altered, he literally collapsed. No more impudent repartee, no more insolent epigram. He became livid, a lividness that changed from grey to green and then to dark purple.

Though the case might be lost, the trial had to continue. Sir Edward Clarke tried desperately to salvage Oscar from the ruins of the case. In a skilful re-examination of his client, he attempted to wrench the case back to Queensberry's vicious and prolonged persecution of Oscar over his relationship with Bosie. He read aloud five of Queensberry's foul letters to Bosie, together with his letter to Alfred Montgomery in which he had classified Oscar as a 'damned cur and coward of the Rosebery type'. Queensberry's comments about the Prime Minister caused a sensation in court.

Carson opened the case for the defence late in the afternoon. He knew that Oscar had already lost the case, but he had to go through the formality of defending Queensberry. Lord Queensberry, said Carson, neither regretted nor withdrew anything he had said or done. He had acted as any father would have acted. 'He has done what he did premeditatedly and he was determined, at all risks and all hazards, to try and save his son.' Carson pointedly referred to the fact that Lord Rosebery's name had cropped up during the trial. 'For my own part,' he told the jury, 'I say with absolute sincerity that I am very glad those letters have been read here.' It was quite clear from the letters, Carson went on, that any suggestion that 'distinguished persons' were in some way 'mixed up' in the charges against Oscar Wilde was entirely groundless. Though it was an accomplished smoothing away of an awkward problem, Carson's protestations clearly failed to convince everyone in court.

Carson turned to boys and young men whose names had come up in the trial. 'You will hear from these witnesses,' declared Carson dramatically, 'and let me say that nothing can be more painful than to ask witnesses . . . to go through

the various descriptions of the manner in which Wilde acted towards them.'
Carson's promise to produce in court the boys that Oscar had had sex with sent
an audible murmur of shock through the court.

Carson had not finished his opening speech when the court rose for the day.
Oscar and Bosie must have debated what to do about the trial with Clarke and
Humphreys long into the night. There was no longer any hope that Oscar
would be spared a criminal prosecution. He could continue to fight a case he
was now bound to lose, or he could flee abroad for his life and hope that he
would not be stopped at Dover. Clarke outlined the stark choices to Oscar:

> I said that, if the case went to its end and the jury found that the accusations
> were justified, the judge would unquestionably order his arrest. He listened
> quietly and gravely, and then thanked me for my advice and said he was
> prepared to act upon it. I then told him that there was no need for his
> presence in Court while the announcement was being made. I hoped and
> expected that he would take the opportunity of escaping from the country,
> and I believe he would have found no difficulty in doing so.

There was not a seat to be had in court the next morning. People had queued
for hours to hear the evidence of the boys Oscar was alleged to have had sex
with. Oscar and Bosie were conspicuous by their absence. They were in fact in
a small room elsewhere in the court. Oscar had seemingly delayed his decision
to withdraw from the case until the very last minute. Carson rose to continue
outlining the case for defence. He had been on his feet for some twenty minutes
when Sir Edward Clarke signalled that he wished to confer with him. The two
counsel whispered inaudibly together, and then Clarke addressed the court.

Mr Oscar Wilde, he said, wished to withdraw from the case and would
accept that he had 'posed as a sodomite' – at least as far as the literary part of
the case was concerned. But Mr Justice Collins was having none of it. If Sir
Edward Clarke for the prosecution wished to accept a verdict of 'Not guilty'
for Queensberry, he was entitled to do so, but there could be no restricting this
verdict to just the literary part of the case. Either Oscar had posed as a sodomite
or he had not. Queensberry was either guilty of libelling Oscar or he was not.
Not only that. Queensberry's Plea of Justification must be found 'true in
substance and fact' and it must be found that his accusations had been
'published for the public benefit'. The jury took only minutes to return a
verdict of 'Not Guilty'. There was loud and prolonged cheering in court from
the public gallery, cheering which Mr Justice Collins made no attempt to
silence. 'Lord Queensberry may be discharged?' Carson enquired of Mr
Justice Collins, shouting above the din in court. 'Oh certainly,' the judge
replied. And with those two very ordinary words, one of the most
extraordinary trials of its time came to a humiliating end.

As soon as he returned to the judge's room, Mr Justice Collins sat down and
wrote a brief note to Carson. 'I never heard a more powerful speech or a more
searching cross-exam,' he wrote. 'I congratulate you on having escaped most of

the filth.' Carson had done his job well, but he was left with an abiding sense of regret at what he knew would be the consequences of his actions. 'I have ruined the most brilliant man in London,' he said sadly to his wife that evening.

Kill the bugger!

'If one tells the truth, one is sure, sooner or later, to be found out.'

As he drove away with Bosie and Robbie from the Old Bailey in his hired carriage and pair, Oscar was in a state of shock and near collapse. He realised that he had been routed by Queensberry and that his life lay in ruins. What made it worse was that he knew he was the architect of his own misfortune. He had embarked blindly and foolishly on the prosecution of Queensberry, and now his blindness and foolishness had come back to haunt him. As in a Greek tragedy, Oscar's arrogance and wanton contempt for the rules of life, his hubris, had been his undoing. 'I am one of those who are made for exceptions, not for laws,' he had once declared. Now he had made the bitter and humiliating discovery that this was not so, that he was, like everyone else, made for laws, and not exceptions. He had tempted providence and paid the price:

> Once I had put into motion the forces of Society, Society turned on me and said 'Have you been living all this time in defiance of my laws? You shall have those laws exercised to the full. You shall abide by what you have appealed to.'

Oscar, Bosie and Robbie drove first to the nearby Holborn Viaduct Hotel, where a private room had been engaged for lunch. They were followed by Queensberry's private detectives, Littlechild and Kearley. From there Oscar hastily dictated a letter to the editor of the *Evening News*, which Robbie took down on two of the hotel's envelopes:

> It would have been impossible for me to have proved my case without putting Lord Alfred Douglas in the witness box against his father. Lord Alfred Douglas was extremely anxious to go into the box, but I would not let him do so. Rather than put him into so painful a position, I determined to retire from the case, and to bear on my own shoulders whatever ignominy and shame might result from my prosecuting Lord Queensberry.

It was, of course, an outright lie. There had never been any question of Bosie taking the stand. It was true Bosie had been extremely anxious to testify to the

374

fact that his father 'was an inhuman brute' who had 'bullied and persecuted' his wife and 'had for twenty years neglected and ill-treated his children'. But Bosie simply failed to grasp that Queensberry's inadequacies as a husband and a parent were not pertinent to the libel case, and his testimony about his father's cruelties would most certainly have been ruled inadmissible by the judge. Bosie always maintained that, had he been allowed to take the stand, Oscar might well have won his case. 'At the very worst,' he told Frank Harris many years later, 'even if he had lost the case, there would have been no subsequent criminal prosecution of Wilde. All the sympathy and all the feeling would have been on our side.' Bosie blamed Sir Edward Clarke for first agreeing to call him as a witness and then reneging on his promise. It was a charge Clarke vigorously refuted.

Oscar also dashed off a short note to Constance, which he sent to Tite Street by special messenger. 'Dear Constance, Allow no one to enter my bedroom or sitting room – except servants – today,' he wrote. 'See no one but your friends.' Oscar was worried that Littlechild and Kearley or even detectives from Scotland Yard would turn up at Tite Street and rifle through his compromising letters and private papers in their search for more evidence.

Percy Douglas arrived and the four of them ate a wretched lunch contemplating the wreck and ruin of the trial. They went over and over the options. Would Oscar face a criminal prosecution, and if so, how soon would the warrant for his arrest be issued? And would Bosie – as Oscar's partner in sexual crime – be arrested too? Should Oscar flee abroad while he still could? Should Bosie flee? Oscar hesitated and wavered. He was in a state of shock and incapable of making a decision. But, in case he could be persuaded to fly to Paris, Robbie was despatched to Oscar's bank to cash a cheque for £200.

Oscar, Bosie and Percy, meanwhile, drove to Ely Place, to the offices of Sir George Lewis, who might, they hoped, be able to advise them what to do. The interview was short and to the point. 'What's the use of coming to me now?' Lewis snapped:

> I am powerless to do anything. If you had had the sense to bring Lord Queensberry's card to me in the first place I would have torn it up and thrown it in the fire, and told you not to make a fool of yourself.

From Ely Place, they set off for the Cadogan Hotel in Sloane Street, where Bosie had been staying for the past couple of weeks. Now, in addition to the carriage containing Littlechild and Kearley, three or four other carriages containing a dozen or so reporters also followed them, making a strange procession.

After cashing the cheque, Robbie went to Tite Street, where he broke the news as gently as he could to Constance, who burst into floods of tears. 'Poor Oscar!' she sobbed, 'Poor Oscar! I hope he is going abroad.' Robbie tried to comfort Constance as best he could but time was short. He needed to go to the Cadogan Hotel and continue to try, if possible, to persuade Oscar to flee while there was still time. He found Oscar collapsed into an armchair determinedly drinking hock and seltzer. He seemed abstracted and was oblivious to the pressing entreaties of his friends to leave at once and catch the boat train. 'The train has gone,' Oscar said in a hollow voice. 'It is too late.' He was waiting for the inevitable.

For Queensberry it was a day of vindication and triumph. As he left the court he delivered a public message to Oscar. 'If the country allows you to leave, all the better for the country!' he snarled. 'But if you take my son with you, I will follow you wherever you go and shoot you like a dog!' But Queensberry actually wanted to see Oscar prosecuted and imprisoned. 'I think he ought not to be allowed to leave the country,' he told reporters at a press conference he held at Carter's Hotel in Albemarle Street that afternoon. 'I think he ought to be placed where he can ruin no more young men.' Queensberry knew he was the hero of the hour and was revelling in his new-found status as guardian of public morals. 'I have done my duty, not only to my family and myself, but also to the community,' he told reporters. 'It has cost me £1,200, and now if the law of England don't step in I must make my own law.' He had been overwhelmed, he said, 'with congratulations from all quarters of the globe' and proudly held up a sheaf of telegrams, singling out one from the actor, Charles Danby, which read simply 'Hearty Congratulations', and another, 'Every man in the City is with you. Kill the bugger!'

While Queensberry basked in moral righteousness, his solicitor, Charles Russell, acting on his client's instructions, had been extremely busy. As soon as the case ended, he wasted no time in sending a letter to Hamilton Cuffe, the Director of Public Prosecutions:

Dear Sir, In order that there may be no miscarriage of justice, I think it is my duty at once to send you a copy of all our witnesses' statements, together with a copy of the shorthand notes of the trial. Yours faithfully, Charles Russell.

Russell's letter was a warning shot to the powers that be. Oscar must not be allowed to slip away into the shadows of a continental exile in Paris or Florence, however congenial to him and however convenient to the authorities such a flight might be. He must be arrested and tried.

Hamilton Cuffe moved with astonishing speed. Immediately he received Russell's letter, Cuffe summoned him to his office. What was said between the two men is not recorded, but Trelawny Backhouse and others believed that it was at this meeting that Russell delivered Queensberry's short and explicit ultimatum to the Liberal government: send Oscar Wilde to prison or face the exposure of several senior Liberal politicians – including the Prime Minister – as sodomites. Certainly, within an hour or two of meeting with Russell, Cuffe had hastily convened a conference at the House of Commons with Asquith, the Home Secretary, Sir Robert Reid, the Attorney-General, and Sir Frank Lockwood, the Solicitor-General. It is hard to think of any convincing reason

– other than the one Backhouse suggests – for this hastily summoned and extraordinary meeting of senior Liberal politicians, other than that there were pressing political considerations in some way connected to the prosecution of Oscar Wilde. Over the coming days and weeks, Bosie and several others became convinced that Queensberry was blackmailing the Liberal government into sending Oscar to prison.

Asquith immediately issued instructions that Oscar was to be stopped wherever he might be found. So much for Oscar's proud boast that the Treasury would always give him twenty-four hours to leave the country before attempting to arrest him. Cuffe summoned Detective-Inspector Brockwell of Scotland Yard to his office in the Treasury building, and, at about half past three, Brockwell and Angus Lewis, a senior Treasury solicitor, proceeded to Bow Street Magistrates Court where they had a private interview with Sir John Bridge, the chief magistrate. Bridge returned with Brockwell and Lewis to Whitehall to pore over the evidence and decide on the charges that Oscar might face. At the end of the deliberations, Oscar was only charged at this stage with various counts of indecency. The damaging conspiracy charges would come later. Despite the allegations of sodomy in Queensberry's Plea of Justification, it was decided not to charge Oscar with this much more serious offence.

At exactly five minutes to five, barely five hours after the collapse of the case against Queensberry, Sir John Bridge signed warrants for the arrest of Oscar Wilde and Alfred Taylor and handed them to Detective-Inspector Brockwell for immediate execution. At some time between five and six o'clock, Thomas Marlowe, a sympathetic reporter from the *Star*, turned up at the Cadogan Hotel and spoke to Robbie. Marlowe told him that the news had come through on the tape that a warrant had been issued for Oscar's arrest. When Robbie told Oscar about the warrant, Oscar went 'very grey in the face'. Robbie begged him to save himself while he still could. But Oscar refused. He had made up his mind. 'I shall stay and do my sentence whatever it is,' he said with quiet dignity.

Bosie was not with Oscar when the news of the warrant broke. He had raced down to the House of Commons to see his cousin, the MP George Wyndham. The news was not good. Wyndham had spoken to Arthur Balfour, a leading Tory politician and future prime minister, who had been told by senior figures in the government's legal machine that Oscar's case was hopeless. He was 'certain to be condemned', Wyndham told Bosie, and 'sure to be imprisoned'. There was no case against Bosie – yet. But Balfour and others, he said, were 'unanimous' in their opinion that Bosie 'had better go abroad for a year or two'. 'Bosie took it very well,' Wyndham told his father, the Hon. Percy Scawen Wyndham, two days later:

> He thought I was going to ask him to go at once, and began saying that nothing on earth would make him leave London until the trial was over. You may be sure that nothing will: he is quite insane on the subject.

Bosie had still not returned from the House of Commons when, at about twenty past six, Detective-Inspector Richards and Detective-Sergeant Allen entered the Cadogan Hotel. 'Is Oscar Wilde staying here?' they asked the hall porter. 'Will you show us to his room?' The two detectives were shown up to room 53 where they knocked and entered and found Oscar sitting in an armchair 'calmly smoking a cigarette and drinking a brandy and soda'. The floor was strewn with copies of the evening newspapers.

'Mr Wilde, I believe?' said Inspector Richards.

'Yes,' he answered. 'Yes.'

'We are police officers, and hold a warrant for your arrest,' said Richards. 'I must ask you to accompany me to the police station.'

'Shall I be able to obtain bail?' Oscar asked plaintively.

'That is a matter for the magistrate.'

'Well,' said Oscar with a deep sigh. 'If I must go I will give you the least possible trouble.' He swayed a little as he got up. Fear, shock, hock and selzer and brandy and soda had made him unsteady on his legs. Robbie helped him on with his overcoat, and Oscar picked up his hat, his gloves and his cane. Drawing himself up to his full height and lighting a cigarette, he said, 'I am now, gentleman, ready to accompany you.'

Oscar was escorted outside and conveyed by hansom cab number 15,034 to Scotland Yard before being transferred to Bow Street Police Court where he was taken into the charge room and formally charged with various counts of indecency with men. Now charged, Oscar was searched. The £200 in cash was found, along with various writs for unpaid bills, and one or two letters. Oscar's cigarettes and matches were also taken away.

Bosie returned from the House of Commons a matter of minutes after Oscar's arrest. He found a note from Oscar scrawled in haste. 'My dear Bosie':

I will be at Bow Street Police Station tonight – no bail possible I am told. Will you ask Percy, George Alexander, and Waller, at the Haymarket, to attend to give bail. Would you also wire Humphreys to appear at Bow Street for me. Wire to 41 Norfolk Square, W. Also, come to see me. Ever yours, Oscar

As Bosie rushed off to Bow Street in pursuit of Oscar, Robbie returned to Tite Street to pack a change of clothes and some toiletries for Oscar. Constance was not there. She had left Tite Street that afternoon and gone to seek refuge at the house of her aunt, Mrs William Napier. With the help of one of the servants, Robbie forced his way into Oscar's locked bedroom and study and gathered up as many of his incriminating letters and papers as he could find. Though the situation seemed hopeless, at least the police would not be able to find more evidence and add further names to the long list of boys Oscar had had sex with.

Bosie arrived at Bow Street at about eight o'clock in the evening 'in a frightful state of despair and consternation'. He had been to see George Alexander, who was playing the lead in *The Importance of Being Earnest*, and Lewis Waller, who was playing the part of Sir Robert Chiltern in *An Ideal*

Husband, about standing bail for Oscar. Both had refused. Now Bosie offered to stand surety for Oscar himself, but the police told him that there could be no question of bail. He wanted to see Oscar, but was peremptorily refused permission.

Bosie's world was fast disintegrating around him. He was powerless to do anything to help Oscar. He went back to the Cadogan Hotel and wrote to everyone he could think of, anyone who might be able to help. 'Can you do anything or suggest anything in this horrible tragedy?' Bosie wrote in pencil to George Ives late that evening:

> I am so miserable and wretched that I am unfit for anything. I cannot see Oscar or give him anything, not even some poison to kill himself with. I should be glad to hear that he is dead, and I wish he had died before this terrible thing happened.

Bosie was almost hysterical with grief and anguish. Suicide, Oscar's and his own, seemed a tempting way out of the hideous nightmare they were in. Ives was sympathetic. 'Poor boy,' he wrote in his diary. 'When I think what he must suffer I am sick at heart.' Ives, too, hoped that Oscar might have committed suicide, and he even melodramatically contemplated suicide himself, going so far as to take out his revolver and rhapsodising how a bullet would save him from 'the force of all the state'.

That evening, as Bosie was desperately trying to see Oscar and get him bailed from Bow Street, Adrian and Laura Hope received an unexpected visit from Constance's aunt, who had come to solicit help from the Wildes' old friends and neighbours. 'A most trying visit from Mrs William Napier,' Laura wrote in her diary, 'in a most frantic state about her poor niece Constance Wilde as the whole verdict has gone against her monstrous husband – the whole episode most terrible.'

As the long day drew to its end, only Queensberry was happy as he celebrated his famous victory with friends and cronies far into the small hours. Constance lay sleepless in her aunt's house, trying to make some sense of the sudden devastation of her life and hopes, and of her children's lives and hopes. Not much more than a mile away, Bosie was alone in his suite at the Cadogan Hotel, his face pale with exhaustion and stained with tears, pacing round and round as he tried desperately to think of a way to save his beloved Oscar. In his narrow, dirty cell in the bowels of the Bow Street Police Court, Oscar lay sleepless on the long narrow bench. He was cold and uncomfortable, despite the blanket handed to him by a friendly policeman. The effects of the afternoon's alcohol had worn off, and he was deprived of his constant supply of cigarettes. He was hungry and alone, caught up in the inexorable process of law, a process he himself had initiated. He could but wonder at the extraordinary fate which had taken him in so short a space from the heady pinnacles of success and fame to the depths of shame and infamy.

Oscar at bay

'Is it not high time that a little charity, Christian or anti-Christian, were imported into this land of Christian shibboleths and formulas? Most sane men listen on in silence while Press and public condemn to eternal punishment and obloquy a supposed criminal who is not yet tried or proved guilty.' – Robert Buchanan to the Star, *16 April 1895*

Oscar ate nothing the next morning, but drank copious quantities of tea ordered in from the Tavistock Hotel in nearby Covent Garden. After a quick wash with cold water, he replaced his soiled collar from the previous day and waited to make the first of his three appearances before Sir John Bridge at Bow Street Police Court in committal proceedings. It was the first time that Oscar would encounter in court some of the key prosecution witnesses against him. Just after the first of these, Charlie Parker, had gone into the witness box, it was announced that Alfred Taylor had been arrested in his rooms at Denbigh Place, Pimlico and was to join Oscar in the dock. Oscar greeted Taylor with a slight bow. Taylor smiled and bowed back.

Charlie Parker, his brother William and Alfred Wood all took the stand and briefly gave their evidence. Charlie went over the events of the night in March 1893 when he and his brother had been introduced to Oscar over a sumptuous dinner at Kettner's, after which he had gone back to the Savoy and spent an hour and a half in bed with Oscar. Alfred Wood told of his dinner with Oscar in a private room in the Florence restaurant, after which he had gone back with Oscar to Tite Street and had sex with him. 'I was the worse for drink,' Wood said, in explanation. Oscar listened impassively. They were an unappetising sight. Max Beerbohm called them 'a knot of renters', and *Reynolds's News* called them 'male strumpets'. 'A something' was how Robert Sherard collectively and contemptuously described them later, 'a multiple something that was giggling and chatting and smoking cigarettes. It was The Evidence.'

The last of the key witnesses to be called was 'Jenny' Mavor. Mavor described his first meeting with Oscar: how he and Taylor had met Oscar and Bosie for dinner, how he had received a present of a silver cigarette case from Oscar a week later, and how he had arranged to meet Oscar at the Albemarle Hotel, where he subsequently spent the night. When Mavor was asked what had taken place that night between Oscar and himself, Mavor boldly replied, 'Nothing'. There was an audible murmur of surprise at his answer.

Bosie was in court and smiled. He had spotted Jenny Mavor in one of the corridors in Bow Street before the proceedings began.

'Surely you are not going to give evidence against Oscar?' Bosie demanded.

'Well, what can I do?' answered Mavor, looking round in a frightened manner. 'I daren't refuse to give evidence now. They got a statement out of me.'

'For God's sake,' said Bosie, 'remember you are a gentleman and a public school boy. Don't put yourself on a level with scum like Wood and Parker. When counsel asks you the questions, deny the whole thing, and say you made the statement because you were frightened by the police. They can't do anything to you.'

'All right,' said Mavor, grabbing Bosie's hand. 'I'll do what you say.'

Jenny Mavor's denial that anything immoral had occurred between himself and Oscar was a small but nevertheless important victory. Unlike the unreliable and decidedly criminal 'male strumpets' who constituted the bulk of the evidence against Oscar, Jenny Mavor was more or less respectable; he worked for his living and was well-educated. His denials might well carry more weight with a jury than the assertions of self-confessed blackmailers and male prostitutes. At the conclusion of the day's proceedings, the magistrate Sir John Bridge flatly turned down a request for bail. 'I think there is no worse crime than that with which the prisoners are charged,' he said. 'I shall therefore refuse bail.'

In the days that followed Oscar's arrest, the air was alive with rumours that more arrests were imminent. 'Sworn informations have been lodged against several persons mentioned in the trial,' reported the *New York Herald*, 'some of whose names were not made public, and the civil officers are only awaiting the authority of the Treasury Department to make the arrests.' The *Star* predicted a 'sensational development', saying that 'Warrants are understood to have been granted for the arrest of four other persons whose names have been canvassed in connection with the case.'

Who could these 'four other persons' be? Bosie was certainly one of them. It was clear from Oscar's cross-examination that Bosie was not just Oscar's lover, but also his willing and energetic accomplice in sexual crime. It was equally clear that Bosie had had dealings with male prostitutes and blackmailers. Not only that. His poems were explicitly sodomitical in sentiment. It seemed only a matter of time before the authorities would arrest him and he would stand in the dock alongside Oscar and Alfred Taylor. Maurice Schwabe was another. He had cropped up several times in the libel trial, his name never being uttered, but instead written down on a scrap of paper. Lord Rosebery's name had also been 'canvassed in connection with the case'. Was this what the *Star* meant by a 'sensational development'? Was it possible that the Prime Minister himself would be arrested and charged? Rumours of Rosebery's imminent resignation kept cropping up in the newspapers, usually immediately adjacent on the page to reports of Oscar's arrest. Was this by accident or design – an example of the time-honoured newspaper trick of saying the unsayable?

Meanwhile, Rosebery's health continued to go from bad to worse. 'Rosebery seems to me to make no way: there being hardly any improvement in his sleeping powers,' Sir Edward Hamilton confided to his diary three days after Oscar's arrest. Over the next few days, Hamilton became even more alarmed. 'The last three nights have been very bad again,' he wrote on Friday 12 April. Rosebery was 'certainly more depressed about himself' and was talking about suicide again.

Oscar's arrest had started a sudden and intense outpouring of hatred against Oscar and his kind. It was, Frank Harris said, 'an orgy of Philistine rancour such as even London had never known before'. The newspapers were almost universally hostile to him. 'Mr Oscar Wilde is damned and done for,' exulted the *Echo*. 'We begin to breathe a purer air,' proclaimed the *Pall Mall Gazette*. The *Daily Telegraph* devoted a lengthy editorial to the subject of the devilish Oscar and all his works:

> We have had enough, and more than enough, of Mr. OSCAR WILDE, who has been the means of inflicting on public patience during the recent episode as much moral damage of the most offensive and repulsive kind as any single individual could well cause.

The *National Observer*, edited by Oscar's former friend W.E. Henley, pulled no punches, describing Oscar as 'the obscene impostor'. The paper was in no doubt that Oscar and everything that he represented must be done away with:

> There must be another trial at the Old Bailey, or a coroner's inquest – the latter for choice; and the Decadents, or their hideous conceptions of the meaning of Art, of their worse than Eleusinian mysteries, there must be an absolute end.

The hostility in the newspapers was matched and reflected by the public at large. 'Public feeling is fiercely hostile to him, among all classes,' George Wyndham told his father. Street ballads and cheap pamphlets attacking Oscar were starting to appear. According to André Raffalovich, there were rumours of a league being formed 'whose goal was to pursue all the suspect individuals, without regard for their wealth, position or merit'. Many of Oscar's friends and acquaintances were quick to turn against him. 'I look forward eagerly to the first act of Oscar's new Tragedy,' Aubrey Beardsley wrote with schoolboy glee to Ada Leverson. 'But surely the title *Douglas* has been used before?' Oscar's letters were burnt, his books thrown away. To his surprise and dismay, Bosie experienced this hostility at first hand the day after Oscar's arrest, when he called on Adrian and Laura Hope to solicit their help. 'Adrian had a most painful interview with Lord Alfred Douglas,' Laura Hope wrote in her diary, 'who came to implore him to go bail for that fiend O.W. which was of course impossible.' In the eyes of both polite and impolite society, Oscar had become a 'fiend'.

There were plenty who exulted in Oscar's arrest and hoped that there would be many more arrests, a wholesale mucking out of the sodomitical Augean Stables. Blanche Crackanthorpe, the wife of the solicitor Montague Crackanthorpe, wrote to her friend, the actress Elizabeth Robins:

> There was an idea on Sunday that many other arrests would follow – I only hope they may – nothing would do so much to purge schools and universities – and sorely they need it – as sentences which should strike terror and dismay into the hearts of the offenders. 'Light, light, more light.'

In the first days after Oscar's arrest, many Uranians began to feel afraid. The climate of hostility towards men who loved men was so intense, so tangible, that they feared they would be the victims of a judicial pogrom. Many decided to go abroad. There was, said Frank Harris, a sudden 'strange exodus' of Uranians swept across the channel by the 'wind of terror' in London. John Gray discreetly slipped out of the country and went to Berlin, where André Raffalovich later joined him. Robbie at first refused to leave Oscar. But his mother was emphatic, and, by dint of contributing £500 to the cost of Oscar's defence and promising to look after Lady Wilde, she persuaded a reluctant Robbie to go to France. Taking Reggie Turner with him, Robbie decamped to the Hotel Terminus in Calais from where they could watch the unfolding drama.

Even though it seemed almost certain that he would be arrested, Bosie was adamant that he would not leave Oscar. 'I have determined to remain here and do what I possibly can,' he told Robert Sherard:

> though I am warned on all hands that my own risk is not inconsiderable, and my family implore me to go away. I do not say this to try and gain credit for myself, for I should be a base coward if I did anything else, considering all I owe to him, and that I am in many ways the innocent cause of this horrible calamity.

Though many among Oscar's large and glittering acquaintance seemed to have simply melted away, there were still a few stalwart friends left. Robert Sherard in Paris rallied to his standard. Ada and Ernest Leverson were steadfast in their loyalty. Max Beerbohm told Reggie Turner that Trelawny Backhouse 'is raising money for the conduct of the case', and that Will Rothenstein 'is most sympathetic and goes about the minor clubs insulting everyone who does not clamour for Hoscar's instant release'. And in a gesture of great generosity, Sir Edward Clarke had volunteered to defend Oscar for no fee.

Bosie was tireless in his efforts to galvanise support for Oscar. He wrote letter after letter to the newspapers protesting at the relentlessly hostile press coverage of the case. 'Mr Oscar Wilde,' Bosie wrote:

has been tried by the newspapers before he has been tried by a jury, that his case has been almost hopelessly prejudiced in the eyes of the public from whom the jury who must try the case will be drawn, and that he is practically being delivered over bound to the fury of a cowardly and brutal mob.

Bosie constituted himself head of an informal committee working to free Oscar and to change public and political attitudes towards sex between men by writing letters and pamphlets. Max Beerbohm sent a jaundiced and amusing sketch to Reggie Turner of a pamphlet-writing evening at Ernest and Ada Leverson's home. 'The scene that evening at the Leversons' was quite absurd,' Beerbohm wrote:

An awful New Woman in a divided skirt (introduced by Bosie) writing a pamphlet at Mrs Leverson's writing-table with the aid of several whiskey-and-sodas; her brother – a gaunt man with prominent cheek-bones from Toynbee Hall who kept reiterating that 'these things must be approached through first principles and through first principles alone:' two other New Women who subsequently explained to Mr Leverson that they were there to keep a strict watch upon New Woman number one, who is not responsible for her actions: Mrs Leverson making flippant remarks about messenger-boys in a faint undertone to Bosie, who was ashen-pale and thought the pamphlet (which was the most awful drivel) admirable: and Mr Leverson explaining to me that he allowed his house to be used for these purposes not because he approved of 'anything unnatural' but by reason of his admiration for Oscar's plays and personality. I myself exquisitely dressed and sympathising with no one.

In *The Importance of Being Earnest*, Oscar had drawn a witty thumbnail sketch of Holloway Prison. 'The surroundings are middle-class,' he wrote, 'but the gaol itself is fashionable and well-aired; and there are ample opportunities of taking exercise at certain stated hours of the day.' The truth, at least for prisoners on remand, was not so very far removed from the theatrical fiction. Oscar spent his four weeks on remand in Holloway in comparative comfort, though it was nothing compared to the luxury of his previous lifestyle. He occupied a 'special cell' at the far end of the east wing of the prison, a larger and more comfortable cell than normal, approximately eleven feet square, which could be hired for a fee by prisoners on remand. Given Oscar's predilection for *grandes dames* and duchesses, it was perhaps appropriate that reputedly this cell's last occupant was a duchess remanded to Holloway for contempt of court. Special cells were unfurnished, and Oscar was able to hire some reasonably comfortable furniture, including an armchair, from a local firm. As a prisoner on remand he was allowed to wear his own clothes and have his meals sent in from a local restaurant. He could also have the daily papers.

But, according to a journalist who wrote a well-informed article about Oscar's daily routine in Holloway, Oscar often had 'moments of very low-spiritedness, and becomes almost despondent'. Bosie managed to visit Oscar almost every day in Holloway. But, he told Robert Sherard, Oscar was always penned in 'a horrible kind of barred cage, separated from him by a space of one yard, and in almost complete darkness with twenty other people talking at the same time'. Oscar would visibly 'brighten up' after Bosie's visits but would become 'very low-spirited and morose' after a consultation with his solicitor. Oscar's greatest misery was in not being allowed to smoke, and he found it hard to sleep. 'He is out of bed most of the night and, in unstockinged feet, paces the room in apparently not too good a mood.'

It was Bosie, and Bosie alone, who sustained Oscar through the misery and loneliness of the first dreadful days on remand in Holloway. 'Nothing but Alfred Douglas's daily visits quicken me into life,' Oscar told Robert Sherard. 'A slim thing, gold-haired like an angel, stands always at my side,' Oscar said of Bosie in a letter to the Leversons. 'His presence overshadows me. He moves in the gloom like a white flower.' Though he was 'dazed with horror', Oscar told an unnamed correspondent that nevertheless 'sometimes there is sunlight in my cell, and every day someone whose name is Love comes to see me, and weeps so much through prison-bars that it is I who have to comfort him.'

Oscar left Holloway only to attend the committal proceedings at Bow Street. The second of these took place on Maundy Thursday, 11 April. The police van 'was received by the motley crowd of roughs, hanging about the entrance to the court, with a hoarse shout which might have been a cheer or a jeer'. When Oscar stepped into the dock, it was evident that his week in prison was beginning to take its toll. He looked paler and thinner, weary and old. 'Yes, Oscar at bay was on the whole a pleasing sight,' W.E. Henley wrote with *schadenfreude* to a fellow journalist of this appearance in court:

Holloway and Bow Street have taken his hair out of curl in more senses than one. And I am pretty sure that he is having a damn bad time.

More witnesses against Oscar were produced: an assortment of landladies, housekeepers and servants, alongside Fred Atkins and Edward Shelley. Now that Jenny Mavor had denied any improprieties between himself and Oscar, the respectable, intellectual-looking Shelley represented by far the greatest danger to Oscar. Oscar listened to Shelley's evidence 'with an inscrutable countenance, his gloves hanging from his fingers while his hands supported and almost covered his face', while his eyes remained fixed blankly on the wall behind Sir John Bridge.

Bosie told Robert Sherard that, during one of the committal proceedings, he managed to spend some time alone with Oscar in a private room. Bosie did not reveal what they discussed, but, significantly, it was after this meeting between them that Bosie first began to claim that there was a political conspiracy ranged against Oscar. Was it Oscar who first sowed the seeds of the idea of a conspiracy against him? And, if so, what had he heard? And from whom? The next day, Bosie told Sherard unequivocally that there was 'a diabolical conspiracy' against Oscar 'which seems almost unlimited in its size and strength'. As if to give credence to Bosie's claim, Hamilton Cuffe, the Director of Public Prosecutions, was in court to watch the proceedings. And there were some strange and disturbing rumours concerning the key witnesses against Oscar. Some of them, it was alleged, had been bought new suits of clothes and, in a highly unusual step, were being lodged with police detectives in secret locations. Not only that, there was talk of them having been paid to testify, not just by Queensberry, but also by the Crown. It was rumoured that each of the witnesses received £5 a week for the duration of the trials. And then there was the fact that Alfred Taylor had been promised immunity from prosecution, if he agreed to turn Queen's Evidence and testify against Oscar. Clearly, the government was going to extraordinary lengths to secure a conviction. 'The government appears determined to obtain a condemnation by all possible means, honest or not, which are in its powers,' Sir Edward Clarke privately told Bosie.

Eight days later, on 19 April, when he made his third and final appearance at Bow Street, it was obvious to everybody that Oscar's health and spirits had deteriorated to 'a startling degree':

> His face was haggard and grey, his cheeks seemed fallen in, his hair unkempt, and his general mien was one of great depression and sudden age. Even his clothes – the grey coat with the velvet collar and cuffs, the silk hat, the gloves – seemed to have deteriorated.

Constance had already left London to go and stay with Lady Mount-Temple at Babbacombe Cliff. Ever since Oscar's arrest, she had been in a state of shock and grief. Her younger son, Vyvyan, recalled his mother 'in tears, poring over masses of press-cuttings'. On the day of Oscar's third appearance at Bow Street, Constance wrote to the Sibyl of Mortimer Street for consolation:

> My dear Mrs Robinson, What is to become of my husband who has so betrayed and deceived me and ruined the lives of my darling boys? Can you tell me anything? You told me that after this terrible shock my life was to become easier, but will there be any happiness in it, or is that dead for me? And I have had so little. My life has all been cut to pieces as my hand is by its lines. As soon as this trial is over I have to get my judicial separation, or if possible my divorce in order to get the guardianship of the boys. What a tragedy for him who is so gifted.

Even in the depths of her own misery, Constance could still feel the enormity of Oscar's tragedy.

On the same day, Charles Gill, the senior Treasury counsel who was in charge of the prosecution of Oscar in the courts, wrote a remarkable letter to Hamilton Cuffe, advising against prosecuting Bosie alongside Oscar.

Though Gill was convinced that 'there is little room for doubt that immoral relations existed' between Bosie and Oscar, nevertheless:

> Having regard to the fact that Douglas was an undergraduate at Oxford when Wilde made his acquaintance – the difference in their ages – and the strong influence that Wilde has obviously exercised over Douglas since that time – I think that Douglas if guilty – may fairly be regarded as one of Wilde's victims.

Not only was Bosie just another of Oscar's young victims, but it would, Gill wrote, be extremely hard to prove in court that Bosie had had sex with Alfred Wood and Charles Parker. But Gill was lying. Wood and Parker had both made statements alleging sex with Bosie. The evidence against Bosie was from the same source, and of the same weight, as the evidence against Oscar. It was clear that the government was willing – indeed eager – to convict Oscar on the evidence of male prostitutes and blackmailers, and yet extremely reluctant to prosecute Bosie on the same testimony.

In turn, Cuffe sent an even more remarkable memorandum to Asquith, the Home Secretary, explaining why Bosie would not be prosecuted:

> We think he fell when a boy at Oxford and has never had the force of will or character to emancipate himself from his degrading submission to Wilde. It may be hoped that if Wilde be convicted and Douglas be thus forcibly separated from him there may be a chance of his abandoning his present course of life.

Cuffe's assessment of the situation flew in the face of even the most cursory examination of the evidence stacked against Bosie. That Bosie was guilty of sexual crimes – with Oscar, with Wood and Parker and almost certainly with others – was not in doubt. But he was a victim, more sinned against than sinning, Cuffe maintained. Cuffe's assessment was remarkably similar – suspiciously similar – to Queensberry's view of the relationship between Oscar and his son. Queensberry believed that Bosie had been 'corrupted' by Oscar and could be 'cured' of his acquired vices if only Oscar's influence was forcibly removed. Cuffe was nevertheless alive to the interpretation that might be put on any decision not to press charges against Bosie. 'Irresponsible persons,' Cuffe warned Asquith, 'very likely will say that he goes unprosecuted because of his position in life.' Gill's letter and Cuffe's memorandum were kept secret until 1999. Why? Was the decision not to prosecute Bosie yet another of Queensberry's demands? Oscar was to be sent to prison, and Bosie was not to be prosecuted – or else Queensberry would make public what he knew about Rosebery and other senior Liberals. Queensberry got his own way again.

Bosie was completely unaware of the secret discussions about whether or not to prosecute him. He lived, he wrote, 'in daily and momentary expectation of being arrested' and sent for trial. Every day he received 'letters of warning imploring me to go and save myself'. Oscar was also fearful that Bosie would be arrested. He begged and pleaded with Bosie to go abroad, to save himself while he still could. Oscar could not bear to think that Bosie might be arrested, tried and sent to rot in prison. He knew, too, that any charges brought against Bosie might well include sodomy, which would mean a minimum sentence of ten years, and a maximum of life. But Bosie still hesitated. He could hardly bear to think of leaving Oscar in his wretched plight. He certainly did not lack courage and was fully prepared to face arrest and imprisonment. It was only at the 'urgent request' of Sir Edward Clarke, who assured him that his presence in the country could only do Oscar 'harm' and 'destroy what small chance he had of acquittal', that Bosie finally and with a heavy heart agreed to go abroad. 'I am so happy that you have gone away!' Oscar wrote to Bosie. 'I know what that must have cost you. It would have been agony for me to think that you were in England when your name was mentioned in court.'

Bosie delayed his departure until the last possible moment, leaving England for France on 25 April, the day before Oscar's trial began at the Old Bailey.

The love that dares to speak its name

*'Misfortunes one can endure – they come from outside, they are
accidents. But to suffer for one's own faults – ah! – there is the
sting of life.'*

Every available seat in the Central Criminal Court at the Old Bailey was
occupied on Friday 26 April when Oscar and Alfred Taylor stepped into the
dock. Oscar looked 'haggard and worn', and his long hair was 'dishevelled'. As
the charges against them were read out, there was, according to André
Raffalovich, a clap of thunder and a flash of lightning, and many of those
present must have wondered if these were rumblings of divine discontent, a
modern-day hail of fire and brimstone, at the moral disobedience of the new
Sodom.

The indictment contained no less than twenty-five counts, eight of them
relating directly to acts of gross indecency committed by Oscar with Charles
Parker, Alfred Wood and Edward Shelley, as well as with a boy or boys
unknown at the Savoy Hotel. Oscar could count himself fortunate that he was
not charged with sodomy, though there were plenty who believed that he
should have been. 'Many people are asking why the indictment has been drawn
under the Act involving the minor penalties,' Mr Dike of Whitehall wrote to
the *Star* on 23 April, dropping a heavy hint as to the true reason. 'If rumour is
but tinged with truth the reason is a good one – and as bad as it could be.'
Ironically, while Bosie and others were convinced that Oscar was being made
the scapegoat to save the careers and reputations of Lord Rosebery and other
senior figures in the Liberal Party, Mr Dike and many of the general public
were equally convinced that he was being treated leniently because Lord
Rosebery's name had been mentioned in connection with the case. This
interpretation gained an even wider currency when it emerged that the single
charge of sodomy against Taylor had been dropped before the case came to
court.

With or without the sodomy charges, it was still a devilish indictment. Oscar
and Taylor were jointly charged with eight counts that they 'did conspire

389

combine confederate and agree together unlawfully' to procure acts of gross
indecency. If the jury failed to convict Oscar on the straightforward counts of
gross indecency, they could always convict him on the counts of conspiring to
commit an act of gross indecency. The different charges carried different
burdens of proof: conspiracy to procure an act of gross indecency did not
require the act to have taken place, merely that it was the *intention* of the
conspirators that it should take place. Oscar was damned if he did have sex with
the boys and, seemingly, damned if he did not. Sir Edward Clarke protested
vigorously at the conspiracy charges, to no avail.

Charles Gill opened the case for the prosecution with a long *résumé* of the
facts. Unlike Edward Carson, Gill was no orator, and his opening speech
seemed to drag on interminably. Oscar 'looked terribly bored', and 'many of
the spectators began to rustle papers, shuffle their feet, and cough loudly',
causing the usher to make several calls for silence. The case for the prosecution
lasted for three days, and the witnesses called were the same who had testified
during the committal proceedings at Bow Street: Charles and William Parker,
Alfred Wood, Fred Atkins, Jenny Mavor and Edward Shelley, along with an
assortment of waiters, housekeepers, chambermaids and landladies. The only
surprise was Charlie Parker's claim that Oscar had 'committed the act of
sodomy on me' the first night they met in the Savoy. Oscar sat in the dock and
listened attentively to the evidence, betraying 'a great deal of nervous anxiety,
now and again heaving deep sighs as some especially incriminating evidence
was brought out'.

In his cross-examinations, Sir Edward Clarke managed to significantly
damage the credibility of the boys. Charlie Parker, Alfred Wood and Fred
Atkins were all exposed as blackmailers who had demanded money with
menaces from the men they slept with. And thanks to some anonymous notes
sent to him at the Old Bailey, Clarke was also able to prove that Fred Atkins
had lied through his teeth under oath. Edward Shelley came across as neurotic,
a young man who had been arrested for assaulting his father and who admitted
to not being in his right mind at the time of the assault.

By the time the prosecution had finished presenting its case against Oscar
and Taylor, it was clear that the evidence for the eight counts of conspiracy was
extremely flimsy. The prosecution's best hope had been Jenny Mavor's
detailed account of how Taylor had arranged for him to meet Oscar at dinner,
and Taylor's celebrated remarks on that evening, 'I'm glad you've made
yourself pretty. Mr Wilde likes nice clean boys!' But Mavor's insistence that
no improprieties had ever taken place between Oscar and himself took the wind
out of the prosecution's sails. On the morning of the fourth day of the trial,
Charles Gill rose and told the judge that the prosecution was withdrawing the
charges of conspiracy. Gill's announcement caused a sensation in court. A
third of the charges had been withdrawn against Oscar and Taylor.

Clarke opened the case for the defence and announced that he would call
Oscar as his first witness. It was a bold and unexpected strategy. It was widely
assumed that, after Oscar's bruising encounter with Carson, Clarke would not

risk putting his client in the witness box again. Having damaged the credibility of the boys, Clarke set out to present Oscar as a man who had behaved with consistent probity and openness. If Oscar was guilty of the offences alleged against him, Clarke asked the jury, why had he bothered to prosecute Queensberry in open court – especially after he had seen Queensberry's Plea of Justification: 'Gentlemen of the jury,' asked Clarke, 'do you believe that had he been guilty he would have stayed in England and faced those accusations?':

> Men guilty of such offences suffer from a species of insanity. What, then, would you think of a man who, knowing himself to be guilty and that evidence would be forthcoming from half-a-dozen different places, insisted on bringing his case before the world? Insane would hardly be the word for it.

The only one rational explanation, said Clarke, was that Oscar was innocent. Clarke's arguments were compelling.

When Charles Gill rose to cross-examine Oscar, he turned to Bosie's Uranian poem 'Two Loves', which had been published in the *Chameleon*.

'Is it not clear that the love described relates to natural and unnatural love?' asked Gill.

'No,' replied Oscar.

'What is the "Love that dare not speak its name"?' Gill demanded with a sneer in his voice.

Gill's question was the opportunity Oscar had been waiting for. It was his chance to justify and explain the nature of the great love that he and Bosie shared. 'The "Love that dare not speak its name",' Oscar replied:

> in this century is such a great affection of an elder for a younger man as there was between David and Jonathan, such as Plato made the very basis of his philosophy, and such as you find in the sonnets of Michelangelo and Shakespeare. It is that deep, spiritual affection that is as pure as it is perfect. It dictates and pervades great works of art like those of Shakespeare and Michelangelo, and those two letters of mine, such as they are. It is in this century misunderstood, so much misunderstood that it may be described as the 'Love that dare not speak its name,' and on account of it I am placed where I am now. It is beautiful, it is fine, it is the noblest form of affection. There is nothing unnatural about it. It is intellectual, and it repeatedly exists between an elder and a younger man, when the elder man has intellect, and the younger man has all the joy, hope and glamour of life before him. That it should be so the world does not understand. The world mocks at it and sometimes puts one in the pillory for it.

Oscar's speech was electrifying. There was a loud and spontaneous outburst of applause from the public gallery, mingled with a few boos and hisses. 'If there is the slightest manifestation of feeling,' said Mr Justice Charles testily,

'I shall have the court cleared. There must be complete silence preserved.' Few who heard the speech could fail to be moved by the dignity and power of Oscar's words, and by the depth of passion with which he spoke them. 'Oscar has been quite superb,' Max Beerbohm wrote to Reggie Turner:

> His speech about the Love that dares not tell his name was simply wonderful, and carried the whole court right away, quite a tremendous burst of applause. Here was this man, who had been for a month in prison and loaded with insults and crushed and buffeted, perfectly self-possessed, dominating the Old Bailey with his fine presence and musical voice. He has never had so great a triumph.

Oscar himself seemed to draw strength and courage from his *apologia*. It was a calculated act of defiance, rather than of defence. The night before, he had written to Bosie in the full expectation that in a few hours 'all will be over', and 'prison and dishonour' would be his destiny. 'Our love was always beautiful and noble,' he told Bosie, 'and if I have been the butt of a terrible tragedy, it is because the nature of that love has not been understood.' Oscar's speech to the jury was a proud proclamation of the beauty and nobility of his love for Bosie. It was to be his last speech as a free man before his incarceration. He did not seek to deny that there was an erotic as well as a spiritual element to his love for Bosie, saying only that it was pure, it was perfect and that there was nothing unnatural about it. When Oscar pleaded 'Not guilty' to the charges levelled against him, he was speaking the truth; not the literal, lawbound truth of the courtroom, but the higher truth, the truth that told him that something so pure, something so perfect as love and sex between men could not be unnatural, could not be a crime.

Mr Justice Charles began his lengthy summing up on 1 May, the fifth day of the trial. It lasted three hours and was scrupulously fair to both the defendants. There were, Mr Justice Charles said, four questions for the jury to consider:

1. Do you think that Wilde committed indecent acts with Edward Shelley and Alfred Wood and with a person or persons unknown at the Savoy Hotel or with Charles Parker?
2. Did Taylor procure or attempt to procure the commission of these acts or any of them?
3. Did Wilde and Taylor or either of them attempt to get Atkins to commit indecencies?
4. Did Taylor commit indecent acts with Charles Parker or with William Parker?

The jury went out to consider their verdict at twenty-five minutes to two. It was widely assumed that their deliberations would be brief and to the point, and that Oscar and Taylor would be found guilty on most, if not all the remaining counts. But the minutes turned into hours, and there was still no sign that the jury had reached a verdict. Just after five, the jury filed back into court. 'Hoscar stood very upright when he was brought up to hear the verdict and looked most leonine and sphinx-like,' Max Beerbohm told Reggie Turner.

The jury were all agreed that Oscar and Taylor had not attempted to persuade Fred Atkins to commit indecencies, but they were unable to agree on the three remaining questions. Consequently they were unable to return a verdict. The next morning a newspaper published what purported to be the voting of the jury. Ten of the twelve jurors believed that Oscar had had sex with Edward Shelley and Charlie Parker, and eight of them believed he had had sex with Alfred Wood. Again, ten jurors believed Taylor was guilty of procuring boys for Oscar to have sex with. Rather surprisingly, only two jurors believed Taylor had had sex with both the Parker brothers.

Under normal circumstances, it was not absolutely certain that there would be a fresh trial. The newspapers were quick to call for justice to be seen to be done. 'Ought the prosecution to stop? asked the *Morning*:

> That is a very grave question. Whatever may be the truth as regards Wilde and Taylor, the evidence given at the Old Bailey seems to affect more reputations than those that have been openly impugned. What are these mysterious names written on slips of paper and passed between counsels' table, the witness-box, and the Bench? If there is a widespread canker in our midst, as the authorities seem to believe, it cannot too soon be thoroughly cauterised.

The message of the *Morning*'s editorial was clear. If a fresh trial failed to materialise, it would be because of political interference. A second trial and a verdict of guilty would, according to Sir Edward Hamilton, 'remove what appears to be a wide-felt impression that the Judge & Jury were on the last occasion *got at,* in order to shield others of a higher status in life'. Hamilton returned to the same theme again, referring to a widespread suspicion that the government was trying to 'hush up' the case. Edward Carson spoke to Sir Frank Lockwood, the Solicitor General on the subject. 'Cannot you let up on the fellow now?' he asked Lockwood. 'He has suffered a great deal.' 'I would,' Lockwood replied, 'but we cannot: we dare not: it would at once be said, both in England and abroad, that owing to the names mentioned in Queensberry's letters we were forced to abandon it.' Lockwood was not telling Carson the whole truth. Not only had he been a party to the original decision taken by senior members of the government to prosecute Oscar, a decision which Bosie and others alleged was taken under the duress of Queensberry's threats, but he was also related to Maurice Schwabe, whose name had been so carefully and so frequently concealed during the trials.

After some complicated legal manoeuvres, Oscar was finally freed on 7 May. He knew that his freedom was temporary. It had already been announced that there was to be a new trial in a fortnight, this time to be led by Sir Frank

Lockwood. It was a quite extraordinary turn of events. For the Solicitor-General to undertake the prosecution of what was a misdemeanour, rather than a felony, revealed the lengths to which the government was prepared to go to secure a conviction.

Oscar was released on bail from Bow Street. A suite of rooms had been engaged for him at the Midland Hotel, a gothic fantasy next to St Pancras Station. But no sooner had Oscar settled in than the manager of the hotel appeared and asked him to leave. It was the same story in half-a-dozen other hotels. Queensberry had had Oscar followed, probably by Littlechild and Kearley again, and a quiet word with the hotel manager was enough to have Oscar sent away like a pariah. At midnight, having shaken off his pursuers, Oscar arrived at 146, Oakley Street, Chelsea, where Lady Wilde lived with Willie and his new wife, Lily. 'Give me shelter, Willie, or I shall die in the streets,' he moaned as he stumbled across the threshold like, as Willie put it, 'a wounded stag'.

Oakley Street was a far from ideal refuge. Oscar said the house was 'depressing', and Willie made things worse by his insensitive and ill-timed comments. 'Willie makes such a merit of giving me shelter,' Oscar said. 'He means well, I suppose, but it is all dreadful.' Oscar was profoundly depressed. 'I am not well today. I have nervous prostration,' he told Ada Leverson shortly after his arrival at Oakley Street. To assuage his misery, he was drinking heavily. Sherard turned up from Paris to find him lying on a narrow camp bed, his face flushed and feverish, and smelling strongly of drink. 'Why have you brought me no poison from Paris?' Oscar moaned to Sherard melo-dramatically. 'As for Hosker,' W.E. Henley wrote to a friend with evident satisfaction:

> the news is that he lives with his brother, and is all day steeping himself in liquor and moaning for Boasy . . . They say he has lost all nerve, all pose, all everything: and is just now so much the ordinary drunkard that he hasn't even the energy to kill himself.

Ada Leverson, Oscar's devoted friend, stepped in and offered to receive him at her home in South Kensington, where the nursery floor was given over to him. At the Leversons, Oscar regained his equilibrium and his dignity. There were fresh flowers in his rooms daily, and Oscar would come down for dinner each evening, dazzling and dominating the dinner table as of old. Ada was more than sympathetic to Oscar's sexual tastes, she was an enthusiast, and Oscar could breathe a freer air in Courtfield Gardens than he could almost anywhere else. There was much discussion of Uranian matters, and some of Oscar's time was spent in attempting to convert and convince his friends of the joys of Uranian love. Oscar told Robert Sherard that he considered 'men who did not like boys for bestowing sexual caresses on were abnormal'. And, according to Sherard, when the journalist and translator Teixeira de Mattos called on him, Oscar repeatedly asked him 'whether truly and honestly he could declare that he had never liked young men, had never wished to fondle and caress them, and seemed almost to doubt Tex's sincerity when he emphatically repudiated the very concept of such a thing'.

The period between Oscar's arrest and his imprisonment was the high water mark of the love affair between Oscar and Bosie. Never had their love seemed so sweet and so selfless, so mysterious and so profound. And never had Oscar's faith in the wonder and nobility of Uranian love been so steadfast. Oscar put his feelings into words in a series of moving and meltingly beautiful letters to Bosie. 'Every great love has its tragedy, and now ours has too,' he wrote just before he was sentenced:

> but to have known and loved you with such profound devotion, to have had you for a part of my life, the only part I now consider beautiful, is enough for me. My passion is at a loss for words, but you can understand me, you alone. Our souls were made for one another, and by knowing yours through love, mine has transcended many evils, understood perfection, and entered into the divine essence of things.

Oscar's great transforming love for Bosie explains why he never took any of the many chances he had throughout March, April and May to flee abroad. His friends pleaded with him to flee. Sherard urged him to jump bail. Frank Harris announced that he had a steam yacht ready and waiting at Erith in Kent to take him to France. Constance journeyed up specially from Torquay and, with tears in her eyes, begged him to flee. And from France Bosie wrote daily urging him to fly. Certainly, Oscar was tempted to flee on several occasions. The prospect of spending years, and perhaps the rest of his life, as a convict, was so daunting that he could hardly bear to think about it. But in the end, he always chose to stay. He knew that by fleeing abroad he would be renouncing his epic love for Bosie. Bosie had, Oscar said, taught him 'the divine secret of the world'. To hide, to run away to safety would be to lose the divine secret, to unlearn what had been so painfully learnt. It would be a betrayal of love. 'A dishonoured name, a hunted life are not for me to whom you have been revealed on that high hill where beautiful things are transfigured,' he told Bosie.

Sacrifice, suffering and death had always been part of Oscar's vision of a great love. It was only through sacrifice and suffering – and sometimes death – that the high hill where beautiful things are transfigured could be ascended and the divine secret of love could be revealed. 'Pleasure hides love from us but pain reveals it in its essence,' he told Bosie. Oscar knew that he would suffer and perhaps even die in prison but he was prepared to pay the price – the highest price to find the philosopher's stone of love, to witness the spiritual alchemy which transformed the base metal of human experience into spiritual gold.

Besides which, Oscar's love for Bosie was part of a wider Uranian Cause which saw itself as embattled and besieged by what George Ives called 'all the powers of evil and ignorance'. Ives, Oscar, Bosie and the other initiates of the Order of Chaeronea were a modern-day Theban Band; warriors and lovers willing and prepared to embrace death rather than surrender. Oscar saw his trials and imprisonment not only as necessary tortures, rites of purification on his revelatory ascent towards the summit of the high hill, but also as trials and tests by fire and water of his Uranian faith. He had lived his Uranian faith and now he was ready to die for it. 'To have altered my life,' he wrote to Robbie three years later, 'would have been to have admitted that Uranian love is ignoble. I hold it to be noble – more noble than other forms.'

Oscar saw his trials and imprisonment as a 'monstrous martyrdom', but nevertheless a glorious one. Seven weeks after Oscar's arrest, in a letter to Henry Labouchère, Bosie declared that Oscar had deliberately chosen martyrdom:

> Mr Oscar Wilde is fulfilling another martyrdom for nature's step-children which if it bears fruit as I think it will, in an outburst of educated feeling which has been smouldering in England for years against laws of senseless cruelty and barbarity will not have been in vain.

Oscar sensed that his trial was historic, the first great battle of the modern age between Uranian love and an uncomprehending, persecuting world. Though he may lose the battle, Oscar hoped and prayed that he – or his Sacred Band of fellow Uranians and their descendants – would at last win the war.

Oscar's second trial began on Wednesday 22 May before the seventy-seven-year-old Mr Justice Wills, who, by a strange coincidence, also lived in Tite Street and must have known Oscar by sight. The day before, in a separate trial, Alfred Taylor had been found guilty of gross indecency with both Charles and William Parker. As four of the eight counts of Oscar's indictment concerned acts of gross indecency with Charles Parker, it was almost certain that Oscar, too, would be found guilty. The trial lasted four days and went over much the same ground as the previous trials. Sir Edward Clarke departed from his usual grave demeanour and went as far as he possibly could to suggest that there was some sort of conspiracy against Oscar. He reminded Lockwood that he was not in court 'to try to get a verdict by any means possible'. Clarke also criticised the witnesses who 'in testifying on behalf of the Crown, have secured immunity for past rogueries and indecencies'.

Oscar gave evidence, but he seemed weary and exhausted by the process. He was resigned to the prospect of prison, as he made clear in his last, exquisite letter as a free man to Bosie. 'My sweet rose, my delicate flower, my lily of lilies,' he wrote:

> It is perhaps in prison that I am going to test the power of love. I am going to see if I cannot make the bitter waters sweet by the intensity of the love I bear you.

His soul, he said, was 'the soul of a man who now weeps in hell, and yet carries heaven in his heart':

O sweetest of all boys, most loved of all loves, my soul clings to your soul, my life is your life, and in all the worlds of pain and pleasure you are my ideal of admiration and joy.

The jury was out for two hours. Oscar stood as they filed back into the court. There was a profound, expectant hush. Oscar's face was white with anxiety. When the first of the seven verdicts of 'Guilty' was delivered, Oscar clutched at the front rail of the dock and his body seemed to shake convulsively. Mr Justice Wills did not mince his words in passing sentence on Oscar and on Alfred Taylor, who had joined him in the dock. 'It is the worst case I have ever tried,' he said. It was impossible to doubt that the prisoner Wilde had been at the 'centre of a circle of extensive corruption of the most hideous kind among young men'. Under the circumstances, he said, he would be expected to pass the severest sentence the law allows: two years with hard labour. 'In my judgement it is totally inadequate for such a case as this,' he added.

There were a few gasps at the sentence and some cries of 'Shame' from the public gallery. Oscar seemed temporarily stunned by the sentence. 'And I?' he said hoarsely. 'May I say nothing, my lord?' But Mr Justice Wills merely waved his hand dismissively to warders who hurried the two prisoners out of sight. Oscar's trials were over. But trials of an entirely different kind awaited him in prison.

A foul and dark latrine

'The Oscar trial is ended, and his dream of love is o'er,
And now in jail, he does bewail.
His funny little capers, he won't cut for two years more,
He'll have to start upon a job, he's never done before,
His very tender feelings will be mangled now and torn,
When he has to rise each morn, and grind the golden corn,
And instead of ham and chicken, and such dainty bits of scran,
For dry toke and pint of skilly, he'll be putting out his can.'
— Anonymous street ballad

Though he had spent four weeks on remand in Holloway, Oscar was utterly unprepared for life as a convict. Many years earlier, he had compared the experience of prison to 'a sickness or a spiritual retreat'. 'It purifies and ennobles,' he wrote, 'and the soul emerges from it stronger and more contained.' Now he was about to find out that there was nothing spiritual about prison, that it contaminated rather than purified, degraded rather than ennobled.

Oscar was transported to Pentonville Prison by Black Maria. On arrival there, he was marched to the reception office where his clothes were removed and his personal belongings taken away and catalogued. He was weighed and measured, and then taken to a room where he was told to strip and immerse himself in a large vat of brownish water which smelt strongly of disinfectant. 'It was a fiendish nightmare, more horrible than anything I had ever dreamed of,' Oscar later told Frank Harris. 'They made me undress before them and get into some filthy water they called a bath and dry myself with a damp brown rag and put on this livery of shame.' Next came the prison barber where, once again, Oscar had to strip while his hair was cropped and then closely shaved to remove any possibility of headlice entering the prison. According to an eye witness, he looked 'an awful sight, more like a well-to-do butcher who has served a sentence for fraud than the great dramatic genius of the nineteenth century'.

After the relative comfort of his large, light and airy 'special' cell at Holloway, into which he had been allowed to bring rented furniture, Oscar's

398

cell in Pentonville came as a shock. It was indescribably bleak. 'The cell was appalling,' Oscar told Harris. 'I could hardly breathe in it.' There was only a plank bed – a bare board with no mattress, raised a few inches above the floor – where Oscar would be forced to sleep for the next three months. He was given a sheet, two blankets and a coverlet. There was a small bucket in which he could urinate and defecate, which had to be slopped out each morning. Often, these buckets became so full and overflowing that many warders reported retching when they first opened the cells in the mornings.

Oscar was examined by the prison doctor and passed as sound for 'first-class hard labour'. Hard labour was designed to punish the prisoner physically and, perhaps more importantly, to elevate him morally. Oscar was forty-one when he went to prison. He had taken no exercise for years and was in no fit state to undergo a gruelling programme of hard labour. During his first month in prison, he was expected to spend no less than six hours each day on the treadwheel, a giant fixed wheel, like the wheel of a watermill, only propelled by the steps of prisoners rather than by the flow of water. It was a pointless exercise, rather like climbing an endless flight of stairs, and never reaching the top. Prisoners were expected to tread the wheel twenty minutes on and five minutes off. For the first three days, Oscar trod the wheel diligently and without complaint. On the fourth day he succumbed to a violent and prolonged attack of diarrhoea. 'The food turned my stomach,' he told Harris. 'The smell and sight of it were enough':

> I did not eat anything for days and days and days, I could not even swallow the bread; and the rest of the food was uneatable; I lay on the so-called bed and shivered all night long . . . After some days I got so hungry I had to eat a little, nibble at the outside of the bread, and drink some of the liquid; whether it was tea, coffee or gruel I could not tell. As soon as I really ate anything it produced violent diarrhoea, and I was ill all day and all night.

When he eventually came out of prison, Oscar met George Ives in Paris and talked extensively about his prison experiences. 'The first year of prison killed me, body and soul,' he told Ives. 'Prison,' he said, 'was a four-fold torture: insomnia from the plank bed, starvation, "sanitation", insanity.' Ives went on to explain in detail what 'dear Oscar' had meant by 'sanitation':

> It seems that diarrhoea is common if not universal from the prison food. And after 5pm no man may leave his cell until the next morning upon any pretext. There are three utensils: one for washing, one for drinking and water, one for purposes of nature. The last only may be used for that purpose and it is too small, so that with bowel trouble pressing there's no means of evacuation.

Oscar's diarrhoea was accompanied by what newspaper reports called 'mental prostration and melancholy'. According to the *Morning* of 6 June, the prison authorities paid little attention to his condition:

It was put down to what is known as 'a prison head' – a complaint most new prisoners suffer from owing to the preliminary dose of bromide of potassium. This drug is said to produce in some people extreme melancholia. As soon as Wilde's case was diagnosed, the doctor discontinued the use of the drug, but his condition did not improve, and he was thought to be in such a bad state that he was removed to the infirmary, where he was placed in a bed surrounded by screens, and watched night and day.

Not for the last time, the prison authorities were worried that Oscar might attempt to take his own life. There was no doubt that he had strong suicidal impulses. 'For the first six months I was so dreadfully unhappy that I longed to kill myself,' Oscar told André Gide after he came out of prison.

It was rumoured in some newspapers that Oscar had already become insane. News of his mental collapse reached the ears of Asquith, the Home Secretary, who had been a friend of Oscar's before the fall. Asquith ordered an immediate medical examination. This was carried out by the prison's Medical Officer, who denied that Oscar had been placed in the prison infirmary or in the padded cell kept for prisoners who were insane or violent. Oscar's condition had 'given no anxiety', the Medical Officer reported to Asquith:

> He was placed under observation on first reception for seven days to be specially watched, as is frequently done with prisoners owing to depression and mental strain of their trial and sentence. With the exception of a little relaxed throat, for which he had been treated, he is in good health and perfectly sane.

But still the rumours persisted that Wilde's physical and mental health were deteriorating. Some of the more experienced prison officers doubted that Oscar would survive his two-year sentence.

As Oscar's health deteriorated, that of Lord Rosebery improved dramatically. Right up to the time of Oscar's imprisonment towards the end of May, it seemed that Rosebery's health was worsening. Newspapers reported that Rosebery's 'memory suddenly failed him in a very painful fashion, leaving him unable to proceed with his argument' in the middle of a speech at the National Liberal Club on 8 May. 'What was I saying?' he floundered. 'What was it I have just said?' To his audience, Rosebery's lapse of memory was disturbing and suggested that he was losing his grip on reality. In the week of Oscar's second trial, the press was full of stories of the Prime Minister's ill-health, and there were strong rumours that he was on the brink of resignation. Then, on Tuesday 28 May, just three days after Oscar's conviction, Sir Edward Hamilton recorded in his diary, 'Rosebery seems better.' On the face of it, it seemed a miracle. But to Bosie, Trelawny Backhouse, More Adey and others who believed that there was a government conspiracy behind Oscar's prosecution and conviction, Rosebery's sudden and coincidental return to health and spirits lent further weight to their case.

Suspicions were fuelled when, after sacrificing Oscar to save himself, a remorseful Rosebery sought to help the man he had destroyed, or so Trelawny Backhouse claimed. Rosebery's closest political ally was Richard Burdon Haldane MP QC, who had recently served on a Parliamentary enquiry into the country's penal system. On 14 June Haldane went, supposedly at Rosebery's request, to Pentonville to see Oscar. 'I had a long talk with him,' Haldane wrote to his mother the same day. 'He broke down and cried. I think I put a little hope into his heart and have been able to make some arrangements for him.' Four days later, on 16 June, Haldane spent the morning closeted with Rosebery before going on to meet with 'the family of Oscar Wilde' in the afternoon. Haldane does not specify which members of the family were present, but Constance was almost certainly there. She had not, in fact, gone abroad but had stayed in London for Oscar's second trial and for the first weeks of his imprisonment. Other family members may well have included Constance's brother Otho and Oscar's brother Willie. 'This is a sordid case,' Haldane told his mother after the meeting, 'and one wishes to lighten the burden as far as one can.'

'Make arrangements' and 'lightening the burden'. Was Haldane carrying out the wishes of his friend and political ally, Rosebery? Certainly what fragments of correspondence remain strongly suggest that Haldane's role during Oscar's imprisonment was much more substantial than he later admitted publicly. He seems to have acted as Oscar's unofficial advocate, quietly pressurising the prison authorities to grant him extra privileges and liaising with Oscar's friends and family, advising them what steps to try and take to secure his early release. 'I have been in private communication with the authorities,' Haldane wrote to More Adey in December 1895. Four weeks later, he wrote to Adey again in terms which suggest that there were behind-the-scenes efforts being made on the part of the government to look after Oscar's health and well-being. 'The authorities are looking carefully after him but they must not be thought to be giving differential treatment further than his condition requires,' wrote Haldane. When Adey sent a copy of this letter to Oscar's friend Adela Schuster, or 'Miss Tiny' as Oscar had dubbed her on account of her largeness, he swore her to secrecy and asked her to destroy the letter.

The following year Adey wrote to Constance suggesting that she make a private appeal to the Home Secretary for Oscar's release. A draft of Adey's letter survives, written in his spidery handwriting with many crossings-out and emendations:

For the last 10 months I have been working hard to obtain Oscar's release and was in private communication with the Home Office as long ago as last November. Circumstances have since placed me in further communication with several Members of Parliament and other influential people who have already done [much] on Oscar's behalf since his imprisonment. They urge me to represent to you that a private letter from you to the Home Secretary *is likely, especially at this particular time*, to have great weight with him. At the same time, they impress upon me the necessity for strict secrecy concerning any appeals, as being essential to their success.

It is clear from this letter that there was a considerable amount of secret political activity to try and free Oscar, or at least to curtail his sentence, as well as to ease the terrible daily discomforts of prison life.

Adey spent the first weeks of Oscar's imprisonment with Bosie and Robbie Ross in Rouen, in the Hôtel de la Poste where a small group of English Uranian exiles had gathered. Like Bosie, Adey was convinced that there had been a conspiracy to send Oscar to prison. From Rouen, he drafted a *résumé* of his theories about Oscar's conviction to an unnamed French journalist, offering 'the following suggestion':

It has long been reported that a person – indeed several persons – *but one in particular, in very high authority* has been implicated in uni-sexual practices which are in England illegal.

Short of spelling out Rosebery's name, Adey could hardly make it any plainer that he was talking about the Prime Minister. 'I am certain,' he continued:

that the Treasury were faced by a body of private persons, some of whose names I know, headed by the infamous Lord Queensberry, to obtain a conviction by some means or other against Mr Wilde. These individuals, I believe, *blackmailed* the Treasury, holding over the Treasury the threat that, if Wilde were not convicted, damning evidence would be produced against important and exalted persons.

'I trust you may see your way to point out clearly and to insist,' Adey wrote to the journalist, 'that whether Mr Wilde was addicted to uni-sexual vice or not, he was convicted on insufficient and tainted evidence for political purposes.'

Adey decided not to send this letter, but kept it, marking it 'letter never sent'. Unlike Bosie, Adey was reasonably discreet and thought that more could be achieved by quiet and persistent lobbying. There was another reason why he may have decided not to send the letter. If he had sought to expose and embarrass a corrupt and conspiratorial Liberal government, he was too late. As Adey was writing his letter, Rosebery's fragile Liberal government imploded and a snap general election was called. Rosebery was voted out of office. If the conspiracy theorists were correct and Oscar's conviction was the consequence of a conspiracy to save Rosebery and keep the Liberal government in power, it had ironically only managed to prolong its life by less than a month.

Bosie, meanwhile, had launched a vigorous campaign, both public and private, to try and ease Oscar's burden, to seek his release and to bring about social and legal emancipation for vexed and persecuted Uranians. After Henry Labouchère had publicly called for Bosie to be given the 'opportunity to meditate' on his crimes 'in the seclusion of Pentonville Prison', Bosie initiated an angry and impassioned private correspondence with Labby on the subject of Uranian love, writing to him on 9 June:

> These tastes are perfectly natural congenital tendencies in certain people (a very large minority) and . . . the law has no right to interfere with these people provided they do not harm other people; that is to say, when there is neither seduction of minors or brutalization and where there is no public outrage on morals.

Bosie ended his letter with a defiantly Uranian clarion call. 'I confess I have not many hopes of the present age,' he wrote, '*but ultimate liberation* from conventional slavery and tyranny is as inevitable as death.'

Three weeks later, Bosie took up the Uranian cudgels again in a letter to the *Review of Reviews*:

> Why on earth in the name of liberty and common sense a man cannot be allowed to love a boy, rather than a woman when his nature and his instinct tell him to do so, and when he has before him the example of such a number of noble and gifted men who have had similar tastes (such as Shakespeare, Marlowe, Michael Angelo, Frederick the Great, and a host of others), is another question and one to which I should like to hear a satisfactory answer.

At the same time he addressed a lengthy petition to Queen Victoria, appealing for her to exercise her power of pardon for Oscar 'the poet and dramatist who now lies in prison, unjustly convicted by the force of prejudice'. Perhaps wisely, Bosie did not suggest to the Queen that senior members of Her Majesty's government had conspired to send Oscar to prison, merely confining himself to a ritual denunciation of his father. Oscar had, he said, fallen victim 'to the spite and unscrupulous cunning of another man, the Marquis of Queensberry, whose son I have the misfortune to be'.

Bosie wrote to his brother Percy urging him to use the family's political contacts to help Oscar. 'As soon as this conservative government comes in something must be done,' he told Percy:

> Please don't give up trying, for my sake. These things can always be managed somehow, only it wants obstinacy. All these relations of ours could do anything.

He also asked Percy to see what could be done in the way of bribery and corruption. 'Do old chap see if you can't do something about bribing the warders at Pentonville. I hear that much can be done, in the way of getting food in et cet: sent in. I have bad moments sometimes when I can neither eat nor sleep for thinking of him.' Percy presumably obliged. A few weeks later, the new Tory Home Secretary, Sir Matthew Ridley, wrote to Evelyn Ruggles-Brise, Chairman of the Prison Commission, and the man in charge of the nation's prisons, to say that his predecessor had been told 'that there were suspicions that the Officers of Pentonville Prison were being tampered with by O. Wilde's friends'. Ridley went on to say that Oscar was 'for this reason removed to Wandsworth'.

Oscar had been moved to Wandsworth on 4 July. His premature removal there also foiled an audacious plot by a group calling themselves 'The Few American Friends' based in New York. In September, the Governor of Pentonville, Mr J.B. Manning, received an extraordinary letter written in pencil from the 'Friends', offering him 'one hundred thousand pounds in English gold' if he would 'set the poet free' – and 'half that sum for the liberation of Taylor'. The 'Friends' said they were concerned about preserving Oscar's literary ability:

> Should Wilde serve his sentence in prison he will get so tainted with the abominations of prison-life so as not to be able to shake it off, and his poetic power will be lost and he will be irretrievably ruined. We think he should be set at liberty.

Whether this was their only motive is unlikely. The 'Friends' were much more likely to be wealthy American Uranians who were prepared to pay almost any price to free a man they regarded as a prophet. 'All you have to do,' they told Manning, 'is to pay some people in the prison to look the other way':

> Use the personal column of the 'New York Herald'. Wipe this communication out, only preserving the piece of paper on which it is written for purposes of identification when we make a full settlement with you. Spare no expense. We will pay all and more than you can use over the amount in full herein stated. Act Promptly, if not forget that you have received this, so the matter will go no further.

Oscar was to spend five months in Wandsworth where, if anything, his condition seemed to worsen. The chaplain at Wandsworth, W.D. Morrison, was an ardent campaigner for prison reform, and took a special interest in Oscar. Morrison wrote that Oscar was in 'an excited flurried condition', when he first arrived at Wandsworth, 'and seemed as if he wished to face his punishment without flinching'. But, after a few weeks there, 'it was easy for the experienced eye to see that this man would break down long before his sentence came to an end'. Morrison preached patience. 'I could be patient, for patience is a virtue,' Oscar retorted. 'It is not patience, it is apathy you want here and apathy is a vice.'

It was not long before Morrison had some disturbing intelligence to report. On 11 September he wrote privately to Haldane to inform him that Oscar was masturbating compulsively in his cell:

He is now quite crushed and broken. This is unfortunate as a prisoner who breaks down in one direction generally breaks down in several, and I fear that from what I hear and see that perverse sexual practices are again getting the mastery over him. This is a common occurrence among prisoners of his class and is of course favoured by constant cellular isolation. The odour of his cell is now so bad that the officer in charge of him has to use carbolic in it every other day.

In Pentonville, Oscar had been dosed with bromide of potassium, which was given to prisoners to suppress their libido. But the drug had been discontinued after a few days because it was thought to be contributing to Oscar's depression. Without bromide of potassium, Oscar's libido would have been as high as ever, and it would, perhaps, have been surprising had he not sought relief from sexual tension through masturbation.

Masturbation was not a trivial issue for the authorities. In the latter half of the nineteenth century, it was regarded as not only a pernicious and debilitating vice, but increasingly as both a symptom and a cause of insanity. David Skae, the eminent Scottish doctor and President of the Association of Medical Officers of Asylums and Hospitals for the Insane, was the first to categorise 'masturbatory insanity' as a separate and distinct mental illness in 1863. Masturbation in prison was regarded as a form of insanity, and the 1895 report from the Departmental Committee on Prisons recorded several cases of prisoners given over to masturbation in Wandsworth and Wormwood Scrubs:

Male aged 48. – Found in an enclosed yard. No insane record. Health good on admission. No morbid symptom for *two months*. On second-class labour. Then symptoms of excitability showed themselves, was self-abuse; soon became acutely maniacal and was removed to asylum.

Male aged 25. – Felony. No insane record. Sound on admission, and so continued for *14 months*. Then became strange in manner and was placed under observation. In a few weeks was certified insane. His disease was connected with self-abuse. His diet was liberal throughout, and he was working in association when the symptoms occurred.

Female aged 20. – Rogue and vagabond. No insane record. Of vicious tendencies and antecedents. Showed moral perversity of a kind that for some time obscured the mental symptoms. These last became however sufficiently aggravated to warrant certificate of insanity.

In each case, masturbation led to a diagnosis of insanity and removal to either a local madhouse or to a prison for the criminally insane – most probably Broadmoor. Oscar's situation was serious. If he was masturbating compulsively, then the prison authorities would have a strong case for declaring him insane and sending him too to Broadmoor.

This outcome would be a disaster for Oscar, but also a terrible embarrassment for the prison service and the government, as Morrison pointed out to Haldane:

The practical question is what should be done? If he were to go off his head under cellular discipline it is almost certain to arouse a good deal of indignation in the public mind and the authorities will no doubt be blamed for allowing such a thing to happen. This contingency should if possible be avoided.

Haldane thought the matter sufficiently serious to inform the Home Secretary, Sir Matthew Ridley, who treated the allegations very seriously, summoning Morrison to the Home Office. Morrison told the Home Secretary that he was convinced that Oscar was masturbating compulsively. After seeing Morrison, Ridley took the extraordinary step of summoning the warder in charge of Oscar's cell to the Home Office to personally cross-question him about Oscar's supposed masturbation. Ridley also instructed the Medical Inspector of Prisons, Dr Gover, to look into the matter. Gover visited Wandsworth on 20 September and examined Oscar in the presence of the prison doctor, Dr Quinton. He reported that there was 'not the slightest evidence that Wilde is yielding to perverse sexual practices – self-abuse is *not* common among prisoners of his class, as Mr Morrison alleges'. On 7 October Ridley wrote to Haldane:

> I have seen Mr Morrison, who adheres to his statements in spite of the medical evidence, which is supported also by that of the Prison Doctor, Dr Quinton, who enjoys a very high reputation for professional acumen. The warder in charge of Oscar Wilde's cell tells me that he had noticed a curious smell, and that he had mentioned it in conversation with the Chaplain. You will see that Dr Gover accounts for this smell by the use of Jeyes purifying fluid.

Ridley's letter smacks of a cover-up. Jeyes purifying fluid was a disinfectant made from coal tar, and it would be hard for Dr Gover to confuse the distinctly balsamic, antiseptic tang of coal tar, with the sickly sweet smell of commingled sweat and semen in a confined space. Besides which, Morrison had no reason to lie. He had sought Haldane's help in the matter knowing that Oscar was at very real risk of being declared insane if it was proved that he was masturbating compulsively.

Nine months later, in a petition to the Home Secretary requesting that his sentence be commuted, Oscar as good as admitted to compulsive masturbation when he described how the system of almost constant solitary confinement made him 'the sure prey of morbid passions, and obscene fancies, and thoughts that defile, desecrate and destroy'. And in his epic poem of prison life, 'The Ballad of Reading Gaol', Oscar obliquely acknowledged the powerful impulse to masturbate in prison:

> Each narrow cell in which we dwell
> Is a foul and dark latrine,

And the fetid breath of living Death
    Chokes up each grated screen,
And all, but Lust, is turned to Dust
    In humanity's machine.

Masturbation may have been the only release for Oscar in the grave new world where he found himself, the only form of pleasure available to him in the living hell of Wandsworth. Not only that. It might have been the only tangible way to affirm his love for Bosie and his identity as a Uranian. 'I sat amidst the ruins of my wonderful life, crushed by anguish, bewildered with terror, dazed through pain,' Oscar recalled in *De Profundis*:

> Every day I said to myself, 'I must keep love in my heart today, else how shall I live through the day?'

Was Oscar's compulsive masturbation an outpouring of lust, a brute and defiant expression of the seed of life in a place where the fetid breath of living Death was omnipresent? Or was it an attempt to recreate and remember the Arcadian erotic landscape of life before the fall, to rekindle what now seemed the far distant echoes of his love for Bosie? Or a strange amalgam of both?

Oscar's mental and physical health continued to deteriorate inexorably. When Oscar left Wandsworth briefly to attend his bankruptcy hearing in early October, his old friend, the solicitor Arthur Clifton, was present and managed to have a short conversation with him:

> I was very much shocked at Oscar's appearance, though scarcely surprised . . . his hair was rather long and he looked dreadfully thin . . . he was very much upset and cried a great deal: he seemed quite broken-hearted and kept on describing his punishment as savage.

A week later, on Sunday 13 October, Oscar collapsed during a service in the prison chapel. He had woken that morning and had been unable to stand. Dr Quinton was called, contented himself with telling Oscar that he would be punished for malingering if he refused to get up. Oscar forced himself to get up, falling over and bruising himself while he was dressing, and managed to walk shakily to the chapel. 'I could hardly stand up,' he told Frank Harris later. 'Everything kept disappearing and coming back faintly; and suddenly I must have fallen.'

Oscar woke up in the prison infirmary with a pain in his ear where he had bumped himself as he had fallen. He was suffering from severe dysentery. 'I saw him at the Infirmary at Wandsworth on Monday,' Robert Sherard told More Adey. 'He is a perfect wreck and says he will be dead before long.' Lily Wilde, Oscar's sister-in-law, also visited him in the infirmary. 'I sat with Oscar yesterday for 3/4 of an hour,' she wrote to More Adey:

He is suffering from dysentery brought on I should say by great bodily weakness. He is hungry but cannot eat the food and at present is only allowed a little beef tea. Mentally he is very unhappy and indeed what else could he be. He is very altered in *every* way more I cannot tell you. He seemed gratified when I told him how you had kindly come up to give me news of him. The whole interview has made me more than sad.

Robbie Ross saw Oscar at the next bankruptcy hearing and managed to speak to him for a few minutes. Oscar's 'mind is considerably impaired', a shocked Robbie told Oscar Browning:

Physically he was much worse than anyone had led me to believe. Indeed I really should not have known him at all. This I know is an ordinary figure of speech, but it exactly describes what I experienced. His clothes hung about him in loose folds and his hands are like those of a skeleton. The contour of his face is completely changed . . . He is still in the infirmary but told me he wanted to leave as he hoped to die very soon. Indeed he only spoke calmly about death. Every other subject caused him to break down.

Oscar's dysentery could be treated with drugs, plenty of rest and a nutritious diet. But his mental state, in particular his obsession with the subject of death and dying, was giving rise to considerable alarm. Haldane again took up the cudgels on Oscar's behalf and alerted the Home Secretary to his mental condition. Sir Matthew Ridley instructed two of the country's leading experts on criminal lunacy, Dr David Nicholson, Superintendent of Broadmoor, and Dr Richard Bryan, also of Broadmoor, to assess Oscar's mental state, paying particular attention to whether or not there was any 'moral derangement', a coded reference to compulsive masturbation. They saw Oscar on 22 October and wrote their report a week later. The report has survived and makes fascinating reading:

His history before imprisonment shows that he had the birth and education of a gentleman, and that his intellectual capacity was of a high order, as evidenced by the success which his novels, plays, and other writings met with. He busied himself in seeing to the rehearsal and proper stage rendering of his own plays, he possessed a great fund both of general information and of worldly knowledge. He also posed as the 'apostle' of art and culture, more especially as was seen in an aestheticism which was the outcome of an almost childish vanity.

On the other hand, with all his ability and while he gloried in being, as he was, in some sort, a social pet and pattern, he lived a life of the grossest self-indulgence, and practised the most disgusting and odious criminal offences with others of his own sex and that too not with one or two individuals of a better station in life, but apparently with the most casual acquaintances of comparatively low social position. He exhibited these depraved tastes and led this double life for years before his arrest and trial.

What seemed to shock Nicholson and Bryan most was that Oscar had enjoyed casual sex with working-class boys. 'During our interview with him,' their report continued, Oscar:

> entered freely into the circumstances of his past history, more especially as they had relation to his present position which he appeared to feel acutely, and upon which he dilated with great fervour and some amount of emotional depression, occasionally accompanied by tears. This display of feeling was no doubt referable, as he himself gave us to understand, to remorseful and bitter thoughts of the blasting of his future by the abominable follies of the past, and we do not regard this as being either unnatural or as indicating moral derangement.

Oscar was not mad, only bad. It was his bodily health which required attention, not his mind. They informed Sir Matthew Ridley that 'with careful treatment and, shortly removal to a Prison in the country, with different work and a greater range of reading there is nothing to indicate that prison will prejudicially affect him'. They also recommended that Oscar 'be allowed such association with other prisoners as may be deemed advisable or desirable or convenient'. But Nicholson and Bryan added a caveat to their recommendation:

> It would not however be right to allow a man with his proclivities and with his avowed love for the society of males, to be in association *except under the continuous supervision of a warder.*

Ridley and Ruggles-Brise accepted the recommendations of the report. 'Oscar Wilde will be removed tomorrow to Reading Prison where suitable occupation in the way of gardening and bookbinding and library work will be found for him,' Ruggles-Brise wrote in a memorandum on 19 November. 'I have so informed Mr Haldane privately sending him a copy of the medical report.'

Reading Gaol was built on the site of a former leper colony and was, perhaps ironically, an appropriate choice for the social and sexual leper that Oscar had become. His first, nightmarish six months in prison were over, and he was to spend the remaining eighteen months of his sentence as prisoner C.3.3, the name taken from the cell he occupied, the third cell on the third-storey gallery of Block C.

Bitter waters

'Those who are faithful know only the trivial side of love: it is the faithless who know love's tragedies.'

Almost from the day of Oscar's arrest in April, Constance had been determined to divorce him. In June, shortly after her arrival in Switzerland where she had gone to live in self-imposed exile with Cyril and Vyvyan, Constance wrote to her old friend Emily Thursfield to tell her of her plans. 'I have to sue for a divorce because the boys must be free,' she wrote:

> and I cannot get a separation. I have not the legal claims for that, and on account of the way he has behaved about money affairs no-one would trust him to look after the boys if anything should happen to me and he got control of my money.

Despite her determination to end the marriage, Constance's generous and forgiving heart was far from being turned to stone. In the midst of her own misfortunes, she could still feel for Oscar. 'I have been quite broken-hearted,' she told Emily. 'It is so terrible to be here free in the heavenly air, and to think of those four walls round him.' She planned to return to London towards the end of the year – hopefully, she said, to give evidence in divorce proceedings.

After three months in prison, Oscar was entitled to receive his first visit, and on 26 August the ever-loyal Robert Sherard – 'the bravest and most chivalrous of all brilliant beings', Oscar called him in *De Profundis* – came to see him. The visiting order was for two people, but Sherard went alone, claiming that he could not find any of Oscar's friends to accompany him. Sherard noticed that Oscar's 'hands were disfigured, and that his nails were broken and bleeding; also that his head and face were untidy with growth of hair'. Oscar was, he realised, 'greatly depressed, and at one time had tears in his eyes'.

Sherard tentatively broached the subject of Constance. He had decided to take upon himself the task of bringing about a reconciliation between Oscar and Constance. He had never been able to comprehend Oscar's sexual attraction to young men, and was convinced that he was suffering from a species of insanity. 'The only hope of salvation in this world for my friend,' Sherard wrote shortly afterwards, 'is in his being able to return to his wife,

410

after the completion of his sentence.' Sherard began his campaign of reconciliation by initiating a correspondence between himself and Constance to try and find out what it would take for her to draw back from the brink of divorce. In his self-appointed mission to save the Wildes' marriage, Sherard was aided – knowingly or unknowingly – by Constance's brother, Otho, who wrote the first letter which Oscar received in prison in late August, at the same time as Sherard's visit. Otho pleaded with Oscar to do everything in his power to avert the threatened divorce. If Oscar 'would only write once' to Constance and beg her forgiveness, he was convinced she would cease proceedings for divorce.

Oscar took Otho's advice and wrote a long letter to Constance, the text of which has not survived. Whatever it was he told her touched her deeply. She was beginning to waver on the question of divorce, but still she doubted whether Oscar's expressions of regret and contrition and his promises for the future were sincere. To resolve the matter, Constance decided she would go and see him in Wandsworth. She had to apply to the Prison Commissioners for exceptional leave to visit him. 'My husband, I have reason to know, is apprehensive of my obtaining a divorce from him within a short time,' she wrote:

> As my mind is not however definitely made up to this step, but is dependent on questions which can only be properly discussed between him and me personally, I am most anxious to be allowed to talk over matters with him and discuss the arrangements, business and others of an intimate nature, by which so extreme a step might be avoided.

Permission was granted, and Constance made the long journey to London in the company of Miss Boxwell, a new friend whom she had met in Switzerland.

Constance saw Oscar on 21 September and was shocked by what she found: shocked at his state, and shocked by the degrading and grim conditions of the convict prison. Immediately on her return to Miss Boxwell's flat where she was staying, Constance sat down and wrote to Sherard:

> It was indeed awful, more so than I had any conception it could be. I could not see him and I could not touch him, and I scarcely spoke . . . When I go again, I am to get at the Home Secretary through Mr Haldane and try to get a room to see him in and touch him again. He says he has been mad these last three years, and he says that if he saw Alfred Douglas he would kill him. So he had better keep away and be satisfied with having marred a fine life. Few people can boast so much.

Constance's description of Oscar's life as 'fine' and her desire to 'touch him again' showed she was still, despite everything, deeply in love with him. It is clear from her letter that they had discussed at least some of those questions of 'an intimate nature' which Constance needed the answers to before she could

411

rescind the divorce proceedings. Bosie was the main bone of contention between them. Did Oscar still love him? And what guarantees could he give her that he would not go back to Bosie and to his old way of life when he was released from prison?

Oscar's answers were satisfactory, more than satisfactory. They were music to her ears. Oscar had been insane, the victim of an erotic madness, for which Bosie was to blame. Now in prison, he could see the truth of things and bitterly repented the past. The love between Oscar and Constance, so profound and precious to her, had survived its darkest hour, and the evil Bosie was seemingly vanquished. Oscar promised her that he would not see or communicate with Bosie or Robbie or with any of his former Uranian friends. Back in Switzerland, Constance confided her hopes and fears to Emily Thursfield:

> I do not wish to sever myself entirely from Mr Wilde who is in the very lowest depths of misery. And he is very repentant and minds most of all what he has brought on myself and the boys. It seems to me (and to many others too) that by sticking to him now, I may save him from even worse, and I believe that he cares now for no-one but myself and the children. This is the opinion of the prison authorities and no-one can just now know him so well. At the same time I am quite aware that I am running a certain, possibly a very great risk . . . But, dearest Emily, I think we women are meant for comforters and I believe no-one can really take my place now, or help him as I can.

It is hard to know whether Oscar's visceral expressions of hatred for Bosie and his repudiation of his Uranian past represented a genuine change of heart, or were merely a calculated expedient designed to soothe Constance's righteous indignation and avert a divorce. A divorce would be catastrophic for Oscar. Not only would it mean severing his links with Cyril and Vyvyan, but it would open up the threat of a further – and perhaps more serious – prosecution against him. Constance would have to produce grounds for the divorce, and new evidence of sexual liaisons might come to light. Oscar faced the appalling prospect of being released from prison, re-arrested and returned to prison. And if the new evidence included allegations of sodomy, he would most likely rot in prison for the rest of his life.

Oscar's instinct for self-preservation must have had some influence on his changed attitudes. But Oscar was going through a profound and painful change in his feelings for Bosie. Faced with the full horror of prison life, its humiliations, its privations and its mental tortures of loneliness and loss of selfhood, he was beginning to feel irritation and resentment at the idea of Bosie flying free under the blue skies of the Mediterranean – even though paradoxically it had been Oscar himself who, before his trial began, had begged Bosie to flee abroad.

Robert Sherard's second visit to Wandsworth, which took place three weeks after Constance had visited Oscar, helped to crystallise Oscar's mood of bitter resentment against Bosie. Using the pseudonym Kennedy, Sherard had applied for special permission to visit Oscar as part of his ongoing mission to try and avert Constance's threatened divorce proceedings. Much of the hour-long visit in a private room was taken up by Sherard's news that Bosie had written, and was about to publish, an article on Oscar in the French literary magazine *Mercure de France*. He had heard rumours that Bosie was intending to quote from some of the love letters Oscar had sent to him during the trials, and that the article was to be 'an apology for, and a glorification of, "The Greek Movement"'. He wanted to know if Oscar knew about it, and whether or not he approved of it. Oscar most certainly did not approve. 'I was greatly taken aback, and much annoyed, and gave orders that the thing was to be stopped at once,' he wrote angrily in *De Profundis*:

> You had left my letters lying about for blackmailing companions to steal, for hotel servants to pilfer, for housemaids to sell. That was simply your careless want of appreciation for what I had written you. But that you should seriously propose to publish selections from the balance was almost incredible to me.

Sherard wrote an indignant and 'violent' letter to Bosie telling him to withdraw the article from publication. He also wrote to the editor of the *Mercure de France* to inform him of Oscar's vehement opposition to the idea.

Sherard's interference was the first of several wedges driven between Oscar and Bosie by himself and by others. But the action turned out to be more timely than anyone had imagined. Bosie had planned his article as a passionate proclamation that he and Oscar were lovers in both a spiritual and a physical sense: 'Let my enemies interpret as they will!' Bosie proudly declared. 'I say now quite frankly that our friendship was love, real love – Love, it is true, perfectly pure but extremely passionate.' There was more. Bosie went on to produce a detailed and full-blooded *exposé* of the government conspiracy against Oscar. 'What then was the secret of this determination to obtain his condemnation at any cost? Why did the government evince such a thirst for his blood?' demanded Bosie:

> I may perhaps be allowed to advance a theory. I give it for what it is worth, but I can say that it is not merely a hypothesis. I did not invent it; I have heard it on good authority that the Government was intimidated. Mr Wilde's enemies and the Queensberry faction threatened to make new revelations incriminating senior members of the ruling party if Mr Wilde would not be condemned . . .

In short, Bosie thundered, Oscar '*was sacrificed to save the reputation of a party*'. It was explosive stuff and, if it had ever been published, would have almost certainly dashed any hopes Oscar might have for a remission of his sentence.

In the days and weeks that followed, Oscar's heart was further hardened against Bosie by various snippets of intelligence about Bosie's private life gleaned from Robbie Ross and More Adey, who had both spent time abroad with Bosie and remained in close contact with him. After several months in prison of almost continuous suicidal thoughts, and suffering from almost constant ill-health in the form of diarrhoea and dysentery, it was galling for Oscar to have to hear the details of Bosie's slow peregrination across Europe, following the sun southwards through France and down to Sorrento, Naples and Capri. It was even more galling for him to make a mosaic from the fragments he heard of Bosie's joyous hedonism and his continuing dedication to the 'eternal quest for beauty'.

Shortly after going over to France, Bosie had spent nearly three weeks in the company of Charlie Hickey, who was by all accounts a delightful young man – 'one of the thousand Charlies of London', Oscar had described him, 'all flowers of the narcissus kind'. Charlie Hickey was very attractive and very generous with his sexual favours. He had certainly slept with Oscar, with Bosie, with Reggie Turner, and quite probably with Robbie Ross and More Adey as well. After Charlie left France and returned to England, Bosie spent some time with Lionel Johnson and with More Adey, before proceeding to Le Havre where he became embroiled in a little local difficulty over two boys he had hired as deckhands for the small yacht he used to take out. Bosie wrote to his brother Percy, telling him that there had been paragraphs in the local newspaper and that he had received a series of anonymous letters:

> warning me that police and detectives were watching me day and night and that at the smallest chance of an excuse they had they would '*désembarquer*' me: that is expel me from France and send me back to England!

Bosie was in Sorrento in August where he wrote his article on Oscar for the *Mercure de France*. Thankfully, there were some Uranian distractions in the form of cock-sucking boys, one of whom was passed on to Robbie. 'Am surprised at not hearing from Bobbie to whom I sent a gourmet of great personal beauty,' he wrote to More Adey. In September Bosie took a small villa in Capri where he wrote a beautiful sonnet, 'To Sleep', which spoke of his inner turmoil. Sleep, Bosie wrote, was not 'a balm for bruised hearts', but rather a nightmare:

> I dread the summons to that fierce assize
> Of all my foes and woes, that waits me when
> Thou mak'st my soul the unwilling denizen
> Of thy dim troubled house where unrest lies.

The poems Bosie wrote during Oscar's imprisonment are among his finest and are replete with mournful images of loss, despair and death. In 'Vae Victis!', also written in Capri, Bosie wrote:

> But vainly, alas!
> Do I hide in the south,
> Kiss close with my mouth
> Red flowers, green grass,
> For Autumn has found me
> And thrown her arms around me.
> She has breathed on my lips and I wander apart,
> Dead leaves in my heart.

But life in Capri also had its share of lighter domestic incident, as Bosie joyfully told Ada Leverson:

> I have just had a slight domestic tragedy. The boy has complained that the advances of the cook have been insupportable, the cook on the other hand declares that life is insupportable to him without love, both are now weeping. What am I to do? I sympathise with the cook, but I am in a responsible position.

As he was settling into the villa in Capri, it gradually became clear to Bosie that there was a problem with Oscar. The first inkling came when the Governor of Wandsworth Prison wrote to inform him that Oscar had declined to receive a letter from him. 'I can't make it out at all,' he told Ada Leverson on 13 September:

> It appears from the letter that Oscar *had* the power to correspond with me but that he deliberately preferred not to. Can you throw any light on the question? . . . I am so upset and perplexed by it all. It seems impossible to find out what is really happening. I am so afraid that some secret influence has been brought to bear on Oscar, or that he has been told some lie about me. It seems to me *quite inconceivable* that he should prefer to correspond with his 'family' than with me without some very strong reason of which I know nothing. Altogether I am in utter misery and despair.

Bosie followed this letter up with several others. 'I have had frantic letters from Bosie,' Ada Leverson told More Adey five days later. 'It seems Oscar had the opportunity of writing to him but reserved the right to correspond with his wife. Bosie is of course much distressed about this. I have just written to him trying to calm him down. I daresay he is very lonely.' And, on 21 September, Bosie wrote to Sherard, unaware that Sherard was intent on breaking up his friendship with Oscar. He included a message for Oscar:

> Tell him from me that I love him and only living to see him again and that if he dies in prison or ceases to love me I shall kill myself too, for I have nothing else to live for, and even as it is the burden of living is almost insupportable . . . I wish you could make Oscar know how much I think of him and how I

long for him. I have taken a villa here: tell him his room is all ready and waiting for him.

Robbie Ross joined Bosie in Capri in November and confirmed all Bosie's worst suspicions. Much to Bosie's fury, Robbie revealed that Oscar's feelings for him had changed and that he was intent on a reconciliation with Constance. 'How can he expect anything from his wife?' demanded Bosie angrily in a letter to More Adey on 30 November. 'What did she do for him when he was in trouble and how can he have changed so?' Bosie pleaded with Adey to intercede on his behalf with Oscar:

I am writing to you now, dear More, unknown to Bobbie, to beg you to do what you can for me with Oscar. If only you could make him understand that though he is in prison he is still the court, the jury, the judge of my life and that I am waiting hoping for some sign that I have to go on living. There is nobody to play my cards in England, nobody to say anything for me, and Oscar depends *entirely* on what is said to him, and they all seem to be my enemies. I won't argue. I will only say one thing and I beg you to believe it, that I shall kill myself if Oscar throws me over . . . The only thing that could make his life bearable is to think that he is suffering for me because he loved me, and if he doesn't love me I can't live and it is so utterly easy to die. Do work for me, More, and even if you cut him to the heart and make him unhappy you will really be doing him good if you can only make him love me again and know that he is being martyred for my sake.

But a thousand miles away, an increasingly bitter and vengeful Oscar saw things slightly differently. In the silence and the solitude of cell C.3.3 in Reading Gaol – 'this tomb for those who are not yet dead', he called it – he no longer saw himself as a martyr to the love of Bosie, but rather as Bosie's victim, bullied and cajoled by a beautiful, immoral and scheming boy into suing his hated father. Nor did Oscar any longer see himself as the first martyr to the great Uranian Cause. On the contrary, he now regarded himself as a victim of diseased and debased passions. In July 1896, and again in November, Oscar addressed two long petitions to the Home Secretary for his release. He had been suffering, he wrote, from 'monstrous sexual perversion', from 'a form of sexual madness', from 'the most horrible form of erotomania', which left him 'prey of the most revolting passions'. And the 'vice' of his sexual lust for young men still infected him like a 'strange disease', was still 'embedded in his flesh', 'spread over him like a leprosy'. Oscar feared that his 'sexual madness' would overwhelm him and that he would become permanently insane. He was not hyperbolising or misrepresenting his views in the hopes of securing an early release on medical grounds. Three weeks after he wrote his first petition, More Adey visited him and was convinced Oscar really believed what he was saying. He noted that Oscar has 'petitioned HS about 3 weeks ago to be treated as erotomaniac and to be sent somewhere to be cured. Has constant fear of breaking down utterly in brain.'

Oscar's removal to Reading Gaol had not produced any noticeable improvements in his mental health. Physically, he had stabilised and had only spent two days in the prison infirmary in his first six months. But mentally, he seemed to be getting worse. Matters had not been helped by the death of his beloved mother on 3 February 1896. Apprehensive about the effect that the news of Lady Wilde's death would have on Oscar, Constance made the long journey from Genoa, where she had now settled, to break the terrible tidings. 'I believe it will half kill him,' she confided to Lily Wilde, and she was right. Oscar was profoundly grief-stricken by 'so irreparable, so irredeemable a loss'. Constance had not seen Oscar for five months and was shocked by what she found. Oscar was 'changed beyond recognition', she told the artist, Edward Burne-Jones:

> They give him work to do in the garden and the work he likes most to do is to cover the books with brown paper – for at least it is books to hold in his hand – but presently the keeper made a sign with his finger and like a dog he obeyed and left the room . . . it is all inexpressibly dreadful.

It was to be the last time that Constance and Oscar ever met.

Over the next weeks and months, Oscar's mental health deteriorated further. In May, when Robbie Ross and Robert Sherard went to visit Oscar, Robbie made notes in pencil immediately after the visit ended. According to Robbie, Sherard was 'much shocked by the change for the worse' in Oscar since the last time he had seen him. 'He is much thinner, is now clean shaven so that his emaciated condition is more apparent,' Robbie recorded:

> His face is dull brick colour. (I fancy from working in the sun in the garden). His eyes were horribly vacant, and I noticed that he had lost a great deal of hair (this when he turned to go and stood in the light). He always had great quantities of thick hair, but there is now a bald patch on the crown. It is also streaked with white and grey . . . He cried the whole time and when we asked *him* to talk more he said he had nothing to say and wanted to hear *us* talk. That as you know is very unlike Oscar.

Oscar's anxieties about his sanity were evident. 'Asked did we think his brain seemed all right?' Robbie wrote in his notes. 'Feared that confinement' might 'deprive him of his mind. It was a constant dread.' Robbie summed up his impression of Oscar's condition. 'I do *not* think they treat him badly,' he wrote:

> but I firmly and honestly believe apart from all prejudice that he is simply wasting and pining away, to use the old cliché he is sinking under a broken heart. I should say that 'Confinement apart from all labour or treatment had made him temporarily *silly*.' That is the mildest word that will describe my meaning.

Robbie concluded on a sombre note. 'I should be less surprised to hear of dear Oscar's death than of Aubrey Beardsley's and you know what he looks like.' Beardsley was dying of tuberculosis.

It was also clear to Robbie that Oscar had turned against Bosie:

> When I told him that Bosie's poems were coming out and that I had messages in a letter which I showed through bars. He said '*I would rather not hear about that just now.*'

Oscar returned to the subject of Bosie in a letter he wrote to Robbie the day after his visit. His once beloved Bosie who, almost exactly a year earlier, he had called 'my sweet rose, my delicate flower, my lily of lilies', he now referred to simply, coldly and curtly, as 'Douglas'. 'You said that Douglas was going to dedicate a volume of poems to me,' Oscar wrote:

> Will you write at once to him and say he must not do anything of the kind. I could not accept or allow such a dedication. The proposal is revolting and grotesque. Also, he has unfortunately in his possession a number of letters of mine.

The very idea that Bosie was in possession of any of his letters or his gifts was, Oscar said, 'peculiarly repugnant to me':

> I cannot of course get rid of the revolting memories of the two years I was unlucky enough to have him with me, or of the mode by which he thrust me into the abyss of ruin and disgrace to gratify his hatred of his father and other ignoble passions. But I will not have him in possession of my letters or gifts.

Bosie's intended dedication was to be in the form of a poem 'To Oscar Wilde', the text of which surfaced in the 1960s:

> 'What shall I say? What thought, what word recall
> What God invoke, what charm, what amulet,
> To make a sonnet pay a hopeless debt,
> Or heal a bruised soul with a madrigal?
>
> O Vanity of words! my cup of gall
> O'erflows with this, I have no phrase to set,
> And all my agony and blood sweat
> Comes to this issue of no words at all.
>
> This is my book, and in my book my soul
> With its two woven threads of joy and pain.
> And both were yours before they were begun.
> Oh! that this dream would like a mist unroll,
> That I might look upon your face again,
> And hear your kind voice say; 'This was well done.'

In his own mind, at least, Bosie was suffering dreadfully. 'I am not in prison,' he told More Adey, 'but I think I suffer as much as Oscar, in fact more, just as I am sure he would have suffered more if he had been free and I in prison.' Bosie's comments were either naive or breathtakingly insensitive. In any event, Oscar's heart was already hardened against him. 'Even if I get out of this loathsome place,' he told Robbie, 'I will have nothing to do with him nor allow him to come near me.'

Bosie refused to accept that Oscar's attitude to him had fundamentally changed. 'I do not believe that he means what he says, and I regard what he says as non-existent,' he wrote defiantly in September 1896 to More Adey:

I ignore the cruel insults and the unmerited reproaches which I am told his lips have uttered against me. I attribute them simply to an evil and lying spirit which at present inhabits Oscar's body, a spirit born in an English prison, out of English 'prison discipline', and which I hope in spite of everybody and everything to ultimately cast out of him.

Oscar had warned him, he said, that 'all sorts of influences would be brought to bear on me to make me change'. And the last time he had seen Oscar in prison, in Holloway:

he kissed the end of my finger through an iron grating . . . and begged me to let nothing in the world alter my attitude and my conduct towards him.

Bosie was convinced that Oscar still loved him and that they would finally be reunited. 'Nothing in the world can keep us apart,' he declared. 'All the friends and relations, all their plots and their plans, will go to the winds when once I am alone with him again and holding his hand.'

While Bosie was professing his faith, Oscar was losing his. His changed attitude to Bosie and his repudiation of Uranian love were symptoms of a profound crisis of faith. Before he went to prison, he told Bosie that he was going to test the power of love, to see if he could not make the bitter waters of shame, ignominy and imprisonment sweet by the sheer intensity of the love he felt. Oscar had indeed tested the power of love and, amidst the terrible sufferings and mental tortures of his first year in prison, had found it wanting. However hard he had tried to keep it alive in his heart, the sacred flame of love had flickered and died, to be replaced by the prison's flaring gas jets. The bitter waters had engulfed him.

From the depths

*'A patriot put in prison for loving his country loves his country,
and a poet in prison for loving boys loves boys.'*

Oscar's salvation – physically, mentally and spiritually – was brought about by a change of Governor at Reading Gaol. When Oscar arrived at Reading, the stern disciplinarian Major Isaacson was in charge. Oscar called Isaacson a 'mulberry-faced Dictator', and Robbie Ross found him 'haughty and impatient' and 'not unlike the headmaster of a public school'. Frank Harris, who visited Reading in June, at the request of Evelyn Ruggles-Brise, Chairman of the Prison Commission, to ascertain the state of Oscar's physical and mental health, thought Isaacson was 'almost inhuman' with his boasts that he was 'knocking the nonsense out of Wilde'. Oscar told Harris that he was 'perpetually being punished for nothing'. 'The Governor loves to punish,' he said, 'and he punishes by taking my books away from me.' In 'The Ballad of Reading Gaol', his great poem of prison life, Oscar was referring to the regime of Isaacson when he wrote:

> The Governor was strong upon
> The Regulations Act.

The concerns expressed by Robbie Ross, More Adey and Frank Harris led to a decision being taken at the highest levels to replace Isaacson. Ruggles-Brise told Harris that the Home Secretary himself thought 'it would be a great loss to English literature', if Oscar 'were really injured by prison discipline'. Accordingly, in July 1896, Major James Osmond Nelson became Governor of Reading Gaol.

The change in Oscar's circumstances was immediate and apparent. The number of punishments meted out to prisoners dropped dramatically, and Ruggles-Brise personally drafted a set of confidential instructions for Nelson on the treatment of Oscar. He was to be allowed paper, pen and ink, and as many books to read as he wanted, within reason. If there were books that Oscar particularly wished to read that were not in the prison library, then these were to be obtained. Oscar was overwhelmed when Nelson told him the news. According to George Ives, Nelson came to Oscar in his cell and said: 'The Home Secretary says you are to have books. Here is one you may like; I have just been reading it myself.' At this, Oscar burst into tears. 'Those are the first kind words that have been spoken to me since I have been in gaol,' he told Nelson.

Oscar put the pen and ink to good use, and in the months before his release from Reading he wrote what has come to be known as *De Profundis*, an epic and extraordinary letter to Bosie of fifty thousand words. According to Thomas Martin, a prison warder who befriended Oscar during his last months in Reading Gaol, Oscar wrote *De Profundis* mostly in the evenings, when he knew he would be undisturbed:

> In his cell were two wooden trestles, across which he placed his plank bed. This was his table, and, as he himself observed: 'It was a very good table, too.'

Oscar wrote *De Profundis* under a severe misapprehension. He believed that Bosie had made no attempt to write to him in prison, that he no longer cared about him and that he had left him to rot in prison, out of sight and out of mind. Oscar's bitterness and resentment at Bosie's apparent neglect is evident at the beginning and the end of *De Profundis*. 'Dear Bosie,' Oscar began:

> After long and fruitless waiting, I have determined to write to you myself, as much for your sake as for mine, as I would not like to think that I had passed through two long years of imprisonment without ever having received a single line from you, or any news or message even, except such as gave me pain.

'What I must know from you,' Oscar wrote in his peroration, 'is why you have never made any attempt to write to me. I waited month after month to hear from you.' Oscar was being grossly unfair. It was he who had refused to countenance a letter from Bosie in the first place, and it was he who became angry and refused to listen whenever visitors told him that they had a message from Bosie for him. Robert Sherard's mischief-making had succeeded only too well. Oscar was completely unaware of Bosie's heartbreak at his sufferings in prison, and at what he perceived as Oscar's changed attitude to him.

After completing *De Profundis*, Oscar told Robbie that he earnestly hoped that reading it would do Bosie 'some good':

> It is the first time that anyone has ever told him the truth about himself . . . the letter is one he thoroughly deserves, and that if it is unjust, he thoroughly deserves injustice. Who indeed deserves it more than he who was always so unjust to others?

Oscar wanted to hurt Bosie, to humiliate him and punish him, just as he himself had been hurt, humiliated and punished. 'You must read this letter right through,' he instructed Bosie at the beginning of *De Profundis*, 'though each word may become to you as the fire or knife of the surgeon that makes the delicate flesh burn or bleed.' He wanted Bosie to confront his 'supreme vice of shallowness' and all his lesser vices of egotism, selfishness, temper, greed and lust. Especially lust.

Oscar excoriated Bosie for opening up to him a world of purely sexual gratification, for luring him, as he put it, 'into the imperfect world of coarse uncompleted passions, of appetite without distinction, desire without limit, and formless greed'. He was again being unfair. Their love affair had always been driven not only by unbridled sexual licence but also by a profoundly idealised, spiritual love. Oscar had been as eager as Bosie to plumb the depths of lust and scale the heights of love. 'Tired of being on the heights I deliberately went to the depths in the search for new sensations,' he wrote in *De Profundis*:

> What the paradox was to me in the sphere of thought, perversity became to me in the sphere of passion.

Oscar began writing *De Profundis* in January 1897 and finished it three months later in March. What started as a letter of recrimination and reproach became, in the course of three months, a kind of autobiography, an *apologia* for Oscar's life and his love affair with Bosie. Oscar recognised it as such. 'Well, if you are my literary executor,' Oscar told Robbie Ross two months before his release from Reading Gaol:

> you must be in possession of the only document that really gives any explanation of my extraordinary behaviour with regard to Queensberry and Alfred Douglas. When you have read the letter, you will see the psychological explanation of a course of conduct that from the outside seems a combination of absolute idiocy with vulgar bravado.

De Profundis was also an exercise in catharsis, an expelling of all the feeling of pain and humiliation, injustice and anger that Oscar experienced in prison. He began writing his letter of 'changing, uncertain moods' in the bleak depths of an endless winter. By the time it was completed, he could look out from the window of his cell and see the first, tremulous signs of spring in 'some poor black soot-besmirched trees that are just breaking out into buds of an almost shrill green'. 'Of the many, many things for which I have to thank the Governor,' he told Robbie:

> there is none for which I am more grateful than for his permission to write to A.D. and at as great a length as I desired. For nearly two years I had within me a growing burden of bitterness, much of which I have now got rid of.

What was begun in bitterness, ended in hope. By the time he had reached the end of *De Profundis*, Oscar had rediscovered his love for Bosie. It was clear, indeed, that he was anticipating a future of sorts with him. 'Incomplete, imperfect, as I am, yet from me you may have still much to gain,' he told Bosie in the closing sentences of the letter:

> You came to me to learn the Pleasure of Life and the Pleasure of Art. Perhaps I am chosen to teach you something much more wonderful, the meaning of Sorrow, and its beauty.

In the course of writing *De Profundis*, Oscar had not only rediscovered his love for Bosie, he had also rediscovered his attraction to other men. The storm of sexual repudiation and self-loathing that had battered him in the first eighteen months of his imprisonment had subsided. The frantic language of sexual self-revulsion that Oscar had used in his petitions to the Home Secretary, his talk of this 'most horrible form of erotomania', his 'monstrous sexual perversion' and his 'most revolting passions', had given way in *De Profundis* to a calmer, altogether more rational acceptance and assessment of his sexual tastes. 'Sins of the flesh are nothing,' he wrote. 'They are maladies for physicians to cure, if they should be cured.' Only 'sins of the soul' were shameful.

Oscar came to realise that, while there was nothing wrong in loving men and in having sex with men, there was a moral choice about how and where love and sex were bestowed. To wallow in the immoral universe of 'coarse uncompleted passions' and unbridled lust which he had inhabited for so long was essentially a sin of the soul. Not only was it behaviour unworthy of an artist, but it was also self-centred and selfish. It revolved around his own sexual pleasure, his own sexual gratification, crucially ignoring the feelings of his sexual partners. 'I grew careless of the lives of others,' he wrote:

> I took pleasure where it pleased me and passed on. I forgot that every little action of the common day makes or unmakes character, and that therefore what one has done in the secret chamber one has some day to cry aloud on the housetops.

But Oscar also rediscovered his faith in the nobility of Uranian love and recognised once again that he was a victim of discriminatory laws against men who loved men: 'Reason does not help me,' he wrote. 'It tells me that the laws under which I am convicted are wrong and unjust laws.' It was a theme Oscar would return to soon after he left prison in 'The Ballad of Reading Gaol'.

Under the benign regime of Major Nelson, it was not long before Oscar started to put his refound sexual attraction to men into practice. It was difficult – if not impossible – for prisoners under the system of cellular isolation to have sex in convict prisons. But there were always ways and means. 'There is no prison on any world into which love cannot force an entrance,' Oscar wrote in *De Profundis*. Despite the best efforts of the prison authorities, sex between prisoners did present a problem. The Report of the Departmental Committee on Prisons in 1895 dealt with the issue circumspectly, concluding that, 'when prisoners of all kinds were collected together', it undoubtedly 'led to much evil':

> It has been generally assumed that the chief risk lay in the corruption of young by old offenders. We are of the opinion that there is at least as much danger of contamination among the younger prisoners. They are of the age when curiosity stimulates the inherited or acquired depravity which is so often found in young criminals. However this may be we agree that great care is necessary with respect to all classes of prisoners, in order to prevent mischief arising from anything like intercourse.

Long after Oscar's release from prison, Warder Martin told Robert Sherard:

> I am well aware that in convict prisons especially this vice is prevalent. When I was at Dartmoor, I heard the warders speak about it. In fact these sexual problems presented a never-ceasing worry to the officials and necessitated constant vigilance.

A year and a half in prison had taught Oscar how to hold conversations with other prisoners without seeming to move his lips. Oscar befriended several prisoners, usually younger and handsome. 'There are many good nice fellows here,' he told Reggie Turner:

> I have seven or eight friends – they are capital chaps. Of course we can't speak to each other, except a word now and then at exercise, but we are great friends, they take their punishment so well, so cheerfully.

One of these friends was a young man called Harry Elvin who was, Oscar wrote, 'the one I liked best; a very handsome soldier of twenty years of age'. With the help of the obliging Warder Martin, Oscar communicated with his friends by notes written on torn scraps of paper. Less than a month after Oscar's release, Robert Sherard wrote to Oscar's old friend Carlos Blacker, who had been one of Oscar's witnesses at his wedding, and to whom Oscar had dedicated *The Happy Prince and Other Tales*. 'I had some interesting things to tell you about Oscar's life in prison,' Sherard wrote:

> Would you believe that he actually *nouait une intrigue* in prison with one of his fellow-prisoners, sending his *billets doux* through the friendly warder?

Forty years later, Sherard returned to this subject, writing to A.J.A. Symons about:

> the prisoners in Reading whom O.W. admired and with whom he carried on a surreptitious correspondence, getting Martin to 'shove' notes from him under the doors of their cells. Two years hard labour had not been able to

cure him of his urge to fondle and caress (without any satisfaction to himself but a mental one) males who appealed to the woman he fancied himself to be when the homosexual craze got hold of him.

Though Warder Martin denied delivering messages to other prisoners on Oscar's behalf, a few fragmentary notes written to him by Oscar from his cell in Reading seem to suggest the opposite. 'You must get me his address some day – he's such a good fellow,' he wrote to Martin in April 1897:

Of course I would not for worlds get such a friend as you into any *danger*. I quite understand your feelings. You must get A.3.2 to come out and clean on Saturday morning and I will give him my note then myself.

On the back of this scrap, Warder Martin replied, 'I will ask him verbally for his address if that would suit you as well.'

After his release Oscar sent money to several of his fellow convicts through Robbie Ross. Robbie kept an account book recording payments of between £1 and £3 to nine former inmates of Reading Gaol: Fleet, Ford, Stone, Eaton, Cruttenden, Bushell, Mullword, Smith and Langley. Oscar wrote letters to each of them, some of them undoubtedly flirtatious. 'Please be careful not to mix the letters,' Oscar instructed Robbie. 'They are all *nuanced*.' At least one of these friendships was not sexually motivated. Arthur Cruttenden visited Oscar in France after his release. 'I had better say candidly that he is not "a beautiful boy"':

He is twenty-nine years of age, but looks a little older, as he inherits hair that catches silver lines early: he has also a slight, but still *real*, moustache. I am thankful and happy to be able to say that I have no feeling for him, nor could have, other than affection and friendship. He is simply a manly simple fellow, with the nicest smile and the pleasantest eyes, and I have no doubt a confirmed '*mulierast*'.

'Mulierast' was the opposite of 'pederast', and meant a lover of women, rather than a lover of boys. Robbie had coined the word from the Latin word 'mulier', meaning a woman or a wife. Oscar was delighted with Robbie's invention and used it frequently.

As the time of his release from prison drew nearer, Oscar and his friends had to decide on his future. The most pressing question was where he was going to live. To stay in England would, of course, be impossible. Oscar had hinted to Bosie in *De Profundis* that they might meet soon after he came out of prison, perhaps in June, 'when all the roses are in their wanton opulence', in 'some quiet foreign town like Bruges'. But Robbie Ross and More Adey had very different ideas. Prompted by the hatred of Bosie that Oscar had expressed throughout his first eighteen months in prison, Robbie and More had agreed that it would be best for Oscar to have nothing more to do with him. It was hard for them not to feel that Bosie was in some way responsible for the appalling situation Oscar now found himself in. And for Robbie, at least, the issue was further clouded by a complex blend of loyalty to Oscar and jealousy of Bosie. More Adey signalled his and Robbie's attitudes at the end of a draft of a long letter he wrote to Constance in July 1896:

> As I have mentioned the name of Alfred Douglas, and as I think that you know he is a friend of mine, I ought to tell you that I and the very few other friends whom he had in common with Oscar, have told him that we should be sorry to see a renewal of (Oscar's and his) their intimacy, and that considering Oscar's expressed wishes to the contrary we could not do anything to forward any renewal, even though Alfred Douglas on his part might wish it.

'On the contrary,' he continued. 'We are anxious to forward Oscar's desire to conform to *your* wishes and atone to you in any way he can for the great sorrow he has caused you.'

More Adey wrote a tactful letter to Bosie in February 1897, suggesting that it would be better if Bosie did not meet with Oscar after his release from prison. Predictably, his letter provoked a storm of invective from Bosie. 'All this about it "being better for Oscar and I not to meet" et cet is canting humbug,' he replied furiously. 'What you are working for I don't know and I don't understand.' Bosie accused More and Robbie, both converts to Catholicism, of succumbing to 'the baleful influence of the Catholic Church':

> The fact of belonging to and really believing in that institution puts such a gulf between you and Bobbie on one hand and real pagans with a real sense of the supremacy of Greek love over everything else such as Oscar and I, that it is impossible for you to understand what I think about, and what Oscar would think if he were in his normal condition. I feel I have been out-witted and out-intrigued all through, and *sans amertume* I tell you both that when I get the chance I will fight with any weapons I can find.

For her part, Constance had no intention of allowing Oscar to see Bosie after his release from prison. Despite the best efforts of Robert Sherard to bring about a reconciliation between Oscar and Constance, relations between them had deteriorated very badly. The cause was money. After his bankruptcy, one of Oscar's few assets was a life interest in Constance's private income of £800 a year. If Constance died, Oscar would be entitled to her annual income for the rest of his life. This asset was put up for auction by the Official Receiver and was bought by Robbie and More on Oscar's behalf. It was a shrewd move. 'I happened to know,' Robbie wrote later, 'that Mrs Wilde was in a very precarious state of health and that it was quite possible that she would die before her husband, in spite of the bad reports of his health in prison.'

Constance was furious. She considered the purchase of Oscar's life interest in her private income as nothing less than trickery and 'double dealing'. Oscar was also furious and instructed Robbie and More to relinquish the life interest and to defer to Constance's wishes in all financial matters. But still they delayed and dithered. By February 1897, as he was writing *De Profundis*, relations between Oscar and Constance had reached a nadir. Constance had instituted divorce proceedings. 'At the present moment,' Oscar told Bosie:

> my wife . . . is preparing a divorce suit, for which, of course, entirely new evidence and an entirely new trial, to be followed perhaps by more serious proceedings, will be necessary. I, naturally, know nothing of the details. I merely know the name of the witness on whose evidence my wife's solicitors rely. It is your own Oxford servant, whom at your special request I took into my service for our summer at Goring.

The 'Oxford servant' was Walter Grainger, with whom Oscar had had sex in Oxford and in Goring. The 'more serious proceedings' which Oscar feared almost certainly refer to a trial for sodomy, and the 'entirely new evidence' suggests that Sir George Lewis, who was acting for Constance in the divorce, had obtained a statement from Walter Grainger alleging that Oscar had sodomised him. When Robbie and More heard about the divorce, they told Oscar that he would be able to defend himself against the charges of sodomy. Oscar was scathing:

> To talk of my defending the case against Sir George Lewis is childish. How can I expect to be believed on a mere detail? What limit is there to the amount of witnesses he may produce? None. He and Queensberry can sweep Piccadilly for them. It makes me sick with rage when I am told of the opportunities I shall have of defending the case.

Eventually a compromise was hammered out. In exchange for the life interest in her private income, Constance agreed to drop divorce proceedings. Instead, a 'Deed of Separation' was drawn up. Oscar was to receive a small annuity of £150 from Constance, in return for which he relinquished all rights over his children, agreed to live always abroad and promised not to 'annoy or molest the said Constance Mary Wilde or in any manner compel or attempt to compel her to cohabit with him or live or attempt to live in the same house with her without her consent'. There was a last sting in the tail. If Oscar were to indulge in 'any moral misconduct or notoriously consort with evil or disreputable companions', his small income would be instantly forfeit.

There was no question as to the meaning of the clause. It referred to Uranians generally, and to Bosie in particular. This was spelt out in a letter Constance's solicitor, H.M. Holman, wrote to More Adey on 10 May. 'I do hope you will impress upon him,' he wrote, 'how absolutely fatal to him any further intercourse with Lord Alfred Douglas will be.' Holman imparted some

427

alarming intelligence. 'Apart from the fact that Lord Alfred is a "notoriously disreputable companion",' he wrote:

> Lord Queensberry has made arrangements for being informed if his son joins Mr Wilde and has expressed his intention of shooting one or both. A threat of this kind from most people could be more or less disregarded, but there is no doubt that Lord Queensberry, as he has shown before, will carry out any threat that he makes to the best of his ability.

When Oscar read the Deed, he knew that he was exchanging one prison for another. 'I am to be deprived of my £150 if I know any "disreputable" people,' he wrote to More Adey:

> As good people, as they are grotesquely termed, will not know me, and I am not to be *allowed* to know *wicked* people, my future life, as far as I can see at present, will be passed in comparative solitude.

Oscar signed the Deed of Separation with a heavy heart on 15 May, just four days before he was released. He had avoided a divorce with its attendant and very real risk of a further, even more spectacular prosecution for sodomy. But he had paid a heavy price for his freedom. He had signed away any chance of a future with Bosie.

Comfort and despair

*'No – what consoles one nowadays is not repentance, but pleasure.
Repentance is quite out of date.'*

At eight-thirty on the evening of 18 May 1897, the night before he was due to
be released from prison, Oscar's cell was unlocked and he was handed a paper
parcel and told to dress himself quickly. The parcel contained the clothes he
had been wearing on the day of his conviction two years earlier. A few minutes
later, dressed incongruously in a frock coat that was now a little too big for him,
a silk top hat and patent leather boots, Oscar was escorted down the three steep
flights of metal stairs and through the echoing central vault of Reading Gaol to
the main entrance, where Major Nelson and his deputy were waiting for him.
Oscar was, he remembered, 'mentally upset and in a state of very terrible
nervous excitement'. There were many things he wanted to say to Major
Nelson: he wanted to express his gratitude for the Governor's kindness to him,
as well as talk to him of the awful, baleful injustices of prison life. But there was
only time for a hurried farewell, and for Major Nelson to hand Oscar a bulky
envelope containing the manuscript of *De Profundis*. Along with the Deputy
Governor and a warder out of uniform, Oscar was hurried into a waiting cab
and driven off at speed to the railway station at Twyford, five miles away. The
station at Reading was much nearer, less than half-a-mile from the prison, but
was considered too risky. Two journalists were already loitering outside the
prison gates, and there might be dozens more at Reading Station, desperately
trying to catch a glimpse of Oscar.

A month before his release, Oscar had petitioned the Home Secretary. He
was anxious, he said, to avoid reporters from the 'many English, French and
American newspapers' who had 'already announced their intention of
attending the ceremony of release'. He considered that 'such interviews at
such a moment would be from every point of view unseemly'. More
importantly, he begged the Home Secretary not to allow him 'under any
circumstances' to be transferred from Reading to another prison immediately
prior to his release. He was anxious to avoid a repeat of the grotesque and
humiliating 'ordeal' he underwent when he was brought 'in convict dress and
handcuffed by a mid-day train from Clapham Junction to Reading' and was
made to stand on the platform at Clapham surrounded by a jeering mob. The

experience was, he wrote in the archaic and stilted third person style of a petitioner:

> so utterly distressing, from the mental no less than the emotional point of view, that he feels quite unable to undergo any similar exhibition to public gaze.

Oscar was relieved that he was at least allowed to wear his own clothes.

There was a wait of fifteen minutes at Twyford, and Oscar and the warder were obliged to sit in the waiting room while the Deputy Governor bought the tickets and booked a compartment. One journalist had managed to follow the cab from the prison, and he walked into the waiting room to observe Oscar. 'He looked very well,' the *Morning* reported the next day. 'His build and general appearance were – as of old – distinguished and attractive.' The journey to London took a little over an hour. Oscar's party left the train at the suburban station of Westbourne Park and proceeded by cab to Pentonville, the prison where Oscar had begun his sentence. The treadwheel had come full circle.

It was still very cold when, at six-fifteen the next morning, a closed carriage swept out from the massive gates of Pentonville Prison and drove off at speed southwards towards the centre of London. In it were Oscar, More Adey and the Reverend Stewart Headlam, the Church of England priest who had bravely stood bail for Oscar two years earlier. There were good reasons for the secrecy surrounding Oscar's release. Oscar needed protecting, not just from the hordes of clamouring journalists who were desperate to see him and talk to him, but rather more seriously from the Marquis of Queensberry. Robbie Ross and More Adey had got wind of a devilish plot by the Scarlet Marquis to ambush and physically attack Oscar on his release from Pentonville. A few days earlier, More Adey had written to the Home Office asking for permission for the carriage that was to collect Oscar to be allowed to drive inside the prison gates. 'We have received several warnings that the Marquis of Queensberry proposes to assault him,' he wrote, and 'we shall be glad to know if suitable protection will be afforded until Mr Wilde reaches the boat for Dieppe.'

Oscar was taken to Stewart Headlam's house in Bloomsbury. It was, Ada Leverson recalled, a house full of:

> Burne-Jones and Rossetti pictures, Morris wallpaper and curtains, in fact an example of the decoration of the early eighties, very beautiful in its way, and very like the Aesthetic rooms Oscar had once loved.

Ada and Ernest Leverson had gone to Headlam's house to mark the occasion of Oscar's return to the world. 'Everyone was intensely nervous and embarrassed,' she recalled. 'We had the English fear of showing our feelings, and at the same time the human fear of not showing our feelings.' Oscar put everyone at their ease immediately. 'He came in with the dignity of a king returning from exile,' Ada wrote:

He came in talking, laughing, smoking a cigarette, with waved hair and a flower in his button-hole, and he looked markedly better, slighter and younger than he had two years previously.

'Sphinx!' Oscar exclaimed. 'How marvellous of you to know exactly the right hat to wear at seven o'clock in the morning to meet a friend who has been away. You can't have got up, you must have sat up.'

Oscar kept up a seemingly effortless flow of inconsequential chatter. But behind the facade, he was nervous, uncertain and anxious. Before his imprisonment he had been supremely confident of his place in the order of things. 'The gods had given me almost everything,' he wrote in *De Profundis*. He had been a dandy and a wit, a poet, a playwright and a prophet of the Uranian gospel. He had been a husband and a father and a lover of young men. But what the gods had given, the gods had taken away. Certainty had been replaced by uncertainty, fame by infamy. Now Oscar was an ex-convict: estranged from his wife, his children and his lover, disgraced and disavowed. He was no longer sure of who or what he was. Constance compared his fate to Humpty Dumpty's: 'quite as tragic and quite as impossible to put right'. His brilliant life had been broken and fractured into a thousand iridescent shards.

Before prison, Oscar had been a joyous pagan, a Greek out of time. Now there were moments when he acted like a penitent Christian. During his first hours of freedom at Headlam's house, he announced on the spur of the moment that he would like to go on a Catholic retreat, and there and then dashed off a letter to the priests of the Jesuit Church in Farm Street asking if he might spend six months on retreat with them. Before he left prison, he had discussed converting to Catholicism with Robbie, who had been very sceptical. 'I did not believe in his sincerity and told him if he really meant it, to go to a priest, and I discouraged him from anything hasty in the matter.' Oscar did not have to wait long for an answer to his request to go on retreat. It was turned down. He could not be accepted on 'the impulse of a moment'. Oscar was distraught at the refusal. According to Ada Leverson, 'he broke down and sobbed bitterly'.

Before he left prison Oscar had decided that he would live abroad under the assumed name of Sebastian Melmoth. It was a resonant and revealing conjunction of names. Sebastian was the beautiful young martyr whom Oscar had spoken of as 'a lovely brown boy with crisp, clustering hair and red lips'. Sebastian was traditionally venerated as the patron saint of men who loved men because of the persistent legend that his martyrdom had not so much involved being pierced by the arrows of the Praetorian Guard as being penetrated by their penises. He was supposed to have been gang-raped and then to have bled to death. The surname Melmoth was taken from the Gothic horror fantasy, *Melmoth the Wanderer*, written by Oscar's maternal great-uncle Charles Maturin, and first published in 1820. In the novel, Melmoth sells his soul in return for a hundred and fifty years of perpetual youth but from then on is doomed to restlessly roam, trying to extend his life even further by stealing the souls of others. As Sebastian Melmoth, Oscar was simultaneously a saint and a sinner, a martyr and the murderer of his own soul. Like Dorian Gray, he had become 'a complex multiform creature that bore within itself strange legacies of thought and passion, and whose very flesh was tainted with the monstrous maladies of the dead'. Oscar must henceforth live, he said, as the 'Infamous St Oscar of Oxford, Poet and Martyr'.

Late in the afternoon on the day of his release, Oscar and More Adey travelled from London to Newhaven. There they caught the overnight steamer to Dieppe, arriving at four-thirty in the morning. Robbie Ross and Reggie Turner were on the jetty, anxiously scanning the horizon for the first sight of the ferry. Robbie wrote a vivid account of the occasion. 'It was a magnificent spring morning,' he recalled. As the steamer glided into the harbour, Oscar's tall figure, dominating the other passengers, was easily recognised:

> We began running to the landing stage and Wilde recognised us and waved his hand and his lips curled into a smile. His face had lost all its coarseness and he looked as he must have looked at Oxford in the early days before I knew him.

When the boat finally docked, Robbie recalled, Oscar 'with that odd elephantine gait which I have never seen in anyone else, stalked off the boat'. He was carrying a large sealed envelope containing the manuscript of *De Profundis*, which he straightaway handed to Robbie. 'This, my dear Bobbie, is the great manuscript about which you know.' They went directly to the Hôtel Sandwich where Robbie and Reggie had filled Oscar's room with flowers and books. After two years of almost continuous solitary confinement, Oscar was desperate to talk. He talked compulsively, a great, raging torrent of words tumbling out of him as fast as they could. By nine in the morning, an exhausted Robbie insisted on lying down. The party reassembled at noon for *déjeuner*, all of them – with the exception of Oscar – still worn out.

In the afternoon they drove to nearby Arques-la-Bataille and sat down on the ramparts of the castle. Robbie remembered how Oscar was overwhelmed by the beauty of nature:

> He enjoyed the trees and the grass and country scents and sounds in a way I had never known him do before, just as a street-bred child might enjoy them on his first day in the country: but of course there was an adjective for everything – 'monstrous', 'purple', 'grotesque', 'gorgeous', 'curious', 'wonderful'.

Later that day, or early the next, Oscar wrote to Constance. It was a long letter, and 'full of penitence', as Constance described it to her brother, Otho. The text has not survived, but it seems that Oscar begged Constance to consider accepting him back as her husband, but, like his wish to enter a Jesuit retreat, Oscar's desire for reconciliation may have been no more than the mood of the moment, a passing impulse. Constance replied on 24 May. Her letter is lost, but an indignant Oscar later told Bosie that the letter was 'calculated to exasperate and embitter him and to make impossible the reunion which she professed to desire'. According to Bosie, Constance offered:

> to 'take him back' on certain conditions. Oscar did not show me the letter . . . but he told me that her 'conditions' were insulting, and he turned pale and trembled with anger when he spoke to me about her letter. That letter finished all chance of reconciliation and finally killed all that was left of his love for her.

Oscar may have been exasperated at the tone of Constance's letter, but he was also rather relieved. To have to return to Constance, indigent, penitent and forever grateful for her forgiveness, was a gloomy prospect. He was beginning to enjoy the sweets of freedom. He was delighted when a group of young French poets and students arrived in Dieppe from Paris to welcome him to France, and he entertained them in grand style at the Café des Tribunaux. It was a noisy, boisterous evening, so much so that Oscar was warned by the Sub-Prefect of Dieppe to comport himself with more dignity.

Much of Oscar's conversation in those first days in Dieppe revolved around his experiences in prison. According to Robbie, he was already beginning to weave them into an exquisite fable:

> Reading Prison had already become for him a sort of enchanted castle of which Major Nelson was the presiding fairy. The hideous machicolated turrets were already turned into minarets, the very warders into benevolent Mamelukes and we ourselves into Paladins welcoming Coeur de Lion after his captivity.

But this enchantment quickly became tarnished when Oscar heard three days later that Warder Martin had been dismissed from the prison service for the heinous crime of giving 'some sweet biscuits to a little hungry child'. Oscar wrote a long and passionate letter to the *Daily Chronicle* on the treatment of children in prison.

Oscar was not allowed to forget for long that he was an ex-convict. He was snubbed by people who before his fall had been proud to know him. The French portrait painter Jacques-Emile Blanche, whom Oscar had known since the early 1880s, was in Dieppe and was out walking with the artist Walter Sickert one day when he spotted Oscar sitting in the Café Suisse. Oscar beckoned to them. 'I pretended not to see,' Blanche recalled. 'I know for a fact that he was wounded to the quick by my action, and the recollection of that episode still fills me with remorse.' There would be other wounding moments. Aubrey Beardsley cut Oscar in the street, as did many other English visitors to Dieppe. He was often the target of ugly disapproving looks and, on several occasions, was asked to leave cafés and restaurants when other customers objected to his presence.

Equally there were those like Mrs Arthur Stannard – the writer John Strange Winter – who made a point of showing great attention to him. Oscar could salute her grace, her courage and her charm, but was unable to admire her novels. 'I breakfast tomorrow with the Stannards,' he told Robbie in high good humour:

> What a great passionate splendid writer John Strange Winter is! How little people understand her work! *Bootle's Baby* is *une oeuvre symboliste*: it is really only the style and the subject that are wrong. Pray never speak lightly of *Bootle's Baby* – indeed, pray never speak of it at all; I never do.

A week in Dieppe was enough. There were too many English people, too many potential slights and embarrassments. Besides which, Oscar needed peace and quiet to write his great poem of prison life, 'The Ballad of Reading Gaol'. He chose the small village of Berneval-sur-Mer, three miles outside Dieppe, taking up residence in the Hôtel de la Plage on 26 May. Reggie Turner had already left Dieppe, but Robbie accompanied Oscar to Berneval and spent a night or two there before returning to London.

It was here that Oscar had sex with Robbie again: the first time in many years. Bosie told Harford Montgomery Hyde that it was Robbie who 'dragged' Oscar back to sex with men while they were staying together at Berneval. Certainly, the day after Robbie left, Oscar wrote him a tender love letter. He was 'dear sweet Robbie'. 'No other friend have I now in this beautiful world,' Oscar told him:

> I want no other. Yet I am distressed to think that I will be looked on as careless of your own welfare, and indifferent of your good. You are made to help me. I weep with sorrow when I think how much I need help, but I weep with joy when I think that I have you to give it to me.

'It is not for nothing that I named you in prison St Robert of Phillimore,' Oscar concluded. 'Love can canonise people.' It was hardly the most passionate of encounters. Oscar was in need of comfort, and Robbie obligingly comforted him. It was sex as consolation, sex born out of long and deep affection. It was loving, but it was not love. It would never, could never, scale the same emotional heights as Oscar's love for Bosie, let alone approach the same fiery heat of passion, danger and excitement that Oscar had experienced in his feastings with panthers. But Oscar was nevertheless grateful, and when Robbie left Berneval, he began, he said, to realise his 'terrible position of isolation'.

But Oscar soon rallied. 'I adore this place,' he declared four days after Robbie's departure. 'The whole country is lovely, and full of forest and deep meadow. It is simple and healthy.' Some of Oscar's enthusiasm for Berneval lay in the fact that he was far removed from the sexual temptations of large cities. 'If I live in Paris I may be doomed to things I don't desire. I am afraid of big towns . . . I am frightened of Paris.' He was also frightened, he said, of the temptations of southern Italy, Egypt and Algiers, all of them in Richard Burton's Sotadic Zone, where sodomy and pederasty were the rule, rather than the exception. 'If I lived in Egypt I know what my life would be,' he said darkly. There were sexual temptations close at hand even in Berneval, but Oscar proudly boasted to Robbie of having resisted them. On the last day of May he had bathed in the sea. 'I went into the water without being a Pagan,' he told Robbie:

> The consequence was that I was *not* tempted by either Sirens or mermaidens, or any of the green-haired following of Glaucus. I really think that this is a remarkable thing. In my pagan days, the sea was always full of tritons blowing conches, and other unpleasant things. Now it is quite different.

A few days later, on 3 June, Oscar entertained the first of many visitors to Berneval. Ernest Dowson, the poet, Charles Conder, the water-colour artist, and Dalhousie Young, a composer who had written a passionate defence of Oscar after his conviction, came together to Berneval to dine and sleep – 'at least I know they dine,' Oscar wrote, 'but I believe they never sleep'. Dowson was thirty years old, and an alcoholic, but still darkly handsome. Oscar had first met him in 1890. He had been an ardent supporter of Oscar, lambasting 'English hypocrisy' and sympathising with Oscar's 'torture'. 'Cher Monsieur le Poète,' Oscar wrote to Dowson after his departure from Berneval:

> It was most kind of you coming to see me, and I thank you very sincerely and gratefully for your pleasant companionship and the many gentle ways by which you recalled to me that, once at any rate, I was a Lord of Language and had myself the soul of a poet.

Dowson enjoyed the visit equally. 'The other day I met Oscar and dined with him at his seaside retreat,' he told a friend:

> I had some difficulty in suppressing my own sourness and attuning myself to his enormous joy in life just at this moment – but I hope I left him with the impression that I had not a care in the world. He was in wonderful form, but has changed a good deal – he seems of much broader sympathies, much more human and simple.

They met frequently, and their friendship suddenly seemed to deepen into love. It is unlikely that the relationship was ever sexual, but there may have been drunken embraces and declarations of undying love. 'There is a fatality about our being together that is astounding – or rather quite probable,' Oscar told Dowson:

Had I stayed at Arques I should have given up all hopes of ever separating from you. Why are you so persistently and perversely wonderful?

A week later Oscar told him that he was 'wonderful and charming all last night'. Dowson's sexual interest lay in young girls, but he appears not to have been disconcerted by Oscar's sexual choices and even introduced Oscar to a young friend of his, a French officer who seemingly shared Oscar's Uranian tastes. On 13 June Oscar wrote to Dowson to tell him how 'charming' he was at Berneval, and how much he liked '*your* friend, *and mine*, the dear Achille', who was 'a most noble and splendid fellow'.

It was Dowson who persuaded Oscar to visit a brothel in Dieppe. Dowson told the poet W.B. Yeats that he had persuaded Oscar of the need to acquire 'a more wholesome taste in sex' and how they had 'pooled their financial resources and proceeded to the appropriate place, accompanied by a cheering crowd'. When Oscar emerged from the brothel, he whispered to Dowson: 'The first these ten years, and it will be the last. It was like cold mutton.' Addressing the crowd of curious onlookers in a louder voice, Oscar added, 'But tell it in England for it will entirely restore my character.'

Another visitor to Berneval was the twenty-one-year-old John Rowland Fothergill, a student at the London School of Architecture, whom Oscar christened poetically – before he even met him – 'the architect of the moon'. Fothergill was a young Uranian, and Oscar had invited him for the pleasure of his company as well as for some professional advice on a house he was thinking of building in Berneval. Fothergill's first impressions of Oscar were not encouraging. Looking down from the railings of the steamer, he saw 'a huge and fat person in white flannels with a comical little red beret on top of it all'. Fothergill thought him 'rather vulgar'. Fothergill met several of Oscar's friends at Berneval. There was Dowson, Oscar's 'first hyacinth since Douglas'. The publisher and pornographer Leonard Smithers was also there. Smithers was 'sea green' with absinthe, Fothergill recalled, and was constantly complaining 'that Aubrey Beardsley with whom he had a contract for all his work had sent him nothing'. Oscar reproved Smithers. 'My dear Leonard,' he said, 'you are a monstrous person. You have bought his soul and what more can you ask for?'

Oscar told Fothergill that he was lonely in Berneval and confided to him that he was missing Bosie desperately. Oscar expressed his feelings in verse to Fothergill:

> Two loves have I:
> the one of comfort;
> the other of despair.
> The one has black;
> the other golden hair.

Oscar was talking about Robbie and Bosie. Robbie represented the comfort of love, Bosie love's despair. Comfort or despair? The safe, predictable and consoling homespun of Robbie's love, versus the dazzling and dangerous love of Bosie Douglas, the love he had so vehemently disavowed. Oscar was literally as well as poetically on the horns of a dilemma.

It had taken just four weeks for Oscar's love for Bosie to re-ignite. Immediately after Oscar's release from Reading Gaol, Bosie had sent him a furious, accusing letter. Though the text does not survive, it was sufficiently unpleasant and vitriolic for Oscar to describe it as 'revolting'. 'I have a real terror now of that unfortunate ungrateful young man with his unimaginative selfishness,' he told Robbie on 28 May:

> I feel him as an evil influence, poor fellow. To be with him would be to return to the hell from which I do think I have been released. I hope never to see him again.

A day or so later he wrote to Robbie again, telling him that he was 'terrified about Bosie'. Bosie had apparently given an interview about Oscar and his prison experiences, sending Oscar into a tailspin of panic. 'Bosie can almost ruin me,' he wrote. 'I earnestly beg that some entreaty be made to him not to do so a second time. His letters to me are infamous.'

Infamous or not, Oscar could not resist the temptation of answering them. He wrote 'a beautiful letter' to Bosie in Paris towards the end of May, which Bosie promptly returned with another letter of his own full of bitter invective. 'My dear boy,' Oscar replied teasingly on 2 June. 'If you *will* send me back beautiful letters, with bitter ones of your own, of course you will never remember my address. It is as above.' Though there could be no question of their meeting, Oscar enjoined Bosie to 'always write to me about your art and the art of others. It is better to meet on the double peak of Parnassus than elsewhere.' By the end of the letter, Oscar was reverting to the Uranian language of love he had so often used with Bosie before the fall, speaking of 'dear Reggie Cholmondeley, with his large faun's eyes and honey sweet smile'.

Just two days later, it was obvious that the embers of Oscar's great love for Bosie were quickening into flame. 'Don't think I don't love you,' he declared:

> Of course I love you more than anyone else. But our lives are irreparably severed, as far as meeting goes. What is left to us is the knowledge that we love each other, and every day I think of you, and I know you are a poet, and that makes you doubly dear and wonderful.

Two more days and Oscar and Bosie were almost as of old, in print at least. Bosie was his 'dearest boy' again. 'I must give up this *absurd* habit of writing to you every day,' Oscar wrote, jokingly declaring that they must try and write to each other only once a week. 'I am so glad you went to bed at seven o'clock,' he wrote, adding a witty allusion to Bosie's predilection for buggering boys:

Modern life is terrible to vibrating delicate frames like yours: a rose-leaf in a storm of hard hail is not so fragile. With us who are modern it is the *scabbard* that wears out the sword.

It was now inevitable that they should meet. On 15 June, barely four weeks after his release from Reading Gaol, Oscar wrote to confirm that his 'dear honey-sweet boy' was to come to Berneval incognito four days later. 'Your name is to be Jonquil du Vallon,' he added insouciantly.

The stage was set for an epic and romantic reconciliation when, on Thursday 17 June, Oscar received a letter from his solicitor warning him that the meeting could not take place. Not only would it be in breach of the terms of the Deed of Separation from Constance and would result in Oscar forfeiting his small allowance, it would also bring down the wrath of Queensberry on his head. 'At present it is impossible for us to meet,' an agitated Oscar told Bosie:

If Q came over and made a scene and a scandal it would utterly destroy my future and alienate all my friends from me . . . I think of you always, and love you always, but chasms of moonless night divide us. We cannot cross it without hideous and nameless peril.

It was almost certainly Robbie who had tipped off Oscar's solicitor about Bosie's planned visit to Berneval, and Bosie was furious, sending a 'long indictment' of Robbie to Oscar. Oscar was forced to steer a middle course. He desperately wanted to see Bosie again, but he knew that Robbie was dead set against the idea. He knew, too, that Robbie effectively controlled what meagre capital he possessed and could easily intervene to stop his allowance from Constance. Oscar tried to keep both of his 'two loves' sweet, telling Robbie how he had written 'a long letter – of twelve foolscap pages – to Bosie to point out to him that I owe everything to you and your friends, and that whatever life I have as an artist in the future will be due to you.'

The summer wore on, with Bosie and Robbie at each other's throats. Bosie wrote to Robbie to inform him that their friendship was at an end. 'He has really left me no choice at all,' Bosie indignantly told More Adey:

He has said things to me which are quite unforgivable and which would make it positively dishonourable for me to continue my friendship for him . . . It seems to me that he is possessed by an extraordinary spirit of animosity and vindictive hatred towards me.

Bosie was right. Robbie had behaved badly and would continue to do so. He was prepared to go to almost any lengths to keep Oscar and Bosie apart. Robbie genuinely believed that Bosie had wreaked havoc in Oscar's life and would continue to do so. He wanted to protect Oscar from Bosie's destructive whirlwind. But there was also no doubt that, after the recrudescence of sexual relations between them, Robbie had cast himself in the role of Oscar's officially beloved, giving balm and succour to a disgraced genius.

Oscar felt increasingly lonely and isolated without Bosie, and Bosie was equally wretched at not being able to see Oscar. On 21 August, Bosie wrote to his brother Percy, threatening suicide:

> I don't even know whether you will get this letter, and if you do I suppose you can't do anything. Unless however something turns up in a few days I shall shoot myself, as I am sick and tired of this miserable life I lead, always alone, always begging people to come and see me who never come.

Neither Oscar nor Bosie could restrain their love for each other, or live with the misery of being forced to stay apart. A week later, they met in Rouen, some fifty miles from Dieppe, and spent the night together. 'The meeting was a great success,' Bosie recalled:

> I have often thought since that if he or I had died directly after that, our friendship would have ended in a beautiful and romantic way. Poor Oscar cried when I met him at the station. We walked about all day arm in arm, or hand in hand, and were perfectly happy.

'Yes I saw Bosie,' Oscar told Robbie after his return from Rouen, 'and of course I love him as I always did, with a sense of tragedy and ruin.' A few days later, Oscar wrote to his 'own Darling Boy' with a passionate declaration of love and longing and need. 'I wish that when we met at Rouen we had not parted at all,' he told Bosie:

> I feel that my only hope of again doing beautiful work in art is being with you. It was not so in old days, but now it is different, and you can really recreate in me that energy and sense of joyous power on which art depends. Everyone is furious with me for going back to you, but they don't understand us. I feel that it is only with you that I can do anything at all. Do remake my ruined life for me, and then our friendship and love will have a different meaning to the world.

The 'chasms of moonless night' had been bridged. A week later, Oscar and Bosie eloped secretly to Naples.

Two outcast men

'Friendship is far more tragic than love. It lasts longer.'

Oscar was careful not to tell anyone of his planned elopement with Bosie. But before he left Berneval, Oscar did announce his intention to spend the winter in southern Italy. 'I cannot stay in the North of Europe: the climate kills me,' he told his old friend Carlos Blacker, who now lived in Switzerland:

> I don't mind being alone when there is sunlight and *joie de vivre* all about me, but my last fortnight at Berneval has been black and dreadful, and quite suicidal. I have never been so unhappy.

Blacker was sceptical. He suspected that Oscar's motives in going to Italy were primarily sexual and wrote to him, accusing him of 'returning to his vomit', as he put it later. 'You are really wrong in your views on the question of my going there,' Oscar replied indignantly. 'It is not perversity but unhappiness that makes me turn my steps to the South.'

Oscar and Bosie arrived in Naples on Monday 19 September. Neither of them had much money, and Oscar had been obliged to borrow the money for the train fare from Vincent O'Sullivan, a rather serious-minded young Irish-American poet and novelist in Paris whom he had first met in London a year or so before his trials. Oscar and Bosie installed themselves in the Hôtel Royal des Étrangers – 'a hotel of absurd prices', Oscar called it – and celebrated their elopement by running up an enormous bill of £68 in just over a week. Naples was Bosie's choice. The climate was delightful, and the cost of living was low – at least in theory. But, most importantly, Naples was a city *simpatico* to the many European Uranians who flocked there – and to nearby Capri – to enjoy what Oscar called the area's 'freedom from morals'.

Two days after his arrival in Naples, Oscar tried to explain in an emotional letter to Robbie why he had eloped with Bosie. 'My going back to Bosie was psychologically inevitable,' he wrote. 'I cannot live without the atmosphere of Love: I must love and be loved, whatever price I pay for it.' He had been lonely – 'so lonely that I was on the brink of killing myself' – and in the midst of his 'loneliness and disgrace' Bosie offered him love which, after three months struggling against a 'hideous Philistine world', he gratefully accepted. Oscar

440

told Carlos Blacker that he knew his decision to return to Bosie would pain his few remaining friends. 'But I cannot help it,' he wrote. 'I must remake my maimed life on my own lines.' He admitted to Reggie Turner that his great love for Bosie was a paradox. 'I love him, and have always loved him. He ruined my life, and for that very reason I seem forced to love him more,' he wrote:

> So when people say how dreadful of me to return to Bosie, do say *no* – say that I love him, that he is a poet, and that, after all, whatever my life may have been ethically, it has always been *romantic*, and Bosie is my romance. My romance is a tragedy of course, but it is none the less a romance, and he loves me very dearly, more than he loves, or can love anyone else, and without him my life was dreary.

Oscar and Bosie quickly set up home together and rented the small and secluded Villa Giudice in Posilippo, a quiet village just to the north of Naples. 'We have a lovely villa over the sea, and a nice piano,' Oscar told Robbie. The Villa Giudice was 'very beautiful', according to one Italian journalist who visited Oscar and Bosie there:

> All around, flower beds kept with the utmost care; farther on, shadowy alleys, and beyond the trees, the vastity of the calm sea, of a livid hue that stretched to the horizon. A deep silence.

They had a cook called Carmine, a maid and two boys to serve them – Peppino and Michele – as well as an infestation of rats. The rats were driven out by the successful ministrations of a 'potent witch' who came to the villa and 'burned odours and muttered incantations'.

'I intend to winter here, if all goes well,' Oscar told the young writer and music critic Stanley Makower, soon after his arrival in Naples. 'I love the place: it is, to me, full of Dorian and Ionian airs.' Oscar was not just referring the city's rich cultural heritage. There were plenty of erotic temptations to which he and Bosie were only too happy to yield. 'The museum is full, as you know, of lovely Greek bronzes,' Oscar told Ernest Dowson:

> The only bother is that they all walk about the town at night. However, one gets delicately accustomed to that – and there are compensations.

Life in Naples was perfect. All was harmony. Oscar and Bosie were both working, separately and together. Oscar was revising 'The Ballad of Reading Gaol', and Bosie was writing sonnets. They were also collaborating on a libretto for an opera – *Daphnis and Chloe* – that Dalhousie Young was composing. 'We are together,' Oscar told Leonard Smithers simply:

> He understands me and my art, and loves both. I hope never to be separated from him. He is a most delicate and exquisite poet, besides – far the finest of

all the young poets in England . . . He is witty, graceful, lovely to look at, loveable to be with.

Smithers had agreed to publish 'The Ballad of Reading Gaol'. He was an extraordinary man. Formerly a solicitor in Sheffield, he had turned to publishing, making his money out of pornography and using it to subsidise the publication of works of a more literary bent. It was Smithers who, in 1893, had published *Teleny*, the highly sexually explicit novel of Uranian love which Oscar had had a hand in writing. He looked like a rather grubby clerk or a commercial traveller. Oscar drew a vivid thumbnail sketch of him for Reggie Turner:

> He is usually in a large straw hat, has a blue tie delicately fastened with a diamond brooch of the impurest water, or perhaps wine, as he never touches water – it goes to his head at once. His face, clean shaven as befits a priest who serves at the altar whose God is literature, is wasted and pale, not with poetry, but with poets, who, he says, have wrecked his life by insisting on publishing with him. He loves first editions, especially of women – little girls are his passion – he is the most learned erotomaniac in Europe. He is also a delightful companion, and a dear fellow, very kind to me.

'My definition of a straightforward publisher is Leonard Smithers,' Robbie Ross told Ada Leverson. 'He always *said* he would cheat you and always *did*. He was the only honest publisher I ever met.'

'The Ballad of Reading Gaol' was to be Oscar's literary swan song. He spent almost six months working on the epic poem of one hundred and nine stanzas, which tells the story of the execution of Trooper Charles Wooldridge, hanged at Reading Gaol – while Oscar was an inmate there – on 7 July 1896, for having slashed his wife's throat in a fit of jealousy. The ballad is a powerful and moving indictment of the futility of capital punishment and of the senseless cruelty of prison life. Oscar fully intended 'Reading Gaol' to be a polemic, even though he considered that this in some way devalued it artistically. 'The poem suffers under the difficulty of a divided aim in style,' he told Robbie. 'Some is realistic, some is romantic, some poetry, some propaganda.'

Behind the story of Trooper Wooldridge's execution, 'Reading Gaol' also reveals Oscar's experiences and feelings about his imprisonment. He drew explicit parallels between his own crime and punishment and that of Trooper Wooldridge. Both were in prison for crimes of passion. Both were being punished for love. And both had become social and sexual outcasts:

> A prison wall was round us born,
> Two outcast men we were:
> The world had thrust us from its heart,
> And God from out His care:
> And the iron gin that waits for Sin
> Had caught us in its snare.

There are deliberate echoes and invocations of Oscar's own experience of love and sex in the lines, 'Some love too little, some too long/ Some sell, and others buy'. Oscar had loved Bosie too much and, by his own admission, loved many others too little. His compulsive masturbation in Wandsworth was invoked in the ballad, as were the storms of sexual doubt and self-loathing that had assailed him in prison. Oscar wrote of the 'crooked shapes of Terror', the reproachful 'sprites' and 'phantoms' of the night, who assume the 'smirking' gait and 'mincing' manners of a nightmarish Uranian underworld. These 'slim shadows' with 'subtle sneer and fawning leer' mock Oscar's sexual past with the significantly worded refrain:

> *'But he does not win who plays with Sin*
> *In the secret House of Shame.'*

There was a clear reference in the ballad to the unjust laws under which Oscar had been convicted and sent to prison:

> I know not whether Laws be right,
>   Or whether Laws be wrong;
> All that we know who lie in gaol
>   Is that the wall is strong;
> And that each day is like a year,
>   A year whose days are long.

But the over-arching theme of 'Reading Gaol' is the death of love: all kinds of love, and all manner of deaths. After life, love is the greatest of all God's blessings because it is made in His own image. And, just as man is born to die, so love must inevitably die, invariably at the hands of the beloved:

> And all men kill the thing they love,
>   By all let this be heard,
> Some do it with a bitter look,
>   Some with a flattering word,
> The coward does it with a kiss,
>   The brave man with a sword!

Though bleak and stark, 'Reading Gaol' is nonetheless a fundamentally optimistic poem. For death is not only the end, but also the beginning. The death of one love also means the birth of another. Oscar had experienced the death of his love for Bosie in prison. Now he was experiencing its rebirth. The warm sun-filled days of the Neapolitan autumn soothed and lulled him. Feeling loved and loving, he slowly began to enjoy life once again. There were long lunches eaten alfresco within sight of the sea, and excursions to Capri where, according to the historian Suetonius, the Emperor Tiberius created an erotic Arcadia where he indulged in abandoned orgies with boys and young men, famously training boys to act as 'minnows' in his swimming pool, nipping and biting his genitals as he swam. 'We go to Capri for three days,' Oscar playfully announced to Reggie Turner. 'I want to lay a few simple flowers on the tomb of Tiberius. As the tomb is of someone else really, I shall do so with the deeper emotion.' And in the spirit of Tiberius, Oscar and Bosie could spend their evenings in Naples drinking to excess and sampling a seemingly unending and exciting range of erotic distractions with beautiful and willing young men. It was in Naples, Robbie said many years later, that Oscar contracted the 'alcoholic habits from which he never recovered and reverted to homosexual excesses, both of which continued until he died'.

They were amused when the obsessively secretive George Ives wrote a carefully coded and consequently almost incomprehensible letter to Oscar in Naples, which prompted Bosie to draft a witty reply, written, he told Ives, 'in your own mysterious style':

My dear G

O showed me your letter. We are here at N or rather at P which is close to N. We met a charming fellow here yesterday. I wonder if you know him; his name is X and he lives at Z. He was obliged to leave R on account of a painful scandal connected with H and T. The weather here is D today but we hope it may soon be L again.

Yours in the strictest privacy
A.B.D.
PS: Have you written to A.C. lately and seen R.S.?

There were, of course, squabbles and arguments. According to Vincent O'Sullivan, plates were thrown by Bosie on at least one occasion. But these arguments were minor eruptions, soon quieted and quickly forgotten. Before the fall, their every attempt at domesticity had invariably ended in disaster. Bosie would descend into one of his epileptic fits of rage and, white with anger, would flounce out, sending Oscar a series of vile letters. But life at the Villa Giudice was different, altogether happier. Oscar and Bosie were content just to be together and to work together. Their love had passed through the valley of the shadow of death and had emerged 'rose-crowned' as of old.

There were still those who violently disapproved of them. 'It is very curious that none of the English colony here have left cards on us,' Oscar wrote. 'Fortunately we have a few simple friends among the poorer classes.' Their presence in Naples quickly became known to the newspapers and a spate of articles and supposed interviews appeared, setting off alarm bells in the British Embassy in Rome. One of the attachés, the 'very witty and talkative' Beauchamp Denis Brown, whom Bosie had known at Oxford, was despatched to the Villa Giudice, where he privately informed Bosie that their ménage in Posilippo was '*mal vu*' by the Embassy.

Brown's visit and coded warning to Bosie to leave almost certainly had something to do with fact that Lord Rosebery had that year paid £16,000 for the beautiful Villa Delahante, also in Posilippo, where he would indulge his passion for sodomising young men for many years to come. There was every reason to fear that the unpredictable and passionate Bosie might confront Rosebery with his allegations of a conspiracy in the Liberal Party, of the plot to sacrifice Oscar in order to save Rosebery and other senior Liberals from exposure as sodomites. It is not clear whether Rosebery was in the Villa Delahante in the autumn of 1897, or whether Oscar and Bosie even knew that Rosebery had bought a villa in Posilippo. But sooner or later the poets and the politician were bound to meet, a prospect which caused Rosebery some trepidation.

When Bosie and Oscar showed no signs of taking any notice of the heavy diplomatic hint to leave Posilippo, Eustace Neville-Rolfe, Rosebery's close friend and the British Consul in Naples, made some circumspect investigations and, in a letter to Rosebery marked 'Very secret', concluded that there was little danger of a confrontation. The Villa Giudice is 'fully two miles from you', he told Rosebery:

> Oscar Wilde calling himself Mr Sebastian Mothwell . . . lives a completely secluded life . . . he looks thoroughly abashed, much like a whipped hound . . . I really cannot think he will be any trouble to you.

But the approval or otherwise of the British Embassy, the British Consul and the British community in Naples was of small moment to Oscar and Bosie. What did matter was the concerted opprobrium of family and friends.

Oscar had written to Constance a few days after his arrival in Naples to let her know that he intended to winter there. Though he made no mention of Bosie, Constance's suspicions were instantly aroused. Angry and upset, she wrote to Carlos Blacker, who had become her trusted advisor: 'Question – has he seen that dreadful person at Capri?' 'That dreadful person' was Bosie. Constance could not bear even to write his name:

> No-one goes to Naples at this time of year. So I see no other reason for his going, and I am unhappy. Write to me and tell me what to do.

Constance was haunted by the very idea of any contact between Oscar and Bosie. Without waiting for Blacker's advice, she sat down and wrote to Oscar that very day. She wrote to Blacker to tell him what she done:

> I have today written a note to Oscar saying that I required an immediate answer to my question whether he had been to Capri or whether he had met anywhere that appalling individual. I also said that he evidently did not care much for his boys since he neither acknowledged their photos which I sent him nor the remembrances that *they* sent him. I hope it was not too hard of me to write this, but it was quite necessary.

Within a day or so of writing to Oscar, Constance was told – by either Blacker or Robbie, or by both – that Oscar and Bosie were living together in Naples. She was in a paroxysm of rage and bitterness and wrote a long and 'terrible' letter to Oscar. 'I *forbid* you to see Lord Alfred Douglas,' she wrote. 'I forbid you to return to your filthy, insane life. I forbid you to live at Naples.'

At first, Oscar's response was scathing and defiant. 'How can she really imagine that she can influence or control my life?' he demanded of Robbie. 'She might just as well try to influence and control my art. I could not live such an absurd life – it makes one laugh.' But when Constance's angry letters were followed by no fewer than three furious letters in as many days from Robbie attacking him for setting up home with Bosie, Oscar tried a conciliatory approach. 'Robbie has written me three unkind and detestable letters,' he told Reggie Turner. 'But he is such a dear, and I love him so much, that I accepted them meekly.' To Robbie himself, Oscar was almost grovelling:

> As you remade my life for me you have a perfect right to say what you choose to me, but I have no right to say anything to you except to tell you how grateful I am to you, and what a pleasure it is to feel gratitude and love at the same time for the same person.

But Oscar's attempts at conciliation were doomed to failure. The brooding, embittered Robbie did not want Oscar's worthy protestations of platonic love, gratitude and friendship. He wanted the joyous, passionate, irrational and unconditional love that Oscar lavished on an unworthy Bosie. If he could not have Oscar's love for himself, he was determined that Bosie should not have it. And if hurting Bosie meant hurting Oscar, so be it.

Robert Sherard also entered the fray. When he heard the news in the Authors' Club in London that Oscar was living with Bosie, he could not resist making some highly critical comments about Oscar's morality. Oscar was told about Sherard's remarks and penned a stinging rebuke to 'that bravest and most chivalrous of all beings':

> When you wish to talk morality – always an amusement – and to attack me behind my back, don't, like a good fellow, talk so loud, as the reverberation reaches from the Club to Naples; also, it is easy – far too easy – for you to find an audience that does not contain friends of mine; before them, play Tartuffe in the style of Termagant to your heart's content; but when you do it in the presence of friends of mine, you expose yourself to rebuke and contempt, and of course I hear all about it.

Constance dropped her bombshell on 16 November. Her solicitor wrote to Oscar to inform him that she was stopping his 'wretched £3 a week' because he had created 'a public scandal' by living with Bosie, a notoriously 'disreputable person'. Oscar was outraged. 'Women are so petty,' he told Robbie, 'and Constance has no imagination.' Besides which, Oscar objected to the description of Bosie as a disreputable person. 'After all,' he told Robbie, 'no charge was made against him at any of my trials, not anything proved, or attempted to be proved.' What did Constance expect him to do? His very existence was a scandal. He could not live alone, and Bosie was the only one of his friends able or willing to share his life. 'If I were living with a Naples renter I would I suppose be all right,' he added bitterly. 'As I live with a young man who is well-bred and well-born, and who has been charged with no offence, I am deprived of all possibility of existence.'

There was another bombshell five days later. The guileless More Adey wrote to Oscar telling him that he and Robbie not only agreed with Constance's decision but that they were a party to making it. 'I said at once,' he wrote:

> that your wife was acting strictly within her legal rights according to the agreement, when I was asked whether your friends wished to oppose your wife's action in withdrawing your allowance.

Oscar was incredulous and furious. He felt utterly betrayed and was for once, as he told Reggie Turner, lost for words:

> For More and Robbie to have done this – More and Robbie of all people in the world! – is so astounding that I cannot comment on the fact. I simply state it.

Oscar could just about comprehend More's role in the affair. More was fussy and over-precise in business matters and might easily have allowed himself to be persuaded that Oscar had contravened the terms of the Deed of Separation. But Robbie's actions were altogether different. It was barely three months since they had resurrected their sexual relationship. Robbie was a hypocrite and a false friend. A Uranian himself, he objected to Oscar's Uranian love for Bosie. And he professed friendship for Oscar at the same time as he sought to destroy his life with Bosie.

Though he was provoked beyond measure, Oscar tried to be conciliatory. He wrote to Robbie to see if there was any possibility of a compromise. 'Do you think that if I engaged not to *live* with Bosie – in the same house – that that would be regarded as a concession of any kind?' he asked:

> To say that I would never see him or speak to him again would of course be childish – out of the question – but I am quite ready, and so will Bosie be, to say that we would not live in the same house again, if that would be regarded as an equitable concession. Or do you think that everything is over, and that my wife will hear of nothing that would enable me to live?

He appealed to More Adey in a similar vein. 'Do, if possible, try to arrange something,' he pleaded:

I know you all think I am wilful, but it is the result of the nemesis of character, and the bitterness of life. I was a problem for which there was no solution.

Bosie was not so diplomatic. He realised that Robbie was jealous of Oscar's love for him and came out and said so in an indignant letter to More, adding for good measure that he thought Robbie 'perfectly capable' of trying to sabotage the publication of 'Reading Gaol' so as to further starve Oscar of money. It was natural that More should show Bosie's letter to Robbie, who immediately went into a huff and wrote stiffly to Smithers to inform him that he could no longer be involved in any plans for the publication of 'Reading Gaol' as he had ceased to enjoy Oscar's confidence in business matters.

Oscar and Bosie were worried about the withdrawal of Oscar's £3 a week, but not unduly so. Bosie received an allowance of £8 a week from his mother, and this, together with what Oscar could beg, borrow or earn from the ballad was enough – more than enough – to keep them in wine and boys for the foreseeable future. Then the third bombshell exploded. In late November, Lady Queensberry, prompted by Robbie and More, wrote to Bosie to tell him that she was stopping his allowance until he parted from Oscar. It was the last straw. Oscar and Bosie knew they were beaten. They had been, as Robbie jubilantly phrased it, 'starved out'. Oscar was bitter. 'It is proposed to leave me to die of starvation, or blow my brains out in a Naples urinal,' Oscar told Smithers in late November. He was outraged by what he saw as the warped morality of his family and friends, who would rather see him dead than in bed with Bosie. 'Moral people, as they are termed, are simple beasts,' he declared:

> I would rather have fifty unnatural vices than one unnatural virtue. It is unnatural virtue that makes the world, for those who suffer, such a premature Hell.

Shortly afterwards, on 3 December, Bosie and Oscar parted. Bosie went to Rome, and Oscar, after a week on his own in the Villa Giudice, went to Taormina in Sicily as the guest of a 'very cultivated' Russian of 'advanced years'. Here he met the German photographer, Baron von Gloeden, who made a living selling photographs to visiting Uranians of naked Sicilian youths disporting themselves in an erotic evocation of ancient Greece and Tiberian Capri. Von Gloeden gave Oscar some of his photographs, two of which still survive.

Neither Oscar nor Bosie appeared to be inconsolable with grief at their enforced parting. Oscar soon acquired a new companion. 'I hear you have a beautiful love in Naples,' Smithers wrote to Oscar in January 1898. Bosie meanwhile had arrived in Paris and was soon writing to Oscar, typically complaining about the cost and difficulties of finding boys in Paris:

> The annoyance of living in this town and not having any money to live the way

one would like is perpetual. The facilities of Naples are so enormously superior. Here I have simply not the energy of going to the trouble of doing that sort of thing. Since I left Rome, there have only been three occasions, and unbridled chastity is telling on my health and spirits.

Publicly, Oscar and Bosie pretended that they had parted in acrimony. Both wrote letters regretting their decision ever to live together in Naples. 'It is, of course, the most bitter experience of a bitter life,' Oscar told Robbie:

It is a blow quite awful and paralysing, but it had to come, and I know it is better that I should never see him again. I don't want to. He fills me with horror.

'I am so glad, O so glad! to have got away,' Bosie told his mother:

I am so afraid you will not believe me, and I am so afraid of appearing to pose as anything but what I am, but I am not a hypocrite and you must believe me. I wanted to go back to him, I longed for it and for him, because I love him and admire him and think him great and almost good, but when I had done it and when I got back, I hated it, I was miserable.

The sentiments of both letters were untrue. Both were deliberately written with the clear purpose of regaining their allowances. Oscar was most certainly not filled with horror at Bosie, and Bosie was far from 'glad, O so glad!' to get away from Oscar. Once their allowances had been restored, they fully intended to see each other again. But with one crucial difference: they would meet as friends, not lovers. As their Neapolitan autumn imperceptibly turned to gentle winter, Oscar and Bosie both came to realise that their epic love for each other had faded into a loving friendship.

A joy-song

JACK: He seems to have expressed a desire to be buried in Paris.
CANON CHASUBLE: In Paris! I fear that hardly points to
any very serious state of mind at the last.

Oscar arrived in the City of Light on 13 February 1898, the very day that 'The Ballad of Reading Gaol' was published to great acclaim in England. Oscar hoped that the publication would ensure his entrée to literary Paris. 'A poem gives one *droit de cité*, and shows that one is still an artist,' he wrote. 'Reading Gaol' was a phenomenal success, quickly selling out of the first edition of four hundred copies. Oscar was exasperated by the meagre print-run and by the failure of the 'absurd' Smithers to advertise the book. 'I fear he had missed a popular "rush",' he told Robbie. 'He is so fond of "suppressed" books that he suppresses his own.' After a coolness lasting three months, during which time neither Oscar nor Robbie had written to the other, Oscar broke the ice the day after he arrived in Paris and sent a short, cordial note to Robbie asking him to come and see him. Within days they were back on the best of terms and, with one or two wobbles, would remain so until Oscar's death.

Relations with Constance were also beginning to thaw. There had been an angry silence between them ever since she had stopped his allowance in mid-November. But Oscar had Smithers send a copy of 'Reading Gaol' to her in Genoa, where she had finally settled. She was moved and 'frightfully upset by this wonderful poem of Oscar's', she told her brother, Otho. 'It is frightfully tragic and makes one cry.' On 4 March she wrote to Carlos Blacker asking him to go and see Oscar. 'He has, as you know, behaved exceedingly badly both to myself and my children,' she said, 'and all possibility of our living together has come to an end, but I am interested in him, as is my way with anyone that I have once known.'

Constance asked Blacker to tell Oscar that she thought the ballad 'exquisite' and that she hoped its huge success would encourage him to write more. To her surprise and consternation, Constance received a less-than-tactful letter from Oscar five days later, requesting the restoration of his allowance. The tone of the letter was far from the abject contrition that Constance had hoped for. He had written, she reported to Blacker, 'more or less demanding money as of right', curtly informing her that she owed him £78 and hoped she would send it. 'I know that he is in great poverty, but I don't care to be written to as though it were my fault,' she told Blacker. Nor was the unapologetic, defiant tone of Oscar's observations on his love affair with Bosie designed to propitiate her. Constance told Blacker:

> He says that he loved too much and that that is better than hate! This is true abstractly, but his was an unnatural love, a madness that I think is worse than hate. I have no hatred for him, but I confess that I am afraid of him.

She refused to reinstate Oscar's allowance. But fortunately for Oscar she had, just before she received his letter, generously sent £40 to Robbie for Oscar, asking him not to tell Oscar where the money had come from.

Oscar was bitter when he heard that his allowance was not to be reinstated. 'I have a sort of idea that she really wants me dead,' Oscar told Blacker:

> It is a horrible and persistent thought, and I daresay she would be relieved to hear you had recognised me at the Morgue.

But it was Constance, not Oscar, who was in the morgue. Three weeks later, on the night of 7 April, Oscar had a vivid dream that Constance had come to Paris to visit him. 'I kept on saying, "Go away, go away, leave me in peace".' The following day he received a telegram from Otho telling him that Constance was dead. She had indeed left him in peace. Constance had died in Genoa following an operation on her spine. In early 1895, she had tripped over a loose carpet at Tite Street and fallen downstairs, damaging her back. An operation in March 1895 – 'not a serious one', she told Robbie at the time – had been unsuccessful, and she had suffered a creeping paralysis ever since. Many years later, Otho said that Constance had died of an internal tumour, 'brought about in the first place by what she went through under her mother', an unassuageable childhood grief compounded by the many later griefs in her marriage. Constance's younger son, Vyvyan Holland, said his mother had died of 'a broken heart'.

Oscar sent a flurry of 'telegraphic tears of Hibernian sorrow' to his friends, bemoaning 'this fresh misery an unkind fate had brought upon him'. 'It really is awful,' Oscar lamented to Carlos Blacker a few days after he heard the news. 'I don't know what to do. If we had only met once, and kissed each other. It is too late. How awful life is.' Robbie was not convinced by Oscar's acute outpouring of grief. He had been great friends with Constance and almost certainly felt her death keenly himself. 'You will have heard of Mrs Wilde's death,' Robbie told Leonard Smithers:

> Oscar of course did not feel it at all. It is rather appalling for him as his allowance ceases and I do not expect his wife's trustees will continue it.

'He is in very good spirits and does not consume too many,' Robbie added, in a reference to Oscar's drinking which was reaching epic proportions.

'Alcohol, taken in sufficient quantities,' Oscar declared, 'produces all the effect of intoxication, but the only proper intoxication is conversation.' He would generally drink the best part of a bottle of brandy a day, in addition to wine, champagne, whisky and absinthe, which then contained thujone, a toxic substance which damaged the brain but produced vivid hallucinations. 'Absinthe stands alone,' Oscar once remarked:

> It is like nothing else; it shimmers like southern twilight in opalescent colouring; it has about it the seduction of strange sins. It is stronger than any other spirit and brings out the subconscious self in man.

Many years later, Bosie recalled that he had 'seen Oscar over and over again so drunk that he couldn't walk, in the last two years of his life'. According to Stuart Merrill, an American poet who lived in Paris, Oscar had 'never been exactly sober', but now he was drinking huge amounts. 'He used to be so overcome that he could scarcely stagger from the Madeleine to the Opera,' Merrill recalled. And Trelawny Backhouse claims that Oscar not only drank huge quantities of absinthe, but that he also used cocaine regularly.

Oscar would spend every night drinking and talking, talking and drinking, as if he could not stop. He would talk brilliantly and prodigiously to anyone who cared to listen, to 'waiters, coachmen, sellers of late papers, beggars, poor street girls'. His conversation was 'like a superhuman burst of fireworks', the writer Ernest La Jeunesse remembered, 'interwoven strands of gold and precious stones, of subtle ideas'. George Ives recorded a meeting with Oscar one evening at the Café de la Paix where they stayed until closing time. Predictably, Ives drank glass after glass of hot milk, while Oscar demolished endless whisky and sodas. Afterwards they went on to another bar, to another café, to anywhere that was open, where Oscar could get another drink. In the small hours, a drunken Oscar staggered back to his hotel, leaving Ives on the boulevard agonising over whether to speak to a beautiful boy who was loitering with erotic intent.

Money, or rather the lack of it, was a constant problem for Oscar, and for those of his friends who tried to ensure that he had enough money to pay for food and lodgings. Fortunately, Robbie was wrong about Oscar's allowance. Constance had added a codicil to her will specifying that he should continue to receive his £3 a week during his lifetime. But £3 a week was meaningless to a man who could spend £30 a day and have nothing to show for it. 'Like dear St Francis of Assisi I am wedded to Poverty,' Oscar wrote to a friend:

> But in my case the marriage is not a success: I hate the Bride that has been given to me: I see no beauty in her hunger and her rags: I have not the soul of St Francis: my thirst is for the beauty of life: my desire for its joy.

Oscar was incapable of managing his money. If he had any cash, he would spend it on fine food, drink and boys. Robbie's solution was to steadily dole out small amounts to Oscar. 'I tell everybody not to give Oscar money,' he said to Vincent O'Sullivan. 'If you give him anything give him clothes.' Oscar regarded Robbie's caution as just plain parsimony. 'Robbie is a dear but he does not understand,' he complained.

Oscar devoted his very considerable talents to begging, borrowing and virtually stealing money from whoever and wherever he could. He sold the scenario of a play, which he called *Love is Law*, to Frank Harris for £175, and then sold the same scenario to several other people. The play was virtually identical to the play he had sketched out to George Alexander in the summer of 1894, which had been provisionally entitled *Constance*. After many misunderstandings and much negotiation, Harris wrote and eventually produced the play – *Mr and Mrs Daventry* – in October 1900, just a month before Oscar died.

Harris was shocked when Bosie described Oscar as 'a fat old prostitute' over his insistent demands for money. Bosie explained later that he had used the words 'when I was hot from an interview with him in which he had alternately whined and wheedled and wept to extract more than the £40 I had just given him'. Bernard Shaw understood perfectly. 'I know that there is no beggar on earth as shameless as an Irish beggar,' he told Bosie forty years later. 'I have seen them when they are perfectly well-off beg from poor people.'

Oscar occasionally lost track of his stratagems for extracting money. He wrote to Robbie beseeching him to send his allowance early. A sudden crisis had arisen:

> A wretched inn-keeper at Nogent to whom I owe 100 francs, out of a bill of 300, threatens to sell Reggie's dressing-case, my overcoat, and two suits, if I don't pay him by Saturday. He has been detaining these things and now threatens a sale.

Two days later Oscar was forced to eat humble pie. 'I am so sorry about my excuse,' he told Robbie. 'I had forgotten I had used Nogent before. It shows the utter collapse of my imagination, and rather distresses me.' But there were times when Oscar was in real need. 'I had a fearful letter from poor Oscar who seems in a dreadful state of poverty even allowing for slight exaggeration,' Robbie wrote to Smithers a month after Constance's death. 'He says he had no dinner on Friday or Saturday.' Robbie was strapped for cash himself and was forced to ask Smithers to sell a picture on his behalf and send Oscar £5. 'Tell Oscar that a *friend* is sending him the money. There is no need to mention my name.'

There was little or no money to be had from writing. After the publication of 'The Ballad of Reading Gaol' and of a long and passionate letter on prison reform to the *Daily Chronicle*, Oscar ceased to write. He did undertake the editing and revision of *An Ideal Husband* and *The Importance of Being Earnest* for publication by Smithers, but wrote nothing else except many wonderful letters to his friends chronicling his life. Despite the encouragement and entreaties of the devoted Robbie, who sent him beautiful blank notebooks to write in, Oscar knew that he would never write again. When he was asked by the Comtesse de Brémont why he no longer wrote, Oscar replied:

> Because I have written all there was to write. I wrote when I did not know life; now that I do know the meaning of life, I have no more to write. Life cannot be written; life can only be lived. I have lived.

At Oxford, a quarter of a century earlier, Oscar had written in his commonplace book that 'the end of life is not action but contemplation, not doing but being.' Oscar sensed that he was reaching the end of his life, both physically and metaphysically. He no longer needed or wanted to write, but merely to contemplate the world he found himself in. He no longer wanted to do. He simply wanted to be.

At the very core of his being was his sexuality. To be at one with himself was to be at one with his Uranian self. In Paris he embraced his sexual urges and was in turn embraced and enveloped by them, achieving an erotic state of grace where desire was balanced by satisfaction, and where the contradictory imperatives of love and sex were resolved, merging into a perfect whole. Many years earlier, in his poem 'Hélas!', Oscar had asked whether the price of Uranian love was too high, whether 'the honey of romance' was worth losing his 'soul's inheritance'. Disgraced, disavowed and harrowed by prison and its thousand humiliations, he now found such debates meaningless. No longer encumbered by a wife or by his position in society, Oscar had no need to conceal his sexual self. He was liberated, emancipated from all internal and external constraints, and he could realise that delicious state of being:

> To drift with every passion till my soul
> Is a stringed lute on which all winds can play.

Among Oscar's many lovers in the last three years of his life, there was one for whom he felt a particular *tendresse*. Oscar met Maurice Gilbert 'by chance' during his first fortnight in Paris. His mother was French and his father English – 'all French lily and English rose' Oscar called him – and he was, or had been, a soldier in the marine infantry. Oscar hymned Maurice's flower-like beauty in letters to his friends. 'His upper lip is more like a rose-leaf than any rose-leaf I ever saw,' Oscar told Reggie Turner, adding that Maurice's 'eyelashes are too long'. He was 'jonquil-like in aspect, a sweet narcissus from an English meadow', and his mouth, he told Robbie, is 'the most beautiful mouth I know. It has the curves of Greek art and English flowers.' When Oscar embraced and kissed Maurice in public, he was rebuked by the journalist Jacques Daurelle, who told him he had *'retourné à son vomissement'*. Oscar was impervious. 'He is beautiful,' he told Daurelle. 'Look at him. He has the profile of Bonaparte.' 'He grows dearer to me daily,' Oscar told Smithers on 5 March.

Maurice was not only beautiful, he was also sweet, gentle, yielding and devoted. He was as happy to have sex with Oscar's friends as he was with Oscar. He was, Oscar said, 'a born Catholic in romance', and Reggie, Robbie and Bosie all had love affairs with Maurice, seemingly concurrently. In May, Maurice went to London where he spent time with Reggie Turner and with Robbie. 'No cheque this morning,' Oscar wrote to Robbie on 24 May, 'but instead my sweet Maurice, *our* sweet Maurice, looking quite charming and as delightful as ever. He seems a little *tired*, but that of course was the journey.' Robbie was particularly taken by Maurice and wrote to Oscar asking him to give Maurice his 'undying love'.

Bosie met Maurice at some point in early April and straight away laid amorous siege to him. Maurice appears to have rejected Bosie's advances, at least at first. 'Bosie is being very angelic and quiet,' Oscar told Robbie. 'It did him a great deal of good being trampled on by Maurice.' But by June, they were having a full-blown affair. 'Bosie is now inseparable from Maurice; they have gone again to Nogent,' Oscar told Robbie on 1 June.

Ever since his arrival in Paris, Oscar had seen Bosie frequently and even helped him choose furniture for his new flat. They were friendly and affectionate, but Oscar sometimes carped at the less attractive sides of Bosie's personality. Bosie had started to gamble heavily. 'He apparently goes to races every day, and loses of course,' Oscar told Robbie. 'He has a faculty of spotting the loser, which, considering that he knows nothing at all about horses, is perfectly astounding.' Oscar also criticised his sense of humour. 'Bosie has no real enjoyment of a joke unless he thinks there is a good chance of the other person being pained or annoyed,' he told Robbie:

It is an entirely English trait, the English type and symbol of a joke being the jug on the half-opened door, or the distribution of orange-peel on the pavement of a crowded thoroughfare.

When he was not betting on the horses or spending time with Maurice, Bosie was, as ever, chasing boys. 'He is devoted to a dreadful little ruffian aged fourteen,' Oscar informed Reggie:

whom he loves because at night, in the scanty intervals he can steal from an arduous criminal profession, he sells bunches of purple violets in front of the Café de la Paix. Also every time he goes home with Bosie he tries to rent him. This, of course, adds to his terrible fascination. We call him the '*Florifer*,' a lovely name. He also keeps another boy, aged twelve! whom Bosie wishes to know, but the wise 'Florifer' declines.

A week or so later, Bosie had 'grown tired of the Florifer but intends using the word in a sonnet', Oscar told Reggie, adding philosophically, 'All romances should end in a sonnet. I suppose all romances do.'

Oscar reported to Robbie his irritation at Bosie's crassness in bringing a young renter to a literary dinner given by the French author and journalist Henry Davray:

> Bosie turned up ten minutes after my arrival with *Gaston!* of all people, and placed him at Davray's table, where he gabbled about bicycles, and was generally offensive. Davray was much annoyed, and so was I. Bosie cannot understand the smallest iota of social tact, and does not see that to thrust 'Giton, the boy-paederast' into a literary reunion, without being invited, is vulgar. So life goes on.

Bosie's life in Paris could be summed up in a phrase. 'Boys, brandy, and betting monopolise his soul,' Oscar wrote. 'He is really a miser: but his method of hoarding is spending: a new type.'

Oscar was not a gambler, but he devoted as much, if not more, time as Bosie to boys and brandy. The boys of the boulevards became Oscar's lovers and friends. Oscar said that they were the only companions he could get. This was not strictly the case. He was far from friendless and rarely lonely or alone. He saw Bosie frequently, usually once or twice a week – sometimes more, sometimes less. He was often with Frank Harris, and Robbie Ross and Reggie Turner regularly came over to Paris to see him. And George Ives, Charles Conder and Will Rothenstein all spent time with him, as did many other friends.

It was true that he was sometimes snubbed by some of his former friends, and shunned by some of literary Paris, but only because of the way he flaunted his friendships and love affairs with the boulevard boys. 'I cannot bear being alone,' he told Robbie:

> While the literary people are charming when they meet me, we meet rarely. My companions are such as I can get, and I of course have to pay for such friendships.

André Gide squirmed with embarrassment when he met Oscar one evening while out strolling along the boulevards. Oscar was sitting at a table on the terrace of a café and begged André and his companion to join him for a drink. André priggishly did not want to be seen talking to Oscar. He tried to take the chair facing Oscar, with only his back visible to the street, but Oscar obliged him to sit next to him, revealing their acquaintance to the world. Both Pierre Louÿs and Henri de Régnier gave Oscar the 'cold shoulder', according to Vincent O'Sullivan, who later recalled that many former friends of Oscar in Paris had begged Robbie to try and make Oscar 'realise that he was ruining what sympathy was left for him among the Parisians by showing himself drunk on the boulevards with Sodomist outcasts'.

Oscar relished the company of the boulevard boys and in the course of his three years in Paris he got to know many of them. He wandered, he said, in 'the

Circle of the Boulevards', invoking the *Inferno* of Dante. But his life on the boulevards was far from a journey through Hell, more a kind of *louche* Heaven. There was Edmond, whom Oscar christened 'Edmond de Goncourt' after the diarist. Oscar introduced the boy to Robbie, and they enjoyed a brief affair. 'Edmond de Goncourt begs to be remembered with love to you,' Oscar wrote to Robbie. 'He adores his sash and your memory.' A month later, Oscar reported that:

> Edmond is very smart, and directs his little band of brigands on the Boulevard with great success. His book, *Les Chevaliers du Boulevard,* is begun, but he says he finds poetry very difficult. That promises well for his future as an artist.

Robbie was not impressed when Oscar announced that he wanted to rent a suite of unfurnished rooms, convinced that he only wanted the rooms to make it easier to have sex with boys. 'I don't wish to be horrid,' Oscar rebuked Robbie wittily:

> but I think you are a little unkind in saying that you cannot explain to people that the object of my taking unfurnished rooms is to enable me to have boys. Boys can be had everywhere. The difficulty I am under is my name, my personality.

There was Casquette of the blue suit; a boy known only as 'Le Premier Consul', to whom Oscar was 'devoted'; and an eighteen-year-old Russian youth called Maltchek Perovinski, 'quite charming and very educated'. And there was Léon, whom Oscar used to meet 'to smoke a cigarette or to weave words about life' and sometimes to sleep with: 'A meeting with *Léon*, whom I found wandering in the moonlit chasm of my little street, ended an admirable Continental Sunday,' he told Reggie. Giorgio was 'a most passionate faun', a young Corsican who worked at the Restaurant Jouffroy. 'His position was menial,' Oscar wrote, 'but eyes like the night and the scarlet flower of a mouth made one forget that.' Eugene was named 'the harvest-moon', a reference to the fact that he was uncircumcised. Georges was a 'beautiful boy of bad character'; Walter was a 'snub-nosed little horror'; and Henri, who plied his trade up and down the boulevard all day, had, Oscar wrote, 'the sweetest and most compromising smiles for me, especially when I am with friends'.

Many of the boys were accomplished and dangerous criminals, a fact which endeared them to Oscar, who saw them as fellow outlaws. 'Edmond de Goncourt' was arrested and sent to prison. But, on his release, he was unabashed and paraded up and down the boulevard in a new straw hat. Joseph, 'a little Dionysiac', was extremely violent and was sent to prison for attempted murder. Alphonse, a lover of both Oscar and Reggie Turner, went in for *chantage*, or blackmail. 'Your little friend Alphonse was arrested last night for *chantage*,' Oscar told Reggie in December 1898:

He demanded fifteen francs, and was only given ten and a cab-fare, so on being expelled from the house he made a scene and was taken up. There is much joy amongst his friends, as his general conduct did not meet with approval. It is a pity he always wanted to behave badly; it gave him a demoniac pleasure. He was quite an imp, though attractive in love scenes.

Despite his own frequent relations with boulevard boys, Robbie was frequently assailed by attacks of conscience and morality and would often urge Oscar to change his ways and stop associating with 'these gutter perverts', as he called them. Oscar gave as good as he got. He was not about to take lessons in moral probity from his 'dear little absurd Robbie'. 'The only thing that consoles me,' Oscar told him:

is that your moral attitude towards yourself is even more severe than your moral attitudes towards others. Yours is the pathological tragedy of the hybrid, the Pagan–Catholic. You exemplify the beauty and the uselessness of Conscience.

Rather more kindly, he sometimes made light of Robbie's confused notions of morality, telling him:

It is quite true that when you talk morals to me, which you do quite beautifully, I always pipe on a reed and a faun comes running out of the thicket. You at once say 'What a lovely faun!' The rest is silence.

Robbie even went so far as to suggest to Oscar that he might consider getting married. Oscar treated Robbie's absurd suggestion with the wit it deserved. 'As regards to my marrying again,' he wrote:

I am quite sure that you will want me to marry this time some sensible, practical, plain, middle-aged boy, and I don't like the idea at all. Besides I am practically engaged to a fisherman of extraordinary beauty, aged eighteen. So you see there are difficulties.

In December 1898, Oscar accepted Frank Harris's invitation to spend three months on the French Riviera as his guest. Oscar was installed at the Hôtel des Bains in Napoule, near Cannes. He took daily walks in the pine woods, and discovered that 'the fishing population of the Riviera have the same freedom from morals as the Neapolitans have'. He had, he said, 'two special friends, one called Raphael, the other Fortuné – both quite perfect, except they can read and write.' 'Yes,' he told Leonard Smithers, 'even at Napoule there is romance: it comes in boats and takes the form of fisher-lads, who draw great nets, and are bare-limbed: they are strangely perfect.' Oscar told Harris that he was thinking of writing a poem to be entitled 'The Ballad of the Fisher-Boy'. It was, he explained, to be a companion piece to 'The Ballad of Reading Gaol', but 'a joy-song' rather than 'a song of sorrow and despair'. It would, he said, 'sing of liberty instead of prison, joy instead of sorrow, a kiss instead of an execution'. Oscar reeled off three wonderful stanzas to Harris but never got round to writing them down.

On a trip to Nice, Oscar bumped into a friend from Paris, eighteen-year-old *le petit Georges*, 'one of the noble army of the Boulevard':

> He is like a very handsome Roman boy, dark, and bronze-like, with splendidly chiselled nose and mouth, and the tents of midnight are folded in his eyes; moons hide in their curtains. He is visiting Nice on speculative business. It is beautiful, and encouraging, to find people who can combine romance with business – blend them indeed, and make them one.

Oscar celebrated Christmas with a new friend, Harold Mellor, who was staying at Cannes and came constantly to Napoule to see Oscar, bringing with him 'a very pretty Italian boy' called Eolo. Mellor was a 'charming fellow', a Uranian, who had been 'sent away from Harrow at the age of fourteen for being loved by the captain of the cricket eleven'. He was extremely wealthy and lived with Eolo in a house in Gland, Switzerland, which he begged Oscar to visit. Oscar accepted Mellor's invitation and left for Gland in late February 1899, travelling there via Genoa, where he stopped off to visit Constance's grave. 'It is very pretty – a marble cross with dark ivy-leaves inlaid in a good pattern,' he told Robbie:

> It was very tragic seeing her name carved on a tomb . . . I brought some flowers. I was deeply affected – with a sense, also, of the uselessness of all regrets. Nothing could have been otherwise, and Life is a very terrible thing.

Oscar took his own comments on the futility of regret to heart. On the same day that he visited Constance's grave, he also picked up 'a beautiful young actor' from Florence:

> whom I wildly loved. He has the strange name of Didaco. He has the look of Romeo, without Romeo's sadness: a face chiselled for high romance. We spent three days together.

The visit to Gland was not a success. Though the villa was pretty and comfortable, Oscar decided that he did not much like Harold Mellor after all:

> He is a silent, dull person, cautious and economical: revolting Swiss wines appear at meals: he is complex without being interesting: has Greek loves, and is rather ashamed of them: has heaps of money, and lives in terror of poverty: so I regard it as a sort of Swiss *pension*, where there is no weekly bill.

A month with Mellor was enough, and Oscar announced to Smithers that he was returning to Genoa 'to try and find a place . . . where I can live for ten francs a day (boy *compris*)'. But by May, Oscar was back in Paris and had resumed the usual pattern of his life there.

In March 1900 Oscar had sufficiently mended his breach with Harold Mellor to accept his invitation to spend two months in Italy. They went to Sicily first, where Oscar befriended Manuele, Francesco and Salvatore. 'I love them all,' he told Robbie, 'but only remember Manuele.' Oscar also became great friends with a fifteen-year-old seminarist, Giuseppe Loverde. Giuseppe was 'most sweet', and every day Oscar 'kissed him behind the high altar' in the cathedral of Palermo. From Sicily they went to Naples and spent three days there. Oscar was disappointed to discover that most of his 'friends' in the city were in prison. 'But I met some of nice memory,' he told Robbie, 'and fell in love with a Sea-God, who for some extraordinary reason is at the Regia Marina School instead of being a Triton.'

Oscar and Mellor arrived in Rome on 12 April. Mellor returned to Switzerland after two days, while Oscar remained in the Eternal City for a month and was joined there for a short visit by Robbie. There was, Oscar reported to Bosie enthusiastically, a plentiful supply of exceptionally beautiful boys. 'I am glad you are enjoying Rome so much,' Bosie replied. 'I quite agree with you that the boys are far more beautiful there. In fact I think they come next to English boys.'

Oscar mentioned several Roman boys in his letters. There was Homer, who talked too much, and Pietro, who was 'dark, and gloomy, and I love him very much'. There was Omero, whom Robbie had picked up and passed on to Oscar. Omero was a guide 'who knows nothing about Rome'. And there were the two friends, Armando and Arnaldo. 'I have given up Armando, a very smart elegant young Roman Sporus,' Oscar told Robbie. 'He was beautiful, but his requests for raiment and neckties were incessant: he really bayed for boots, as a dog moonwards.' Oscar promptly took up with Arnaldo. There was Philippo, a student, and another boy, Dario, to whom Oscar presented a ticket to see the Pope:

> It was the first time he had ever seen the Pope: and he transferred to me his adoration of the successor of Peter: would I fear have kissed me on leaving the Bronze Gateway had I not sternly repelled him. I have become very cruel to boys, and no longer let them kiss me in public.

Just before he left Rome, Oscar wrote to Robbie to tell him that he had bidden goodbye 'with tears and one kiss, to the beautiful Greek boy' Robbie had introduced him to.

In the same letter, Oscar spoke about the erotic intensity of his life since his release from prison. 'In the mortal sphere, I have fallen in and out of love, and fluttered hawks and doves alike,' he wrote:

> How evil it is to buy Love, and how evil to sell it! And yet what purple hours

one can snatch from that grey slowly-moving thing we call Time! My mouth is twisted with kissing, and I feed on fevers.

It was almost as if Oscar sensed that time was running out, that he would soon pass from the mortal to the immortal sphere. Death had stalked him ever since he had gone to prison. Speranza had died, and Trooper Wooldridge had been executed in prison. Aubrey Beardsley had died – 'at the age of a flower', Oscar wrote – in March 1898, less than a month after Oscar's arrival in Paris. Three weeks later, Constance was dead. The following year, Oscar's older brother, Willie, died of alcoholism. Ernest Dowson had died in February 1900, two months before Oscar's trip to Rome. Even Queensberry, the scarlet Marquis, had died, convinced to the last that he was being 'persecuted by the Oscar-Wilders'.

'You must not think of me as being morbidly sad, or wilfully living in sadness,' Oscar had told Carlos Blacker soon after he came out of prison. 'I often find myself strangely happy.' During the last three years of his life Oscar was to remain strangely happy. According to Vincent O'Sullivan, who knew him well during the last years, the legend of Oscar's life 'ebbing out in squalor and destitution and abandonment' was wrong. 'I give it as my firm opinion that Oscar Wilde was, on the whole, fairly happy during the last years of his life,' Bosie wrote later:

He had an extraordinarily buoyant and happy temperament, a splendid sense of humour, and an unrivalled faculty for enjoyment of the present. Of course, he had his bad moments, moments of depression and sense of loss and defeat, but they were not of long duration.

There were times when Oscar was penniless and went hungry for a day, or even two, but such occasions were rare. He lived in cheap but clean and comfortable hotels, and ate well in inexpensive – and sometimes expensive – restaurants. His appetite for life was undimmed. Everything he did, he did to excess. He drank prodigiously, because he wanted to. He was a self-declared and unapologetic sexual pagan who indulged his appetite to the full. He was an outcast, an outlaw, but he gloried in his notoriety. His life was, for the most part, joyous and affirming.

Yet occasionally, the shadow of death would pass over him and his face would, according to Vincent O'Sullivan, sometimes 'be swept with poignant anguish and regret' when he talked about the past, or contemplated with apprehension his future:

which he saw as a mountain-pass under darkling shadows falling ever thicker – becoming in fact, save by miracle, impracticable for him. At such moments he would pass his large hand with a trembling gesture over his face and stretch out his arm as though to ward off the phantom of his destiny.

At other times, Oscar would ponder his future with equanimity, almost curiosity, and his large grey-blue eyes would take on an abstracted faraway look. It was, O'Sullivan wrote, 'a looking out, a looking beyond, a stare that would penetrate to the invisible'.

The end of life was indeed contemplation.

November 1900

Late on the evening of 29 November 1900, a printed visiting card bearing the name 'Mr Robert Ross, Reform Club' was brought up to Father Cuthbert Dunne, a young Irish priest at St Joseph's Church in the Avenue Hoche. On the back of the card, Robbie had written:

> Can I see one of the fathers about a very urgent case or can I hear of a priest elsewhere who can talk English to administer the sacraments to a dying man?

In great haste, Father Dunne went with Robbie to the Hotel d'Alsace in the Rue des Beaux-Arts, where Oscar had lived since August 1899. As they drove through the dark, wintry streets of Paris, Robbie told Father Dunne that the man he was about to see was Oscar Wilde. Reggie Turner and a male nurse were asked to leave Oscar's small room while Father Dunne, assisted by Robbie, administered baptism and the last rites.

Earlier that day, Robbie had rushed back to Paris from the South of France in response to a telegram from Reggie Turner telling him that Oscar's condition was 'almost hopeless'. After what was supposed to be a routine operation on his ear on 10 October, Oscar had gradually become sicker, but then appeared to be slowly recovering and was well enough to get up and take several drives in the Bois de Boulogne. He was managing to consume as much champagne as he wanted, as well as the occasional glass of absinthe. On one of these drives, in early November, Oscar caught a chill and developed an abscess in his ear, which eventually led to cerebral meningitis.

Oscar knew that he was going to die. 'Somehow I don't think I shall survive to see the new century,' he told Robbie. 'If another century began and I was still alive, it would really be more than the English could stand.' He woke one day and said to Reggie Turner, 'I dreamt I was supping with the dead.' 'My dear Oscar,' Reggie answered. 'You were probably the life and soul of the party.' To another visitor he remarked, 'My wallpaper and I are fighting a duel to the death. One or the other of us has to go.' By 25 November, it was clear that Oscar was not going to recover. He was being injected with morphine and lapsed in and out of consciousness, his mind seeming to wander.

When Robbie arrived on the morning of 29 November, Oscar's appearance was 'very painful':

He had become quite thin, his flesh was livid, his breathing heavy. He was trying to speak. He was conscious that people were in the room, and raised his hand when I asked him whether he understood. He pressed our hands.

At dawn on 30 November, Oscar's final struggle began. 'There was the so-called death-rattle, or roughness of breathing in his throat,' Reggie recalled. 'I have never heard anything like it before,' Robbie told More Adey. 'It sounded like the horrible turning of a crank, and it never ceased until the end.' At approximately a quarter to two that afternoon, Oscar's breathing eased. Robbie held his hand and felt his pulse fluttering. Five minutes later, Oscar heaved a profound sigh. He exhaled one last, long, deep breath, and then was silent.

Bosie arrived too late to be with Oscar at the end but was the chief mourner at his funeral four days later. 'I am miserable and wretched about darling Oscar,' he told More Adey afterwards:

It seems so beastly that I couldn't have seen him before he died . . . It seems to get worse every day. I try to think that perhaps it is better than when he was in prison, but then one had the hope of seeing him again, and now I don't believe I ever shall.

Oscar was only forty-six when he died. He had lived 'more lives than one', vividly, intensely and passionately. 'I was a man who stood in symbolic relations to the art and culture of my age,' he wrote in a remarkable and prophetic passage of self-obituary in *De Profundis*:

The gods had given me almost everything. I had genius, a distinguished name, high social position, brilliancy, intellectual daring: I made art a philosophy, and philosophy an art: I altered the minds of men and the colours of things: there was nothing I said or did that did not make people wonder . . . to truth itself I gave what is false no less than what is true as its rightful province, and showed that the false and the true are merely forms of intellectual existence. I treated Art as the supreme reality and life as a mere mode of fiction: I awoke the imagination of my century so that it created myth and legend around me: I summed up all systems in a phrase, and all existence in an epigram.

A year after Oscar's death, Bosie composed his personal obituary in the form of a moving sonnet, 'To Oscar Wilde', which perhaps comes close to capturing the billowing cloud of infectious joy and wonder that surrounded Oscar:

> I dreamed of him last night, I saw his face
> All radiant and unshadowed of distress,
> And as of old, in music measureless,
> I heard his golden voice and marked him trace
> Under the common thing the hidden grace,

And conjure wonder out of emptiness,
Till mean things put on beauty like a dress

And all the world was an enchanted place.
And then methought outside a fast locked gate
I mourned the loss of unrecorded words,
Forgotten tales and mysteries half said,
Wonders that might have been articulate,
And voiceless thoughts like murdered singing birds.
And so I woke and knew that he was dead.

Above all else, for Bosie, Oscar was the first and the greatest 'martyr' to the cause of Uranian love. In 'The Ballad of Reading Gaol', Oscar wrote what was to become his own Uranian epitaph:

And alien tears will fill for him
Pity's long-broken urn,
For his mourners will be outcast men,
And outcasts always mourn.

Oscar died an outcast and was mourned by 'outcast men'. But he also knew that he was a martyr in an epic struggle for the freedom of men to love men, and he was confident that Uranian love would, in time, be seen as 'noble'. 'Yes. I have no doubt we shall win,' he told George Ives, 'but the road is long, and red with monstrous martyrdoms.'

A hundred years and many monstrous martyrdoms later, Oscar's men are outcast men no more and the love that dared not speak its name has at last found its joyful voice.

Permissions and picture Credits

Permissions

The author would like to thank the following: Merlin Holland for permission to quote extensively from Oscar's letters, to reproduce Oscar's unpublished poem 'Choir Boy', and to use other materials copyright to his family; HarperCollins Publishers for permission to reprint from *The Complete Letters of Oscar Wilde* (copyright 2000 Merlin Holland); the literary estate of Lord Alfred Douglas for permission to quote from Bosie's published and unpublished writings; Caroline Gould for permission to quote from the letters of Robbie Ross; the Trustees of the National Library of Scotland for permission to quote from the letters of Richard Burdon Haldane; to Father Bede Bailey for permission to quote from the letters and writings of John Gray and André Raffalovich; to Chris Furse for permission to quote from the writings of John Addington Symonds; and to Marie-Jaqueline Lancaster for permission to quote from the diaries of Laura Troubridge, and from the letters of Laura Troubridge and Adrian Hope; and to Editions Gallimard in Paris for permission to quote from the journals and letters of André Gide.

Every effort has been made to trace all the copyright holders, but if any have been inadvertently overlooked the publishers will be pleased to make any necessary arrangements.

Picture credits

'Oscar and friend, c.1877', 'Oscar and Bosie in Norfolk', 'Oscar and Bosie in Oxford, Spring 1893', 'Oscar and Bosie in Naples', 'Constance two years before her death' all courtesy of the William Andrews Clark Memorial Library, Los Angeles; 'Neronian Oscar' courtesy of the Harry Ransom Humanities Research Center, University of Texas at Austin; 'Robbie Ross' courtesy of the late Mary Viscountess Eccles; 'John Gray' and 'André Raffalovich' courtesy of Father Bede Bailey; '"Stella" Boulton, "Fanny" Park and Lord Arthur Clinton' courtesy of the Essex Record Office; 'a card with hideous words' courtesy of the Public Record Office; 'Oscar c.1890' and 'Oscar's Uranian photograph of two boys' courtesy of the Neil Bartlett Collection; 'Oscar's Uranian photograph of five boys' courtesy of Simon Watney; 'Oscar in Rome' courtesy of the National Portrait Gallery.

Notes

Abbreviations
Ellmann: Richard Ellmann, *Oscar Wilde* (New York, 1988)
Letters: *The Complete Letters of Oscar Wilde*, edited by Merlin Holland and Rupert Hart-Davis (London, 2000)
Works: *Collins Complete Works of Oscar Wilde*, Centenary Edition (Glasgow, 1999)

May 1895
'crowded to suffocation': *Illustrated Police Budget*, 1 June 1895, in *The Oscar Wilde File* compiled by Jonathan Goodman (London, 1988), page 128.
'You'll dine your man in Paris': Stuart Mason, *Oscar Wilde: Three Times Tried* (London, [1912]), page 459.
'eagerly scanning the faces': *Illustrated Police Budget*, in *The Oscar Wilde File*, pages 128–130.
'It is the worst case', 'Shame': Mason, *Oscar Wilde: Three Times Tried*, page 464.
'And I?': the *Star*, 27 May 1895.
'It is perhaps in prison': *Letters*, page 651.
'this tomb': *Letters*, page 656.
'scarlet threads': *Letters*, page 706.
'The two great turning points': *Letters*, page 732.

Wonder and remorse
'Oxford is the capital': Frank Harris, *Oscar Wilde* (Michigan, 1959), page 26.
'much too long': G.T. Atkinson, 'Oscar Wilde at Oxford', *Cornhill Magazine*, volume LXVI, number 395 (May 1929), page 559.
'moonlike': Atkinson, 'Oscar Wilde at Oxford', page 559.
'singularly mild': Ellmann, page 75.
'He did not come': Atkinson, 'Oscar Wilde at Oxford', page 563.
'like a man': Ellmann, page 75.
'a Celebrity': Davis Coakley, *Oscar Wilde: The Importance of Being Irish* (Dublin, 1995), page 22.
'sex-awakening': Frank Harris, *My Life and Loves* (New York, 2000), pages 4–5.
'sentimental friendships': Barbara Belford, *Oscar Wilde: A Certain Genius* (London, 2000), page 29.
'There was one boy': Harris, *Oscar Wilde*, page 19.
'the romantic medium of': Philip E. Smith II and Michael S. Helford, *Oscar Wilde's Oxford Notebooks* (New York and Oxford, 1989), page 115.
'that strange and to us revolting perversion': Coakley, *Oscar Wilde*, page 156.
'These things are so repugnant': W.B. Stanford and R.B. McDowell, *Mahaffy: A*

Biography of an Anglo-Irishman (London, 1971), pages 156–157.
'As to the epithet *unnatural*': Coakley, *Oscar Wilde*, page 157.
'my old pupil Mr Oscar Wilde of Magdalen College': Richard Pine, *The Thief of Reason* (Dublin, 1995), page 125.
'my first and my best teacher': *Letters*, page 562.
'who has the most Greek': *Letters*, page 42.
'left leg is a Greek poem': Atkinson, 'Oscar Wilde at Oxford', page 563.
'Greek sensuous delicate lips': *Letters*, page 50.
'a beautiful boy': Wilde, 'Historical Criticism in Antiquity', in Ellmann, page 1.
'White says old Wilde': Shane Leslie, *Memoir of John Edward Courtenay Bodley*, (London, 1930), pages 24–25.
'who leaves foolish letters': diary of J.E.C. Bodley, 4 December 1875, in Ellmann, page 59.
'this psychological question': *Letters*, page 27.
'is charming': *Letters*, page 40.
'Ah God, it is a dreary thing': Oscar Wilde, manuscript of unpublished poem 'Choir Boy', Clark Library, Los Angeles.
'I had been taught': John Addington Symonds, *Memoirs*, edited by Phyllis Grosskurth (London, 1984), page 128.
'divert my passions': Symonds, *Memoirs*, page 135.
'I was very much pained': Ellmann, page 58.
'dear Eva': 'The Diner-Out', A.J.A. Symons, *Essays and Biographies* (London, 1969) page 161.
'an *exquisitely pretty girl*': *Letters*, page 29.
'two sweet years': *Letters*, page 71.
'something of mine': *Letters*, page 107.
'a cloak to hide his secret': *Works*, page 438.

Tea and beauties
'It is a dreadful thing': from a conversation with Edgar Saltus, Christie's, *The Prescott Collection: Printed Books and Manuscripts*, New York, 6 February 1981, page 200.
'a very pleasant, handsome, young fellow': *Oscar Wilde: Interviews and Recollections*, edited by E.H. Mikhail (London, 1979), volume I, page 30.
'By early train': diary of Lord Ronald Gower, 4 June 1876, in H. Montgomery Hyde, *Oscar Wilde* (London, 1976), page 19.
'I came down here on Monday': *Letters*, page 21.
'Life's aim': *Works*, page 497.
'dallying in the enchanted isle': *Letters*, page 28.
'a charming little fishing lodge': *Letters*, page 30.
'We had a delightful day': *Letters*, pages 34–35.
'I saw a great deal of Arthur May': *Letters*, page 36.
'the bloom and vitality': *Dublin University Magazine*, July 1877, in Ellmann, page 83.
'A counted number of pulses': Walter Pater, *Studies in the History of the Renaissance*, in Michael Patrick Gillespie, 'Ethics and Aesthetics in *The Picture of Dorian Gray*', in *Rediscovering Oscar Wilde*, edited by C. George Sandulescu and Colin Smythe (Gerrards Cross, 1994), pages 143–144.
'might possibly mislead': Robert Aldrich, *The Seduction of the Mediterranean* (London, 1993), page 76.

'All flames are pure': George Ives materials, 26 February 1894, Humanities Research Center, Austin, Texas.

'an early call': *Letters*, page 59.

'timid and afraid': Vincent O'Sullivan to A.J.A. Symons, 26 May 1937, in Vincent O'Sullivan, *Some Letters to A.J.A. Symons* (Edinburgh, 1975).

'a Philistine like you': Leslie, *Memoir of John Edward Courtenay Bodley*, page 17.

'extreme aesthete': *New York Times*, 20 June 1882, in Ellmann, page 84.

'my blue china': Atkinson, 'Oscar Wilde at Oxford', page 562.

'When a young man says': *Interviews and Recollections*, volume I, page 40.

'the absolute stupidity': *Interviews and Recollections*, volume I, page 40.

'A fair slim boy': *Works*, page 775.

'rose-red youth': *Works*, page 29.

'Youth! Youth!': *Works*, page 31.

'the mere fact of youth': Mason, *Oscar Wilde: Three Times Tried*, page 79.

'confession': Father Sebastian Bowden to Oscar Wilde, 16 April 1878, in Symons, *Essays and Biographies*, page 169.

'Mr Soddington Symonds': H. Montgomery Hyde, *The Other Love* (London, 1970), page 101.

'As a Catholic': Father Sebastian Bowden to Oscar Wilde, 16 April 1878, in Pine, *Oscar Wilde*, page 22.

'this untidy but romantic house': *Letters*, page 85.

'tea at Oscar Wilde's': Laura Troubridge, *Life Among the Troubridges*, edited by Jacqueline Hope-Nicholson (London, 1966), page 152.

'his strange appearance': *Interviews and Recollections*, volume II, page 257.

'discovered Mrs Langtry': Ellmann, page 266.

'There is only one thing in the world': *Works*, pages 18–19.

'Anyone could have done that': Boris Brasol, *Oscar Wilde: The Man – The Artist* (London, 1938), page 183.

'a supper party the night before': *Interviews and Recollections*, volume I, page 14.

'And many a maiden will mutter': 'A verse on the Grosvenor Gallery', *The Oscar Wilde File*, page 9.

'Maudle': Golnitz, 'The Artist's Studio', in Gary Schmidgall, *The Stranger Wilde* (New York, 1994), page 58.

'I am the original of *Maudle*': *Interviews and Recollections*, volume I, page 40.

'My attitude': *Interviews and Recollections*, volume I, page 40.

'a very clever play': Wolf Von Eckardt, Sander L. Gilman and J. Edward Chamberlain, *Oscar Wilde's London* (London, 1987), page 180.

'the utterly utter': Gerard Manley Hopkins to Robert Bridges, 1881, in Frances Winwar, *Oscar Wilde and the Yellow Nineties* (1940) page 65.

'a curious toadstool': Ellmann, page 161.

'Fancy Portrait': Belford, *Oscar Wilde*, page 89.

'Aesthete of Aesthetes': *Punch*, 25 June 1881, in Schmidgall, *The Stranger Wilde*, page 59.

'The cover is consummate': Robert Sherard, *The Life of Oscar Wilde* (London, 1911), pages 172–173.

'a volume of echoes': Sherard, *The Life of Oscar Wilde*, pages 172–173.

'poems are thin': Hesketh Pearson, *The Life of Oscar Wilde* (Middlesex, 1960), pages 59–60.

'terror and misery': *Interviews and Recollections*, volume II, page 275.

'advise a separation': R. Miles to Oscar Wilde, 1881, Clark Library.

'bored you': *Letters*, page 89.

'a poet's face': John Stokes, 'Wilde the Journalist', *The Cambridge Companion to Oscar Wilde*, edited by Peter Raby (Cambridge, 1997), page 77.

'a very charming time': *Letters*, page 101.

A little in love

'Men marry': *Works*, page 46.

'a good marriage': Lady Wilde to Oscar Wilde, in Joy Melville, *Mother of Oscar* (London, 1999), page 145.

'distressed beyond words': *Letters*, page 82.

'I am so glad': *Letters*, page 82.

'Alfred Milner': *Letters*, page 83.

'become very close': *Letters*, page 82.

'I want to see you': *Letters*, pages 82–83.

'Charlotte': *Letters*, page 82.

'a wonderful young Irishman': 'My Oscar', unpublished papers of Violet Hunt, in Robert Secor, 'Aesthetes and Pre-Raphaelites', *Texas Studies in Language and Literature*, volume XXI, number 3 (fall 1979), page 401.

'Letitia's young men!': Hunt, 'My Oscar', in Secor, 'Aesthetes and Pre-Raphaelites', page 401.

'Botticelli by Burne-Jones': Hunt, 'My Oscar', in Secor, 'Aesthetes and Pre-Raphaelites', page 397.

'In ten minutes': Hunt, 'My Oscar', in Secor, 'Aesthetes and Pre-Raphaelites', page 401.

'slip of a girl': Hunt, 'My Oscar', in Secor, 'Aesthetes and Pre-Raphaelites', page 397.

'big lusty fellow': Hunt, 'My Oscar', in Secor, 'Aesthetes and Pre-Raphaelites', page 401.

'The Bernhardt': Hunt, 'My Oscar', in Secor, 'Aesthetes and Pre-Raphaelites', page 402.

'fine, true voice': Hunt, 'My Oscar', in Secor, 'Aesthetes and Pre-Raphaelites', page 402.

'Beautiful women like you': Hunt, 'My Oscar', in Secor, 'Aesthetes and Pre-Raphaelites', page 402.

'We will rule the world': Hunt, 'My Oscar', in Secor, 'Aesthetes and Pre-Raphaelites', page 403.

'and a little in love': Hunt, 'My Oscar', in Secor, 'Aesthetes and Pre-Raphaelites', page 405.

'the sweetest Violet': *Letters*, page 89.

'really in love with me': diary of Violet Hunt, 25 February 1891, in Belford, *Oscar Wilde*.

'as nearly as possible escaped': Violet Hunt, *The Flurried Years* (London, 1926), page 168, in Belford, *Oscar Wilde*, pages 78 and 327.

'a single white Eucharist': 'My Oscar', unpublished papers of Violet Hunt, in Belford, *Oscar Wilde*, pages 79 and 327.

'the brutality of strong lights': Eric Lambert, *Mad With Much Heart* (London, 1967), page 155.

'a most amusing description': Otho Holland Lloyd to A.J.A. Symons, 22 May 1937, Clark Library, Los Angeles.

'Lady Wilde has sold': Joyce Bentley, *The Importance of Being Constance* (London, 1983), page 32.

'O.W. came yesterday': *Letters*, page 221.
'Grandpa, I think': Merlin Holland, *The Wilde Album* (London, 1997), page 112.
'By the by, Mama': Ellmann, page 234.
'There are some lives': Otho Holland Lloyd to Carlos Blacker, 13 January 1901, in Sotheby's, *English Literature and History*, London, 10 and 11 June 1986.
'a tragedy': Otho Holland Lloyd to A.J.A. Symons, 22 May 1937, Clark Library.
'Two women cousins living': Otho Holland Lloyd to A.J.A. Symons, 22 May 1937, Clark Library.
'she could not say': Otho Holland Lloyd to A.J.A. Symons, 27 May 1937, Clark Library.
'I shall always think': Otho Holland Lloyd to A.J.A. Symons, 22 May 1937, Clark Library.
'at my insistence': Otho Holland Lloyd to A.J.A. Symons, 22 May 1937, Clark Library.
'A most intense': Winwar, *Oscar Wilde and the Yellow Nineties*, page 61.

Nothing but my genius
'Strange that a pair': Ellmann, page 164.
'His outer garment': *New York World*, 3 January 1882, in *Oscar Wilde: Interviews and Recollections* volume I, page 36.
'I am not exactly pleased': Ellmann, page 158.
'disappointed with the Atlantic': Ellmann, page 158.
'lashed to the bowsprit': Hyde, *Oscar Wilde*, page 51.
'nothing to declare but my genius': Ellmann, page 160.
'I stand at the top': *Letters*, page 126.
'Caricature is the tribute': Hyde, *Oscar Wilde*, page 53.
'sepulchral': Hyde, *Oscar Wilde*, page 53.
'womanish': *Newport Mercury and Weekly News*, 22 January 1882, in Mary Warner Blanchard, *Oscar Wilde's America* (New Haven and London, 1998), page 10.
'mamma's boy': *New York Times*, 24 January 1882, in Blanchard, page 10.
'neat, delicate and arched': *Newark Daily Advertiser*, 31 January 1882, in Blanchard, page 10.
'Is he manne': *Boston Evening Transcript*, 4 February 1882, in Blanchard, page 11.
'epicene': *New York Times*, 21 January 1882, in Ellmann, page 178.
'fatuous fool': Oscar Cargill, 'Mr. James's Aesthetic Mr. Nash', *Nineteenth-Century Fiction*, volume XII, number 3 (December 1957), pages 180–181.
'undecided': Ellmann, page 179.
'Where is *she?*': Winwar, *Oscar Wilde and the Yellow Nineties*, page 78.
'pallid and lank': *Brooklyn Daily Eagle*, 3 January 1882, in Blanchard, page 13.
'act effeminately': George Chauncey, *Gay New York* (New York, 1994), page 33.
'many pallid': *Tribune*, 9 January 1882, in Winwar, *Oscar Wilde and the Yellow Nineties*, page 80.
'young men painting': *Washington Post*, 22 January 1882, in Blanchard, page 13.
'What a little Ganymede': *Letters*, page 124.
'absorbed the Whitmanesque': *Philadelphia Press*, 19 January 1882, *Interviews and Recollections*, volume I, page 47.
'calamite': Richard Jenkyns, *The Victorians and Ancient Greece* (New York, 1981), page 283.
'high towering love': John Addington Symonds, *Sexual Inversion* (New York, 1984), page 183.

'The chief value': *Pall Mall Gazette*, 25 January 1889, in Gary Schmidgall, *Walt Whitman: A Gay Life* (New York, 1998), page 294.
'There is something so Greek': *Interviews and Recollections*, volume I, page 47.
'Oscar Wilde has expressed': J.M. Stoddart to Walt Whitman, 11 January 1882, in Schmidgall, *Walt Whitman*, page 286.
'hearty salutations': Ellmann, page 167.
'Walt Whitman will be in': Ellmann, page 167.
'I have come to you': *Interviews and Recollections*, volume I, page 47.
'If you are willing': Schmidgall, *Walt Whitman*, page 286.
'"thee and thou" terms': *Interviews and Recollections*, volume I, pages 46–47.
'We had a jolly good time': *Interviews and Recollections*, volume I, page 46.
'Everyone who knew Whitman': Harrison Reeves, *Mercure de France*, 1 June 1913.
'he just resented': George Ives, 19 November 1893, HRC.
'I have the kiss': George Ives, 6 January 1901, in John Stokes, *Oscar Wilde: Myths, Miracles and Imitations* (Oxford, 1996), page 69.
'Unto thy martyrdom': Winwar, *Oscar Wilde and the Yellow Nineties*, page 70.
'There is none': Symons, *Essays and Biographies*, page 177.
'too effusive': Pearson, *The Life of Oscar Wilde*, page 71.
'Among the "many young men"': Ellmann, page 200.
'Have you read the *Saturday*': Ellmann, page 200.
'My friends criticised': Pearson, *The Life of Oscar Wilde*, page 64.
'the true poet': Ellmann, pages 212–213.
'I send you the young Greek': *Letters*, page 176.
'a lovely bas-relief': *Letters*, page 228.
'by a thin-faced youth': Pearson, *The Life of Oscar Wilde*, page 83.
'America is a land': Hyde, *Oscar Wilde*, page 81.

Freedom from sordid care
'The proper basis for marriage': *Works*, page 163.
'Are you in love?': Melville, *Mother of Oscar*, page 180.
'Miss Ward Howe': Violet Hunt, 21 November 1882, in Secor, 'Aesthetes and Pre-Raphaelites', page 399.
'praised Constance immensely': Lady Jane Wilde to Oscar Wilde, 1882, in Melville, *Mother of Oscar*, page 181.
'I think she would kill you': Otho Holland Lloyd to Nellie Hutchinson, 28 February 1883, in Melville, *Mother of Oscar*, page 187.
'At present I am deep': *Letters*, pages 204–205.
'mes premières fleurs': *Letters*, page 207.
'*cet individu*': Hyde, *Oscar Wilde*, page 85.
'honey-coloured': *Letters*, page 211.
'suppurating syphilitic sores': Kevin H.F. O'Brien, 'Robert Sherard', *English Literature in Transition*, volume XXVIII, number 1, page 10.
'moonlit meanderings': *Letters*, page 210.
'How could I refuse': *Letters*, page 210.
'Priapus was calling': H. Montgomery Hyde, *Famous Trials 7: Oscar Wilde* (London, 1962), pages 53–54.
'The only reflection': Robert Sherard to A.J.A. Symons, 3 June 1937, in Belford, *Oscar Wilde*, page 117.
'He is grown': Laura Troubridge, July 1883, in Troubridge, *Life Among the Troubridges*,

page 164.

'His amber-coloured hair': Richard Le Gallienne, *The Romantic '90s* (London, 1951), page 141.

'You will think': Otho Holland Lloyd to Nellie Hutchinson, May 1883, in Melville, *Mother of Oscar*, page 188.

'I don't believe that he means': Otho Holland Lloyd to Nellie Hutchinson, June 1883, in Melville, *Mother of Oscar*, page 189.

'wherever she went': Otho Holland Lloyd to Nellie Hutchinson, June 1883, in Melville, *Mother of Oscar*, page 190.

'If the man were': Otho Holland Lloyd to Nellie Hutchinson, June 1883, in Melville, *Mother of Oscar*, page 190.

'this is his way': Otho Holland Lloyd to Nellie Hutchinson, June 1883, in Melville, *Mother of Oscar*, page 189.

'an epicene youth': Ellmann, page 240.

'You know everybody says': Ellmann, page 236.

'I am afraid you and I': Ellmann, page 244.

'I told the Atkinsons': Ellmann, page 244.

'though decidedly extra': *Letters*, page 221.

'Such stupid nonsense': *Letters*, page 272.

'Prepare yourself': *Letters*, page 222.

'shaking with fright': *Letters*, page 221.

'three good proposals': Bentley, *The Importance of Being Constance*, page 33.

'Grandpapa will, I know, be nice': *Letters*, page 232.

'I am so dreadfully nervous': *Letters*, page 222.

'I won't stand opposition': *Letters*, page 222.

'My father': Emily Lloyd to Oscar Wilde, 30 November 1883, Clark Library.

'I am intensely pleased': Melville, *Mother of Oscar*, pages 191–192.

'growing quite rich': *Letters*, page 224.

'The best work in literature': *Letters*, page 265.

'I hear that Oscar's fiancée only has £400 a year': Laura Troubridge, 1884, in Secor, 'Aesthetes and Pre-Raphaelites', page 399.

'as nearly as possible escaped': Hunt, *The Flurried Years*, page 168.

'is not a matter for affection': *Works*, page 559.

'A hundred and thirty thousand pounds!': *Works*, page 409.

'a very nice, pretty, sensible girl': Lady Jane Wilde to Mrs Knott, February 1884, in Melville, *Mother of Oscar*, page 194.

'What causes him some uneasiness': Emily Lloyd to Oscar Wilde, 6 December 1883, Clark Library.

'He had an interview in chambers with Mr Hargrove': Otho Holland Lloyd to A.J.A. Symons, 27 May 1937, Clark Library.

'I think it likely': Emily Lloyd to Oscar Wilde, 17 December 1883, Clark Library.

'should be made to understand': Emily Lloyd to Oscar Wilde, 17 December 1883, Clark Library.

The marriage cure

'LADY BRACKNELL: To speak frankly': Oscar Wilde, *Works*, page 410.

'He certainly had been very much': Lord Alfred Douglas, *The Autobiography of Lord Alfred Douglas* (London, 1929), pages 59–60.

'force and depth of character': Bentley, *The Importance of Being Constance*, page 87.

'I'm going to be married to': *Letters*, page 224.

'mystical': *Letters*, page 225.

'Madonna Mia': *Works*, page 836.

'a fair slim boy': *Works*, page 755.

'Impervious as Cyprian was': André Raffalovich, *A Willing Exile* (London, 1890), page 20.

'It was not love': Raffalovich, *A Willing Exile*, page 22.

'marrying that girl': Ellmann, page 235.

'can't help liking him': *Letters*, page 221.

'She scarcely ever speaks': Louise Jopling, *Twenty Years of My Life* 1867–1887 (London, 1925), page 79.

'It is horrid': *Letters*, page 224–225.

'I am with Oscar when': *Letters*, page 225.

'My darling love': Constance Lloyd to Oscar Wilde, in Winwar, *Oscar Wilde and the Yellow Nineties*, pages 126–127.

'all very pretty indeed': *Letters*, pages 21–22.

'a very good age': *Works*, page 368.

'When I have you': Constance Lloyd to Oscar Wilde, in Winwar, *Oscar Wilde and the Yellow Nineties*, page 127.

'certainly the most immoral': W.H. Auden, *Forewords and Afterwords*, in *An Improbable Life*, selected by Edward Mendelson (London), pages 307–308.

'prayers, struggles, all means used': Havelock Ellis, *Studies in the Psychology of Sex* (Philadelphia, 1902), page 57.

'was the excitation': Symonds, *Memoirs*, page 136.

'there had been connection': Ellis, *Studies in the Psychology of Sex*, page 164.

'I sought out a scarlet woman': Ellis, *Studies in the Psychology of Sex*, page 74.

'used to dream': Ellis, *Studies in the Psychology of Sex*, page 88.

'If only you were a boy': Melville, *Mother of Oscar*, page 264.

'the boyish appearance': Schmidgall, *The Stranger Wilde*, page 106.

'another means': Oscar Wilde and Others, *Teleny* (London, 1986), pages 86–87.

'the slender lithesomeness': Wilde and Others, *Teleny*, page 87.

'Could I but have felt': Wilde and Others, *Teleny*, page 87.

'youthful': Anne Amor Clark, *Mrs Oscar Wilde* (London, 1983), page 59.

'You say you love': Alan Sheridan, *André Gide: A Life in the Present* (London, 1998), page 129.

'Physicians often strongly tempted': Ellis, *Studies in the Psychology of Sex*, page 198.

'I felt the necessity': Symonds, *Memoirs*, page 135.

'recommended cohabitation': Symonds, *Memoirs*, page 152.

'great mistake – perhaps the great crime': Symonds, *Memoirs*, pages 184–185.

'I married without passion': Symonds, *Memoirs*, page 185.

'found, to his disappointment': Ellis, *Studies in the Psychology of Sex*, page 88.

'Bachelors are not fashionable': *Works*, page 556.

'There is only this much': Sherard, *Life of Oscar Wilde*, page 233.

'No woman': Sherard, *Life of Oscar Wilde*.

Against nature

'The only way to behave to a woman': *Works*, page 371.

'a silly and thoroughly characteristic letter': Ellmann, page 251.

'stopped and rifled': Brasol, *Oscar Wilde*, page 176.

'It's so wonderful': Robert Sherard to A.J.A. Symons, 3 June 1937, Clark Library.
'I pointed out': Robert Sherard to A.J.A. Symons, 3 June 1937, Clark Library.
'Such a great event': in Phyllis Grosskurth, *John Addington Symonds* (London, 1964), pages 94–95.
'annulée et tendre': in Ellmann, page 252.
'Of course I need not tell you': *Letters*, page 229.
'the most splendid acting I ever saw': *Letters*, page 228.
'the show-places of the Paris inferno': Sherard, *Oscar Wilde*, page 94.
'the saddest daughters of joy': Sherard, *Oscar Wilde*, page 96.
'The criminal classes': Sherard, *Oscar Wilde*, page 95.
'Stretched out in every posture of pain': Sherard, *Oscar Wilde*, pages 96–97.
'the favourite spectacle': Sherard, *Oscar Wilde*, page 96.
'the breviary of decadence': introduction to J.K. Huysmans, *Against Nature*, translated by Robert Baldick (London, 1959), page 13.
'Bible and bedside book': Ellmann, page 252.
'a sudden storm of wind and rain': *Letters*, page 227.
'Dear Sir, the book': *Letters*, page 524.
'taking up the volume': *Works*, page 96.
'After a few minutes': *Works*, page 98.
'progressively less manly': Huysmans, *Against Nature*, page 17.
'In the days when he had belonged': Huysmans, *Against Nature*, pages 22–23.
'a young scamp of sixteen or so': Huysmans, *Against Nature*, page 80.
'has a supple figure, sinewy legs': Huysmans, *Against Nature*, page 110.
'as blunt-witted and brutish': Huysmans, *Against Nature*, page 112.
'yearning for her': Huysmans, *Against Nature*, page 111.
'rough, athletic caresses': Huysmans, *Against Nature*, page 112.
'timid and appealing': Huysmans, *Against Nature*, page 116.
'This last book of Huysmans': *Morning News*, 20 June 1884.
'The whole book seemed to him': *Works*, page 97.

An ideal wife
'What nonsense people talk': *Works*, page 131.
'I am thinking of becoming': *Letters*, page 230.
'What should be the distinguishing': on display at *Oscar Wilde: A Life in Six Acts*, British Library, London, 2000.
'the divine joy of sacrifice': Melville, *Mother of Oscar*, pages 65–66.
'A woman has a strong tendency': Melville, *Mother of Oscar*, page 69.
'It is better to have loved and lost': Coakley, *Oscar Wilde*, page 178.
'more of a sedative': Wilde and Others, *Teleny*, page 58.
'succeeded in accomplishing': Symonds, *Sexual Inversion*, pages 168–169.
'Did you see the Wildes': diary of Laura Hope, 8 June 1886, in P. Jullien, 'The Wildes at No 16 Tite Street', *London Magazine*, volume IX, page 70.
'Mr and Mrs Oscar Wilde to tea': diary of Laura Troubridge, 8 July 1884, *Life Among the Troubridges*, page 169.
'Oscar Wilde and his wife': Adrian Hope and Laura Troubridge, *Letters of Engagement*, edited by Marie-Jaqueline Lancaster (London, 2002), page 38.
'Mrs Oscar Wilde is utterly devoid': Marie Corelli, in Clark, *Mrs Oscar Wilde*, page 73.
'Burne-Jones and': Marion Mainwaring, *Mysteries of Paris* (London, 2001), page 45.
'so cold and undemonstrative outwardly': Ellmann, page 246.

'said during dinner': Hope and Troubridge, *Letters of Engagement*, page 115.

'simply revolting': Hope and Troubridge, *Letters of Engagement*, page 117.

'a pretty young woman': Le Gallienne, *The Romantic '90s*, page 144.

'She was sentimental': Arthur Ransome, *Oscar Wilde: A Critical Study* (London, 1912), page 36.

'I knew a case': Ada Leverson, in Julie Speedie, *Wonderful Sphinx* (London, 1993), pages 87–88.

'How passionately I worship': Ellmann, page 246.

'really very fond': *Letters*, page 785.

'There is only one thing': Coakley, *Oscar Wilde*, page 178.

'She could not understand me': *Letters*, page 785.

'*Ennui* is the enemy!': *Letters*, page 1131.

'Women are always on the side of morality': *Works*, page 469.

'the only way a woman': *Works*, page 80.

'Then turning to my love I said': *Works*, page 867.

'When I married': Harris, *Oscar Wilde*, page 284.

'Ugliness I consider a malady': Sherard, *Oscar Wilde*, page 57.

'I can sympathise': *Works*, page 42.

'Pity! Pity has nothing to do with love': Harris, *Oscar Wilde*, page 285.

'many men find': André Raffalovich, *Uranisme et Unisexualité* (Lyon, 1896), page 125, translated by Sian Jones.

'must love indeed': Wilde and Others, *Teleny*, page 131.

'Don't talk to me of the other sex': Harris, *Oscar Wilde*, page 270.

'Oscar had no illusions': Robert Sherard to A.J.A. Symons, 31 May 1937, Hyde Collection.

'Act dishonourably, Robert': Robert Sherard to A.J.A. Symons, 31 May 1937, Hyde Collection.

'glutted their lust': Hyde, *Oscar Wilde*, page 183.

'Mr Wilde told me': Hyde, *Famous Trials 7*, page 185.

'Mr Wilde spoke several times': Hyde, *Famous Trials 7*, page 185.

'A woman's passion': Harris, *Oscar Wilde*, page 272.

'Get hence, you loathsome Mystery!': *Works*, page 882.

'Her thighs were bare': Wilde and Others, *Teleny*, page 80.

'I am afraid that women appreciate cruelty': *Works*, page 82.

Playing with fire

'Marriage is a sort of forcing-house': Robert Hichens, *The Green Carnation* (London, 1961), page 30.

'Dear and Beloved': *Letters*, pages 241–242.

'best Olympian': Ellmann, page 265.

'My dear Philip': *Letters*, page 239.

'Yes. I always call': Hyde, *Famous Trials 7*, page 125.

'charmed. I have a very vivid': *Letters*, page 266.

'Harry, why did you let me': *Letters*, page 267.

'I find the earth as beautiful as the sky': *Letters*, page 267.

'you have the power': *Letters*, page 268.

'Do you know him?': *Letters*, page 268.

'There is no sin': Timothy d'Arch Smith, *Love in Earnest* (London, 1970), page 77.

'What is Harry doing?': *Letters*, page 269.

'What is your real ambition in life': *Interviews and Recollections*, volume I, page 5.

'Nothing is good in moderation': Ellmann, page 268.

'Enough is as bad as a meal': Pearson, *The Life of Oscar Wilde*, page 171.

'Moderation is a fatal thing': *Works*, page 498.

'Does it all seem a dream, Harry?': *Letters*, page 269.

'How much more poetic': Pearson, *The Life of Oscar Wilde*, page 79.

'You too have the love': *Letters*, page 272.

'not the fruit of experience': Ellmann, page 139.

'I wanted to eat of the fruit': *Letters*, page 739.

'most fiery moment of ecstasy': *Letters*, page 272.

'Strangely enough': *Letters*, page 272.

'To be master of these moods is exquisite': *Letters*, page 272.

'To drift with every passion till my soul': *Works*, page 864.

'an unknown land full of strange flowers': *Letters*, page 272.

'Let us live like Spartans': *Letters*, page 274.

'Come at 12 o'c on Sunday': *Letters*, page 276.

'Dear Douglas, I have lost your note': *Letters*, page 281.

'We must have many evenings together': *Letters*, page 281.

'I hope you and Osborne are reading hard': *Letters*, page 281.

'young Oxonians are very delightful': *Letters*, page 278.

Mad and coloured loves

'Love is all very well': *Works*, page 286.

'Oscar's star has been low': Ellmann, page 281.

'Give me the luxuries': Harris, *Oscar Wilde*, page 36.

'A word from you': *Letters*, page 280.

'In mad and coloured loves': Ian Small, *Oscar Wilde Revalued* (Buckinghamshire, 1993), page 131.

'consistency is the last refuge': Oscar Wilde, 'The Relation of Dress to Art', in *The Artist as Critic*, edited by Richard Ellmann (Chicago, 1982).

'the best writer in Europe': Jean Graham Hall and Gordon D. Smith, *Oscar Wilde: The Tragedy of Being Earnest* (Chichester, 2001), page 33.

'epicene youth': *Truth*, 18 July 1883.

'I have never seen anything like it before': Neil Bartlett, *Who Was That Man?* (London, 1988), pages 136–137.

'on the increase': H. Montgomery Hyde, *The Cleveland Street Scandal* (London, 1976), page 17.

'The increase of these monsters': Hyde, *The Other Love*, page 120.

'a criminal confederacy': Hyde, *The Other Love*, page 129.

'a disgrace to legislation': John Addington Symonds to Charles Kains Jackson, 18 December 1892, in John Addington Symonds, *Letters*, edited by Herbert M. Schueller and Robert L. Peters (Detroit, 1969), page 791.

'The only way to get rid of a temptation': *Works*, pages 28–29.

'the face of Puck': Pearson, *The Life of Oscar Wilde*, pages 354–355.

'a rather pathetic-looking little creature': Douglas, *Autobiography*, page 70.

'had known Ross': new preface to Frank Harris and Lord Alfred Douglas, *The Life and Confessions of Oscar Wilde* (London, 1925), pages 49–50.

'copping for a steamer': Rupert Croft-Cooke, *Feasting with Panthers* (London, 1968), page 264.

'flattery laid on with a trowel': Douglas, *Autobiography*, pages 72–73.

Poets and lovers
'How much more poetic': Pearson, *The Life of Oscar Wilde*, page 79.
'highest form of literature': *Letters*, page 265.
'too busy to lecture': *Letters*, page 304.
'a certain taint of vulgarity about it': *Letters*, page 317.
'The sin was mine': Stuart Mason, *Bibliography of Oscar Wilde* (London, 1914), page 47.
'a virtual divorce': Otho Holland Lloyd to Arthur Ransome, 28 February 1912, in Ellmann, page 278.
'heavenly hills': Symonds, *Memoirs*, page 203.
'nothing base': Symonds, *Memoirs*, page 204.
'But who is this that cometh by the shore?': Mason, *Bibliography*, page 47.
'leaders of Hellas': diary of George Ives, 31 March 1894, HRC.
'Bosie, from his friend the author': inscription made by Oscar Wilde, in Winwar, *Oscar Wilde and the Yellow Nineties*, page 189.
'Shelley with a chin': *Interviews and Recollections*, volume II, pages 303–304.
'full of much that is dainty': *Letters*, page 327.
'I can recognise a whole life': *Letters*, page 351.
'fanning out': *Interviews and Recollections*, volume II, pages 303–304.
'a most charming fellow': *Letters*, page 327.
'With Oscar Wilde, a summer day': *Letters*, page 367.
'To Richard Le Gallienne, poet and lover': Ellmann, page 283.
'This copy of verse': Ellmann, page 283.
'Oscar Wilde, sweet "Fancy's child"': Karl Beckson, *The Oscar Wilde Encyclopedia* (New York, 1998), page 193.
'Bother space and time!': *Letters*, page 368.
'Yea! Dear Poet': Small, *Oscar Wilde Revalued*, pages 77–78.
'To say of these poems': Oscar Wilde, *Pall Mall Gazette*, 27 March 1885, in d'Arch Smith, *Love In Earnest*, pages 30–31.
'The first is beauty': André Raffalovich, 'Two Loves', in d'Arch Smith, *Love in Earnest*, page 31.
'Of all sweet passions': Lord Alfred Douglas, *Sonnets* (London, 1935), page 23.
'You could give me a new thrill': Ellmann, page 282.
'the more dangerous affections': Jerusha Hull McCormack, *John Gray: Poet, Dandy & Priest* (London, 1991), page 148.
'Oscar says he likes you so much': Alexander Michaelson, 'Oscar Wilde', *Blackfriars*, volume VIII, number 92 (November 1927), page 700.
'Never again did I speak': Michaelson, 'Oscar Wilde', page 700.
'We'd like a table for six, please': Rupert Croft-Cooke, *The Unrecorded Life of Oscar Wilde* (London, 1972), page 10.
'he came to London with the intention': *Letters*, page 256.
'a foetus in a bottle': Sherard, *The Life of Oscar Wilde*, page 97.
'a dislike, not of a friendship': Hull McCormack, *John Gray*, page 47.

Æolian harps
'This passion for beauty': unpublished notebook of Oscar Wilde at Princeton in Hull McCormack, *John Gray*, page 53.

'You will find him everything': *Letters*, page 360.

'My reception was semi-royal': *Letters*, page 360.

'a violent brain attack': Oscar Browning to his mother, March 1889, in H.E. Wortham, *Oscar Browning* (London, 1927), page 222.

'fair sailor': Ian Anstruther, *Oscar Browning* (London, 1983), page 134.

'his admiring cohort': *Max Beerbohm's Letters to Reggie Turner*, edited by Rupert Hart-Davis (New York, 1965), page 287.

'sons': Raffalovich, *Uranisme et Unisexualité*, translated by Sian Jones.

'the exquisite Æolian harps that play': 'Oscar Wilde by an American [Max Beerbohm]', in *Max Beerbohm's Letters to Reggie Turner*, page 287.

'I wish you would send me': *Letters*, page 375.

'My dear Adonis': *Letters*, page 282.

'I send you your necktie': *Letters*, page 482.

'What a pretty name you have!': *Letters*, page 418.

'Dear Mr Hill, Come and have tea on Friday': *Letters*, page 380.

'What do you allow': *Letters*, page 347.

'I wish I could draw like you': *Letters*, page 347.

'What a charming time we had at Abbott's Hill': *Letters*, page 352.

'For people whom one has had': *Letters*, page 1095.

'terrible': Ellmann, page 283.

'There is something about them': Ellmann, page 283.

'You are completely without feeling': Ellmann, page 283.

'a literary tavern': Max Beerbohm to Reginald Turner, 29 September 1893, in *Max Beerbohm's Letters to Reggie Turner*, pages 71–72.

'Vociferous young writers': Rupert Croft-Cooke, *Bosie: Lord Alfred Douglas* (New York, 1963), page 43.

'I hasten to write': Frederick Althaus to Oscar Wilde, 12 November 1888, Clark Library.

'I never told you': Frederick Althaus to Oscar Wilde, 12 November 1888, Clark Library.

'I shall as soon as I get them': Frederick Althaus to Oscar Wilde, 12 November 1888, Clark Library.

'I have heard from Barnes': Frederick Althaus to Oscar Wilde, 1889, Clark Library.

'Dear Oscar, I could not help': Frederick Althaus to Oscar Wilde, 1889, Clark Library.

'Dear Oscar, I shall be at the Lyric': Frederick Althaus to Oscar Wilde, 1889, Clark Library.

'My dear Oscar, I have an invitation': Frederick Althaus to Oscar Wilde, 19 March 1889, Clark Library.

'The other evening': Frederick Althaus to Oscar Wilde, 19 March 1889, Clark Library.

'The afternoon post': Frederick Althaus to Oscar Wilde, 4 June 1889, Clark Library.

'Your letter just received': Frederick Althaus to Oscar Wilde, 4 June 1889, Clark Library.

'How furious you will be': Frederick Althaus to Oscar Wilde, 4 June 1889, Clark Library.

Spiritualised sodomy

'Literature has always anticipated life': *Works*, pages 1083–1084.

'To the onlie begetter': *Works*, page 315.

'Mr W. Hall happinesse': William Shakespeare, *Sonnets*, edited by Stephen Booth (New York, 1977), page 548.
'Indeed the story is half yours': *Letters*, pages 407–408.
'subtle and secret poisoner': *Works*, page 1093.
'He loves Greek gems, and Persian carpets': *Works*, page 1095.
'determined to startle the town as a dandy': *Works*, page 1095.
'sought to be somebody': *Works*, page 1095.
'had that curious love of green': *Works*, page 1095.
'remarks that he cannot': Ellis, *Studies in the Psychology of Sex*, page 61.
'It has also been remarked': Ellis, *Studies in the Psychology of Sex*, page 166.
'The colour green and Hell': *Interviews and Recollections*, volume I, page 355.
'whose personality for some reason': *Works*, page 307.
'a full-length portrait of a young man': *Works*, pages 302–303.
'effeminate': *Works*, page 304.
'People who did not like him': *Works*, page 304.
'as a sacrifice to the secret of the Sonnets': *Works*, page 311.
'I believe in Willie Hughes': *Works*, page 312.
'His very name fascinated me': *Works*, pages 319–320.
'as some fair-haired English lad whom': *Works*, page 332.
'the mystery of his sin or of the sin': *Works*, page 320.
'deciphering the story': *Works*, page 343.
'cause': *Works*, page 348.
'I still believe in Willie Hughes': *Works*, page 348.
'was explaining why': Margot Oxford, *More Memories* (London, 1933), page 116.
'the ambiguity of the sexes': *Works*, page 330.
'It is only when we recognise': *Works*, page 325.
'young Roman': *Works*, page 327.
'kind of mystic transference': *Works*, page 325.
'the soul, the secret soul': *Works*, page 344.
'a rapture on "the golden hair"': *The World*, 10 July 1899, in Beckson, *The Oscar Wilde Encyclopedia*, page 290.
'Our English homes': Pearson, *The Life of Oscar Wilde*, page 148.
'did Oscar incalculable injury': Harris, *Oscar Wilde*, page 69.

Shadow and song
'My weakness is that I do': Frank Benson to Robert Sherard, MS1047, University of Reading.
'gross bodily appetite': *Works*, page 325.
'Love had, indeed, entered': *Works*, page 325.
'the quenchless flame': *Works*, page 839.
'very aesthetic and romantic looking': Montrose J. Moses and Virginia Gerson, *Clyde Fitch and His Letters* (Boston, 1924), pages 46–47.
'slight, dark': Moses and Gerson, *Clyde Fitch and His Letters*, pages 85–86.
'many of the more charming qualities': Moses and Gerson, *Clyde Fitch and His Letters*, page xii.
'dire consequences': Moses and Gerson, *Clyde Fitch and His Letters*, pages 17–18.
'I believe myself that the Romance': Clyde Fitch to Kate Douglas Wiggin, 30 November 1894, in Moses and Gerson, *Clyde Fitch and His Letters*, page 97.
'What a charming day': *Letters*, page 403.

'You precious maddening man': Clyde Fitch to Oscar Wilde, July 1889, in Melissa Knox, *Oscar Wilde: A Long and Lovely Suicide* (London, 1994), page 151.

'invent me a language': Clyde Fitch to Oscar Wilde, July 1889, in Knox, *Oscar Wilde*, page 151.

'*Nobody* loves you as *I* do': Clyde Fitch to Oscar Wilde, in Knox, *Oscar Wilde*, page 151.

'You are my poetry': Clyde Fitch to Oscar Wilde, in Knox, *Oscar Wilde*, page 151.

'Wisden is obvious': *Letters*, page 408.

'Somebody I used to like is at Ostend': *Letters*, page 409.

'It is 3. And you are not coming': Clyde Fitch to Oscar Wilde, in Knox, *Oscar Wilde*, page 151.

'I *am* so glad': Clyde Fitch to Oscar Wilde, in Knox, *Oscar Wilde*, page 151.

'Out of the mid-wood's twilight': *Works*, page 874.

'These men are mad': *Works*, page 595.

'In some parts of Ireland': Pine, *The Thief of Reason*, page 255.

'magic mirror of the moon': *Letters*, page 709.

'Romance is a profession plied beneath the moon': *Letters*, page 1119.

'Clyde Fitch from his friend Oscar Wilde': Beckson, *The Oscar Wilde Encyclopedia*, page 102.

'It is quite delightful': Ellmann, page 307.

'I saw Mr Ricketts on Saturday': *Letters*, page 410.

'Oh, nonsense, Oscar': Pearson, *The Life of Oscar Wilde*, page 193.

'a decaying piece of oak and framed it in': *Letters*, page 412.

'My dear Ricketts, It is not a forgery at all': *Letters*, page 412.

'the one house in London': *The Cambridge Companion to Oscar Wilde*, page 39.

'Somebody pointed out to her': Brocard Sewell, *In the Dorian Mode: A Life of John Gray* (Cornwall, 1983), page 14.

'And Beauty is a form of genius': *Works*, page 31.

'passionate adoration', *Works*, page 307.

John and Dorian

'There is something tragic': *Works*, page 1245.

'father then commands': Hull McCormack, *John Gray*, page 17.

'I have lost my father': Hull McCormack, *John Gray*, page 97.

'at one of those Soho': Frank Liebich, 'Oscar Wilde', Clark Library.

'hinted, rather vaguely': Liebich, 'Oscar Wilde', Clark Library.

'John Gray and I talked but little': Liebich, 'Oscar Wilde', Clark Library.

'complex multiform creature': *Works*, page 107.

'Dorian': Ernest Dowson to Arthur Moore, 2 February 1891, Ernest Dowson, *Letters*, edited by Desmond Flower and Henry Maas (London, 1967), page 182–183.

'I have made great friends': Lionel Johnson to Campbell Dodgson, 5 February 1891, in Hull McCormack, *John Gray*, page 55.

'As I came downstairs': Arthur Symons, *The Memoirs of Arthur Symons* (London, 1975), page 136.

'Dorian': Croft-Cooke, *Feasting With Panthers*, page 209.

'Dorian': *Letters*, page 625.

'The Dorians gave': Symonds, *Sexual Inversion*, page 24.

'extraordinary personal beauty': *Works*, pages 18–19.

'little more than a lad': *Works*, page 23.

'boy': Oscar Wilde, *The Picture of Dorian Gray* [*Lippincott's Monthly Magazine*], edited by Donald L. Lawler (New York and London, 1988), page 180.
'I turned half-way round': *Works*, page 21.
'terrible joy and no less terrible despair': *Works*, page 307.
'white purity of his boyhood': *Works*, page 40.
'made to be worshipped': *Works*, page 90.
'From the moment I met you': *Works*, page 89.
'idolatry': *Works*, page 89.
'There was love in every line': Wilde, *The Picture of Dorian Gray*, edited by Lawler, pages 232–233.
'the secret of his soul': *Works*, page 20.
'He likes me': *Works*, page 24.
'selfish, over-concerned': Hull McCormack, *John Gray*, pages 151–152.
'beautiful voice': *Works*, page 28.
'could not help liking': *Works*, page 30.
'The aim of life is self-development': *Works*, page 28.
'To realise one's nature perfectly': *Works*, page 28.
'Courage has gone out of our race': *Works*, page 28.
'We are punished': *Works*, pages 28–29.
'You, Mr Gray, you yourself': *Works*, page 29.
'Stop!': *Works*, page 29.
'Of all sweet passions': Lord Alfred Douglas, 'In Praise of Shame', *Sonnets*, page 23.
'life's mystery': *Works*, page 30.
'touched some secret chord': *Works*, page 29.
'touched my backside': E.M. Forster, terminal note to *Maurice* (London, 1971), page 217.
'To project one's soul': *Works*, page 40.

Scarlet threads
'There is no such thing': *Works*, page 17.
'to gather up the scarlet threads of life': *Works*, page 77.
'Why is your friendship': *Works*, page 112.
'Why is it that every': Wilde, *The Picture of Dorian Gray*, edited by Lawler, page 258.
'Does not this passage': Merlin Holland, *Irish Peacock and Scarlet Marquess* (London, 2003), page 102.
'The passion I had tried to stifle': Wilde and Others, *Teleny*, pages 109–110.
'I do not think': Symonds, *Sexual Inversion*, page 150.
'Then there are other stories': *Works*, page 113.
'old acquaintance': Symonds, *Memoirs*, page 253.
'intimacy': *Works*, pages 121–122.
'musical': d'Arch Smith, *Love in Earnest*, page 53.
'stretched out a hand, took a piece of a paper': *Works*, pages 124–125.
'I am so glad you like': *Letters*, page 585.
'Imagine a girl, hardly seventeen years of age': *Works*, page 49.
'a beautiful young girl': *Letters*, page 224.
'sudden mad love': *Works*, page 54.
'shallow and stupid': *Works*, page 72.
'All excess': *Letters*, page 435.
'a life of mere sensation': *Letters*, page 430.

'I want to eat of the fruit of all the trees': *Letters*, page 739.

'I don't regret': *Letters*, page 739.

'in an unbroken chain of events': Sewell, *In the Dorian Mode*, page 12.

'I went through instruction': John Gray to André Raffalovich, early February 1899, in Sewell, *In the Dorian Mode*, page 89.

'There are moments, psychologists tell us': *Works*, page 137.

'The hero, the wonderful': *Works*, page 97.

'a New Hedonism': *Works*, page 99.

'The future would be the same as our past': *Works*, page 54.

'Romance lives by repetition': *Works*, page 142.

'preaching corruption': Raffalovich, *Uranisme et Unisexualité*, translated by Sian Jones.

'He was interested': Raffalovich, *Uranisme et Unisexualité*, translated by Sian Jones.

'He knew the little anecdotes': Raffalovich, *Uranisme et Unisexualité*, translated by Sian Jones.

'I felt that this gray': *Works*, page 47.

'The more he knew': *Works*, page 98.

'As I lounged in the park': *Works*, page 47.

'the downward path': Raffalovich, *Uranisme et Unisexualité*, translated by Sian Jones.

Outlawed noblemen

'Not a year passes': *Works*, page 528.

'It is quite tragic for me': *Letters*, page 569.

'a certain immoral': *The Trials of Oscar Wilde*, edited by H. Montgomery Hyde (London, 1949), page 344.

'very dangerous': Walter Pater to Frank Harris, 1890, in Frank Harris, *Contemporary Portraits* (New York, 1919), pages 215–216.

'Even in the precincts': Robert Ross to Oscar Wilde, 1890, Clark Library.

'Oscar once talked to me': Michaelson, 'Oscar Wilde', page 700.

'Oscar really is too bold': Walter Pater to Frank Harris, 1890, in Harris, *Contemporary Portraits*, pages 215–216.

'is an odd and very audacious': John Addington Symonds to Horatio Forbes Brown, in Symonds, *Letters*, page 477.

'a great wobbly blancmange': Douglas Murray, *Bosie: A Biography of Lord Alfred Douglas* (London, 2000), page 47.

'He had been at Oxford': Ellmann, page 320.

'It hardly seemed fair': Ellmann, page 320.

'insane heat': Harris, *Contemporary Portraits*, pages 215–216.

'unmanly, sickening, vicious': Stuart Mason, *Art and Morality* (London, 1912), page 200.

'Ganymede-like': Mason, *Art and Morality*, page 159.

'Dullness and dirt are the chief feature of': Mason, *Art and Morality*, page 65.

'Whether the Treasury': Mason, *Art and Morality*, page 28.

'I am quite incapable of understanding how': *Letters*, page 428.

'We have received': Ward, Lock & Co to Oscar Wilde, 10 July 1890, CRIM 1 41/6, Public Record Office.

'What is the use of writing of': Ellmann, pages 321–322.

'Why go grubbing in muck heaps?': Mason, *Art and Morality*, page 75.

'The story – which deals with matters': Mason, *Art and Morality*, page 78.

'I got it doing some private work': Colin Simpson, Lewis Chester and David Leitch,

The Cleveland Street Affair (Toronto, 1976), page 16.

'I will tell you the truth': Simpson, Chester and Leitch, *The Cleveland Street Affair*, page 16.

'I made the acquaintance': Simpson, Chester and Leitch, *The Cleveland Street Affair*, page 17.

'He said – good evening': Simpson, Chester and Leitch, *The Cleveland Street Affair*, page 18.

'On one or two occasions': Hyde, *The Cleveland Street Scandal*, pages 21–22.

'another nice little boy': Hyde, *The Cleveland Street Scandal*, page 22.

'On one occasion at least': Hyde, *The Cleveland Street Scandal*, page 22.

'I think it is hard': Hyde, *The Cleveland Street Scandal*, page 25.

'Observation has been kept': Hyde, *The Cleveland Street Scandal*, page 26.

'I am *told* that Newton': Simpson, Chester and Leitch, *The Cleveland Street Affair*, pages 73–74.

'Prince Eddy and I must': Lord Arthur Somerset to Reginald Brett, in Hyde, *The Cleveland Street Scandal*, page 59.

'a travesty': Hyde, *The Cleveland Street Scandal*, page 53.

'This afternoon Sir Dighton Probyn': the Hon. Hamilton Cuffe to the Lord Chancellor, 16 October 1889, in Hyde, *The Cleveland Street Scandal*, page 90.

'see Lord Salisbury if necessary': the Prince of Wales to Sir Dighton Probyn, October 1889, in Hyde, *The Cleveland Street Scandal*, page 90.

'Just seen Francis K': Lord Arthur Somerset to Reginald Brett, 17 October 1889, in Hyde, *The Cleveland Street Scandal*, page 91.

'I felt that in writing to you': Sir Dighton Probyn to Lord Salisbury, in Hyde, *The Cleveland Street Scandal*, page 96.

'I am still a professional Mary-Ann': Simpson, Chester and Leitch, *The Cleveland Street Affair*, page 52.

'since the 1st May, 1879': Simpson, Chester and Leitch, *The Cleveland Street Affair*, page 49.

'I complained to Hammond': Hyde, *The Cleveland Street Scandal*, page 145.

'a tall, fine-looking man': Simpson, Chester and Leitch, *The Cleveland Street Affair*, page 50.

'I picked him up': Hyde, *The Cleveland Street Scandal*, page 146.

'Where did you meet': Hyde, *The Cleveland Street Scandal*, page 144.

'an actual Sodomite': Hyde, *The Cleveland Street Scandal*, page 108.

'Be sure, if you see me': Hyde, *The Cleveland Street Scandal*, page 146.

'prompted': Hyde, *The Cleveland Street Scandal*, page 136.

'I rang the bell': Simpson, Chester and Leitch, *The Cleveland Street Affair*, page 144.

'a more melancholy': Hyde, *The Cleveland Street Scandal*, page 153.

'of this dreadful scandal': Hyde, *Oscar Wilde*, page 118.

Apples of Sodom
'In the study hall': Stokes, *Oscar Wilde*, page 58.

'What about the young': in Max Beerbohm, 'Dorian Gray: An Examination Paper', Clark Library.

'Bless you, Oscar': Lionel Johnson, 'In Honour of Dorian and his Creator', in Ellmann, page 324.

'I lunched with Pater': Lionel Johnson to Campbell Dodgson, 15 April 1889, in Rev. Raymond Roseliep, *Some Letters of Lionel Johnson* (Indiana, 1957).

'Their eyes on fire': Linda Dowling, *Hellenism and Homosexuality in Victorian Oxford* (London, 1994), page 136.
'Dear Mr Johnson': *Letters*, page 423.
'On Saturday at mid-day': *Letters*, page 423.
'more like the head boy': in Lionel Johnson, *Collected Poems*, edited by Ian Fletcher (New York and London, 1982), page xxxi.
'a learned snowdrop': Michael Field, *Works and Days: From the Journal of Michael Field*, edited by T. and D. Sturge Moore (London, 1933), page 120.
'I hope you will let me know when': *Letters*, page 423.
'new boy': Raffalovich, *Uranisme et Unisexualité*, page 247, translated by Sian Jones.
'intoxicating': Lord Alfred Douglas to A.J.A. Symons, 8 July 1935, Clark Library.
'inordinately proud': the Marquess of Queensberry, *Oscar Wilde and the Black Douglas* (London, 1949), page 49.
'I have not been able to find a trace': H. Montgomery Hyde, *Lord Alfred Douglas* (London, 1984), page 7.
'to be worth two pence to anybody': Hyde, *Lord Alfred Douglas*, page 6.
'delicate features': Hyde, *Lord Alfred Douglas*, page 9.
'beautiful face': Hyde, *Lord Alfred Douglas*, page 9.
'good abilities and good principles': Murray, *Bosie*, page 9.
'After Bosie's birth': Croft-Cooke, *Bosie*, page 26.
'When he was a child': Queensberry, *Oscar Wilde and the Black Douglas*, page 63.
'a row': Hyde, *Lord Alfred Douglas*, page 14.
'a plot': Croft-Cooke, *Bosie*, page 33.
'filled with disgust and loathing': Symonds, *Memoirs*, page 94.
'Barber, annoyed and amused me': Symonds, *Memoirs*, pages 94–95.
'a sink of iniquity': Douglas, *Autobiography*.
'I remember thinking': Lord Alfred Douglas, *Without Apology* (London, 1938), page 316.
'at least ninety per cent': Douglas, *Autobiography*, page 26.
'own personal experience': *Introduction to my Poems with Some Considerations on the Oscar Wilde Case*, Clark Library.
'Six years at Winchester': unpublished manuscript of 'The Dead Past' by Sir Edmund Trelawny Backhouse, MS Eng misc. d1225, Bodleian Library, Oxford.
'In my time perhaps': Backhouse, 'The Dead Past'.
'Bozie, as he was commonly called': Backhouse, 'The Dead Past'.
'Young fellows are quite as much': Anonymous, *The Sins of the Cities of the Plain: or the Recollections of a Mary Ann* (London, 1881), page 65.
'the great public schools of England': Stokes, *Oscar Wilde*, page 57.
'If all persons guilty': *The Trials of Oscar Wilde*, pages 359–360.
'In the streets': Hyde, *The Cleveland Street Scandal*, page 222.
'Did you ever hear': Anonymous, *The Sins of the City of the Plain*, page 119.
'which were neither pure': Douglas, *Autobiography*, page 26.
'Bosie, I love you more now': Murray, *Bosie*, page 62.
'bedfellow of Douglas at Winchester': Robert Ross to Frank Harris, 17 May 1914, HRC.
'I left Winchester': Queensberry, *Oscar Wilde and the Black Douglas*, page 26.
'the Temple of Eros': Queensberry, *Oscar Wilde and the Black Douglas*, page 26.
'a frank and natural pagan': Douglas, *Autobiography*, pages 76–77.
'pagan ethics': Douglas, *Autobiography*, page 28.

'quite certain of the truth': Lord Alfred Douglas to Lady Queensberry, 6 January 1894, in Croft-Cooke, *Bosie*, page 94.

Wild and terrible music

'I have never sowed': Barry Day, *Oscar Wilde: A Life in Quotes* (London, 2000), page 246.

'His was a peculiarly English': Queensberry, *Oscar Wilde and the Black Douglas*, page 25.

'gifted, or cursed': Queensberry, *Oscar Wilde and Black Douglas*, page 25.

'grass-gorged': Field, *Works and Days*, pages 139–140.

'Poke him and he would bleed': Elizabeth Robins, 'Oscar Wilde: An Appreciation', *Nineteenth Century Theatre*, volume XXI, number 2 (1993), page 108.

'A big man, with a large pasty face': Marcel Schwob, December 1891, in Ellmann, page 346.

'Luxury – gold-tipped matches': Pine, *Oscar Wilde*, page 143.

'remarkable and arresting': Douglas, *Without Apology*, page 75.

'We had tea in his little writing-room': Douglas, *Autobiography*, page 59.

'just the ordinary interchange': Douglas, *Autobiography*, page 84.

'Oscar took a violent fancy': Douglas, *Without Apology*, page 122.

'Alfred Douglas from his friend': *Letters*, page 461.

'From the second time he saw me': Lord Alfred Douglas to Frank Harris, 20 March 1925, HRC.

'He "made up to me"': Douglas, *Autobiography*, page 75.

'Bosie, from his friend the author': Winwar, *Oscar Wilde and the Yellow Nineties*, page 189.

'the one topic': *Letters*, page 692.

'the gutter and the things': *Letters*, page 684.

'I was always on the best of terms': Douglas, *Autobiography*, page 59.

'Cyprian was, or seemed to be': Raffalovich, *A Willing Exile*, page 79.

'Honesty compels me to say': Douglas, *Autobiography*, pages 59–60.

'Constance was here': Speranza Wilde to Oscar Wilde, 3 November 1891, in Clark, *Mrs Oscar Wilde*, page 105.

'I would like you home': Speranza Wilde to Oscar Wilde, late 1891, in Joy Melville, *The Life of Jane Francesca Wilde* (London, 1994), page 235.

'quite unsympathetic': Otho Holland Lloyd to A.J.A. Symons, 27 May 1937, Clark Library.

'Oscar always said': Charles Ricketts to an unnamed correspondent, 1928, in Charles Ricketts, *Self-Portrait: Taken From the Letters & Journals of Charles Ricketts*, edited by Cecil Lewis (London, 1939), page 403.

'I believe that women appreciate cruelty': *Works*, page 82.

'Always! That is a dreadful word': *Works*, page 32.

'Of course you would have': *Works*, page 80.

'confidence in you': Emily Lloyd to Oscar Wilde, 30 November 1883, Clark Library.

'The one charm of marriage': *Works*, page 20.

'The only way a woman': *Works*, page 80.

'bored to death with married life': *Letters*, page 785.

'if you will give us two rooms': Frank Liebich, 'Oscar Wilde', Clark Library.

'There's nothing in the world': *Works*, page 451.

'When I have you for my husband': Constance Lloyd to Oscar Wilde, 1883, Winwar,

Oscar Wilde and the Yellow Nineties, page 127.
'the symbolic incarnation': Huysmans, *Against Nature*, page 66.
'obsessed by the spirit': *Interviews and Recollections*, volume I, page 192.
'If the blank book': Vincent O'Sullivan, *Aspects of Wilde* (London, 1978), page 32.
'I am writing a play': O'Sullivan, *Aspects of Wilde*, page 33.
'bed of abominations': *Works*, pages 588–596.
'Daughter of adultery': *Works*, page 591.
'I will kiss your mouth: *Works*, page 590.
'abnormal predominance': Richard Krafft-Ebing, *Psychopathia Sexualis* (London, 1959), page 75.
'The latest turn': Krafft-Ebing, *Psychopathia Sexualis*, page 82.
'Thou wouldst not suffer me': *Works*, pages 604–605.
'Her lust must be an abyss': *Interviews and Recollections*, volume I, page 193.
'Paris is a city that pleases me greatly': *Interviews and Recollections*, volume I, page 170.
'To the young man': Jonathan Fryer, *André & Oscar: Gide, Wilde and the Gay Art of Living* (London, 1997), page 63.
'There were four of us': in André Gide, *Oscar Wilde* (London, 1951), page 18.
'Wilde, Wilde': Nancy Erber, 'The French Trials of Oscar Wilde', *Journal of History and Sexuality*, volume VI (1996), page 556.
'I love André personally very deeply': *Letters*, page 874.
'the egoist without an ego': Lord Alfred Douglas to Robert Sherard, 1933, in Brasol, *Oscar Wilde*, page 257.
'Gide est amoureux d'Oscar Wilde': journal of Jules Renard, 1891, in Sheridan, *André Gide*, page 76.
'Wilde is piously setting about': André Gide to Paul Valéry, 4 or 11 December 1891, in Fryer, *André & Oscar*, page 33.
'Wilde, I believe': André Gide, 1 January 1892, in Fryer, *André & Oscar*, page 34.

Strange green flowers
'One should always be in love': *Works*, page 81.
'A *green* carnation?': W. Graham Robertson, *Time Was: The Reminiscences of W. Graham Robertson* (London, 1931), pages 135–136.
'I invented that magnificent flower': *Letters*, page 617.
'were wearing make-up': Raffalovich, *Uranisme et Unisexualité*, page 247, translated by Sian Jones.
'unspeakable animal': Belford, *Oscar Wilde*, pages 188–189.
'Ladies and Gentlemen': Pearson, *The Life of Oscar Wilde*, page 224.
'impudent': Belford, *Oscar Wilde*, pages 188–189.
'People of birth': Brasol, *Oscar Wilde*, page 262.
'addressed from the stage': Schmidgall, *The Stranger Wilde*, page 11.
'Quite too-too puffickly precious': Schmidgall, *The Stranger Wilde*, page 11.
'Mr Oscar Wilde and a suite': Sewell, *In the Dorian Mode*, page 23.
'unmanly': Bartlett, *Who Was That Man?*, page 50.
'these strange green': Richard Gallienne, *English Poems* (London, 1892).
'a thin scarlet thread': d'Arch Smith, *Love in Earnest*, page 60.
'The green carnation to which': Bartlett, *Who Was That Man?*, page 50.
'Do try to be present': Lady Wilde to Oscar Wilde, 8 February 1892, in Melville, *Mother of Oscar*, page 239.
'hard and fast rules': *Works*, page 423.

'Morality does not help me': *Letters*, page 732.

'Constance will be away': Michaelson, 'Oscar Wilde', page 700.

'You would feel that he was lying': *Works*, page 438.

'that the perfect harmony': W.B. Yeats, *Autobiographies* (London, 1950), page 135.

'Life is a wide stormy sea': Oscar Wilde, *A Wife's Tragedy*, in R. Shewan, 'A Wife's Tragedy', *Theatre Research International*, volume VII (1982), pages 99–101.

'I am told there is hardly a husband': *Works*, page 430.

'Tell me why, sad and sighing': Lord Alfred Douglas, *Lyrics* (London, 1935), page 58.

'Boys are so wicked': *Works*, page 427.

'an intellectual face': Holland, *Irish Peacock and Scarlet Marquess*, page 134.

'M was in such an ill-temper': Edward Shelley to John Lane, February 1891, in J.W. Lambert and Michael Ratcliffe, *The Bodley Head 1887–1987* (London, 1987), pages 52–53.

'with his coat off': Edward Shelley to John Lane, 4 June 1891, in Thomas Mallon, 'A Boy of No Importance', *Biography*, volume I, number 3 (summer 1978), page 68.

'I should like to have a few minutes': Edward Shelley to John Lane, December 1890, in Lambert and Ratcliffe, *The Bodley Head*, page 52.

'A Physical Impossibility': Backhouse, 'The Dead Past'.

'He seemed to take notice of me': Lambert and Ratcliffe, *The Bodley Head*, pages 53–54.

'We dined together in a public room': Lambert and Ratcliffe, *The Bodley Head*, pages 53–54.

'The lighter forms of literature': *The Trials of Oscar Wilde*, pages 296–297.

'I had met no one': William Rothenstein, *Men and Memories: Recollections of William Rothenstein* (New York, 1931), page 87.

'Will you come into my bedroom?': *The Trials of Oscar Wilde*, page 213.

'stupor': Edward Shelley's statement, witness statements, private collection.

'flattered, inebriated, terrified': Raffalovich, *Uranisme et Unisexualité*, pages 262–263, translated by Sian Jones.

'placed his hand on the private parts': *The Shame of Oscar Wilde: From the Shorthand Reports* (Paris, 1906), page 94.

'I was weak of course': *The Trials of Oscar Wilde*, page 296.

'a peculiar sort of exaltation': Hyde, *Oscar Wilde*, page 281, and in Hyde, *Famous Trials 7*, page 239.

'I was entrapped': *The Trials of Oscar Wilde*, page 296.

'What a triumph was yours last night!': Edward Shelley to Oscar Wilde, 21 February 1892, in *The Trials of Oscar Wilde*, page 297.

'To Edward Shelley': Mason, *Oscar Wilde: Three Times Tried*, page 385.

'I have longed to see you': Edward Shelley to Oscar Wilde, 27 October 1892, in *The Shame of Oscar Wilde*, page 95.

'I saw Edward Shelley': John Gray to Pierre Louÿs, 1 August 1892, in *A Friendship of the Nineties*, edited by Alan Walter Campbell (Edinburgh, 1984), page 17.

'intolerable': Hyde, *Famous Trials 7*, page 191.

'that viper': Mason, *Oscar Wilde: Three Times Tried*, page 390.

'I have had a very horrible interview': Holland, *Irish Peacock and Scarlet Marquess*, page 233.

'I am most anxious to see you': Edward Shelley to Oscar Wilde, 27 October 1892, in *The Shame of Oscar Wilde*, page 95.

'I am afraid sometimes': 'Oscar Wilde Retried', *New York Herald*, 23 May 1895, page 9.

'I am determined': Edward Shelley to Oscar Wilde, 25 October 1894, in *The Shame of Oscar Wilde*, page 95.

'Shelley was in the habit': Croft-Cooke, *Feasting with Panthers*, page 264.

'a foolish young man': Raffalovich, *Uranisme et Unisexualité*, pages 262–263, translated by Sian Jones.

'I used to be utterly reckless of young lives': *Letters*, page 905.

Hyacinth and Narcissus

'In this world': Pearson, *The Life of Oscar Wilde*, page 242.

'a very pathetic letter': *Letters*, page 795.

'very fair and pretty': Jack Saul, *Recollections of a Mary-Ann* (London, 1881), pages 112–114.

'into the hands': Symonds, *Sexual Inversion*, pages 149–150.

'God forgive the past': Edward Shelley to Oscar Wilde, in Croft-Cooke, *Feasting With Panthers*, page 263.

'their infamous war against life': *Letters*, page 759.

'infamous conduct at Oxford': Croft-Cooke, *Bosie*, page 57.

'a most pathetic and charming letter': *Letters*, page 795.

'Oh, he knows everything about us': Penelope Fitzgerald, *Edward Burne-Jones: A Biography* (London, 1989), page 196.

'When I was deprived of his advice': *Letters*, page 702.

'When Edwin Levy': *Letters*, page 725.

'the Fates were weaving': *Letters*, page 706.

'his soul with honey': Lord Alfred Douglas to Lady Queensberry, 10 December 1843, in Croft-Cooke, *Bosie*, page 91.

'I was fascinated by Wilde': Lord Alfred Douglas to Frank Harris, 1925, HRC.

'wilful, fascinating, irritating': *Letters*, page 961.

'young Adonis': *Works*, page 19.

'the visible incarnation': *Works*, page 89.

'boyhood': Lord Alfred Douglas to Frank Harris, 1925, in H. Montgomery Hyde, 'Oscar Wilde and Lord Alfred Douglas', *Essays by Divers Hands*, edited by Sir Angus Wilson (Suffolk, 1984) page 146.

'Say that I love him': *Letters*, page 948.

'I was filled up with drinks': Lord Alfred Douglas to Frank Harris, 1925, HRC.

'My dearest Bobbie': *Letters*, page 526.

'pollution labiale': Laurence Housman to George Ives, 17 October 1933, HRC.

'That man is a cock sucker': the Marquis of Queensberry to Percy Douglas, in Murray, *Bosie*, page 74.

'practised penis-sucking': Raffalovich, *Uranisme et Unisexualité*, page 119, translated by Sian Jones.

'inspiration': Hyde, *Oscar Wilde*, page 187.

'Love is a sacrament': George Ives materials, HRC.

'most distasteful observance': Robert Sherard to A.J.A. Symons, 8 June 1937, Clark Library.

'penis-sucking': Raffalovich, *Uranisme et Unisexualité*, page 119, translated by Sian Jones.

'sensual, without being debauched': Raffalovich, *Uranisme et Unisexualité*, pages 121–122, translated by Sian Jones.

'It is hateful to me now to speak': Lord Alfred Douglas to Frank Harris, 1925, HRC.
'never seen anything like it': Bartlett, *Who Was That Man?*, pages 136–137.
'did not shrink': Ellis, *Studies in the Psychology of Sex*, page 89.
'a vulgar error': Symonds, *Sexual Inversion*, page 107.
'It is the common belief': Symonds, *Sexual Inversion*, page 106.
'Anal intercourse (active or passive)': P.W.J. Healy, 'Uranisme et Unisexualité: A Late Victorian View of Homosexuality', *New Blackfriars* (February 1978), page 59.
'Oh, it was so little that': Douglas, *Autobiography*, page 75.
'faithfully, loyally, devotedly, unselfishly': Lord Alfred Douglas to Lady Queensberry, March 1894, in Hyde, *Oscar Wilde*, page 167.
'perfect love': Lord Alfred Douglas, unpublished article for *Mercure de France*.
'all a question for physiology': *Works*, pages 35–36.
'Sins of the flesh are nothing': *Letters*, page 714.
'Those who are faithful': *Works*, page 25.

Gay, gilt and gracious
'Be careful to choose': O'Sullivan, *Aspects of Wilde*, page 93.
'From Oscar to the Gilt-mailed boy': displayed in *Wilde and the Nineties: An Essay and an Exhibition* edited by Charles Ryskamp, New Jersey, 1966.
'the gilt and graceful boy': *Letters*, page 599.
'the gay, gilt and gracious lad': *Letters*, page 588.
'slim gilt soul': Hyde, *Famous Trials 7*, page 245.
'gilt silk hair': *Letters*, page 589.
'a miracle of impudence': Edward Pigott to Spencer Ponsonby, in Regenia Gagnier, *Idylls of the Marketplace* (Stanford, 1986), pages 170–171.
'I shall leave England': interview with Wilde in *Pall Mall Budget*, in *Oscar Wilde: Interviews and Recollections*, volume I, page 186.
'And wilt thou, Oscar, from us flee': *Spectator*, 9 July 1892, in Beckson, *The Oscar Wilde Encyclopedia*, page 325.
'There is not enough fire': Pearson, *The Life of Oscar Wilde*, page 229.
'I do not know exactly which course': Max Beerbohm to Reginald Turner, early July 1892, in *Max Beerbohm's Letters to Reggie Turner*, page 23.
'violent and invincible': Croft-Cooke, *Bosie*, page 61.
'Oscar is at Homburg under a regime': *Letters*, page 530.
'Oscar had a pony cart': Lord Alfred Douglas to A.J.A. Symons, 14 March 1939, Clark Library.
'I am so sorry about Lord Alfred Douglas': private collection.
'an underpaid clerk in a small provincial bank': *Works*, page 490.
'a great fancy': *Works*, page 470.
'It is because I like you so much': *Works*, page 475.
'He is certainly not natural': Ellmann, page 380.
'Ah, every day dear Herbert': Pearson, *The Life of Oscar Wilde*, page 237.
'How you delight in your disciples!': Alan Sinfield, *The Wilde Century* (London, 1994), page 73.
'the queerest mixture': Lytton Strachey to Duncan Grant, 1907, in Ellmann, page 378.
'It is perfectly monstrous': *Works*, page 469.
'Nothing is serious except passion': *Works*, page 471.
'There is no secret of life': *Works*, page 497.
'frequently came to my mother's house': Douglas, *Autobiography*, page 59.

'endless little notes': *Letters*, page 763.

'two long interviews': *Letters*, page 763.

'She told me of your chief faults': *Letters* page 687.

'I asked her why': *Letters*, page 763.

'The first time': *Letters*, page 763.

'one of my children': *Letters*, page 694.

'I have in my blood': Brian Roberts, *The Mad Bad Line* (London), page 193.

'Those incessant scenes': *Letters*, page 689.

'loyal, kind and forgiving': Lord Alfred Douglas to Lady Queensberry, 6 January 1894, in Croft-Cooke, *Bosie*, page 93.

'eccentricities and peculiar views': Lord Alfred Douglas to Lady Queensberry, 6 January 1894, in Croft-Cooke, *Bosie*, page 93.

'acted the part': Croft-Cooke, *Bosie*, page 93.

'the murderer of your soul': Croft-Cooke, *Bosie*, page 93.

'People's mothers bore me to death': *Works*, page 487.

'looked unhappy': the Marquess of Queensberry's statement, witness statements, private collection.

'part-read': the Marquess of Queensberry's statement, witness statements, private collection.

'a desirable companion': witness statements, private collection.

'All through my childhood': Douglas, *Autobiography*, page 16.

'My father suddenly': Douglas, *Autobiography*, page 93.

'some strained feelings': Holland, *Irish Peacock and Scarlet Marquess*, page 30.

Prophets and priests

'How can you have the flower': Harris, *Oscar Wilde*, page 270.

'the only one that ever': Douglas, *Without Apology*, page 165.

'rapt I gaze upon': d'Arch Smith, *Love in Earnest*, page 51.

'His lips are sweet and red': Douglas, *Lyrics*, page 60.

'A.R.B. – I like your story': d'Arch Smith, *Love in Earnest*, page 53.

'unholy, decadent academy': Lord Alfred Douglas, *Halcyon Days: Contributions to the Spirit Lamp* selected and introduced by Caspar Wintermans (New Hampshire, 1995).

'I never got the *Spirit Lamp*': *Letters*, pages 545–546.

'all who are interested': Gagnier, *Idylls of the Marketplace*, page 147.

'monstrous laws': *Works*, page 29.

'the new Individualism': *Works*, page 1197.

'new culture': Lord Alfred Douglas to Charles Kains Jackson, 10 September 1893, HRC.

'Perhaps nobody knows': Lord Alfred Douglas to Charles Kains Jackson, 10 September 1893, HRC.

'dived': diary of George Ives, 21 November 1899, HRC.

'Our meeting was quite droll': diary of George Ives, 30 June 1892, HRC.

'having obtained permission': diary of George Ives, 14 October 1893, HRC.

'establish a Pagan Monastery': diary of George Ives, 26 October, 1892, HRC.

'moving very rapidly': diary of George Ives, 14 October 1893, HRC.

'time has been so full': diary of George Ives, 26 October 1893, HRC.

'all creativity, laying plans': Stokes, *Oscar Wilde*, page 72.

'A Religion, A Theory of Life': Jeffrey Weeks, *Coming Out* (London, 1990), page 123.

'The vow that shall make you': George Ives materials, HRC.

'Thou knowest the two': Weeks, *Coming Out*, page 123.
'is forbidden On Duty': diary of George Ives, 26 February 1894, HRC.
'Oscar Wilde's influence': diary of George Ives, 26 October 1893, HRC.
'Love is a sacrament': George Ives materials, HRC.
'He was very beautiful': diary of George Ives, 14 October 1893, HRC.
'Love is the only': diary of George Ives, 15 March 1894, HRC.
'Oscar, you were right': diary of George Ives, 5 December 1899, HRC.
'our dear brother of the Faith': diary of George Ives, 12 January 1894, HRC.
'cataract-blinded': John Addington Symonds to Edward Carpenter, 21 January 1893, in Weeks, *Coming Out*, page 41.
'The blending of Social Strata': John Addington Symonds to Edward Carpenter, 21 January 1893, in Weeks, *Coming Out*, page 41.
'the high towering love': Symonds, *Sexual Inversion*, page 183.
'I conceive of a millennium of earth': Edward Carpenter, *Towards Democracy* (Manchester, 1896).
'Among the working masses': Ellis, *Studies in the Psychology of Sex*, page 13.
'patent to all observers': Ellis, *Studies in the Psychology of Sex*, page 15.
'He had made advances': Ellis, *Studies in the Psychology of Sex*, page 15.
'What is called the vice': Philippe Jullian, *Oscar Wilde* (London, 1979), page 179.
'Manliness has become': Knox, *Oscar Wilde*, page 73.
'all body and no soul': Backhouse, 'The Dead Past'.
'a pledge of comradeship': Symonds, *Memoirs*, pages 277–278.
'I deliberately': *Letters*, page 730.
'like feasting with panthers': *Letters*, page 758.
'imperfect world of coarse': *Letters*, page 726.
'the brightest of gilded snakes': *Letters*, page 759.
'the mire': *Letters*, page 692.
'sprawling in the mire': *Gil Blas*, 22 November 1897, in Schmidgall, *The Stranger Wilde*, page 268.
'not Destiny, merely': *Letters*, page 701.
'Nemesis has caught': *Letters*, page 921.
'cure the soul': *Works*, page 134.
'Only in the mire': *Letters*, page 921.

For love or money
'What a fuss people make': *Works*, page 35.
'Are there beautiful people': *Letters*, pages 541–542.
'You are my ideal Gerald': *Letters*, page 540.
'Tired of the passion': Douglas, *Sonnets*, page 19.
'undying love': *Letters*, page 544.
'My Own Boy': *Letters*, page 544.
'Was it not repugnant': Hyde, *Famous Trials 7*, page 230.
'a marriage': Pierre Louÿs to André Gide, in Gide, *Oscar Wilde*, page 72.
'I hope marriage': *Letters*, page 603.
'Charlie, dear': Hyde, *Famous Trials 7*, page 179.
'a very girlish boy': statement of Fred Atkins, 1895, witness statements, private collection.
'What was the attraction': Mason, *Oscar Wilde: Three Times Tried*, page 355.
'very civil and friendly': Hyde, *Famous Trials 7*, pages 188–189.

'I know a man': Hyde, *Famous Trials 7*, pages 188–189.
'It was arranged': *The Trials of Oscar Wilde*, page 211.
'Our little lad': Croft-Cooke, *Feasting with Panthers*, page 270.
'in Oscar's room': witness statement, private collection.
'It was quite a surprise': Hyde, *Famous Trials 7*, page 189.
'I have a great fancy': Hyde, *Famous Trials 7*, page 248.
'penetrated the dim-lit': *Evening News*, 5 April 1895, in Christopher Craft, 'Alias Bunbury: Desire and Termination in *The Importance of Being Earnest*', in *Representations*, volume XXI (summer 1990), page 30.
'a cigarette is the perfect type': *Works*, page 67.
'Instead of simply offering': Pierre Louÿs to André Gide, June 1892, in Hull McCormack, *John Gray*, page 91.
'pale-eyed and pimply-faced': *The Star*, 11 April 1895.
'Mr Wilde kissed the waiter': Hyde, *Famous Trials 7*, pages 184–185.
'not to go see those woman': Hyde, *Famous Trials 7*, page 185.
'Shall I come into bed': Hyde, *Famous Trials 7*, page 185–186.
'perform certain operations': statement of Fred Atkins, 1895, witness statements, private collection.
'Are you Alfred Wood?': Mason, *Oscar Wilde: Three Times Tried*, page 211.
'one of the best to be got': *The Trials of Oscar Wilde*, pages 201–202.
'put his hand inside': *The Shame of Oscar Wilde*, page 29.
'"kissing &c" had taken place': witness statements, private collection.
'It was a long time': *The Shame of Oscar Wilde*, page 29.
'£3 or £4 at a time': statement of Alfred Wood, 1895, witness statements, private collection.
'did not fulfil his promises': witness statements, private collection.
'several times': witness statements, private collection.
'Familiarities': statement of Alfred Wood, 1895, witness statements, private collection.
'Bosie's whims have led me': Campbell Dodgson to Lionel Johnson, 8 February 1893, British Library.
'that we were going to Torquay': Campbell Dodgson to Lionel Johnson, 8 February 1893, British Library.
'If you knew': Croft-Cooke, *Bosie*, page 364.
'Babbacombe Cliff has become': *Letters*, page 547.
'succeeded in combining': *Letters*, page 555.
'Babbacombe School': *Letters*, page 556.
'Our life is lazy and luxurious': Campbell Dodgson to Lionel Johnson, 8 February 1893, British Library.
'When you left': *Letters*, page 691.
'with a heart of lead': *Letters*, page 560.

Feasting with panthers
'Moderation is a fatal thing': Pearson, *Life of Oscar Wilde*, page 171.
'begged': *Letters*, page 691.
'food and drink': Oscar Wilde's Bankruptcy Proceedings, High Court of Bankruptcy B9/428, PRO.
'I really am not going to be imprisoned': *Works*, page 380.
'How grossly materialistic!': *Works*, page 380.
'the clear turtle soup': *Letters*, pages 774–775.

'Suppose I like a food that is poison': Harris, *Oscar Wilde*, page 292.

'the honey of thy sugar lips': Lord Alfred Douglas, 'A Port on the Aegean', in Murray, *Bosie*, page 50.

'I am sorry to say that Oscar': Max Beerbohm to Reggie Turner, 12 April 1893, in *Max Beerbohm's Letters to Reggie Turner*, page 35.

'It was like feasting with panthers': *Letters*, page 758.

'I can't understand sensible men': CG [Charles Grolleau], *The Trial of Oscar Wilde from the Shorthand Reports* (Paris, 1906).

'Now you, you could get money': CG, *The Trial of Oscar Wilde*.

'Darling': CG, *The Trial of Oscar Wilde*.

'paid all his attention to my brother': in Hyde, *Famous Trials 7*, page 177.

'My brother took it into his': Hyde, *Famous Trials 7*, page 177.

'He showed curiosity': Mason, *Oscar Wilde: Three Times Tried*, pages 203–204.

'This is the boy for me!': statement of Charles Parker, 1895, witness statements, private collection.

'Your brother is lucky!': Hyde, *Famous Trials 7*, pages 177–8.

'I was there about two hours': Anonymous, 'The Life of Oscar Wilde as Prosecutor and Prisoner', 1895.

'toss him off': CG, *The Trial of Oscar Wilde*.

'He suggested two or three times': CG, *The Trial of Oscar Wilde*.

'I don't suppose boys': Hyde, *Famous Trials 7*, page 172.

'You say positively': Hyde, *Famous Trials 7*, page 175.

'certain operations with his mouth': statement of Charles Parker, 1895, witness statements, private collection.

'a common boy': statement of Jane Margaret Cotta, 1895, witness statements, private collection.

'close-cropped hair': Hyde, *Famous Trials 7*, page 194.

'were stained in a peculiar way': *The Trials of Oscar Wilde*, page 220.

'soil': statement of Jane Margaret Cotta, 1895, witness statements, private collection.

'How disgusting!': statement of Jane Margaret Cotta 1895, witness statements, private collection.

'One of the housemaids came to me': *The Trials of Oscar Wilde*, pages 210–211.

'I do not wish to enlarge': *The Trials of Oscar Wilde*, page 261.

'the sodomistic act': *The Shame of Oscar Wilde*, pages 39–40.

'You deny that the bed-linen': CG, *The Trial of Oscar Wilde*.

'On going to the room': statement of Antonio Migge, 1895, witness statements, private collection.

'I know nothing about the Savoy': Hyde, *Famous Trials 7*, page 267.

'come and smoke a cigarette': Craft, 'Alias Bunbury', page 30.

'not to be a beast': *The Shame of Oscar Wilde*, page 64.

'Hello! Here's my Herbert': statement of Herbert Tankard, 1895, witness statements, private collection.

'is always kissing me': statement of Herbert Tankard, 1895, witness statements, private collection.

'ocular and most horrible proofs': Backhouse, 'The Dead Past'.

'What the paradox was to me': *Letters*, page 730.

'the sins of another': *Letters*, page 714.

'carefully coached': *Letters*, page 714.

'It was not me they spoke about': Harris, *Oscar Wilde*, page 166.

'He wanted to': Harris, *Oscar Wilde*, page 166.
'giving him certain information': Douglas, *Autobiography*, page 111.
'was not in prison': *Letters*, page 784.
'nothing irritated him more': Hyde, *Oscar Wilde*, page 347.
'a stinking scandal': the Marquis of Queensberry to Alfred Montgomery, 6 July 1894, in St John Irvine, *Oscar Wilde: A Present Time Appraisal* (London, 1951), pages 251–252.
'You were both kicked out': Hyde, *Oscar Wilde*, page 193.
'Isn't that Mr. Oscar Wilde?': Harris, *Oscar Wilde*, page 97.
'live his own life to the utmost': Douglas, *Autobiography*, page 76.

The madness of kisses
'The criminal classes': *Works*, page 1243.
'Ah! You don't know?': diary of Edmond de Goncourt, 30 April 1893, in Erber, 'The French Trials of Oscar Wilde', page 561.
'I now hear on good authority': the Marquess of Queensberry to Lord Alfred Douglas, 1 April 1894, in Croft-Cooke, *Bosie*, page 97.
'This one's quite hot enough': Mason, *Oscar Wilde: Three Times Tried*, page 393.
'stolen': Mason, *Oscar Wilde: Three Times Tried*, page 34.
'to get away from': *The Trials of Oscar Wilde*, page 202.
'I suppose you think': Mason, *Oscar Wilde: Three Times Tried*, page 34.
'I don't consider these letters': Mason, *Oscar Wilde: Three Times Tried*, page 35.
'I'm very much afraid': Mason, *Oscar Wilde: Three Times Tried*, page 35.
'infernal nuisance': Vyvyan Holland, *Son of Oscar Wilde* (London, 1954), page 192.
'I am making some slight changes': O'Sullivan, *Aspects of Wilde*, page 11.
'royalties and bigwigs': *Letters*, page 560.
'The first night': *Max Beerbohm's Letters to Reginald Turner*, page 37.
'I pointed this case out': Cheiro, *Cheiro's Memoirs: The Reminiscences of a Society Palmist* (London, 1912), page 57.
'Kindly give this letter ': Mason, *Oscar Wilde: Three Times Tried*, page 57.
'I told him that I was rehearsing': Mason, *Oscar Wilde: Three Times Tried*, page 57.
'I was told by my servant': Mason, *Oscar Wilde: Three Times Tried*, pages 35–36.
'empty with fear': Harris, *Oscar Wilde*, page 94.
'notorious boy scoundrel': diary of George Ives, 4 June 1903, HRC.
'his strong love of nature study': diary of George Ives, 23 December 1893, HRC.
'I suppose this means': diary of George Ives, 23 December 1893, HRC.
'Vague whispers': *New York Herald*, 7 April 1895, page 2.
'evil rumours': Sherard, *Oscar Wilde*, page 113.
'vulgar appearance': Harris, *Oscar Wilde*, page 90.
'very unpleasant stories': *Interviews and Recollections*, volume II, page 287.
'a dangerous situation': *Interviews and Recollections*, volume II, pages 287–288.
'Poor Oscar!': Max Beerbohm to Robert Ross, 1893, in Ellmann, page 394.
'Nothing is serious except passion': *Works*, page 471.
'The real enemy of modern life': Hyde, *Oscar Wilde*, page 155.
'The wildest profligate': Hyde, *Oscar Wilde*, page 155.
'the most learned erotomaniac': *Letters*, page 924.
'The work is, undoubtedly': Wilde and Others, *Teleny*, page 10.
'He was usually accompanied by': Wilde and Others, *Teleny*, page 9.
'A friend of mine': Wilde and Others, *Teleny*, page 9.

'It was evident to me': Wilde and Others, *Teleny*, page 10.
'I can easily see why': Wilde and Others, *Teleny*, pages 9–10.
'always struggled against': Wilde and Others, *Teleny*, pages 51–52.
'musical': d'Arch Smith, *Love in Earnest*, page 53.
'Far from being ashamed': Wilde and Others, *Teleny*, pages 129–130.
'Then, Heaven': Wilde and Others, *Teleny*, page 188.
'About the falling out with Oscar': John Gray to Pierre Louÿs, 16 March 1893, in Hull McCormack, *John Gray*, page 105.
'corrupting the youth': *Max Beerbohm's Letters to Reggie Turner*, page 290.
'preaching corruption': Raffalovich, *Uranisme et Unisexualité*, page 248, translated by Sian Jones.
'a young man with a promising career': d'Arch Smith, *Love in Earnest*, page 187.
'the tiniest rivulet of text': Sewell, *In the Dorian Mode*, page 40.
'Oscar Wilde has been charming': Pierre Louÿs to Georges Louÿs, 22 April 1893, in Ellmann, page 393.
'fatal connection': Hull McCormack, *John Gray*, page 106.
'I wanted to have a friend': Fryer, *André & Oscar*, page 67.
'that sexual relations': Backhouse, 'The Dead Past'.
'better, saner, finer philosophy': Hyde, *Oscar Wilde*, page 155.
'a mock marriage': Backhouse, 'The Dead Past'.

Brazen candour
'Really, if the lower orders': *Works*, page 358.
'Ossian Savage': *Interviews and Recollections*, volume I, pages 221–222.
'missing word competition': Mason, *Art and Morality*, page 22.
'a peculiarly plain boy': Holland, *Irish Peacock and Scarlet Marquess*, pages 207–208.
'private parts': statement of Walter Grainger, 1895, witness statements, private collection.
'placed his penis': statement of Walter Grainger, 1895, witness statements, private collection.
'very serious trouble': statement of Walter Grainger, 1895, witness statements, private collection.
'I really don't care twopence': d'Arch Smith, *Love in Earnest*, page 53.
'under the circumstances': *Letters*, page 702.
'acted as before to me': statement of Walter Grainger, 1895, witness statements, private collection.
'frightened': statement of Walter Grainger, 1895, witness statements, private collection.
'the *fun* of being with Oscar': Croft-Cooke, *Bosie*, page 364.
'I have done no work here': *Letters*, page 566.
'finding that life in meadow and stream': *Letters*, page 567.
'You've no idea the sort of face': Harris, *Oscar Wilde*, page 104.
'peculiar': statement of Gertrude Simmonds, 1895, witness statements, private collection.
'Much to my surprise Mr Wilde': statement of Gertrude Simmonds, 1895, witness statements, private collection.
'punch him': statement of Ernest Mitchelmore, 1895, witness statements, private collection.
'The morning of the day': *Letters*, page 692.

'sullenly': *Letters*, page 692.

'four wire baskets filled': Oscar Wilde's Bankruptcy Proceedings, High Court of Bankruptcy, B9/428, PRO.

'Ross was by way of being devoted': Douglas, *Autobiography*, pages 70–71.

'Freddie is the one friend': Robert Ross to Christopher Millard, 6 September 1913, in Maureen Borland, *Wilde's Devoted Friend: A Life of Robert Ross 1869–1918* (Oxford, 1990), page 194.

'slender, attractive, impulsive boy': Douglas, *Autobiography*, page 71.

'one of my greatest friends': Lord Alfred Douglas to Percy Douglas, 'The Constant Nymph', Maggs Brothers Limited, no date.

'contains a great deal': Ricketts, *Self-Portrait*, page 124.

'a woman of grave, Greek beauty': *Works*, page 515.

'Suppose when I leave': *Works*, page 529.

'Yours is a very nasty scandal': *Works*, page 528.

'He and I are closer than friends': *Works*, page 551.

'the game of life': *Works*, page 528.

'high character, high moral tone, high principles': *Works*, page 577.

'my secret and my shame': *Works*, page 562.

'Do you think that it is weakness': *Works*, page 538.

'pitiless in her perfection': *Works*, page 561.

'The ten commandments': *Works*, page 558.

'any secret dishonour or disgrace': *Works*, page 534.

'Women are not meant to judge us': *Works*, page 579.

A pugilist of unsound mind

'The basis of every scandal': *Works*, page 472.

'we shall have you Prime Minister': *Works*, page 581.

'a man of forty': *Works*, page 518.

'a nervous temperament': *Works*, page 518.

'A personality of mark': *Works*, page 518.

'firmly-chiselled mouth': *Works*, page 518.

'undisciplined temper': Lord Acton to George Murray, Whit Sunday 1892, bundle 1674, Atholl Archive, Blair Castle.

'an excellent, amiable young man': Murray, *Bosie*, page 66.

'brightness and good temper': George Murray to Lord Acton, 19 October 1894, MS10049, National Library of Scotland, Edinburgh.

'cultured, charming and generous': Backhouse, 'The Dead Past'.

'there was something very winning': Sir Edward Walter Hamilton, 19 October 1894, BL Add MSS 48665, British Library.

'he was much liked': Sir Edward Walter Hamilton, 19 October 1894, BL Add MSS 48665, British Library.

'the most loveable youth': Arthur Ellis to Lord Rosebery, 22 October 1894, MS10049, National Library of Scotland.

'every boy of good looks': Symonds, *Memoirs*, page 94.

'little bandbox': Robert Rhodes James, *Rosebery* (London, 1985), page 56.

'devoted': Brian Roberts, *The Mad Bad Line: The Family of Lord Alfred Douglas* (London, 1981), page 159.

'became attracted': Backhouse, 'The Dead Past'.

'Like the Arabs and the Ottomans': Backhouse, 'The Dead Past'.

'considering some of the things': Lewis Harcourt, 1891, in Roberts, *The Mad Bad Line*, pages 184–185.
'Brookfield's zeal in the pursuit of homosexuals': H. Montgomery Hyde to Rupert Hart-Davis, 27 May 1967, HRC.
'One eminent personage': 'Xavier Mayne' (pseudonym), *The Intersexes: A History of Similisexualism as a Problem in Social Life* (Rome, 1908), page 237.
'soirée': Backhouse, 'The Dead Past'.
'the very eccentric': Backhouse, 'The Dead Past'.
'homosexual to the fingertips': Backhouse, 'The Dead Past'.
'Lord Douglas took me aside': Backhouse, 'The Dead Past'.
'He was extremely and ideally handsome': Backhouse, 'The Dead Past'.
'Lord Queensberry was for the moment furious': diary of Sir Algernon West, 5 June 1893, in Roberts, *The Mad Bad Line*, page 160.
'Scarlet Marquis': *Letters*, page 621.
'I have quite given up': Roberts, *The Mad Bad Line*, page 157.
'drunken, declassé and half-witted': *Letters*, page 707.
'Any possibility there may have been': Rhodes James, *Rosebery*, page 300.
'the paramount influence': Backhouse, 'The Dead Past'.
'Many scandalous anonymous letters': Backhouse, 'The Dead Past'.
'Cher Fat Boy': Queensberry to Lord Rosebery, 22 August 1893, MS 10170 f255, National Library of Scotland.
'Jew nancy boy': Queensberry to Lord Rosebery, 22 August 1893, MS 10170 f255, National Library of Scotland.
'peerage business': Queensberry toy Lord Rosebery, 22 August 1893, MS 10170 f255, National Library of Scotland.
'I have a punching ball': Queensberry to Lord Rosebery, 22 August 1893, MS 10170 f255, National Library of Scotland.
'The Marquis of Queensberry, in consequence': Rhodes James, *Rosebery*, page 287.
'It is a material and unpleasant': Rhodes James, *Rosebery*, page 287.
'God help the country': Queensberry to Lord Rosebery, 22 August 1893, MS 10170 f255, National Library of Scotland.

A schoolboy with wonderful eyes
'Little boys should be obscene': *Interviews and Recollections*, volume II, page 373.
'rich clusters of vine leaves': Murray, *Bosie*, page 49.
'Nor have I ever seen Oscar': *Max Beerbohm's Letters to Reginald Turner*, page 53.
'scenes': *Letters*, page 692.
'I suspected that': Lord Alfred Douglas, *Without Apology*.
'no intellectual obligation': *Letters*, page 692.
'the one really true thing': *Letters*, page 692.
'Ultimately the bond': *Letters*, page 692.
'trivial in thought and action': *Letters*, page 692.
'The froth and folly': *Letters*, page 692.
'the eternal quest for beauty': Lord Alfred Douglas to Charles Kains Jackson, 9 April 1894, in Hyde, *Lord Alfred Douglas*, page 55.
'a malady, or a madness, or both': *Letters*, page 730.
'You were extremely angry': *Letters*, page 692.
'But in reality, I could not': *Letters*, page 693.
'a good opportunity': *Letters*, page 693.

'I have just finished translating': Lord Alfred Douglas to Charles Kains Jackson, 31 August 1893, HRC.

'The general philistine attacks': Lord Alfred Douglas to Charles Kains Jackson, 10 September 1893, HRC.

'I am bored to death': Lord Alfred Douglas to Charles Kains Jackson, 31 August 1893, HRC.

'What I said about the 'Straw Hat'': Lord Alfred Douglas to Charles Kains Jackson, 10 September 1893, HRC.

'Straw Hat, No Band (for Friend)': Janet Taylor and Kenneth Cliff, 'Mr Lock: Hatter to Oscar Wilde and Associates', *The Wildean*, number 22 (January 2003), page 21.

'and I saw thee': Lord Alfred Douglas, 'A Port in the Aegean', in Murray, *Bosie*, page 50.

'I was so fascinated by the expression': Lord Alfred Douglas to Charles Kains Jackson, 31 August 1893, HRC.

'I am held fast by the lassoo of desire': Lord Alfred Douglas to Robbie Ross, 11 February 1895, Hyde Collection.

'really very fond': *Letters*, page 785.

'no matter what you wrote': *Letters*, page 693.

'It was represented to me': *Letters*, page 693.

'March '93, for Aubrey': Matthew Sturgis, *Aubrey Beardsley: A Biography* (London, 1998), pages 131–132.

'the most monstrous of orchids': *Interviews and Recollections*, volume II, page 270.

'Absinthe is to all other drinks': Harris, *Oscar Wilde*, page 75.

'certain forms of crime': Max Beerbohm to Reginald Turner, 10 October 1892, in *Max Beerbohm's Letters to Reggie Turner*, page 26.

'Yes, yes, I look like a sodomite': Belford, *Oscar Wilde*, pages 204–205.

'made advances to upwards': Ellis, *Studies in the Psychology of Sex*, page 15.

'advances on Beardsley': Robert Sherard to A.J.A. Symons, 31 May 1937, Hyde Collection.

'boasted of having had': Backhouse, 'The Dead Past'.

'I don't mind his morals': Backhouse, 'The Dead Past'.

'Sales sont tes parties secrètes': Backhouse, 'The Dead Past'.

'like a mad woman': *Works*, page 592.

'like the naughty scribbles': Paul Raymond and Charles Ricketts, *Oscar Wilde: Recollections* (London, 1932), page 52.

'used to inspect': Backhouse, 'The Dead Past'.

'I can tell you I had a warm time': Aubrey Beardsley to Robert Ross, late November 1893, in Aubrey Beardsley, *Letters*, edited by Henry Maas, J.L. Duncan and W.G. Good (London, 1970), page 58.

'There have been very great': Max Beerbohm to Reginald Turner, 19 December 1893, in *Max Beerbohm's Letters to Reggie Turner*, page 84.

'frequently': Biscoe Hale Wortham to Oscar Browning, 12 October 1893, ALS King's College.

'a nice-looking, well-mannered': Biscoe Hale Wortham to Oscar Browning, 12 October 1893, ALS King's College.

'there was something suspicious': Biscoe Hale Wortham to Oscar Browning, 12 October 1893, ALS King's College.

'the desire of his soul': Max Beerbohm to Reginald Turner, 19 December 1893, in *Max Beerbohm's Letters to Reggie Turner*, page 84.

'the letter contained the word "Boy"': Oscar Browning to Frank Harris, 3 November 1919, HRC.
'On Saturday the boy slept': Oscar Browning to Frank Harris, 3 November 1919, HRC.
'formed the acquaintance': Biscoe Hale Wortham to Oscar Browning, 12 October 1893, ALS King's College.
'The schoolboy Helen': Max Beerbohm to Reginald Turner, 19 December 1893, in *Max Beerbohm's Letters to Reggie Turner*, page 84.
'a pretty sharp lookout': Biscoe Hale Wortham to Oscar Browning, 12 October 1893, ALS King's College.
'left absolutely no doubt': Biscoe Hale Wortham to Oscar Browning, 12 October 1893, ALS King's College.
'in its naked hideousness': Biscoe Hale Wortham to Oscar Browning, 12 October 1893, in Anstruther, *Oscar Browning*, pages 133–134.
'I am miserable about poor Toddy': Mina Wortham to Oscar Browning, 16 October 1893, in Anstruther, *Oscar Browning*, page 135.
'Ross is simply one of a gang': Biscoe Hale Wortham to Oscar Browning, 15 October 1893, in Borland, *Wilde's Devoted Friend*, page 34.
'Biscoe was surprised last evening': Mina Wortham to Oscar Browning, 16 October 1893, in Anstruther, *Oscar Browning*, page 135.
'very unsatisfactory': Robert Ross to Oscar Browning, 16 October 1893, in Anstruther, *Oscar Browning*, pages 135–136.
'It is frightfully dull here': Lord Alfred Douglas to Lord Percy Douglas, 16 October 1893, 'The Constant Nymph', Maggs Brothers Limited, no date.
'Please don't let Mamma': Lord Alfred Douglas to Lord Percy Douglas, 16 October 1893, 'The Constant Nymph', Maggs Brothers Limited, no date.
'decidedly ruffled': diary of George Ives, 19 October 1893, HRC.
'The fact is that': Mina Wortham to Oscar Browning, 16 October 1893, in Anstruther, *Oscar Browning*, page 135.
'Col. D– has been like many': Biscoe Hale Wortham to Oscar Browning, 25 October 1893, ALS King's College.
'They will doubtless get two years': Oscar Browning to Frank Harris, 3 November 1919, HRC.
'At length I am thankful': Biscoe Hale Wortham to Oscar Browning, 25 October 1893, in Anstruther, *Oscar Browning*, page 136.

On a gilded barge
'I don't think England': *Works*, page 467.
'I am not allowed to live': Robert Ross to Lord Alfred Douglas, October 1893, in Borland, *Wilde's Devoted Friend*, pages 35–36.
'blackmailing': *Max Beerbohm's Letters to Reggie Turner*, page 84.
'going in for the wildest folly': William Rothenstein to Margaret Woods, 28 October 1893, in Hyde, *Lord Alfred Douglas*, page 47.
'a long chat with O.W.': diary of George Ives, 28 October 1893, HRC.
'is sleepless, nervous': *Letters*, page 575.
'Why not try and make arrangements': *Letters*, page 575.
'knowledge and concurrence': *Letters*, page 694.
'Douglas went to Egypt': Robert Ross to Frank Harris, 17 May 1914, HRC.
'I understand that': diary of George Ives, 29 November 1893, HRC.

'the Sotadic Zone': Elaine Showalter, *Sexual Anarchy* (Middlesex, 1990), pages 81–82.

'classical region of all abominations': Richard Burton, *Terminal Essay* (London, 1885).

'the highdried and highly respectable': Burton, *Terminal Essay*.

'I want to ask if you': Lord Alfred Douglas to Charles Kains Jackson, 29 November 1893, HRC.

'I am very unhappy': Lord Alfred Douglas to Charles Kains Jackson, 29 November 1893, HRC.

'culminating in one': *Letters*, page 693.

'I remember that afternoon': *Letters*, page 693.

'The usual telegrams': *Letters*, page 693.

'and under the influence': *Letters*, page 694.

'darling': statement of Gertrude Simmonds, 1895, witness statements, private collection.

'with a sense of tragedy': *Letters*, page 934.

'sadly and seriously trying': *Letters*, page 694.

'I am happy in the knowledge': *Letters*, page 577.

'ruining his soul': Lord Alfred Douglas to Lady Queensberry, 6 June 1894, in Croft-Cooke, *Bosie*, page 91.

'I should also like to tell you': Lord Alfred Douglas to Lady Queensberry, 6 January 1894, in Croft-Cooke, *Bosie*, page 94.

'I am passionately fond of him': Lord Alfred Douglas to Lady Queensberry, 10 December 1893, in Croft-Cooke, *Bosie*, page 92.

'There is nothing I would not do': Lord Alfred Douglas to Lady Queensberry, ?March 1894, in Hyde, *Oscar Wilde*, page 167.

'will be remembered and written about': Lord Alfred Douglas to Lady Queensberry, 10 December 1893, in Croft-Cooke, *Bosie*, page 92.

'I went as far as I could': *Letters*, page 694.

'At twelve o'clock you drove up': *Letters*, page 686.

'for luncheon, dinner, suppers, amusements': *Letters*, page 688.

'work undisturbed': *Letters*, page 686.

'had a great number of callers': statement of Thomas Price, 1895, witness statements, private collection.

'I would not allow him': statement of Ernest Scarfe, 1895, witness statements, private collection.

'I remember him because': statement of Thomas Price, 1895, witness statements, private collection.

'Frank': *Letters*, page 570.

'You must tell me': *Letters*, page 570.

'I am so glad you like': *Letters*, page 585.

'deeply moved': *Letters*, page 586.

'I am enjoying this place very much': Lord Alfred Douglas to Lady Queensberry, 10 December 1893, in Croft-Cooke, *Bosie*, page 89.

'a pretty, interesting boy': diary of W.S. Blunt, 13 December 1893, Fitzwilliam Museum, Cambridge.

'Here comes Cromer!': Robert Hichens, *Yesterday* (London, 1947), page 60.

'the boy-snatcher of Clement's Inn': *Letters*, page 878.

'the last word in comfort': Douglas, *Autobiography*, page 73.

'More fair than any flower is thy face': Douglas, *Autobiography*, page 73.

'a piece of perfidy': Lord Alfred Douglas to Hesketh Pearson, 13 November 1944, HRC.

The Scarlet Marquis

'A typical Englishman': Day, *Oscar Wilde*, page 68.
'hurled out of the official residence': Robert Ross to Frank Harris, 17 May 1914, HRC.
'the fleshpots of Egypt': *Letters*, page 704.
'a romantic encounter': Queensberry, *Oscar Wilde and the Black Douglas*, page 33.
'I know that on the sand': Douglas, *Sonnets*, page 21.
'I confess I was astounded': *Letters*, page 695.
'Finally you actually telegraphed': *Letters*, page 695.
'I said that time healed every wound': *Letters*, page 695.
'passionate telegrams': *Letters*, page 695.
'a threat of suicide': *Letters*, page 695.
'When I arrived in Paris': *Letters*, page 696.
'flame-coloured': *Works*, page 280.
'Love is wiser than Philosophy': *Works*, page 280.
'love to him was always a sacrifice': diary of George Ives, 4 June 1903, HRC.
'completely got round': Douglas, *Autobiography*, page 99.
'Dear Bosie is with us': Max Beerbohm to Reginald Turner, 12 March 1894, in *Max Beerbohm's Letters to Reggie Turner*, pages 91–92.
'caressed': statement of the Marquis of Queensberry, 1895, witness statements, private collection.
'exceedingly distressed': statement of the Marquis of Queensberry, 1895, witness statements, private collection.
'Your disgusted so-called father': the Marquis of Queensberry to Lord Alfred Douglas, in Ellmann, page 417.
'No wonder people are talking': the Marquis of Queensberry to Lord Alfred Douglas, in Ellmann, pages 417–418.
'Sir I would request of you': statement of the Marquis of Queensberry, 1895, witness statements, private collection.
'What a funny little man': statement of the Marquis of Queensberry, 1895, witness statements, private collection.
'a telegram of which the commonest street-boy': *Letters*, pages 707–708.
'You impertinent young jackanapes': the Marquis of Queensberry to Lord Alfred Douglas, 1894, in Croft-Cooke, *Bosie*, page 98.
'some withdrawal': statement of the Marquis of Queensberry, 1895, witness statements, private collection.
'save': Statement of the Marquis of Queensberry, 9 March 1895, CRIM 1 41/6, PRO.
'I cried over you': Holland, *Irish Peacock and Scarlet Marquess*, page 218.
'malformation of the parts of generation': Ellmann, page 405.
'I wish you would write': Lord Alfred Douglas to Charles Kains Jackson, 9 April 1894, HRC.
'the slave of beauty': *Works*, pages 312–313.
'Beauty-Spirit': diary of George Ives, 23 December 1893, HRC.
'to get a glimpse': diary of George Ives, 26 October 1893, HRC.
'the gay, gilt and gracious lad': *Letters*, page 588.
'I had a frantic telegram': *Letters*, page 589.
'ugly rumours': Martin Birnbaum, *Oscar Wilde: Fragments and Memories* (London, 1920), page 9.
'Stop to let this man out!': Birnbaum, *Oscar Wilde*, page 9.
'He has nothing to say': *Pall Mall Gazette*, 30 March 1889, in d'Arch Smith, *Love in Earnest*, page 27.

'Who did I meet here?': Sheridan, *André Gide*, page 100.

'a burly friend': statement of the Marquis of Queensberry, 1895, witness statements, private collection.

'I am off to the country': *Letters*, page 592.

'"Sit down!" said Queensberry curtly': Mason, *Oscar Wilde: Three Times Tried*, pages 37–39 and Holland, *Irish Peacock and Scarlet Marquess*, pages 57–58.

'waving his small hands': *Letters*, page 699.

'I am not and have never been ashamed': Douglas, *Autobiography*, page 102.

'Under these circumstances': George Lewis to Oscar Wilde, 7 April 1894, in Ellmann, page 420.

'I do not see why I should': the Marquis of Queensberry to Alfred Montgomery, 6 July 1894, in Roberts, *The Mad Bad Line*, page 199.

'plausible George Wyndham': Roberts, *The Mad Bad Line*, pages 198–199.

'gradually drop': Roberts, *The Mad Bad Line*, pages 198–199.

'My Lord Marquis': C.O. Humphreys to the Marquis of Queensberry, 11 July 1894, in statement of Marquis of Queensberry, 1895, witness statements, private collection.

'I have received your letter': the Marquis of Queensberry to C.O. Humphreys, 13 July 1894, in statement of Marquis of Queensberry, 1895, witness statements, private collection.

'I now made up my mind': statement of Marquis of Queensberry, 1895, witness statements, private collection.

'As you return my letters unopened': statement of Marquis of Queensberry, 1895, witness statements, private collection.

'outrageous libels': statement of Marquis of Queensberry, 1895, witness statements, private collection.

'If I am to be openly defied': Roberts, *The Mad Bad Line*, page 200.

'a maniac': *Letters*, page 598.

The boys on the beach

'When you really want love': Day, *Oscar Wilde*, page 158.

'own dear boy': *Letters*, page 594.

'own dearest boy': *Letters*, page 601.

'dear, wonderful boy': *Letters*, page 594.

'I want to see you': *Letters*, page 594.

'You are more to me': *Letters*, page 602.

'the Elect': *Letters*, page 1127.

'Their ideals are so different': diary of George Ives, 5 July 1894, in Stokes, *Oscar Wilde*, pages 72–73.

'brilliant as a shining jewel': diary of George Ives, 15 October 1893, HRC.

'Was awake till past 3': diary of George Ives, 16 October 1893, HRC.

'bright as Apollo': diary of George Ives, 24 October 1893, HRC.

'a difficult character': diary of George Ives, 16 October 1893, HRC.

'the Cause must not be injured': diary of George Ives, 16 October 1893, HRC.

'the original of Dorian Gray': diary of George Ives, 24 August 1894, HRC.

'is staying here tonight': diary of George Ives, 24 August 1894, HRC.

'That miserable traitor': diary of George Ives, 24 August 1894, HRC.

'I love superstitions': Coakley, *Oscar Wilde*, page 101.

'Always when they prophesy': Pearson, *The Life of Oscar Wilde*, pages 284–285.

'the Sibyl of Mortimer Street': *Letters*, page 594.

'The only thing that consoles me': *Letters*, page 594.

'I have been deeply impressed': *Letters*, page 595.

'Your father is on the rampage': *Letters*, page 598.

'Your new Sibyl is really wonderful': *Letters*, page 602.

'curious and interesting': Edward Carpenter, *Intermediate Types Among Primitive Folk* (London, 1919), page 15.

'prophets or priests': Carpenter, *Intermediate Types Among Primitive Folk*, page 16.

'spiritual sight': diary of George Ives, 26 October 1893, HRC.

'positively prophetic in his power': diary of George Ives, 27 July 1894, HRC.

'"C" was very nervous': diary of George Ives, 27 July 1894, HRC.

'I am overdrawn £41': *Letters*, page 598.

'The house, I hear, is small': *Letters*, page 598.

'Dearest Bosie, I have just come in': *Letters*, page 598.

'I had great fun': Lord Alfred Douglas to Robert Ross, 1894, in Ellmann, page 421.

'distinctly strained': Douglas, *Autobiography*, pages 59–60.

'I feel as tho' I must write': Constance Wilde to Arthur Humphreys, 1 June 1894, in Sotheby's, *English Literature and History*, London, 22 and 23 July 1985.

'I liked you': Constance Wilde to Arthur Humphreys, 1 June 1894, in Sotheby's, *English Literature and History*.

'I spoke to you': Constance Wilde to Arthur Humphreys, 1 June 1894, in Sotheby's, *English Literature and History*.

'Your marriage was made': Constance Wilde to Arthur Humphreys, 1 June 1894, in Sotheby's, *English Literature and History*.

'My Darling Arthur': Constance Wilde to Arthur Humphreys, 11 August 1894, in Sotheby's, *English Literature and History*.

'of rank and fashion': *Letters*, page 599.

'bored to death': *Letters*, page 785.

'invites down a lot of fashionable': *Letters*, page 599.

'prudish': *Letters*, page 599.

'an absurd experiment': *Letters*, page 599.

'extremely strong': *Letters*, page 600.

'I love him as I always did': *Letters*, page 934.

'Eighteen men were taken': Croft-Cooke, *Feasting with Panthers*, page 277.

'known': Hyde, *Oscar Wilde*, page 187.

'Oscar has at length been arrested': Max Beerbohm to Reginald Turner, 12 August 1894, in *Max Beerbohm's Letters to Reggie Turner*, page 97.

'I was very sorry to read': *Letters*, page 603.

'Do tell me all about Alfred?': *Letters*, page 603.

'the vilest possible character': Croft-Cooke, *Feasting with Panthers*, page 278.

'helping the two boatmen': Holland, *Irish Peacock and Scarlet Marquess*, page 144.

'Percy left the day after': *Letters*, page 602.

'a youth of about eighteen': Hyde, *Famous Trials 7*, page 121.

'loafer': Hyde, *Famous Trials 7*, page 121.

'nearly always with': statement of Alfonso Harold Conway, 1895, witness statements, private collection.

'took hold': statement of Alfonso Harold Conway, 1895, witness statements, private collection.

'spent': statement of Alfonso Harold Conway, 1895, witness statements, private collection.

'took me to his bedroom': statement of Alfonso Harold Conway, 1895, witness statements, private collection.
'I promised him': Hyde, *Famous Trials 7*, pages 122–123.
'in order that he shouldn't be ashamed': Holland, *Irish Peacock and Scarlet Marquess*, page 149.
'He acted as before': statement of Alfonso Harold Conway, 1895, witness statements, private collection.

The arsenic flower
'It is perfectly monstrous': *Works*, page 469.
'immaculately dressed': Hichens, *Yesterday*, pages 69–70.
'I thought him rather pleasant': Harris, *Oscar Wilde*, page 106.
'unrelieved by any flashes': *Letters*, page 615.
'saw a good deal': Harris, *Oscar Wilde*, page 106.
'it was a sort of photograph': Harris, *Oscar Wilde*, page 106.
'an undisguised portrait': Backhouse, 'The Dead Past'.
'It is so interesting to be wonderful': Hichens, *The Green Carnation*, page 16.
'"What a pity my poor father is so plain"': Hichens, *The Green Carnation*, page 17.
'a young Greek god': Hichens, *The Green Carnation*, page 94.
'one of the most utterly vicious': Hichens, *The Green Carnation*, page 58.
'worshipped the abnormal': Hichens, *The Green Carnation*, page 17.
'There are moments': Hichens, *The Green Carnation*, pages 20–21.
'a very pretty woman': Hichens, *The Green Carnation*, page 18.
'quite £20,000 a year': Douglas, *Autobiography*, page 188.
'tall and largely built man': Hichens, *The Green Carnation*, page 17.
'I was born epigrammatic': Hichens, *The Green Carnation*, page 28.
'Prolonged purity wrinkles': Hichens, *The Green Carnation*, page 25.
'There are only a few people': Hichens, *The Green Carnation*, in Bentley, *The Importance of Being Constance*, page 104.
'The bows and salutations': *Letters*, page 622.
'the arsenic flower of an exquisite life': Hichens, *The Green Carnation*, page 26.
'All the men who wore them': Hichens, *The Green Carnation*, page 24.
'followers of the higher philosophy': Hichens, *The Green Carnation*, pages 73–74.
'The philosophy to be afraid': Hichens, *The Green Carnation*, pages 73–74.
'the one awkwardness': Hichens, *The Green Carnation*, page 90.
'Do you love this carnation': Hichens, *The Green Carnation*, page 96.
'He will be for me': Gide, *Oscar Wilde*, page 79.
'How exquisite rose-coloured youth is': Hichens, *The Green Carnation*, page 80.
'The refining influence': Hichens, *The Green Carnation*, page 101.
'Kindly allow me to contradict': *Letters*, page 617.
'the Sphinx of Modern Life': *Letters*, page 568.
'I am not surprised': Max Beerbohm to Ada Leverson, September 1894, in Speedie, *Wonderful Sphinx*, page 48.
'Esmé and Reggie are delighted': *Letters*, page 615.
'a doubting disciple': *Letters*, page 615.
'*The Green Carnation* ruined': Harris, *Oscar Wilde*, page 107.
'invisible city of Sodom': André Raffalovich, *L'Affaire Oscar Wilde*, in Pine, *Oscar Wilde*, page 108.
'really raised the hue and cry': Sherard, *Oscar Wilde*, page 117.

'the book did me a lot of harm': Douglas, *Autobiography*, page 74.
'the Treasury will always give me': Backhouse, 'The Dead Past'.
'an elderly gentleman with a red face': Hichens, *The Green Carnation*, page 17.
'What is his father about': the Marquis of Queensberry to Minnie Douglas, 18 February 1895, in Roberts, *The Mad Bad Line*, page 206.
'You suddenly appeared': *Letters*, page 697.
'The next day, a Monday': *Letters*, page 697.
'bored': *Letters*, page 697.
'that dreadful low fever': *Letters*, page 697.
'In London you meet a friend': *Letters*, page 697.
'irritable voice and ungracious manner': *Letters*, page 698.
'At three in the morning': *Letters*, page 698.
'new pleasures were waiting': *Letters*, page 698.
'with renewed emphasis': *Letters*, page 698.
'It was an ugly moment for you': *Letters*, page 699.
'a common dinner knife': *Letters*, page 699.
'a very serious quarrel': Max Beerbohm to Ada Leverson, 7 July 1894, HRC.
'Oscar does not answer': Max Beerbohm to Ada Leverson, 7 July 1894, HRC.
'I am so pressed for money': *Letters*, page 597.
'My play is really very funny': *Letters*, page 602.
'in and out of his study': Marie Stopes, March 1939, in Murray, *Bosie*, page 302.
'To tell you *a great secret*': Robert Ross to Adela Schuster, 23 December 1900, in *Robert Ross: Friend of Friends* edited by Margery Ross (London, 1952), page 68.
'that we should treat all the trivial things': *St James's Gazette*, 18 January 1895, in Pearson, *The Life of Oscar Wilde*, page 254.
'a simple, unspoiled nature': *Works*, page 368.
'If I ever get married': *Works*, page 359.
'I thought you had come up': *Works*, page 359.
'a very high moral tone': *Works*, page 361.
'Nothing will induce me': *Works*, page 363.
'Exploded! Was he the victim': *Works*, page 408.
'the sure prey of morbid passions': *Letters*, page 658.
'I am off to the country': *Letters*, page 592.
'I was going to tell you': Aleister Crowley to Robert Lockhart, 1913, in Timothy d'Arch Smith, *Bunbury: Two Notes on Oscar Wilde* (Wiltshire), pages 7–8.
'I hope some of the faithful': *Letters*, page 1127.
'One name can make my pulses bound': John Gambril Nicholson, 'Of Boys' Names', in Christopher Craft, 'Alias Bunbury', page 45.
'Have you read a volume': John Addington Symonds to an unnamed correspondent, 2 July 1892, in Craft, 'Alias Bunbury', page 46.
'produces vibrations': *Works*, page 366.
'I love scrapes': *Works*, page 374.
'I don't know a single chap': *Works*, page 374.
'a lady considerably advanced': *Works*, page 368.
'This treatise, "The Green Carnation"': *Works*, page 418.
'a most sweet and interesting': diary of George Ives, 13 November 1894, HRC.
'the most dreadful scrapes': *Works*, pages 361–362.
'I really am not going to be imprisoned': *Works*, pages 386.
'reckless extravagance': *Works*, page 385.

'farce': William Archer, *The World*, 20 February 1894, in Beckson, *The Oscar Wilde Encyclopedia*, page 157.
'bitter trials': *Works*, page 382.

Love's sacrifice
'A kiss may ruin a human life': *Works*, page 511.
'partaken of out of doors': *The Taunton Mail*, 24 October 1894, British Newspaper Library.
'a very deadened report': *The Taunton Mail*, 24 October 1894, British Newspaper Library.
'Where can his Lordship be?': *The Taunton Mail*, 24 October 1894, in Roberts, *The Mad Bad Line*, page 183.
'I hope he hasn't shot himself': *The Taunton Mail*, 24 October 1894, British Newspaper Library.
'I will walk along beside the hedge': *The Taunton Mail*, 24 October 1894, British Newspaper Library.
'lying in the hedge': *The Taunton Mail*, 24 October 1894, British Newspaper Library.
'head was very much sprinkled': in Roberts, *The Mad Bad Line*, page 183.
'On my arrival I found': *The Taunton Mail*, 24 October 1894, British Newspaper Library.
'terrible news': Harry Toley to Lord Rosebery, 1894, MS 10097, National Library of Scotland.
'Drumlanrig is going to marry': Lewis Harcourt, 1894, in Roberts, *The Mad Bad Line*, page 186.
'What the result': Lord Drumlanrig to Lord Rosebery, 1894, MS 10097, National Library of Scotland.
'by setting private detectives': Backhouse, 'The Dead Past'.
'Queensberry wrote to the Prime Minister': Backhouse, 'The Dead Past'.
'had not met or spoken frankly': the Marquis of Queensberry to Alfred Montgomery, 1894, in Murray, *Bosie*, pages 69–70.
'a noble sacrifice': Backhouse, 'The Dead Past'.
'an appalling tragedy': diary of W.S. Blunt, 25 October 1894, Fitzwilliam Museum.
'It seems unlikely': diary of W.S. Blunt, 25 October 1894, Fitzwilliam Museum.
'positive that his uncle Drumlanrig': Hyde, *Oscar Wilde*, page 171.
'a scandal lay behind it': personal communication by Sheila Colman.
'stained with a darker suggestion': *Letters*, page 700.
'There is no reason to suppose': Sir Edward Walter Hamilton, 19 October 1894, BL Add MSS 48665, British Library.
'prostrate on the earth': in Trevor Fisher, *Oscar and Bosie: A Fatal Passion* (London, 2002), page 1.
'Dear Lord Rosebery': George Murray to Lord Rosebery, 19 October 1894, MS 10049, National Library of Scotland.
'the Snob Queers like Rosebery': the Marquis of Queensberry to Lord Alfred Douglas, 1 November 1894, in Murray, *Bosie*, pages 69–70.
'polluted': *Letters*, page 700.
'I settled myself to go': *Letters*, page 700.
'I telegraphed at once': *Letters*, page 700.
'Wickedness is a myth': *Works*, page 1244.
'"I am Shame"': Lord Alfred Douglas, 'In Praise of Shame', Douglas, *Sonnets*, page 22.

'nothing on earth to do': Lord Alfred Douglas, 'Foreword' to Winwar, *Oscar Wilde and the Yellow Nineties*, page xvi.
'I am the Love': Douglas, *Lyrics*, page 56.
'the good luck to meet Oscar': John Francis Bloxam to Charles Kains Jackson, 19 November 1894, Clark Library.
'gaze': Mayne, *The Intersexes*, pages 426–427.
'The Priest and the Acolyte is not by Dorian': *Letters*, page 625.
'There is no sin': *The Chameleon*, volume I, number 1 (1894).
'too direct': *Letters*, page 625.
'certainly a case for the police': Jerome K. Jerome, *To-Day*, 29 December 1894, in d'Arch Smith, *Love in Earnest*, page 58.
'That young men are here': Jerome, *To-Day*, 29 December 1894, in d'Arch Smith, *Love in Earnest*, page 58.
'I have now in my possession': the Marquis of Queensberry to Minnie Douglas, 11 March 1895, in Queensberry, *Oscar Wilde and the Black Douglas*, page 59.
'this hideous monster': the Marquis of Queensberry to Minnie Douglas, 4 March 1895, in Queensberry, *Oscar Wilde and the Black Douglas*, page 58.

Passionate fauns
'You do not feel the beauty': John Addington Symonds to Charles Kains Jackson, 24 April 1892, in Symonds, *Letters*, pages 682–683.
'the year of the Faith 2233': diary of George Ives, 1 January 1895, HRC.
'After going among that set': diary of George Ives, 1 January 1895, HRC.
'roaring successes': Henry James to William James, Beckson, *The Oscar Wilde Encyclopedia*, page 170.
'in a moment of weakness': statement of Edward Shelley, 1895, witness statements, private collection.
'I saw a knife': Speedie, *Wonderful Sphinx*, page 75.
'a long voyage': *Letters*, page 594.
'Yes. I fly to Algiers': *Letters*, page 629.
'little white walled-in house': *Works*, page 106.
'There is a great deal of beauty here': *Letters*, page 629.
'full of villages': *Letters*, page 629.
'I have the feeling': André Gide to his mother, January 1895, in Sheridan, *André Gide*, page 116.
'ashamed': Jonathan Dollimore, 'Different Desires: Subjectivity and Transgression in Wilde and Gide', *Textual Practice*, volume I, number 1 (spring 1987), page 48.
'that terrible man': André Gide to his mother, 28 January 1895, in Sheridan, *André Gide*, page 116.
'less softness in his look': Gide, *Oscar Wilde*, page 27.
'adore': Gide, *Oscar Wilde*, page 27.
'vile procurer': Gide, *Oscar Wilde*, page 74.
'as beautiful as bronze statues': Gide, *Oscar Wilde*, page 74.
'All these guides are idiots': Gide, *Oscar Wilde*, page 74.
'On the whole': Gide, *Oscar Wilde*, page 75.
'I have a friend': Gide, *Oscar Wilde*, page 76.
'in a hissing, withering, savage': Gide, *Oscar Wilde*, page 77.
'overweening': Gide, *Oscar Wilde*, page 77.
'laid great stress': Gide, *Oscar Wilde*, page 79.

'twelve or thirteen': André Gide to his mother, 2 February 1895, in Fryer, *André & Oscar*, page 129.

'elope': Gide, *Oscar Wilde*, page 79.

'But to run away': Gide, *Oscar Wilde*, page 79.

'Lulled by the strange torpor': Gide, *Oscar Wilde*, pages 82–83.

'The song of the flute': Gide, *Oscar Wilde*, page 83.

'*Venez*': Gide, *Oscar Wilde*, page 83.

'Dear, would you like': Gide, *Oscar Wilde*, pages 83–84.

'a dreadful effort of courage': Gide, *Oscar Wilde*, pages 83–84.

'two enormous policemen': Gide, *Oscar Wilde*, page 86.

'Oh no, dear, on the contrary': Gide, *Oscar Wilde*, page 86.

'A young Arab': Laurence Housman to George Ives, 17 October 1933, HRC.

'transports of delight': in Sheridan, *André Gide*, page 119.

'Since then, whenever': in Sheridan, *André Gide*, pages 118–119.

'blackened': André Gide to his mother, 30 January 1895, in Fryer, *André & Oscar*, pages 114–115.

'ambiguous distinction': André Gide to his mother, 30 January 1895, in Fryer, *André & Oscar*, pages 114–115.

'with disgusting obstinacy': André Gide to his mother, January 1895, in Sheridan, *André Gide*, page 120.

'who seeks shame': André Gide to his mother, 30 January 1895, in Fryer, *André & Oscar*, pages 114–115.

'a young prince': Sheridan, *André Gide*, page 120.

'I have been trying to read': Lord Alfred Douglas to André Gide, 1929, in Murray, *Bosie*, pages 288–289.

'a mass of lies': Lord Alfred Douglas to Robert Sherard, 25 May 1933, in Brasol, *Oscar Wilde*, page 256.

'My dear Bobbie': Lord Alfred Douglas to Robbie Ross, 11 February 1895, private collection.

'Finally we made it up': Lord Alfred Douglas to Robbie Ross, 11 February 1895, private collection.

'I am far too occupied': Lord Alfred Douglas to Robbie Ross, 11 February 1895, private collection.

'Boys, yes boys': Fryer, *André & Oscar*, page 130.

'I am really having': Lord Alfred Douglas to Robbie Ross, 11 February 1895, private collection.

Hideous words

'If your sins find you out': Day, *Oscar Wilde*, page 253.

'monstrous doses': Stephen Yeldham, *The Homeopathic Treatment of Syphilis and Gonorrhoea* (London, 1860).

'disgusting hodgepodge': Yeldham, *The Homeopathic Treatment of Syphilis and Gonorrhoea*.

'Let a man take a turn': Yeldham, *The Homeopathic Treatment of Syphilis and Gonorrhoea*.

'You were kind enough': *Letters*, page 630.

'What I wanted however': Algy Bourke to Lady Queensberry, in Queensberry, *Oscar Wilde and the Black Douglas*, page 41.

'this hideous scandal of Oscar Wilde': the Marquis of Queensberry to Minnie Douglas,

4 March 1895, in Queensberry, *Oscar Wilde and the Black Douglas*, page 58.
'dark, sinister, winter's night': *Interviews and Recollections*, volume II, page 267.
'Wilde fanatics': *Interviews and Recollections*, volume II, page 267.
'with elaborate dandyism': *Interviews and Recollections*, volume II, page 270.
'the very breath of success': *Interviews and Recollections*, volume II, page 267.
'the lily of the valley': *Interviews and Recollections*, volume II, page 267.
'a single green carnation': *Interviews and Recollections*, volume II, page 270.
'beaming with euphoria': *Interviews and Recollections*, volume II, page 270.
'What a contrast': *Interviews and Recollections*, volume II, page 270.
'I had all Scotland Yard': *Letters*, page 632.
'I don't think I should': in Pearson, *The Life of Oscar Wilde*, page 255.
'Yes: the Scarlet Marquis': *Letters*, page 632.
'He prowled about': *Letters*, page 632.
'Upon investigating the case': C.O. Humphreys to Oscar Wilde, 28 February 1895, in Roberts, *The Mad Bad Line*, pages 205–206.
'Such a persistent persecutor': C.O. Humphreys to Oscar Wilde, 28 February 1895, in Roberts, *The Mad Bad Line*, page 206.
'I may say that as Percy': the Marquis of Queensberry to Minnie Douglas, 18 February 1895, in Queensberry, *Oscar Wilde and the Black Douglas*, page 55.
'You must all be mad': the Marquis of Queensberry to Minnie Douglas, 4 March 1895, in Queensberry, *Oscar Wilde and the Black Douglas*, page 58.
'I am greatly touched': *Letters*, page 633.
'You thought simply': *Letters*, page 709.
'A.D. brought to my hotel': *Letters*, pages 795–796.
'bombard': *Letters*, page 796.
'Lord Queensberry desired me': Examination of Oscar Wilde, 9 April 1895, CRIM 1 41/6, PRO.
'Give this card to Oscar Wilde': Evidence of Sydney Wright – Hall Porter, CRIM 1 41/6, PRO.
'For Oscar Wilde ponce and somdomite': Evidence of Sydney Wright – Hall Porter, CRIM 1 41/6, PRO.
'the action of Lord Queensberry': Hyde, *Famous Trials 7*, pages 9–10.
'loathsome letter': *Letters*, page 796.
'Dearest Bobbie': *Letters*, page 634.
'Dear Constance': *Letters*, page 633.
'My only chance of resisting': *Letters*, page 787.
'forgiveness with a condition': Napoleon Argles, *How to Obtain a Divorce* (London, 1895).
'I now learn that no condonation': *Letters*, page 784.
'I live in a world of puppets': Pearson, *The Life of Oscar Wilde*, page 278.
'most unusual destiny': Cheiro, *Cheiro's Memoirs*, page 57.
'What curious things': Pearson, *The Life of Oscar Wilde*, page 279.
'Blindly I staggered': *Letters*, page 690.
'My judgement forsook me': *Letters*, page 690.
'What is loathsome to me': *Letters*, page 759.
'You said that your own family': *Letters*, pages 703–704.
'If you are innocent': Hyde, *Oscar Wilde*, page 197.
'booby-trap': Roberts, *The Mad Bad Line*, page 198.

Raking Piccadilly
'One should never make': Small, *Oscar Wilde Revalued*, page 129.
'Dear Mr Dunn': Lord Alfred Douglas to James Nicol Dunn, 2 March 1895, Clark Library.
'Are you the Marquis of Queensberry?': Statement of Det. Insp. Thomas Creet, CRIM 1 41/6, PRO.
'publishing a certain defamatory libel': 'Oscar Wilde and the Marquis', *New York Herald*, 3 March 1895, page 9.
'fifty years of age', *New York Herald*, 3 March 1895, page 9.
'most cruel persecution': Mason, *Oscar Wilde: Three Times Tried*, page 1.
'For Oscar Wilde ponce and somdomite': Evidence of Sydney Wright – Hall Porter, CRIM 1 41/6, PRO.
'posing as somdomite': Evidence of Sydney Wright – Hall Porter, CRIM 1 41/6, PRO.
'to pose as a thing': the Marquis of Queensberry to Lord Alfred Douglas, 1 April 1894, in Croft-Cooke, *Bosie*, page 97.
'I venture to say': Mason, *Oscar Wilde: Three Times Tried*, page 3.
'temporarily exalted': Robbie Ross, unpublished preface to 'After Reading', no date, Clark Library.
'a somewhat nervous': *New York Herald*, 3 March 1895, page 9.
'Poor, poor Oscar!': Max Beerbohm to Reginald Turner, 3 March 1895, in *Max Beerbohm's Letters to Reggie Turner*, page 100.
'used to walk about with him': Stokes, *Oscar Wilde*, page 45.
'Hullo, Ned Carson': Edward Marjoribanks, *The Life of Lord Carson* (London, 1932), volume I, page 171.
'deep moral indignation': Marjoribanks, *The Life of Lord Carson*, page 171.
'No doubt he will perform': Sir Travers Humphreys, 'Foreword' to Hyde, *Famous Trials 7*, page 14.
'concrete proofs': Backhouse, 'The Dead Past'.
'go and speak to Cook': the Marquis of Queensberry to Minnie Douglas, 26 February 1895, in Queensberry, *Oscar Wilde and the Black Douglas*, page 56.
'constituted himself': Hyde, *Famous Trials 7*, page 89.
'With Brookfield alas!': O'Sullivan, *Aspects of Wilde*, pages 105–106.
'Nature was in this matter': *Letters*, page 670.
'a fine old Irish Commissionaire': *Interviews and Recollections*, volume II, pages 288–289.
'hatbox full of papers': statement of Sophia Gray, 1895, witness statements, private collection.
'Obliged to see Tree': Mason, *Oscar Wilde: Three Times Tried*, page 357.
'My dear Alfred': Charles Mason to Alfred Taylor, 30 November 1891, in Mason, *Oscar Wilde: Three Times Tried*, page 361.
'terrified into giving evidence': diary of George Ives, 2 May 1895, HRC.
'to forewarn Mr Wilde': Caspar Wintermans, *Oscar Wilde: A Plea and a Reminiscence* (Woobrugge, 2002), page 20.
'We are very worried just now': Constance Wilde to Marie Belloc Lowndes, March 1895, in Ellmann, page 441.
'in matters of grave importance': *Works*, page 406.
'very much agitated': Douglas, *Autobiography*, page 59.
'Have no fear': Roberts, *The Mad Bad Line*, page 217.

Vexed and persecuted lovers
'A short primer, *When to Lie and How*': *Works*, page 1090.
'God knows I never sought': Rhodes James, *Rosebery*, page 366.
'The whole thing came': John Wodehouse, 19 February 1895, in *The Journal of John Wodehouse, First Earl of Kimberley for 1862–1902* edited by Angus Hawkins and John Powell (London, 1997), pages 430–431.
'George Murray says': journal of Lewis Harcourt, 20 February 1895, Bodleian Library.
'insomnia': 'Lord Rosebery's Health', *New York Herald*, 10 March 1895, page 9.
'I cannot forget 1895': Rhodes James, *Rosebery*, page 373.
'for the first time in his life': Rhodes James, *Rosebery*, page 373.
'long-continued derangement': Roberts, *The Mad Bad Line*, page 248.
'the most obstinate and puzzling case': Roberts, *The Mad Bad Line*, page 248.
'thinks Rosebery's illness': journal of Lewis Harcourt, 16 February 1895, Bodleian Library.
'fatal termination': Rhodes James, *Rosebery*, page 370.
'with reference to one': Holland, *Irish Peacock and Scarlet Marquess*, page 14.
'the white feather': the Marquis of Queensberry to Albert Montgomery, 6 July 1894, in Roberts, *The Mad Bad Line*, page 199.
'a buzz of conversation': *Evening News*, 9 March 1895, in 'It is 1895', *The Oscar Wilde File*, page 40.
'taking wise counsel': *Letters*, page 690.
'I saw Humphreys today': Lord Alfred Douglas to Lord Percy Douglas, 11 March 1895, in 'The Constant Nymph', Maggs Brothers Limited, no date.
'I can only accept this brief': Hyde, *Oscar Wilde*, page 203.
'absolutely false and groundless': Hyde, *Lord Alfred Douglas*, pages 73–74.
'is quite another thing': *Interviews and Recollections*, volume I, page 188.
'a very great favour': *Letters*, page 635.
'We have been to the Sibyl Robinson': *Letters*, page 636.
'people of importance': Harris, *Oscar Wilde*, page 115.
'For God's sake man': Harris, *Oscar Wilde*, page 338.
'a haughty indignant silence': Harris, *Oscar Wilde*, page 338.
'Such advice': Harris, *Oscar Wilde*, page 117.
'sticking place': Lord Alfred Douglas to Frank Harris, 1925, in Harris and Douglas, *The Life and Confessions of Oscar Wilde*, page 38.
'a little tired': Douglas, *Autobiography*, pages 121–122.
'vexed and persecuted lovers': George Ives materials, HRC.
'I told him it was': Cheiro, *Cheiro's Memoirs*, page 58.
'a knock-down blow': Reginald Turner to G.J. Renier, 22 March 1933, Clark Library.
'bravely, wondrously bravely': Reginald Turner to G.J. Renier, 22 March 1933, Clark Library.

Fighting with panthers
'rarely pure': *Works*, pages 361–362.
'All trials': *Letters*, page 777.
'that tiger life': Knox, *Oscar Wilde*, page 84.
'fight with panthers': *Letters*, page 635.
'a gayer tie': Sachaverell Sitwell to H. Montgomery Hyde, 25 July 1948, HRC.

'commonplace-looking': *The Star*, 3 April 1895, in *The Oscar Wilde File*, page 43.
'a nonconformist parson': Harris, *Oscar Wilde*, page 120.
'again and again': Holland, *Irish Peacock and Scarlet Marquess*, page 29.
'the very grave responsibility': Holland, *Irish Peacock and Scarlet Marquess*, page 28.
'a sort of prose sonnet': Holland, *Irish Peacock and Scarlet Marquess*, page 34.
'epigrammatic statements': Holland, *Irish Peacock and Scarlet Marquess*, pages 40–41.
'upon the bookstalls': Holland, *Irish Peacock and Scarlet Marquess*, pages 40–41.
'ponderous and fleshy': *The Oscar Wilde File*, page 48.
'You stated': Holland, *Irish Peacock and Scarlet Marquess*, pages 40–41.
'Each man sees his own sin': Mason, *Art and Morality*, page 81.
'you left it open': Holland, *Irish Peacock and Scarlet Marquess*, pages 78–79.
'I quite admit that I *adored* you': Holland, *Irish Peacock and Scarlet Marquess*, pages 90–91.
'undying love': Holland, *Irish Peacock and Scarlet Marquess*, page 107.
'determined to face him': Holland, *Irish Peacock and Scarlet Marquess*, pages 121–124.
'an intellectual treat': Hyde, *Famous Trials 7*, pages 119–120.
'My Lord': Holland, *Irish Peacock and Scarlet Marquess*, page 138.
'a young lad named Conway?': Mason, *Oscar Wilde: Three Times Tried*, page 60.
'You dressed him up': Holland, *Irish Peacock and Scarlet Marquess*, page 149.

So very ugly
'betray myself with a kiss': *Letters*, page 615.
'Pray excuse us from dinner tonight': *Letters*, page 636.
'anything and everything': Hyde, *Famous Trials 7*, pages 137–138.
'Nemesis has caught me in her net': *Letters*, page 921.
'not so fresh or so bright': Mason, *Oscar Wilde: Three Times Tried*, page 70.
'How many young men': Holland, *Irish Peacock and Scarlet Marquess*, page 163.
'How old was Parker?': Holland, *Irish Peacock and Scarlet Marquess*, pages 164–165.
'What I would like to ask you': Holland, *Irish Peacock and Scarlet Marquess*, pages 174–175.
'even a young boy': Hyde, *Famous Trials 7*, pages 129–130.
'familiar terms with Grainger?': Holland, *Irish Peacock and Scarlet Marquess*, pages 207–209.
'anything so horrible': Elizabeth Robins to Blanche Crackanthorpe, ?9 April 1895, in Elizabeth Robins, 'Oscar Wilde: An Appreciation', page 111.
'premeditatedly': Holland, *Irish Peacock and Scarlet Marquess*, page 149.
'You will hear from these witnesses': *The Trials of Oscar Wilde*, page 168.
'I said that': Hyde, *Oscar Wilde*, page 221.
'Lord Queensberry': *The Trials of Oscar Wilde*, page 178.
'a more powerful speech': R. Henn Collins to Edward Carson, 5 April 1895, in Marjoribanks, *The Life of Lord Carson*, page 229.
'I have ruined': Pine, *Oscar Wilde*, page 105.

Kill the bugger!
'If one tells the truth: *Works*, page 1244.
'made for exceptions': *Letters*, page 732.
'Once I had put into motion': *Letters*, page 758.
'It would have been impossible': *Letters*, page 637.
'was an inhuman brute': Lord Alfred Douglas to Frank Harris, 1925, in Harris and

Douglas, *The Life and Confessions of Oscar Wilde*, page 29–30.
'At the very worst': Lord Alfred Douglas to Frank Harris, in Harris and Douglas, *The Life and Confessions of Oscar Wilde*, pages 29–30.
'Dear Constance': *Letters*, page 637.
'What's the use': Douglas, *Autobiography*, page 104.
'Poor Oscar! Poor Oscar!': Pearson, *The Life of Oscar Wilde*, page 288.
'The train has gone': Harris, *Oscar Wilde*, page 140.
'If the country allows you': *New York Times*, 6 April 1895.
'I think he ought not': *New York Herald*, 6 April 1895, page 9.
'I have done my duty': *New York Herald*, 6 April 1895, page 9.
'Dear Sir': Charles Russell to Hon. Hamilton Cuffe, 5 April 1895, PRO.
'very grey in the face': in Ellmann, page 456.
'certain to be condemned': George Wyndham to Hon. Percy Scawen Wyndham, 7 April 1895, in Hyde, *Lord Alfred Douglas*, pages 83–84.
'Is Oscar Wilde staying here?': *Illustrated Police Budget*, 13 April 1895, in *The Oscar Wilde File*, page 84,
'My dear Bosie': *Letters*, page 637.
'in a frightful state': Douglas, *Autobiography*, page 106.
'Can you do anything': Lord Alfred Douglas to George Ives, ?7 April 1895, Clark Library.
'Poor boy when I think': diary of George Ives, 8 April 1895, HRC.
'A most trying visit': diary of Laura Hope, 5 April 1895, in Hyde, *Oscar Wilde*, page 227.

Oscar at bay

'I was the worse for drink': Mason, *Oscar Wilde: Three Times Tried*, page 154.
'a knot of renters': Max Beerbohm to Reginald Turner, 3 May 1895, in *Max Beerbohm's Letters to Reggie Turner*, pages 103–104.
'male strumpets': *Reynolds's News*.
'A something': Sherard, *Oscar Wilde*, page 188.
'Nothing': Mason, *Oscar Wilde: Three Times Tried*, page 150.
'Surely you are not': Douglas, *Autobiography*, page 119.
'I think there is no worse crime': Roberts, *The Mad Bad Line*, page 231.
'Sworn informations have been lodged': *New York Times*, 6 April 1895.
'sensational development': *The Star*, 8 April 1895.
'Rosebery seems to me': diary of Sir Edward Hamilton, 8 April 1895, in *The Destruction of Lord Rosebery*, edited by David Brooks (London, 1986), page 237.
'an orgy of Philistine rancour': Harris, *Oscar Wilde*, page 144.
'Mr Wilde is damned': *Echo*, 6 April 1895, in *The Oscar Wilde File*, page 79.
'We begin to breathe': *Pall Mall Gazette*, in *The Oscar Wilde File*, page 79.
'We have had enough': *Daily Telegraph*, 6 April 1895, in *The Oscar Wilde File*, page 75.
'the obscene imposter': *National Observer*, 6 April 1895, in Pine, *The Thief of Reason*, page 13.
'There must be another trial': Michael S. Foldy, *The Trials of Oscar Wilde* (London, 1997), page 55.
'Public feeling is fiercely hostile': George Wyndham to Hon. Percy Scawen Wyndham, 7 April 1895, in Hyde, *Lord Alfred Douglas*, pages 83–84.
'whose goal was to pursue': Raffalovich, *Uranisme et Unisexualité*, page 267, translated by Sian Jones.

'I look forward eagerly': Aubrey Beardsley to Ada Leverson, April 1895, in Beardsley, *Letters*, page 82.

'Adrian had a most painful': diary of Laura Hope, 6 April 1895, in Hyde, *Oscar Wilde*, page 227.

'There was an idea': Blanche Crackanthorpe to Elizabeth Robins, 9 April 1895, in Kerry Powell, 'Oscar & Two Women', *Rediscovering Oscar Wilde*, page 314.

'I have determined to remain': Lord Alfred Douglas to Robert Sherard, April 1895, in Sherard, *Oscar Wilde*, pages 126–127.

'is raising money': Max Beerbohm to Reginald Turner, 3 May 1895, in *Max Beerbohm's Letters to Reggie Turner*, pages 103–104.

'Mr Oscar Wilde has been tried': Lord Alfred Douglas to the *Star*, 19 April 1895, in Hyde, *Famous Trials 7*, page 158.

'The scene that evening': Max Beerbohm to Reginald Turner, 3 May 1895, in *Max Beerbohm's Letters to Reggie Turner*, page 104.

'The surroundings are middle-class': *Works*, page 386.

'special cell': Leonard Creswell Ingleby, *Oscar Wilde: Some Reminiscences* (London, 1912), page 83.

'moments of very low-spiritedness': Ingleby, *Oscar Wilde*, page 88–89.

'a horrible kind of barred cage': Lord Alfred Douglas to Robert Sherard, April 1895, in Sherard, *Oscar Wilde*, pages 125–126.

'brighten up': Ingleby, *Oscar Wilde*, pages 90–91.

'Nothing but Alfred Douglas's': *Letters*, page 644.

'A slim thing': *Letters*, page 641.

'dazed with horror': *Letters*, page 644.

'was received by': Mason, *Oscar Wilde: Three Times Tried*, page 160.

'Yes, Oscar at bay': W.E. Henley to Charles Whibley, 13 April 1895, in Hyde, *Famous Trials 7*, pages 162–163.

'with an inscrutable countenance': Mason, *Oscar Wilde: Three Times Tried*, page 168.

'a diabolical conspiracy': Lord Alfred Douglas to Robert Sherard, April 1895, in Sherard, *Oscar Wilde*, pages 125–126.

'The government appears': Lord Alfred Douglas, 'Oscar Wilde', Clark Library, translated by Christopher Millard.

'a startling degree': Mason, *Oscar Wilde: Three Times Tried*, page 170.

'in tears, poring': Holland, *Son of Oscar Wilde*, page 61.

'My dear Mrs Robinson': *Letters*, page 642.

'there is little room': Charles Gill to Hamilton Cuffe, 19 April 1895, PRO.

'We think he fell': Charles Gill to Hamilton Cuffe, 19 April 1895, PRO

'Irresponsible persons': Charles Gill to Hamilton Cuffe, 19 April 1895, PRO.

'in daily and momentary': Lord Alfred Douglas to Henry Labouchère, 31 May 1895, Clark Library.

'letters of warning': *The Morning Post*, 18 April 1913.

'urgent request': Lord Alfred Douglas to Henry Labouchère, 31 May 1895, Clark Library.

'I am so happy': *Letters*, page 647.

The love that dares to speak its name
'Misfortunes one can endure': *Works*, page 429.

'haggard and worn': *The Shame of Oscar Wilde*, page 16.

'Many people are asking': *The Star*, 23 April 1895, in *The Oscar Wilde File*, page 99.

'looked terribly bored': Mason, *Oscar Wilde: Three Times Tried*, page 214.

'committed the act of sodomy': CG, *The Trials of Oscar Wilde from the Shorthand Reports*.

'a great deal of nervous anxiety': Mason, *Oscar Wilde: Three Times Tried*, page 214.

'Gentleman of the jury': Mason, *Oscar Wilde: Three Times Tried*, pages 266–267.

'Is it not clear that': Mason, *Oscar Wilde: Three Times Tried*, pages 271–272.

'If there is the slightest manifestation': Mason, *Oscar Wilde: Three Times Tried*, page 272.

'Oscar has been quite superb': Max Beerbohm to Reginald Turner, 3 May 1895, in *Max Beerbohm's Letters to Reggie Turner*, page 102.

'all will be over': *Letters*, page 646.

'1. Do you think': Mason, *Oscar Wilde: Three Times Tried*, page 312.

'Hoscar stood very upright': Max Beerbohm to Reginald Turner, 3 May 1895, in *Max Beerbohm's Letters to Reggie Turner*, pages 102–103.

'Ought the prosecution': *The Morning*, 2 May 1895, in *The Oscar Wilde File*, pages 117–118.

'remove what appears': diary of Sir Edward Hamilton, 21 May 1895, in Sir Edward Hamilton, *The Destruction of Lord Rosebery*, edited by David Brooks (London, 1986), page 250.

'Cannot you let up': Hyde, *Famous Trials 7*, page 224.

'Give me shelter': Hyde, *Oscar Wilde*, page 224.

'depressing': Hyde, *Famous Trials 7*, pages 222–223.

'I am not well today': *Letters*, page 649.

'Why have you brought me': Sherard, *Oscar Wilde*, page 157.

'As for Hosker': W.E. Henley to Charles Whibley, early May 1895, in Hyde, *Oscar Wilde*, page 271.

'men who did not like boys': Robert Sherard to A.J.A. Symons, 8 June 1937, Clark Library.

'Every great love': *Letters*, page 650.

'the divine secret of the world': *Letters*, page 651.

'A dishonoured name': Oscar Wilde to Lord Alfred Douglas, ?May 1895, in Hyde, *Oscar Wilde*, page 272.

'Pleasure hides from us': *Letters*, page 651.

'To have altered my life': *Letters*, page 1019.

'monstrous martyrdom': *Letters*, page 1044.

'to try to get a verdict': Hyde, *Famous Trials 7*, page 253.

'My sweet rose': *Letters*, page 651.

'the soul of a man': *Letters*, page 651.

'It is the worst case': Mason, *Oscar Wilde: Three Times Tried*, page 464.

'And I? May I say': O'Brien, 'Robert Sherard', page 14.

A foul and dark latrine

'The Oscar trial is ended': in John Stokes, *In the Nineties* (Hemel Hempstead, 1989), page 5.

'sickness or spiritual retreat': Pine, *The Thief of Reason*, pages 295–296.

'It was a fiendish nightmare': Harris, *Oscar Wilde*, page 194.

'special': Ingleby, *Oscar Wilde*, page 83.

'The cell was appalling': Harris, *Oscar Wilde*, page 194.

'The food turned my stomach': Harris, *Oscar Wilde*, page 194.

'The first year of prison': diary of George Ives, 12 March 1898, HRC.

'mental prostration': *The Morning*, 6 June 1895, in *The Oscar Wilde File*, page 136.

'given no anxiety': H. Montgomery Hyde, *Oscar Wilde: The Aftermath* (London, 1963), page 7.

'memory suddenly failed him': *New York Herald*, 21 May 1895, page 9.

'Rosebery seems better': diary of Sir Edward Hamilton, 28 May 1895, in Hamilton, *The Destruction of Lord Rosebery*, page 251.

'I had a long talk': R.B. Haldane to his mother, National Library of Scotland.

'the family of Oscar Wilde': Haldane to his mother, National Library of Scotland.

'I have been in private': Haldane to More Adey, 6 December 1895, Clark Library.

'The authorities are looking': Haldane to More Adey, 8 January 1895, Clark Library.

'For the last 10 months': More Adey to Constance Wilde, 30 July 1896, Bodleian Library.

'the following suggestion': More Adey to an unnamed French correspondent, June 1895, Clark Library.

'opportunity to meditate': Ellmann, page 473.

'These tastes are perfectly': Lord Alfred Douglas to Henry Labouchère, 9 June 1895, Clark Library.

'Why on earth': in Croft-Cooke, *Bosie*, page 132.

'the poet and dramatist': in Hyde, *Lord Alfred Douglas*, pages 91–92.

'As soon as this conservative': Lord Alfred Douglas to Lord Percy Douglas, 11 July 1895, in 'The Constant Nymph'.

'Capt. Stopford informs me': Sir Matthew Ridley to E. Ruggles-Brise, 30 September 1895, PRO.

'The Few American Friends': William White, 'A Bribe for Oscar Wilde', Fales Library, New York.

'an excited flurried condition': Ellmann, page 495.

'it was easy for': *Sir Evelyn Ruggles-Brise: A Memoir of the Found of Borstal* compiled by Shane Leslie (London, 1938), pages 135–136.

'He is now quite crushed': W.D. Morrison to R.B. Haldane, 11 September 1895, PRO.

'Male aged 48': Prisons Committee, *Report From the Departmental Committee on Prisons* (London, 1895), page 581.

'The practical question': W.D. Morrison to R.B. Haldane, 11 September 1895, PRO.

'not the slightest evidence': E. Gover to E. Ruggles-Brise, 23 September 1895, PRO.

'I have seen Mr Morrison': Sir Matthew Ridley to R.B. Haldane, 7 October 1895, PRO.

'the sure prey': *Letters*, page 658.

'Each narrow cell': *Works*, page 897.

'I sat amidst the ruins': *Letters*, page 715.

'I was very much shocked': *Letters*, page 665.

'I could hardly stand up': Harris, *Oscar Wilde*, page 196.

'I saw him at the Infirmary': Robert Sherard to More Adey, 18 October 1895, Clark Library.

'I sat with Oscar yesterday': Lily Wilde to More Adey, 18 October 1895, Clark Library.

'mind is considerably impaired': Robert Ross to Oscar Browning, 12 November 1895, in ALS King's College, Cambridge.

'Physically he was much worse': Robert Ross to Oscar Browning, 12 November 1895, in ALS King's College, Cambridge.

'His history before imprisonment': report by Drs D Nicholson and Richard Bryan, 29 November 1895, PRO.
'Oscar Wilde will be removed': PRO.

Bitter waters
'Those who are faithful': *Works*, page 25.
'I have to sue': Constance Wilde to Emily Thursfield, 25 June 1895, Clark Library.
'I have been quite broken-hearted': Constance Wilde to Emily Thursfield, 25 June 1895, Clark Library.
'the bravest and most chivalrous': *Letters*, page 716.
'hands were disfigured': Sherard, *Oscar Wilde*, page 199.
'The only hope of salvation': Robert Sherard to Matthew Ridley, 12 September 1895, in O'Brien, 'Robert Sherard', page 17.
'would only write once': Hyde, *Oscar Wilde: The Aftermath*, page 24.
'My husband': Hyde, *Oscar Wilde: The Aftermath*, page 28.
'It was indeed awful': Sherard, *Oscar Wilde*, pages 201–202.
'I do not wish to sever': Constance Wilde to Emily Thursfield, 12 October 1895, Clark Library, in Clark, *Mrs Oscar Wilde*, page 190.
'an apology for': Sherard, *Oscar Wilde*, page 204.
'I was greatly taken aback': *Letters*, page 716.
'let my enemies interpret': Wintermans, *Oscar Wilde*, pages 20 and 27.
'one of the thousand Charlies': Leonard J. Leggett, 'Reginald Turner: The Friend in the Background', Clark Library, in Stanley Weintraub, *Reggie: A Portrait of Reginald Turner* (New York, 1965), page 98.
'all flowers of the narcissus kind': in Weintraub, *Reggie*, page 98.
'warning me that police': 'The Constant Nymph', page 16.
'Am surprised at not hearing': Hyde, *Lord Alfred Douglas*, page 92.
'a balm for bruised hearts': Douglas, *Sonnets*, page 28.
'But vainly, alas!': Douglas, *Lyrics*, page 43.
'I have just had a slight': Lord Alfred Douglas to Ada Leverson, 1895, in Speedie, *Wonderful Sphinx*, pages 96–97.
'I can't make it out': Lord Alfred Douglas to Ada Leverson, 13 September 1895, Clark Library.
'I have had frantic letters': Ada Leverson to More Adey, 19 September 1895, Clark Library.
'Tell him from me': Lord Alfred Douglas to Robert Sherard, 22 September 1895, University of Reading.
'How can he expect': Lord Alfred Douglas to More Adey, 30 November 1895, Clark Library.
'this tomb for those': *Letters*, page 658.
'petitioned HS about 3 weeks ago': More Adey's notes on a visit to Oscar Wilde, Bodleian Library.
'I believe it will': Constance Wilde to Lily Wilde, February 1896, Clark Library, in Melville, *Mother of Oscar*, pages 274–275.
'much shocked': Robert Ross to More Adey in *Robert Ross: Friend of Friends*, page 9.
'changed beyond recognition': Fitzgerald, *Edward Burne-Jones*, page 266.
'You said that Douglas': *Letters*, page 654.
'What shall I say?': Lord Alfred Douglas, 'To Oscar Wilde', Hyde Archive, Magdalen College, Oxford.

'I am not in prison': Lord Alfred Douglas to More Adey, 30 November 1895, in Hyde, *Lord Alfred Douglas*, page 95.

'Even if I get out': *Letters*, page 655.

'I do not believe': Lord Alfred Douglas to More Adey, September 1896, in Hyde, *Lord Alfred Douglas*, page 102.

'Nothing in the world': Richard Ellmann and John Espey, *Oscar Wilde: Two Approaches* (Los Angeles, 1977), pages 15–16.

From the depths

'A patriot put in prison': *Letters*, page 1019.

'haughty and impatient': Robert Ross to More Adey, 1896, in *Robert Ross: Friend of Friends*, pages 42–43.

'The Governor loves to punish': Harris, *Oscar Wilde*, page 193.

'The Governor was strong upon': *Works*, page 887.

'it would be a great loss': Harris, *Oscar Wilde*, page 192.

'The Home Secretary says': diary of George Ives, 24 May 1896, HRC.

'In his cell': Sherard, *The Life of Oscar Wilde*, page 351.

'Dear Bosie': *Letters*, pages 683–684.

'some good': found as 'do him good': *Letters*, page 782.

'You must read this letter': *Letters*, page 685.

'into the imperfect world': *Letters*, page 726.

'Tired of being': *Letters*, page 730.

'Well, if you are my literary executor': *Letters*, page 780.

'Of the many, many things': *Letters*, pages 782–783.

'Incomplete, imperfect': *Letters*, page 780.

'Sins of the flesh': *Letters*, page 714.

'I grew careless': *Letters*, page 730.

'I used to be utterly': *Letters*, page 905.

'Reason does not help me': *Letters*, page 732.

'I know not whether': *Works*, page 896.

'There is no prison': *Letters*, page 779.

'when prisoners of all kinds': Report from the Departmental Committee on Prisons, 1895, page 20.

'There are many nice fellows': *Letters*, page 830.

'the one I liked best': *Letters*, page 976.

'I had some interesting things': Robert Sherard to Carlos Blacker, 8 June 1897, in Anjali Gallup-Diaz, 'The Author, His Friends, and the Ballad of Reading Gaol', *Reading Wilde: Querying Spaces* (New York, 1995), page 83.

'the prisoners in Reading': Robert Sherard to A.J.A. Symons, 25 August 1938, in Hyde, *Oscar Wilde: The Aftermath*, page 212.

'You must get me his address': *Letters*, page 798.

'Please be careful': *Letters*, page 861.

'I had better say candidly': *Letters*, page 887.

'when all the roses': *Letters*, page 778.

'As I have mentioned': More Adey to Constance Wilde, 30 July 1896, Bodleian Library.

'All this about': Lord Alfred Douglas to More Adey, 8 February 1897, in Hyde, *Lord Alfred Douglas*, page 103.

'I happened to know': Robert Ross, 'Statement of Evidence in His Case Against

Douglas', Clark Library.
'At the present moment': *Letters*, page 704.
'To talk of my defending': *Letters*, page 787.
'Deed of Separation': Sotheby's, *English Literature and History*, London, 22–23 July 1985.
'I do hope you will': H. Martin Holman to More Adey, 10 May 1897, in Hyde, *Oscar Wilde: The Aftermath*, pages 134–135.
'I am to be deprived': *Letters*, page 808.

Comfort and despair
'No – what consoles one nowadays': *Works*, page 460.
'mentally upset': *Letters*, page 862.
'many, English, French': *Letters*, page 803.
'so utterly distressing': *Letters*, page 803.
'He looked very well': *The Morning*, 19 May 1897, in *The Oscar Wilde File*, page 142.
'We have received several': More Adey to Sir Edward Clayton, 16 May 1893, Clark Library.
'of Burne-Jones and Rossetti': *Interviews and Recollections*, volume II, page 342.
'The gods had given me': *Letters*, page 729.
'quite as tragic': Constance Wilde to Otho Holland Lloyd, 26 March 1892, in Clark, *Mrs Oscar Wilde*, page 207.
'I did not believe': Robert Ross to Wilfrid Scawen Blunt, in Borland, *Wilde's Devoted Friend*, pages 155–156.
'the impulse of a moment': *Interviews and Recollections*, volume II, page 343.
'a lovely brown boy': 'The Tomb of Keats', in Ellmann, *The Artist as Critic*, page 5.
'a complex multiform creature': *Works*, page 107.
'Infamous St Oscar of Oxford': *Letters*, page 1041.
'It was a magnificent': *Letters*, page 842.
'He enjoyed the trees': *Letters*, page 842.
'full of penitence': in Ellmann, page 535.
'calculated to exasperate': *Interviews and Recollections*, volume II, page 432.
'Reading Prison had already': *Letters*, page 844.
'some sweet biscuits': *Letters*, page 847.
'I pretended not to see': *Interviews and Recollections*, volume II, page 352.
'I breakfast tomorrow': *Letters*, page 869.
'dragged': Lord Alfred Douglas to A.J.A. Symons, 3 June 1937, Clark Library.
'dear sweet Robbie': *Letters*, page 858.
'terrible position of isolation': *Letters*, page 858.
'I adore this place': *Letters*, page 869.
'I went into the water': *Letters*, page 866.
'at least I know': *Letters*, page 877.
'English hypocrisy': Ernest Dowson to Arthur Moore, June 1896, in Dowson, *Letters*, page 369.
'Cher Monsieur Le Poète': *Letters*, page 883.
'The other day I met Oscar': Ernest Dowson to Conal O'Riordan, 10 June 1897, in Dowson, *Letters*, pages 384–385.
'There is a fatality': *Letters*, page 901.
'wonderful and charming': *Letters*, page 907.
'*your* friend, and *mine*': *Letters*, page 908.

'a more wholesome taste': Pearson, *The Life of Oscar Wilde*, pages 335–336.
'the architect of the moon': *Letters*, page 1075.
'a huge and fat person': David Sox, *Bachelors of Art: Edward Perry Warren and The Lewes House Brotherhood* (London, 1991), pages 139–140.
'first hyacinth since Douglas': Sox, *Bachelors of Art*, page 141.
'that Aubrey Beardsley': Sox, *Bachelors of Art*, pages 140–141.
'Two loves have I': Sox, *Bachelors of Art*, page 141.
'revolting': *Letters*, page 858.
'terrified about Bosie': *Letters*, page 865.
'My dear Boy': *Letters*, page 872.
'dear Reggie Cholmondeley': *Letters*, page 874.
'Don't think I don't love you': *Letters*, page 880.
'I must give up': *Letters*, page 885.
'dear honey-sweet boy': *Letters*, page 898.
'At present it is impossible': *Letters*, page 901.
'long indictment': *Letters*, page 908.
'a long letter': *Letters*, page 909.
'He has really left me': Lord Alfred Douglas to More Adey, 30 June 1897, in Croft-Cooke, *Bosie*, page 156.
'I don't even know': Lord Alfred Douglas to Lord Percy Douglas, in 'The Constant Nymph'.
'The meeting was a great success': Hyde, *Lord Alfred Douglas*, page 110.
'Yes I saw Bosie': *Letters*, page 934.
'own Darling boy': *Letters*, page 932.

Two outcast men
'Friendship is far more': *Works*, page 1242.
'I cannot stay': *Letters*, page 935.
'returning to his vomit': Carlos Blacker to Otho Holland Lloyd, 21 December 1900, in Maguire, 'Oscar Wilde and the Dreyfus Affair', *Victorian Studies*, volume XLI, number 1.
'You are really wrong': *Letters*, page 936.
'a hotel of absurd prices': *Letters*, page 949.
'freedom from morals': *Letters*, page 1112.
'My going back to Bosie': *Letters*, page 942.
'But I cannot help it': *Letters*, page 947.
'I love him, and have': *Letters*, page 948.
'We have a lovely villa': *Letters*, page 950.
'very beautiful': *Il Pungolo parlamentare*, 9–10 October 1897, in Masolino d'Amico, 'Oscar Wilde in Naples', *Rediscovering Oscar Wilde*, page 78.
'potent witch': Douglas, *Autobiography*, pages 158–159.
'I intend to winter here': *Letters*, page 947.
'The museum is full': *Letters*, page 958.
'We are together': *Letters*, page 952.
'He is usually': Hyde, *Oscar Wilde*, pages 331–332.
'My definition of a straightforward': Robert Ross to Ada Leverson, in Ellmann and Epsey, *Oscar Wilde: Two Approaches*, page 42.
'The poem suffers': *Letters*, page 956.
'A prison wall was round us born': *Works*, page 887.

'we go to Capri': *Letters*, page 962.

'alcoholic habits': Robert Ross, 'Statement of Evidence in His Case Against Douglas', Clark Library.

'in your own mysterious style': Lord Alfred Douglas to George Ives, 22 October 1897, Clark Library.

'It is very curious': *Letters*, page 955.

'very witty and talkative': *Letters*, page 976.

'*mal vu*': Hyde, *Lord Alfred Douglas*, pages 115–116.

'Very secret': E. Neville-Rolfe to Lord Rosebery, 30 December 1897, in 'A Note on Oscar Wilde, Alfred Douglas and Lord Rosebery', in *English Language Notes*, volume XXIII, number 1 (1985), page 43.

'Question – has he seen': Constance Wilde to Carlos Blacker, 26 September 1897, in J. Robert Maguire, 'An Oscar Wilde Autograph Envelope at Auction', *Antiquarian Book Monthly* (October 2000), page 31.

'I have today written': *Letters*, page 955.

'I *forbid* you to see': *Letters*, page 994.

'How can she really imagine': *Letters*, page 955.

'Robbie has written me': *Letters*, page 951.

'As you remade my life': *Letters*, page 950.

'When you wish to talk': *Letters*, page 963.

'wretched £3 a week': *Letters*, page 955.

'a public scandal': Oscar Wilde to More Adey, 20 November 1897, in Hyde, *Lord Alfred Douglas*, pages 115–116.

'Women are so petty': *Letters*, page 955.

'After all, no charge': *Letters*, page 979.

'If I were living': *Letters*, page 979.

'I said at once that your wife': *Letters*, page 989.

'For More and Robbie': *Letters*, page 990.

'Do you think that if ': *Letters*, page 991.

'Do, if possible, try': *Letters*, page 995.

'perfectly capable': Lord Alfred Douglas to More Adey, in Croft-Cooke, *Bosie*, page 167.

'starved out': Robert Ross, 'Statement of Evidence in His Case Against Lord Alfred Douglas', Clark Library.

'It is proposed to leave me': *Letters*, page 996.

'Moral people': *Letters*, page 996.

'very cultivated': *Letters*, page 1008.

'I hear you have': Leonard Smithers to Oscar Wilde, 26 January 1898, MS Walpole, Bodleian Library.

'The annoyance of living': Lord Alfred Douglas to Oscar Wilde, 7 January 1898, in Hyde, *Lord Alfred Douglas*, page 231.

'It is, of course, the most bitter': *Letters*, page 1029.

'I am so glad!': Lord Alfred Douglas to Lady Queensberry, 7 December 1897, in Ellmann, page 554.

A joy-song

'JACK: He seems to have': *Works*, page 381.

'A poem gives one': *Letters*, page 1022.

'I hear he had missed': *Letters*, page 1019.

'frightfully upset by this': *Letters*, page 1027.

'He has, as you know': *Letters*, page 1035.

'exquisite': *Letters*, page 1035.

'more or less demanding': *Letters*, page 1038.

'He says that he loved': *Letters*, page 1038.

'I have a sort of idea': *Letters*, page 1039.

'I kept on saying': Pearson, *The Life of Oscar Wilde*, page 346.

'not a serious one': Constance Wilde to Robert Ross, 12 March 1895, Clark Library, in Clark, *Mrs Oscar Wilde*, pages 159–160.

'brought about in the first place': Otho Holland Lloyd to A.J.A. Symons, 22 May 1937, Clark Library.

'a broken heart': Vyvyan Holland to Frank Harris, 9 May 1926, HRC.

'telegraphic tears': Vyvyan Holland to Frank Harris, 9 May 1926, HRC.

'It is really awful': *Letters*, page 1055.

'You will have heard': *Letters*, page 1054.

'Alcohol taken in sufficient': Belford, *Oscar Wilde*, page 281.

'Absinthe stands alone': Harris, *Oscar Wilde*, page 75.

'seen Oscar over and over again': Lord Alfred Douglas to A.J.A. Symons, 8 March 1937, Clark Library.

'never been exactly sober': Stuart Merrill, 'Some Unpublished Recollections', *Adam International Reviews*, numbers 241–243 (1954), page 12.

'waiters, coachmen, sellers': Jean-Joseph Renaud, 'The Last Months of Oscar Wilde in Paris', Clark Library.

'like a superhuman burst': Nancy Erber, 'The French Trials of Oscar Wilde', pages 586–587.

'Like dear St Francis of Assisi': *Letters*, page 1145.

'I tell everybody not to': O'Sullivan, *Aspects of Wilde*, page 56.

'a fat old prostitute': Harris, *Oscar Wilde*, page 305.

'when I was hot': Lord Alfred Douglas to Frank Harris, no date given, in Harris and Douglas, *The Life and Confessions of Oscar Wilde*, page 54.

'I know that there is no beggar': George Bernard Shaw to Lord Alfred Douglas, 18 April 1938, in *Bernard Shaw and Alfred Douglas: A Correspondence* edited by Mary Hyde (London, 1982), pages 30–32.

'A wretched inn-keeper': *Letters*, page 1101.

'I am so sorry': *Letters*, page 1102.

'I had a fearful letter': *Letters*, page 1061.

'Because I have written': Pearson, *The Life of Oscar Wilde*, page 367.

'the end of life': *Oscar Wilde's Oxford Notebooks*, pages 141–142.

'the honey of romance': *Works*, page 864.

'To drift with every passion': *Works*, page 864.

'by chance': *Letters*, page 1025.

'all French lily and English rose': *Letters*, page 1077.

'His upper lip': *Letters*, page 1066.

'jonquil-like in aspect': *Letters*, page 1074.

'most beautiful mouth I know': *Letters*, page 1083.

retourné à son vomissement: Ellmann, pages 562–563.

'He grows dearer to me daily': *Letters*, page 1031.

'a born Catholic in romance': *Letters*, page 1076.

'No cheque this morning': *Letters*, page 1073.

'Bosie is being very angelic': *Letters*, page 1057.
'Bosie is now inseparable': *Letters*, page 1081.
'He apparently goes': *Letters*, pages 1057–1058.
'Bosie has no real': *Letters*, page 1081.
'He is devoted': *Letters*, page 1066.
'grown tired of the Florifer': *Letters*, page 1075.
'Bosie turned up': *Letters*, page 1070.
'Boys, brandy, and betting': *Letters*, page 1192.
'I cannot bear being alone': *Letters*, page 1068.
'cold shoulder': O'Sullivan, *Aspects of Wilde*, pages 184–185.
'realise that he was ruining': O'Sullivan, *Some Letters to A.J.A. Symons*, page 45.
'the Circle of the Boulevards': *Letters*, page 1064.
'Edmond de Goncourt': *Letters*, page 1056.
'Edmond is very smart': *Letters*, page 1058.
'I don't wish to be horrid': *Letters*, page 1078.
'quite charming': *Letters*, page 1157.
'to smoke a cigarette': *Letters*, page 1074.
'A meeting with *Léon*': *Letters*, page 1078.
'a most passionate faun': *Letters*, page 1104.
'the harvest-moon': *Letters*, page 1106.
'beautiful boy of bad character': *Letters*, page 1108.
'snub-nosed little horror': *Letters*, page 1110.
'the sweetest': *Letters*, page 1144.
'a little Dionysiac': *Letters*, page 1107.
'Your little friend Alphonse': *Letters*, page 1107.
'these gutter perverts': Hyde, *Lord Alfred Douglas*, page 204.
'dear little absurd Robbie': *Letters*, page 1088.
'It is quite true': *Letters*, pages 1105–1106.
'As regards to my marrying': *Letters*, page 1116.
'the fishing population': *Letters*, page 1112.
'two special friends': *Letters*, page 1113.
'Yes, even at Napoule': *Letters*, page 1119.
'joy-song': Harris, *Oscar Wilde*, page 281.
'one of the noble army': *Letters*, page 1114.
'a very pretty Italian boy': *Letters*, page 1112.
'charming fellow': *Letters*, page 1116.
'It is very pretty': *Letters*, page 1128.
'a beautiful young actor': *Letters*, page 1132.
'He is a silent, dull person': *Letters*, page 1132.
'to try and find a place': *Letters*, page 1139.
'I love them all': *Letters*, page 1179.
'most sweet': *Letters*, page 1179.
'friends': *Letters*, page 1179.
'But I met some': *Letters*, page 1179.
'I am glad you are enjoying': Lord Alfred Douglas to Oscar Wilde, early May 1900, in Hyde, *Lord Alfred Douglas*, pages 231–232.
'dark and gloomy': *Letters*, page 1181.
'who knows nothing': *Letters*, page 1185.
'I have given up Armando': *Letters*, page 1182.

'It was the first time': *Letters*, page 1186.
'with tears and one kiss': *Letters*, page 1187.
'In the mortal sphere': *Letters*, page 1187.
'at the age of a flower': *Letters*, page 1040.
'You must not think': *Letters*, page 912.
'ebbing out in squalor': O'Sullivan, *Aspects of Wilde*, page 41.
'I give it as my firm opinion': *The Shame of Oscar Wilde*, page 117.
'be swept with poignant anguish': O'Sullivan, *Aspects of Wilde*, page 54.
'a looking out': O'Sullivan, *Aspects of Wilde*, page 155.

November 1900
'Can I see one of the fathers': Rupert Croft-Cooke, 'Oscar Wilde Discoveries', *Books and Bookmen* (February 1974), page 40.
'almost hopeless': *Letters*, page 1219.
'I dreamt I was supping': *Letters*, page 1213.
'My wallpaper and I': Ellmann, page 581.
'very painful': *Letters*, page 1219.
'There was the so-called': Harris and Douglas, *The Life and Confessions of Oscar Wilde*, page 23.
'I have never heard': *Letters*, page 1220.
'I am miserable': Lord Alfred Douglas to More Adey, December 1900, in Hyde, *Lord Alfred Douglas*, page 128.
'more lives than one': *Works*, page 892.
'I was a man': *Letters*, pages 737–738.
'I dreamed of him': Douglas, *Sonnets*, page 38.
'And alien tears': *Works*, page 896.
'Yes. I have no doubt': *Letters*, page 1044.

Index